PETRI NETS – MANUFACTURING AND COMPUTER SCIENCE

Edited by **Pawel Pawlewski**

Petri Nets – Manufacturing and Computer Science
http://dx.doi.org/10.5772/2578
Edited by Pawel Pawlewski

Contributors

Dejan Gradišar, Gašper Mušič, Belhassen Mazigh, Abdeljalil Abbas-Turki, Yen-Liang Pan, Gen'ichi Yasuda, Tiago Facchin, Miguel Afonso Sellitto, Chongyi Yuan, Liangbing Feng, Masanao Obayashi, Takashi Kuremoto, Kunikazu Kobayashi, Iwona Grobelna, Ivo Martiník, Pece Mitrevski, Zoran Kotevski, Razib Hayat Khan, Poul E. Heegaard, Kazi Wali Ullah, Hussein Karam Hussein Abd El-Sattar, Wlodek M. Zuberek, Gustavo Callou, Paulo Maciel, Dietmar Tutsch, Julian Araújo, João Ferreira, Rafael Souza, J. Dassow, G. Mavlankulov, M. Othman, S. Turaev, M.H. Selamat, R. Stiebe, José Reinaldo Silva, Pedro M. G. del Foyo, Sangita Kansal, Mukti Acharya, Gajendra Pratap Singh, Samir Hamaci, Karim Labadi, A. Moumen Darcherif, Gi Bum Lee, Han Zandong, Jin S. Lee, Parisa Heidari, Hanifa Boucheneb, Taha Benarbia

Published by InTech

Janeza Trdine 9, 51000 Rijeka, Croatia

Publishing Process Manager Marina Jozipovic
Technical Editor InTech DTP team
Cover InTech Design team

Additional hard copies can be obtained from orders@intechopen.com

Petri Nets – Manufacturing and Computer Science, Edited by Pawel Pawlewski
p. cm.
ISBN 978-953-51-0700-2

Meet the editor

Paweł Pawlewski, PhD, is Assistant Professor at the Faculty of Engineering Management at Poznan University of Technology. His area of interest comprises: modeling, process simulation and optimization, organization of manufacturing processes, operational management, reengineering and IT applications in logistics. He is the author or co-author of more than 100 scientific papers. He is also co-author of the book "Reengineering". In 1994-2008 he managed a team performing a software for design and optimization of mechanical structures implemented among other things in VW-Wolsburg, VW-Shanghai, Audi-Ingolstadt, Seat-Barcelona, Porsche-Stuttgart, BMW–Munchen. All actions were taken within vMACH Engineering company. In 2009-2011 he cooperated with AMC Polska company in the scope of process simulation and optimization with the usage of Witness. Since 2011 he is a Manager of Simulation and Optimization Center in Logistic and Production Processes (SOCILAPP) at Poznan University of Technology. Habilitation dissertation titled "Methodology of modeling dynamic changes of production process' resource structure in mechanical engineering industry" is under accreditation procedure. Since 2011 he cooperates with Cempel Consulting. He is also a Flexsim Software Products Inc. (USA) Partner in Poland. Since 2012 he is member of Editorial Board (as Associate Editor) of International Journal of Artificial Intelligence (IJAI).

Contents

Preface

Manufacturing and Computer Science – these are major usage fields for applications using Petri Nets, which are the subject of the present monograph.

Manufacturing, i.e. producing goods, is one of the realms of human activity which has greatly affected the development of civilization. Over centuries, the large-scale manufacturing of goods changed the social relations, created new lifestyles and contributed to the improvement of life conditions of whole societies. The economic development has become an objective realized by states and commonwealths of states. It includes both quantitative changes referring to the growth in production, employment, investments, the scale of operating capital, incomes, consumption as well as other economic values describing the quantitative character of the economy (economic growth) and qualitative changes (changes in the organization of society). The improvement of life standards, the increase in production, a better social situation and greater public security are the basic benefits resulting from economic growth and development. Nowadays, owing to the increasingly complex products and technologies, the manufacturing still strongly stimulates development. It considerably affects other fields, e.g. computer science, as it creates new challenges. The role of production in the world is still crucial. When comparing the crisis in the automotive industry with the IT companies crisis (the so-called dot-com bubble burst), we can see that the first one had a more widespread effect over the world. The growing role of China, the leader in the scale and growth of production, changes the global distribution of power.

Pawel Pawlewski
Department of Management Engineering, Poznan University of Technology,
Poznan,
Poland

Section 1

Manufacturing

Chapter 1

Automated Petri-Net Modelling for Batch Production Scheduling

Dejan Gradišar and Gašper Mušič

Additional information is available at the end of the chapter

http://dx.doi.org/10.5772/48467

1. Introduction

Production scheduling is a fundamental function in production control. It has an immediate and considerable impact on the efficiency of related manufacturing processes and significantly influences the overall production performance.

The primary characteristic of batch production is that the output of the process appears in quantities of materials or lots called batches. All components are completed at a workstation before they move to the next one. These kinds of production environments appear in chemical, pharmaceutical, food and similar industries.

The control of batch processes poses difficult issues as these processes are neither continuous nor discrete, but have the characteristics of both. ISA society introduced a multi-part S88 standard where the first part [1] defines the models and terminology for batch plants and control systems. S88 provides a framework for the development of technologies that not only support control activities of batch processes but also management activities, such as scheduling. This is illustrated in [14] where a generic framework is defined for interpreting a multi-purpose/product batch plant in terms of S88 constructs for scheduling purposes.

In order to cope with the behaviour of a batch production process an appropriate mathematical model is needed. When the behaviour is described by such a model, formal methods can be used, which usually improve the understanding of systems, allow their analysis and help in implementation. MILP based formulations of batch process features are typically used as shown in [12]. Nevertheless, Petri nets have also been applied in different aspects of modelling, qualitative and quantitative analysis, control, planning and scheduling of batch processes [4]. Independently of the chosen framework, the modelled behaviour is often extremely complex. Within the changing production environment the effectiveness of batch production modelling is, therefore, a prerequisite for the effective design and operation of batch systems.

To determine a model, data from different existing information systems could be used. From production management systems, such as Manufacturing Resource Planning (MRP II) and Enterprise Resource Planning (ERP), data about the needs, product structure and process structure could be gained [21]. On the other hand, data from the production process could be used to determine the actual resource availability. MRP II and ERP systems are commonly used in discrete manufacturing for upper level production control, such as production planning. Standard production management tools, such as MRP, are also used in batch production environment [20]. As defined with standard S88.01 the required raw materials and their quantities are determined from a dedicated data structure named *Formula*. This way the formula can be linked to standard Bill of Materials (BOM) used within MRP II concept [7].

While in a discrete manufacturing processes BOM are used to determine process materials and their quantities needed for production of finished products, in batch production processes these data are given with Formula. The same is with information that defines a sequence of operations required to produce an item. In discrete manufacturing processes these are defined with Routing, and Manufacturing recipes are used in batch production.

These two groups of data items, together with the given resource units, form the basic elements of the production process. These data can be effectively used to build up a model of the batch production system with timed Petri nets. An algorithm will be introduced, which builds a Petri-net model from the existing data. The model is built directly in a top-down manner, starting from the Formula (BOM) and the Manufacturing recipes (routings) [21].

First a class of Petri nets used is presented in a formal manner with detailed discussion on time representation. Next a method to describe a Formula with Petri net structure is given. Root item, representing the product, is composed of sub-items (sub-processes). Later a method of describing the basic production activities with timed Petri net is presented. The obtained model is applied in optimisation of batch scheduling problem.

2. Timed PN

In the Petri net literature, three basic ways of representing time in Petri nets are used [2]: firing durations (FD), holding durations (HD) and enabling durations (ED). When using FD principle the transition firing has duration [23]. In contrast, when using HD principle, a firing has no duration but a created token is considered unavailable for the time assigned to transition that created the token, which has the same effect. With ED principle, the firing of the transitions has no duration while the time delays are represented by forcing transitions that are enabled to stay so for a specified period of time before they can fire. This is a more general concept since it allows for modelling of task interruption. Some authors use an even more general concept, which assigns delays to individual arcs, either inputs or outputs of a transition [10].

When modelling several performance optimisation problems, e.g. scheduling problems, such a general framework is not needed. It is natural to use HD when modelling most scheduling processes as operations are considered non-preemptive. The timed version of CPNs defined by [9] uses a HD equivalent principle, where the unavailability of the tokens is defined implicitly through the corresponding time stamps. While CPNs allow the assignment of delays both to transition and to output arcs, we further simplify this by allowing time delay inscriptions to transitions only. This is sufficient for the type of examples investigated here, and can be generalised if necessary.

To include a time attribute of the marking tokens, which determines their availability and unavailability, the notation of timed CPN will be adopted. Tokens are accompanied with a timestamp, which is written next to the token number and separated from the number by @. E.g., two tokens with time stamp 10 are denoted 2@10. A collection of tokens with different time stamps is defined as a multiset, and written as a sum (union) of sets of timestamped tokens. E.g., two tokens with time stamp 10 and three tokens with timestamp 12 are written as $2@10 + 3@12$. The timestamp of a token defines the time from which the token is available.

Time stamps are elements of a time set TS, which is defined as a set of numeric values. In many software implementations the time values are integer, i.e., $TS = \mathbb{N}$, but will be here admitted to take any positive real value including 0, i.e., $TS = \mathbb{R}_0^+$. Timed markings are represented as collections of time stamps and are multisets over TS : TS_{MS}. By using HD principle the formal representation of a P/T timed Petri net is defined as follows. $TPN = (\mathcal{N}, M_0)$ is a timed Petri net system, where: $\mathcal{N} = (P, T, Pre, Post, f)$ is a Timed Petri net structure, $P = \{p_1, p_2, ..., p_k\}, k > 0$ is a finite set of places, $T = \{t_1, t_2, ..., t_l\}, l > 0$ is a finite set of transitions. $Pre : (P \times T) \rightarrow \mathbb{N}$ is the input arc function. If there exists an arc with weight k connecting p to t, then $Pre(p,t) = k$, otherwise $Pre(p,t) = 0$. $Post : (P \times T) \rightarrow \mathbb{N}$ is the output arc function. If there exists an arc with weight k connecting t to p, then $Post(p,t) = k$, otherwise $Post(p,t) = 0$. $f : T \rightarrow TS$ is the function that assigns a non-negative deterministic time delay to every $t \in T$. $M : P \rightarrow TS_{MS}$ is the timed marking, M_0 is the initial marking of a timed Petri net.

To determine the availability and unavailability of tokens, two functions on the set of markings are defined. The set of markings is denoted by $\mathbb{M}$. Given a marking and model time, $m : P \times \mathbb{M} \times TS \rightarrow \mathbb{N}$ defines the number of available tokens, and $n : P \times \mathbb{M} \times TS \rightarrow \mathbb{N}$ the number of unavailable tokens for each place of a TPN at a given time τ_k. Note that model time also belongs to time set TS, $\tau_k \in TS$.

Using the above definitions, addition and subtraction of timed markings, and the TPN firing rule can be defined. Given a marked $TPN = (\mathcal{N}, M)$, a transition t is time enabled at time τ_k, denoted $M[t\rangle_{\tau_k}$ iff $m(p, M, \tau_k) \geq Pre(p,t)$, $\forall p \in \bullet t$. An enabled transition can fire, and as a result removes tokens from input places and creates tokens in output places. The newly created tokens are accompanied by timestamps depending on the model time and the delay of transition that created the tokens. If marking M_2 is reached from M_1 by firing t at time τ_k, this is denoted by $M_1[t\rangle_{\tau_k} M_2$. The set of markings of TPN $\mathcal{N}$ reachable from M is denoted by $R(\mathcal{N}, M)$.

3. Modelling procedure

Petri nets are a family of tools that provide a framework, which can be used for various problems that appear during the life-cycle of a production system [18]. In this section we present the modelling of production system using timed Petri nets for the purpose of performance control. When timed Petri nets are used, it is possible to derive performance measures such as makespan, throughput, production rates, and other temporal quantities. The Petri net model is built based on the data stored in production management information systems, i.e., ERP system.

3.1. The class of production systems

With the method presented here several scheduling problems that appear in various production systems can be solved. In a discrete manufacturing different jobs are needed to produce a final product that is composed of several components. Similarly in batch production different activities have to be performed in order to produce a final product. However, here the resultant product is produced with some irreversible change, e.g. products are mixed from quantities of ingredients.

Different management systems (*ERP*) can be applied for different types of production systems to plan the production process activities. We are assuming here a management system that can provide plan for both, discrete and batch process. The system generates work orders that interfere with the demands for the desired products. Different jobs/procedures are needed to produce a desired product. Set of operations needed to produce one item represent a job. In general, more operations have to be performed using different resources in order to complete a specific job. To complete a specific product, more sub-products may be needed. To list these components a BOM is used in discrete manufacturing and formulas in batch manufacturing. These components determine sub-jobs that are needed to manufacture a parent item. In this way the general scheduling problem is defined that can be applied both in discrete or batch production environment and can be given as:

- n jobs are to be processed: $J = \{J_j\}, j = 1, ..., n$,
- r resources are available: $M = \{M_i\}, i = 1, ..., r$,
- each job J_i is composed of n_j operations: $O_j = \{o_{jk}\}, k = 1, ..., n_j$,
- each operation can be processed on (more) different sets of resources $S_{jkl} \in R$; l determines the number of different sets,
- the processing time of each operation o_{jkl}, using resource set S_{jkl}, is defined with T_{jkl},
- precedence constraints are used to define that some operations within one job has to be performed before a set of operations in another job.

Using this definition, the following assumptions have to be considered:

- Resources are always available and never break down.
- Each resource can process a limited number of operations. This limitation is defined by the capacity of resources.
- Operations are non pre-emptive.
- When an operation is performed, it is desirable to free the resources so that they can become available as soon as possible. Intermediate buffers between processes are common solutions. It is common for batch processes that successive operations need to be performed on the same resource as predecessor. In this case the resource is free when the last operation is finished.
- Processing times are deterministic and known in advance.
- Work orders define the quantity of desired products and the starting times. Orders that are synchronised in time are considered jointly.

3.2. Modelling of production activities

Here we present a method of describing the production-system activities with timed Petri nets using the holding-duration representation of time. The places represent resources and jobs/operations, and the transitions represent decisions or rules for resources assignment/release and for starting/ending jobs.

To make a product, a set of operations has to be performed. We can think of an operation as a set of events and activities. Using a timed PN, events are represented by transitions and activity is associated with the presence of a token in a place.

An elementary operation can be described with one place and two transitions, see Figure 1. When all the input conditions are met (raw material and resources are available) the event that starts the operation occurs, t_1. This transition also determines the processing time of an operation. During that time the created token is unavailable in place p_2 and the operation is being executed. After that time the condition for ending the operation is being satisfied and t_2 can be fired. Place p_1 is not a part of the operation, it determines the input condition, e.g. the availability of the input material.

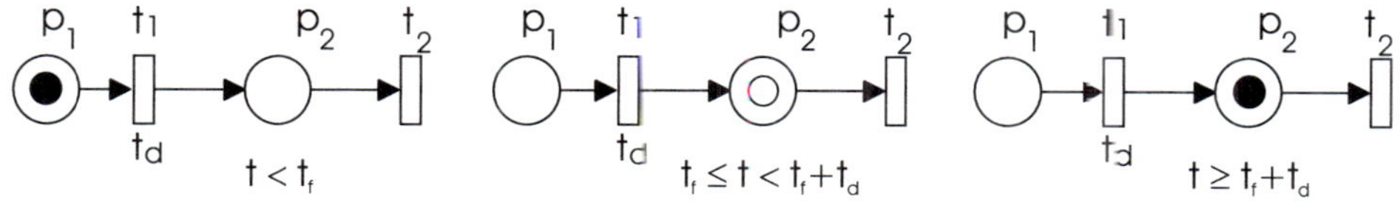

Figure 1. Operation described with timed Petri net.

When parallel activities need to be described the Petri-net structure presented in Figure 2 is used. Transition t_0 sets the input conditions for the parallel execution of two operations. In places p_{01} and p_{02} operations can wait for the available resource(s). The time delays of the transitions t_{11in} and t_{12in} define the duration of each operation. An available token in place p_{11} (p_{12}) indicates that operation is finished. Transition t_1 is used to synchronise both operations.

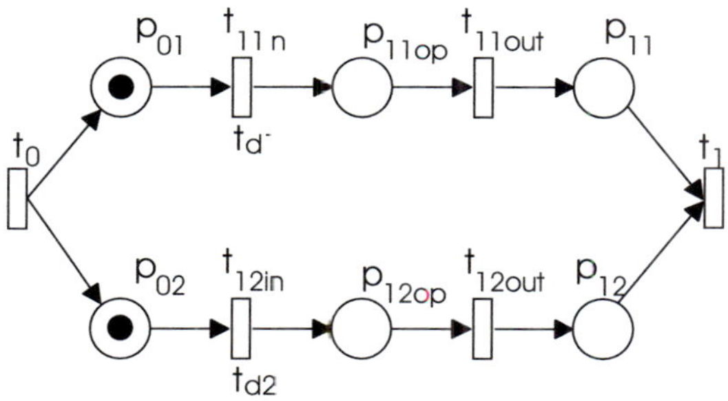

Figure 2. Two parallel operations.

An operation might need resources, usually with a limited capacity, to be executed; this is illustrated in Figure 3. Place p_{R1} is used to model a resource R_1. Its capacity is defined with the initial marking of that place. The resource is available to process the operation if there are enough available tokens in it. When the resource is used at the start of the operation the unavailable token appears in place p_{1op}. After the time defined by transition t_{1in} the token becomes available, t_{1out} is fired, and the resource becomes free to operate on the next job. For this reason zero time needs to be assigned to the transition t_{1out}. An additional place p_1 models the control flow. When the token is present in this place, the next operation can begin.

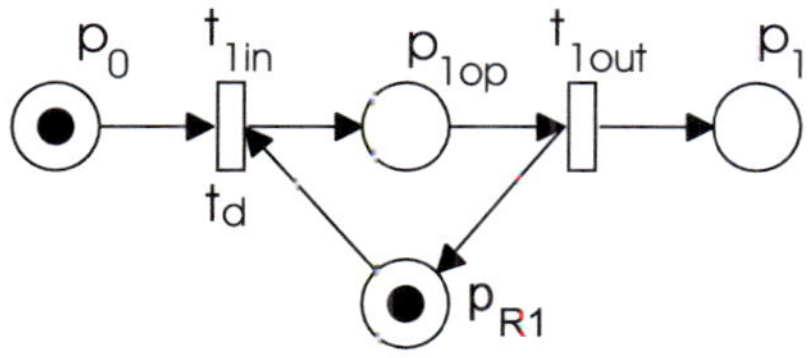

Figure 3. Operation that uses a resource with finite capacity.

A particular operation can often be done on more different (sets of) resources with different availability, and the time duration can be different on each set of resources. An example where an operation can be executed on two different sets of resources is shown in Figure 4. If the operation chooses resource R_3, its time duration is determined with the transition $f(t_{2in}) = t_{d2}$. Otherwise the set of resources, composed of R_1 and R_2, is being selected and its operation time is defined with $f(t_{1in}) = t_{d1}$.

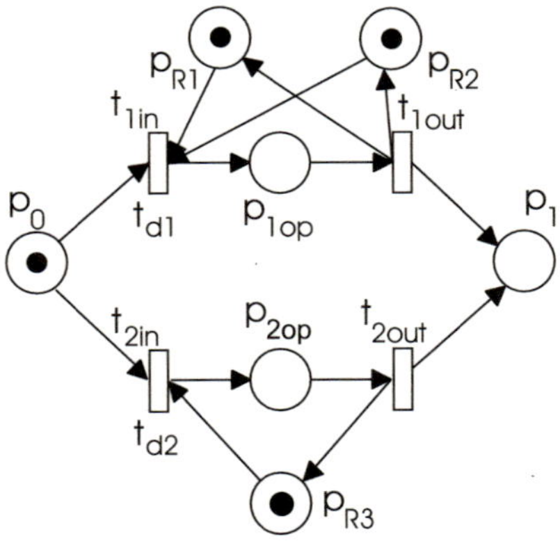

Figure 4. Operation that can be performed on two different sets of resources.

There are common situations where more operations use the same resource, e.g., an automated guided vehicle (AGV) in a manufacturing system or a mixing reactor in a batch system. This can be modelled as shown in Figure 5.

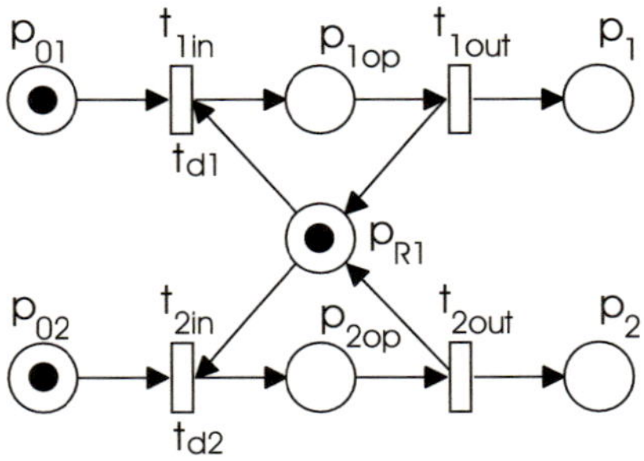

Figure 5. Shared resource.

Precedence constraints are used to define technological limitations and the sequence of operations. An example of two successive operations is shown in Figure 6, depicted as $Op1$ and $Op2$. In this figure an example of technological limitations is also shown. Here, the situation where operation $Op1$ precedes operation $Op3$ is considered. For this purpose an additional place p_{pr1} is inserted between the transition t_{1out} (ending $Op1$) and the transition t_{3in} (starting $Op3$). The weight n of the arc, which connects p_{pr1} to t_{3in}, prescribes how many items need to be produced by the first operation before the second operation can begin.

3.3. Modelling using the data from production-management systems

The most widely used production-management information system in practice are MRP II and ERP. Data stored in those systems can be used to build up a detailed model of the production system with Petri nets. In discrete manufacturing these data are bills of material and routing, while in batch manufacturing master formula and recipe are used to determine the production

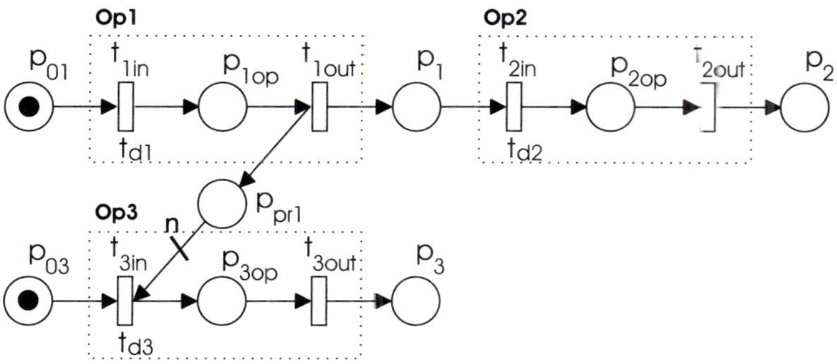

Figure 6. Precedence constraint.

process. Work orders are used to determine which and how many of finished products have to be produced.

3.3.1. Bill of materials (Formula)

The Bill of materials (BOM) is a listing or description of the raw materials and items that make up a product, along with the required quantity of each. In batch manufacturing other terms are used instead, i.e. Formula.

The BOM used in this work is defined as:

$BOM = (R, E, q, pre)$, where:

- $R = \{r_1\}$ is a root item.
- $E = \{e_1, ..., e_i\}$ is a finite set of sub-items,
- $q : E \to \mathbb{N}$ is the function that defines the quantities for each sub-item e_i. $\mathbf{q}$ represents an $i \times 1$ column vector whose ith entry is $q(e_i)$.
- $pre : (E \times E) \to \{0, 1\}$ is a precedence-constraints function It defines the precedence-constraints matrix **pre**, where $\mathbf{pre}(i, j) = 1$ indicates that the i-th item precedes the j-th item. It can also be interpreted as a directed graph.

R is a root item and represents the product that is composed of sub-items described with $e_i \in E$. The number of required sub-items is determined with the vector $\mathbf{q}$. When any sub-item has to be produced before another, the precedence function pre is used to define it. All the sub-items have to be finished before the operation for the subsequent sub-items can begin. A required property of **pre** is that only zero values can be on its diagonal, i.e. a sub-item cannot precede itself. An item is never allowed to become (indirectly) a component of itself. In other words, if the BOM structure is seen as a directed graph, this graph should be cycle-free [21].

If any of the sub-items e_i are composed of any other sub-items, the same BOM definition is used to describe its dependencies. The items at the highest level of this structure represent a finished product, and those at the lower level represent raw materials. The items that represent raw materials do not have a BOM.

Table 1 shows an example of a BOM describing the production of product I, which is composed of three components, i.e., three items of J, one item of K and and two items of

Item	Sub-item	Quantity	Precedence constraints
I	J	3	0 1 0
	K	1	0 0 0
	L	2	0 0 0

Table 1. Example of the BOM structure.

L. From the precedence-constraint matrix it is clear that all of the items J has to be completed before the production of item K can begin.

The mathematical representation of the BOM of item I would be represented as:

$$BOM = (R, E, \mathbf{q}, \mathbf{pre}), \text{ where } R = \{I\},$$

$$E = \{J\ K\ L\}, \quad \mathbf{q} = \begin{bmatrix} 3\ 1\ 2 \end{bmatrix} \quad \text{and} \quad \mathbf{pre} = \begin{bmatrix} 0\ 1\ 0 \\ 0\ 0\ 0 \\ 0\ 0\ 0 \end{bmatrix}.$$

To start with building a model, let us assume that, for each item from the BOM, only one operation is needed. As stated before, each operation can be represented with one place and two transitions (Figure 1). To be able to prescribe how many of each item is required the transition t_{Rin} and the place p_{Rin} are added in front, and p_{Rout} and t_{Rout} are added behind this operation. The weight of the arcs that connect t_{Rin} with p_{Rin} and p_{Rout} with t_{Rout} are determined by the quantity q_0 of the required items. In this way an item I is represented with a Petri net as defined in Figure 7.

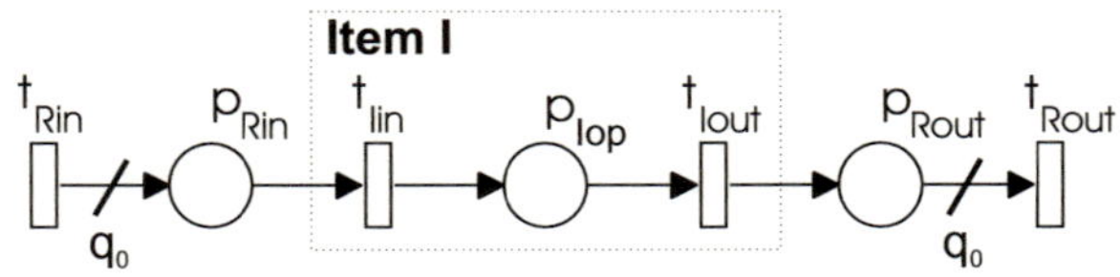

Figure 7. PN structure representing one item in the BOM.

As finished product is defined with a structure of BOMs, the construction of the overall Petri net is an iterative procedure that starts with the root of the BOM and continues until all the items have been considered. If the item requires any more sub-assemblies (i.e., items from a lower level) the operation, the framed area of the PN structure presented in Figure 7, is substituted with lower-level items. If there are more than one sub-items, they are given as parallel activities.

The substitution of an item with sub-items is defined as follows:

- Remove the place p_{Iop} and its input/output arcs.
- Define the PN structure for sub-components, as it is defined with a BOM. Consider the precedence constraints.
- Replace the removed place p_{Iop} by the sub-net defined in the previous step. The input and output transitions are merged with the existing ones.

The result of building the PN model of this example (Table 1) is given in Figure 8, where item I is composed of three subitems: J, K and L.

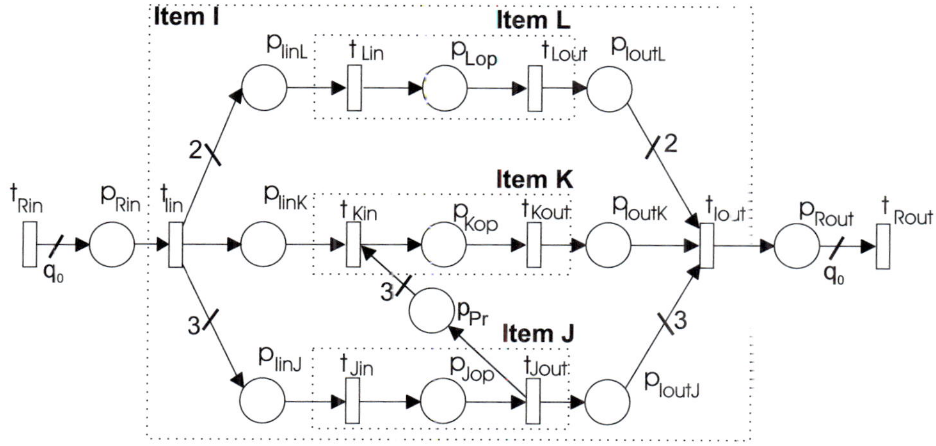

Figure 8. BOM structure defined by PN.

3.3.2. Routings (Recipe)

For each item that can appear in production process, and does not represent a raw material, a routing is defined. It defines a job with sequence of operations, each requiring processing by a particular resource for a certain processing time, which are needed for transforming raw material into the (sub)product. This information are provided by routing tables in discrete manufacturing, and by recipes in batch manufacturing industries. The table contains a header, where the item that is being composed is defined and the lines where all the required operations are described. For each operation one line is used.

As an example, the routing table for item K is given as presented in Table 2. Three operations are needed to produce this item; the first of these operations can be done on two different resources. Similar notation is used for other possible cases, e.g. an operation that needs three resources R_1 and two R_2, or one resource R_1 and three R_3 would be presented by $(3 \times R_1, 2 \times R_2)/(R_1, 3 \times R_3)$.

Operations	Duration	Resources
Op10	10s/9s	R1/R3
Op20	20s	R2
Op30	12s	R1

Table 2. Routing of product K.

The implementation of the routing data in one item of a BOM is defined as follows:

- Remove the place p_{Xop} and its input/output arcs.
- Define a PN structure for the sub-components, as it is defined with routing data. Also precedence constraints are considered here.
- Place p_{Xop} is replaced with the sub-net defined in previous step, where input and output transitions are merged with the existing ones.

Function that defines PN structure for every sub-component yields the corresponding sequence of production operations from the routing table and for each operation a timed Petri net is built as defined in section 3.3.1. All the placed operations are connected as prescribed by the required technological sequence, and each operation is assigned to the required places representing appropriate resources.

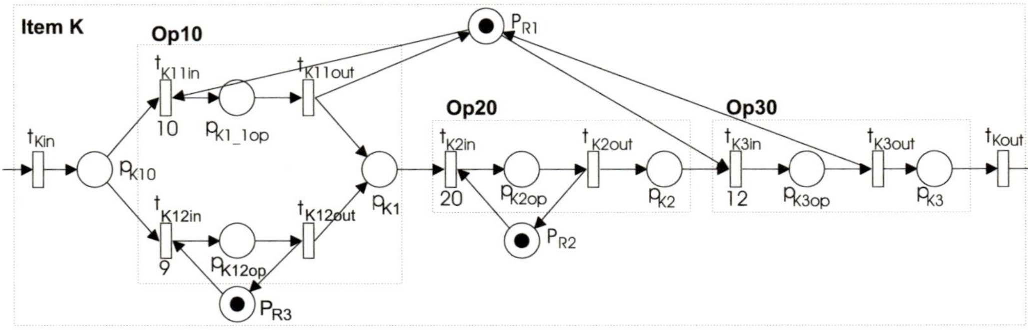

Figure 9. Routing of product *K* modelled with timed Petri net.

The PN structure in Figure 9 is achieved if the sequence of operations described with a routing table (Table 2) is modelled. The resulting PN structure is inserted into the main PN model, on the place where item *K* (p_{Kop}) was.

The routings/recipes are submodels that are inserted (by substitution, as defined previously) into the main model defined with the BOM structure. However, some activities of any sub-item may also be described with a BOM, i.e., in the case they are composed of semi-products. The construction of the overall Petri-net model can be achieved by combining all of the intermediate steps.

3.3.3. Work order

The work order ($WO = [R, q_0, st]$) determines which and how many of the finished products have to be produced. Each product (R) can be represented with a Petri-net model, shown in Figure 7, where one place is added in front and one at the end of the structure to determine the start and end of the work. As usually more products are produced at one time (one product is represented with one batch), the weight of the arc that connects t_{Rin} and p_{Rin} are used to determine the number of required batches (q_0). To be able to consider different starting times for different quantities of one product the general structure shown in Figure 10 is used. q_0 determines the number of products to be finished. Orders for products which should start with the production at the same time are merged and every group of products with the same starting time is modelled with places $p_1, p_2, ...p_n$ and with tokens located in them. The timestamps, which are assigned to these tokens determine the starting time of every group of products. Wights $q_1, q_2, ...q_n$ determine the number of products, where $q_1 + q_2 + ... + q_n$ is equal to q_0. The token in the place p_{end} implies that WO is finished.

3.4. Specifics of batch production processes

In previous sections (3.3.1 – 3.3.3) we present methods to represent formula, recipe and work orders with Petri nets. As given so far these elements can be equally used for discrete and batch process environments. However, as mentioned in 3.1 there are some specifics in batch production processes.

Actually batch production is more complicated and formula and recipe are more connected as are BOM and routings [7]. There are common situations where precedence constraints

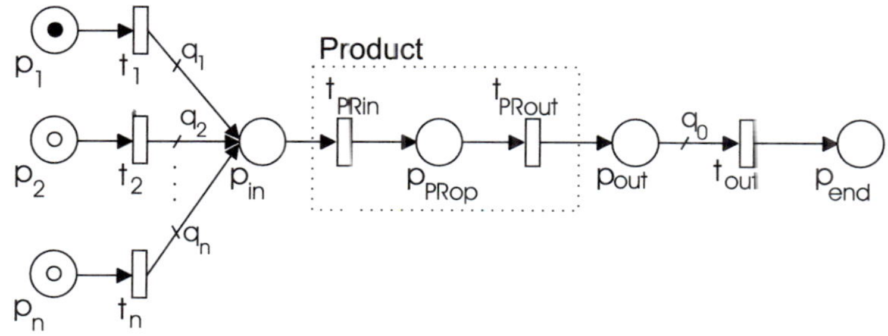

Figure 10. Petri net structure of a work order.

are not used only to define interdependencies between different (finished) items, but also for interdependencies between job operations of various items that are defined with recipes. In this situations the definition of BOM (Formula) has to be extended.

Definition of a sub-items set E is extended in a way that it contain also the information about operations that produce that item: $E = \{(e_1, o_{1k}), ...(e_i, o_{in_j})\}$.

Further also a precedence-constraint function *pre* is extended in order to include information about how many operations are needed for every item. As defined in 3.1, set of operations needed to produce j-th item is given as $O_j = \{o_{jk}\}$, where $k = 1, ..., n_j$. Size of the matrix is therefore defined with $[m \times m]$, where $m = \sum n_j$, $j = 1...n$. Here n is number of items that make up a product. In this way we can define an extended precedence-constraints function pre as $pre : ((E \times O) \times (E \times O)) \rightarrow \{0, 1\}$. Element from constraint matrix $pre(p_{ij}, p_{kl}) = 1$ indicates that the j-th operation from i-th item precedes l-th operation from k-th item. Here index p_{ij} in a matrix **pre** presents j-th operation of i-th item and p_{kl} l-th operation of k-th item.

3.5. Procedure for building the PN model

With WO demands for product to be finished are passed. For each WO a Petri net model has to be defined. The modelling procedure can be summarised in the Algorithm 1.

Algorithm 1 Read BOM

```
[R, q, st] = readWO()
For i = 1 to length(R)
    E = readBOM(R(i))
    PN = placePN(R(i), E, q(i), [ ], st(i), x0, y0)
    PN = routing(PN, R(i))
end
```

First, the data about the WO are read. The products that are needed to be produced are given in R; in vector **q** the quantities of the desired products are passed; and vector **st** is used to determine the starting time of each product. For each product the Petri-net structure, shown in Figure 10, is determined and placed on the model. The step when the $routing()$ is called is described in more detail with algorithm 2.

First, the routing and the BOM data are read from the database (functions *readRouting()* and *readBOM()*). For each operation that comprises the routing, the algorithm checks whether it is made up of sub-item(s) or this is an operation. In the first case, the function *placePN()* is used to determine the PN structure of the given structure BOM. Precedence constraints are added

Algorithm 2 Read Routing

```
function PN = routing(PN, R)
datRoute = readRouting(R)
[E, q, pre] = readBOM(R)
for i = 1 to length(datRoute.Op)
    if datRoute.Resources ==BOM
       PN1 = placePN(R, E, q, pre, [ ])
       PN = insertPN(PN, PN1)
       for j = 1 to length(E)
          PN1 = routing(PN1, E(j))
       end
    else
       PN = constructPN(PN, datRoute(i))
       PN = insertPN(PN, PN1)
    end
 end
```

if they exist. With the function *insertPN()* the resulting subnet is inserted into the main PN structure. If the operation represents the production operation, the function *constructPN*() is called. With it, basic elements (Figures 1–6) are recognised, joined together and placed in the model, again using the function *insertPN()*. All the data about resources and time durations are acquired from the routing table. The described algorithm has been implemented in Matlab.

The resulting model is stored in a XML-based format employing Petri Net Markup Language (PNML) [6].

3.6. Verification

When the model is built up, it should be verified to see whether it reflects the system operation as defined with data about the production process. Some interesting properties of the model can be checked with the P-invariant analysis. Several P-invariants can be identified in the model. Their number is defined with the sum of all the resources, the number of product routes and the number of all precedences that are present in the model. It can be stated that the weighted sum of tokens that belongs to every P-invariant, which is a consequence of a resource, is equal to the capacity of that resource. The weighted sum of all other invariants is defined with the common number of batches of demanded product.

If possible, the model is later simplified in a way, that eliminated nodes do not influence the model behaviour.

4. Scheduling

Scheduling is one of the most important management functions and is a fundamental problem in the control of any resource-sharing organisation. Scheduling problems are very complex and many have been proven to be NP hard [8].

Literature on deterministic scheduling classifies the manufacturing scheduling problems according to machine environment structure, processing characteristics and constraints, and objectives. Standard machine environment structures lead to standard scheduling problems, e.g., open shop, flow shop and job shop problems, which are commonly studied. All three problem classes address a problem of sequencing n jobs (tasks) through a set of r machines (resources) where every job has to be processed once on every machine and every such job operation requires a specified processing time. The problems differ in restrictions on the job routings.

The scheduling problems related to batch plants possess a more complicated structure compared to standard scheduling problems. Batch plants are flexible and alternative resources can be used for conveying recipe operations. There may be different operation processing time assignments based on which equipment is used for processing and there may be specific requests on precedences or allowable intermediate storage time. This significantly complicates the problem of operations scheduling in batch processes. A comprehensive review of the state-of-the art of short-term batch scheduling is presented in [12]. Different types of batch scheduling problems are specified and the types of optimization models are reviewed. The presented models result in a formulation of MILP optimization problem and its solution yields an optimal schedule.

Petri nets can be used to effectively model all standard deterministic scheduling problem classes. Furthermore, the modelling power of Petri nets allows for derivation of models also for problems, which do not have standard problem structure but are closer to real process specifics. This is typical e.g. in batch systems where complex interconnections among process equipment are possible and vary considerably with used batch recipes. Even when the models are not as general as the above mentioned MILP problem representations, Petri nets can be used to model main model components of a two stage batch scheduling approach as defined in [12]. In contrast to monolithic approach the two stage approach assumes that the number of batches of each size is known in advance. The scheduling stage therefore concentrates on the allocation of processing resources to the batches while the plant work load is determined in a previous stage.

4.1. Petri net based derivation of optimal or sub-optimal schedules

To derive a feasible schedule, the obtained Petri net model can be simulated by an appropriate simulation algorithm. During the simulation, the occurring conflicts are resolved 'on the fly', e.g. by randomly choosing a transition in conflict that should fire. Instead, heuristic dispatching rules [5], such as Shortest Processing Time (SPT), can be introduced when solving the conflicting situations. The schedule of process operations can be determined by observing the marking evolution of the net. Depending on the given scheduling problem a convenient rule should be chosen. Usually, different rules are needed to improve different predefined production objectives (makespan, throughput, production rates, and other temporal quantities).

A more extensive exploration of the reachability tree is possible by PN-based heuristic search method proposed by [11]. It is based on generating parts of the Petri net reachability tree, where the branches are weighted by the time of the corresponding operations. The chosen transition firing sequence corresponds to a schedule, and by evaluating a number of sequences a (sub)optimal schedule can be determined. The method is further investigated in [22], where a modified heuristic function is proposed and tested on a number of benchmark tests. The problems of the approach are in the complexity of the reachability tree, which can generally not be completely explored. The search has to be limited to predefined maximum tree size in order to complete in a reasonable time. In addition to that, the heuristic function used within the search has to be chosen such that the search is directed more into the depth of the tree, which makes the obtained solution very sensitive to decisions taken at initial levels of the tree and in many cases the quality of the obtained solutions is rather low.

Recent reports in scheduling literature show an increased interest in the use of meta-heuristics, such as genetic algorithms (GA), simulated annealing (SA), and tabu search (TS). Meta-heuristics have also been combined with Petri net modelling framework to solve complex scheduling problems [19]. With such an approach, the modelling power of Petri nets can be employed, and relatively good solutions of scheduling problems can be found with a reasonable computational effort, although the convergence to the optimum can not be guaranteed. Compared to reachability tree based search methods, meta-heuristics require less memory.

The problem is that these methods require a sort of neghbouring solution generation strategy. This is easily accomplished for well structured problems, e.g. standard scheduling problems, but may be problematic for general models. In contrast, reachability tree methods as well as priority rule based methods can be used with any type of Petri net model. This motivates the investigation of combined methods, such as the combination of dispatching rules and local search [13].

Dispatching rules, however, do not always enable to reach the optimum even if combined with optimization methods. Using the rule based conflict resolution strategy the solution space is explored in a time driven manner where a transition is fired whenever at least one transition is enabled. In contrast, the reachability tree based methods enable to explore the solution space in an event driven manner. It is possible that a chosen firing sequence imposes one or more intervals of idle time between transitions, i.e. some transitions are enabled but do not fire due to waiting for enablement of another transition in accordance to the chosen sequence. The difference is important in cases when the optimal solution can be missed unless some idle time is included in the schedule as shown in [15]. In other words, the optimal solution generally belongs to the class of semi-active schedules [16]. The schedules generated by an event-driven reachability tree search are semi-active schedules.

4.2. Algorithmically generated Petri net models and schedules

In contrast to academic investigation of static scheduling problems the real manufacturing environment is far more dynamic. Planned work orders are often changing, priority orders are inserted, planned resources may become unavailable. A fast derivation of models that adequately represent the current situation in the process is therefore of extreme importance for a usable scheduling system. The above described automatic generation of Petri net models can be effectively used for these purposes.

The proposed algorithm also allows for specific process sequence structures typical for batch processes. E.g., the scheduling literature typically addresses a type of problems where a resource required by an operation is released as soon as the operation is finished. This is typical in the discrete industry, where intermediate products are stored in buffer zones in between machines. In batch processes the situation is different in the sense that a resource, e.g. a reactor is used both for processing and intermediate storage. The resource can be occupied by a number of successive operations, which can be easily modelled by Petri nets. Furthermore, the use of timestamped tokens provides a convenient representation of the time status of the processed work orders.

4.3. Evaluation of schedules

As the majority of commonly used scheduling objective functions are based on completion times of the jobs or work orders and due dates, the timed Petri net modelling framework yields a possibility to use the same kind of model with an objective function tailored to the needs of the particular production scenario.

In the field of deterministic scheduling the objective to be minimised is always a function of the completion times of the jobs or work orders [16]. This fits well in the timed Petri net scheduling framework where the time evolution of the net marking depends on timestamps associated with the tokens. If the schedule is modelled properly, the work order completion times can be read from the timestamps of tokens in the final marking obtained by timed Petri net simulation.

Let o_{ji} denote the i-th operation of work order j. Let C_{ji} denote the completion time of the operation o_{ji}. The completion time of the work order, i.e. the completion of the last operation of the work order is denoted by C_j.

During the timed Petri net marking evolution, start of o_{ji} corresponds to triggering of a related transition t_{ji}. Associated delay $f(t_{ji})$ corresponds to duration of o_{ji}. Following the firing rule, the transition output places are marked with tokens whose time attribute is set to $@(\rho_{ji} + f(t_{ji}))$ if ρ_{ji} denotes the moment of transition firing, i.e., the release time of o_{ji}. The generated timestamp equals the completion time of o_{ji}: $C_{ji} = \rho_{ji} + f(t_{ji})$.

Assuming the timed Petri net model of scheduling problem as described above, let $p_{WO\_j\_end} \subset P$ denote the j-th work order end place, i.e. the place that holds a token representing finished status of the work order. Let M_f denote the final marking reached after all the operations had been finished. If a token in $p_{WO\_j\_end}$ corresponds to finishing the last operation of work order WO_j then $M_f(p_{WO\_j\_end}) = 1@C_j$. Therefore the completion times can be read from $M_f(p_{WO\_j\_end})$: $C_j = M_f(p_{WO\_j\_end}) \subset TS_{MS}$.

4.3.1. *Makespan*

Makespan C_{max} is equivalent to the completion time of the last finished work order: $C_{max} = max(C_1, \ldots, C_n)$. Considering the above notation

$$C_{max} = max(M_f(p_{WO\_j\_end})), j = 1 \ldots n \tag{1}$$

4.3.2. *Total weighted completion time*

The sum of weighted completion times gives an indication of the inventory costs related to a schedule [16]. Given a final marking M_f the cost can be calculated as

$$\sum w_j C_j = \sum_{j=1}^{n} w_j M_f(p_{WO\_j\_end}) \tag{2}$$

4.3.3. *Tardiness*

If a set of due dates d_j is adjoined to the work orders, the tardiness of a work order is defined as the difference $C_j - d_j$ if positive, and 0 otherwise:

$$T_j = max(M_f(p_{WO\_j\_end}) - d_j, 0) \tag{3}$$

In contrast to objective measures, which are related to final marking, the initial marking can be used to specify release dates of work orders. If a token in $p_{WO\_j\_st}$ corresponds to the initial request of work order WO_j, and r_j is a corresponding release date then $M_0(p_{WO\_j\_st})$ should contain a token $1@r_j$.

5. A case study: Multiproduct batch plant

The applicability of our approach will be demonstrated on the model of a multiproduct batch plant designed and built at the Process Control Laboratory of the University of Dortmund. The demonstration plant is relatively simple compared to industrial-scale plants, but poses complex control tasks. A detailed description of the plant can be found in [17].

In the following a brief description of the plant will be given. From the data given in production management systems a timed Petri-net model is built. With the help of a simulator/scheduler using different scheduling rules, different schedules can be achieved. At the end the results for the given problem are presented and compared with the results achieved with other techniques.

5.1. Description of the plant

The process under consideration is a batch process that produces two liquid substances, one blue, one green, from three liquid raw materials. The first is coloured yellow, the second red and the third is colourless. The colourless sodium hydroxide (NaOH) will be referred to below as white. The chemical reaction behind the change of colours is the neutralisation of diluted hydrochloric acid (HCl) with diluted NaOH. The diluted HCl acid is mixed with two different pH indicators to make the acid look yellow if it is mixed with the first one and red when mixed with the second one. During the neutralisation reaction the pH indicators change their colour when the pH value reaches approximately 7. The first indicator changes from yellow to blue, and the second from red to green.

The plant consists of three different layers, see Figure 11. The first layer consists of the buffering tanks B11, B12 and B13, which are used for holding the raw materials "Yellow", "Red" and "White". The middle layer consists of three stirred tank reactors, R21, R22 and R23. Each reactor can be filled from any raw-material buffer tank. The production involves filling the reactor with one batch of "Yellow" or "Red" and then neutralising it with one batch of "White". The lower layer consists of two buffer tanks, B31 and B32, in which the products are collected from the middle layer. Each of them is used exclusively for "Blue" or "Green" and can contain three batches of product. The processing times of the plant are presented in Table 3. The system can be influenced through different inputs, pumps P1-P5 and valves V111-V311.

5.2. The scheduling problem

The plant provides a variety of scheduling problems. In our case we are dealing with a problem, where we have a demand to produce a certain amount of finished products. Also the starting times of every work order are given. Our task is to determine when raw materials must be available and when the overall production process will be finished. Our goal is to finish the production in the shortest time.

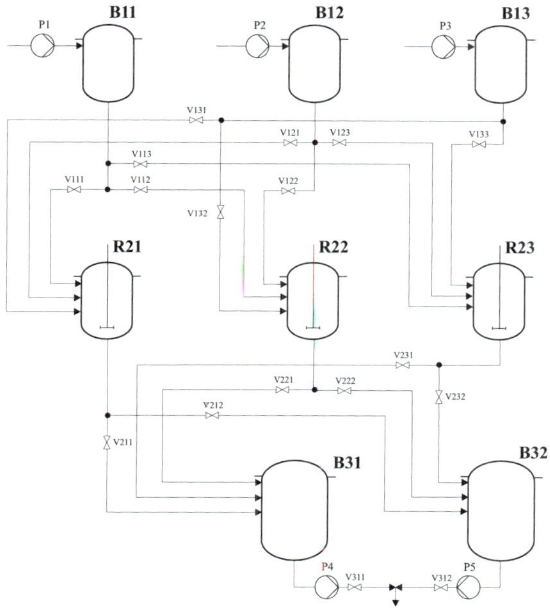

Figure 11. Multiproduct batch plant.

Process	Time(s)
Pumping 1 batch "Yellow" into B11	12
Pumping 1 batch "Red" into B12	12
Pumping 1 batch "White" into B13	12
Draining 1 batch "Yellow" into R21	15
Draining 1 batch "Red" into R21	11
Draining 1 batch "White' into R21	10
Draining 1 batch "Yellow" into R22	12
Draining 1 batch "Red" into R22	13
Draining 1 batch "White" into R22	9
Draining 1 batch "Yellow" into R23	12
Draining 1 batch "Red" into R23	14
Draining 1 batch "White" into R23	13
Draining 1 batch "Blue" from R21 into B31	12
Draining 1 batch "Green" from R21 into B32	13
Draining 1 batch "Blue" from R22 into B31	12
Draining 1 batch "Green" from R22 into B32	12
Draining 1 batch "Blue" from R23 into B31	12
Draining 1 batch "Green" from R23 into B32	12
Pumping 3 batches "Red" out of B31	30
Pumping 3 batches "Green" out of B32	30

Table 3. Processing times.

Work orders, given in table 4, illustrate the problem, where six batches of "Blue" (PB) and six batches of "Green" (PG) products have to be produced. It follows that we need six batches of "Yellow" and "Red" raw materials and twelve batches of "White" raw material.

Product	Code	Amount	Starting time
Blue	PB	6	0
Green	PG	6	0

Table 4. Work orders.

5.3. Structure of the production facility given in production management system

Data about the production process and its structure can be obtained from the production management information systems. These data can be presented in a form of a recipe and the formula as described in chapter 3.4.

There are two recipes available, which are specifying a sequence of operations needed to produce product "PB" and product "PG". They are given with tables 5 and 6.

	Operation	Duration	Resources
PB	Op10	–	BOM_B
	Op20 draining R2x in B31	12/12/12	[R_1](R21/R22/R23), B31
	Op30 pumping from B31	30	$(3 \times 1) \times$B31
Y	Op10 pumping Y in B11	12	[BY_1](B11)
	Op20 draining B11 in R2x	15/12/12	[R_3](R21/R22/R23), [BY_2](B11)
WB	Op10 pumping W in B13	12	[BW_1](B13)
	Op20 draining B13 in R2x	10/9/13	[R_2](R21/R22/R23), [BW_2](B13)

Table 5. Recipe of a product "PB".

	Operation	Duration	Resources
PG	Op10	–	BOM_ G
	Op20 draining R2x in B32	13/12/12	[R_ 1](R21/R22/R23), B32
	Op30 pumping from B32	30	$(3 \times 1) \times$B32
R	Op10 pumping Y in B12	12	[BR_ 1](B12)
	Op20 draining B12 in R2x	11/13/14	[R_ 3](R21/R22/R23), [BR_ 2](B12)
WG	Op10 pumping W in B13	12	[BW_ 1](B13)
	Op20 draining B13 v R2x	10/9/13	[R_ 2](R21/R22/R23), [BW_ 2](B13)

Table 6. Recipe of a product "PG".

To produce Blue product ("PB"), firstly operation *Op10* has to be carried out. This operation determines only that a sub-product, defined with formula "B", is needed. When this sub-product is ready, two more operations are needed. *Op20* gives information about draining the product into the buffer tank *B31* and *Op30* about pumping the final product out of that buffer tank. The fact, that buffer tank could not be emptied before three batches of sub-product "B" are poured in it, is described with this notation: $(3 \times 1) \times B31$.

In batch manufacturing situations when one task has to be executed with a (group of) resource(s), that were used to execute a previous task already are common. These resources are in our case labelled with an additional mark, i.e. code with serial number in square brackets is added in front of this resource(s). For example, this occurs in our case when one of the reactor is being used. Code $[R\_1]$ is assigned to the reactor (from a group of reactors $R2x$) which is needed for operation $Op20$ when producing product "B" and indicates that this resource can now be released. Note, that this resource was assigned with an operation where code $[R\_3]$ was used already (*Op10* of a sub-product "Y").

Formula given in Table 7 lists the raw materials needed to produce items "B" and "G". Item "B" represents a sub-product that is needed for operation *Op10* of a recipe "PB". The production of one item "B" requires one "Yellow" ("Y") and one "White" ("WB") batches (items). Each of these two items are produced with two operations. Note that some batch-specific precedence constraints exists. Operation *Op20* of item "Y" precede operation *Op20* of item "WB". The structure of item "G" is given in a similar way.

Item	Sub-item	Quantity	Preced. constr.
B	Y, Op10	1	0 0 0 0
	Y, Op20		0 0 0 1
	WB, Op10	1	0 0 0 0
	WB, Op20		0 0 0 0
G	R, Op10	1	0 0 0 0
	R, Op20		0 0 0 1
	WG, Op10	1	0 0 0 0
	WG, Op20		0 0 0 0

Table 7. Formula for the items "B" and "G".

5.4. Modelling

In this subchapter production process described previously is modelled with timed Petri nets. To build a model the algorithm from Chapter 3.5 is used. This model can later be used to schedule all the tasks, that are necessary to produce as much final products as required by work orders.

From work orders, given in table 4 it is recognised which and how much of each products are required. Let start with the procedure on building the Blue product ("PB"). When applying the first step of our algorithm, the PN structure shown in figure 12 is achieved.

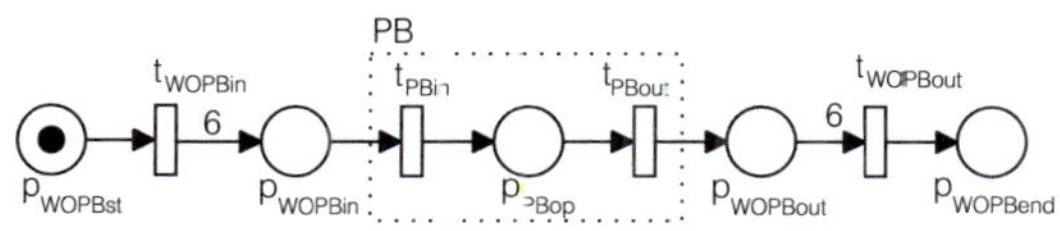

Figure 12. PN model of PB product.

In the second step, additional information are added into this model (framed part of figure 12). Data about all the details are gathered from recipe list of product "PB" (table 5). Information about emptying the buffer tank *B*31 (*Op30*) and draining the reactor *R2x* (*Op20*) are added. As operation (*Op20*) needs resources, that are used by previous operations, not all details are added yet at this place. A model, shown in Figure 13 is achieved.

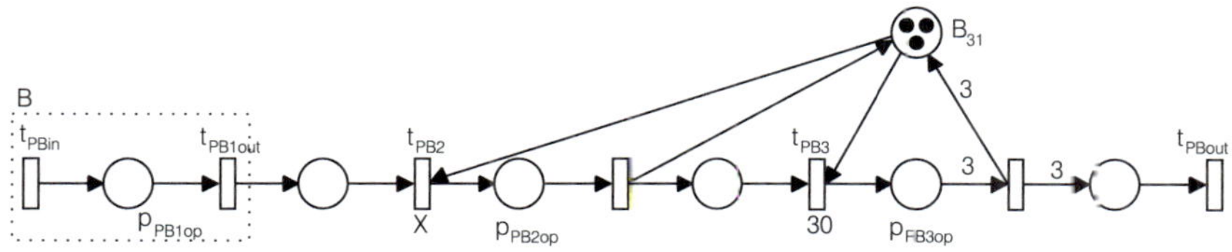

Figure 13. PN model of PB product.

Operation *Op10* (place P_{PB1op}) is defined with formula for item "B" (see table 7). It represents a mixing operation of two raw materials "Y" and "WB". Both sub-items are described with two operations, where precedence constraints are included as given with formula. Figure 14 shows how this formula information is modelled with Petri nets.

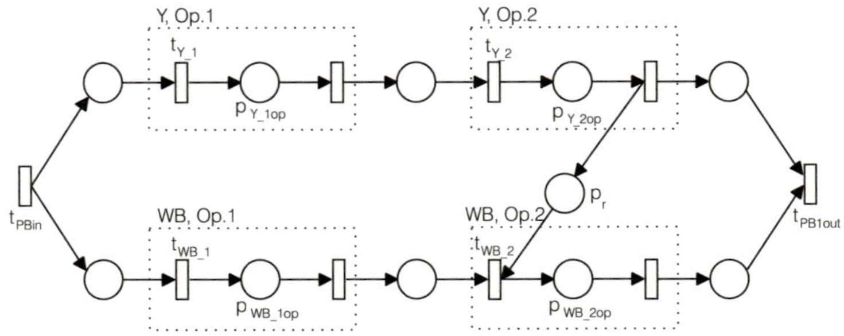

Figure 14. PN model of PB product with inserted BOM information.

In figure 15 some parts of a model given in figure 14 are simplified and information about the usage of rectors R_{2x} is added.

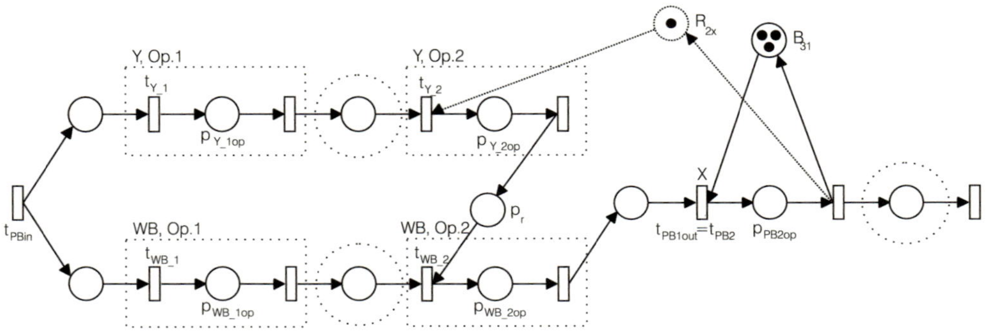

Figure 15. PN model of PB product.

As there are three possible reactors (R_{21}, R_{22} or R_{23}) that can be used to perform these operations this model is extended with the structure given in figure 16.

With this procedure a detailed timed Petri-net model of the production of the blue product ("PB") is obtained. The same procedure was performed to model also the production of green product ("PG"), and a Petri net model given in figure 17 is achieved.

5.5. Results

The resulting model was at the end verified using P-invariant analysis. We can find out eleven P-invariant, where eight of them refer to resources and three of them to the production routes.

In this way a Petri net model of a multiproduct batch plant was achieved on which different scheduling algorithms can be performed in order to obtain the most effective production. Petri-net simulation was used to evaluate different schedules of tasks that are needed to produce the desired amount of final products. Makespan was the performance measure of interest. The schedule allows an easy visualisation of the process and ensures that sufficient raw materials ("Yellow", "Red" and "White" batches) are available at the right time. It respects

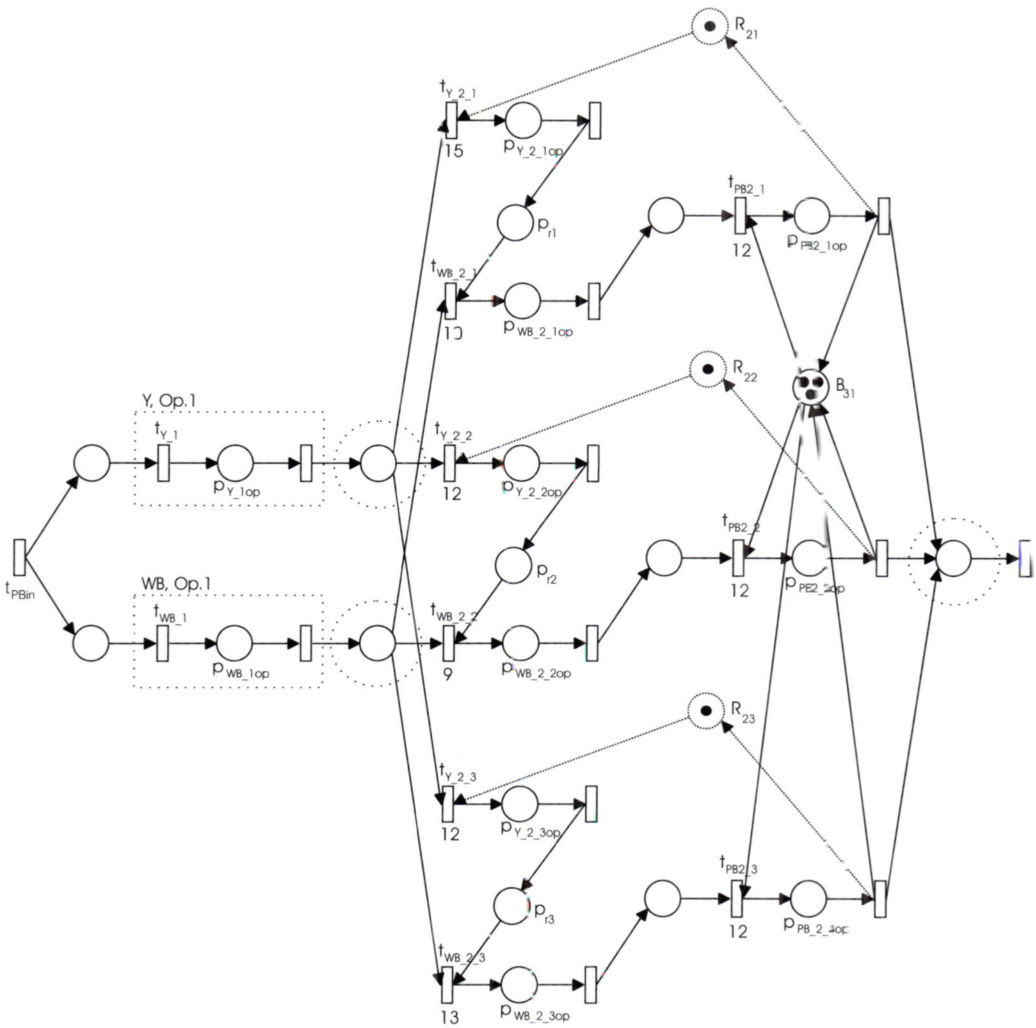

Figure 16. PN model of PB product.

all the production constraints and the duration of the whole process can be identified. A schedule of the batch process using SPT priority rule is given with Gantt chart (figure 18).

The results were compared with the results obtained using various algorithms and are presented in table 8.

Algorithm	Makespan
SPT rule	315s
LPT rule	331s
Branch and Bound ([17])	323s
MS Project ([3])	329s

Table 8. Results.

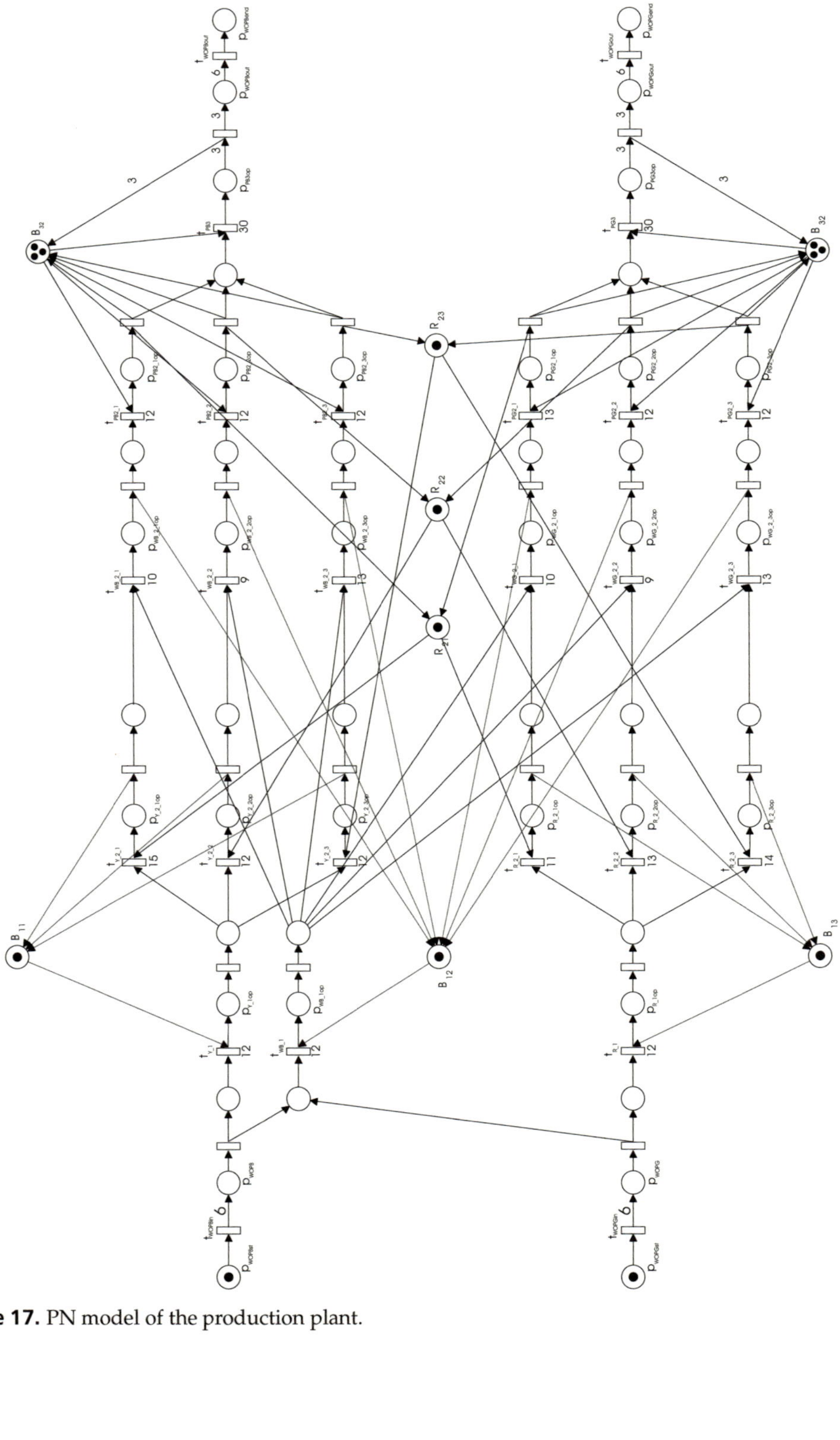

Figure 17. PN model of the production plant.

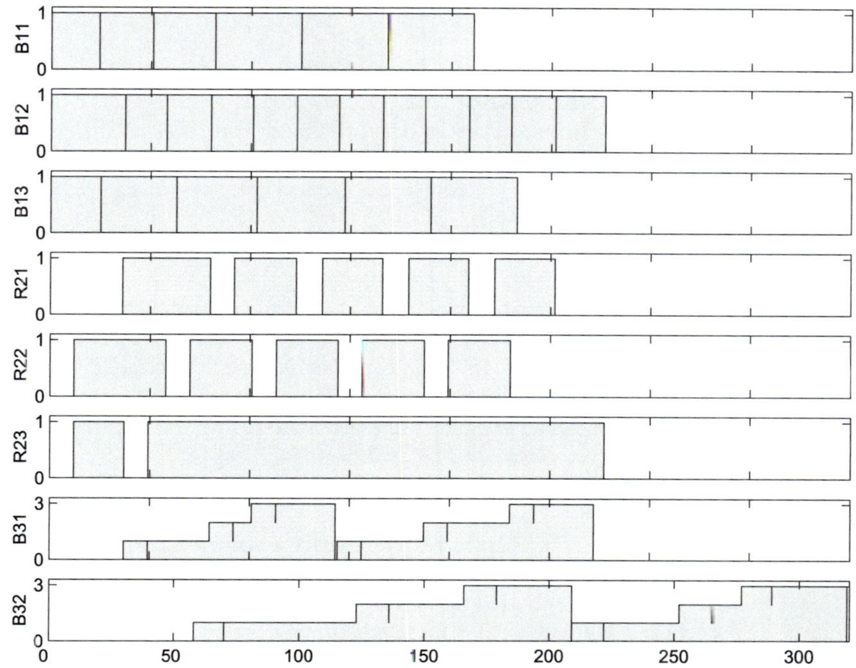

Figure 18. Production schedule.

6. Conclusion

A procedure for using existing data from production management systems to build the Petri-net model was developed. Timed Petri nets with the holding-duration principle of time implementation were used to model basic production activities. For the purposes of scheduling, different heuristic rules can be used within Petri net simulation. The applicability of the proposed approach was illustrated on a practical scheduling problem, where the data about the production facility is given with the formula and recipe. The model achieved with the proposed method was used to determine a schedule for production operations. The proposed method is an effective way to get an adequate model of the production process, which can be used to develop different analyses of the treated system, e.g. schedules.

Acknowledgements

The work was done in the frame of the Competence Centre for Advanced Control Technologies. Operation is partly financed by the Republic of Slovenia, Ministry of Education, Science, Culture and Sport and European Union (EU) - European Regional Development Fund.

Author details

Dejan Gradišar
Jožef Stefan Institute, Slovenia

Gašper Mušič
Faculty of Electrical Engineering, University of Ljubljana, Slovenia

7. References

[1] ANSI/ISA [1995]. *ANSI/ISA-88.01-1995 Batch Control Part 1: Models and Terminology (Formerly ANSI/ISA-S88.01-1995)*, ANSI/ISA.

[2] Bowden, F. D. J. [2000]. A brief survey and synthesis of the roles of time in Petri nets, *Mathematical and Computer Modelling* 31(10-12): 55–68.

[3] Gradišar, D. & Mušič, G. [2004]. Scheduling production activities using project planning tool, *Electrotechnical Review* 71(3): 83–88.

[4] Gu, T. & Bahri, P. A. [2002]. A survey of Petri net applications in batch processes, *Computers in Industry* 47(1): 99–111.

[5] Haupt, R. [1989]. A survey of priority rule-based scheduling, *OR Spectrum* 11(1): 3–16.

[6] Hillah, L., Kindler, E., Kordon, F., Petrucci, L. & Treves, N. [2009]. A primer on the Petri net markup language and ISO/IEC 15909-2, *Petri Net Newsletter* 76: 9–28.

[7] ISA [2008]. *ISA-TR88.95.01 Using ISA-88 and ISA-95 Together*, ISA.

[8] Jain, A. & Meeran, S. [1999]. Deterministic job-shop scheduling: Past, present and future, *European Journal of Operational Research* 113(2): 390–434.

[9] Jensen, K. [1997]. *Coloured Petri nets. Basic concepts, analysis methods and practical use*, Springer-Verlag, Berlin.

[10] Lakos, C. & Petrucci, L. [2007]. Modular state space exploration for timed Petri nets, *International Journal on Software Tools for Technology Transfer* 9: 393–411.

[11] Lee, D. & DiCesare, F. [1994]. Scheduling flexible manufacturing systems using Petri nets and heuristic search, *IEEE Trans. on Robotics and Automation* 10(2): 123–132.

[12] Méndez, C., Cerdá, J., Grossmann, I. E., Harjunkoski, I. & Fahl, M. [2006]. State-of-the-art review of optimization methods for short-term scheduling of batch processes, *Computers & Chemical Engineering* 30(6-7): 913–946.

[13] Mušič, G. [2009]. Petri net base scheduling approach combining dispatching rules and local search, *21st European Modeling & Simulation Symposium*, Vol. 2, Puerto de La Cruz, Tenerife, Spain, pp. 27–32.

[14] Nortcliffe, A. L., Thompson, M., Shaw, K. J., Love, J. & Fleming, P. J. [2001]. A framework for modelling in S88 constructs for scheduling purposes, *ISA Transactions* 40(3): 295–305.

[15] Piera, M. A. & Mušič, G. [2011]. Coloured Petri net scheduling models: Timed state space exploration shortages, *Math.Comput.Simul.* 82: 428–441.

[16] Pinedo, M. L. [2008]. *Scheduling: Theory, Algorithms, and Systems*, 3rd edn, Springer Publishing Company.

[17] Potočnik, B., Bemporad, A., Torrisi, F., Mušič, G. & Zupančič, B. [2004]. Hybrid modelling and optimal control of a multi product bach plant, *Control Engineering Practice* 12(9): 1127–1137.

[18] Silva, M. & Teruel, E. [1997]. Petri nets for the design and operation of manufacturing systems, *European Journal of Control* 3(3): 182–199.

[19] Tuncel, G. & Bayhan, G. [2007]. Applications of petri nets in production scheduling: a review, *The International Journal of Advanced Manufacturing Technology* 34(7-8): 762–773.

[20] Wijngaard, J. & Zijlstra, P. [1992]. MRP application the batch process industry, *Production Planning & Control* 3(3): 264–270.

[21] Wortmann, H. [1995]. Comparison of information systems for engineer-to-order and make-to-stock situations, *Computers in Industry* 26(3): 261–271.

[22] Yu, H., Reyes, A., Cang, S. & Lloyd, S. [2003]. Combined Petri net modelling and AI based heuristic hybrid search for flexible manufacturing systems-part II: Heuristic hybrid search, *Computers and Industrial Engineering* 44(4): 545–566.

[23] Zuberek, W. M. [1991]. Timed petri nets: definitions, properties and applications, *Microelectronics and Reliability* 31(4): 627–644.

Chapter 2

Specifying and Verifying Holonic Multi-Agent Systems Using Stochastic Petri Net and Object-Z: Application to Industrial Maintenance Organizations

Belhassen Mazigh and Abdeljalil Abbas-Turki

Additional information is available at the end of the chapter

http://dx.doi.org/10.5772/50229

1. Introduction

In Industrial Maintenance Company (IMC) a vast number of entities interact and the global behaviour of this system is made of several emergent phenomena resulting from these interactions. The characteristics of this system have increased both in size and complexity and are expected to be distributed, open and highly dynamic. Multi-Agent Systems (MAS) are well adapted to handle this type of systems. Indeed, the agent abstraction facilitates the conception and analysis of distributed microscopic models [9]. Using any holonic perspective, the designer can model a system with entities of different granularities. It is then possible to recursively model subcomponents of a complex system until the requested tasks are manageable by atomic easy-to-implement entities. In multi-agent systems, the vision of holons is someway closer to the one that MAS researchers have of Recursive or Composed agents. A holon constitutes a way to gather local and global, individual and collective points of view. A holon is a self-similar structure composed of holons as sub-structures. A hierarchical structure composed of holons is called a holarchy. A holon can be seen, depending on the level of observation, either as an autonomous atomic entity or as an organisation of holons (this is often called the Janus effect [12]). Holonic systems have already been used to model a wide range of systems, manufacturing systems [15, 16, 33], health organizations [32], transportation [2], etc. The different organisations which make up an IMC must collaborate in order to find and put in place various strategies to maintain different production sites. In order to honour its contracts, the IMC should handle the whole of its resources (human and material), ensure the follow up in real time the equipment in different production sites and plan actions to be executed. A part of the maintenance could be remotely achieved (tele-maintenance and/or tele-assistance [17], e-maintenance [13], etc.). Several constraints should be integrated in the process of strategy search and decision making before mobilizing operation teams. Concretely, the search for an efficient maintenance strategy should be found while taking into account the following constraints: (a) The urgency level of the maintenance task requested by a given production site, (b) A distance between mobile teams and production sites, (c) The estimated intervention duration, (d) The respect of the legal daily working time of maintenance crew, (e) Verification of the availability of the stored spare parts, (f) The reconstitution of new teams in view of the mentioned constraints.

To satisfy some of these constraints, we propose a formal holonic approach for modelling and analysis all the entities that constitutes an IMC. We use Holonic Multi-Agent Systems (HMAS) in which holons are agents that may be composed of agents for developing complex systems. To this end, we use an Agent-oriented Software Process for Engineering Complex Systems called ASPECS [8]. The process is considered by their authors as an evolution of the PASSI [3] process for modelling HMAS and it also collects experiences about holon design coming from the RIO (Role, Interaction and Organization) approach [11]. It is sufficient to say that the definition of the MAS meta-model adopted by the new process has been the first step and from this element all the others (activities, guidelines and workflow) have been built according to this guideline [4, 30, 31]. This meta-model defines the underlying concepts. A step-by-step guide from requirements to code allows the modelling of a system at different levels of details. Going from each level to the next consists in a refinement of the meta-model concepts. The objective of this work consists in consolidating the ASPECS methodology by using a formal specification and analysis of the various organizations and the interactions between them. This phase will facilitate the code production of organizations, roles and holons. In addition, it will be possible to test each organization, their roles and each holons independently. This type of analysis, will allow checking certain qualitative properties such as invariants and deadlock, as well as a quantitative analysis to measure the indicators of performance (cost of maintenances, average duration of the interventions, average time to reach a site of production, etc). In this chapter, our extended approach will be used to model and analyze an Industrial Maintenance Company (IMC). After a brief presentation of the framework, the maintenance activities in a distributed context are presented. ASPECS process and modelling approach will be introduced in section 3. Analysis and conception phase of this process and their associated activities are then described in order to identify the holonic IMC organisation. In section 4, first we present our specification formalism and second we assign an operational semantics to it. Additionally, we illustrate how to use the operational semantics as a basis for verification purposes. The specification formalism we intend to present combines two formal languages: Stochastic Petri Nets and Object-Z. Finally, Section 5 summarises the results of the chapter and describes some future work directions.

2. Industrial maintenance company distributed context

For economic and/or efficacy reasons, many companies are being implanted in geographically wide spread areas. Hence, many IMC are compelled to represent their organisations so as to meet efficiently the demands of their clients. Therefore this activity is among those witnessing a rise on the word market in spite of the economic moroseness (particularly large scale and multiple competence maintenance companies). In this distributed context, the maintenance activities are divided on two following structures: (a) Central Maintenance Teams (CMT) which realizes the process of reparation - corrective maintenance, (b) Mobile Maintenance Teams (MMT) which carries out inspections, replacement and several other actions on the various production sites.

To ensure the maintenance of several production sites, many teams specialized in various competence fields should be mobilized. Those in charge of handling these resources should overcome complex logistical problems thereby the need to develop aiding methods and tools for decision making to efficiently manage this type of organizations. Among the services proposed by an IMC, we can mention: (a) On site intervention, (b) Technical assistance via telephone or distance intervention, (c) The study and improvement of equipment, (d) Organisation and engineering, (e) Formation in industrial maintenance, (f) The search for and the development of new maintenance methods. The focus in this research is to find an efficient maintenance policies taking into account multiples alias. We propose a formal approach, based on the paradigm HMAS, to specify and analyze an efficient and adaptive IMC. As such, a specification approach based on HMAS to be a promising approach to deal with the unpredictable request of maintenance due to their decentralization, autonomy, cooperation features and their hierarchical ability to react to unexpected situation. For this specification, we use ASPECS methodology to identify holonic organization of a steady system and we combine two formal languages: Object-Z and Petri Nets for modeling and analysis specification of an IMC.

3. A holonic specification approach of an IMC

3.1. A quick overview of ASPECS process

The ASPECS process structure is based on the Software Process Engineering Metamodel (SPEM) specification proposed by OMG [25]. This specification is based on the idea that a software development process is collaboration between abstract active entities, called Roles that perform operations, called Activities, on concrete, tangible entities, called Work Products. Such as it was proposed by [4], ASPECS is a step-by-step requirement to code software engineering process based on a metamodel, which defines the main concepts for the proposed HMAS analysis, design and development. The target scope for the proposed approach can be found in complex systems and especially hierarchical complex systems. The main vocation of ASPECS is towards the development of societies of holonic (as well as not-holonic) multi-agent systems. ASPECS has been built by adopting the Model Driven Architecture (MDA) [25]. In [5] they label the three meta-models "domains" thus maintaining the link with the PASSI meta-model. The three definite fields are: (a) The Problem Domain. It provides the organisational description of the problem independently of a specific solution. The concepts introduced in this domain are mainly used during the analysis phase and at the beginning of the design phase, (b) The Agency Domain. It introduces agent-related concepts and provides a description of the holonic, multi-agent solution resulting from a refinement of the Problem Domain elements, (c) The Solution Domain is related to the implementation of the solution on a specific platform. This domain is thus dependent on a particular implementation and deployment platform.

Our contribution will relate to the consolidation of the Problem Domain and the Agency Domain. We propose a formal specification approach for analysis the various organizations and the interactions between them facilitating therefore the *Solution Domain*.

3.2. Requirements analysis

The analysis phase needs to provide a complete description of the problem based on the abstractions defined in the metamodel problem domain CRIO (Capacity, Role, Interaction and Organization). All the activities that make up this first phase and their main products can be identified. Indeed, this phase shows the different steps that can be used for the requirements since the description of the field requirements to capacities identification. It also shows how documents and UML diagrams must be constructed for each step. In the following, we present objective, description and diagrams for each step used in the requirements analysis phase.

3.2.1. Requirements domain description

The aim of this phase is to develop a first description of the application context and its functionalities. This activity aims to identify, classify and organize in hierarchy all functional and non functional requirements of different project actors. It must also provide a first estimated scope of the application as well as its size and complexity. In this work, the analysis approach adopted is based on the use case UML diagrams. To facilitate the analysis and reduce the complexity of the system studied, we decomposed the system studied into three modules: Mobile Maintenance Teams (MMT), Maintenance Policies (MP) and Maintenance Mediation (MM) which plays the role of mediator between the first two as shown in Figure 1. Let us now explain the role of each part of the system. The objective of "Mobile Maintenance

Figure 1. Set parts associated to the IMC

Teams" (MMT) is: (a) Receive maintenance requests from "Mediation Maintenance", (b) Planning for maintenance actions, (c) Execute maintenance tasks, (d) Generate maintenance report. The role of "Mediation Maintenance" (MM) is: (a) Receive maintenance requests of different production sites, (b) Diagnosing problems, (c) Classify problems, (d) Responding to customers, (e) Send request maintenance to MMT or MP, (f) Receive execution plans of maintenance from MT or MP if necessary. The objective of "Maintenance Policies" (MP) is: (a) Receive maintenance requests from "Mediation Maintenance", (b) Scheduling maintenance tasks, (c) Execute maintenance tasks, (d) Generate maintenance report, (e) Send report to maintenance "Mediation service", (f) Develop new maintenance methods, (g) Provide training maintenance.

As an example, we'll just show the use case diagram of different scenarios associated to the MMT (Figure 2.). Similarly, we can use identical approach to describe other roles and establish their use case diagrams.

3.2.2. Problem ontology description

First, problem ontology provides a definition of the application context and specific domain vocabulary. It aims to deeper understanding the problem, completing requirements analysis and use cases, with the description of the concepts that make up the problem domain and their relationships. Ontology plays a crucial role in ASPECS process development. Indeed, its structure will be a determining factor for identifying organizations. The ontology is described here in terms of concepts, actions and predicates. It is represented using a specific profile for UML class diagrams. The ontology of the IMC is described in Figure 3.

This ontology represents the knowledge related to the Mobile Maintenance Teams, Mediation Maintenance, Maintenance Policies, the different concepts that compose and the relationships between these components.

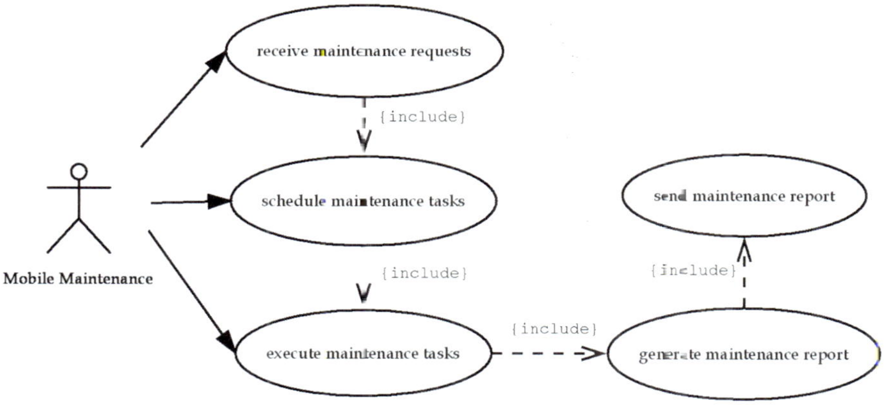

Figure 2. Use case diagram of Mobile Maintenance Teams

3.2.3. *Identifying organizations*

This action must establish a decomposition of the organizational system and define the objectives of each organization. Every needs identified in the first activity, has an associated organization incarnating the global behavior in charge to satisfy or to realize. Identified organizations are added directly to the use case diagram, in the form of packages including stereotyped use cases diagram that are responsible to satisfy. The Mobile Maintenance Teams organization can be decomposed into three sub-organizations: MMT Forwarding, Tasks Planning and Tasks Execution as shown in Figure 4.

The same process can be used to describe Mediation and Mobile Maintenance Teams organization. According to this decomposition, we can obtain organizational hierarchy of the IMC (Figure 5).

In this hierarchy, MMT Forwarder serves as an intermediary between Mediation Maintenance and Mobile Maintenance Teams. Similarly, CMT Forwarding is directly linked to both organizations Mediation Maintenance and Maintenance Policies.

3.2.4. *Identification of roles and interactions*

The context and objectives of each organization are now identified. The identification of roles and interactions aims to decompose the global behavior incarnated by an organization into a set of interacting roles. This activity must also describe the responsibilities of each role in satisfying the needs associated with their respective organizations. Each role is associated with a set of concepts in the ontology and generally a subset of those associated with his organization. Roles and interactions that constitute each organization are added to their class diagrams as described in Figure 6. A role is represented by a stereotyped class, and an interaction between two roles is represented by an association between classes of roles. Note also that in this figure, the link "Contributes to" means that an organization contributes in part to the behavior of a role at a higher level of abstraction.

3.2.5. *Description of interaction scenarios*

The objective of this activity is to specify the interactions between roles to induce higher level behavior. This activity describes the interactions between the roles defined within a given

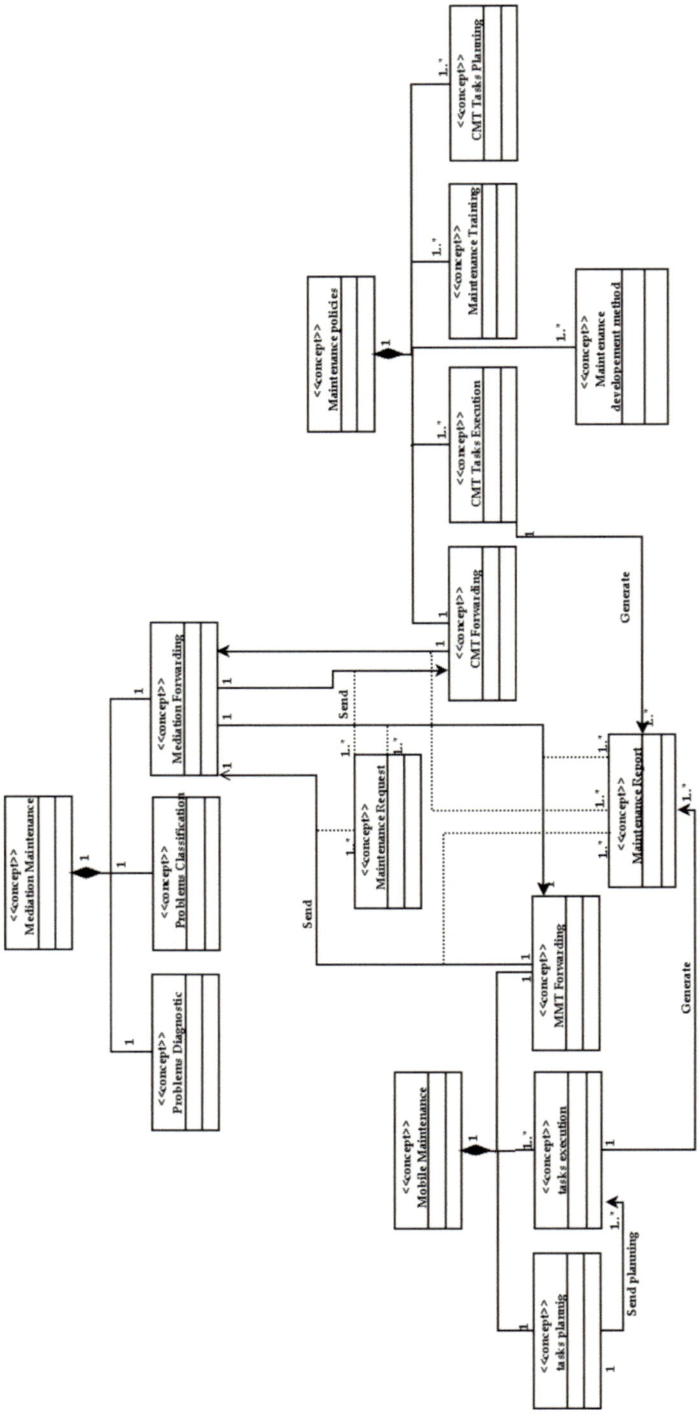

Figure 3. Ontology of the IMC system

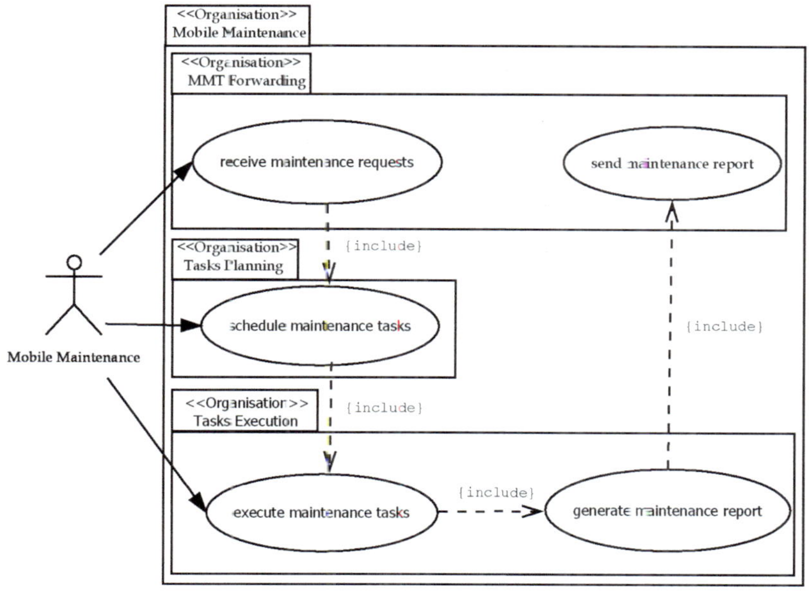

Figure 4. Mobile Maintenance Teams Organization

organization and specifies the means of coordination between them to meet the objectives of their organization. Consequently, each organization is associated with at least one scenario and it may involve defined roles in different organizations. Indeed, an organization usually requires information from other organizations at different level of abstraction. The scenarios detail the sequence of arrival or transfer of such information. Describing interaction scenarios is supported by a set of UML sequence diagrams. An example of interaction scenario associated with the organization IMC system is shown in Figure 7. This diagram above describes possible scenarios within the organization "Mobile Maintenance Teams". For each received request, "Planning Tasks" will schedule maintenance tasks and "Tasks Execution" executes maintenance tasks and finally generates a maintenance report. Scenarios of "Mediation Maintenance" and "Maintenance Policies" organization are not complicated and are not represented here.

3.2.6. Behavioral roles plans of organizations

The description of the behavior plans of roles specify the behavior of each role adapted with the objectives assigned to it and interactions in which it is implicated. Each plan describes the combination of behavior and sequencing of interactions, external events and tasks that make up the behavior of each role. Figure 8 shows the behavior plans of the roles that constitute the IMC organizations.

3.2.7. Identification of capacities

This activity aims to increase the generic behavior of roles by separate clearly the definition of these behaviors of their external dependencies organizations. It is particularly to refine the behavior of roles, to abstract the architecture of the entities that will play them, and ensuring

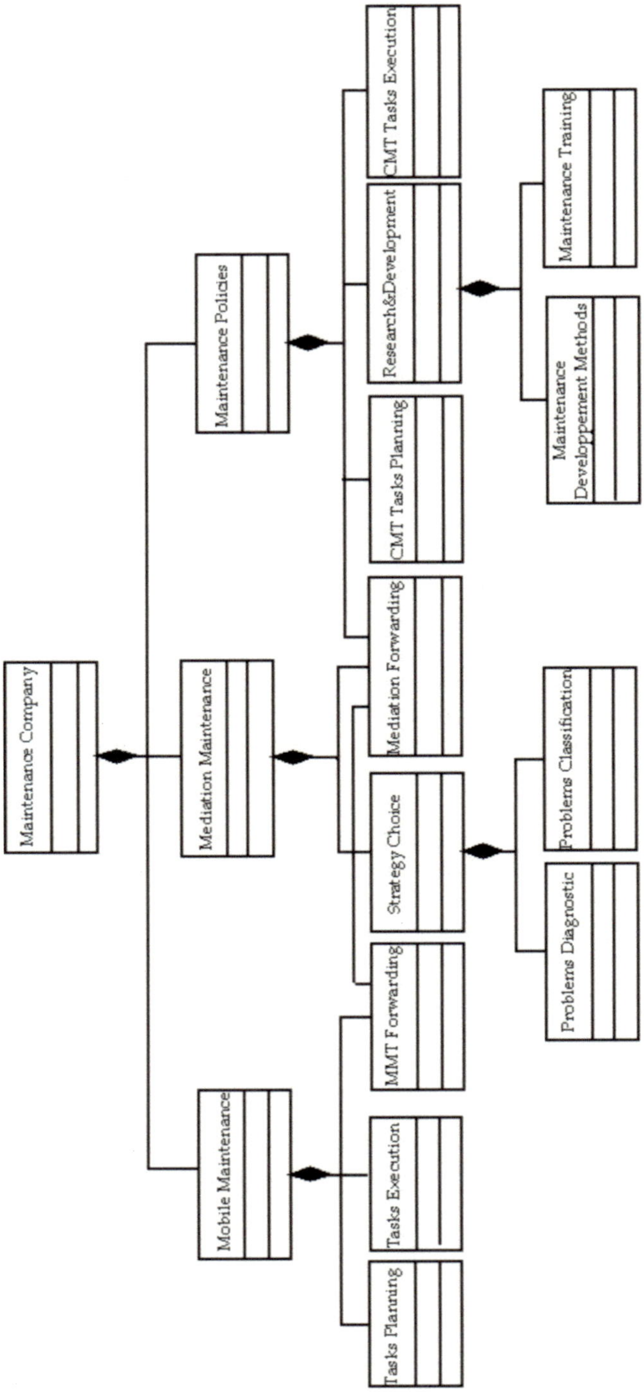

Figure 5. Organizational hierarchy of the IMC

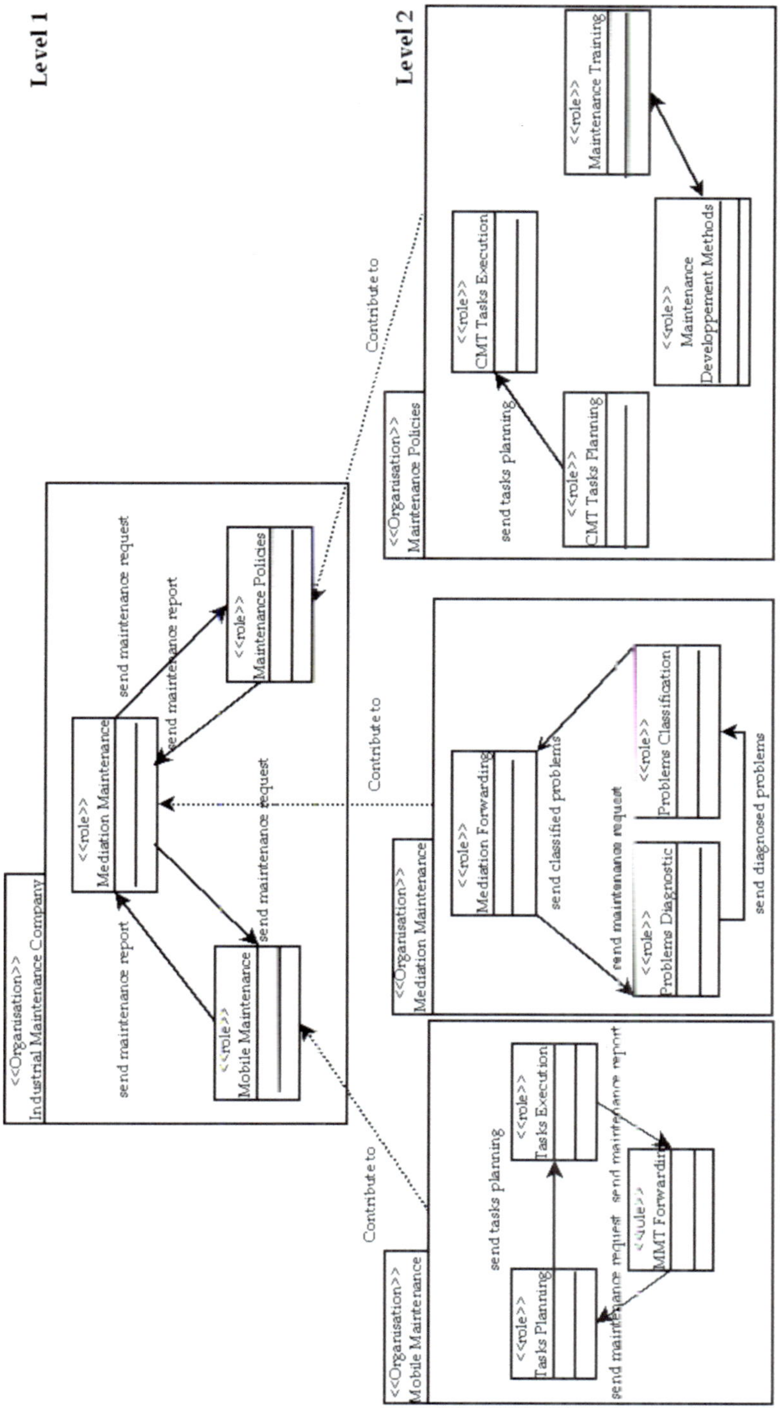

Figure 6. Description of a few roles and interactions of the IMC organization

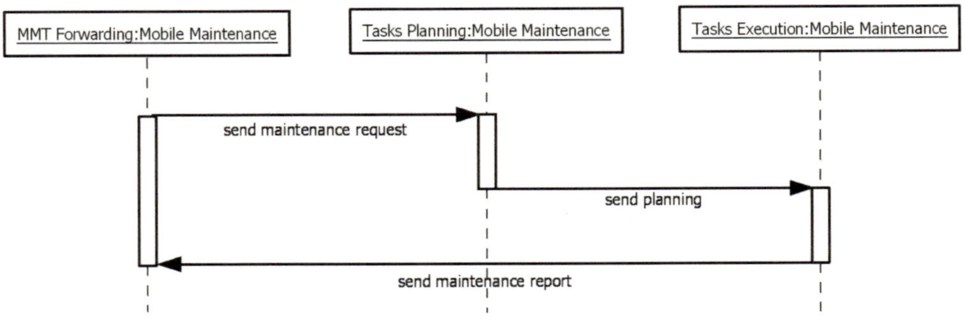

Figure 7. Description of interaction scenarios for MMT

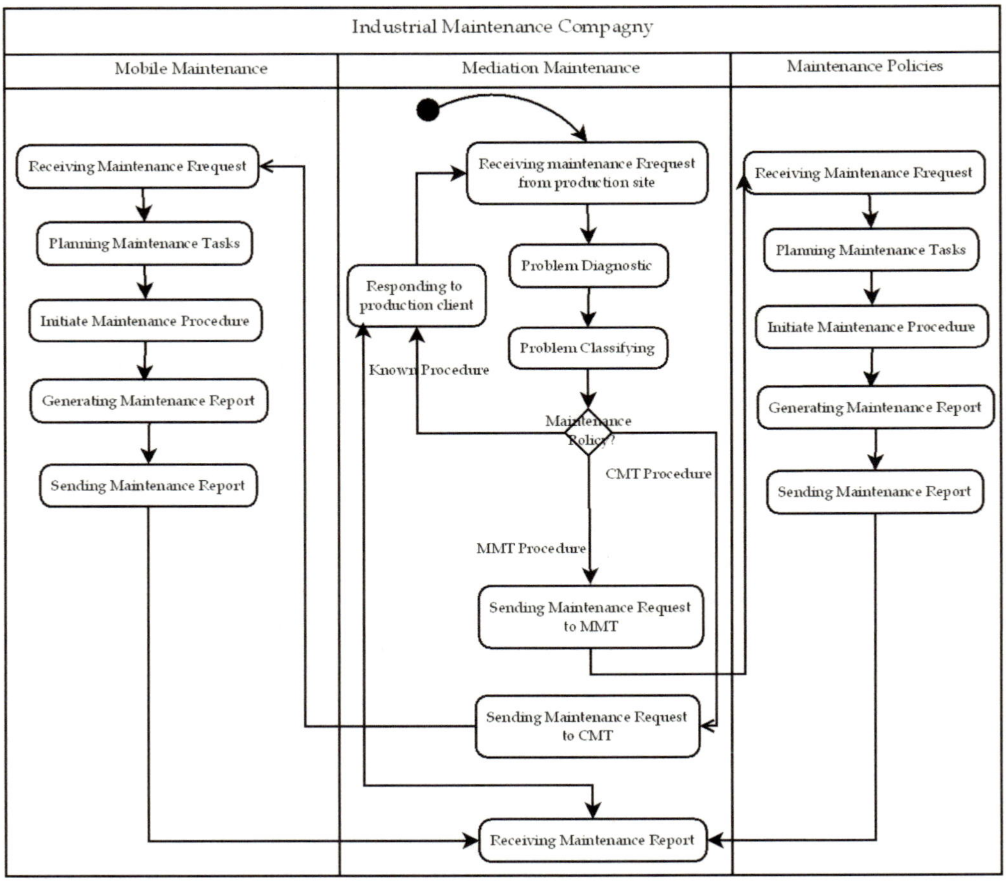

Figure 8. Behavioral roles plans description of the IMC organization

their independence from any external element not associated to them. The identification of capacity needs to determine the competences set required for each role. Capacities are added as stereotyped classes in UML class diagrams of the organizations concerned. In our case, we will identify the capacities required by the roles of the IMC organization (Figure 9).

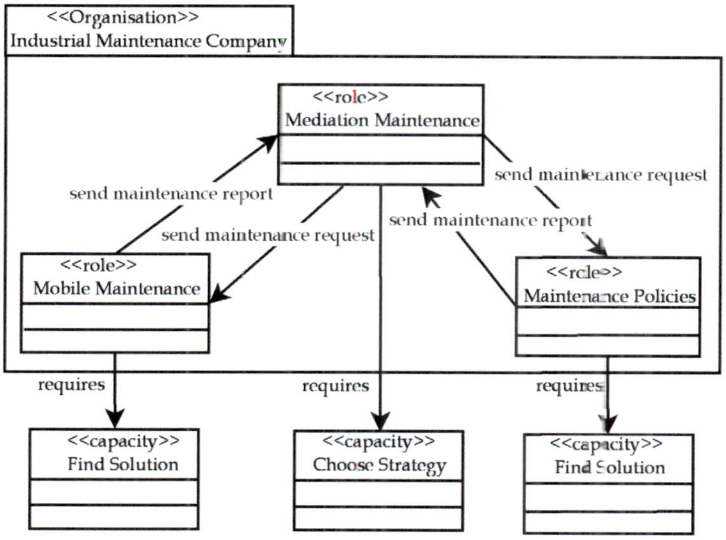

Figure 9. Identification of capacities required by the roles of the IMC organization

3.3. Holarchies design

At this stage of the process, all system organizations, their roles and associated communications are now fully described and specified. Holarchies design is the last activity of the design phase. It performs a global synthesis in which the results of all previous work are summarized and combined in one product. It is devoted to the agentification of the organizational hierarchy and the definition of the entities in charge of running it. Its objective is to define holons system and deduce the holarchy structure. To build the holarchy of the system, the organizations that compose the system are instantiated as groups. A set of holons is then created at each level, each playing one or more roles in one or more groups in the same level. Composition relations between super-holons and sub-holons are then specified in accordance with the contributions from the organizations defined in the organizational hierarchy. The organizational hierarchy is directly associated with the hierarchy of holons (or holarchy). The dynamics governing rules of holons, and the types of governance of each composed holon, are also described. All these elements are then synthesized to describe the structure of the initial holarchy system. To represent static structure of holarchy, the notation used is inspired from the "cheese board' diagrams proposed by [7]. However, it was adapted to better represent the holonic approach. The holonic structure of the IMC is presented in Figure 10.

At level 0 of the holarchy, we find three super-colons H1, H2 and H3, which play respectively Mobile Maintenance, Mediation Maintenance and Maintenance Policies in the group g0: Industrial Maintenance Company. It is reminded that this name means that the group g0 is an instance of the organization Industrial Maintenance Company. The super-holon H1 contains an instance of the Mobile Maintenance organization (g2 group), the super-holon H2 contains an instance of the Maintenance Mediation organization (g4 group) and the super-holon H3 contains an instance of the Maintenance policies (g8 group). The holon H7 of Mediation organization is also a super-holon strategy Choice who plays in the group g4 (Mediation Maintenance). This super-holon contains an instance of the organization strategy Choice (g5 group). Holon H11, of the Maintenance Policies organization, is also a super-holon which acts in the Research & Development group g8.

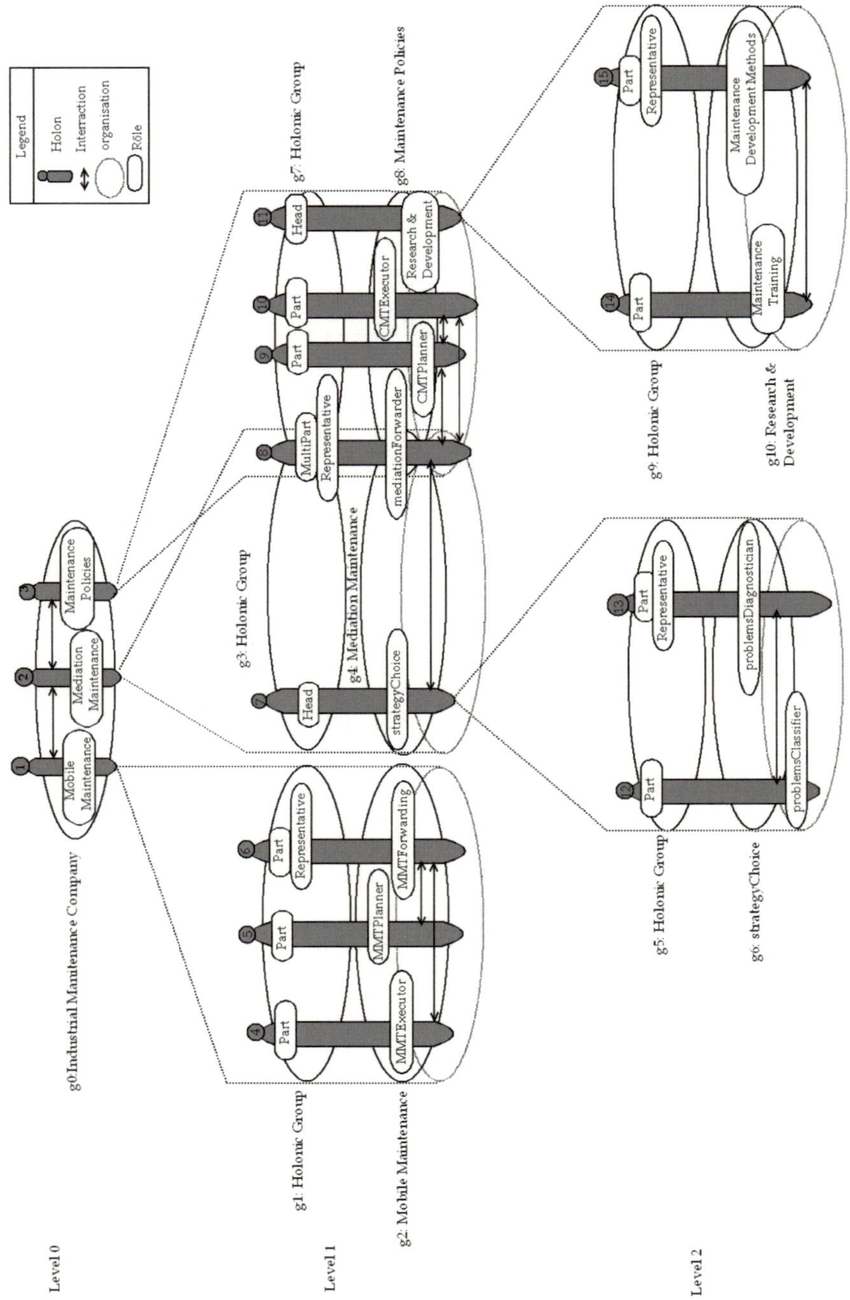

Figure 10. Holonic Structure of the IMC

This super-holon contains an instance of the Research & Development organization (g10 group). Holon H8 Playing Mediation role is named Multi-part role since sharing between Maintenance Policies and Maintenance Mediation organizations. In different organizations, interactions between holons are represented by arrows.

4. Heterogeneous formal specification and verification of holonic organisation based on SPN and object-Z language

In this section, we present an integration method of Stochastic Petri Nest (SPN) and Object-Z (OZ) by define coherent formalism called SPNOZ. This formalism is an extension of our formalism which was first defined and based on Z language [14] and GSPN called ZGSPN [19]. Petri nets (PN) are an excellent graphic formal model for describing the control structures and dynamic behaviour of concurrent and distributed systems, but Petri nets lack modelling power and mechanisms for data abstraction and refinement [22, 28].

OZ [6] is a formal notation for specifying the functionality of sequential systems. It is based on typed set theory and first order logic and thus offers rich type definition facility and supports formal reasoning. However, OZ does not support the effective definition of concurrent and distributed systems and OZ specifications often do not have an explicit operational semantics. The benefits of integrating SPN with OZ include: (a) a unified formal model for specifying different aspects of a system (structure, control flow, data types and functionality), (b) a unified formal model for specifying different types of systems (sequential, concurrent and distributed systems), (c) a rich set of complementary specification development and analysis techniques. Our approach consists in giving a syntactic and semantic integration of both languages. Syntactic integration is done by introducing a behaviour schema into OZ schema. The semantic integration is made by translating both languages towards the same semantic domain as shown in (Figure 11). An operational semantics is aimed to the description of how the system evolves along the time.

The semantic entity associated to a given specification can be seen as an abstract machine capable of producing a set of computations. Because of this, we believe that an operational semantics is a suitable representation for verification and simulation purposes. The approach consists in using a pre-existent model checker rather than developing a specific one. Both transition system models of a SPNOZ class can be used for verification purposes by model checking. In this work, the resulting specification is model-checked by using the Symbolic Analysis Laboratory (SAL) [23]. One of the reasons for choosing SAL is that it also includes verification tools and procedures that support from deductive techniques and theorem proving.

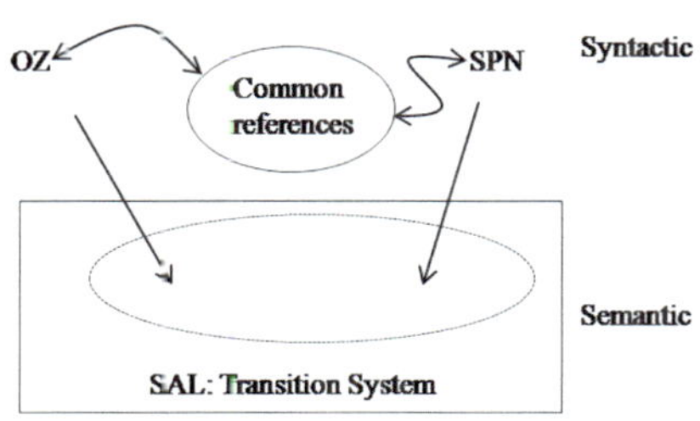

Figure 11. Composition formalisms Approach

4.1. Our syntactic integration method

To be able to build a multi-formalisms specification system, it is necessary to establish a relation of composition between partial specifications. Indeed, any whole of partial specifications must at one moment or another indicates or calls upon part of the system specified by another whole of partial specifications. As the process of composition that we use is based in type integration, the formalism of the Petri Nets is integrated into Object-Z formalism to specify schema with dynamic aspects. This composition can be expressed in several ways: sharing variables with the constraints expressed on the same entity or with translation into a single formalism for all formalisms used. SPN formalism is integrated into the formalism Object-Z to specify classes with behavioral aspects. This integration from the syntactically point of view, is based on a shared syntactic domain which consists of two parts: (a) A set of types and classes Object-Z specifying the main aspects of the SPN, (b) A function that converts a SPN in syntactic elements of the shared domain. This syntactic domain does not share instead of translation of Petri nets to Object-Z but is used to reference within the class Object-Z the elements of the Petri nets included. For instance, the approach presented here assigns to Object-Z the description of data structures and functions, and to the Stochastic Petri Nets the description of behavioral aspects. This section presents a simplified description of the operational semantics of SPNOZ [20] specification models. To express the aspects of SPN in Object-Z, we must have rules to translate a SPN into syntactic elements of the domain. For this, we use a function like relationship between PN and Object-Z scheme.

4.1.1. From PN to SPN

In [19], we proposed some syntactic integration of different classes of Petri Nets with abbreviations and extensions. We remind here that corresponding to SPN after recalling the semantic of ordinary PN. Inherently, the basic components of a Petri net, the concepts of marking and firing. Petri nets (PNs) introduced by C. A. Petri [27] were originally intended as a means for the representation of the interaction, logical sequence and synchronization among activities which are only of a logical nature [26]. A PN is a directed bipartite graph which comprises a set of places P, a set of transitions T, and a set of directed arcs defined by input and output incidence application (Pre and Post). Each place contains an integer (positive or zero) number of tokens or marks. The number of tokens contained in a place P_i will be called either $m(P_i)$ or m_i. The net marking, m, is defined by the vector of these markings, i.e., $m = \{m_1, m_2, \ldots, m_{|P|}\}$. The marking defines the state of the PN, or more precisely the state of the system described by the PN. The evolution of the state thus corresponds to an evolution of the marking, an evolution which is caused by firing of transitions, as we shall see. Generalized PN is a PN in which weights (noted by w, strictly positive integers) are associated with the arcs. When an arc $P_i \rightarrow T_j$ has a weight w, this means that transition T_j will only be enabled (or firable) if place P_i contains at least w tokens. When this transition is fired, w tokens will be removed from place P_i. When an arc $T_i \rightarrow P_j$ has a weight w, this means that when T_j is fired; w tokens will be added to place P_i.

The graph of markings (or reachability graph) is made up of summits which correspond to reachable markings and of arcs corresponding to firing of transitions resulting in the passing from one marking to another. The specification of a PN is completed by the initial marking m0. Since standard Petri nets did not convey any information about the duration of each activity or about the way in which the transition, which will fire next in a given marking, is actually selected among the enabled transitions, a lot of research effort has been made to exploit the modeling power of PNs. Most efforts were concerned with embedding PN models into timed environments. Stochastic Petri Nets (SPN) was introduced independently by [21, 24]. Both efforts shared the common idea of associating an exponentially distributed firing time with each transition in a PN, but differed in delays.

This random variable expresses the delay from the enabling to the firing of the transition. A formal definition of a SPN is given by the following 8-tuple [18]:

$SPN = (P, T, Pre, Post, C, Ih, R, m_0)$; where
$P = \{P_1, P_2, ..., P_n\}$ is a finite, not empty, set of places;
$T = \{T_1, T_2, ..., T_m\}$ is a finite, not empty, set of transitions;
$P \cap T = \emptyset$ is the sets P and T are disjointed;
$Pre : P \times T \longrightarrow N$ is the input incidence application;
$Post : P \times T \longrightarrow N$ is the output incidence application;
$C : P \longrightarrow N^+ \cup \{\infty\}$ is the capacity of places;
$Ih \subset \{P \times T\}$ is the set of k-inhibitor arcs;
$R : T \rightarrow \{\text{firing rate expressions}\}$ associated with timed transitions;
$m_0 = \{m_{01}, m_{02}, ., m_{0n}\}$ is the initial marking , with $m_{0i} = m_0(P_i)$.

Basically, a Stochastic PN may be considered as a timed PN in which the timings have stochastic values. The firing of transition T_j will occur when a time d_j has elapsed after its enabling and this time is a random value. In this basic model, usually called stochastic PN, the random variable d_j follows an exponential law of rate $\lambda_j \in \lambda(\lambda = \{\lambda_1, \lambda_2, \ldots, \lambda_{|T|}\})$. Noted that firing rates may depend on places markings, and in this case, firing rate expression is used. This means that: $Pr[d_j \leq t + dt | d_j > t] = \lambda_j.dt$. The probability density and the distribution function of this law are, respectively, $h(t) = \lambda_j e^{-\lambda_j t}$ and $H(t) = Pr[d_j \leq t] = 1 - e^{-\lambda_j t}$.

The average value of this law is $1/\lambda_j$ and its variance $1/\lambda_j^2$. It is clear, from the previous equations, that this law is completely defined by the parameter λ_j. A fundamental feature of an exponential law is the memoryless property, i.e.: $Pr[d_j \leq t_0 + t | d_j > t_0] = Pr[(d_j \leq t)$.

This property may be interpreted in the following way: let d_j be a random variable exponentially distributed, representing for example the service time of a customer. The service of this customer begins at time $t = 0$. If at time t_0 the service is not yet completed, the distribution law of the residual service time is exponential with the same rate as the distribution law of d_j. This property is important since it implies the following one.

Property: If transition T_j, whose firing rate is λ_j, is q-enabled at time t and if $q > 0$:

$$q \leq min_{i:P_i \in {}^0T_j} \left(m(P_i)/Pre(P_i, P_j) \right) < q + 1$$

${}^0T_j$ is the set of input places of T_j, then $Pr[\lambda_j$ will be fired between t and $t + dt] = q.\lambda_j.dt$, independently of the times when the q enabling occurred (simultaneously or not). The product $q.\lambda_j = \lambda_j(m)$ is the firing rate associated with T_j for marking m. It results from the previous property, that the marking $m(t)$ of the stochastic PN is an homogeneous Markovian process, and thus an homogeneous Markov chain can be associated with every SPN. From the graph of reachable markings, the Markov chain isomorphic to SPN is obtained. A state of the Markov chain is associated with every reachable marking and the transition rates of the Markov chain are obtained from the previous property. Note that there is no actual conflict in a SPN. For example, the probability that firing transition T_i occurs simultaneously with transition T_j is zero since continuous time is considered. One approach may be used to analyze a SPN consists of analyzing a continuous time, discrete state space Markov process (bounded PN). Let $T(m)$, denote the set of transitions enabled by m. If $T_k \in T(m)$, the conditional firing probability of T_k from m is: $Pr[T_k \text{ will be fired } |m] = \lambda_k(m)/\sum_{j:T_j \in T(m)} \lambda_j(m)$; the dwelling time $\lambda(m)$ follows an exponential law, and the mean dwelling time in marking m is $1/\lambda(m)$ with $\lambda(m) = \sum_{j:T_j \in T(m)} \lambda_j(m)$.

4.1.2. SPN expressed in OZ

This section discusses aspects of SPN expressed in OZ. These aspects can be obtained by successive refinements starting from formal definition of ordinary PN. Figure 12 shows the specification of a SPN expressed by the OZ syntax. The class schema SPN includes, from top to bottom, an abbreviation declaration and two free types [1] places and transitions. After that, comes an unnamed schema generally called the state schema, including the declaration of all class attributes. Next schema INIT includes a predicate that characterize the initial state of the class. The last schema defines specific operation of the SPN class. The first two lines in the predicates determine the input and output places of a transition. The third and fourth predicate verifies if the transition is firable (enable): input places contain enough tokens and output places have not reached their maximum capacity. The fifth verifies inhibitor arc between P and T authorizes the firing. Finally, the last two predicates express the marking change after firing timed transition. At the end, we specify the invariants of the SPN model. Now that we have expressed aspects of SPN in OZ, we must have rules for translating any PN of syntactic elements. For this we inspired from [11] using a function like relationship between PN and the types and patterns of the OZ domain. This function transforms any PN into OZ specification written with the schemas defined in the previous section. The function we call $\aleph$ is the basis of the mechanism of syntactic integration of our multi-formalisms. This function is defined inductively $\aleph$ as follows: (a) If ψ is an ordinary Petri Nets then $\aleph(\psi)$ is a PN scheme, (b) If ψ is a Stochastic Petri Nets then $\aleph(\psi)$ is a SPN scheme.

4.2. Syntactic integration based in SPNOZ formalism

4.2.1. The case of the IMC organisation

In order to illustrate syntactic integration of our approach, we specify a part of our Industrial Maintenance Company (IMC-Part). We have limited our work to the specification of the Mobile Maintenance Teams Organization which is a part of the holonic structure of the system studied with two MMT. We assume that the choice of the intervening teams depends on the following information: the availability of the MMT, the distance at which the MMT is from the production site and spare parts stock level of MMT. We suppose that our system can be in three different states: Mobile Team(i) Available (MTA(i)), Mobile Team(i) on Production Site (MTPS(i)) and Mobile Team(i) with Critical Level of Stock (MTCLS(i)). For this reason, we use a free or built type to describe the system state:

STATE_IMC-Part ::= MTA | MTPS | MTCLS.

SPN

place
transition

$Place : \mathbb{P}\ place$
$Transition : \mathbb{P}\ transition$
$Pre : place \times transition \rightarrow \mathbb{N}$
$Post : transition \times place \rightarrow \mathbb{N}$
$Ih : place \times transition \rightarrow \mathbb{N}$
$R : transition \rightarrow \mathbb{R}_{+}^{*}$
$C : place \rightarrow \mathbb{N}^{+}$
$R : transition \rightarrow \mathbb{R}_{+}^{*}$
$M_0 : place \rightarrow \mathbb{N}$
$M : place \rightarrow \mathbb{N}$

INIT

SPN

M=M0

Firing Transitions

Δ SPN
$T : Transition$
$P : Place$
$InP : transition \leftrightarrow place$
$OutP : transition \leftrightarrow place$
$D : \mathbb{R}_{+}^{*}$

$\forall T : Transition \cdot InP(\{T\}) = \{P : Place \mid P \mapsto T \in Pre \cdot P\}$
$\forall T : Transition \cdot OutP(\{T\}) = \{P : Place \mid T \mapsto P \in Post \cdot P\}$
$\forall P : InP(\{T\}) \cdot M\ P \geqslant Pre(P \mapsto T)$
$\forall P : OutP(\{T\}) \mid M\ P + Post\ T \mapsto P \leqslant C\ P$
$\forall P : InP(\{T\}) \mid P \mapsto T \in Ih \cdot M\ P < Pre(P \mapsto T) \wedge M'\ P = M\ P$
$\forall P : InP(\{T\}) \cdot M'\ P = M\ P - Pre(P \mapsto T) \wedge D = 1/(R\ T)$
$\forall P : OutP(\{T\}) \cdot D = 0 \Rightarrow M'\ P = M\ P + Post(T \mapsto P)$

#Place≠0
#Transition ≠0

Figure 12. Specification SPN based on OZ class syntax

The system to be specified is described by its state and following average times, estimated by the Maintenance Policies organization, such as: t_{DMMTi} the average time Displacement of Mobile Maintenance Team(i) to reach Production site, associated to transition T(i); $t_{RepMMTi}$ the average time for intervention of Mobile Maintenance Team(i), associated to transition T′(i); t_{SD} the time limit to which Maintenance Team must arrive on a production site; t_{RepCMT} the average time for Repairing the defective parts by Central Maintenance Team, associated to transition T″(i). Other parameters are introduced to supplement the specification such as: Ci the level stock of Mobile Maintenance Team(i); Cmin(i) the minimum level stock of Mobile Maintenance Team(i) (below this value, MMT(i) must re-enters to the IMC); *m* and *n* the initial state of stocks. Syntactically, SPNOZ specification IMC-Part is like OZ class, with the addition of a behaviour schema, which includes a SPN. The IMC-Part class on Figure 13 specifies a part of the IMC system. The class IMC-Part includes an abbreviation declaration and the behaviour schema which containing SPN. The state system is presented with class schema IMC-Part. In the initial state, all the MMT are available and the spare parts stock level is at its maximum (m and n). The initial state is presented with Init_IMC-Part schema.

In Figure 13, transitions in dotted lines (T1, T2, T"1 and T"2) are transition that interact with MMT forwarding and Tasks Planning organizations.

4.2.2. SPNOZ syntax

Formally, an SPNOZ class C is defined by giving a triple (V_C, B_C, O_C). The set V_C includes the variables of the class, as named in the state schema. B_C is the behaviour SPN and O_C is the set of operations of the class, the names of the operation schemas of the class. For the IMC-Part class, variables and operations are:

$$V_{IMC-Part} = \{S, t_{DMMT1}, t_{DMMT2}, t_{RepMMT1}, t_{RepMMT2}, t_{RepCMT}, t_{SD}, C1, C2, Cmin1, Cmin2\}$$

$$O_{IMC-Part} = \{SelectTeam1, SelectTeam2\}$$

Operation Select Team1 and Select Team2 can select a mobile team to involve on a production site. This selection will be made according to predefines criteria (availability of MMT, the average time Displacement of MMT and his spare parts stock level). If a team meets the different criteria, it will be chosen and its associated SPN model will be instantiated with different values for the new crossing rates $(\lambda_i, \lambda'_i, \lambda''_i)$. Otherwise MMT will not be selected and its associated model will be blocked (Pre(MTAi $\mapsto$ T_i)=∞) and second team will be solicited. Finally, Select Team1 and Select Team2 expressions translate the fact that if the level of the inventories of MMTi teams with reached critical level, it will not have the possibility of intervening on any site of production (probably it will turn over to IMC).

4.3. SPNOZ semantics

The semantic integration is made by translating both languages towards the same semantic domain. The semantic entity associated to a given class takes the form of a transition system, in two possible versions, timed or untimed. As the approach proposed in [10], rather thaninsert one language into the other produces their semantic integration by adopting a common semantic domain, i.e., transition systems. The semantic description of a SPNOZ class C consists in representing the set of computations that C can take. Computations are sequences of states subject to causal restrictions imposed by the structure and the elements of C. The state of class C, which we call a situation, is essentially a pair $s = (v, m)$. Symbol $v : V_C \rightarrow D$ denotes a estimation of all the variables of C, with D denoting the super domain where all the variables take values, each one according to its type. Symbol m represents a state configuration of the behavior Stochastic Petri Nets. A state configuration is a state that can be active multiple transitions. The initial situation $s_0 = (v_0, m_0)$, is determined as follows. The initial valuation v_0 is a valuation that satisfies the predicates of the INIT scheme. Variables that do not appear in the INIT scheme usually are given default values m_0 is the initial state configuration. The basic evolution stage is the situation change, called firing, which we describe now. Step $i + 1$ takes the system from situation i to situation $i + 1$ and is noted

IMC-Part

STATE_IMC-Part := S_MTA | S_MTPS | S_MTCLS

Behavior

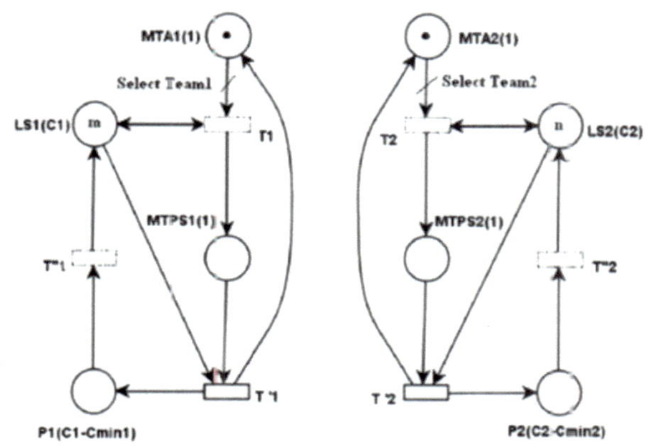

S : STATE_IMC-Part
Pre : place × transition → N
t_{DMMT1}, t_{DMMT2}, $t_{RepMMT1}$, $t_{RepMMT2}$, t_{RepCMT}, t_{SD}: Z+
C1, C2, Cmin1, Cmin2: N

$t_{RepMMT1} < t_{RepCMT}$
$t_{RepMMT2} < t_{RepCMT}$
$Cmin1 < C1 \leq m$
$Cmin2 < C2 \leq n$

Init_IMC-Part

S = S_MTA
C1 = m
C2 = n

Select Team1

Δ(S)

if $S = S\_MTA \wedge C1 > Cmin1 \wedge t_{DMMT1} \leqslant t_{SD}$
then $Pre(MTA1 \mapsto T1) = 1$ [T1 franchissable]
$\wedge \lambda_1 = \frac{1}{t_{DMMT1}} \wedge S' = S\_MTPS \wedge \lambda_1' = \frac{1}{t_{RepMMT1}} \wedge \lambda_1'' = \frac{C1 - Cmin1}{t_{RepCMT}}$
else $Pre(MTA1 \mapsto T1) = \infty$ [T1 infranchissable]

Select Team2

Δ(S)

if $S = S\_MTA \wedge C2 > Cmin2 \wedge t_{DMMT1} \leqslant t_{SD}$
then $Pre(MTA2 \mapsto T2) = 1$ [T2 franchissable]
$\wedge \lambda_2 = \frac{1}{t_{DMMT2}} \wedge S' = S\_MTPS \wedge \lambda_2' = \frac{1}{t_{RepMMT2}} \wedge \lambda_2'' = \frac{C2 - Cmin2}{t_{RepCMT}}$
else $Pre(MTA2 \mapsto T2) = \infty$ [T2 infranchissable]

$m \neq 0$
$n \neq 0$

Figure 13. IMC-Part system specification based on SPNOZ syntax

$(v_i, m_i) \overset{T(m_i)}{\rightarrow} (v_{i+1}, m_{i+1})$ where $T(m_i)$ is the set of transitions activated at step i. (marking m_i). The step occurs when at least one of the SPN's transitions is enable. To describe the situation transformation produced by a step, we adopt the formalism of transition systems, particularly the Mana and Pnueli notation style by means of predicates. With class C, we associate the transition system $Tr_{sys} = (V, \phi, T_{sys})$. Symbol $V = V_C \cup \{m\}$ represents the set of variables. Variable m takes value in the graph of markings. The states of the transition system Tr_{sys} are the situations of C, i.e., valuations of the variables in V. If s denote a state of Tr_{sys}, we simplify notation as follows: for all $v \in V, s[v]$ denotes the value of v at s. Symbol ϕ represents the initial state predicate. Any valuation of V that satisfies ϕ is an initial state of the system: s is an initial state if $s[\phi] = true$ (where $s[\phi]$ denotes the valuation of formula ϕ from the value of its variables in s). Symbol $T_{sys} = T_{B_C} \cup T_{O_C}$ represents the set of transitions of PNOZ class where T_{B_C} represent the set of PN shown in behavior scheme of the class and T_{O_C} represent the set of transition generated from the operation liste O_C of the class C. A transition $T_i \in T_{sys}$ defines an elementary change of the state of the transition system. Such a change is described by a transition relation: $\rho_i = V \times V' \rightarrow \{TRUE, FALSE\}$. To the set V of variable symbols we add the set V' of variable symbols decorated with a prime character ('). For any $x \in V$, an occurrence of symbol x in ρ_i represents the valuation of x in the source state of transition T_i and an occurrence of x' the valuation of x in the destination state of T_i. The couple of states (s, s') can be a couple (source; destination) of transition T_i if $\rho_i(s[V], s'[V']) = true$, where $s[V]$ denotes the valuation of unprimed variables in the state s and $s'[V']$ the valuation of primed variables in state s'.

Concerning Timed transition system (TTS) associated to the SPNOZ class C, from the transition system the transition system $Tr_{sys} = (V, \phi, T_{sys})$ previously defined, we define $TTS_{sys} = (V^t, \phi^t, T^t_{sys})$ obtained as follows: (a) Augment variables set V with time variable t;$V^t = V \cup \{t\}$ which takes value in some totally ordered set with a lowest bound. Typically, $\mathbb{N}$ (the natural integers) is used to model discrete time and $\mathbb{R}^+$ to model dense time, (b) Let $\phi^t = \phi \wedge (t = 0)$, (c) For each transition $T_i \in T^t_{sys}$, add a variable that represents the real-time in the system. Next, we define the set of computations that a timed transition system can yield, which is to be considered as the timed semantics of a SPNOZ classes. We note $m_i \overset{T_i}{\rightarrow} m_{i+1}$ to assert that the transition system goes from state m_i to state m_{i+1} by means of transition T_i and take time $t = 1/\lambda_i$, (with λ_i : firing rate of T_i). We define a finite macro-step to be a finite succession $m_0, m_1, \ldots, m_n$ of state that: (a) $m_0 \models \phi^t$, (b) For every state m_i of TTS_{sys}, there is a transition $T_i \in T^t_{sys}$ such that $m_i \models Pre(T_i)$ and $m_i \models Post(T_i)$ and $t = 1/\lambda_i$.

In [19], more details about the full semantic integration is presented.

4.4. Validation and simulation of SPNOZ specification

SALenv contains a symbolic model checker called sal-smc allows users to specify properties in Linear Temporal Logic (LTL), and Computation Tree Logic (CTL). However, in the current version, SALenv does not print counter examples for CTL properties. When users specify an invalid property in LTL, a counter example is produced. LTL formulas state properties about each linear path induced by a module. For instance, the formula G(p⇒F(q)) states that whenever p holds, q will eventually hold. The formula G(F(p)) states that p often holds infinitely. The example illustrated by Figure 14 shows some properties of the system written in the form of theorems with the LTL and CTL formulas. The SAL language includes the clause theorem for declaring that a property is valid with respect to a modeled system by a

```
IMC: CONTEXT =
BEGIN

        Time : Real;
         Vals : TYPE = [0 .. n];
        STATE_IMC-Part : TYPE = {S_MTA, S_MTPS, S_MTCLS};
        IMC-Part : MODULE =
        BEGIN
             INPUT tDMMT1 ,tDMMT2, tRepMMT1, t RepMMT2, tRepCMT1, tRepCMT2, tSD : Time
             INPUT  C1, C2, Cmin1, Cmin2, n, m : INTEGER
             INPUT Select Team1, Select Team2 : BOOLEAN
             OUTPUT  S : STATE_IMC-Part
             OUTPUT  λ1, λ2 : Time
            OUTPUT  M : ARRAY[MTA1, LS1, P1, MTPS1, MTCLS1, MTA2,
LS2, P2, MTPS2, MTCLS2] OF Vals
             LOCAL Trans_sys IN {T1, T'1, T''1,  T2, T'2, T''2}

INITIALIZATION
       S = S_MTA,
       M0 = {1, m, 0, 0, 1, n, 0, 0},
       C1 = m,
       C2 = n,
       t RepMMT1 < tRepCMT , t RepMMT2 < tRepCMT , Cmin1 < C1 ≤ m, Cmin2 < C2 ≤ n

     TRANSITION  [
        Pre (S : STATE_IMC-Part , T : Trans_sys ) : INTEGER
       t_Select Team1 :
            IF  (S  =  S_MTA   AND   M[MTA1]  =  1  AND   C1  >  Cmin1  AND
tDMMT1≤ tSD )
            THEN
                S'  =  S_MTPS   AND  M[MTPS1]  =  1  AND  λ1 = 1/tDMMT1  AND
λ'1 = 1/tRepMMT1  AND  λ''1 = (C1−Cmin1)/tRepCMT1
             ELSE
                 Pre (S_MTA , T1) = ∞
            ENDIF
       []

    t_Select Team2 :
          IF (S= S_MTA AND  M[MTA2]= 1 AND  C2 > Cmin2  AND tDMMT1≤
tSD )
            THEN
               S'  =  S_MTPS   AND  M[MTPS 2]=  1  AND   λ2 = 1/tDMMT2  AND
λ'2 = 1/tRepMMT2  AND  λ''2 = (C2−Cmin2)/tRepCMT2
            ELSE
               Pre (S_MTA , T2) = ∞
            ENDIF
   END;

       %------------------------
       % system properties
       %-----------------------
      th1 : THEOREM  IMC-Part|- G(S = S_MTA AND  M[LS1] > Cmin1  AND
λ1 = (1/ tDMMT1) AND  t_Select Team1 => F( S' = S_MTPS));
     Liveness : THEOREM  IMC-Part |- G(M[LS1] /= 0 AND M[LS2] /=0);
     Boundedness : THEOREM  IMC-Part |- G(M[MTA1]+M[MTPS1]=1 AND
M[P1]+M[LS1]= m);

END
```

Figure 14. SAL CONTEXT associated to the SPNOZ IMC

CONTEXT. The first theorem th1 can be interpreted as whenever the system in state S_MTA and Select Team1 is true, transition holds, the system will probably in S_MTPS state. The following command line is used:

./sal-smc IMC th1
proved.

SALenv also contains a Bounded Model Checker called sal-bmc. This model checker only supports LTL formulas, and it is basically used for refutation, although it can produce proofs by induction of safety properties. The following command line is used:

./sal-bmc IMC th1
no counterexample between depths [0, 10]

Remark: The default behavior is to look for counterexample up to depth 10. The option -depth=<num> can be used to control the depth of the search. The option -iterative forces the model checker to use iterative deepening, and it is useful to find the shortest counterexample for a given property. Before proving a liveness property, we must check if the transition relation is total, that is, if every state has at least one successor. The model checker may produce unsound result when the transition relation is not total. The totality property can be verified using the sal-deadlock-checker. The following command line is used:

/sal-deadlock-checker IMC IMC-Part
Ok (module does NOT contain deadlock state).

The liveness theorem can be interpreted as always, the quantity of stock of piece is not null in the two teams. Now, we use sal-smc to check the property liveness with the following command line:

./sal-smc -v 3 IMC-Part liveness
proved.

The Boundedness theorem can be interpreted as always, the state space system is bounded. Now, we use sal-bmc to check the property Boundedness with the following command line:

./sal-bmc IMC Boundedness
no counterexample between depths [0, 10]

5. Conclusion

In this chapter we showed that HMAS is well adapted to analyse and design an IMC holarchy. The meta-model utilized can be exploited in the implantation stage with the advantage of having formally validated its structure and its behaviour by using Heterogeneous formal specification based on Stochastic Petri Nets and Object-Z. For the moment, we are now refining our SPNOZ tool to establish a semantic-based in Markov chain isomorphic to SPN. This semantic seems best adapted to be transformed into Transition systems. Our future works will focus on a finer analysis of this system type and on a formal modelling of the various scenarios associated with the analysis stage. The notion of multi-views should be integrated. Indeed, the search for and the choice of strategy depends on the point of view of the person or the team required to take decisions according not only the constraints linked to the system but also to their environments. At the same time, it will be interesting to use HMAS which proposes multi-view holarchy introduced in [29] and consequently integrate it in the different existing meta-models.

Author details

Belhassen Mazigh
Faculty of sciences, Department of Computer Sciences, 5000, Monastir, Tunisia

Abdeljalil Abbas-Turki
Laboratoire SET, Université de Technologie de Belfort Montbéliard, Belfort, France

6. References

[1] Arthan, R.D. (1992) On Free Type Definitions in Z, Published in the Proceedings of the 1991 Z User Meeting, Springer Verlag.
[2] Burckert, H.-J., Fischer, K., Vierke, G. (1998) Transportation scheduling with holonic MAS-the teletruck approach, Proceedings of the Third International Conference on Practical Applications of Intelligent Agents and Multi-agent. pp. 577-590.
[3] Cossentino, M. (2005) From requirements to code with the PASSI methodology, In B. Henderson-Sellers & P. Giorgini (Eds.), Agent-oriented methodologies, Hershey, PA, USA: Idea Group Publishing, Chap. IV, pp. 79-106.
[4] Cossentino, M., Gaglio, S., Garro, A., Seidita, V. (2007) Method fragments for agent design methodologies: From standardization to research, In international Journal on Agent Oriented Software Engineering, 1(1), pp. 91-121.
[5] Cossentino, M., Gaud, N., Hilaire, V., Galland, S., Koukam, A. (2010) ASPECS: an agent-oriented software process for engineering complex systems How to design agent societies under a holonic perspective, Auton Agent Multi-Agent System.
[6] Duke, R., Rose, G., Smith, G. (1995) Object-Z: A specification Language Advocated for Description of Standards, Technical report Software Verification Research Center, Departement of Computer Science, University of Queensland, AUSTRALIA.
[7] Ferber, J., Gutknecht, O., Michel, F. (2004) From agents to organizations: an organizational view of multi-agent systems, In Agent-Oriented Software Engineering 4th International Workshop, volume 2935 of LNCS, Melbourne, Australia, Springer Verlag, pp. 214-230.
[8] Gaud, N. (2007) Systèmes Multi-Agents Holoniques : de l'analyse à l'implantation, Ph.D. thesis, Université de Technologie de Belfort-Montbéliard, France.
[9] Gruer, J.P., Hilaire, V., Koukam, A. (2001) Multi-agent approach to modeling and simulation of urban transportation systems, IEEE International Conference on Systems, Man, and Cybernetics, IEEE 4, 2499-2504.
[10] Gruer, P., Hilaire, V., Koukam, A., Rovarini, P. (2003) Heterogeneous formal specification based on Object-Z and statecharts: semantics and verification, In journal Systems and Software, Elsevier Science.
[11] Hilaire, V., Koukam, A., Gruer, P., Müller, J.-P. (2000) Formal specification and prototyping of multi-agent systems, In A. Omicini, R. Tolksdorf, & F. Zambonelli (Eds.), ESAW, LNAI (No. 1972), Springer Verlag.
[12] Koestler, A. (1967) The Ghost in the Machine, Hutchinson.
[13] Lebold, M., Thurston, M. (2001) Open standards for Condition-Based Maintenance and Prognostic Systems, In Proceedings Of 5th Annual Maintenance and Reliability Conference, Gatlinburg, USA.
[14] Lightfoot, D. (2000) Formal Specification Using Z, Palgrave MacMillan, United Kingdom, 2nd Revised edition.

[15] Maturana, F. (1997) Metamorph: an adaptive multi-agent architecture for advanced manfacturing systems, Ph.D. thesis, The University of Calgary.
[16] Maturana, F., Shen, W., Norrie, D. (1999) Metamorph: An adaptive agent-based architecture for intelligent manufacturing, International Journal of Production Research 37 (10) (1999) 2159-2174.
[17] Mayer, G., Wan Abdullah, Z., Lim Ai, M. (2003) Tele-Maintenance for Remote Online Diagnostic and Evaluation of Problems at Offshore Facilities, Sarawak, SPE Asia Pacific Oil and Gas Conference and Exhibition, Jakarta, Indonesia.
[18] Mazigh, B. (1994) Modeling and Evaluation of Production Systems with GSPN, Ph.D. thesis, Institut Polytechnique de Mulhouse, France.
[19] Mazigh, B. (2006) ZGSPN: Formal specification using Z and GSPN, Technical Report MAZ-SPEc-01-06, Department of Computer Science, University of Monastir, Tunisia.
[20] Mazigh, B., Garoui, M., Koukam, A. (2011) Heterogeneous Formal specification of a Holonic MAS methodology based on Petri Nets and Object-Z, In Proceedings of the Federated Conference on Computer Science and Information Systems, 5th International Workshop on Multi-Agent Systems and Simulation, IEEE Computer Society Press,Pologne, pp. 661-668.
[21] Molloy, M. K. (1981) On the Integration of Delay and Throughput Measures in Distributed Processing Models, Ph.D. thesis, UCLA, Los Angeles, CA, USA.
[22] Natarajan, S. (1989) Petri nets: Properties, analysis and applications, Computer Science Laboratory SRI International, Proceedings of IEEE, 77(4).
[23] Natarajan, S. (2000) Symbolic Analysis of Transition Systems, Computer Science Laboratory SRI International.
[24] Natkin, S. (1980) Réseaux de Petri Stochastiques, Ph.D. thesis, CNAM, Paris.
[25] Object Management Group. (2003) MDA guide, v1.0.1, OMG/2003-06-01.
[26] Peterson, J. L. (1982) Petri Net Theory and the Modeling Systems, Prentice-Hall, Englewood Cliffs, NJ.
[27] Petri, C. A. (1966) Communication with Automata, Ph.D. thesis, Technical Report RADC-TR-65-377, New York.
[28] Reisig, W. (1985) Petri Nets an Introduction, EATCS Monographs on Theoretical Computer Science 4.
[29] Rodriguez, S., Hilaire, V., Koukam, A. (2007) Towards a holonic multiple aspect analysis and modeling approach for complex systems: Application to the simulation of industrial plants, In journal Simulation Modelling Practice and Theory 15, pp. 521-543.
[30] Seidita, V., Cossentino, M., Hilaire, V., Gaud, N., Galland, S., Koukam, A (2009) The metamodel: A starting point for design processes construction, In international Journal of Software Engineering and Knowledge Engineering (IJSEKE).
[31] SPEM. (2007) Software process engineering metamodel specification, v2.0, final adopted specification, ptc/07-03-03, Object Management Group.
[32] Ulieru, M., Geras, A. (2002) Emergent holarchies for e-health applications: a case in glaucoma diagnosis, IECON 02 28th Annual Conference of the Industrial Electronics Society, IEEE, vol. 4, pp. 2957-2961.
URL: people.mech.kuleuven.ac.be/jwyns/phd/order.html
[33] Wyns, J. (1999) Reference architecture for holonic manufacturing systems-the key to support evolution and reconfiguration, Ph.D. thesis, Katholieke Universiteit Leuven.

Chapter 3

A Computationally Improved Optimal Solution for Deadlocked Problems of Flexible Manufacturing Systems Using Theory of Regions

Yen-Liang Pan

Additional information is available at the end of the chapter

http://dx.doi.org/10.5772/50873

1. Introduction

While competing for a finite number of resources in a flexible manufacturing system (FMS), e.g., robots and machines, each part has a particular operational flow that determines the order in which such resources are needed. However, such competition for shared resources by concurrent job processes can lead to a system deadlock. It occurs when parts are blocked waiting for shared resources held by others that will never be granted. Its related blocking phenomena often incur unnecessary overhead cost, e.g., a long downtime and low utilization rate of some critical and expensive resources, possibly leading to a catastrophic outcome in some highly automated FMS. Therefore, an efficient deadlock control policy must be developed to ensure that deadlocks do not occur. Having received considerable attention in literature, deadlock is normally prevented by using an offline computational mechanism to control the resource requests in order to avert deadlocks. Fanti and Zhou[1] introduce three fundamental methods (i.e. prevention, detection and avoidance) to solve the deadlock problems. Deadlock prevention aims to impose system constraints to prevent a deadlock. Importantly, deadlock prevention algorithms do not require run-time costs since the problems are solved in system design and planning stages. This study belongs to the deadlock prevention field.

Petri nets (PN)[2] have been recognized as one of the most powerful formal methods for modeling FMS. The reason is that they are well suited to represent such FMS characteristics as precedence relations, concurrence, conflict and synchronization. Their analysis methods used for deadlock prevention in FMS include structural analysis and reachability graphs. Deadlock prevention and avoidance schemes have been developed for controlling FMS[3-8] by using the former. In particular, deadlock prevention problems are solved using the concept of siphons[3-6]. Li & Zhou propose an elementary siphon control policy (ESCP) to reduce the redundant siphons to obtain structurally simpler controllers[9-10]. However, they cannot obtain optimal ones. Reachability graph methods are used to obtain the live system behavior[11-14]. Without confining to a certain class of FMS, they can provide an optimal deadlock controller by adopting the theory of regions[15]. The theory is originally developed for a transition system (TS). A state-based representation with arcs labeled with symbols from an alphabet of events in a TS can be mapped into a PN model. For an elementary TS (ETS) there exists a PN with minimum transition count (one transition for each label) with a reachability graph isomorphic to the original TS.

Uzam[12] follows the theory of regions[15] to define a deadlock-zone (DZ) and deadlock-free zone (DFZ) for preventing deadlocks. Hence, the concept of DZ and DFZ is used to solve ESSPs. An optimal controller can be obtained but suffers from many redundant control places. Ghaffari *et al.*[13] propose a unique interpretation of the theory of regions and define M_F (*forbidden marking*), M_D (*dangerous marking*), M_L (*legal marking*), and Ω (the set of *marking/transition-separation instances* or MTSI). An optimal PN controller synthesis method for FMS is proposed based on both MTSI and the theory of regions. Unfortunately, redundant MTSIs cannot be entirely avoided for large FMS cases.

To reduce redundant control places, Li *et al.*[16] adopt a combined algorithm based on siphon control and the theory of regions[15]. Its advantage is that the number of separation instances is significantly reduced after some sets of elementary siphons of a system are controlled. However, it fails to determine all sets of MTSIs and its application seems limited to some special nets only.

Uzam and Zhou propose an iterative control policy of liveness enforcement for PNs based on the theory of regions[17]. Less computation is required to obtain a controller. However, as indicated by Li et al[18], it requires the repeated calculation of reachability graphs. Piroddi *et al.* propose a combined selective siphons and critical markings in a reachability graph algorithm to obtain optimal controllers via iterations[19]. They successfully identify the critical uncontrolled siphons and control them to make a deadlock-prone PN live. However, their algorithm also requires the repeated calculation of reachability graphs. Eventually, the controllers are not ordinary (i.e. they contain weighted arcs).

This work in this chapter aims to develop a computationally more efficient optimal deadlock control policy by using the theory of regions. It focuses on dead markings in a reachability graph. The concept of a crucial MTSI (CMTSI) is proposed to synthesize optimal controllers. The proposed method can reduce the computational burden of the MTSI method[13] and redundant control places[12-13]. The experimental results indicate that it is the most efficient policy among all known ones[12-13, 16] that can design optimal controllers.

Section 2 presents the basic definitions and properties of PNs and the theory of regions. Section 3 describes the proposed policy. Section 4 presents the experimental results. Section 5 gives the comparisons. Conclusions are made in Section 6.

2. Preliminaries

2.1. Petri nets[2]

A Petri net (*PN*) is a 5-tuple $N = (P, T, F, W, M_0)$ where *P* is a finite set of places; *T* is a finite set of transitions, with $P \cup T \neq \varnothing$ and $P \cap T = \varnothing$; $F \subseteq (P\times T) \cup (T\times P)$ is the set of all directed arcs, $W: (P\times T) \cup (T\times P) \rightarrow \mathbf{N}$ is the weight function where $\mathbf{N} = \{0, 1, 2, \ldots\}$, and $M_0: P \rightarrow \mathbf{N}$ is the initial marking. A *PN* is said to be ordinary, denoted as (P, T, F), if $\forall f \in F$, $W(f) = 1$. $[N]^+(p, t) = W(p, t)$ is the input function that means the multiplicity of a directed arc from *p* to *t* if $(p, t)\in F$. $[N]^-(p, t) = W(t, p)$ is the output function that means the multiplicity of a directed arc from *t* to *p* if $(t, p)\in F$. The set of input (resp., output) transitions of a place *p* is denoted by $\bullet p$ (resp., $p\bullet$). Similarly, the set of input (resp., output) places of a transition *t* is denoted by $\bullet t$ (resp., $t\bullet$). A PN structure (P, T, F, W) is denoted by *N*. A PN with a given initial marking is denoted by (N, M_0).

A PN is said to be pure if no place is both input and output places of the same transition. The so-called incidence matrix $[N]$ of a pure Petri nets is defined as $[N] = [N]^- - [N]^+$. A transition *t* is said to be enabled at marking *M*, if $\forall p\in \bullet t$, $M(p) \geq W(p, t)$, *or p* is marked with at least $W(p, t)$ tokens, as denoted by $M[t>$. A transition may fire if it is enabled. In an ordinary net, it is enabled iff $\forall p \in \bullet t$, $M(p) \geq 1$. Firing *t* at *M* gives a new marking M' such that $\forall\, p \in P$, $M'(p) = M(p) - W(p, t) + W(t, p)$. It is denoted as $M[t>M'$. *M* indicates the number of tokens in each place, which means the current state of the modeled system. When M_n can be reached from M_0 by firing a sequence of transitions σ, this process is denoted by $M\, [\sigma > M_n$ and satisfies the *state equation* $M_n = M + [N]\vec{\sigma}$. Here, $\vec{\sigma}$ is a vector of non-negative integers, called a *firing vector*, and $\vec{\sigma}(t)$ indicates the algebraic sum of all occurrences of *t* in σ. The set of all reachable markings for a PN given M_0 is denoted by $R(N, M_0)$. Additionally, a definition of linearized reachability set (using the state equation) is defined as $\mathbf{R}(N, M_0)=\{M\!: M = M_0 + [N](\bullet\, \vec{\sigma})\}$. This definition is suitable for the incorporation of the state equation into a set of linear constraints. The markings in $\mathbf{R}(N, M_0)$ - $R(N, M_0)$ are called *spurious ones* (with respect to the state equation)[20]. They may also be the solutions of the state equation but not reachable markings. In this work, ones just focus on the reachable markings.

A transition *t* is said to be *live* if for any $M\in R(N, M_0)$, there exists a sequence of transitions whose firing leads to M' that enables *t*. A PN is said to be *live* if all the transitions are live. A PN contains a *deadlock* if there is a marking $M \in R(N, M_0)$ at which no transition is enabled. Such a marking is called a dead marking. Deadlock situations are as a result of inappropriate resource allocation policies or exhaustive use of some or all resources. Liveness of a PN means that for each marking $M \in R(N, M_0)$ reachable from M_0, it is finally possible to fire *t*, $\forall t \in T$ through some firing sequence. (N, M_0) is said to be *reversible*, if $\forall\, M \in R(N, M_0)$, $M_0 \in R(N, M)$. Thus, in a reversible net it is always possible to go back to initial marking (state) M_0. A marking M' is said to be a *home state*, if for each marking $M \in R(N, M_0)$, M' is reachable from *M*. Reversibility is a special case of the home state property, i.e if the home state $M' = M_0$, then the net is reversible.

2.2. Theory of regions and synthesis problem[13]

The theory of regions is proposed for the synthesis of pure nets given a finite TS[15], which can be adopted to synthesize the liveness-enforcing net supervisor (LENS) for a plant model[12-13]. For convenience, our method follows the interpretation of the theory of regions in[13].

First of all, let T be a set of transitions and G be a finite directed graph whose arcs are labeled by transitions in T. Assume that there exists a node v in G such that there exists a path from it to any node. The objective of the theory of regions is to find a pure PN (N, M_0), having T as its set of transitions and characterized by its incidence matrix $[N](p, t)$ and its initial marking M_0, such that its reachability graph is G and the marking of node v is M_0. In the following, M denotes both a reachable marking and its corresponding node in G.

Consider any marking M in net (N, M_0). Because (N, M_0) is pure, M can be fully characterized by its corresponding incidence vector $[N](p, \cdot)\vec{\Gamma}_M$ where $\vec{\Gamma}_M$ is the firing vector of path Γ_M. For any transition t that is enabled at M, i.e., t is the label of an outgoing arc of the node M in G

$$M'(p) = M(p) + [N](p, \cdot)\vec{\Gamma}_{M\to M'}, \forall (M, M') \in G \wedge M[t > M' \quad (1)$$

Consider now any oriented cycle γ of a reachability graph. Applying the state equation to a node in γ and summing them up give the following cycle equation:

$$\sum_{t\in T}[N](p,t)\vec{\gamma}(t) = 0, \forall \gamma \in C \quad (2)$$

where γ is an oriented cycle of G, $\vec{\gamma}(t)$ is a firing vector corresponding to γ, and C is the set of oriented cycles of G.

According to the definition of G, there exists an oriented path Γ_M from M_0 to M. Applying (1) along the path leads to $M(p) = M_0(p) + [N](p,\cdot)\vec{\Gamma}_M$. There are several paths from M_0 to M. Under the cycle equations, the product $[N](p,\cdot)\vec{\Gamma}_M$ is the same for all these paths. As a result, Γ_M can be arbitrarily chosen. The reachability of any marking M in G implies that

$$M(p) = M_0(p) + [N](p,\cdot)\vec{\Gamma}_M \geq 0, \forall M \in G \quad (3)$$

The above equation is called the reachability condition. Notably, (3) is necessary but not sufficient. Hence, spurious markings are beyond this paper.

It is clear that the cycle equations and reachability conditions hold for any place p. For each pair (M, t) such that M is a reachable marking of G and t is a transition not enabled at M, t should be prevented from happening by some place p. Since the net is pure, t is prevented from happening at M by a place p iff

$$M_0(p) + [N](p,\cdot)\vec{\Gamma}_M + [N](p,t) \leq -1 \quad (4)$$

The above equation (4) is called the event separation condition of (M, t). The set of all possible pairs (M, t) where M is a reachable marking and t is not enabled at M is called the *set of event separation instances* or *marking/transitions-separation instances* (MTSI)[13]. Symbol Ω is used to represent the set of MTSI in this paper. To solve the control problem, Ω is identified. The corresponding control places can then be found to prevent the transitions of the controlled system from firing in order to keep all legal markings only.

3. Controller synthesis method

In this section, an efficient controller synthesis method is developed based on the theory of regions. Please note that all transitions of the PN models are regarded as controllable ones.

3.1. Supervisory control problem

It is assumed that a deadlock-prone PN model contains at least a dead marking in its reachability graph at which no transition is enabled. Its reachability graph contains dead and live zones. Consequently, this study attempts to propose a method to prevent the controlled systems from entering a dead zone/marking.

A dead marking cannot enable any transition and thus cannot go to any other markings. We can formally define the dead marking M_D as follows.

Definition 1: The set of *dead markings* $M_D = \{M \in R(N, M_0) \mid$ at M, no transition is enabled$\}$.

Definition 2: A zone consisting of all dead markings is called a *dead zone*, denoted by Z_D.

Once a marking enters a dead zone, the system is dead. If there is no dead zone in a reachability graph, the system is called a live one.

The goal of the work is to control a deadlock-prone system such that it is live. All markings of a reachability graph can be divided into three groups: legal markings (M_L), quasi-dead markings (M_Q), and dead markings (M_D).

Definition 3: The set of *quasi-dead markings* $M_Q = \{M \in R(N, M_0) \mid M$ must eventually evolve to a dead one regardless of transition firing sequences$\}$.

Definition 4: A zone consisting of all quasi-dead markings is called a *quasi-dead zone*, denoted by Z_Q.

Definition 5: A zone consisting of all quasi-dead and dead markings, i.e., $Z_I = Z_D \cup Z_Q$, is called an *illegal zone*.

Markings except quasi-dead and dead markings are legal ones. Once a legal marking is enforced into the illegal zone, the net will eventually become deadlock.

Definition 6: A zone consisting of all legal markings is called a *legal zone*, i.e., $Z_L = R(N, M_0) - Z_I$.

Ramadge and Wonham show that a system has the maximally permissive behavior if the system behavior equals Z_L[21]. In other words, one must remove all the markings in illegal zone (i.e. quasi-dead and dead markings) from $R(N, M_0)$ if one wants to obtain the maximally permissive behavior. Ghaffari *et al.* propose the MTSI method to achieve their deadlock prevention based on the theory of regions[13]. However, the set of all MTSIs from the reachability graph must be identified. As a result, we can conclude that their method is computationally inefficient. A more efficient method is thus needed as described next.

3.2. Crucial MTSI (CMTSI)

Two types of CMTSIs are defined as follows.

Definition 7: Type I CMTSI: $\Omega' = \{(M, t) | M \in M_L, t \in T$, and $\exists M' \in M_D, M'' \in M_L$, and $t' \in T$ such that $M [t > M'$ and $M [t' > M''\}$. Denote the set of all the dead markings related to Ω' as M'_D, i.e., $M'_D = \{M' \in M_D \mid \exists (M, t) \in \Omega'$ such that $M [t > M'\}$. They are called type I deadlocks.

Definition 7 explains a legal marking that can evolve into a dead or legal zone as shown in Figure 1 through a single transition's firing. For those dead markings that are not type I deadlocks, we need to introduce Type II CMTSI and deadlocks.

Definition 8: A zone consisting of all type I deadlocks (M'_D) is called type I dead zone, denoted by Z'.

Definition 9: σ_k is defined as a transition firing sequence starting in a quasi-dead marking (M_Q) and ending in a deadlock marking in M_D where $i = |\sigma_k|$ is the number of transitions in σ_k, called its length. Denote a firing sequence with the shortest length (i.e., smallest i) from any quasi-dead marking to M' as $\sigma^*(M')$ given $M' \in M_D - M'_D$.

Definition 10: Type II CMTSI : $\Omega'' = \{(M, t) | M \in M_L, t \in T$, and $\exists M' \in M_Q, M'' \in M_L, M''' \in M_D, t' \in T$, and a firing sequence $\sigma = \sigma^*(M''')$ from M' to M''' such that $M [t > M', M [t' > M''$, and $M' [\sigma > M'''\}$. The set of dead markings associated with Type II CMTSI is denoted as M''_D, called type II deadlocks. $M''_D = \{M''' \in M_D \mid \exists (M, t) \in \Omega'', M' \in M_Q$ and a firing sequence σ from M' to M''' such that $M[t>M'$ and $\sigma = \sigma^*(M''')\}$.

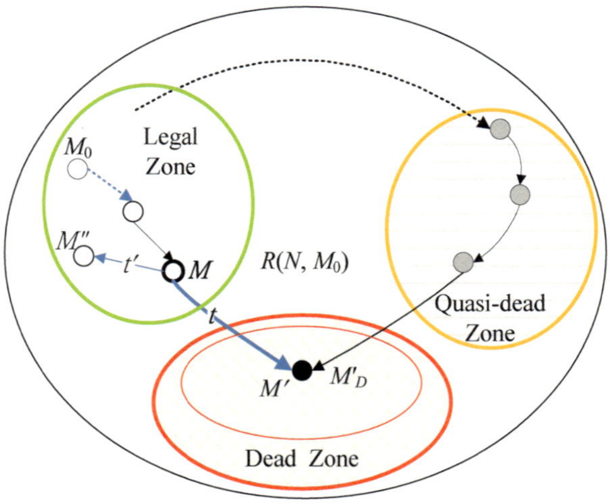

Figure 1. A structure of Type I CMTSI.

Definition 11: A zone consisting of all type II deadlocks (M''_D) is called type II dead zone, Z''.

A Type II CMTSI contains a legal marking that cannot reach a dead marking with one single transition's firing as shown in Figure 2. Given a dead marking in M''_D, the shortest transition firing sequence needs to be found. The main reason is based on the fact that, for a dead marking, the length of the firing sequence from the initial marking to CMTSI is the longest path than those from the initial marking to MTSIs. Hence, the solutions of MTSIs will be totally covered by the solution of CMTSI. For example, as shown in Figure 3, σ^* is the shorter path since $|\sigma^*| < |\sigma'|$ (i.e. $|\sigma^*| =1$ and $|\sigma'| = 3$).

Remark 1: A dead marking is always with its corresponding CMTSI. As a result, the corresponding CMTSI is of either Type I or II. Type I may be viewed as a special case of Type II CMTSI by defining $\sigma^* = 0$ (no need to enter Z_Q but directly to Z_D). Type I CMTSI will be processed first in our proposed method. In the following, Theorems 1-3 will help readers to understand how to choose CMTSIs, which are with the same firing sequence of legal markings, from Types I and II.

Theorem 1: If a dead marking $M \in M'_D$ is associated with two different CMTSIs, only one CMTSI needs to be controlled.

Proof: Assume that a dead marking M is with both CMTSIs $\{M_i, t_n\}$ and $\{M_j, t_n\}$ as shown in Figure 4. According to the state equation, $M_i + [N](\bullet t_m) = M_j + [N](\bullet t_n) = M$. Arranging the above equation, $M_0 + [N](\bullet \vec{\sigma}_{M_0 \to M_i}) + [N](\bullet t_m) = M_0 + [N]\,(\bullet \vec{\sigma}_{M_0 \to M_j}) + [N](\bullet t_n)$. According to (4), realizing either CMTSI, e.g., $\{M_i, t_m\}$, leads to $M_0 + [N](\bullet \vec{\sigma}_{M_0 \to M_i}) + [N](\bullet t_m) \le -1$, which in turn implies $M_0 + [N](\bullet \vec{\sigma}_{M_0 \to M_j}) + [N](\bullet t_n) \le -1$ and vice versa. Hence, only one CMTSI needs to be controlled.

Remark 2: Based on Theorem 1, if a dead marking $M \in M'_D$ is associated with more than two CMTSIs, only one of them needs to be controlled.

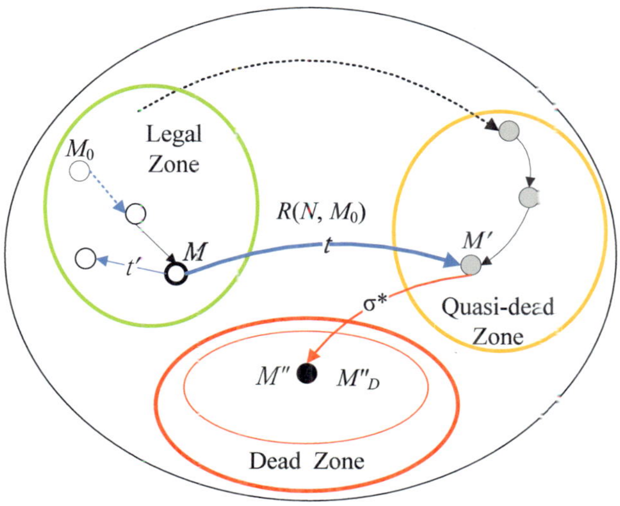

Figure 2. A structure of Type II CMTSI.

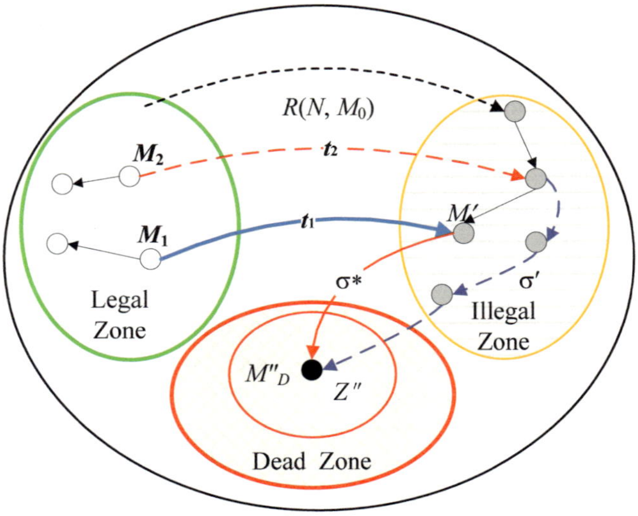

Figure 3. The shorter path σ^* in Type II CMTSI given a dead marking.

Theorem 2: If a dead marking $M \in M''_D$, is associated with two CMTSIs whose markings can reach a same quasi-dead marking M' via their respective single transition's firing, only one CMTSI needs to be controlled.

Proof: Assume that a dead marking M is associated with Type II CMTSIs $\{M_p, t_r\}$ and $\{M_q, t_s\}$. M_p and M_q reaches a quasi-dead markings M' via t_r and t_s's firing, respectively as shown in Figure 5.

According to the state equation, $M_p + [N](\bullet t_r) + [N](\bullet \vec{\sigma}^*) = M_q + [N](\bullet t_s) + [N](\bullet \vec{\sigma}^*)$ M. Arranging the above equation, one can realize that $M_p + [N](\bullet t_r) = M_q + [N](\bullet t_s)$. According to (4), realizing either CMTSI, e.g., $\{M_p, t_r\}$, leads to $M_0 + [N](\bullet \vec{\sigma}_{M_0 \to M_p}) + [N](\bullet t_r) \leq -1$, which in turn implies $M_0 + [N](\bullet \vec{\sigma}_{M_0 \to M_q}) + [N](\bullet t_s) \leq -1$ and vice versa. Hence, only one CMTSI needs to be controlled.

Theorem 3: A dead marking $M \in M''_D$, is associated with two CMTSIs whose markings can reach two different quasi-dead markings M'_p and M'_q via two different single transitions' firing. Both need to be controlled if $[N](\bullet \vec{\sigma}_r^*) \neq [N](\bullet \vec{\sigma}_s^*)$.

Proof: Assume that a dead marking M is associated with both Type II CMTSIs $\{M_p, t_r\}$ and $\{M_q, t_s\}$. M_p and M_q reach two different quasi-dead markings M'_p and M'_q via t_r and t_s's firing, respectively as shown in Figure 6.

According to the state equation, $M_p + [N](\bullet t_r) + [N](\bullet \vec{\sigma}_r^*) = M_q + [N](\bullet t_s) + [N](\bullet \vec{\sigma}_s^*) = M''_D$. Arranging the above equation, $M'_p + [N](\bullet \vec{\sigma}_r^*) = M'_q + [N](\bullet \vec{\sigma}_s^*)$. Since $[N](\bullet \vec{\sigma}_r^*) \neq [N](\bullet \vec{\sigma}_s^*)$, M'_p is not equal to M'_q. And also according to the definition of the event separation condition equation, the first set of CMTSI $\{M_p, t_r\}$ leads to the first event separation condition equation is $M_0 + [N](\bullet \vec{\sigma}_{M_0 \to M_p}) + [N](\bullet t_r) \leq -1$; and the second set of CMTSI $\{M_q, t_s\}$ leads to the another event separation condition equation is $M_0 + [N](\bullet \vec{\sigma}_{M_0 \to M_q}) + [N](\bullet t_s) \leq -1$. Hence, one can infer that M'_p and M'_q are two different quasi-dead markings if $[N](\bullet\vec{\sigma}_r^*) \neq [N](\bullet\vec{\sigma}_s^*)$. It hints the two event separation condition equations are different. As a result, both CMTSIs need to be controlled.

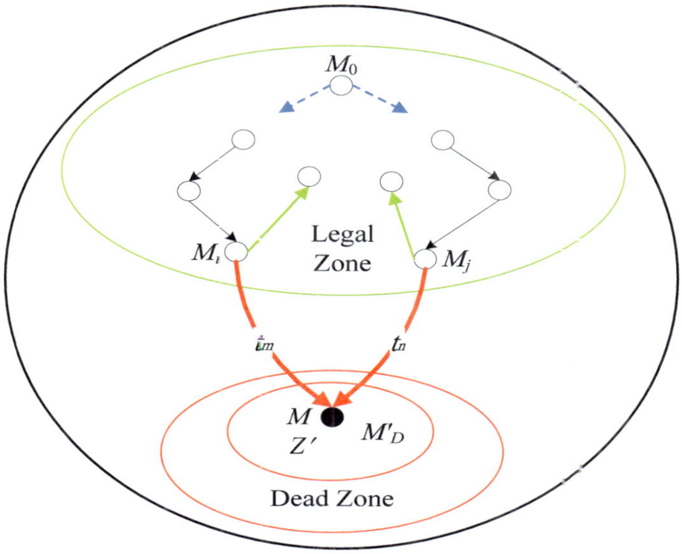

Figure 4. A type I deadlocks associated with two CMTSIs.

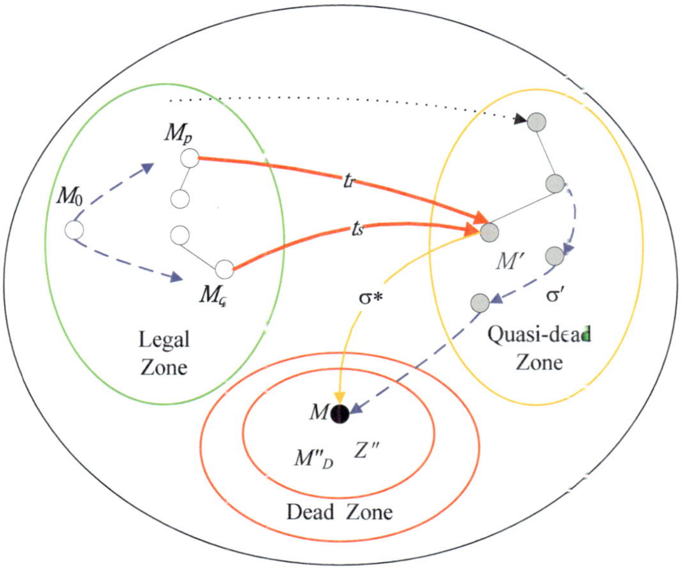

Figure 5. Two CMTSIs connected to the same quasi-dead marking.

Definition 12: A legal marking $M \in M_L$ can be led to a quasi-dead marking M_q via a single transition firing. M_q must eventually evolve to a dead one M_d (i.e. $M_d \in M_D$) after a sequence $\sigma_n = t_1t_2\ldots t_n$ fires. Denote the set of all the markings on the path from M_q to M_d as $M_{q\text{-}d}$.

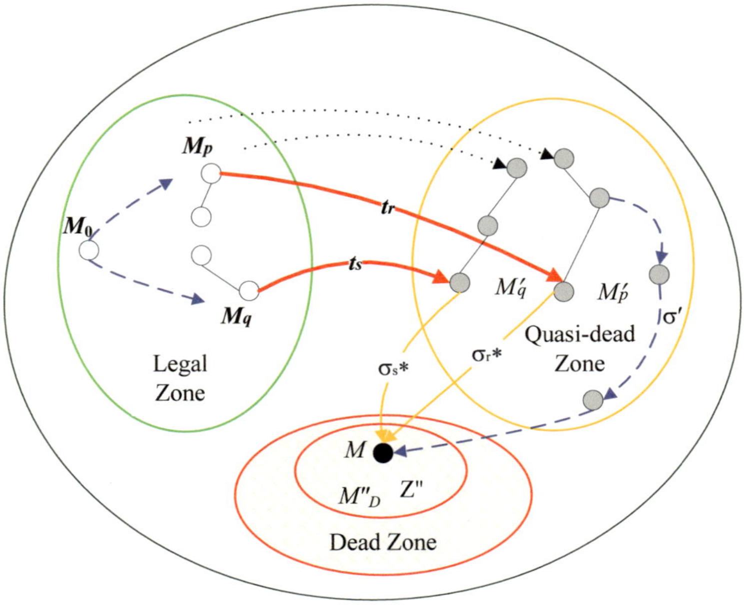

Figure 6. Two CMTSIs connected to two quasi-dead markings.

Remark 3: Based on Theorem 3, both CMTSIs still need to be controlled even if $M_P = M_q$ for the case shown in Figure 7.

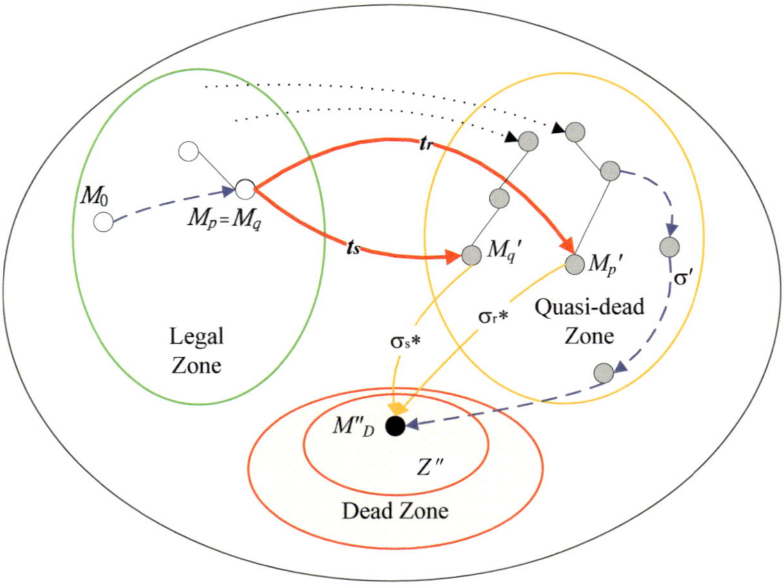

Figure 7. Two CMTSIs connected to two quasi-dead markings M'_p and M'_q with $\sigma_r^* = \sigma_s^* = \sigma^*(M''_D)$.

Control places are then found after CMTSIs. They are used to keep all markings of the controlled system within the legal zone.

Theorem 4: $(\Omega' \cup \Omega'') \subseteq \Omega$

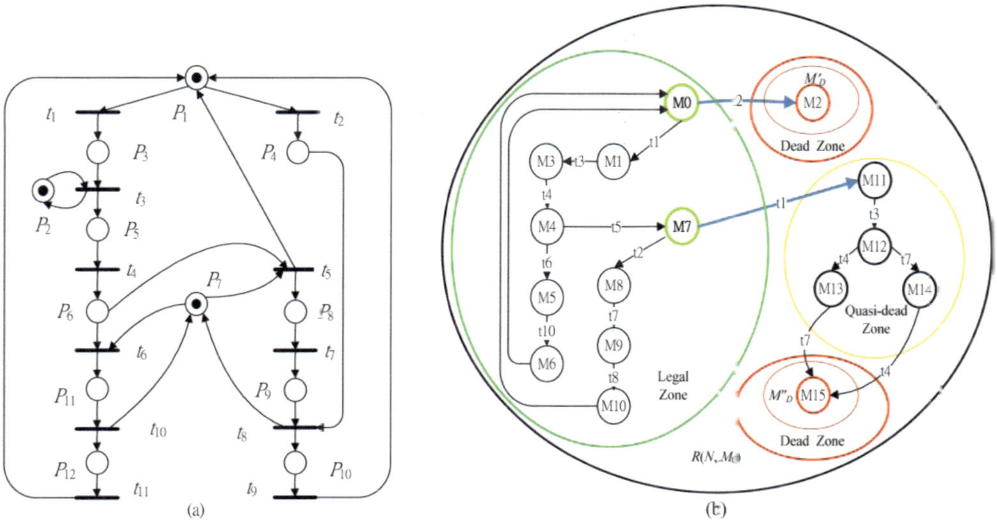

Figure 8. (a) A Petri net model.[22] (b) Its reachability graph.

Here, Figure 8(a) taken from existing literatures[22] is used to demonstrate how to identify two types of CMTSIs from its reachability graph (i.e. Figure 8(b)). Assume that all transitions of PN models are immediately in this case. Therefore, one can easy identify there are two dead markings M'_D (i.e. M_2) and M''_D (i.e. M_{15}) and four quasi-dead markings (i.e. M_{11}, M_{12}, M_{13} and M_{14}). Additionally, the markings M_0, M_1, M_3-M_{10} are the legal markings. Based on the mentioned above, there are two sets of CTMSIs in the reachability graph system due to the two dead markings in the system. As a result, one can infer that $\{M_0, t_2\}$ belongs to type I CMTSI and $\{M_7, t_1\}$ belongs to type II. In this Petri net system model, there are only one type I CMTSI and only one type II.

3.3. Procedure of deadlock prevention policy

Next, quasi-dead, dead, and legal markings are identified. Based on[12-13], the maximally permissive behavior means all of legal markings (M_L) and the number of reachability condition equations equals $|M_L|$. Additionally, all CMTSIs can be obtained such that the legal markings do not proceed into the illegal zone. The proposed deadlock prevention algorithm is constructed as Figure 9.

Theorem 5: The proposed deadlock prevention policy is more efficient than the method proposed by Ghaffari et al.[13]

Proof: The theory of regions is used to prevent the system deadlocks by both our deadlock prevention policy and the conventional one. All MTSIs can be controlled by the two control policies. Since $(\Omega' \cup \Omega'') \subseteq \Omega$, the use of CMTSI can more efficiently handle the synthesis problem than that of MTSI[13].

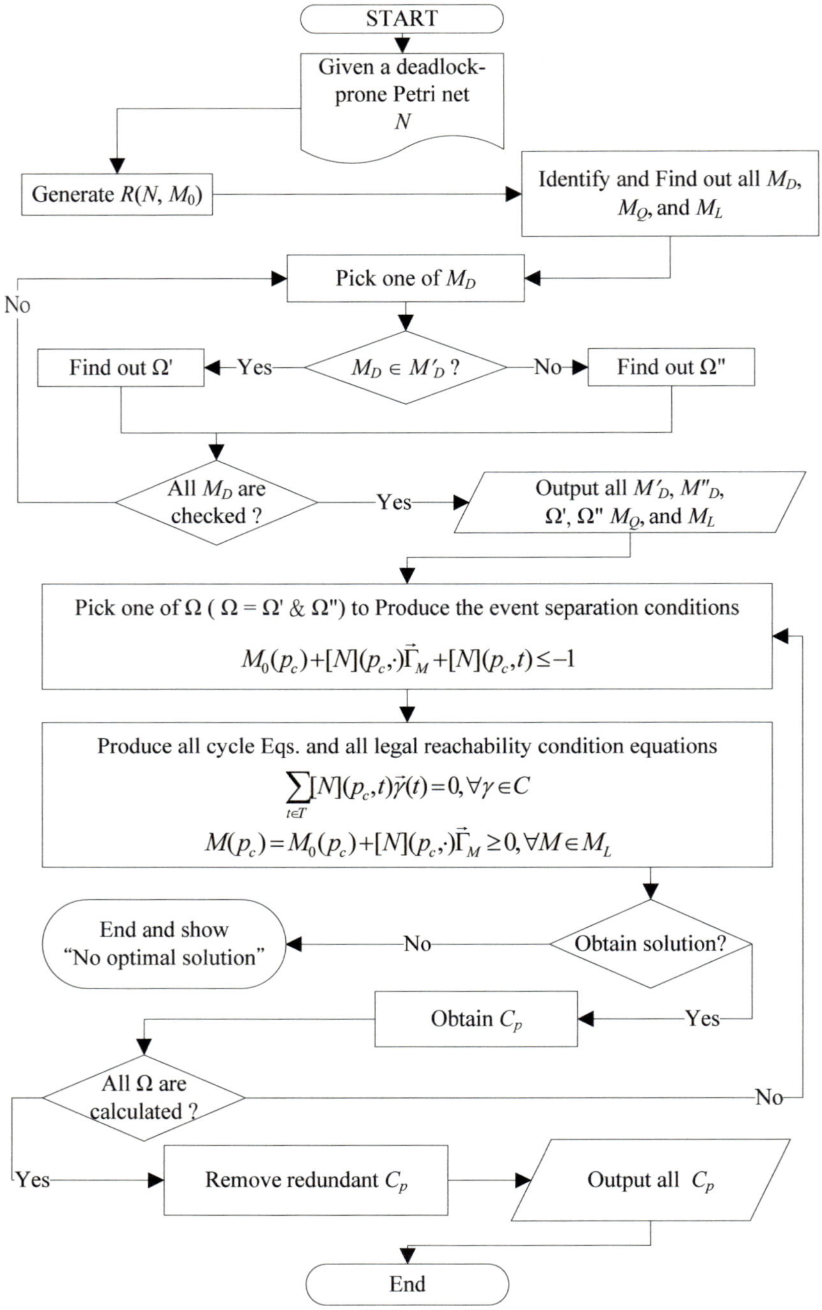

Figure 9. The Proposed Deadlock Prevention Flowchart.

4. Experimental results

Two FMS examples are used to evaluate our deadlock prevention policy[12-23].

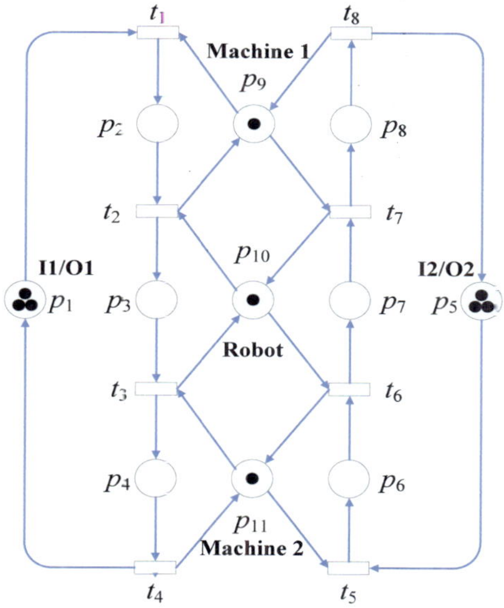

Figure 10. An FMS PN Model[12].

Example I: An FMS is shown in Figure 10[12]. This PN is a system of simple sequential processes with resources (S^3PR), denoted by (N_1, M_0). To do our deadlock prevention policy, $R(N_1, M_0)$ of the PN system can be constructed as shown in Figure 11.

Two dead markings (i.e. M_7 and M_{12}) can then be identified. Next, $\Omega'_1 = \{(M_3, t_5)\}$ and $\Omega'_2 = \{(M_{15}, t_1)\}$ are obtained. The event separation condition equations can be obtained through them as follows.

$$M_7(p_c) = M_0(p_c) + 2[N](p_c, t_1) + [N](p_c, t_2) + [N](p_c, t_5) \leq -1 \tag{5}$$

$$M_{12}(p_c) = M_0(p_c) + [N](p_c, t_1) + 2[N](p_c, t_5) + [N](p_c, t_6) \leq -1 \tag{6}$$

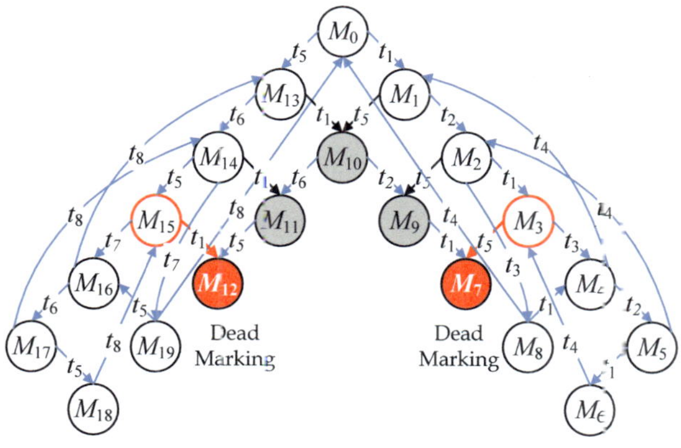

Figure 11. $R(N, M_0)$ of Example I.

Two cycle equations are as follows.

$$[N](p_c, t_1)+[N](p_c, t_2)+[N](p_c, t_3)+[N](p_c, t_4)=0 \quad (7)$$

$$[N](p_c, t_5)+[N](p_c, t_6)+[N](p_c, t_7)+[N](p_c, t_8)=0 \quad (8)$$

After listing all reachability conditions, all legal markings can be determined. In detail, M_0-M_6, M_8, and M_{13}-M_{19} are legal. Hence, the following reachability conditions are obtained.

$$M_0(p_c) \geq 0 \quad (9)$$

$$M_1(p_c) = M_0(p_c) + [N](p_c, t_1) \geq 0 \quad (10)$$

$$M_2(p_c) = M_0(p_c) + [N](p_c, t_1) + [N](p_c, t_2) \geq 0 \quad (11)$$

$$M_3(p_c) = M_0(p_c) + 2[N](p_c, t_1) + [N](p_c, t_2) \geq 0 \quad (12)$$

$$M_4(p_c) = M_0(p_c) + 2[N](p_c, t_1) + [N](p_c, t_2) + [N](p_c, t_3) \geq 0 \quad (13)$$

$$M_5(p_c) = M_0(p_c) + 2[N](p_c, t_1) + 2[N](p_c, t_2) + [N](p_c, t_3) \geq 0 \quad (14)$$

$$M_6(p_c) = M_0(p_c) + 3[N](p_c, t_1) + 2[N](p_c, t_2) + [N](p_c, t_3) \geq 0 \quad (15)$$

$$M_8(p_c) = M_0(p_c) + [N](p_c, t_1) + [N](p_c, t_2) + [N](p_c, t_3) \geq 0 \quad (16)$$

$$M_{13}(p_c) = M_0(p_c) + [N](p_c, t_5) \geq 0 \quad (17)$$

$$M_{14}(p_c) = M_0(p_c) + [N](p_c, t_5) + [N](p_c, t_6) \geq 0 \quad (18)$$

$$M_{15}(p_c) = M_0(p_c) + 2[N](p_c, t_5) + [N](p_c, t_6) \geq 0 \quad (19)$$

$$M_{16}(p_c) = M_0(p_c) + 2[N](p_c, t_5) + [N](p_c, t_6) + [N](p_c, t_7) \geq 0 \quad (20)$$

$$M_{17}(p_c) = M_0(p_c) + 2[N](p_c, t_5) + 2[N](p_c, t_6) + [N](p_c, t_7) \geq 0 \quad (21)$$

$$M_{18}(p_c) = M_0(p_c) + 3[N](p_c, t_5) + 2[N](p_c, t_6) + [N](p_c, t_7) \geq 0 \quad (22)$$

$$M_{19}(p_c) = M_0(p_c) + [N](p_c, t_5) + [N](p_c, t_6) + [N](p_c, t_7) \geq 0 \quad (23)$$

Furthermore, two optimal control places C_{P1} and C_{P2} can be obtained when (5) and (7)-(23) are solved. Their detailed information is: $M_0(C_{P1}) = 1$, $t_1 = t_5 = -1$, $t_2 = t_6 = 1$, $t_3 = t_4 = t_7 = t_8 = 0$; and $M_0(C_{P2})=1$, $t_2 = t_5 = -1$, $t_3 = t_6 = 1$, $t_1 = t_4 = t_7 = t_8 = 0$. By the same way, using (6) and (7)-(23), one can find two optimal control places, C_{p3} and C_{p4}. $M_0(C_{P3}) = 1$, $t_1 = t_6 = -1$, $t_2 = t_7 = 1$, $t_3 = t_4 = t_5 = t_8 = 0$; and $M_0(C_{P4}) = 1$, $t_1 = t_5 = -1$, $t_2 = t_6 = 1$, $t_3 = t_4 = t_7 = t_8 = 0$. Notably, C_{P1} and C_{P4} are the same. Therefore, a redundant control place (C_{P4}) can be removed. As a result, the system net can be controlled with the three control places C_{P1}, C_{P2} and C_{P3}. The optimally controlled system net (N_{1H}, M_0) is obtained as shown in Table 1.

It is worthy to emphasize that the three control places are obtained by using two CMTSIs and 36 equations under our control policy. However, six MTSIs/ESSPs and 108 equations have to be solved in two existing literatures[12, 24].

Additional Control Places	$M_0(C_{pi})$	$\bullet(Cp)$	$(Cp)\bullet$
Cp_1	1	t_2, t_6	t_1, t_5
Cp_2	1	t_3, t_6	t_2, t_5
Cp_3	1	t_2, t_7	$t_{[illegible]}$, t_6

Table 1. Control Places of the Net (N_{1H}, M_0)

Example II: This example is taken from[23] and is used in [12, 16, 24]. Here, the PN model of the system, denoted as (N_2, M_0), is shown in Figure 12.

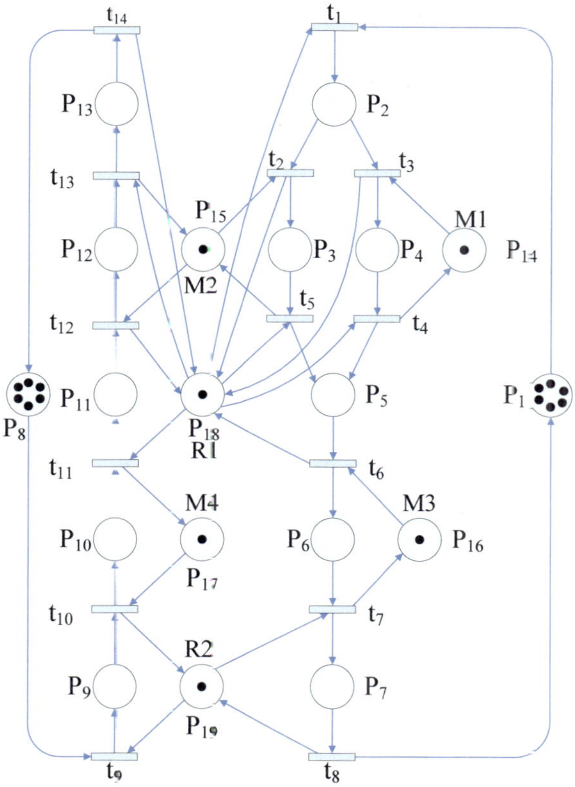

Figure 12. The Petri nets model of example II.

To prevent deadlock, 282 reachable markings (M_1 to M_{282}) are identified according to the software INA[25]. 16 dead markings M_9, M_{19}, M_{70}, M_{71}, M_{76}, M_{77}, M_{78}, M_{83}, M_{84}, M_{94}, M_{99}, M_{100}, M_{105}, M_{106}, M_{112}, and M_{113} are then located. Next, 61 quasi-dead markings M_6, M_7, M_8, M_{14}, M_{15}, M_{16}, M_{17}, M_{18}, M_{25}, M_{48}, M_{66}, M_{67}, M_{68}, M_{69}, M_{72}, M_{73}, M_{74}, M_{75}, M_{79}, M_{80}, M_{81}, M_{82}, $M_{8[illegible]}$, M_{101}, M_{102}, M_{103}, M_{104}, M_{108}, M_{109}, M_{110}, M_{111}, M_{124}, M_{130}, M_{135}, M_{136}, M_{141}, M_{142}, M_{143}, M_{150}, $M_{16[illegible]}$, M_{198}, M_{203}, M_{204}, M_{210}, M_{250}, M_{251}, M_{257}, M_{258}, M_{259}, M_{260}, M_{261}, M_{262}, M_{263}, M_{265}, M_{269}, M_{270}, $M_{27[illegible]}$, M_{273}, M_{274}, M_{277}, and M_{278} are found based on Definition 3 in this paper. Hence, the number of legal markings (i.e. 288 – (16 + 61) = 205) can be determined. Type I and II CMTSIs can be obtained as shown in Table 2. Notice that $\{(M_{56}, t_9)\}$ in M_{77} is a redundant one.

M'_D	Ω'_C	M''_D	Ω''_C
M_9	$\{(M_{65}, t_1)\}$	M_{19}	$\{(M_{56}, t_1)\}$
			$\{(M_{56}, t_9)\}$
M_{70}	$\{(M_{43}, t_9)\}$	M_{76}	$\{(M_{65}, t_{11})\}$
M_{71}	$\{(M_{51}, t_9)\}$	M_{77}	$\{(M_{56}, t_9)\}$
			$\{(M_{56}, t_{11})\}$
M_{78}	$\{(M_{171}, t_9)\}$	M_{83}	$\{(M_{128}, t_{11})\}$
M_{94}	$\{(M_{93}, t_1)\}$	M_{84}	$\{(M_{60}, t_9)\}$
			$\{(M_{60}, t_{11})\}$
M_{99}	$\{(M_{98}, t_1)\}$	M_{105}	$\{(M_{93}, t_{11})\}$
M_{100}	$\{(M_{98}, t_4)\}$	M_{106}	$\{(M_{98}, t_{11})\}$
		M_{112}	$\{(M_{122}, t_{11})\}$
		M_{113}	$\{(M_{96}, t_{11})\}$

Table 2. The Dead Markings and Their Relative CMTSIs.

M'_D	Event Separation Condition Equations
M_9	$M_0 + 3t_1 + t_2 + t_3 + 2t_9 + t_{10} \leq -1$
M_{70}	$M_0 + 3t_1 + t_2 + 2t_3 + 2t_4 + t_6 + 2t_9 + t_{10} \leq -1$
	$M_0 + 3t_1 + 2t_2 + t_3 + t_4 + t_5 + t_6 + 2t_9 + t_{10} \leq -1$
M_{71}	$M_0 + 3t_1 + t_2 + 2t_3 + t_4 + t_5 + t_6 + 2t_9 + t_{10} \leq -1$
	$M_0 + 3t_1 + 2t_2 + t_3 + 2t_5 + t_6 + 2t_9 + t_{10} \leq -1$
M_{78}	$M_0 + 2t_1 + t_2 + t_3 + t_4 + t_5 + t_6 + 2t_9 + t_{10} \leq -1$
	$M_0 + 2t_1 + 2t_2 + 2t_5 + t_6 + 2t_9 + t_{10} \leq -1$
	$M_0 + 2t_1 + 2t_3 + 2t_4 + t_6 + 2t_9 + t_{10} \leq -1$
M_{94}	$M_0 + 2t_1 + t_3 + 3t_9 + 2t_{10} + t_{11} + t_{12} \leq -1$
M_{99}	$M_0 + 3t_1 + 2t_3 + t_4 + t_6 + 3t_9 + 2t_{10} + t_{11} + t_{12} \leq -1$
	$M_0 + 3t_1 + t_2 + t_3 + t_5 + t_6 + 3t_9 + 2t_{10} + t_{11} + t_{12} \leq -1$

Table 3. The Dead Markings and Relative Event Separation Condition Equations of Type I CMTSI.

Tables 3-4 show the event separation condition equations based on 18 CMTSIs. Here, the procedure of our method is introduced as follows. Due to the space limitation, we use only one example (i.e. dead marking M_9) to illustrate how to prevent legal markings from leading to dead one M_9 by using a CMTSI. To do so, $\Omega'_{C1} = \{(M_{65}, t_1)\}$ can be located due to M_9. The event separation condition equation can then be identified as follows.

$$M_9(C_{P1}) = M_0(C_{P1}) + 3t_1 + t_2 + t_3 + 2t_9 + t_{10} \leq -1 \tag{24}$$

Next, three different cycle equations are:

$$t_1 + t_2 + t_5 + t_6 + t_7 + t_8 = 0 \tag{25}$$

$$t_1 + t_3 + t_4 + t_6 + t_7 + t_8 = 0 \tag{26}$$

$$t_9 + t_{10} + t_{11} + t_{12} + t_{13} + t_{14} = 0 \tag{27}$$

Finally, 205 reachability condition equations can be listed. They represent the sequence of all legal markings from the initial one. Moreover, control place C_{P1} can be computed, i.e., $M_0(C_{P1}) = 2$, $\bullet C_{P1} = \{t_6, t_{13}\}$, and $C_{P1}\bullet = \{t_1, t_{11}\}$. Similarly, other control places are obtained as shown in Tables 5-6.

M''_D	Event Separation Condition Equations
M_{19}	$M_0 + 4t_1 + t_2 + 2t_3 + t_4 + t_6 + t_9 + t_{10} \leq -1$
	$M_0 + 4t_1 + 2t_2 + t_3 + t_5 + t_6 + t_9 + t_{10} \leq -1$
	$M_0 + 3t_1 + t_2 + 2t_3 + t_4 + t_6 + 2t_9 + t_{10} \leq -1$
	$M_0 + 3t_1 + 2t_2 + 2t_3 + t_5 + t_6 + 2t_9 + t_{10} \leq -1$
M_{76}	$M_0 + 2t_1 + t_2 + t_3 + 2t_9 + t_{10} + t_{11} \leq -1$
M_{77}	$M_0 + 3t_1 + t_2 + 2t_3 + t_4 + t_6 + t_9 + t_{10} + t_{11} \leq -1$
	$M_0 + 3t_1 + 2t_2 + t_3 + t_5 + t_6 + t_9 + t_{10} + t_{11} \leq -1$
M_{83}	$M_0 + t_1 + t_2 + 2t_9 + t_{10} + t_{11} \leq -1$
M_{84}	$M_0 + 2t_1 + t_2 + t_3 + t_4 + t_6 + t_9 + t_{10} + t_{11} \leq -1$
	$M_0 + 2t_1 + 2t_2 + t_5 + t_6 + t_9 + t_{10} + t_{11} \leq -1$
	$M_0 + 3t_1 + t_2 + 2t_3 + t_4 + t_6 + 2t_9 + t_{10} \leq -1$
	$M_0 + 3t_1 + 2t_2 + t_3 + t_5 + t_6 + 2t_9 + t_{10} \leq -1$
M_{105}	$M_0 + t_1 + t_3 + 3t_9 + 2t_{10} + 2t_{11} + t_{12} \leq -1$
M_{106}	$M_0 + 2t_1 + 2t_3 + t_4 + t_6 + 3t_9 + 2t_{10} + 2t_{11} + t_{12} \leq -1$
	$M_0 + 2t_1 + t_2 - t_3 + t_5 + t_6 + 3t_9 + 2t_{10} + 2t_{11} + t_{12} \leq -1$
M_{112}	$M_0 + 3t_9 + 2t_{10} + 2t_{11} + t_{12} \leq -1$
M_{113}	$M_0 + t_1 + t_3 + t_4 + t_6 + 3t_9 + 2t_{10} + 2t_{11} + t_{12} \leq -1$
	$M_0 + t_1 + t_2 + t_5 + t_6 + 3t_9 + 2t_{10} + 2t_{11} + t_{12} \leq -1$

Table 4. The Dead Markings and Relative Event Separation Condition Equations of Type II CMTSI.

M'_D	Ω'_C	$M_0(C_{pi})$	$\bullet(C_{pi})$	$(C_{pi})\bullet$
M_9	$\{(M_{65}, t_1)\}$	2	t_6, t_{13}	t_1, t_{11}
M_{70}	$\{(M_{43}, t_9)\}$	3	t_6, t_{11}	t_2, t_4, t_9
		3	t_5, t_7, t_{11}	t_2, t_6, t_9
		3	t_7, t_{11}	t_4, t_5, t_9
M_{71}	$\{(M_{51}, t_9)\}$	3	t_7, t_{11}	t_4, t_5, t_9
M_{78}	$\{(M_{171}, t_9)\}$	3	t_7, t_{11}	t_4, t_5, t_9
M_{94}	$\{(M_{93}, t_1)\}$	2	t_6, t_{13}	t_1, t_{11}
M_{99}	$\{(M_{98}, t_1)\}$	4	t_7, t_{11}	t_1, t_9
M_{100}	$\{(M_{98}, t_4)\}$	3	t_7, t_{11}	t_4, t_5, t_9

Table 5. Control Places from TYPE I CMTSI.

Finally, the controlled net is obtained by adding the six control places as shown in Table 7. It is live and maximally permissive with 205 reachable markings. However, 59 ESSPs and nine control places are required in [12]. It hints that 59 sets of inequalities are needed in [12], while only 18 sets of inequalities suffice using our algorithm. Hence, our policy is more efficient than that in [12].

Li *et al.* solve this problem by using elementary siphons controlled policy (ESCP) and the theory of region [16]. A two-stage deadlock prevention method is used. First, ESCP is used to replace a siphon control method[5]. Therefore, the number of dead markings is reduced. Second, the theory of regions is used to obtain the optimal solution. Three elementary siphons (i.e. $S_1 = \{p_2, p_5, p_{13}, p_{15}, p_{18}\}$, $S_2 = \{p_5, p_{13}, p_{14}, p_{15}, p_{18}\}$ and $S_3 = \{p_2, p_7, p_{11}, p_{13}, p_{16}–p_{19}\}$) can be identified. As a result, three control places $V_{S1}–V_{S3}$ as shown in Table 8 are needed to handle three elementary siphons. Then a partially controlled PN system, denoted as (N_{2L1}, M_0), can be obtained after the first stage.

M''_D	Ω''_C	$M_0(C_{pi})$	$\bullet(C_{pi})$	$(C_{pi})\bullet$
M_{19}	$\{(M_{56}, t_1)\}$	2	t_6, t_{13}	t_1, t_{11}
		4	t_7, t_{11}	t_1, t_9
	$\{(M_{56}, t_9)\}$	3	t_5, t_7, t_{11}	t_2, t_6, t_9
		4	t_7, t_{11}	t_1, t_9
M_{76}	$\{(M_{65}, t_{11})\}$	1	t_5, t_{13}	t_2, t_{11}
M_{77}	$\{(M_{56}, t_{11})\}$	1	t_5, t_{13}	t_2, t_{11}
M_{83}	$\{(M_{128}, t_{11})\}$	1	t_5, t_{13}	t_2, t_{11}
M_{84}	$\{(M_{60}, t_9)\}$	3	t_5, t_7, t_{11}	t_2, t_6, t_9
	$\{(M_{60}, t_{11})\}$	1	t_5, t_{13}	t_2, t_{11}
M_{105}	$\{(M_{93}, t_{11})\}$	1	t_5, t_{13}	t_2, t_{11}
M_{106}	$\{(M_{98}, t_{11})\}$	1	t_5, t_{13}	t_2, t_{11}
M_{112}	$\{(M_{122}, t_{11})\}$	1	t_5, t_{13}	t_2, t_{11}
M_{113}	$\{(M_{96}, t_{11})\}$	1	t_5, t_{13}	t_2, t_{11}

Table 6. Control Places from TYPE II CMTSI.

Additional Control Places	$M_0(C_{pi})$	$\bullet(C_{pi})$	$(C_{pi})\bullet$
Cp_1	1	t_5, t_{13}	t_2, t_{11}
Cp_2	2	t_6, t_{13}	t_1, t_{11}
Cp_3	3	t_6, t_{11}	t_2, t_4, t_9
Cp_4	3	t_5, t_7, t_{11}	t_2, t_6, t_9
Cp_5	3	t_7, t_{11}	t_4, t_5, t_9
Cp_6	4	t_7, t_{11}	t_1, t_9

Table 7. Control Places for the Net (N_{2H}, M_0).

However, (N_{2L1}, M_0) has a dead marking. Figure 13 shows a partial reachability graph and the deadlock marking M_{57} is included. M_{57} is one of the 210 reachable markings (i.e. the reachable markings M_1-M_{210} as denoted in [16]. In [16], 210 reachable markings are divided into two categories: legal and illegal zones. The illegal zone consists of quasi-dead markings (i.e. M_{54}, M_{55}, M_{56} and M_{60}) and a dead marking (i.e. M_{57}). Obviously, some legal markings (i.e. M_{43}, M_{44}, M_{47}, M_{48}, M_{49}, M_{53}, M_{59} and M_{74}) can enter the illegal zone (i.e. $Z_I = Z_Q \cup Z_D$). One can realize that they use the theory of regions to prevent these legal markings from entering Z_I. Therefore, they must resolve 8 MTSIs (i.e. $\{(M_{43}, t_9)\}$, $\{(M_{44}, t_9)\}$, $\{(M_{47}, t_9)\}$, $\{(M_{48}, t_9)\}$, $\{(M_{49}, t_9)\}$, $\{(M_{53}, t_4)\}$, $\{(M_{59}, t_1)\}$, $\{(M_{74}, t_2)\}$) and many equations in this example. Then the additional three control places can be obtained as shown in Table 9. Eight MTSIs are needed. Hence, their control policy[16] does not seem efficiently enough when the MTSI at the second stage is used to obtain control places.

To compare the efficiency of the deadlock prevention methods, the proposed one is examined in the system net (N_{2L1}, M_0). One can realize that M_{57} is the only deadlock marking in $R(N_{2L1}, M_0)$. Based on our method, only the dead marking M_{57} needed to be controlled. Here, only one $\Omega' = \{(M_{44}, t_9)\}$ is needed. Obviously, the involved necessary equations are much less than those of the conventional one. We can obtain the same controlled net as that in [16]. Hence, the proposed concept of CMTSIs can be used in their approach [16] to improve its computational efficiency significantly as well.

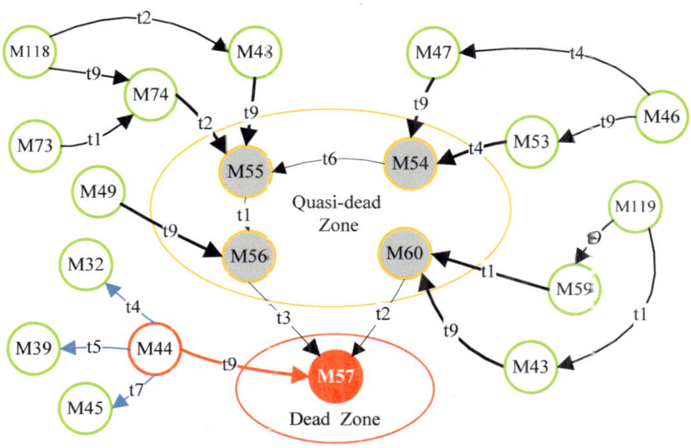

Figure 13. A Partial Reachability Graph of the Net (N_{2L1}, M_0)[16].

Additional Control Places	$M_0(C_{pi})$	$\bullet(C_{pi})$	$(C_{pi})\bullet$
Vs_1	1	t_5, t_{13}	t_2, t_{11}
Vs_2	2	t_4, t_5, t_{13}	t_1, t_{11}
Vs_3	3	t_7, t_{11}	t_4, t_5, t_9

Table 8. Additional Control Places for the Net (N_{2L1}, M_0)

Additional Control Places	$M_0(C_{pi})$	$\bullet(C_{pi})$	$(C_{pi})\bullet$
Cp_1	3	t_6, t_{11}	t_2, t_4, t_9
Cp_2	3	t_5, t_7, t_{11}	t_2, t_6, t_9
Cp_3	4	t_2, t_4, t_7, t_{11}	t_1, t_6, t_9

Table 9. Control Places for (N_{2L1}, M_0) by Two-Stage Method.

5. Comparison with existing methods

One can attempt to make a comparison with the previous methods[12, 16, 24] in terms of efficiency. The first one proposed by Uzam[12], called *Algorithm U*, is totally based on the theory of regions. It solves six ESSPs in Example I. Then three control places are added on the net such that the controlled net is live and reversible. As for Example II, it solves 59 MTSIs. Nine control places are obtained. However, the proposed deadlock prevention policy called *Algorithm P* solves only two and 18 CMTSIs in Examples I and II, respectively.

The other one is proposed by Li *et al.*[16, 24] called *Algorithm L* in which only the theory of regions is used in Example I. Notice that both the controlled results of *Algorithms L* and *U* are the same in Example I. In Example II, using *Algorithm L*, eight MTSIs are solved and six control places are computed. However, under the two-stage control policy, only one set of MTSI is needed by using our new policy to obtain the controlled result that is as the same as *Algorithm L* in Example II. Note that both the definitions of ESSP and MTSI are the same. Hence, ESSP and CMTSI can be regarded as MTSI for the comparison purpose. The detailed comparison results are given in Table 10. However, only 18 MTSIs among 59 MTSIs are needed by using *Algorithm P*.

Example	# of Places	# of Resource Places	MTSI *U, L, P*	Control Places *U, L, P*	Reachable Markings
I	11	3	6, 6, 2	3, 3, 3	15
II	19	6	59,/,18	9,/, 6	205
II (two stages)			/, 8, 1	/, 6, 6	

Table 10. Comparison of the Controlled Systems.

For Example II, eight MTSIs are required to obtain the six control places under *Algorithm L*. Hence, one can infer that its performance is better than that of *Algorithm U*. Only one set of CMTSI is needed to obtain the same control result by *Algorithm P*. As a result, one can conclude that our proposed policy is more efficient than the other two methods.

To examine and compare the efficiency of the proposed method with those in[16, 24] in a system with large reachability graphs, one can use eight different markings of p_1, p_8, p_{15}, p_{18}, and p_{19}: $[6, 5, 1, 1, 1]^T$, $[7, 6, 2, 1, 1]^T$, $[7, 6, 1, 2, 1]^T$, $[7, 6, 1, 1, 2]^T$, $[9, 8, 2, 2, 2]^T$, $[12, 11, 3, 3, 3]^T$, $[15, 14, 4, 4, 4]^T$, and $[18, 17, 5, 5, 5]^T$. Tables 11 and 12 show various parameters in the plant and partially controlled net models, where $M(p_{15})$, $M(p_{18})$, and $M(p_{19})$ vary; $|R|$, $|M_L|$, $|R_D|^U$, $|R_D|^L$, indicate the number of reachable markings (states), legal markings, and dead markings under *Algorithms U* and *L*, respectively. Additionally, MTSIs of *Algorithms U, L,* and *P* are symbolized by $|\psi|^U$, $|\psi|^L$ and $|\psi|^P$, respectively. The last column is $r_a = |\psi|^P / |\psi|^U$ in Table 11, and $r_b = \psi|^P / |\psi|^L$ in Table 12. Notably, *Algorithm G*[13] can be regarded as

Algorithm U in Table 11 since the number of MTSIs and ESSPs are the same. In table 11, here, N_{sep} represents the number of MTSIs, and the N_{sep}/U, N_{sep}/L and N_{sep}/P represent the number of MTSIs of *Algorithms U, L,* and *P*, respectively. Obviously, the number of $|\psi|^U$ in the plant model grows quickly from cases 1 to 8. For instance, when M (p_{15}) = M (p_{18}) = M (p_{19}) = 5, $|\psi|^U$ = 4311, meaning that one must solve 4311 MTSIs when *Algorithm U* is used. However, since $|\psi|^P$ = 228, only 228 equations (MTSIs) need to be solved under *Algorithm P*. As a result, *Algorithm P* is more efficient than *Algorithm U* in a large system.

CASES	$\|R\|$	$\|M_L\|$	$\|R_D\|^U$	$\|\psi\|^U$	$\|\psi\|^P$	r_a
1	282	205	16	59	18	30.5%
2	600	484	27	95	28	29.5%
3	972	870	26	103	26	25.2%
4	570	421	16	107	19	17.8%
5	4011	3711	42	288	42	14.6%
6	27152	26316	84	886	84	9.5%
7	124110	122235	145	2115	145	6.9%
8	440850	437190	228	4311	228	5.3%

Table 11. Parametersin the Plant and Partially Controlled Models with Varying Markings: *U* vs. *P*.

CASE	$\|R\|$	$\|M_L\|$	$\|R_D\|^L$	$\|\psi\|^L$	$\|\psi\|^P$	r_b
1	282	205	1	8	1	12.5%
2	600	484	1	8	1	12.5%
3	972	870	6	10	6	60.0%
4	570	421	1	8	1	12.5%
5	4011	3711	9	15	9	60.0%
6	27152	26316	28	48	28	58.3%
7	124110	122235	60	105	60	57.1%
8	440850	437190	108	192	108	56.3%

Table 12. Parametersin the Plant and Partially Controlled Models with Varying Markings: *L* vs. *P*.

In Table 12, the number of MTSIs calculated by *Algorithm L* can be controlled, but *Algorithm P* is more efficient in these cases. For instance, when M (p_{15}) = M (p_{18}) = M (p_{19}) = 5, $|\psi|^L$ = 192, meaning that one still has to solve 192 MTSIs when *Algorithm L* is used. However, $|\psi|^P$ =108. Only 108 MTSIs need to be solved by using *Algorithm P*. Importantly, the computational cost can be reduced by using our proposed method when it is compared with those in[12, 16]. In conclusion, *Algorithm P* is more efficient in large reachability graph cases than those in[12-13].

6. Conclusion

The proposed policy can be implemented for FMSs based on the theory of regions and Petri nets, where the dead markings are identified in its reachability graph. The underlying notion of the prior work is that many inequalities (i.e. MTSIs) must be solved to prevent legal markings from entering the illegal zone in the original PN model. One must generate all MTSIs in a reachability graph and require high computation. This work proposes and uses CMTSI to overcome the computational difficulty. The detail information is also obtained in existing literatures.[26-29] The proposed method can reduce the number of inequalities and thus the computational cost very significantly since CMTSIs are much less than MTSIs in large models. Consequently, it is optimal with much better computational efficiency than those existing optimal policies[12-13, 16]. More benchmark studies will be desired to establish such computational advantages of the proposed one over the prior ones. It should be noted that the problem is still NP-hard the same as other optimal policies due to the need to generate the reachability graph of a Petri net. The future research is thus much needed to overcome the computational inefficiency of all these methods.

Author details

Yen-Liang Pan
Department of Avionic Engineering, R.O.C. Air Force Academy, Taiwan, R.O.C.

Acknowledgement

The author is grateful to Prof. Yi-Sheng Huang and Prof. MengChu Zhou whose comments and suggestions greatly helped me improve the presentation and quality of this work.

7. References

[1] Fanti MP, Zhou MC. Deadlock control methods in automated manufacturing systems. IEEE Trans Syst Man Cybern A Syst Humans, 2004;34(1):5-22.
[2] Murata T. Petri nets: Properties, analysis and applications. In Proc IEEE. 1989;77(4):541-580.
[3] Ezpeleta J, Colom JM, Martinez J. A Petri net based deadlock prevention policy for flexible manufacturing systems. IEEE Trans Robot Autom. 1995;11(2):173-184.
[4] Jeng MD. A Petri net synthesis theory for modeling flexible manufacturing systems. IEEE Trans Syst Man Cybern B Cybern. 1997;27(2):169-183.
[5] Huang YS, Jeng MD, Xie XL, Chung SL. Deadlock prevention policy based on Petri nets and siphons Int J Prod Res. 2001;39(2):283-305.
[6] Li ZW, Hu HS, Wang AR. Design of liveness-enforcing supervisors for flexible manufacturing systems using Petri nets. IEEE Trans Syst Man Cybern C Appl Rev. 2007;37(4):517-526.
[7] Iordache MV, Moody JO, Antsaklis PJ. A method for the synthesis liveness enforcing supervisors in Petri nets. Procceedings of the 2001 American Control Conference; 2011 Jun 25-27; Arlington, VA, USA. P. 4943-8. (ISBN:0-7803-6495-3)

[8] Park J, Reveliotis SA. Algebraic synthesis of efficient deadlock avoidance policies for sequential resource allocation systems IEEE Trans Autom Control. 2000;16(2):190-195.

[9] Li ZW, Zhou MC. Elementary siphons of Petri nets and their application to deadlock prevention in flexible manufacturing systems. IEEE Trans Syst Man Cybern A Syst Humans. 2004 Jan;34(1):38-51.

[10] Li ZW, Zhou MC. On siphon computation for deadlock control in a class of Petri nets. IEEE Trans Syst Man Cybern A Syst Humans. 2008;38(3):667-679.

[11] Cho H, Kumaran TK, Wysk RA. Graph-theoretic deadlock detection and resolution for flexible manufacturing systems. IEEE Trans Robot Autom. 2000;11(2):190-195.

[12] Uzam M. An optimal deadlock prevention policy for flexible manufacturing systems using Petri net models with resources and the theory of regions. Int J Adv Manuf Technol. 2002;19(3):192-208.

[13] Ghaffari A, Rezg N, Xie XL. Design of a live and maximally permissive Petri net controller using the theory of regions IEEE Trans Robot Autom 2003;19(1):137-142.

[14] Reveliotis SA, Choi JY. Designing reversibility-enforcing supervisors of polynomial complexity for bounded Petri nets through the theory of regions. Lecture Notes in Computer Science. 2006;4024:322-341.

[15] Badouel E, Darondeau P. Theory of Regions. Third Advance Course on Petri Nets. Springer-Verlag, 1998.

[16] Li ZW, Zhou MC, Jeng MD. A maximally permissive deadlock prevention policy for FMS based on Petri net siphon control and the theory of regions. IEEE Trans Autom Sci Eng. 2008;5(1):183-188.

[17] Uzam M, Zhou MC. An iterative synthesis approach to Petri net-based deadlock prevention policy for flexible manufacturing systems. IEEE Trans Syst Man Cybern A Syst Humans. 2007;37(3):362-371.

[18] Li ZW, Zhou MC, Wu NQ. A survey and comparison of petri net-based deadlock prevention policies for flexible manufacturing systems. IEEE Trans Syst Man Cybern C Appl Rev. 2008 ;38(2):173-188.

[19] Piroddi L, Cordone R, Fumagalli I. Selective siphon control for deadlock prevention in Petri nets. IEEE Trans Syst Man Cybern A Syst Humans. 2008;38(6):1337-1348.

[20] Silva M, Teruel E, Colom JM. Linear algebraic and linear programming techniques for the analysis of P/T net systems. LNCS, 1998;1491:303-373.

[21] Ramadge PJ, Wonham WM. The control of discrete event systems. Proc IEEE. 1989;77(1):81-98.

[22] Viswanadham N, Narahari Y, Johnson TL. Deadlock prevention and deadlock avoidance in flexible manufacturing systems using Petri net models. IEEE Trans Robot Autom. 1990;6(6):713-723.

[23] Abdallah IB, ElMaraghy HA. Deadlock prevention and avoidance in FMS: A Petri net based approach. Int J Adv Manuf Technol. 1998;14(10):704-715.

[24] Li ZW, Wang A, Lin H. A deadlock prevention approach for FMS using siphon and the theory of regions. Proceeding of the IEEE International Conference on Systems, Man and Cybernetics; 2004 Oct 10-13; The Hague, Netherlands. P. 5079-84. (ISBN:0-7803-8566-7)

[25] INA. (Integrated Net Analyzer), A Software Tool for Analysis of Petri Nets. Version 2.2, 31.07. 2003. [Online]. Available: http://www.informatik.hu-berlin.de/~starke/ina.html.

[26] Huang YS, Pan YL. Enhancement of An Efficient Liveness-Enforcing Supervisor for Flexible Manufacture Systems. Int J Adv Manuf Technol. 2010;48:725-737. (DOI: 10.1007/s00170-009-2299-x)

[27] Huang YS, Pan YL. An Improved Maximally Permissive Deadlock Prevention Policy Based on the Theory of Regions and Reduction Approach. IET Control Theory Appl. 2011;5(9):1069-1078. (DOI: 10.1049/iet-cta.2010.0371.)

[28] Pan YL, Huang YS. Solutions for Deadlocked Problem of FMSs Using Theory of Regions. Adv Mat Res. 2011 ;314-346 :535-538. (DOI:10.4028/www.scientific.net/AMR.314-316.535.)

[29] Huang YS, Pan YL, Zhou MC. Computationally Improved Optimal Deadlock Control Policy for Flexible Manufacturing Systems. IEEE Trans Syst Man Cybern A Syst Humans. 2012; 42(2):404-415.

Chapter 4

Implementation of Distributed Control Architecture for Multiple Robot Systems Using Petri Nets

Gen'ichi Yasuda

Additional information is available at the end of the chapter

http://dx.doi.org/10.5772/50577

1. Introduction

Because of the generality of the robot's physical structure, control and reprogrammability, it is expected that more and more robots will be introduced into industry to automate various operations. This flexibility can be exploited if the robot control system can be programmed easily. Anyway, it is quite obvious that a single robot cannot perform effective tasks in an industrial environment, unless it is provided with some additional equipment. For example, in building a component, two robots are required to cooperate, one holding some part while the other attaches some other part to it. In other tasks, robots may pursue different goals, making sure that they both don't attempt to use the same resource at the same time. Such synchronization and coordination can only be achieved by getting the robots to talk to each other or to some supervising agent. However, for large-scaled and complicated manufacturing systems, from the viewpoint of cost-performance and reliability appropriate representation and analysis methods of the control system have not sufficiently been established [1]. The lack of adequate programming tools for multiple robots make some tasks impossible to be performed. In other cases, since the control requirements are diversified and often changed, the cost of programming may be a significant fraction of the total cost of an application. Due to these reasons, the development of an effective programming method to integrate a system which includes various robots and other devices that cooperate in the same task is urgently required [2].

In programming by the well-known teaching-playback or teaching by showing, the programmer specifies a single execution for the robot: there are no loops, no conditionals, no data retrieval, nor computations. This method can be implemented without a general-purpose computer, and it is especially adequate for some applications, such as spot welding, painting, and simple materials handling. In other applications such as mechanical assembly and inspection, robot-level languages provide computer programming languages with commands to access sensors and to specify robot motions, enabling the data from external sensors, such as vision and force, to be used in modifying the robot's motion. Many recent methods in robot programming provide the power of robot-level languages without requiring deep programming knowledge, extending the basic philosophy of teaching to include decision-making based on sensing. Another method, known as task-level programming [3], [4], requires specifying goals for the positions of objects, rather than the motions of the robot needed to achieve those goals. A task-level specification is meant to be completely robot-independent; no positions or paths specified by the user depend on the robot geometry or kinematics. This method requires complete geometric models of the environment and of the robot, referred to as world-modeling systems. An object oriented approach has been held for modeling, simulation and control of multiple robot systems and intelligent manufacturing systems [5]-[9]. The main drawback of these methods relative to teaching is that they require the robot programmer to be an expert in computer programming and in the design of sensor-based motion strategies. Hence, this method is not accessible to the typical worker on the factory floor [10], [11].

Robot program development is often ignored in the design of robot control systems and, consequently, complex robot programs can be very difficult to debug. The development of robot programs has several characteristics which need special treatment. Because robot programs have complex side-effects and their execution time is usually long, it is not always feasible to re-initialize the program upon failure. So, robot programming systems should allow programs to be modified on-line and immediately restarted. Sensory information and real-time interactions are crucial and not usually repeatable. The ability to record the sensor outputs, together with program traces should be provided as a real-time debugging tool. Further, because complex geometry and motions are difficult to visualize, 3D graphic simulators can play an important role. Another difficulty comes from the fact that each robot has its own programming system, and it is often undesirable to alter or substitute it with something else. Besides cost considerations, this is because each robot programming language is tailored to the machine it has to control, and it would be simply impossible, for example to obtain a good performance from an articulated robot using a language designed for a Cartesian one. To attend the above requirements, a universal robot programming method with real-time automatic translation from a robot language to another one is required in integrated manufacturing systems.

The decision was then taken to develop a robot programming method for multiple robot systems that would provide the following characteristics. All the activities of the global system should be supervised by the control system, which is the method suitable to the integrated management that is necessary in manufacturing systems. So the integral controller with the strong computational power to do the complex task of the coordination system is needed. According to the parallelism among the subtasks in the multi-robot coordination system, advantage of the parallel architecture of the control system is taken to reach the good control capabilities [12]. To give a prior attention to the requirements about the part flow control, the control algorithm is designed based on the Petri net [13]. The Petri net can describe parallel flows, design and implement real-time robot control tasks [14]-[16], so that the process schedule is easily and effectively laid down, inspected and corrected. Each robot may be programmed in its own language in order to maintain best performance of each machine. Each step of the programming procedure can be verified by graphic simulation in order to improve the interaction between the operator and the robots and to make possible the off-line programming.

In this chapter, the method described in the previous work [17] is applied to program cooperative tasks by multiple robots and to concurrently control real robots. The aim of this chapter is to describe and implement a programming and execution system based on Petri nets that allows easy programming of a control system which includes multiple different robots and a variety of auxiliary devices. The problem how the control and coordination algorithms based on Petri nets are realized in an example of two robots carrying parts cooperatively is resolved.

2. Net models of robotic processes

Because discrete event robotic systems are characterized by the occurrence of events and changing conditions, the type of Petri net considered here is the condition-event net, in which conditions can be modeled by places whilst events can be modeled by transitions. A token is placed in a place to indicate that the condition corresponding to the place is holding. Because a condition-event net should be safe, which means that the number of tokens in each place does not exceed one, all of its arc weights are 1's and it has no self-loops. Condition-event nets can be easily extended and can efficiently model complex robotic processes. By the Petri nets extension, some capabilities which connect the net model to its external environment are employed. A gate arc connects a transition with a signal source, and an output arc connects a place with an external robot to send a command. The marking of a net changes, when a transition, which is enabled, eventually is fired. The place and gate variables involved in transition firing are shown in Figure 1.

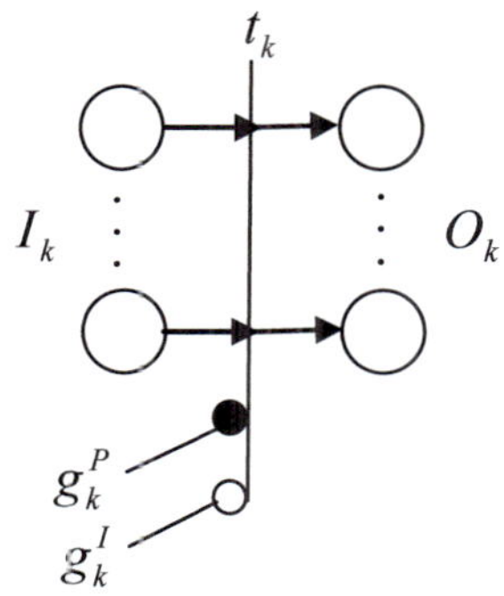

Figure 1. Place and gate variables involved in transition firing test

The firing condition of transition t_k can be written as

$$t_k = (\bigcap_{i \in I_k} p_i \cdot \bigcap_{j \in O_k} \overline{p_j} \cdot g_k^P \cdot \overline{g_k^I}) \tag{1}$$

where $\bigcap$ denotes the logical product operation, and

I_k : set of input places of transition t_k

O_k : set of output places of transition t_k

g_k^P : logical variable of permissive gate condition of transition t_k

g_k^I : logical variable of inhibitive gate condition of transition t_k

The marking change of input and output places of transition t_k can be written as follows:

$$\begin{aligned} &For \quad p_i \in I_k, \quad p_i = \overline{t_k} \cdot p_i \\ &For \quad p_j \in O_k, \quad p_j = t_k + p_j \end{aligned} \tag{2}$$

If a place has two or more input transitions or output transitions, these transitions may be in conflict for firing. When two or more transitions are enabled only one transition should be fired using some arbitration rule. Well-known properties of the condition-event net are as follows. From (1), if the directions of the input and output arcs of a place and the existence of token in the place are reversed, the firing conditions of all the transitions in the net are unchanged. If there is no conflict place in a net, then the net can be transformed into a net with no loop. If there is a loop with no conflict place in a net, the number of tokens in the loop is unchanged. In case that initially there is no token in a net marking, if there are parallel paths between two transitions, the maximum number of tokens in each path is equal to the minimum number of places in each path. So, by addition of a dummy path with a specified number of places, the number of tokens in each path can be controlled.

The dynamic behavior of the system represented by a net model is simulated using the enabling and firing rules. One cycle of the simulation comprises the following steps, which are executed when some gate condition is changed.

1. Calculate the logical variable of the transition associated with the new gate condition using (1).
2. If the transition is fired, calculate the logical variables of its input and output places using (2).
3. Then the marking is changed and a new command is sent to the corresponding robot.

In any initial marking, there must not be more than one token in a place. According to these rules, the number of tokens in a place never exceeds one; the net is essentially a safe graph. A robotic action is modeled by two transitions and one condition as shown in Figure 2. At the "Start" transition the command associated with the transition is sent to the corresponding robot or machine. At the "End" transition the status report is received. When a token is present in the "Action" place, the action is in progressive. The "Completed" place can be omitted, and then the "End" transition is fused with the "Start" transition of the next action. Activities can be assigned an amount of time units to monitor them in time for real performance evaluation. In case of "Waiting" place for a specified timing, after the interval the end signal is sent by the timer. In case of "Waiting" place for a specified signal, the logical function is tested and the resultant signal is sent as a gate condition in place of end signal by the sensing module.

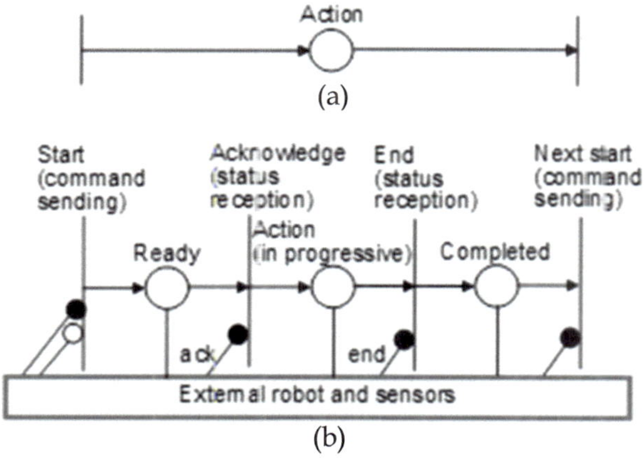

Figure 2. Net representation of robotic action: (a) macro representation, (b) detailed representation

Figure 3 shows the net representation of real-time control of a chucking operation with an external device. Each action place represents a subtask. The "Loading" place represents the macro model of the operation and indicates that, when a token is in the place, only one token exists in the path of places from "Grasp" to "Return".

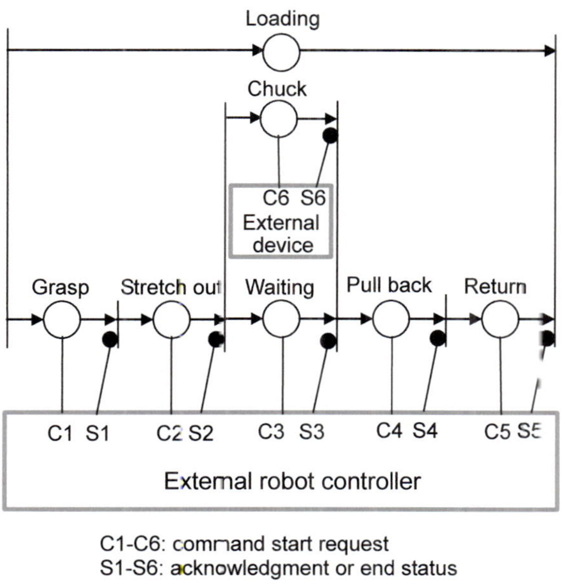

Figure 3. Net representation of chucking operation with a robot and an external device

Figure 4 shows the procedure of macro representation of a pick-and-place operation by a single robot. Figure 4 (a) shows the detailed net model, where if the first transition fires it never fires until the last transition fires. So, a dummy place "Robot" can be added as shown in Figure 4 (b) and a token in the place indicates that the state of the robot is "operating", because a real robot may load or unload only one part at a time. Thus, the place represents the macro state of the task without the detailed net as shown in Figure 4 (c).

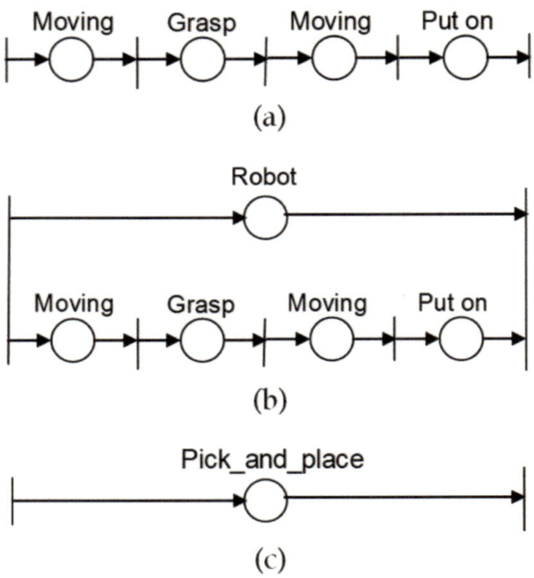

Figure 4. Macro representation of Pick_and_place operation by a robot: (a) detailed representation, (b) parallel representation with dummy place in direct path, (c) macro representation

A dummy place is used to control the maximum number of tokens in the paths parallel to the direct path. In case that the hardware of a robotic system is composed of one or more motion units or axes, the number of tokens in the dummy place indicates the maximum number of processing or parts processed by each motion unit. The overall action is decomposed into detailed actions of constituent motion units by the coordinator.

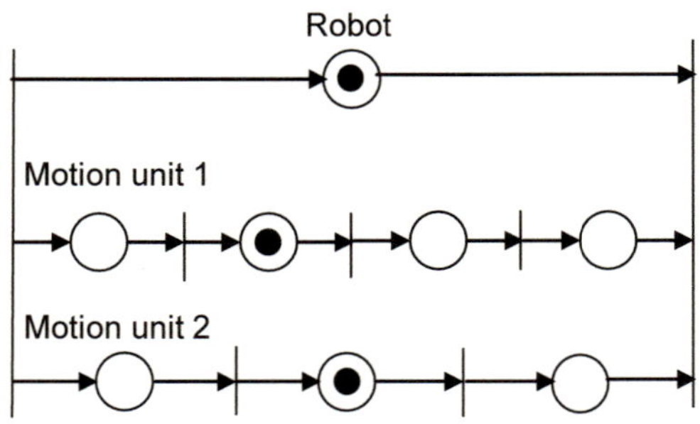

Figure 5. Net representation of robotic system composed of two motion units

A single task executed by a robot or machine is represented as a sequential net model. The places are connected via transitions, each having a Boolean condition or gate condition. This condition is tested while the transition is enabled, i.e., when the preceding place is active. If the condition is true, the succeeding place becomes active, and the preceding place becomes inactive. Places for motion and computational actions have a unique output transition. Decision actions introduce conflict into the net. The choice can either be made non-deterministically or may be controlled by some external signal or command from the upper level controller. Figure 6 shows a basic net structure with task selection. Figure 7 shows a net model with task selection and its corresponding VAL program [18], which is written using direct commands for the hardware robot controller and implies the lowest level detailed representation of the subtasks.

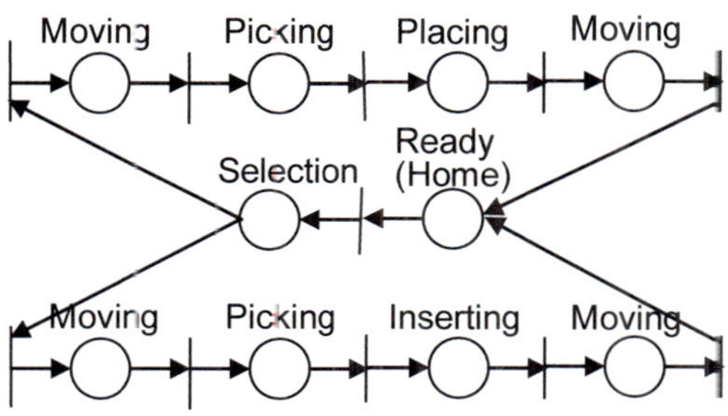

Figure 6. Basic structure of macro net model with task selection

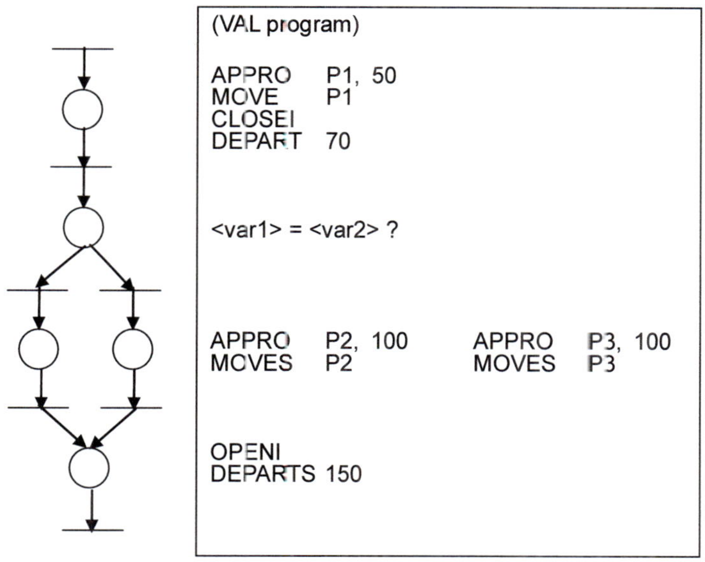

Figure 7. Example net model with task selection and robot language program

Cooperation which requires the sharing of information and resources between the processes, is usefully introduced into the composite net which is simply the union of such sequential nets. Figure 8 shows two equivalent net representations of concurrent tasks with synchronization. In Figure 9, a loop with no token implies that the net falls into a deadlock because of inconsistency with respect to transition firing.

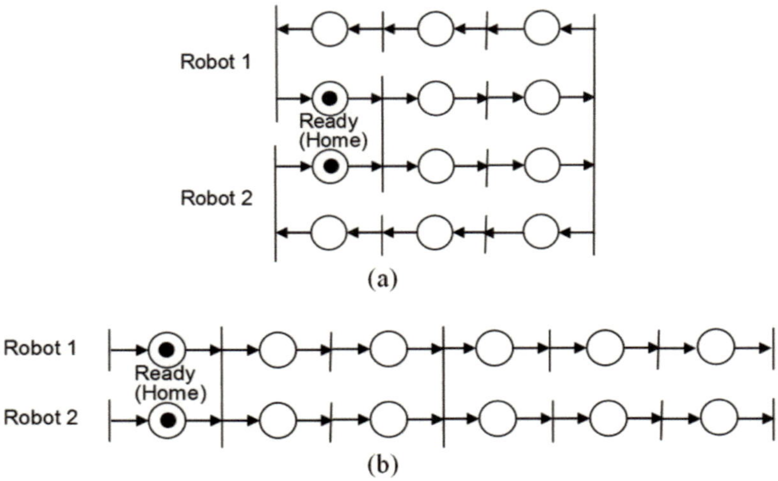

Figure 8. Net representations of basic structure of cooperation between two robots: (a) cyclic, (b) parallel

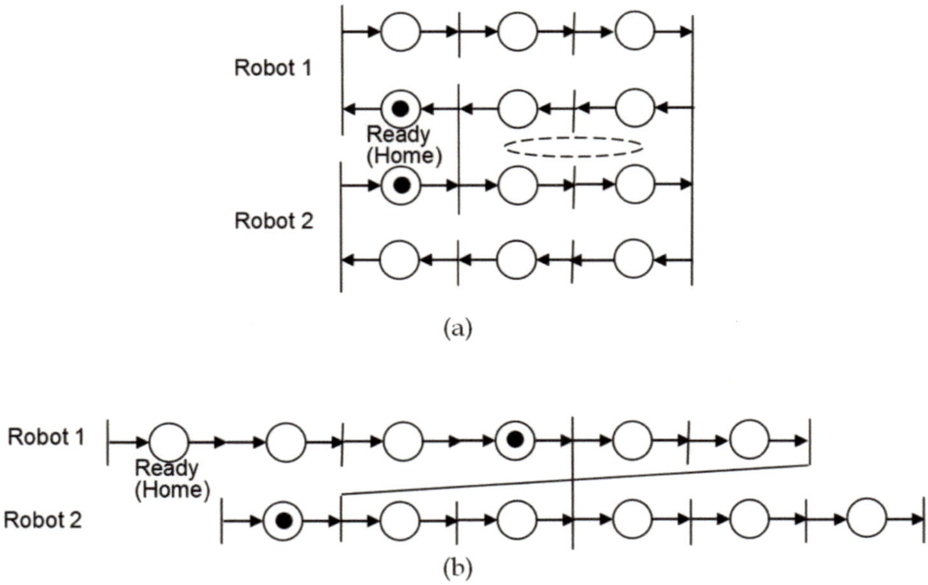

Figure 9. (a) Example net which has a loop with no token, (b) parallel representation which indicates a deadlock situation

3. Synchronization and coordination

A net representation of cooperative operation using synchronization mechanism with permissive and inhibitive gate arcs is shown in Figure 10, where the shared transition requires mutual synchronization between two tasks [19]. Synchronization of transitions is also employed for decomposition of a complex task into simple tasks cooperatively executed by two robots, as shown in Figure 11.

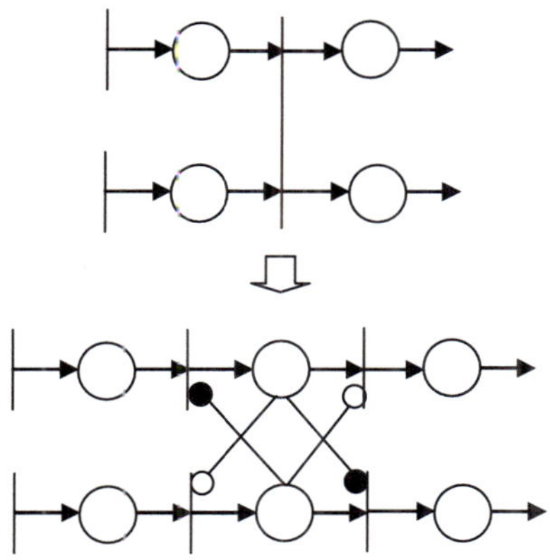

Figure 10. Distributed implementation of synchronization between two machines

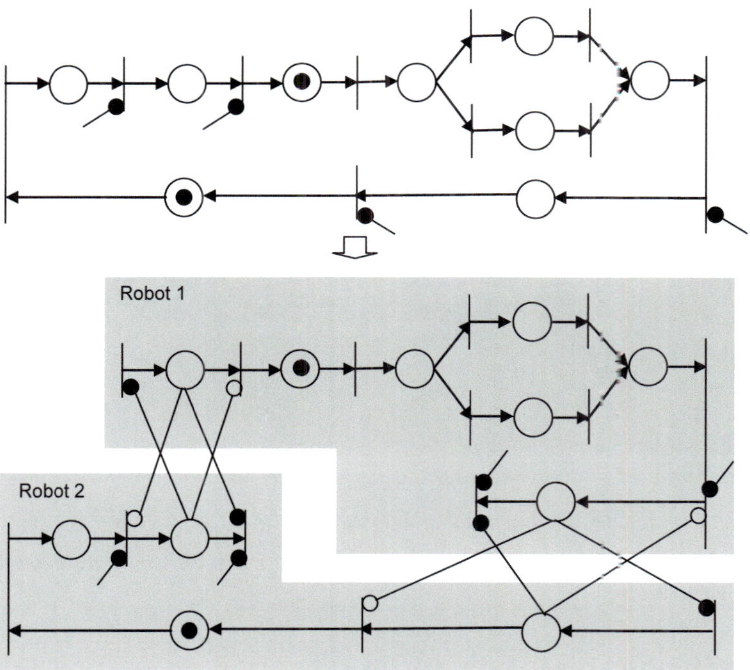

Figure 11. Decomposition of a complex net into two simple nets using synchronization mechanism of transitions

The decomposition procedure of a net is as follows. First, a new place is added in parallel to the input place of the decomposed transition. Then, transitions are added in the input and output of the two places. The input transition of the new place is a source transition. Each place exchanges internal gate signals to input and output transitions with the other place when a token is in the place. The gate arcs are implemented using asynchronous communication between different robots.

4. Net based multiple robot coordination

A coordination task of carrying parts from a machining station to depository is considered as an example application using multiple robots. An arm robot picks up a part from the station and loads it into a mobile robot by which the part is sent to the storehouse. The arm robot is equipped with a visual sensor via which it can recognize the parts as well as their positions and also equipped with a force sensor which is necessary for grasping and loading the parts. On the mobile robot, a radio transceiver is used for its communication sending back feedback information from the sensors and receiving the control information from the main controller. The visual sensor is used for landmark recognition in the environment and infra-red sensors are used for obstacle avoidance. Figure 12 shows the arm robot and the mobile robot.

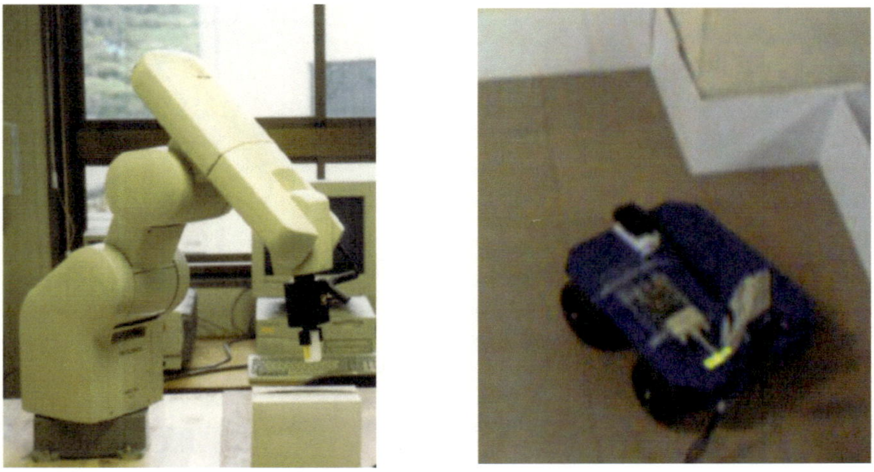

(a) (b)

Figure 12. View of experimental robot systems: (a) arm robot, (b) autonomous mobile robot with radio transceiver and visual sensor

4.1. Task specification based on work flow

Based on robot task level programming of the specified part flow, the coordination task of carrying parts from a machining station to depository is represented as a work flow graph for a part sequentially processed by the arm robot and the mobile robot · In the work flow graph, each node represents a place where any processing is performed on the part, while an arc represent physical processing such as picking, loading, transfer or machining. The work flow comprises the following three arcs as shown in Figure 13.

1. picking from the station pallet by the arm robot
2. loading into the mobile robot by the arm robot
3. transfer from the station to the depository by the mobile robot

Figure 13. Task specification based on work flow processed on parts

The picking, loading, or transfer is specified using a local path in the neighborhood of the start and end place and a global path from the two places. Mutual exclusive resources or shared workspace such as buffers are also considered to avoid robot collision. The work flow diagram is transformed into a conceptual net model considering machines in charge of each processing. Figure 14 illustrates the net model of the coordination task between the two robots. At this point, associated processing such as object identification, alarm processing, exception handling is added. Then each processing is translated into detailed operations or actions. At each step of detailed specification, places of the net are substituted by a subnet in a manner which maintains the structural property such as liveness and safeness. Hierarchical decomposition assures detailed net models free from deadlock.

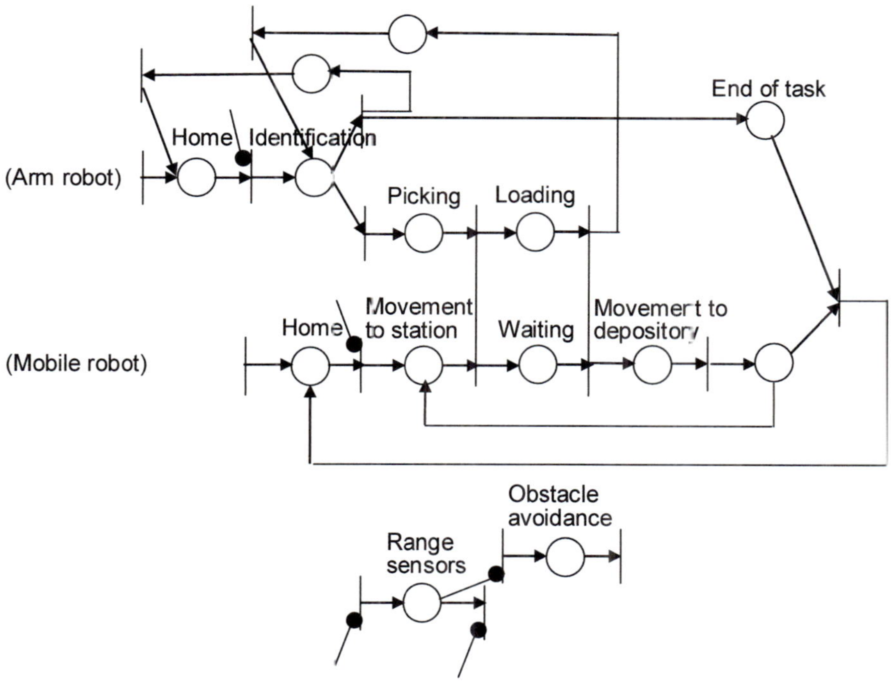

Figure 14. Net model of carrying task by two robots

The conceptual coordination task is specified as follows. First, after the reception of a start command, in "Identification" place, the arm robot judges whether or not there are still parts in the station using the visual sensor. If not, the arm robot informs the mobile robot that the task has been finished with "End of task" place and returns back to its home position. On the contrary, the arm robot starts to get the position of a part and grasp it. The mobile robot moves to the station, and the arm robot, after the completion of the "Grasp" subtask and the "Movement to station" subtask, starts "Loading" subtask while the mobile robot waits at the specified position. After the completion of loading, the mobile robot moves to the depository, and the arm robot executes the "Identification" subtask repeatedly. If the signal of "End of task" is on, the mobile robot returns back to its home position, and if not it moves to the station. From the "Movement to station" and "Movement to depository" places, the gate signal is sent to repeatedly execute the "Obstacle avoidance" subtask using infrared range sensors. In the coordination task, synchronization is represented as a shared transition which is implemented using a sequence of asynchronous communications as shown in Figure 10.

4.2. Subtask control of arm robots

For net based control of the arm robot, unit actions or motions should be defined in a task coordinate system. The trajectories can be free (point to point), straight or circular. The speed of forward movement of a trajectory is specified in the main coordinate of the task coordinate system. The movements in the other coordinates are compensated based on errors. At the end of a trajectory, it can be stopped or continued while turning the direction. When a trajectory is circular, the end-effector can have either of two orientations, that is, to the center of the circle or fixed. In the case of control of the end-effector, there are commands to represent the coordinate frames, open the hand, close the hand, and grasp. The grasp command assumes that the hand has a proximity sensor to autonomously grasp a workpiece in an appropriate direction. Synchronous actions by the arm and the wrist or sequences of unit actions by the arm, the wrist and the fingers are also specified using commands. The reference positions for arm movement are set by a separated teaching method, as well as desired positions of parts known at the programming time. The other positions relative to these positions are computed on-line. In this way, using these commands the final point and the trajectory of the motion can be specified in the task coordinate system. Figure 15 shows the block diagram of the trajectory tracking control in the task coordinate system.

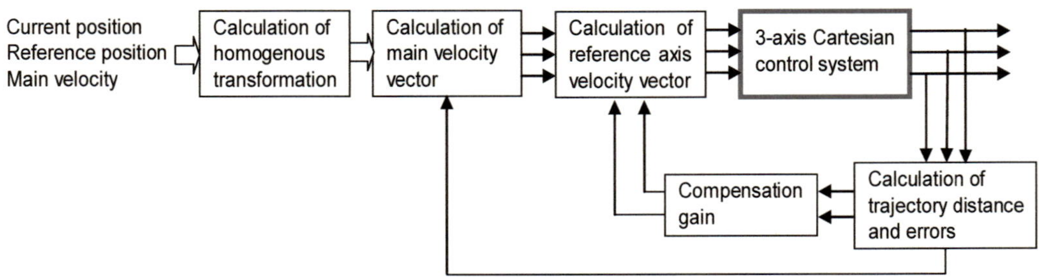

Figure 15. Block diagram of 3-axis Cartesian coordinate arm control system

The command system can be extended to execute actions specified based on information from the external sensors such as visual sensors, proximity sensors or slippage sensors.

Figure 14 shows the hardware structure of the microcontroller-based control system. The visual sensor detects the coordinates of the center of an object and the orientation of an edge of the object. The proximity sensors, which are composed of several LED arrays attached to the fingers can detect the distance and orientation of the object with respect to the planes of the fingers. For the grip command, the grip action raises the grip force till the signal from the slippage sensor becomes zero. When the hand is moving down vertically, if the signal from the slippage sensor rises inversely, then the hand is opened.

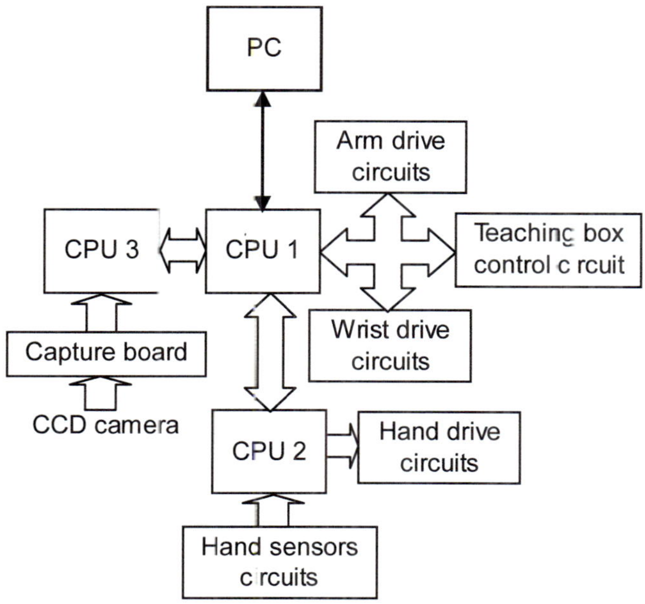

Figure 16. Block diagram of multi-axis arm control system

When programming a specific task, the task is broken down into subtasks through task planning. These subtasks are composed of the position data and the programs that are edited using the robot motion simulator. Each subtask is represented as a place. A place can also represent the internal state of the robot, which is operating or idle, and the state of external devices. The relations of these places are explicitly represented by interconnections of transitions, arcs and gates that are edited with the robot task program editor and simulator. For places that represent subtasks, the following parameters are necessary: 1) the code of the controller such as the vehicle, arm, hand or sensor etc., that executes the subtask, 2) the file name where the subtask such as MOVE, GRASP, RELEASE, or HOLD, etc., is explicitly written with some programming language, and 3) the file name of a set of position data that will be used to execute the subtask. The procedures of editing and simulating of the net model are done interactively until certain specifications are satisfied. At this point, it is expected that problems such as deadlock, conflict resolution, concurrency, synchronization, etc., have been well studied and analyzed. If some error is found, that is if the net model does not satisfy the specification, it can be easily amended by reediting the net model and simulating again.

4.3. Subtask control of mobile robots

The decomposition of "Movement to station" place and the associated control structure are illustrated in Figure 17. In movement control of the mobile robot using state feedback based on pose sensors, the robot's planning task is reduced to setting some intermediate positions (subgoals), with respective control modes, lying on the requested path. The global path planner in the trajectory controller determines a sequence of subgoals to reach the goal. Given a set of subgoal locations, the target tracking controller plans a detailed path to the closest subgoal position only and executes this plan. In the target tracking control, the distance between the robot and the specified target position and the angle between the forward direction and the target is computed based on the current location detected by the internal pose sensors (accelerators and gyros) and the current target. And then, the reference tangent and angular velocities of the mobile robot is determined to meet the target tracking using a state feedback algorithm, and the reference wheel velocities are computed based on inverse kinematics. The new velocity setpoints are sent to the respective wheel velocity controller, which executes proportional plus integral control of its wheel velocity using the rotary encoder.

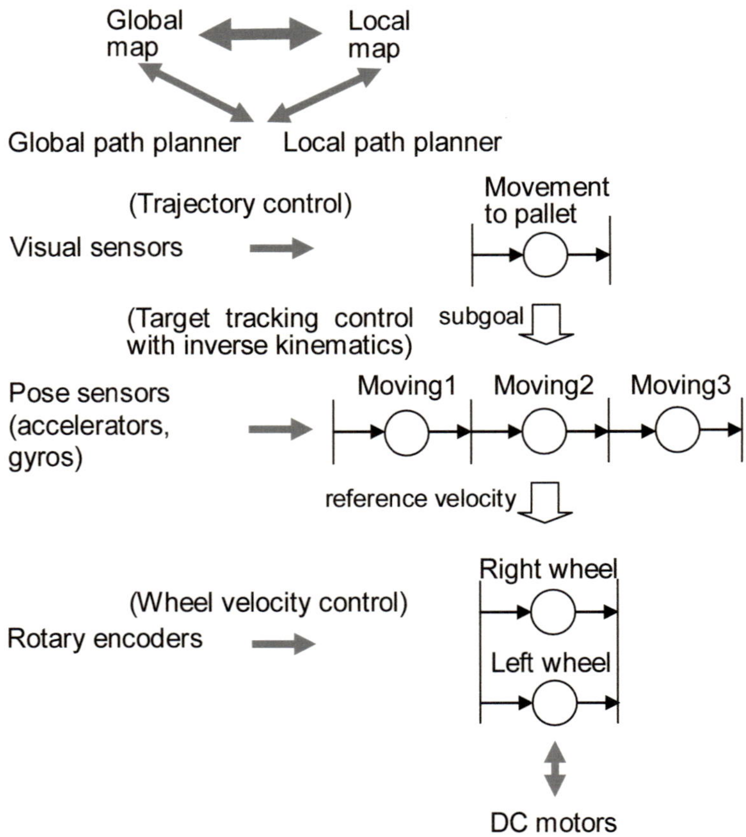

Figure 17. Hierarchical decomposition of net model of mobile robot control system

In case of detection of a blockage on the intended path, the trajectory controller receives a failure notification from the visual sensor, then modifies the subgoals and the short term local knowledge of the robot's surroundings and triggers the target tracking in view of this change to the local environment knowledge. The trajectory controller has the dynamic map with global and local representation that becomes more accurate as the robot moves. Upon reaching this subgoal location, its local map will change based on the perceptual information using the PSD data extracted during motion. Then the target tracking controller triggers the local path planner to generate a path from the new location to the next subgoal location. When the lowest-level wheel velocity control fails to make progress, the target tracking controller attempts to find a way past the obstacle by turning the robot in position and trying again. The trajectory controller decides when and if new information integrated into the local map can be copied into the global map.

The current subgoal and current location are shared by the trajectory controller and the target tracking controller. In the coordinator program, a place is assigned to each shared variable to be protected from concurrent access. Mutual exclusive access to a shared variable is represented by a place, which is identical to the P and V operations on the semaphore, as shown in Figure 18.

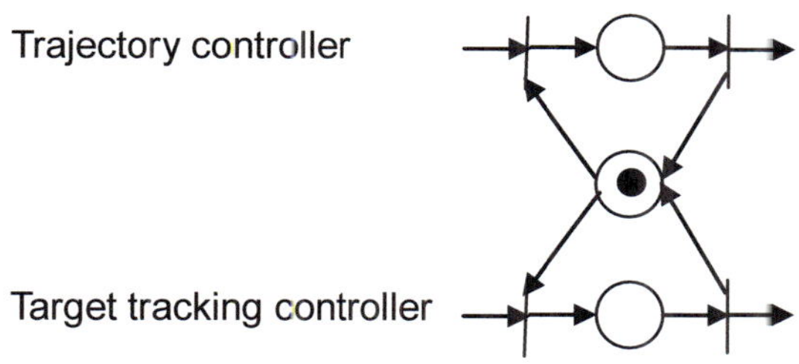

Figure 18. Net representation of mutual exclusive access

If a time-out in real-time control, communication, or sensing data acquisition, is brought about, an alarm signal is sent to the upper controller. When an alarm is processed, a signal is sent to stop any active controller. These signals are implemented by places, as shown in Figure 19. If the final goal is reached, the target tracking controller sends an "End" signal to the trajectory controller, which then sends end signals to the rest of the system.

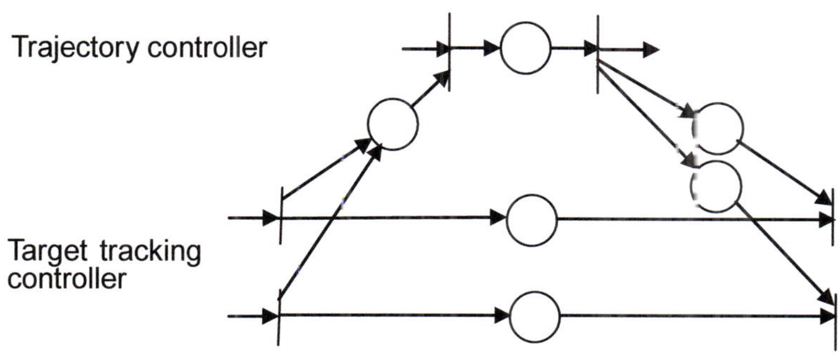

Figure 19. Net representation of signaling between controllers

5. Implementation of net based control system

Based on net models, a programming and execution system is implemented. A whole task is edited with a net based robot task program editor and simulator. In parallel, a robot motion simulator is used to edit the subtask programs. Using these systems, the net program file, the sequence program file, and the position data file are created and used by the multi-robot controller to execute the coordination task. A schematic of the functions of the robot programming system is illustrated in Figure 20. The connections of the robots and devices with PC are shown in Figure 21.

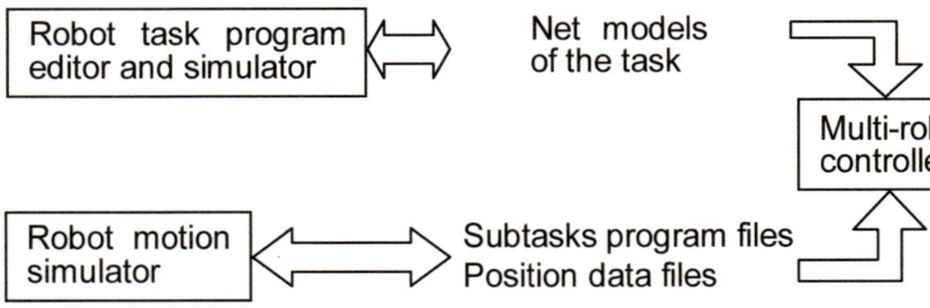

Figure 20. Structure of the robot programming system

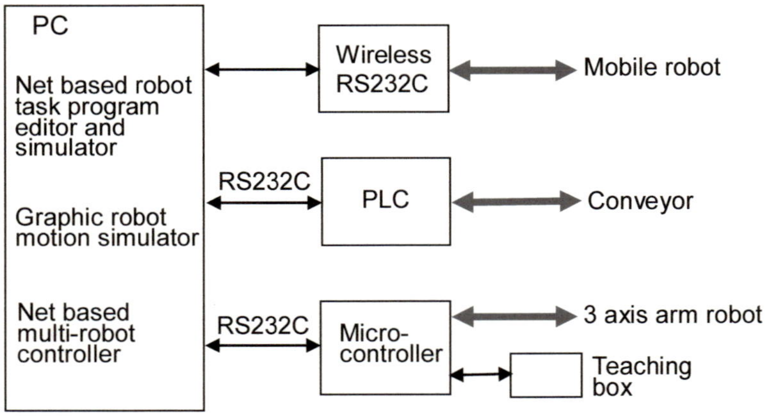

Figure 21. Connections of robots and devices with PC

The geometric data of the robot and workspace are specified using the length of the links of the robot, the geometric parameters of workpiece as well as input and deletion positions, and the form of the end-effector. The simulator constructs the three dimensional model of the robot and the workspace. The numerical data of the joint angles, absolute position and orientation of the robot are displayed on the terminal. The operator inputs the sequence of unit motion commands and position data. Then, the motion data are computed with consideration to the geometric parameters of the robots and workpieces. The net model file, the subtask program files and position data files are simulated with the robot task program editor and simulator and robot motion simulator respectively to test the programs and data that will be used to control the robots. The robot behavior is displayed graphically on a terminal step by step. Then the completed net model is transformed into the tabular form, and these files are loaded into the multi-robot controller that executes the programs. Example views of 3D graphic simulation of the arm robot and the mobile robot are shown in Figure 22. The flow chart of the net based programming method of multi-robot tasks using the separated teaching method is shown in Figure 23.

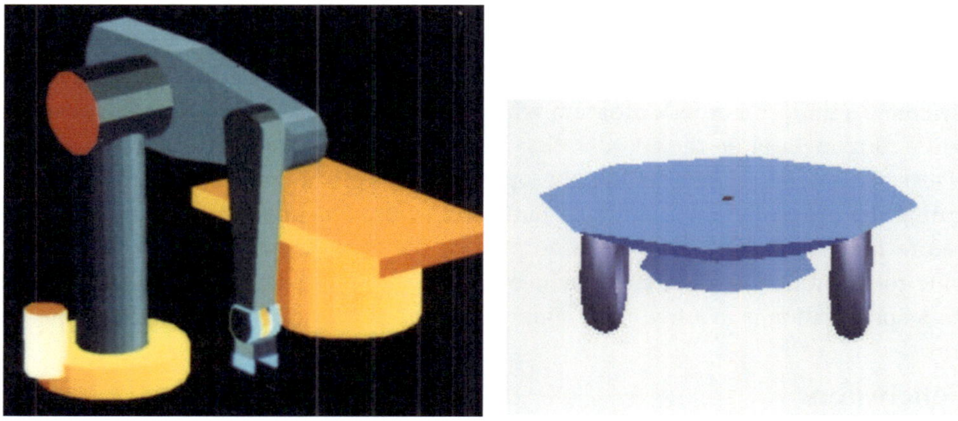

(a) (b)

Figure 22. View of 3D graphic simulation of (a) arm robot and (b) mobile robot

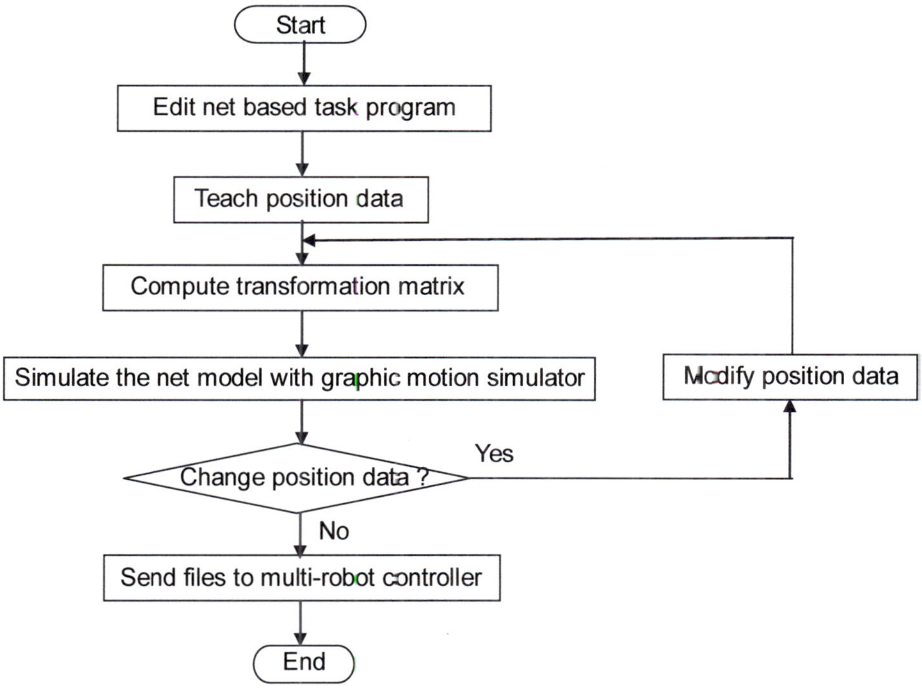

Figure 23. Flow chart of net based programming method using separated teaching method

The multi-robot controller accomplishes the specified task by executing the net model constructed above. Unit actions in a net model used for lowest level controllers are defined in a specified task space, where the action is executed. In the control software the position and orientation in the task space is transformed to the robot coordinate system using the homogeneous transformation matrix. The controller coordinates and supervises the individual controllers based on information explicitly represented by places, place parameters, transitions, arcs, and gates. That is, when a token enters a place that represents a subtask, immediately the controller defined by the control code is informed to execute the subtask with a specified data. Because of the proper nature of the Petri net, the designer can easily create a multi-robot task program which is free of logical errors. The method acts as a programming method on the coordination level and on the organization level [20]. That is, the Petri net is applied as a tool to the operator who plans the multi-robot task, and by executing the net model the individual hardware controllers are regulated and supervised. If, before moving the real robot, the outputs of the robot controller are linked with the graphic robot motion simulator, the whole task programmed can be tested off-line. When the task specification is required to be changed, the net model can be modified on-line.

6. Conclusions

It was confirmed that the multi-robot controller developed based on tasks programmed in the net form controls the equipment according to the programmed net model. The method provides concurrent movement of all robots and machines in the system, and it provides synchronization commands to allow coordination of their movements to accomplish user defined tasks. The commands used by this system are not based on any specific existing robot language. So, the method can be used in any real robot by translating it to the appropriate robot language, and it acts as a programming tool on the coordination level and on the organization level in multiple robot systems.

Author details

Gen'ichi Yasuda
Nagasaki Institute of Applied Science, Japan

7. References

[1] Martinez, J., Muro, P. & Silva, M. (1987). Modeling, Validation and Software Implementation of Production Systems Using High Level Petri Nets, *Proceedings of IEEE International Conference on Robotics and Automation* , pp. 1180-1185

[2] Sakane, S. (1993). Distributed Sensing System with 3D model-based agents, *Proceedings of IEEE/RSJ International Conference on Intelligent Robots and Systems*, pp. 1157-1163

[3] Bonner, J. & Shin, K. G. (1982). A Comparative Study of Robot Languages. *Computer Magazine*, IEEE, Vol. 14, No. 12, pp. 82-96

[4] Lozano-Perez, T. (1983). Robot Programming. *Proceedings of the IEEE*, Vol. 71, No. 7, pp. 821-841

[5] Yasuda, G. (1996). An Object-oriented Network Environment for Computer Vision Based Multirobot System Architectures, *Proceedings of 20th International Conference on Computers & Industrial Engineering*, pp. 1199-1202

[6] Yasuda, G. & Tachibana, K. (1996). An Integrated Object-oriented Expert System for Welding Procedure Selection and Process Control, *CRITICAL TECHNOLOGY: Proceedings of the Third World Congress on Expert Systems*, pp. 186-193

[7] Yasuda, G. (1997). Intelligent Manufacturing and Engineering, In: Jay Liebowitz Ed. *The Handbook of Applied Expert Systems*, CRC Press, Chapter 22, pp. 22.1-22.14

[8] Bussmann, S. (1998). Agent-Oriented Programming of Manufacturing Control Tasks, *Proceedings of the 3rd International Conference on Multi-Agent Systems*, pp. 57 - 63

[9] Yasuda, G. (1999). A Multiagent Architecture for Sensor-Based Control of Intelligent Autonomous Mobile Robots, *ACTA IMEKO 1999 (Proceedings of the 15th World Congress of the International Measurement Confederation (IMEKO))*, Vol.X (TC-17), pp. 145-152

[10] Cassinis, R. (1983). Hierarchical Control of Integrated Manufacturing Systems, *Proceedings of the 13th International Symposium on Industrial Robots and Robots 7*, pp. 12-9 - 12-20

[11] Wood, B. O. & Fugelso, M. A. (1983). MCL, The Manufacturing Control Language, *Proceedings of the 13th International Symposium on Industrial Robots and Robots 7*, pp. 12-84 - 12-96

[12] Yasuda, G., Takai, H. & Tachibana, K. (1994). Performance Evaluation of a Multimicrocomputer-Based Software Servo System for Real-Time Distributed Robot Control, *AUTOMATIC CONTROL 1994 (Proceedings of the 12th Triennial World Congress of IFAC)*, Pergamon, Vol. 2, pp. 673-678

[13] Murata, T. (1989). Petri Nets: Properties, Analysis and Applications. *Proceedings of the IEEE*, Vol. 77, No. 4, pp. 541-580

[14] Simon, D., Espiau, B., Kapellos, K. & Pissard-Gibolette, R. (1997). Orccad: Software Engineering for Real-Time Robotics. A Technical Insight. *Robotica*, Vol. 15, pp. 111-115

[15] Caloini, A., Magnani, G. & Pesse, M. (1998). A Technique for Designing Robotic Control Systems Based on Petri Nets. *IEEE Transactions on Control Systems Technology*, Vol. 6, No. 1, pp. 72-87

[16] Oliveira, P., Pascoal, A., Silva, V. & Silvestre, C. (1998). Mission Control of the Autonomous Underwater Vehicle: System Design, Implementation and Sea Trials. *International Journal of Systems Science*, Vol. 29, No. 4, pp. 1065-1080

[17] Yasuda, G. (2010). Design and Implementation of Hierarchical and Distributed Control for Robotic Manufacturing Systems using Petri Nets. In: Pawel Pawlewski Ed. *Petri Nets: Applications*, InTech Education and Publishing, Chapter 19, pp. 379-392

[18] Unimation Inc. (1979). *User Guide to VAL – A Robot Programming and Control System Version II*

[19] Yasuda, G. & Tachibana, K. (1991). A Parallel Processing Control Approach to the Design of Autonomous Robotic Manufacturing Systems, *Proceedings of the XIth International Conference on Production Research*, pp. 445-449

[20] Graham, J. H. & Saridis, G. N. (1982). Linguistic Decision Structures for Hierarchical Systems. *IEEE Transaction on Systems, Man, and Cybernetics*, Vo. 12, No. 3, pp. 325-329

Chapter 5

Measurement of Work-in-Process and Manufacturing Lead Time by Petri Nets Modeling and Throughput Diagram

Tiago Facchin and Miguel Afonso Sellitto

Additional information is available at the end of the chapter

http://dx.doi.org/10.5772/50288

1. Introduction

A proper planning and the search for better results in the production processes are important for the competitiveness that manufacturing can add to business operations. However, changes in manufacturing involve risks and uncertainties that may affect the company's operations. In this case, modeling and simulation of the production line can assist the decision-making process, avoiding unnecessary expenses and risks before making a decision. A model that can be simulated in the computer is a mechanism that turns input parameters, known and associated requirements of the process, into output parameters and performance metrics that have not yet happened in the real world (Law; Kelton, 1991).

Thereby, a line production model, which can be used in a computer simulation, can be a tool for decision support, because, before the results will crystallize in the real world manufacturing, it can be predicted, with a given reliability, in virtual simulation.

Inventory in process and throughput time that a production plan will generate are quantities that may be useful in decision making in manufacturing and can be predicted by computer simulation. The inventory process (work in process or WIP) consists of materials that have already been released for manufacture (have already left the warehouse or have been received from suppliers), but their orders still not been completed. Lead time is the time between release manufacture order and the product availability for shipment to the customer (Antunes et al., 2007). Some decisions in internal logistics of manufacturing may be related to these quantities: choosing alternatives for compliance with scheduled delivery dates, intermediate storage areas for processing of applications, equipment for internal movement; resources for tool changes and machinery preparation. The most important decision that can be supported by the proposed method is the definition of in-process inventory level that will be allowed in manufacturing. This should not be so low as to generate idle nor so high as to increase the throughput time.

In the first two chapters will be presented basic concepts for modelling the proposed system using Petri Nets and throughput diagram, these methods will be applied in a real manufacturing and the results compared with the real manufacturing outputs.

The aim of this paper is to measure in advance in-process inventory and lead time in manufacturing that a production plan will generate. Knowing the magnitudes of the plan prior to release, a manager can predict and possibly prevent problems, changing the plan. The specific objectives were: i) mapping manufacturing, ii) model building for PN, refining and validated by field data, iii) with the results simulated by throughput diagram, calculate the inventory in process and expected lead time; and iv) discuss the application. Computer simulation is the research method. Delimitation is that made in a single application in shoe manufacturing, in a period of two weeks. The working method includes two operations research techniques, Petri nets (PN) and the throughput diagram and was tested in a production plan already performed, whose results served to refine and validate the model, which can be used in plans not yet released for manufacturing.

The main contribution of this paper is the method of working, replicable to other applications: simulation PN, validated by data field and use the throughput diagram results to calculate the performance metric. The method can be useful in ill-structured problems, as may occur in manufacturing.

2. Petri Nets

The PN describes the system structure as a directed graph and can capture precedence relations and structural links of real systems with graphical expressiveness to model conflicts and queues. Formally, it can be defined as a sixfold (P, T, A, M_0, W, K) in wich: P is a set of states/places, T is a set of transitions, A is a set of arcs subject to the constraint that arcs do not connect directly two positions or transitions, M_0 is the initial state, which tells how many marks/tokens there are in each position to the beginning of the processing, W is a set of arc weights, which tells, for each arc, how many marks are required for a place by the transition or how many are placed in a place after the respective transition; and K is a set of capacity constraints, which reports to each position, the maximum number of marks which may occupy the place (Castrucci; Moraes, 2001). Applying the definition in the PN of Figure 1, $P = [p_0, p_1]$; $T = [t_0]$; $A = [(p_0, t_0), (t_0, p_1)]$; W: $w(p_0, t_0) = 1$, $w(t_0, p_1) = 1$ e $M_0 = [1; 0]$. The token in p_0 enables the transition t_0. After firing, $M = [0; 1]$.

The transitions correspond to changes of states and places correspond to state variables of the system. In the firing of a transition, the tokens move across the network in two phases: enabling and firing transition. A transition $t_j \in T$ is enabled by a token m if $\forall\, p_i \in P$, $m(p_i) \geq w(p_i, t_j)$, i.e., the token in place pi is greater than or equal to the arc weight that connects p_i to t_j.

Some variations are allowed in Petri Nets and were used for modeling, for example, the use of inhibitor arcs.

Figure 1. Symbolic representation of Petri Nets

3. Throughput diagram in manufacturing

In manufacturing, a queue arises when, for variability, at a given instant, the number of orders to be implemented is greater than the available job centers. The manufacturing arrives at the work position (or center), waiting its turn, is processed and proceeds. The sequence is subject to change priorities and interruptions for maintenance or lack of materials (Silva; Morabito, 2007; Papadopoulos et al., 1993).

A work center (machine, production line or manufacturing plant) can be compared to a funnel, in which orders arrive (input), waiting for service (inventory) and leave the system (output). When the work center is observed for a continuous period, the reference period, the cumulative results can be plotted. In Figure 2, it is possible to observe strokes representing the accumulated input and output, measured in amount of work (Wiendahl, 1995). This quantity may be in parts, numbers of hours or another unit value which represents a significant manufacturing effort (Sellitto, 2005).

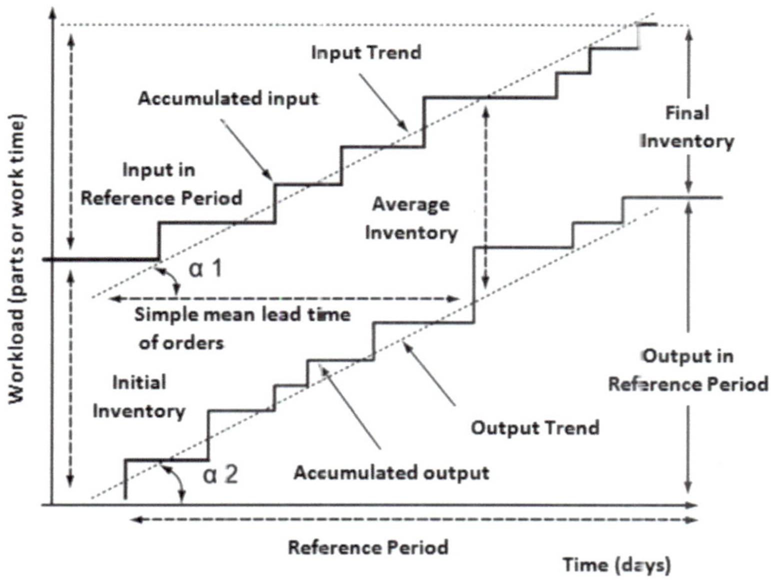

Figure 2. Throughput diagram of a work center

To obtain the line that represents input is necessary knowing the amount of work waiting in the initial inventory at the beginning of the reference period and the output is plotted summing the completed work orders. Wiendahl (1995) presents an analytical development related to the throughput diagram and calculates various quantities of interest to workload control (WLC) such as: lead time, average performance, autonomy, work progress and delays in delivery of orders. For this study case, the funnel formula will be applied:

$$TL_m = I_m / P_m \quad (1)$$

Where, TL_m = simple mean lead time of orders (days); I_m = mean inventory (parts); and P_m = mean performance (parts per day).

For the demonstration, the author uses the figure and considers steady state, i.e., the balance between input and outputs ($\alpha 1 = \alpha 2$) and tan $\alpha 1$ = Im / TLm e tan $\alpha 2$ = Pm. Wiendahl (1995) suggests that the equation can be used for measurement and control of manufacturing.

4. Research - characterization

The research method was a computer simulation. Simplifications have been admitted, but without losing the replicability. The work method was: i) choice of manufacturing,

process mapping and data collection; ii) model construction by Petri Nets; iii) feeding the model with the initial situation of load in a production plan already executed, run and use the results to fit the model; iv) with the results, calculate the mean lead time of orders; and v) discussing and refining the method, analysis of the implications of its use in manufacturing management.

4.1. Manufacturing process mapping

The production process consists of modeling, cutting, sewing, assembling, packing and delivery (dispatching process). Some works use multitasking labour, that moves between closer stages. The manufacturing was divided in three different process: i) Process 1 (cutting, splitting and chamfer); ii) Process 2 (preparation and sewing); and iii) Process 3 (assembling and dispatching).

Basically, the first process consists in cutting operations of the pre-fabricated (insole and sole) and the upper part of the shoes (leather upper). In pre-fabricated, the model was simplified grouping sequential operations. The input of the system is the place "INPUT – m1", all the orders should be loaded in this place, the transition Separation Table (after place m41) is only enabled when all the parts arrive at the place "Separation Table – m41", and is guaranteed by the auxiliary places (m78, m82, m79, m28, m83, m84, m85). The cutting of leather upper was detailed, this process is sequential because the parts should be cutted in different parts of the leather. The input of this process is the place "m42", observe that some operations are performed by the same operators, which explains the use of inhibitor arcs. The third process includes the assembling and dispatching, after this, the shoe process will be finished and ready to leave the factory. The output of the system is the place "BOX OUTPUT – m16".

4.2. Transition time assignments

To assign time to the transitions, all the processes were timed. With the orientation of the production supervisor, the start/end time of each task was defined. It was considered a confidence level of 95% and used the calculation model suggested by Vaz (1993) and AEP (2003). As an example, for the sole cutting operation the average time was 18.13 seconds and the standard deviation was 2 seconds. The minimum number of samples to ensure the confidence level was 19.5, adopting 20 samples. The time for each transition is the average values collected.

4.3. Simulation, inventory and lead time calculations

To test and refine the model was chosen a plan already done, two weeks and nine production orders. It was informed the load for each place, resulting from earlier orders, at the moment of the first evaluated order will enter the system. A new order is queued of previous processing orders, which explains why the lead time in manufacturing is much higher than the standard manufacturing time. The queuing discipline adopted was FIFO (First-In-First-Out). Table 1 shows data from nine manufacturing orders contained in the production plan (dates are considering working days – 8h40m/day = 3.200s/day). In the last column, there is the order lead time, calculated by simulation, and their average.

Order (pairs)	Real Input Date (days)	Real Output Date (days)	Real Input Date (s)	Real Output Date (s)	Simulated Output Date (s)	Simulated Lead Time of Order (s)
1,000	0	2.5	0	78,000	66,480	66,480
500	1	3.5	31,200	109,200	104,450	73,250
1,500	2	6.5	62,400	202,800	174,860	112,460
800	4	7.5	124,800	234,000	233,872	109,072
800	5	9	156,000	280,800	280,704	124,704
400	7	10	218,400	312,000	313,763	95,363
1,000	10.2	12.5	318,240	390,000	361,404	43,164
500	11.2	13	349,440	405,600	399,304	49,864
500	11.7	14	365,040	436,800	428,504	63,464
TOTAL 7,000 Pairs			AVERAGE 81,980 s = 2,627 days			

Table 1. Information for inventory and mean lead time calculation in manufacturing

Wiendahl (1995) presents a method that considers the size of the order Qi. By this method, TLm = [ΣQi x TLorder I] / ΣQi = 2.73 days, close to the calculated 2.63 days. The correlation between real and simulated outputs (column 5 and 6) is 0.99 and the absolute error | real - simulated | average is 9,821s (2.27% of the largest real value). Figure 3 shows the comparison of information from real and simulated outputs, order to order.

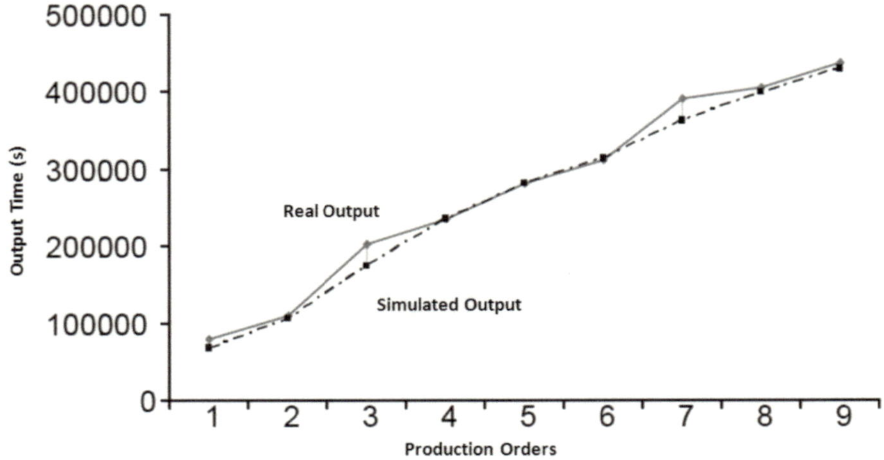

Figure 3. Comparison of information from real and simulated outputs

The simulated mean performance is Pm = 31,200 x [7,000 / (428,504 – 66,480)] = 583 pairs of shoes per day. The calculation basis is: in (428,504 - 66,480) seconds, were delivered 7,000 pairs. The real mean performance is Pm = 31,200 x [7,000 / (428,504 – 78,000)] = 608 pairs of shoes per day.

The time interval between simulated outputs is Δt = [(428,504 – 66,480) / 7,000] = 51.7s and the real is Δt = [(436,800 – 78,000) / 7,000] = 51,25s. The expected mean inventory is Im =Pm.TLm = 583 pairs / day x 2.627 days = 1,531 pairs.

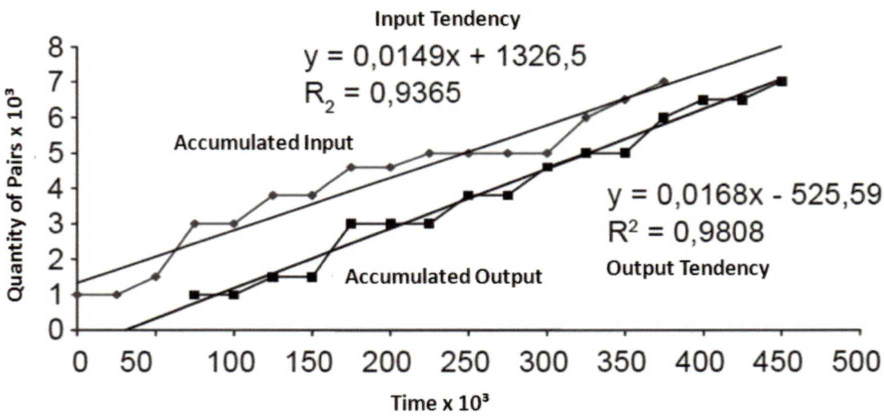

Figure 4. Throughput diagram for real inputs and simulated outputs (at intervals of 25,000s)

The instantaneous numbers of pairs in the system is N(t) = I(t) – O(t). The average, an indicator of mean inventory, calculated by this method is close than the one calculated by the funnel method (1,546 and 1,531 pairs respectively).

Time x 10^3 (s)	Accumulated Inputs I(t)	Accumulated Outputs O(t)	Number of Pairs in Manufacturing N(t)
0	1,000	-	-
25	1,000	-	-
50	1,500	-	-
75	3,000	1,000	2,000
100	3,000	1,000	2,000
125	3,800	1,500	2,300
150	3,800	1,500	2,300
175	4,600	3,000	1,600
200	4,600	3,000	1,600
225	5,000	3,000	2,000
250	5,000	3,800	1,200
275	5,000	3,800	1,200
300	5,000	4,600	400
325	6,000	5,000	1,000
350	6,500	5,000	1,500
375	7,000	6,000	1,000
400	-	6,500	-
425	-	6,500	-
450	-	7,000	-
AVERAGE: 1,546 Pairs			

Table 2. Accumulated inputs and outputs of each order presented in Table 1 (at the same interval)

5. Applications in manufacturing management – results discussion

The simulation can generate data for all processes, individually. For instance, Figure 5 shows the results in place INPUT Sewing Process – m44, the operator at this place is overloaded, also observed in the real process. An alternative would be a redistribution of tasks, adopting parallelisms, without overloading the following posts.

A different situation is shown in Figure 6, the time that the operator is idle in this place is low, and there are no accumulations of tasks over time. This represents that, for this place, the tasks are well distributed.

Other screens allow similar analyzes in all manufacturing places. It is important to analyze the changes in the manufacturing and the impacts that an action causes in each process (for instance, allocate more operators to develop a specific task).

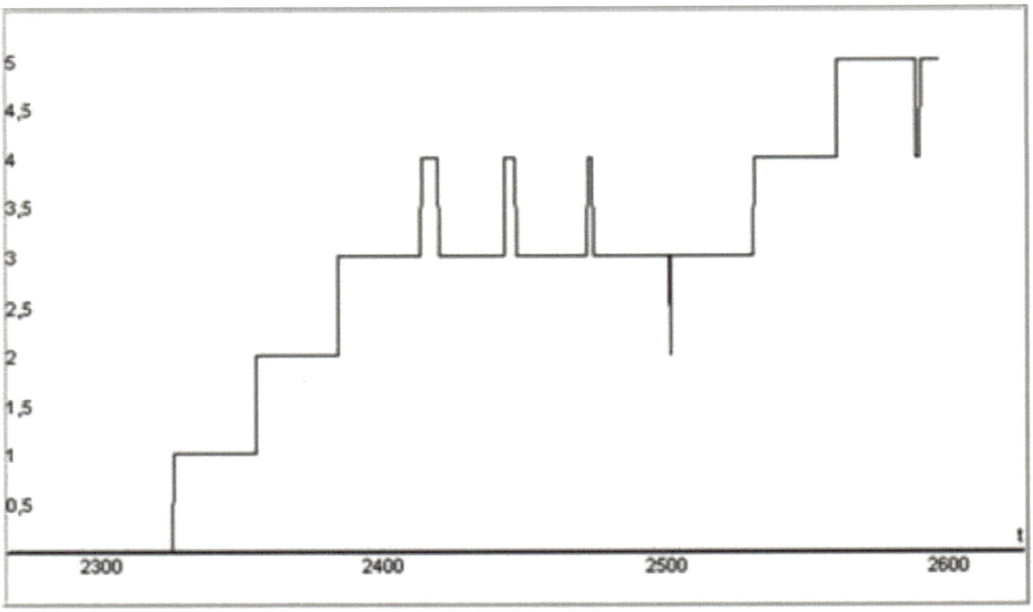

Figure 5. Place: "INPUT Sewing Process – m44"– Results obtained with the simulation

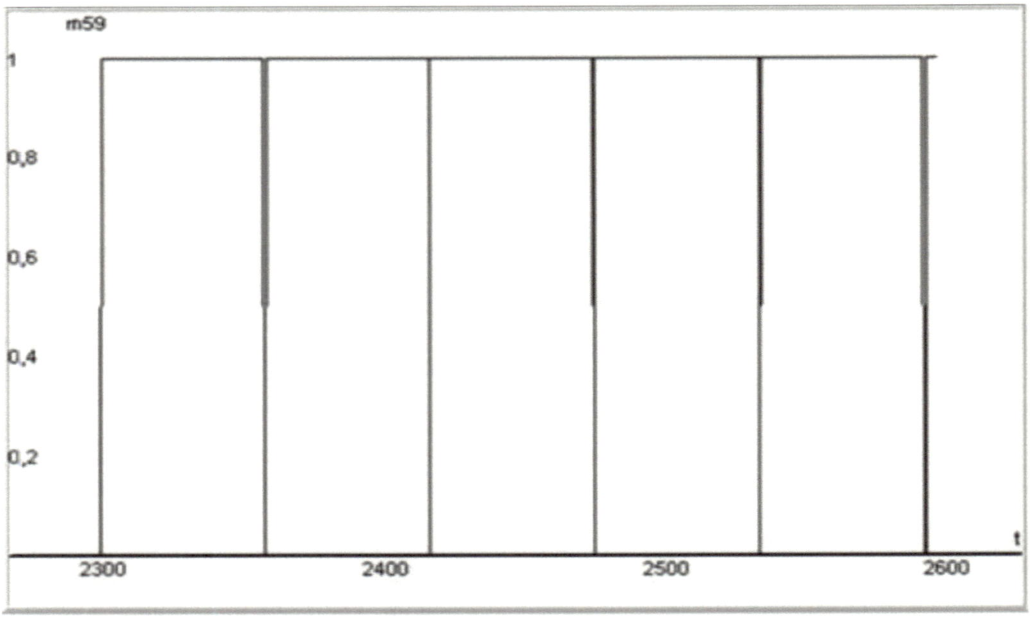

Figure 6. Place: Eyelets verification – m59– Results obtained with the simulation

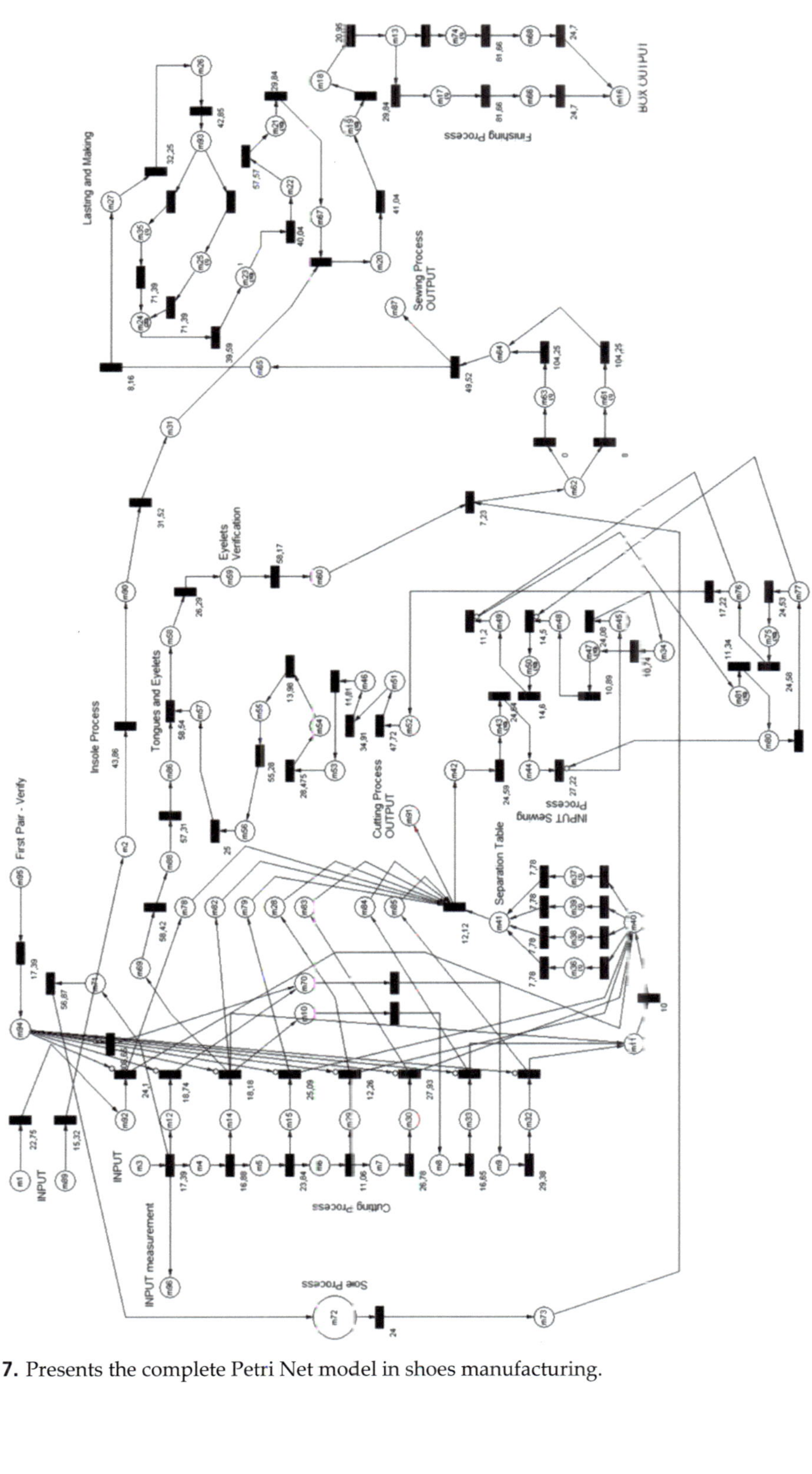

Figure 7. Presents the complete Petri Net model in shoes manufacturing.

6. Final considerations

It was presented and tested a method based on modelling an simulation by Petri Nets and Throughput Diagram for the calculation of two important indicators in manufacturing management: in process inventory and lead time. With the simulation results (provided by the Petri Net model outputs and the throughput diagram) the manufacturing process can be predicted, as well as some modification can be measured and analyzed to optimize the production. As well as save money on alterations that could produce losses in production processes and often, in the real world, are hard to be perceived.

Author details

Tiago Facchin and Miguel Afonso Sellitto
Universidade do Vale do Rio do Sinos - UNISINOS, Brazil

7. References

AEP- Associação Empresarial de Portugal. Métodos e Tempos: Manual Pedagógico. Leça da Palmeira, 2003.

Antunes, J.; Alvarez, R.; Klippel, M.; Bortolotto, P.; Pellegrin, I. Sistemas de Produção. Porto Alegre: Bookman, 2007.

Askin, R.; Krisht, A. Optimal Operation of Manufacturing Systems with Controlled Work-in-Process Levels. International Journal of Production Research, London, v.32, n.7, p.1637-1653, 1994.

Banaszak, Z.; Krogh, B. Deadlock avoidance in flexible manufacturing systems with concurrently competing process flows.

IEEE Transactions on Robotics and Automation, v.6, n.6, p.724-734, 1990.

Bechte, W. Load-oriented manufacturing control just-in-time production for job shops. Production Planning & Control, London, v.5, n.3, p.292-307, 1994.

Breithaupt, J.; Land, M.; Nyhuis, P. The workload control concept: theory and practical extensions of Load Oriented Order Release. Production Planning & Control, London, v.13, n.7, p. 625-638, 2002.

Bitran, G.; Sarkar, D. Throughput Analysis in Manufacturing Networks. European Journal of Operational Research, v.74, n.3, p.448-465, 1994.

Bitran, G.; Morabito, R. Um exame dos modelos de redes de filas abertas aplicados a sistemas de manufatura discretos: Parte I. Gestão & Produção, São Carlos, v. 2, n.2, p.192-219, 1995.

Bitran, G.; Morabito, R. Um exame dos modelos de redes de filas abertas aplicados a sistemas de manufatura discretos: Parte II. Gestão & Produção, São Carlos, v. 2, n.3, p.297-320, 1995A.

Bitran, G.; Dasu, S. A review of open queueing network models of manufacturing systems. Queuing Systems, v.12, n.1-2, p. 95-133, 1992.

Castrucci, P.; Moraes, C. Engenharia de automação industrial. Rio de Janeiro: LTC, 2001.

Boucher, T.; Jafari, M.; Meredith, G. Petri net control of an automated manufacturing cell. Computers and Industrial Engineering, Tarry Town, NY, USA, v. 17, n.1, p.459-463, 1989.

Dallery, Y.; Gershwin, S. Manufacturing flow line systems: a review of models and analytical results. Queuing Systems, v. 12, n.1-2, p. 3-94, 1992.

Dicesare, F.; Harhalakis, G.; PROTH, J. M.; Silva, M.; Vernadat, F. B. Practice of Petri nets in manufacturing. London: Chapman & Hall, 1993.

Drath, R.; Schwuchow, S. Modellierung diskretkontinuierlicher Systeme mit Petri-Netzen. In: Schneider, E. (Org.). Entwurf komplexer Automatisierungssyteme.

Braunschweig: Technische Universität Braunschweig, Institut für Regelungs-und-Automatisierungstechnick, 1997.

Fung, R.; Jiang, Z.; Zuo, M.; TU, P. Adaptive production scheduling of virtual production systems using object-oriented Petri nets with changeable structure. International Journal of Production Research, v. 40, n.8, p.1759-1785, 2002.

Govil, M.; FU, M. Queuing theory in manufacturing: a survey. Journal of Manufacturing Systems, v. 18, n.3, p.210-214, 1999.

Jeng, M. A Petri net synthesis theory for modeling flexible manufacturing systems.

IEEE Transactions on Systems, Man and Cybernetics Part B, v. 27, n. 2, p.169-183, 1997.

Jeng, M.; Xie, X.; Huang, Y. Manufacturing modeling using process nets with resources. In: IEEE International Conference on Robotics and Automation. April. 2000, San Francisco, USA. Proceedings… San francisco, USA: IEEE, 2000.

Law, A.; Kelton, W. Simulation modeling and analysis. New York: McGraw-Hill, 1991.

Lee, D.; Dicesare, F. Scheduling flexible manufacturing systems using Petri nets and heuristic search. IEEE Transactions on Robotics and Automation, New York, NY, v.10, n.2, p.123-133, 1994.

Maciel, P.; Lins, R.; Cunha, P. Introdução às redes Petri e aplicações. Campinas: Instituto de Computação - UNICAMP, 1996.

Martinez, J.; Muro, P.; Silva, M. Modeling, validation and software implementation of production systems using high level Petri nets. IEEE International Conference on Robotics and Automation. Março – Abril, 1987, Raleigh, North Carolina. Proceedings… Raleigh, North Carolina: I3E Comput. Soc., v.4, p. 1180-1185.

Murata, T. Petri Nets: Properties, Analysis and Applications. Proceedings of the IEEE. Chicago, IL, USA, v. 77, n.4, p.541-580, 1989.

Papadopoulos, H. T.; Heavey, C.; Browne, J. Queuing theory in manufacturing systems analysis and design. London: Chapman & Hall, 1993.

Papadopoulos, H.; Heavey, C. Queuing theory in manufacturing systems analysis and design: a classification of models for production and transfer lines. European Journal of Operational Research, v.92, n.1, p.1-27, 1996.

Peterson, J. Petri Net Theory and the modelling of system. Englewood Cliffs, NJ: Prentice-Hall Editions, 1981.

Proth, J.; Wang, L.; XIE, X. A class of Petri nets for manufacturing system integration.

IEEE Transactions on Robotics and Automation, Valbonne, v.13, n.3, p.317-326, 1997.

Reisig, W. Elements of distributed algorithms: modeling and analysis with Petri Nets. Berlim: Springer Verlag, 1998.

Sellitto, M. Medição e controle de desempenho em sistemas de manufatura. Porto Alegre, 2005. Tese – (Doutorado em Engenharia de Produção), UFRGS.

Silva, A. Modelagem de custos em sistemas de manufatura utilizando Redes de Petri. São Carlos, 2002. Dissertação – (Mestrado em Engenharia Mecânica), USP São Carlos.

Silva, C.; Morabito, R. Aplicação de modelos de redes de filas abertas no planejamento do sistema job-shop de uma planta metal-mecânica. Gestão & Produção, São Carlos, v.14, n.2, p.393-410, 2007.

Vaz, A. Cronometragem e a nova realidade. Tecnicouro, Novo Hamburgo, v. 3, n.4, p.34-35, 1993.

Visual Object Net. Software e guia de usuário. Disponível em: http://www.systemtechnik.tu-ilmenau.de/~drath. Acesso em: março 2005.

Xing, K.; Hu, B.; Chen, H. Deadlock avoidance policy for Petri-net modeling of flexible manufacturing systems with shared resources. IEEE Transactions on Automatic Control, New York, NY, USA, v.41, n.2, p.289-295, 1996.

Xiong, H.; Zhou, M. Deadlock-free scheduling of an automated manufacturing system based on Petri nets. IEEE International Conference on Robotics and Automation, Abril 1997, Albuquerque, New Mexico. Proceedings... Albuquerque, New Mexico: IEEE, v.2, p. 945 – 950.

Wiendahl, H. Load-oriented manufacturing control. Berlim: Springer, 1995.

Wiendahl, H.; Breithaupt, J. Automatic production control applying control theory. International Journal of Production Economics, Amsterdam, v. 63, n.1, p.33-46, 2000.

Wu, N.; Zhou, M. Avoiding deadlock and reducing starvation and blocking in automated manufacturing systems. IEEE Transactions on Robotics and Automation, Guang Zhou, v.17, n.5, p.658-669, 2001.

Zhou, M.; Dicesare, F. Parallel and sequential mutual exclusions for Petri net modeling of manufacturing systems with shared resources. IEEE Transactions on Robotics and Automation, Newark, NJ, USA, v.7, n.4, p.515-527, 1991.

Chapter 6

Workflow Modelling Based on Synchrony

Chongyi Yuan

Additional information is available at the end of the chapter

http://dx.doi.org/10.5772/48375

1. Introduction

Prof. Carl Adam Petri wrote: "In order to apply net theory with success, a user of net theory can just rely on the fact that every net which he can specify explicitly (draw on paper) can be connected by a short (≤ 4) chain of net morphisms to the physical real word; your net is, in a very precise sense, physically implementable." (Status Report On Net Theory, 1989, a forward for my book Petri Nets in Chinese[1]).

Why a net is physically implementable? The reason is, every concept in net theory is carefully chosen based on nature laws, and well defined in terms of precise mathematics and logic. For example, the concept of global time does not belong to net theory. Time measured with real numbers exists only in theories like theoretical physics. Logical time does not exist in the real world. For net theory, time is just "clock reading", a measurement of physical changes. Global time is not realistic for systems in which a shared clock is not available.

On the other hand however, it is easy to find in the literature, that many an author introduces new concepts into his or her Petri net with implementation totally forgotten. "Timed Petri Net" is just one of such examples.

As one of the chapters in this book on Petri nets, implementable concepts and only implementable concepts will be introduced.

We start with the definition of a directed net, which is the most fundamental concept in net theory. The next two sections serve to keep this chapter self-reliant.

This chapter is organized as below:

Sections 2 and 3 recall basic definitions of Petri Nets: The concept of directed net deserves a separate section since it is the foundation of the whole net theory. Section 3 is mainly about Place/Transition-systems, based on which workflow models are to be constructed.

Section 4 is an introduction of synchrony, a branch in net theory on transition synchronization that provides theoretical support to workflow modelling.

Section 5 talks about business processes, the subject of workflow research. A full understanding of the concept of business processes makes a good start.

Section 6 proposes the concepts of synchronizers and workflow logic. A synchronizer connects transitions in two consecutive steps in a business process, and workflow logic is obtained when all transitions in a business process are so connected. Properties and analysis methods of workflow logic are defined and proposed. A transition in workflow logic represents a business task while a synchronizer represents a task in workflow management. Workflow logic specifies all possible routes a business case may take when it is processed. An individual business case corresponds to a unique route among all routes given by workflow logic. This route is considered as the semantics of that case. Section 7 defines the concept of case semantics.

Section 8 is about business process management, or automatic management. The dual net of workflow logic is exactly the logic of management, based on which workflow engine conducts the process of individual cases.

Section 9 concludes this chapter with acknowledgement, and the last section is a list of references.

This chapter is about Petri nets and workflow modelling.

There are many ways in the literature to define nets and net systems. For example, the concept of flow relation, namely F, has been made implicit by many researchers. It is often combined with weight function W. Without the flow relation, the concept of directed nets would disappear; and without the concept of directed nets, the whole theoretical part of Petri nets would be without a foundation. Thus, this chapter starts from the definition of directed nets given by C. A. Petri himself.

Petri net systems have been considered as one of the adequate and promising candidates for workflow modelling. The concept of WF-nets proposed by Prof. Aalst from Holland has become popular in the last 10 to 20 years. A team in the Software Development Company of Peking University tried to use WF-nets as a formal model to develop software for a government organization at a time around the year 2000. The WF-nets didn't work, and they didn't know why. The author joint them, and we found problems of WF-nets, leading to failure. The concept of WF-nets was proposed without theoretical foundation. These problems were discussed in our paper titled "A Three Layer Model for Business process" [7]. The concepts of synchronizers, workflow logic and case semantics etc were defined in this paper for the first time. After so many years since then, people interested in workflow modelling remain sticking to WF-nets. Many people do not even know our work, it seems. The reason is, the author guess, General Net Theory (theoretical part of Petri nets) is not popular yet. This chapter shows how important "Synchrony" is to a successful application of Petri nets in the area of workflow modelling.

2. Directed net

Definition 1

A triple N=(S,T;F) is a directed net if $S \cup T \neq \emptyset \land S \cap T = \emptyset \land F \sqsubseteq (S \times T \cup T \times S) \land dom(F) \cup cod(F) = S \cup T$ Where $dom(F)=\{x \mid \exists y: (x, y) \in F\}$ and $cod(F)=\{y \mid \exists x: (x, y) \in F\}$.◆

A directed net used to be called "Petri net". We keep the term "Petri net" to mean "net theory", a term Carl Adam Petri used in *Status Report*. "Net" is often used to mean "directed net" if it causes no ambiguity.

$S \cup T \neq \emptyset \land S \cap T = \emptyset$ demands that a net consists of at least one element, and its elements are clearly classified.

$F \sqsubseteq S \times T \cup T \times S$ indicates that direct dependence does not exist between elements in the same class. $dom(F) \cup cod(F) = S \cup T$ excludes isolated elements from a net.

A directed net has a graphical presentation as shown in Figure 1, in which elements in S and T appear as circles and boxes respectively while elements in F appear as arrows (arcs). The arrow from x to y represents (x,y) in F.

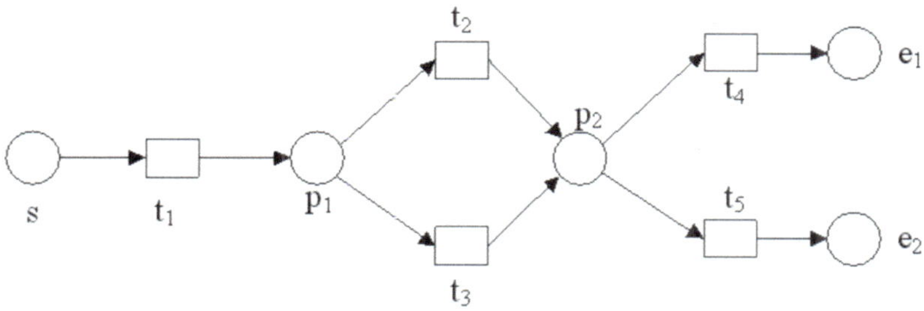

Figure 1. A Directed Net

Petri net (net theory) consists of Special Net Theory and General Net Theory. Special Net Theory focuses on system modelling and General Net Theory focuses on theories supporting system modelling. The concept of directed nets is their common foundation.

Definition 2

Let N=(S,T;F) be a directed net and $X=S \cup T$, For x in X, $^{\cdot}x=\{y \mid (y,x) \in F\}$ is the pre-set of x, $x^{\cdot}=\{y \mid (x,y) \in F\}$ is the post-set of x. For $t \in T$, $^{\cdot}t \cup t^{\cdot}$ is the extension of t.◆

Special Net Theory (SNT for short) and General Net Theory (GNT for short) are derived from Directed Net based on pre-sets and post-sets of elements as described below.

The concept of extensions of transitions leads to the principle of local determinism.

The S-complementation operation on a net leads to the removal of contact. The T-complementation operation on a net leads to the removal of differences between forward and backward flow of tokens (SNT).

The S-completion operation on a net leads to Synchrony while the T-completion operation on a net leads to Enlogy(GNT).

A directed net implies a unique undirected net that leads to Net Topology (GNT).

A special class of directed nets is the occurrence nets that lead to Concurrency (GNT).

Synchrony will be briefly introduced in Section 3, since it provides guidance to workflow modelling. It is impossible in this chapter to go any further on SNT and GNT. The point is, successful applications of Petri nets rely on both SNT and GNT, not only SNT.

3. Net system

Definition 3

A 6-tuple $\Sigma = (S,T;F,K,W,M_0)$ is a net system if (S,T;F) is a directed net and:

$K: S \rightarrow \{1,2,\cdots\} \cup \{\infty\} \wedge W: F \rightarrow \{1,2,\cdots\} \wedge M_0: \rightarrow \{0,1,2,\cdots\}$ such that $\forall s \in S: M_0(s) \leq K(s)$, where K,W,M0 are respectively the capacity function, the weight function and the initial marking. ◆

A mapping $M: \rightarrow \{0,1,2,\cdots\}$ is a marking if it satisfies

$$\forall s \in S: M(s) \leq K(s).$$

Conventionally, elements in S are called places and elements in T are transitions. A place is capable to hold certain kind of resources, with an allowance given by K. Infinite capacity does not mean infinite space for resources. It is just an indication that the capacity of that place is not a factor for a transition to become enabled (see definition below). A transition resembles a change of resource quantities (consumed or produced) and a change in kind. The precise change is given by transition rules. In the rest of this chapter, Σ is always assumed finite, i.e. Σ has a finite number of places and transitions.

Definition 4

1. Transition t is enabled by marking M if $\forall s \in {}^{\cdot}t: W(s,t) \leq M(s) \wedge \forall s \in t^{\cdot}: M(s)+W(t,s) \leq K(s)$. This fact is denoted by M[t>.
2. Transition t may fire, if M[t>, to yield a successor marking M′ given by $M'(s) = M(s) - W(s,t)$ for s in ${}^{\cdot}t - t^{\cdot}$, $M'(s) = M(s)+W(t,s)$ for s in $t^{\cdot} - {}^{\cdot}t$, and $M'(s) = M(s) + W(t,s) - W(s,t)$ for s in ${}^{\cdot}t \cap t^{\cdot}$, and $M'(s) = M(s)$ otherwise. This fact is denoted by M[t>M′.◆

It is easy to prove that the successor M′ is indeed a marking.

A marking represents a resource distribution on S. A transition firing causes the flow of resources along arcs in F, and thus F is called the flow relation of Σ.

It is easy to see that M[t> is determined by ${}^{\cdot}t \cup t^{\cdot}$, the extension of t, and the change from M to M′ is confined to ${}^{\cdot}t \cup t^{\cdot}$. This is the principle of local determinism. A marking is a global state, but the transition rules refer to only the extension of a single transition, not the complete marking. Many system models take global states as a means of system control. But this is not always implementable, since a global state is not always instantly known. It takes time to know the current global state, and this delay may be significant to an effective real time control.

Figure 2 illustrates how to represent a net system graphically. The black dot inside place s is a token, denoting $M_0(s) = 1$. Empty places have no token (resource). Conventionally, $M(s)=0$, $W(x,y) = 1$ and $K(s) = \infty$ are shown by default.

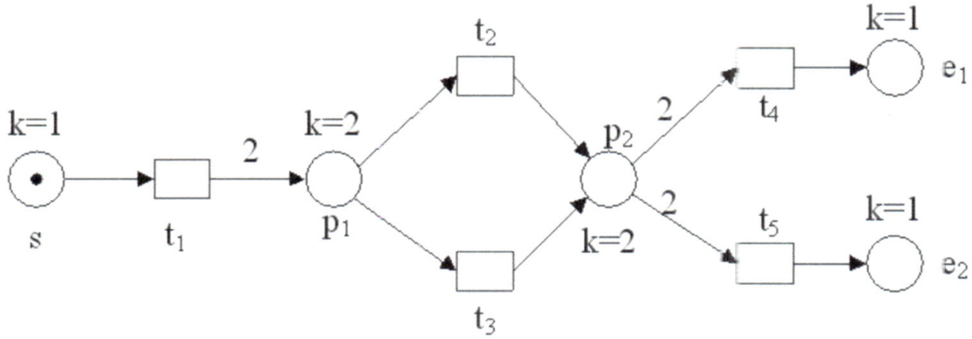

Figure 2. A Net System

Definition 5

Let $\Sigma = (S,T;F,K,W,M0)$ be a net system, M is a marking and t1, t2 are transitions.

1. If $M[t_1>M' \wedge M'[t_2> \wedge \neg M[t_2>$, then t_1 and t_2 are in sequential relation at M, denoted by $M[t_1,t_2>$.
2. If $M[t_1> \wedge M[t_2>$, and $\forall s \in {}^{\bullet}t_1 \cap {}^{\bullet}t_2 : M(s) \geq W(s,t_1) + W(s,t_2)$ and $\forall s \in t_1^{\bullet} \cap t_2^{\bullet} : M(s) + W(t_1,s) + W(t_2,s) \leq K(s)$, then t_1 and t_2 are in concurrent relation at M, denoted by $M[\{t_1,t_2\}>$.
3. If $M[t_1> \wedge M[t_2> \wedge \neg M[\{t_1, t_2\}>$, then t_1, t_2 are in conflict at M, denoted by $cf(t_1,t_2,M)$.
4. If there is a transition t and a place b such that $\forall s \in {}^{\bullet}t : M(s) \geq W(s,t) \wedge M(b) + W(t,b) > K(b)$, then t leads to a contact in b at M, denoted by $ct(t,b,M)$. ◆

Two concurrently enabled transitions can fire either concurrently or one after another.

Theorem 1

The marking reached by concurrently fired transitions can also be reached by the transitions fired one after another.◆

This theorem guarantees that the next definition includes markings reached by concurrent transition firings.

Definition 6

The set of markings reachable from M_0 by consecutive transition firings is usually denoted by $[M_0>$.◆

The set [M_0> may be infinite for a finite system. The algorithm for computing [M_0> produces a finite tree, denoted by T(Σ), and this tree can be re-structured to become a graph, denoted by G(Σ). G(Σ) will be used for the computing of synchronous distances later on. All these concepts and algorithms are in the category of techniques, we will go no further here.

So far we have not said a word about how to relate a net to the real world. This reflects an important aspect of Petri net, that is, a net is unexplained. This nature of nets has its good point and bad point. The good point is: the same net or net system may be explained in different application areas to solve different problems; the bad point is: unexplained transition firings lead to general analysis methods that are bound to be of low efficiency, since they cannot make use of application specific properties.

A net is "physically implementable" when every element in $S \cup T$ has an explaination for a fixed application problem, and every transition firing describes real changes in that application area. A net describes how real changes relate with each other. This chapter aims to show how to build, with the guidance of GNT, net systems for workflow modelling and how to find efficient analysis methods.

Some transitions are defined as "instant transitions" in Timed Petri Nets, for they fire instantly when they become enabled. What would happen when two instant transitions are in conflict? Conflict resolution takes time since it needs to be detected and it requires a decision from the system environment. Generally speaking, an enabled transition may be disabled (by others) without firing.

4. Synchrony

Careful observation reveals that sequential relation, concurrent relation and conflict relation are not relations between two transitions, but rather, they are relations between transition firings, i.e. two transitions may fall into one relation at a marking and fall into a different relation at another marking. Thus, a more precise way to denote these relations is: sq(M[t1>, M[t2>), cn(M[t1>, M[t2>), and cf(M[t1>, M[t2>) respectively. Note that sq(M[t1>, M[t2>) is asymmetry.

Synchrony is about how transitions themselves are synchronized. It describes laws exhibited in the course of transition firings. For example, the sunrise and the sunset are alternating "transitions" while a hand-clapping "transition" consists of simultaneous actions of the two hands. One may observe one more sunrise or one more sunset, depending on the times the observation starts and ends, but one always counts the same number of actions of the two hands for hand clapping. The laws exhibited by alternating transitions and simultaneous transitions are given by "the synchronous distance is 1" and "the synchronous distance is 0" respectively.

The concept of synchronous distance was originally defined in terms of events in a C/E-system, which is a model describing changes in the nature, like the changes of 4 seasons. A C/E-system has no initial marking. Instead, it has a current marking. This chapter is about artificial systems. We have to redefine this concept of synchronous distance to serve our need.

4.1. Synchronous distance in a P/T-system

A net system as defined by Definition 3 and 4 is conventionally called a Place/Transition-system, P/T-system for short.

Definition 7

Let Σ= (S,T;F,K,W,M_0) be a P/T-system. A sequence of transitions δ= $t_1 t_2 \cdots t_n$ is called a transition sequence if they can fire one after another in the given order, starting from the initial marking. The length of δ is n.

An infinite sequence of transitions is a transition sequence if any of its finite prefix is a transition sequence. ◆

In what follows ρ denotes the set of all transition sequences of Σ.

Definition 8

Let Σ=(S,T;F,K,W,M_0) be a P/T-system and T_1, T_2 be subsets of T, $T_1 \neq \emptyset$, $T_2 \neq \emptyset$. Let $\boldsymbol{\delta}$ be a finite transition sequence, i.e. $\delta \in \rho$. Let $\#(\delta, T_1)$, $\#(\delta, T_2)$ denote the numbers of firings of transitions in T_1,T_2 respectively, and $\#(\delta, T_1,T_2) = \#(\delta, T_1) - \#(\delta, T_2)$. The synchronous distance between T_1 and T_2, denoted by $\sigma(T_1,T_2)$, is defined by

$\sigma(T_1,T_2) = \max\{\#(\delta, T_1,T_2) \mid \delta \in \rho\} - \min\{\#(\delta, T_1,T_2) \mid \delta \in \rho\}$ if exists, other wise $\sigma(T_1,T_2) = \infty$. ◆

Figure 3 (a) is P/T-system $\Sigma 1$ and its set of transition sequences is {a, ab, b, ba}. We have, for T_1 = {a} and T2 ={b}, $\max\{\#(\delta, T_1,T_2) \mid \delta \in \rho\} = 1$ and $\min\{\#(\delta, T_1,T_2) \mid \delta \in \rho\} = -1$, so $\sigma(T_1,T_2)$ = 2.

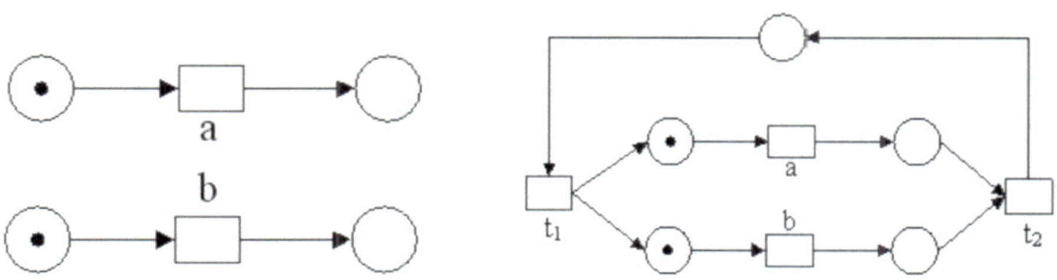

(a) Σ_1, (b) Σ_2

Figure 3. σ(a,b) =2

Note that we write σ(a,b) =2 instead of $\sigma(T_1,T_2)$ =2 in figure 3 by convention when both T_1,T_2 are singletons.

The set of transition sequences of Σ_2 is infinite and it contains infinite sequences. It is easy to check that any repeatable portion in a finite or infinite transition sequence contains the same number of firings of transition b and transition a. This is why σ(a,b) is finite. The consecutive firings of transition a count at most to 2, so do the consecutive firings of transition b. This is the physical meaning of σ(a,b) =2 for Σ_2.

The distance (i.e. synchronous distance from now on) between left hand action and right hand action is 0, since it is impossible to see only an action of either hand in the course of hand clapping.

Figure 4 (a) shows another situation of σ(a,b) =2, where transitions a and b are in conflict at the initial marking. Figure 4 (b) is still another case of σ(a,b) =2.

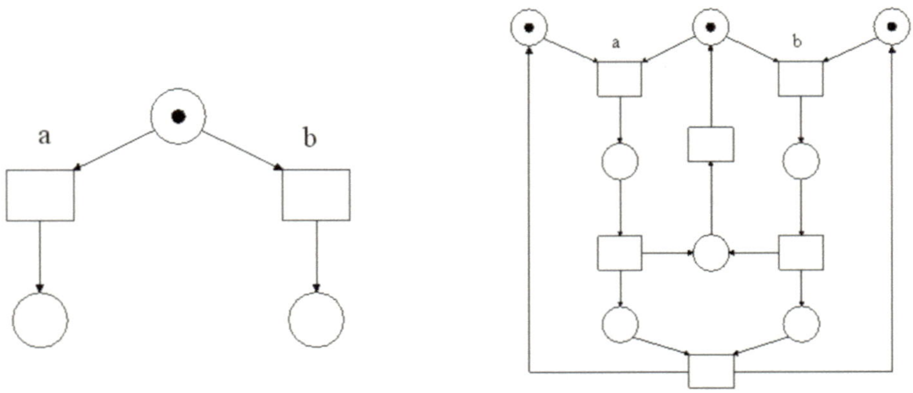

(a) Σ_3 (b) Σ_4

Figure 4. σ(a,b) =2: a and b in conflict

Theorem 2

The synchronous distance defined by Definition 8 satisfies distance axioms:

$\sigma(T_1,T_2) = 0$ if and only if $T_1 = T_2$; $\sigma(T_1,T_2) \geq 0$; $\sigma(T_1,T_2) = \sigma(T_2,T_1)$; $\sigma(T_1,T_2) + \sigma(T_2,T_3) \geq \sigma(T_1,T_3)$. ◆

This theorem explains why the concept is called distance. It is assumed that $T_1 \cap T_2 = \emptyset$ when $\sigma(T_1,T_2) > 0$, since $\sigma(T_1,T_2) = \sigma(T_1 - T_2, T_2 - T_1)$ by definition.

Theorem 3

$\sigma(T_1,T_2) < \infty$ if and on ly if for any repeatable portion δ of any sequence in ρ, $\#(\delta, T_1,T_2) = 0$. ◆

It is easy to prove the above two theorems, so omitted here.

4.2. Transition synchronization and place synchronization

People would think, based on experiences in daily life, that synchronization is something participated by different parties like hand clapping, or some events occurring at the same time like a live casting on TV with an on-going game. Such synchronization is characterized by distance 0, since one cannot see one hand clapping or see the TV show without the game.

We have said that hand clapping is a single transition consisting of actions of two hands; A live show and the on-going game would appear in a net as one transition as well since if they were separated as different transitions in parallel, ordered firings would produce the same effect , but this cannot be true. Synchronization characterized by distance 0 is "transition synchronization". Synchronization with $\sigma(T_1,T_2) > 0$ is "place synchronization" since such synchronization is achieved via places and it can be observed by taking an added place as an observation window.

System Σ_5 in Figure 5 (a) is the same system as shown in Figure 3 (b) with an added place p denoted by a dotted circle and connected to transitions by dotted arrows. This added place does not belong to Σ_5, it is to be used for observations.

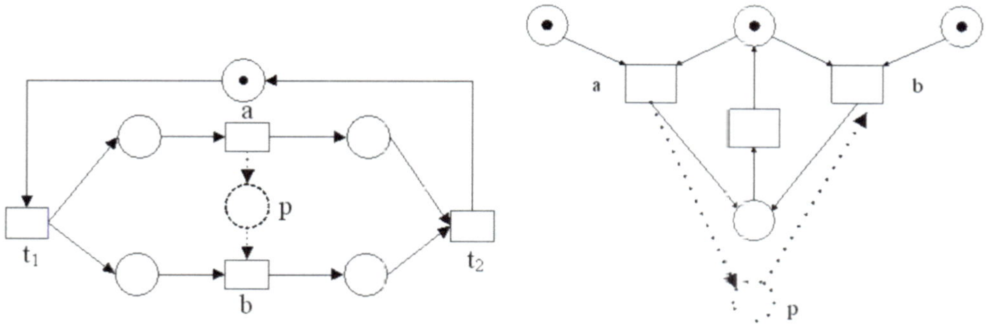

(a) Σ_5 (b) Σ_6

Figure 5. Added Place as Observation Window

An observer records what he finds through the window by putting a token into p when transition a fires and removing a token from p when transition b fires. It is assumed that place p has enough tokens, say n tokens, to start with, so the recording would not be interrupted. The maximum number of tokens in p is n+1 while the minimum is n-1. So the difference is 2 between transition b and transition a. The same observation applies to Σ_6 to get the same distance.

The observation window p for disjoint transition sets T_1 and T_2 is an added place whose input arcs are from T_1 and output arcs are pointing to T_2. Place p gets a token whenever a transition in T_1 fires and loses a token whenever a transition in T2 fires. Place p has enough tokens to start with to ensure a smooth observation. In case the number of tokens in p is not bounded, the distance between T_1 and T_2 is ∞. Otherwise, the difference between the maximum and the minimum is the distance.

It is easy to find that $\sigma(a,b) = \infty$ for the P/T-system in Figure 6 (a), since the repeatable sequence t_1abat_2 contains two firings of a and only one firing of b. The added place p as shown in Figure 6 (b) has weight 2 on the arc from p to transition b, it would have n+1 tokens after the first firing of a and n-1 tokens after the firing of b. The difference is 2.This is a weighted distance between b and a: $\sigma(a,2b) = 2$, the weight for a is 1 while the weight for b is 2. The concept of weighted synchronous distances makes a distinction when infinite distance is encountered. For simplicity, the formal definition of weighted synchronous distances is omitted here.

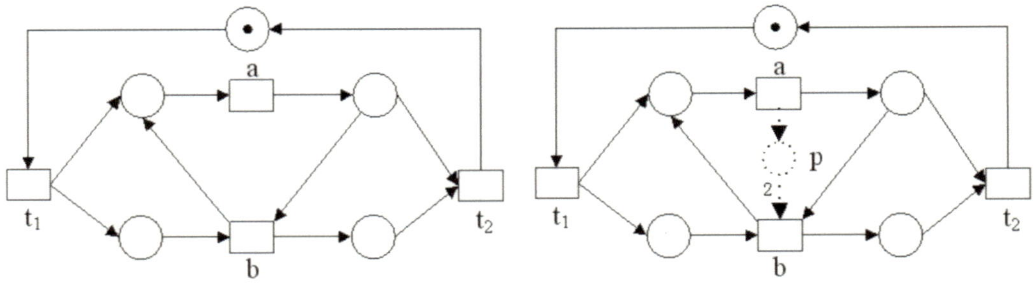

(a) Σ_7 (b)Σ_8

Figure 6. Weighted Synchronous Distance

Generally speaking, T_1 and T_2 may have more than one transition. It is possible that all transitions in the same set share the same weight, it is also possible that different transitions need different weights. It is assumed that the weights, if exist, would take the smallest possible values. For simplicity, we write $\sigma'(T_1,T_2)$ for weighted distance between T_1 and T_2 when the weights for individual transitions are known. The restriction on weights to be smallest leads to uniqueness of the distance.

Theorem 4

For an arbitrary place s in S in P/T-system Σ, as long as s has disjoint pre-set and post-set, $\sigma'(T_1,T_2) = \max\{ M(s) \mid M\in[M_0>\} - \min\{ M(s) \mid M\in[M_0>\}$ if exists, otherwise $\sigma'(T_1,T_2) = \infty$, where T_1 and T_2 are respectively the pre-set and post-set of s and $\sigma'(T_1,T_2)$ denotes a weighted distance with W(s,t) as the weight of transition t in T_2 and W(t,s) as the weight of transition t in T_1.◆

This theorem is true since what the added place records is exactly what happens in s.

In case there are no weights that yield a finite distance between T_1 and T_2, T_1 and T_2 are asynchronous.

4.3. Computing synchronous distance

All transition sequences can be found on the graph G(Σ). Synchronous distances, weighted or not, are defined in terms of transition sequences. Thus, it is possible to design algorithms for the computing of distances. Firstly, if a ring exists on G(Σ) that contains different numbers of firings of T_1 transitions and T_2 transitions, the distance is ∞. All algorithms are designed for computing finite distances only. The book in Chinese entitled *Petri Net Applications* by the author will soon appear, in which an algorithm for the computing of synchronous distances in P/T-systems can be found. It is easy to design an algorithm for computing weighted distances based on this algorithm.

We go no further on synchronous distances in this chapter since what concerns us is workflow modelling and what has been said about synchronous distances is already sufficient.

5. Business process

A successful application of Petri nets requires a full understanding of the application problem.

The term "workflow" was used as a synonym for "business process" in the book *Workflow Management* by W. Aalst and K. Hee. The terminology was developed by the Workflow Management Coalition (WFMC), an organization dedicated to develop standard terminology and standard interfaces for workflow management systems components.

As the first step towards workflow modelling, we make a clear distinction between "workflow" and "business process".

5.1. Business process vs. workflow

A business process is a pre-designed process in an enterprise or an organization for conducting the manipulation of individual cases of a business. It existed even before the birth of computers. The manipulation of individual business cases consists of business tasks and management tasks. The concept of "workflow" aims at "computerized facilitation or automation of a business process, in whole or part" (WFMC). To this end, the separation of business tasks and management tasks is of first importance. In a way, this is similar to the separation of data processing from a program, leading to the concepts of databases and database management systems.

A single business task may be carried out by a computer program. But "computerized automation of a business process" focuses on management automation rather than task automation. Management automation relies on clearly specified management rules. Most of the rules apply to all cases while some of the rules apply to individual cases. The former is "workflow logic" and the latter is "case semantics". The purpose of workflow modelling is nothing but to establish a formal specification of management rules to serve as a guide in the design, implementation and execution of a computer system called "workflow engine". It is the execution of the engine that conducts the processing of business cases. Figure 7 illustrates how workflow is related to business process.

The workflow logic specifies how business tasks are ordered (for causally dependent tasks) and/or synchronized. But, ordering is also a way of synchronization. Thus, workflow logic specifies how business tasks are synchronized for all conceivable cases in a business. In other words, workflow logic specifies all possible routes that a business case may take when being processed. What workflow logic cares about a single business task is not what data it requires or what data it will produce, let along what exact values are inputted or outputted. In this sense, workflow logic is concerned with abstract business tasks only.

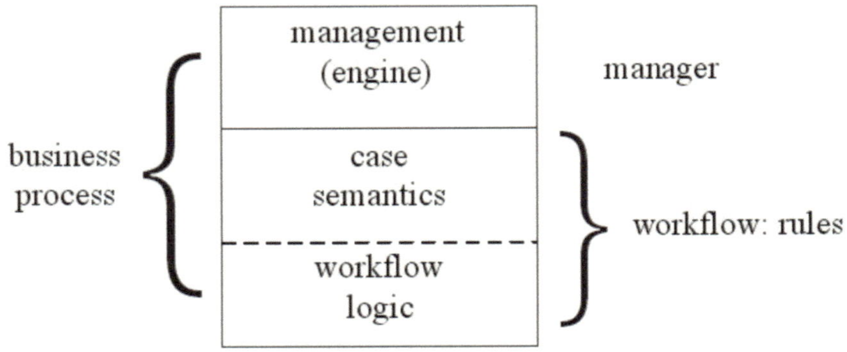

Figure 7. Business Process vs. Workflow

A selection is required at a crossing point of different routes. Concrete data of a given case determine the selection. The so selected route is the "semantics" of the given case. Thus, case semantics is concerned with those data that are used to decide whether a business task is on the route to be selected. These data are called explicit data since they should appear explicitly in the model of case semantics.

5.2. Management task vs. business task

A business must have a pre-designed form (paper form or electronic form) to record how an individual case is initiated and processed. Such a form is called a business form, B-form for short.

A business task can be characterized by

1. It requires professional knowledge, skill and/or experience related to the business.
2. It fills in at least one blank assigned to it on the B-form to tell what has been done.

A management task, on the other hand, requires knowledge on management rules. If it fills in blanks on the B-form at all, the written content is for management need only, e.g. a serial number for sorting and searching B-forms later on.

In the book *Workflow Management*, 16 tasks have been listed for "insurance claim" business in a (fictional) insurance company, among them, the first two tasks are:

1. Recording the receipt of the claim;
2. Establishing the type of claim (for example, fire, motor vehicle, travel, professional).

The first task may assign a serial number to the claim. Otherwise, it would leave no trace on a B-form. In fact, it is even not concerned with what B-form to be used. The second task must fill in the blank "type of claim" at least. Thus, the first task is a management task (may be shared by all businesses in a company) while the second task is a business task. In other words, the first task should be excluded from the workflow logic for "insurance claim", but the second task must be included.

5.3. Iteration vs. no iteration

The author of *Workflow Management* wrote: "This example of a process (i.e. insurance claim) also includes iteration or repetition — namely, the repeated assessment of an objection or the revision of the amount to be paid. In theory, this could go on forever."

As a management rule, an objection to a claim may need to be assessed more than once, but it must be a fixed number of times and by different persons; furthermore, the conclusion of each assessment must be recorded on the B-form. In other words, reassessment is a different task rather than a repetition of assessment.

Mathematically or logically, repetition could go on forever, but not for a theory of management. Endless repetition is not even thinkable in a management theory.

Iteration or repetition implies "redo" of the same task, i.e. what has been written on the B-form should be erased. "Redo" caused by wrong doings could, in theory, occur for every single task since human beings are erroneous by nature. No one would suggest a repetition for every task in a workflow model. "Redo" is nothing but a management measure to heal wrong doings, not a normal portion in a business process. Besides, workflow logic is about abstract tasks, but iteration is case dependent.

Endless redo could not occur since it is under control of the engine.

The execution of a single business task may include iteration. For example, when the amount of goods exceeds the truck load, the truck(s) would have to return after unloading. Such iteration is the detail of task execution, not a measure of management. Besides, it is case dependent. Iteration has nothing to do with workflow logic. What case semantics is concerned with is whether a task is on the route, not how a task is executed.

5.4. Set of tasks vs. set of blanks on B-form

Let $T = \{t_1,t_2,\cdots,t_n\}$ and $B = \{b_1,b_2,\cdots,b_m\}$ be the set of business tasks and respectively the set of blanks on the B-form for a give business process. The investigation here aims at properties of T and B for a well-defined business process.

There must be a correspondence between T and B, telling which blank(s) each task is responsible for. This correspondence should guarantee that no more than one task is responsible for the same blank in the course of processing a single case, and no blank is left empty upon termination of the case processing (those blanks that are not in relation with a given case are assumed to have been crossed out by the engine). Such correspondence has become common sense today. We will say no more about it.

Causal dependence among tasks in T leads to a combinatorial acyclic partial order on $T: < \sqsubseteq T\times T$, and a sub-relation $<\cdot$ of $<$: $x<\cdot y \equiv x<y \wedge \forall z\in T:\neg(x<z\wedge z<y)$. $<\cdot$ is the "immediate successor" relation: y is the immediate successor of x. Since the ordering relation $<$ is derivable from $<\cdot$ by transitivity of $<$, we will talk about $(T, <\cdot)$ instead of $(T, <)$. No iteration among tasks in T leads to acyclic partial order.

Let u be a task in T, u is a start task if it is before every other task, i.e. $\forall t \in T: \neg(t <\cdot u)$; u is an end task if u has no immediate successor. It is assumed that there is a unique start task, i.e. all cases share a unique beginning to recognize and to accept a case.

Let T_1, T_2 be nonempty subsets of T. T_2 is called an immediate successor set of T_1 , denoted by $T_1 <\cdot T_2$, if $\forall u \in T1 \forall v \in T_2 : u <\cdot v$. It is easy to prove that T_1 and T_2 are disjoint, and tasks in T_1 (T_2) are not ordered. Synchronization for management need can only be introduced between T_1 and T_2. Here, the synchronization between T_1 and T_2 must be place synchronization since they are different transitions. In case T_1 and T_2 are both singletons, the synchronization can only be the immediate successor relation. As an example, let be $T_1 = \{a, b\}$ and $T_2 = \{c, d\}$, $\sigma(T_1,T_2)=2$ and $\sigma(T_1,2T_2\ )=2$ are two different ways of synchronization. Taking into account the fact that every task, if it is included on a route, can only be (effectively, redo is not counted) executed once, $\sigma(T_1,T_2)=2$ requires that tasks a ,b being executed in parallel followed by tasks c, d being executed in parallel; $\sigma(T_1,2T_2)=2$ requires that tasks a, b being executed in parallel followed by either task c or task d being executed alone. Data from a given case will be used for the selection between task c and task d. It is clear that synchronous distances would be of no use if redo is taken into account.

Now the processing of a given case goes like this: it begins from the unique start task, each task on the route carries out its duty and fills in blank(s) it is responsible for on the B-form, and passes it to its immediate successor(s) via the engine. The engine takes care of quality checking, successor selection and appointing executer(s) for selected task(s); and finally, the engine passes the B-form to appointed executer(s).

6. Synchronizer and workflow logic

P/T-systems will be used for the modelling of workflow logic. A synchronizer is a special place to connect transitions (tasks) with immediate successor relation ($<\cdot$).

To capture the fact that every task (transition) is executed (effectively) at most once for a single business case and workflow logic contains no iteration, a concept of restricted P/T-systems, RP/T-systems for short, is proposed.

Definition 9

A P/T-system $\Sigma=(S,T;F,K,W,M_0)$ is a RP/T-system if it is acyclic ($F^+ \cap (F^{-1})^+) = \emptyset$) and any transition is restricted to fire at most once. ◆

The P/T-system in Figure 2 is a good example: as a normal P/T-system, transition t_2 can fire twice when p_1 has 2 tokens; but as a RP/T-system, t_2 can fire only once at the same marking. In fact, transitions t_2 and t_3 would fire when p_1 has 2 tokens for a RP/T-system, though t2 remains enabled after its first firing.

Note that RP/T-systems are not a new class of net systems. If we introduce a control place c for every transition t such that c has an empty pre-set and {t} is its post-set, and initially it has one token. Apparently, with an added control place for every transition, every transition can fire at most once by conventional transition rules.

6.1. Synchronizer

Definition 10

A place p in a RP/T-system is a synchronizer if T_1 and T_2 are the pre-set and post-set of p and they are not empty; and $\forall t \in T_1$: $W(t, p) = b$ and $\forall t \in T_2$: $W(p, t) = a$ where b and a are integers such that $0 \le a \le n$ and $0 \le b \le m$; n, m are respectively the numbers of transitions in T_1 and T_2; and $K(p) = ab$.◆

The RP/T-system in Figure 2 has two synchronizers p_1 and p_2 since $K(p_1) = 2$ and $K(p_2) = 2$.

The synchronizer defined by Definition 10 is usually denoted by $p = (T_1, T_2, (a, b))$ or $p = ({}^{\bullet}p, p^{\bullet}, (a, b))$. Figure 8 (a) is the graphical presentation of a synchronizer p and (b) is the detail of p, explaining how synchronization is achieved. Theorem 4 concludes that $\sigma(bT_1, aT_2) = ab$, i.e. the weighted synchronous distance between T_1 and T_2 are ab where b is the weight for all transitions in T_1 and a is the weight for all transitions in T_2.

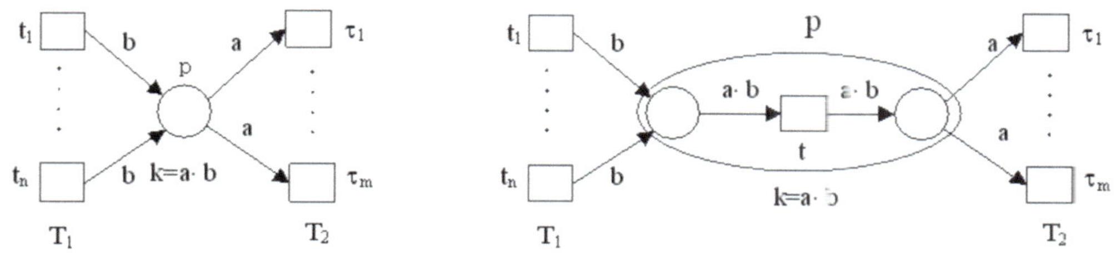

Figure 8. A Synchronizer and its Detail

Definition 11

Let $p = (T_1, T_2, (a, b))$ be a synchronizer and n, m be the numbers of transitions in T_1 and T_2. P can be classified as below:

n=m=1, p is sequential synchronizer,
m>1, p is a split,
n>1, p is a join,
a>1 and a=n, p is an ALL-join,
1<a<n, p is an OR-join,
a=1 and a<n, p is a XOR-join,
b>1 and b=n, p is an ALL-split,
1<b<m, p is an OR-split,
b=1 and b<m, p is a XOR-split.

Here we have deliberately chosen terms used by Prof. Aalst for WF-net. The difference is: our synchronizers are places while synchronization is achieved via transitions in WF-net. Synchrony in Section 3 has made it clear that synchronization with a distance greater than zero is place synchronization. We will see what advantages the concept of synchronizers brings with it when we approach to management logic.

Figure 9 shows how to achieve mixed synchronization where p_1 is an XOR-split and p_2 is an ALL-split. What follows task t would be one of t_1 and t_2 plus both t_3 and t_4.

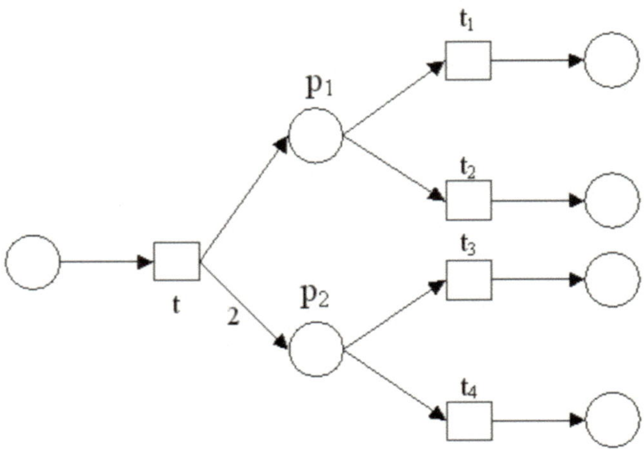

Figure 9. ALL-split and XOR-split mixture

Definition 12

Let x, y be variables of integer type. The place $p_1 = (T_1, T_2, (a, y))$, $p_2 = (T_1, T_2, (x, b))$ and $p_3 = (T_1, T_2, (x, y))$ are variations of synchronizer $p = (T_1, T_2, (a, b))$ as long as $0 < x \leq n$ and $0 < y \leq m$. p_1, p_2 and p3 are flexible synchronizers, since x and y can take different values.◆

Figure 10 explains how flexible synchronizers work: x may take 1 or 2 as its value to achieve different synchronization.

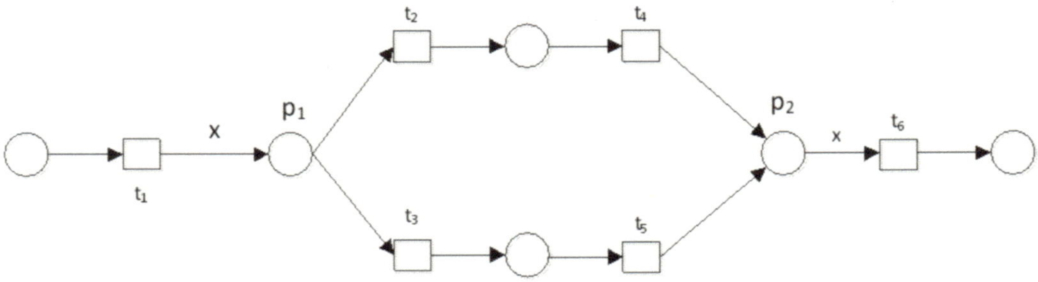

Figure 10. Flexible Synchronizers p_1 and p_2

We have not found a way to express flexible synchronization in terms of WF-net since an OR-split or OR-join transition in WF-net does not tell the exact number "OR" represents.

6.2. Workflow logic

RP/T-systems are candidates for modelling workflow logic, but not every RP/T-system is suitable.

Definition 13

For RP/T-system $\Sigma = (S,T;F,K,W,M_0)$, relation next$\subseteq T \times T$ is given by next = $\{(t, t') \mid t^{\bullet} \cap {}^{\bullet}t' \neq \emptyset\}$. We write next(t, t′) for (t, t′) ∈ next. Σ is well ordered if, for any t, t′ in T, next(t, t′) implies $\forall u \in T: \neg(next(t,u) \wedge next(u, t'))$.

The system in Figure 11 is not well-ordered, since we have next(t_1, t_3) and next(t_1, t_2)∧ next(t_2, t_3).

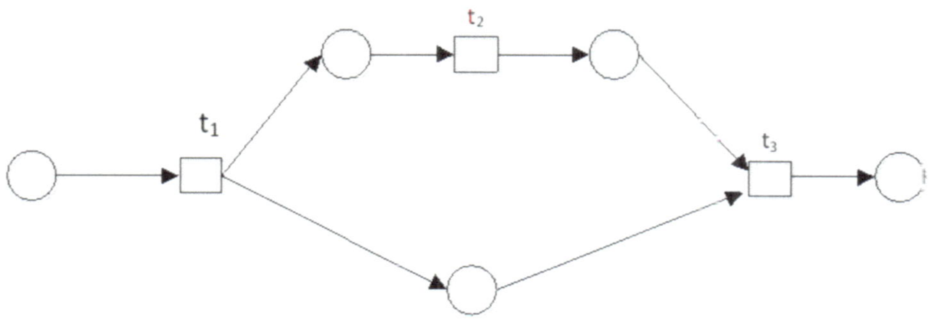

Figure 11. A System not Well-ordered

Remember that we are seeking for net systems that are suitable for modelling workflow logic. If t_1, t_2 and t_3 are tasks, then the B-form would be passed from t_1 to t_3 twice: one directly and one via t_2. This redundancy leads to structure complexity and analytical difficulty. Besides, there might be semantic inconsistency for this or that reason.

Definition 14

A well-ordered RP/T-system $\Sigma = (S,T;F,K,W,M_0)$ is a workflow logic if:

Every transition has nonempty pre- and post- sets; there is a unique place s_0 such that it has an empty pre-set and its post-set is a singleton $\{t_0\}$ and $K(s_0) = 1$, $W(s_0, t_0) = 1$; every intermediate place p is a synchronizer; every end-place, i.e. a place with an empty post-set, has a capacity 1 and its input arc(s) has 1 as its weight; The initial marking has a unique token in s_0.◆

A task is initiated upon receiving a B-form, and passes it over to its successor upon termination. Thus, its pre-set and post-set are nonempty. The unique place s_0 is the place to receive initiated B-forms one by one and one at a time. Transition t_0 is the unique start task. An end-place is to receive completed B-forms, one by one and one at a time. All tasks must be well synchronized, so intermediate places are synchronizers. The weight on an input arc (t, p) of synchronizer p represents that W(t, p) immediate successors need the B-form completed by t, and the weight on an output arc of p represents that B-forms completed by W(p, t) different immediate predecessors of t are needed by t. The unique token in s_0 represents an abstract single case. It is an abstract case since no data is needed. An abstract case resembles all conceivable cases.

The system in Figure 2 is workflow logic. The conventional transition rules would apply to a workflow logic if a control place is added to each of the transitions (so, no transition can fire for the second time for one case) and the detail of every synchronizer as given in Figure 8 is also made explicit. But, this would make workflow logic too complicated for practical use. The following is the transition rules for workflow logic.

Definition 15

Let $\Sigma = (S,T;F,K,W, M_0)$ be a workflow logic, t in T is a transition and M is a marking (i.e. the initial marking M_0 or reachable from M_0 by rules given here).

1. t is enabled by M (or at M), denoted by M[t≫, if $\forall s \in {}^{\bullet}t: M(s)=K(s)$,
2. Once M[t≫ is true, it remains true until either t occurs or t is not enabled according to conventional transition rule.
3. The successor marking, when t fires, is computed according to the conventional rule.◆

It is recommendable to compute the set of reachable markings for the workflow logic given in Figure 2. We denote with $[M_0 \gg$ the set of reachable markings.

Redundancy is always closely connected to complexity. The property of being well-ordered has removed certain redundancy. The next definition reveals different redundancy.

Definition 16

A workflow logic is well-structured if for every synchronizer p and a reachable marking M, M(p) = K(p) implies the fact that either all transitions in the post-set of p are enabled, or none of them is enabled.◆

Figure 12 illustrates this definition: the workflow logic in (a) is not well- structured, since t_3 is enabled but t_4 is not when p_2 has a token (the capacity of a synchronizer is known without saying). On the other hand, transitions t_3, t_4 and t_5 are all enabled when p_2 has 2 tokens in the system in (b).

Careful readers may have noticed that p_2 in (b) is not a synchronizer. No, it is not. It is a variation of a synchronizer. The two transitions t_3 and t_5 in (b) are viewed as twins: either both of them to be on a route, or none of them to be selected since t_4 requires 2 tokens. Thus, as far as route selection is concerned (workflow logic aims at the description of all possible routes), twin transitions could and should be combined as shown in Figure 13. Variations of synchronizers may be allowed in practice for convenience. But for the analysis of workflow logic, combined twins are preferred.

If the system in Figure 12 (b) is taken as workflow logic with a synchronizer variation, it reveals another problem: there would be two tokens upon the completion of one case when t_3 and t_5 are on its route. This is inconsistent with common knowledge: A single case cannot have two separated conclusions. This observation raises a question: what properties a well-defined workflow logic should have, in addition to being well-ordered and well-structured?

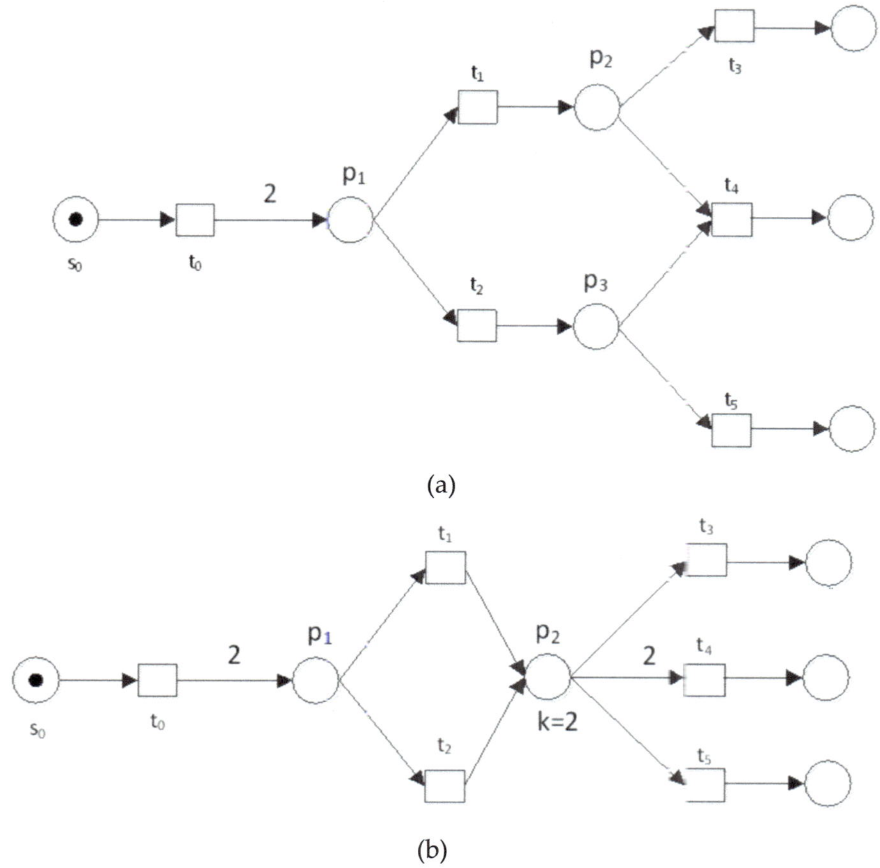

Figure 12. Not well- structured workflow logic

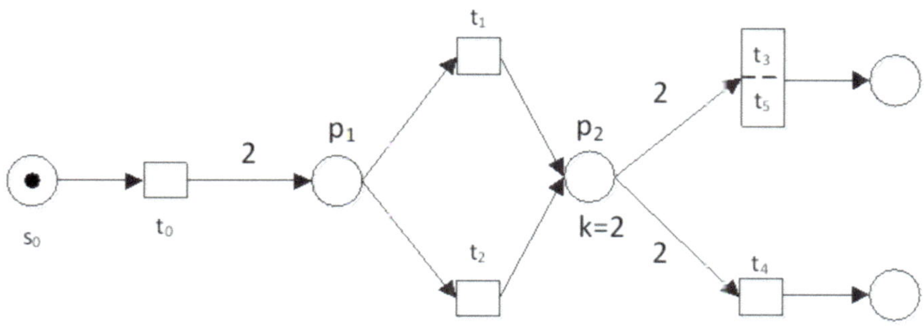

Figure 13. Combined Twins

Soundness! This is the answer from WF-net. Soundness requires:

"A process contains no unnecessary tasks and every case submitted to the process must be completed in full and with no references to it (that is case tokens) remaining in the process."

What we propose is throughness: the token in s_0 (an abstract case) will be passed over by transition firings (tasks) via the engine, to a unique end-place. All properties required by soundness are covered by being through.

In what follows, workflow logic is always assumed well-structured.

6.3. Throughness and reduction rules

Let Σ = (S,T; F, K, W, M_0) be a well-structured workflow logic, and M is a reachable marking.

Definition 17

1. M is a termination marking if it enables no transition; M is an end-marking if there is a unique end-place e such that M(e) = 1 and M(s) = 0 for all places s other than e.
2. Σ is through if every termination marking is an end-marking and every end-marking is also a termination marking. ◆

The workflow logic in Figure 2 is through.

Theorem 5

If workflow logic Σ is through, then for every transition t, there is a reachable marking M that enables t and there is a route to which t belongs.◆

From the fact that Σ is acyclic and s_0 is unique, we know that there is a directed path from s_0 to t. By mathematical reduction on the length of this path, this theorem is easy to prove.

Soundness of a WF-net is proved via computing T-invariant by adding an extra transition between its unique place o and its unique initial place i. This method applies to workflow logic as well. But we do it differently.

Keep in mind the principle of local determinism. Our attention focuses on local structures of workflow logic rather than global properties like T-invariants.

Characteristics of local structures bring up the following reduction rules for proving throughness of workflow logic.

Reduction Rule 1

Synchronizer $p_1 = (T_1,T_0,(a_1, a_2))$ and $p_2 = (T_0,T_2,(b_1,b_2))$ can be reduced to synchronizer $p = (T_1,T_2,(a_1,b_2))$ if $a_2 = b_1$. ◆

Figure 14 illustrates this rule.

Let Σ be the workflow logic to which rule 1 is applied and Σ' is resulted by replacing p_1, T_0, p_2 with p in Σ. We have

Theorem 6

Σ is through if and only if Σ' is through.◆

Synchronizer p_1 requires that a_2 transitions from T_0 to fire after the firings of a_1 transitions from T_1 while synchronizer p_2 requires that b_1 transitions from T_0 to be fired before any transition firing from T_2. Given $a_2 = b_1$, p_1 and p_2 are consistent with each other on T_0: a_1 transitions from T_1 followed by b_2 transitions from T_2. Thus, the theorem is true. (p_1,T_0, p_2) is in fact the detail of p. This reduction of omitting consistent detail is a net morphism in net topology. No wonder the property of being through is reserved. All reduction rules are in fact to conceal local details, and as such, they reserve throughness. But there will be no more theorems and proofs to be given below for simplicity.

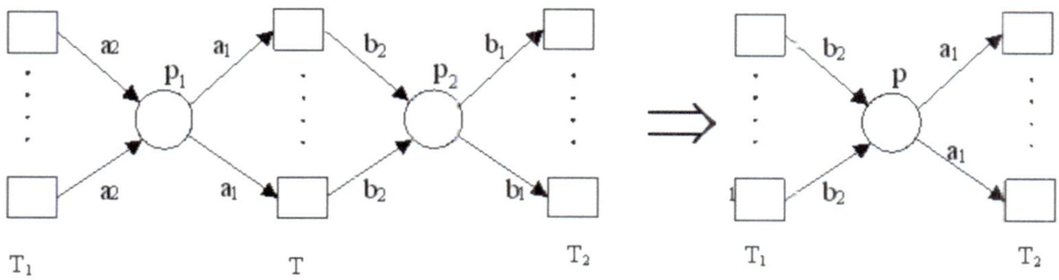

Figure 14. Reduction Rule 1

Reduction Rule 2

For synchronizer p = ({t_1}, {t_2}, (1,1)), if $t_1^{\bullet} \cap {}^{\bullet}t_2 = \{p\}$, then ($t_1$, p, t_2) can be replaced by a single transition t with ${}^{\bullet}t = {}^{\bullet}t_1 \cup {}^{\bullet}t_2 - \{p\}$ and $t^{\bullet} = t_1^{\bullet} \cup t_2^{\bullet} - \{p\}$. All weights on remaining arcs remain.◆

Figure 15 illustrates this rule.

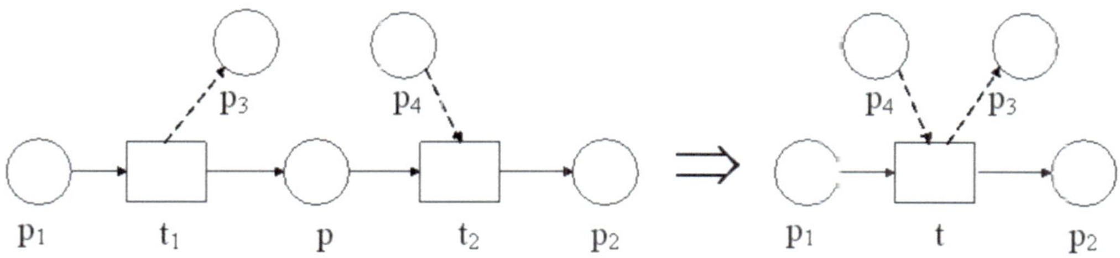

Figure 15. Reduction Rule 2

It is easy to see that the combined effect of t_1 and t_2 on all places other than p is the same as the effect of t. The dotted circles and arcs may exist, but not necessarily.

Reduction Rule 3

For transition t and places p_1, p_2, if $p_1^{\bullet} \cap {}^{\bullet}p_2 = \{t\}$ and W(p_1, t) = W(t, p_2) = 1, then (p_1,t,p_2) can be replaced by p, ${}^{\bullet}p = {}^{\bullet}p_1 \cup {}^{\bullet}p_2 - \{t\}$ and $p^{\bullet} = p_1^{\bullet} \cup p_2^{\bullet} - \{t\}$. All weights on remaining arcs remain. ◆

Note that places p_1 and p_2 are not necessarily synchronizers, i.e. it is possible ${}^{\bullet}p_1 = \emptyset$ and/or $p_2^{\bullet} = \emptyset$.

Figure 16 (a) illustrates this rule.

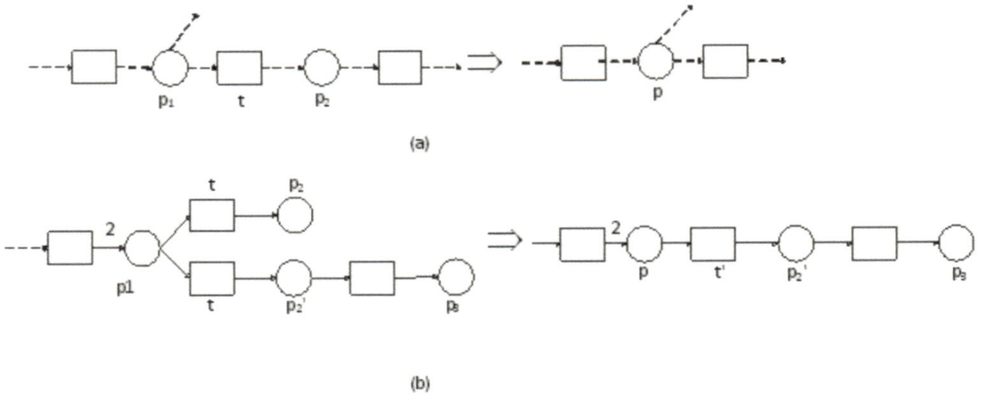

Figure 16. Reduction Rule 3

The workflow logic in Figure 16 (b) is not through since the termination marking would have two tokens at two different end-places. Rule 3 can be applied to reduce it in size, but the resulted place p turns out to be inconsistent between its pre-set and its post-set.

Reduction Rule 4

For $T_1 = \{t_1, t_2,\cdots, t_a\}$ and $T_2 = \{t_1', t_2',\cdots, t_b'\}$, if $p_i = (\{t_i\}, T_2, (1, b))$ is a synchronizer, $i = 1, 2,\cdots, a$, then $p_1, p_2,\cdots$ pa can be reduced to a single synchronizer $p = (T_1,T_2, (a, b))$; If $p_i' = (T_1, \{t_i'\}, (a,1))$ is a synchronizer $i = 1,2,\cdots, b$, then $p_1', p_2',\cdots p_b'$ can be reduced to the same single synchronizer $p = (T_1,T_2, (a, b))$.◆

Figure 17 illustrates this rule where a = 3 and b = 2.

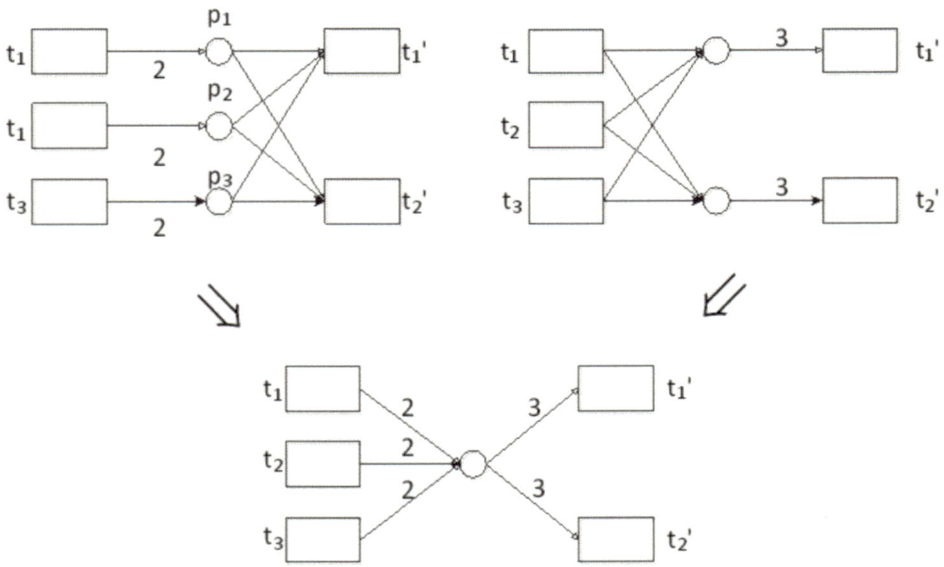

Figure 17. Redaction Rule 4

We will see the significance of this rule and the rule next when management logic is discussed, since separated managements before the rule is applied become centralized management after it.

Reduction Rule 5

If $p_i = (\{t\}, \{t_i\}, (1, 1))$ is a synchronizer for every i, i = 1, 2, ⋯, a, then these synchronizers can be reduced to a single synchronizer $p = (\{t\}, \{t_1, t_2, \cdots, t_a\}, (1, a))$.

If $p_j = (\{t_j\}, \{t\}, (1, 1))$ is a synchronizer for every j, j = 1, 2, ⋯, b, then these synchronizers can be reduced to a single synchronizer $p = (\{t_1, t_2, \cdots, t_b\}, \{t\}, (b, 1))$.◆

Figure 18 illustrates this rule, where a = b = 3. .

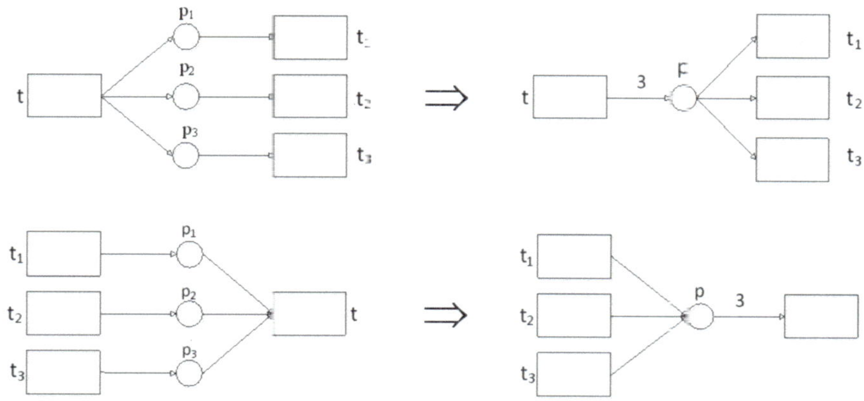

Figure 18. Reduction Rule 5

The next reduction rule reserves throughness, but a place element rather than a synchronizer is used for reduction.

Reduction Rule 6

In this rule, i = 1, 2, ⋯, a and j = 1, 2, ⋯, b. For transition sets $T = \{t_1, t_2, \cdots, t_a\}$ and $T_i = \{t_{i1}, t_{i2}, \cdots, t_{ib}\}$, if $p_i = (\{t_i\}, T_i, (1, b))$ is a synchronizer for every i, then these synchronizers can be reduced to the place p: $^{\cdot}p = T$, $p^{\cdot} = \bigcup_{i=1}^{a} T_i$, $K(p) = ab$, $W(t_i, p) = b$ and $W(p, t_{ij}) = 1$, If $p_i' = (T_i, \{t_i\}, (b, 1))$ is a synchronizer for every i, then these synchronizers can be reduced to the place q: $^{\cdot}q = \bigcup_{i=1}^{a} T_i$, $q^{\cdot} = T$, $K(q) = ab$, $W(t_{ij}, q) = 1$, $W(q, t_i) = b$.◆

Figure 19 illustrates this rule, where a = 3 and b = 2.

A noticeable fact is: places p and q are different from a synchronizer at two aspects. Firstly, their capacities are both ab instead of the product of the input weight and the output weight. Secondly, transitions in T_i and T_j , $i \neq j$, maybe enabled at different times before reduction, but they will be enabled at the same time by p; similarly, transitions in T will be enabled at the same time by q, but maybe not before reduction. The important point is, the number of transitions to be selected for a route remain unchanged (real selection is to be determined by concrete data from a practical case later by case semantics.) due to the fact that all synchronizers in question are either ALL-split or ALL-join. This means that the property of being through is reserved.

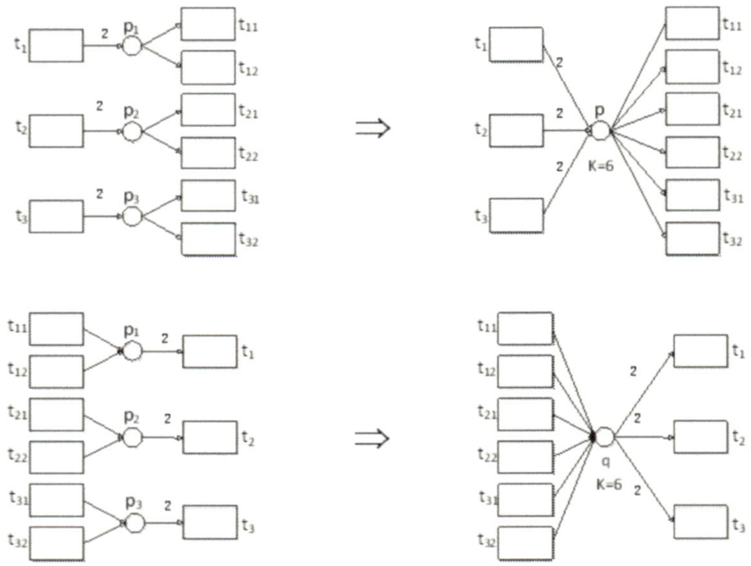

Figure 19. Reduction Rule 6

Definition 18

A place p with $\cdot p = T_1$ and $p\cdot = T_2$, $T_1 \neq \emptyset$, $T_2 \neq \emptyset$, is called a virtual synchronizer if there exist integers a and b such that $\forall t \in T_1$:$W(t,p)=b$,$\forall t \in T_2$:$W(p, t)=a$, $K(p) \neq ab$, but $K(p)/b = n$, $K(p)/a = m$, where n, m are respectively the numbers of transitions in T_1 and T_2. For virtual synchronizer p, we also write $p = (\cdot p, p\cdot, (a,b))$.◆

The two places p and q in Figure 19 are virtual synchronizers. It is easy to check that the two places used for reduction by Rule 6 are virtual synchronizers in general.

For further reduction when a virtual synchronizer is involved, we have the revised version of Reduction Tule 1:

Reduction Rule 1′:

Let each of $p_1 = (T_1, T_0, (a_1, a_2))$ and $p_2 = (T_0, T_2, (b_1, b_2))$ be a synchronizer or a virtual synchronizer. As long as $K(p_1)/a_1 = K(p_2)/b_2$, (p_1, T_0, p_2) can be reduced to $p = (T_1, T_2, (a, b))$, where $a = K(p_1)/b_1$ and $b = K(p_2)/a_2$, and $K(p) = ab$, $\forall t \in T_2$: $W(t, p) = b$ and $\forall t \in T_2$: $W(t, p) = a$. ◆

This rule is applicable when the involved virtual synchronizer is of ALL-join and ALL-split nature. Otherwise, local consistence should be checked since a virtual synchronizer is more flexible than a synchronizer. Figure 20 explains: the workflow logic on top is not through since just one of p_2 and p_3 may have 2 tokens while p_4 requires the two of them to have two tokens each. As shown in the figure, a virtual synchronizer p_5 is obtained when rule 6 is applied. The resulted system after rule 6 remains being not through. If rule 1′ is further applied to p_5 and p_4, we get a system that is through. Inconsistence between p_1 and p_4 is concealed. The virtual synchronizer p_5 does not tell whether it is ALL-split or OR-split. It inherits property of being ALL-split or OR-split from p_1.

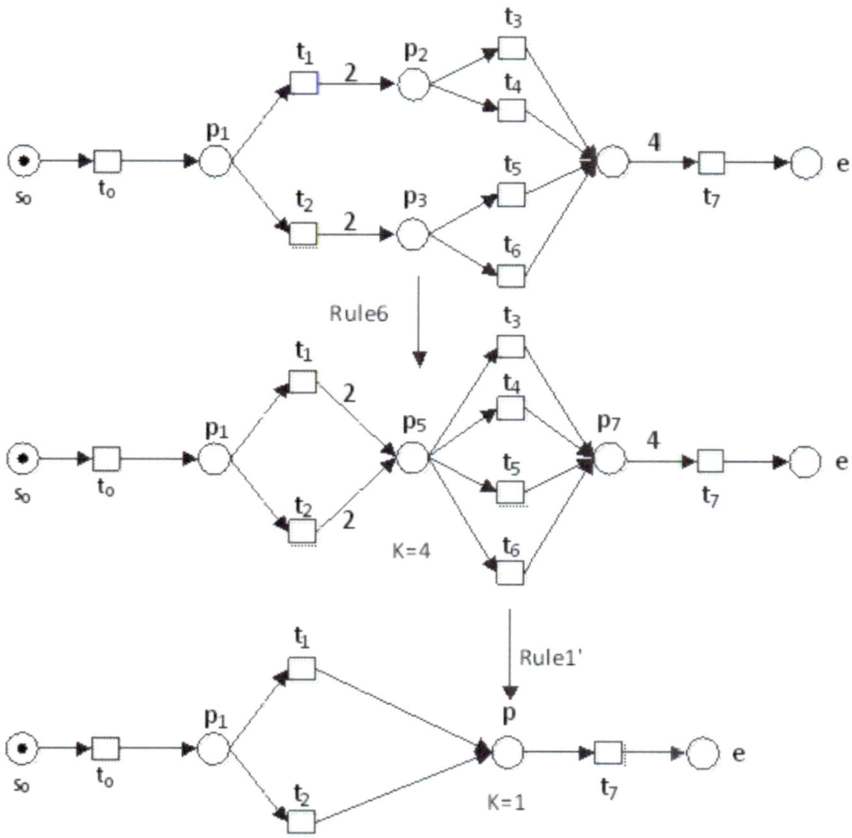

Figure 20. Reduction Rule 1′ leads to Error

Figure 21 illustrates Reduction Rule 1′, in which the workflow logic on top is apparently through. After twice applications of rule 6, the resulted p_6 and p_7 are virtual synchronizers both. By reduction rule 1′, these two virtual synchronizers are replaced by p, which is a synchronizer. This time the property of being through is reserved.

Reduction Rule 6 is suggested not to be used as long as there is a different reduction rule applicable.

Theorem 7

A well-structured workflow logic has the property of being through if it can be reduced to a single isolated place, i.e. a place whose pre-set and post-set are both empty.◆

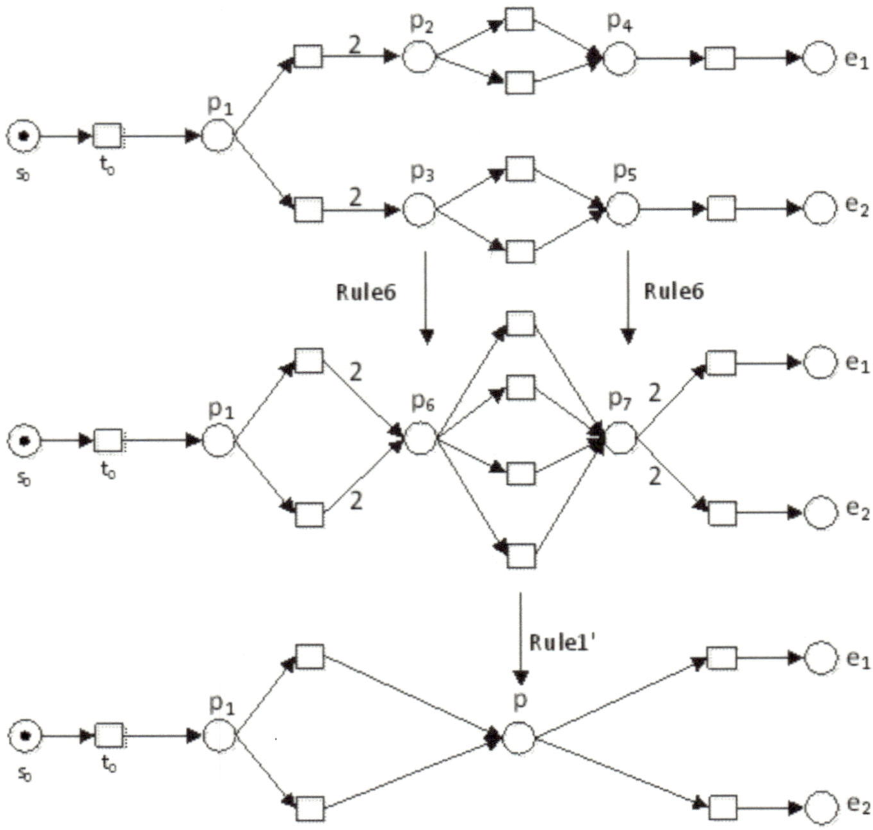

Figure 21. Reduction Rule 1′

This theorem is true since all reduction rules (including carefully used rule 1′) reserve throughness . The isolated place is the start-place and the end place at the same time, thus the concealed detail has the property of being through.

This isolated place represents "harmony" as far as workflow logic is concerned. An interesting fact is, the isolated transition represents "contradiction" when it is resulted by applying the Resolution Rule and the Expansion Rule in Enlogy (a branch in GNT, net logic) for logical reasoning. A pair of dual elements, i.e. a place and a transition, lead to opposite concepts in philosophy, could this happen by chance? In fact as we will see soon, the dual of workflow logic is exactly the logic for workflow management.

We do not claim the completeness of this set of reduction rules. Whenever a user finds workflow logic not reducible to "harmony" though it is indeed through, please try to figure out new reduction rules and to let us know. Reduction rules would be enriched this way, we hope.

Figure 22 shows how to reduce to harmony the workflow logic for insurance claim where t_0, t_1, t_2, t_3 and t_4 are respectively the tasks "accept", "check policy", "check claim", "send letter" and "pay" (See *Workflow Management*).

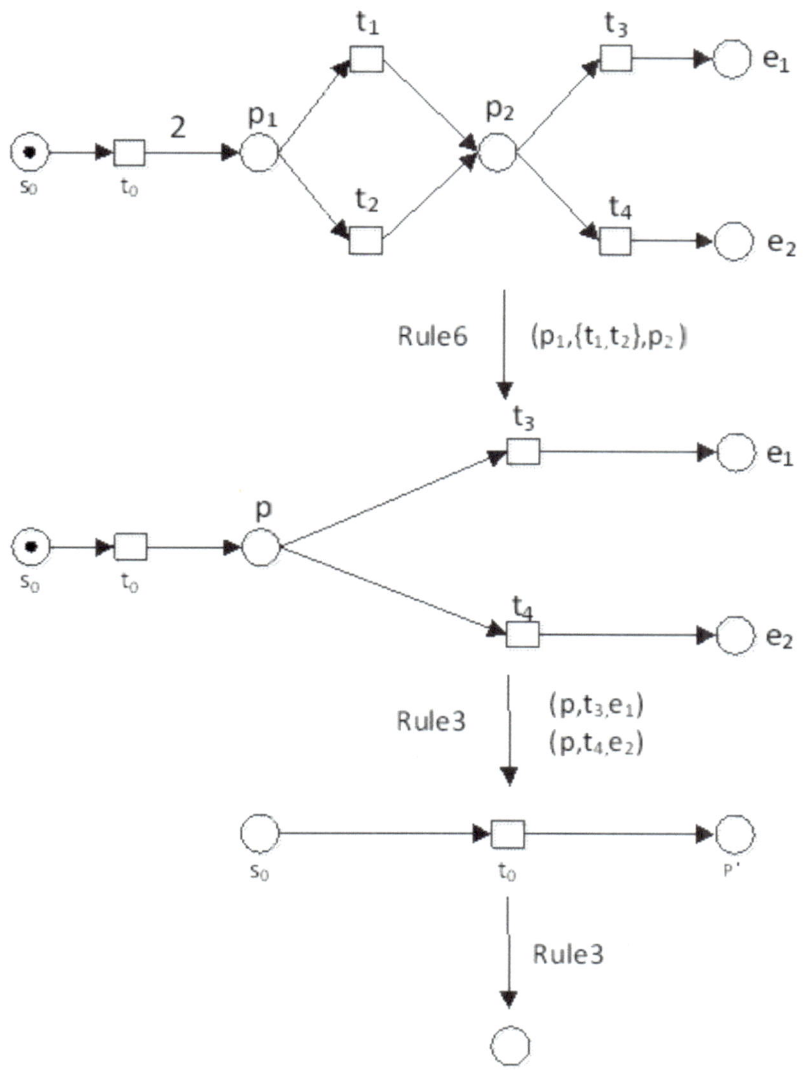

Figure 22. Reducing Workflow to Harmony

Figure 23 is a more complicated net from Dr. Aalst during his visit to Tsinghua University (Beijing, China) in 2004, where (a) is the original net in which every place has the capacity 1 and all weights on arcs are also 1, i.e. a WF-net. The author would suggest to take (b) as the workflow logic for whatever business in mind. Note that (c) contains virtual synchronizers.

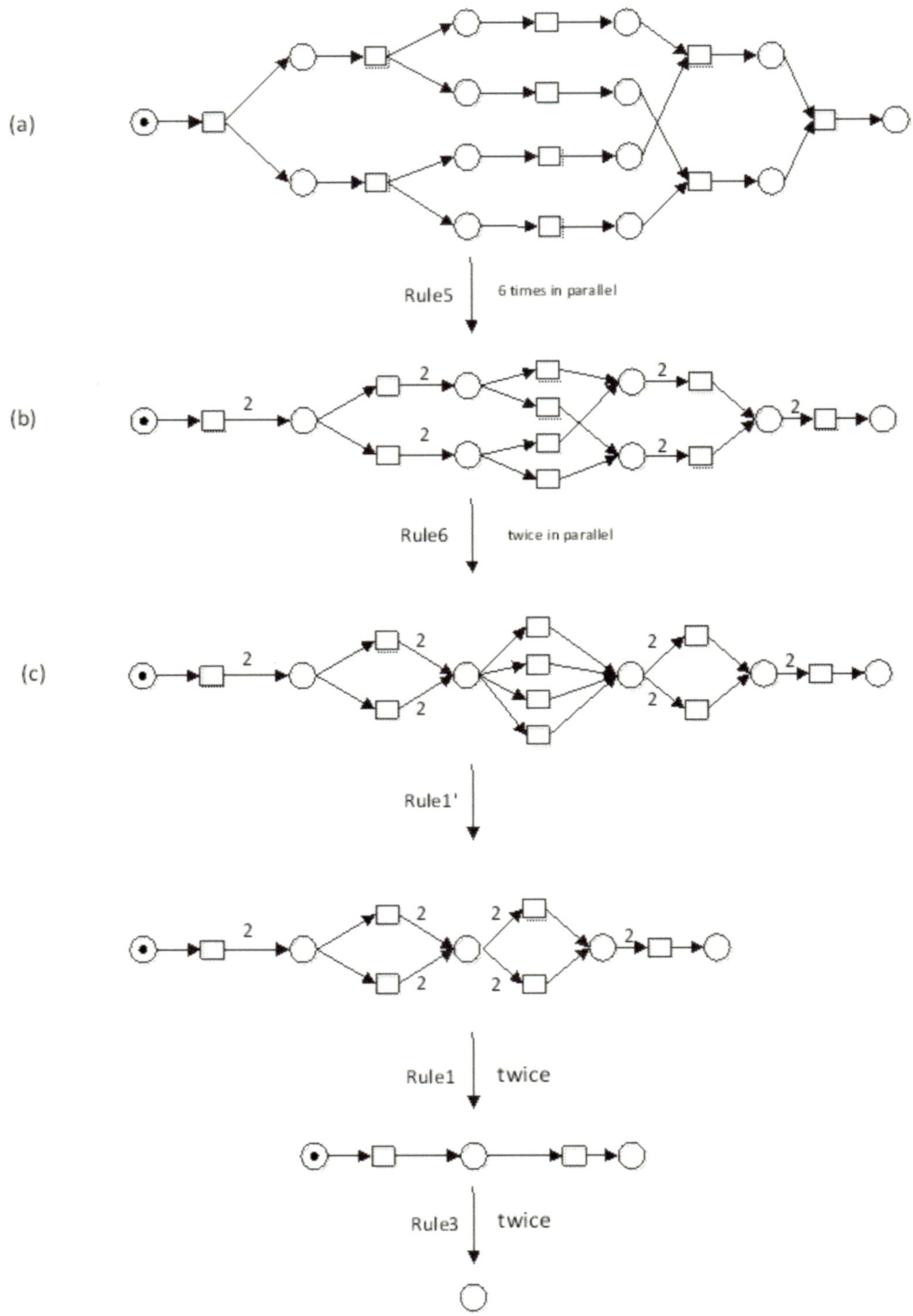

Figure 23. Reduction Process

6.4. Develop a workflow logic for a given business

Let $T = \{t_1, t_2, \cdots t_n\}$ and $B = \{b_1, b_2, \cdots b_m\}$ be respectively the set of business tasks with $<\cdot$ as its immediate successor relation, and the set of blanks on the B-form for a well-designed business. There should be a fixed correspondence between T and B to make clear responsibilities for each of the tasks in T. This correspondence will not be mentioned any more.

Let $\Sigma = (S,T;F,K,W,M_0)$ be the net system such that T is the task set and $S = \{p_1, p_2, \cdots p_k\} \cup \{s_0\} \cup E$ where for each i, i = 1, 2, ⋯, k, k is the number of non-end tasks $t_1, t_2, \cdots t_k$ in T, $\cdot p_i = \{t_i\}$, $p_i\cdot$ is the set of immediate successors of t_i. Let ai be the number of tasks in this immediate successor set, a_i' is the intended number of tasks to be executed after t_i, then $K(p_i) = a_i'$, and $W(t_i, p_i) = a_i'$ for every immediate successor t of t_i, $W(p_i, t) = 1$. It is easy to see that p_i is a synchronizer: $p_i = (\{t_i\}, p_i\cdot' (1, a_i'))$.

The place named s_0 is the unique start place: it has an empty pre-set and its post-set contains the unique start task with arc weight 1.

For every end-task in T, there is a unique end place e in E with 1 as the arc weight between them. E contains nothing else.

$M_0(s_0) = 1$ and all other elements in S have no token.

As a workflow logic of a business process, transition rules for RP/T-systems are assumed for Σ.

Σ must be well-ordered since $<\cdot$ is exactly its next relation among transitions.

Σ may be not well-structured as shown by Figure 12 (a). In this case, measures must be taken as suggested from Figure 12 (a) to (b), then to Figure 13.

Redundant synchronizers may be removed by Reduction Rule 3.

As an example, Let $T = \{t_1, t_2, t_3, t_4, t_5\}$ and $<\cdot = \{(t_1, t_2), (t_1, t_3), (t_2, t_4), (t_2, t_5), (t_3, t_4), (t_3, t_5)\}$. There are 3 non-end tasks in T, namely t_1, t_2 and t_3. So there 3 synchronizers: p_1, p_2 and p_3. Figure 24 shows the developed workflow logic.

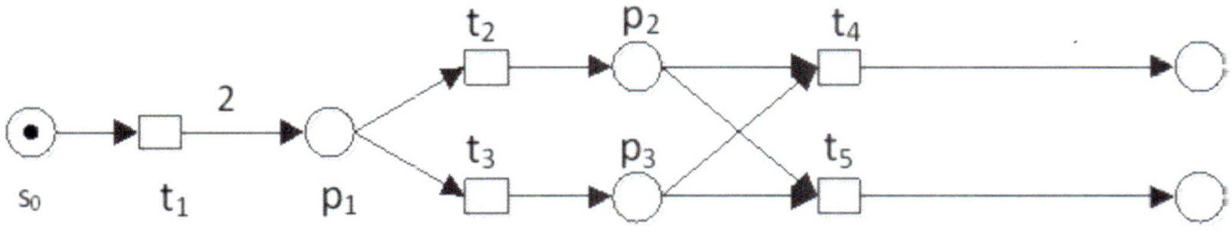

Figure 24. A developed Workflow Logic

There is redundancy in the developed system at p_2 and p_3. By Reduction Rule 3, these two synchronizers are reduced to a single synchronizer $p = (\{t_2, t_3\}, \{t_4, t_5\}, (2, 1))$. This is the workflow logic for insurance claim, as shown in Figure 22, there it was reduced to harmony.

7. Case semantics

Let $\Sigma = (S,T;F,K,W,M_0)$ be the workflow logic developed for a business process. Case semantics is to select a route for the processing of a given case.

A healthy enterprise should have new cases arrive every day. It is impossible to have different routes for different cases. Cases must be classified so that one route for one case class.

Let $C = \{c_1, c_2, \cdots c_k\}$ be the set of conditions for case classification. For example, let Boolean variable x, y be used to record conclusions given by tasks "check policy" and "check claim" respectively for insurance claim i.e. x and y are blanks on the B-form. One way to specify case classes is: $c_1 = x \wedge y$, $c_2 = \neg x \vee \neg y$. This classification is consistent with the workflow logic developed in Figure 24. Another way of case classification is to have 4 classes: $c_1 = x \wedge y$, $c_2 = \neg x \wedge y$, $c_3 = x \wedge \neg y$, $c_4 = \neg x \wedge \neg y$. This classification leads to a different task set: there have to be 4 end tasks. Thus the workflow logic is also different. The B-form should as well be changed accordingly.

Before going on from conditions to routes, a definition of routes is needed.

Definition 19

A route on a workflow logic $\Sigma = (S,T;F,K,W,M_0)$ is a RP/T-system $\Sigma' = (S',T';F',K',W',M_0')$ such that S',T', and F' are subsets of S,T and F respectively:

S 'contains the start place s, a unique end place e, and all synchronizers in S that have a directed path to e

T' consists of the start transition (task), the transition in the pre-set of e, and for every synchronizer $p = (^{\cdot}p, p^{\cdot}(a, b))$ in S', a transitions from $^{\cdot}p$ and b transitions from $p^{\cdot}$.

$F' = \{(x,y) \mid x,y \in S' \cup T' \wedge (x,y) \in F\}$.

For $x \in S'$, $K'(x) = K(x)$; For $(x, y) \in F'$, $W'(x, y) = W(x, y)$; $M_0'(x) = M0(x)$ for all x in S' .◆

The difference between $\Sigma = (S,T;F,K,W,M_0)$ and $\Sigma' = (S',T';F',K',W',M_{0'})$ appears when a synchronizer p is an OR-join and/or OR-split. Conditions $c_1, c_2, \cdots c_k$ will be used to select a transitions from $^{\cdot}p$ and b transitions from $p^{\cdot}$. Thus, variables (blanks in B) used in these conditions are explicit variables, since they will appear explicitly in the system model for case semantics.

7.1. C-net: Net with variables [5,8]

C-net was originally defined for programming, i.e. for computation and communication. Variables are essentially different from conventional place elements of directed nets. A conflict between transitions in a net system is caused by either the lack of tokens in a shared place, or by the limited capacity of a shared place; a conflict between operations on a variable is read-write conflict: simultaneous read-write on the same variable is impossible by nature regardless of the exact value of that variable. Besides, there is a rich variety of data types and operations for data types. Conditions for case classification cannot be formally expressed without variables and operations on variables. The example of insurance claim explains: $c_1 = x \wedge y$, $c_2 = (\neg x \wedge y) \vee (x \wedge \neg y)$, $c_3 = \neg x \wedge \neg y$ provide a third way of case classification.

When variables are introduced into a net as another kind of state elements, a net becomes a C-net. A simplified version of C-net is introduced next, just to serve the need of modeling case semantics.

Definition 20

$\Sigma = (S,V,T;F,K,W,R,Wr, M_T, M_0)$ is a C-net system if

S,V,T are the sets of places, variables and transitions respectively; F,R,Wr are respectively the flow relation, the read relation and the write relation; K,W are the capacity function and the arc weight function; M_T is a marking on T and M_0 is a marking (initial marking) on S.◆

A transition may read and/or write a variable, but not must. The marking on a transition has a Boolean expression as its guard and assignments as its body when it writes. The guard and the body must be consistent in relation to read and write. For example, the guard can only refer to variables that are to be read by the transition.

If a transition has nothing to do with variables, conventional transition rules apply. If a transition has nothing to do with places, it is enabled when its guard is true. If a transition is related with places as well as variables, it is enabled if it is enabled by places and its guard is true.

Isolated transitions are excluded in a C-net.

An enabled transition may fire to produce a successor marking on S, the marking on T remains like the weight function and the capacity function; variables in write relation with this transition are assigned values by the assignments.

A c-net transition in general has a figure called "status" as part of M_T. Transition firings may change "status". But this does not concern us.

To save space, detailed formal definitions are avoided. Figure 25 illustrates them, including graphical presentation of C-nets.

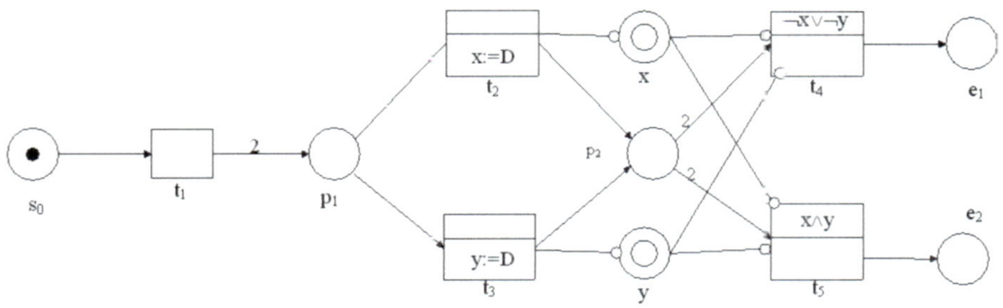

Figure 25. A C-net System: Case Semantics for Insurance Claim

The case semantics of insurance claim given in Figure 25 divides conceivable cases into 2 classes. Variables like x and y are drawn as double circles, write relation is represented by a zero-headed arc from transition to variable, reversed zero-headed arc represents read relation. For example, t_2 writes x and t_4 , t_5 read x.

The start transition t_1 is in no relation with x and y, it has no guard, no body. The guards of both t_2 and t_3 are "true", denoted by default. The write operations of these two transitions are to be performed by their executers, denoted as x:= D where D is the abbreviation of "default". Transitions t_4 and t_5 have conditions for case classification as their guards. They have empty body since they write no variables.

Apparently, the case semantic contains two routes: one for each class. As long as the classification of cases is complete and consistent (every case falls into exactly one class), there would be a unique route for each case.

7.2. Workflow logic and its case semantics

Let $(T,<\cdot)$, $B=\{b_1, b_2, \cdots b_m\}$ and $C=\{c_1, c_2, \cdots c_k\}$ be the main constituents of a business process. There is a precise correspondence between tasks in T and blanks (on B-form) in B; Condition set C is complete and consistent; the immediate successor relation $<\cdot$ is implied by a combinatorial acyclic partial order on T. With all these requirements satisfied, $((T,<\cdot), B, C)$ is a well-designed business process. We will not put all these into formal definitions since that would be cumbersome and uninteresting.

Definition 21

The C-net system $\Sigma'=(S,V,T;F,K,W,R,Wr,M_T,M_0)$ is a case semantics of the workflow logic $\Sigma=(S,T;F,K,W,M_0)$ developed for well-designed business process $((T,<\cdot), B, C)$, if the marking M_T (which is constant) satisfies that for those t in T that have a guard, the guard is a condition in C, and every condition in C is the guard of some transition.◆

Definition 22

Let C-net system $\Sigma'=(S,V,T;F,K,W,R,Wr,M_T,M_0)$ be a case semantics of the workflow logic $\Sigma=(S,T;F,K,W,M_0)$ developed for well-designed business process $((T,<\cdot), B, C)$. If Σ is through, and for every OR-split synchronizer $p=({}^{\cdot}p, p^{\cdot\cdot}(a, b))$, $b<|p^{\cdot}|$, for every condition ci in C, $i=1,2,\cdots k$, $|\{t|t\in p^{\cdot}\wedge guard(t)=c_i\}|=b$, then Σ' is consistent with Σ.◆

Theorem 8

If Σ is a through workflow logic and Σ' is a case semantics consistent with Σ, then there is a unique route for every conceivable case. ◆

For a case in class c_i, the route it will take is obtained by deleting from Σ all transitions whose guard is not c_i together with their successor elements.

Figure 26 shows another case semantics of the insurance claim business process where cases are divided into 3 classes by conditions $c_1 = x\wedge y$, $c_2 = (x\wedge\neg y)\vee(\neg x\wedge y)$ and $c_3 = \neg x\wedge\neg y$. The task set has one more end-task for this classification.

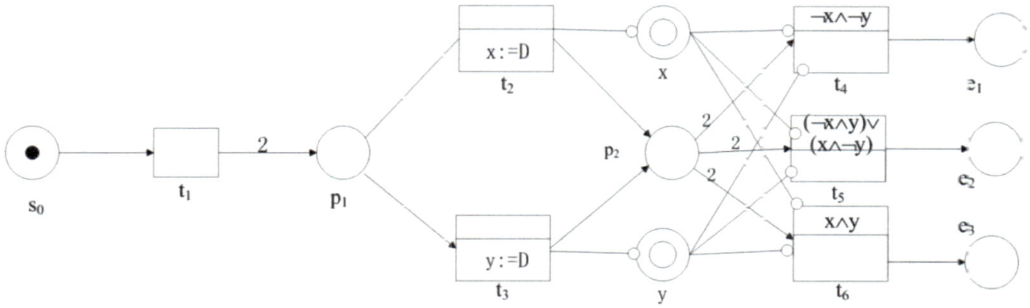

Figure 26. Another Case Semantics for Insurance Claim

The only OR-split synchronizer in Figure 26 is p_2. It has 3 tasks in its post-set and each of which bears a different condition as its guard. This is consistent with p_2: p_2 is a XOR-split synchronizer.

8. Business process management

So far we have proposed a formal model as workflow logic and a formal model as case semantics for a well-designed business process. Case semantics in embedded in a Workflow logic when they are consistent with each other. There is a unique route for every conceivable case as the semantics of that case. Thus, a firm foundation has been laid for management automation. The computer system that conducts the processing of each given case based its semantics is the workflow engine.

8.1. Management logic

As suggested by Figure 8 (b), every synchronizer p = (·p, p·, (a, b)) requires management (transition t in the detail of the synchronizer) to keep tasks in ·p well synchronized with transitions in p·. The start-place requires management, so do all end-places. At the start-place, the engine must recognize the proper business process when a case (B-form) arrives, and to have the corresponding workflow logic ready, and to appoint an executer for the start-task and passes the B-form to the executer. At an end-place, the engine must check whether the case is well processed and to put the completed B-form in place.

All in all, places and synchronizers are exactly where the engine does its duty. In other words, the dual of workflow logic is the management logic, and the dual of case semantics with given condition c_i in C produces the route for all cases classified by c_i.

Definition 22

1. The directed net N′ = (T,S;F) is the dual net of directed net N = (S,T;F).
2. Σ'= (T, S; F,K′,W′, $\mathbf{M}_0$) is the workflow management logic for workflow logic Σ= (S, T; F,K,W, M_0), where $K'(t) = \sum W(p,t)$ for every t in T, i.e. the capacity of t is the sum of all weights on its input arcs; W′(x, y) = W(x, y) for all (x, y) in F; $\mathbf{M}_0$(t) = 0 for t in T.
3. (Σ,Σ') is the logic pair for the business process in question.◆

Figure 27 is the logic pair for insurance claim with two case classes.

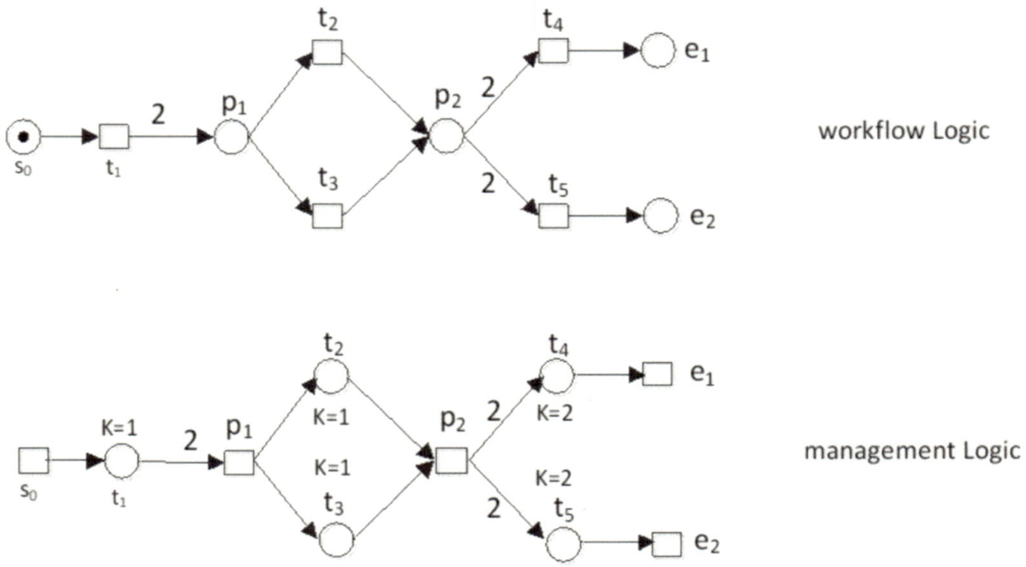

Figure 27. Logic Pair

Management tasks (transitions in Σ') and business tasks (transitions in Σ) are executed in turn: whenever a place (including synchronizers) in Σ has a full capacity of tokens, the transition with the same name in Σ' is enabled. The enabled transition fires to put tokens into its output places in Σ', whenever a place in Σ' has a full capacity of tokens, the transition with the same name in Σ is enabled. This interactive transition firings continue till a transition named with an end-place is fired to move the case token out of the pair. This is the way how management tasks and business tasks interact with each other.

8.2. Route for cases in the same class

A logic pair specifies, for a given business process, how individual cases are processed under the conduction of the engine (the manager). Figure 28 shows a case semantics and its dual, that is a semantic pair, a pair of C-net systems. The guard on a transition (task) will be used by the engine (transitions named after a synchronizer) for the selection of routes. We will not give a formal definition of this pair, since it is clearly specified by the figure. The interaction between this pair is the same with the logic pair, except details given by guards.

Figure 27 and Figure 28 serve as the main part of a formal specification for a workflow engine. The rest of the engine is enterprise specific (personal, organizational division etc.).

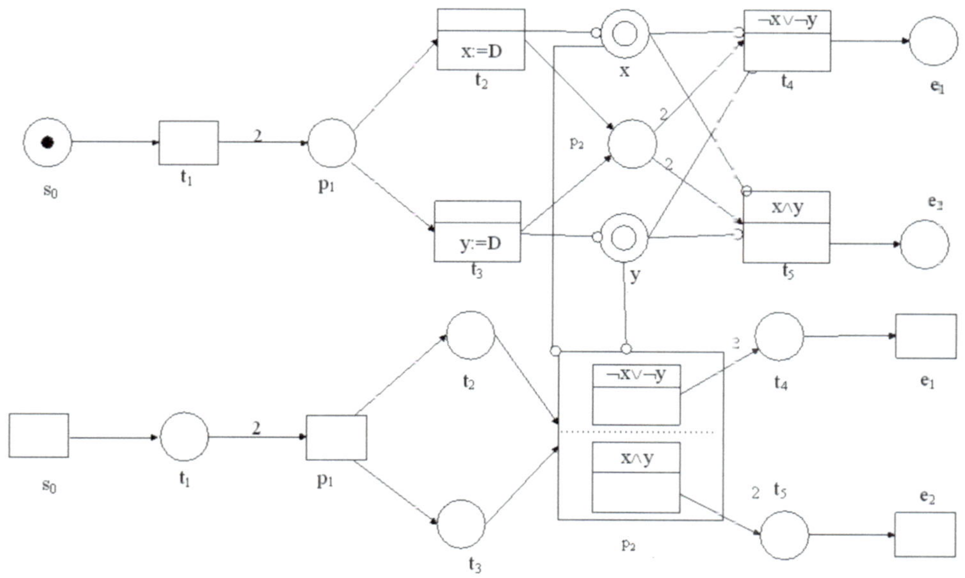

Figure 28. Semantic Pair

8.3. Duty of the engine

The main duty of the engine is to conduct the manipulation of individual cases based on the logic pair (before the class to which the case belongs is known) and the semantic pair (transitions named after an OR-split synchronizer), including appointing executers for selected tasks.

In addition to this major duty, other duties include (not exclusive):

- Set a time upper bound for each task to be executed next, and to remind before expiration, check whether it is done on time;
- Check whether a task is properly done (e.g. whether the content filled in a blank matches its type);
- Decide, based on given rules, what to do when an expiration or quality failure is detected (e.g. redo for quality failure, bad record on the due person for expiration);
- Other thinkable duties, especially enterprise specific ones.

An engine carries out its duty properly if and only if it has predefined management rules to follow. In addition to global rules specified by the logic pair and the semantic pair, local rules are also necessary, i.e. rules for every management task (every place in workflow logic). Remember that all places in workflow logic are where the engine can and must put a hand on.

Some management rules are closely related to individual enterprises, some are even secrete to outsiders. Current and historical business data, business partners data, conventions or traditions etc. All rules related to these must be carefully established and checked together with a well-designed business process, a well-structured workflow logic of the process, a case semantics consistent with the logic. The two pairs are derivable from the logic and semantics. We go no further here in this chapter.

9. Conclusions and acknowledgement

Prof. Carl Adam Petri wrote: "In order to apply net theory with success, a user of net theory can just rely on the fact that every net which he can specify explicitly (draw on paper) can be connected by a short (≤ 4) chain of net morphisms to the physical real world; your net is, in a very precise sense, physically implementable".

We have seen this quotation at the very beginning of this chapter. This chapter tries to make clear how to specify a net that is "in a very precise sense physically implementable". A successful application of net theory starts from a full understanding of the application problem. A well designed business process ((T,<·), B ,C) leads to the discovery of workflow logic, case semantics and management pairs, a tree-layer model for workflow modeling.

Without theory, full understanding of application problems becomes hard. Well-structured business process ((T,<·), B , C) starts from a clear distinction between business process and workflow, a clear distinction between business tasks and management tasks, and a clear distinction between transition synchronizations and place synchronizations. Business process and workflow are not synonym of each other.

A full understanding of application problems and a good grasp of theories in Petri nets that build a road to success.

The author is grateful to the editors of this book. It is a great honor to me as well as a good chance for me to exchange ideas on Petri nets with friends outside my country.

Author details

Chongyi Yuan
School of Electronics Engineering and Computer Science, Peking University, Beijing, China

10. References

[1] C.Y. Yuan: *Petri Nets* in Chinese, Southeast University Press,(1989).
[2] W. Brauer (editor): Net Theory and Applications, Springe LNCS Vol.84.
[3] C. A. Petri: Nonsequential Processes GMD-ISF Report 77, (1977).
[4] C.A. Petri: Concurrency incl. in 2 (in Theoretical Computer Science).
[5] C.Y. Yuan: Principles and applications of Petri Net. Beijing, China: Publishing house of electronics industry, 2005.
[6] W. Aalst, K. Hee: *Workflow Management*, The MIT Press (2000).
[7] C.Y. Yuan, W. Zhao, S.K. Zhang, Y. Huang: A Three Layer Model for Business Process —Process Logic, Case Semantics and Workflow Management, Journal of Computer Science & Technology, Vol.22 No.3, 410-425 (2007).
[8] C.Y. Yuan: *Petri Net Application*, to appear .

Chapter 7

Construction and Application of Learning Petri Net

Liangbing Feng, Masanao Obayashi,
Takashi Kuremoto and Kunikazu Kobayashi

Additional information is available at the end of the chapter

http://dx.doi.org/10.5772/48398

1. Introduction

Petri nets are excellent networks which have great characteristics of combining a well-defined mathematical theory with a graphical representation of the dynamic behavior of systems. The theoretical aspect of Petri nets allows precise modeling and analysis of system behavior, at the same time, the graphical representation of Petri nets enable visualization of state changes of the modeled system [32]. Therefore, Petri nets are recognized as one of the most adequate and sound tool for description and analysis of concurrent, asynchronous and distributed dynamical system. However, the traditional Petri nets do not have learning capability. Therefore, all the parameters which describe the characteristics of the system need to be set individually and empirically when the dynamic system is modeled. Fuzzy Petri net (FPN) combined Petri nets approach with fuzzy theory is a powerful modeling tool for fuzzy production rules-based knowledge systems. However, it is lack of learning mechanism. That is the significant weakness while modeling uncertain knowledge systems.

At the same time, intelligent computing is taken to achieve the development and application of artificial intelligence (AI) methods, i.e. tools that exhibit characteristics associated with intelligence in human behaviour. Reinforcement Learning (RL) and artificial neural networks have been widely used in pattern recognition, decision making, data clustering, and so on. Thus, if intelligent computing methods are introduced into Petri nets, this may make Petri nets have the learning capability, and also performance and the applicable areas of Petri nets models will be widely expanded. The dynamic system can be modeled by Petri nets with the learning capability and then the parameters of the system can be adjusted by online (data-driven) learning. At the same way, if the generalized FPNs are expanded by adding neural networks and their leaning capability, then FPNs are able to realize self-adapting and self-learning functions. Consequently, it achieves automatic knowledge reasoning and fuzzy production rules learning.

Recently, there are some researches for making the Petri net have learning capability and making it optimize itself. The global variables are used to record all state of colored Petri net when it is running [22]. The global variables are optimized and colored Petri net is updated according to these global variables. A learning Petri net model which combines Petri net with a neural network is proposed by Hirasawa et al., and it was applied to nonlinear system control [10]. In our former work [5, 6], a learning Petri net model has been proposed based on reinforcement learning (RL). RL is applied to optimize the parameters of Petri net. And, this learning Petri net model has been applied to robot system control. Konar gave an algorithm to adjust thresholds of a FPN through training instances [1]. In [1], the FPN architecture is built on the connectionism, just like a neural network, and the model provides semantic justification of its hidden layer. It is capable of approximate reasoning and learning from noisy training instances. A generalized FPN model was proposed by Pedrycz et al., which can be transformed into neural networks with OR/AND logic neuron, thus, parameters of the corresponding neural networks can be learned (trained) [24]. Victor and Shen have developed a reinforcement learning algorithm for the high-level fuzzy Petri net models [23].

This chapter focuses on combining the Petri net and fuzzy Petri net with intelligent learning method for construction of learning Petri net and learning fuzzy Petri net (LFPN), respectively. These are applied to dynamic system controls and a system optimization. The rest of this paper is organized as follow. Section 2 elaborates on the Learning Petri net construction and Learning algorithm. Section 3 describes how to use the Learning Petri net model in the robots systems. Section 4 constructs a LFPN. Section 5 shows the LFPN is used in Web service discovery problem. Section 6 summarizes the models of Petri net described in the chapter and results of their applications and demonstrates the future trends concerned with Learning Petri nets.

2. The learning Petri net model

The Learning Petri net (LPN) model is constructed based on high-level time Petri net (HLTPN). The definition of HLTPN is given firstly.

2.1. Definition of HLTPN

HLTPN is one of expanded Petri nets.

Definition 1: HLTPN has a 5-tuple structure, $HLTPN = (NG, C, W, DT, M_0)$ [9], where

i. $NG = (P, Tr, F)$ is called "net graph" with P which called "Places". P is a finite set of nodes. ID: $P \rightarrow N$ is a function marking P, $N = (1, 2, \ldots)$ is the set of natural number. $p_1, p_2, \ldots, p_n$ represents the elements of P and n is the cardinality of set P;

Tr is a finite set of nodes, called "Transitions", which disjoints from *P*, $P \cap Tr = \varnothing$; $ID: Tr \rightarrow N$ is a function marking *Tr*. $tr_1, tr_2, \ldots, tr_m$ represents the elements of *Tr*, *m* is the cardinality of set *Tr*;

$F \subseteq (P \times Tr) \cup (Tr \times P)$ is a finite set of directional arcs, known as the flow relation;

ii. *C* is a finite and non-empty color set for describing different type of data;
iii. $W: F \rightarrow C$ is a weight function on *F*. If $F \subseteq (P \times Tr)$, the weight function *W* is W_{in} that decides which colored Token can go through the arc and enable *T* fire. This color tokens will be consumed when transition is fired. If $F \subseteq (Tr \times P)$, the weight function *W* is W_{out} that decides which colored Token will be generated by *T* and be input to *P*.
iv. DT: $Tr \rightarrow R$ is a delay time function of a transition which has a *Time* delay for an enable transition fired or the fire of a transition lasting time.
v. M_0: $P \rightarrow \cup_{p \in P} \mu C(p)$ such that $\forall p \in P$, $M_0(p) \in \mu C(p)$ is the initial marking function which associates a multi-set of tokens of correct type with each place.

2.2. Definition of LPN

In HLTPN, the weight functions of input and output arc for a transition decide the input and output token of a transition. These weight functions express the input-output mapping of transitions. If these weight functions are able to be updated according to the change of system, modeling ability of Petri net will be expanded. The delay time of HLTPN expresses the pre-state lasting time. If the delay time is able to be learnt while system is running, representing ability of Petri net will be enhanced. RL is a learning method interacting with a complex, uncertain environment to achieve an optimal policy for the selection of actions of the learner. RL suits to update dynamic system parameters through interaction with environment [18]. Hence, we consider using the RL to update the weight function and transition's delay time of Petri net for constructing the LPN. In another word, LPN is an expanded HLTPN, in which some transition's input arc weight function and transition delay time have a value item which records the reward from the environment.

Definition 2: LPN has a 3-tuple structure, *LPN*= (*HLTPN*, *VW*, *VT*), where

i. *HLTPN*= (*NG*, *C*, *W*, *DT*, M_0) is a High-Level Time Petri Net and *NG*= (*P*, *Tr*, *F*).
ii. *VW* (value of weight function): $W_{in} \rightarrow R$, is a function marking on W_{in}. An arc $F \subseteq (P \times Tr)$ has a set of weight function W_{in} and each W_{in} has a reward value item *VW* ∈real number.
iii. VT (value of delay time): DT→R, is a function marking on DT. A transition has a set of DT and each *DT* has a reward value item *VT* ∈real number.

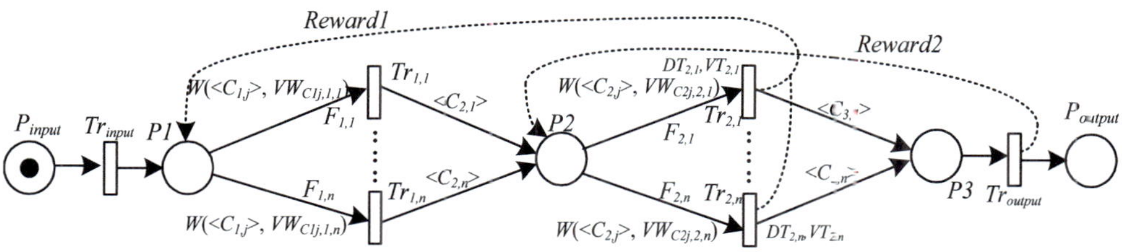

Figure 1. An example of LPN model

An example of LPN model is shown in Figure 1 Using LPN, a mapping of input-output tokens is gotten. For example, in Figure 1, colored tokens C_{ij} (i=1;j=1, 2, …, n) are input to P_1 by Tr_{input}. There are n weight functions $W(<C_{1j}>, VW_{C1j,1,j})$ on a same arc $F_{1,j}$. it is according to the value $VW_{Cij,i,j}$ that token C_{1j} obeys what weight functions in $W(<C_{ij}>, VW_{Cij,i,j})$ to fire a transition. After token C_{1j} passed through arc $F_{i,j}$ (i=1; j=1, 2, …, n), one of $Tr_{i,j}$ (i=1; j=1, 2, …, n) fires and generates Tokens C_{ij} (i=2; j=1, 2, …, n) in P_2. After P_2 has color Token C_{ij} (i=2; j=1, 2, …, n), $Tr_{i,j}$ (i=2; j=1, 2, …, n) fires and different colored Token C_{ij} (i=3; j=1, 2, …, n) is generated. Then, a mapping of C_{1j} – C_{3j} is gotten. At the same time, a reward will be gotten from environment according to whether it accords with system rule that C_{3j} generated by C_{1j}. These rewards are propagated to every $VW_{Cij,i,j}$ and adjust the $VW_{Cij,i,j}$. After training, the LPN is able to express a correct mapping of input-output tokens.

Using LPN to model a dynamic system, the system state is modeled as Petri net marking which is marked for a set of colored token in all places of Petri net, and the change of the system state (i.e. the system action) is modeled as fired of transitions. Some parameters of system can be expressed as token number and color, arc weight function, transition delay time, and so on. For example, different system signals are expressed as different colored of token. When the system is modeled, some parameters are unknown or uncertain. So, these parameters are set randomly. When system runs, the system parameters are gotten gradually and appropriately through system acting with environment and the effect of RL.

2.3. Learning algorithm for LPN

In LPN, there are two kinds of parameters. One is discrete parameter — the arc's weight function which describes the input and output colored tokens for transition. The other is continuous parameter — the delay time for the transition firing. Now, we will discuss two kinds of parameters which are learnt using RL.

2.3.1. Discrete parameter learning

In LPN, RL is used to adjust VW and VT through interacting with environment. RL could learn the optimal policy of the dynamic system through environment state observation and improvement of its behavior through trial and error with the environment. RL agent senses the environment and takes actions. It receives numeric award and punishments from some reward function. The agent learns to choose actions to maximize a long term sum or average of the future reward it will receive.

The arc weight function learning algorithm is based on Q-learning – a kind of RL [18]. In arc weight function learning algorithm, $VW_{Cij,i,j}$ is randomly set firstly. So, the weight function on the arc is arbitrary. When the system runs, formula (1) is used to update $VW_{Cij,i,j}$.

$$VW_{Cij,i,j} = VW_{Cij,i,jj} + \alpha[r + \gamma(\overline{VW_{ci+1j,i+1,j}}) - VW_{Cij,i,j}] \quad (1)$$

where,

i. $\acute{a}$ is the step-size,is a discount rate.

ii. r is reward which $W(<C_{ij}>, VW_{Cij,i,j})$ gets when $Tr_{i,j}$ is fired by $<C_{ij}>$. Here, because environment gives system reward at only last step, so a feedback learning method is used. If $W(<C_{ij}>, VW_{Cij,i,j})$ through $Tr_{i,j}$ generates Token $<C_{i+1,j}>$ and $W(<C_{i+1j}>, VW_{Ci+1j,i+1,j})$ through $Tr_{i+1,j}$ generates Token $<C_{i+2,j}>$, $VW_{Ci+1j,i+1,j}$ gets an update value, and this value is feedback as $W(<C_{ij}>, VW_{Cij,i,j})$ next time reward r.

iii. $\overline{(VW_{ci+1j,i+1,j})}$ is calculated from feedback value of all $W(<C_{i+1j}>, VW_{Ci+1j,i+1,j})$ as formula (2).

$$\overline{(VW_{ci+1j,i+1,j})}_t = \gamma \overline{(VW_{ci+1j,i+1,j})}_{t-1} + r_t \qquad (2)$$

where t is time for that $<C_{i+1j}>$ is generated by $W(<C_{ij}>, VW_{Cij,i,j})$.

When every weight function of input arc of the transition has gotten the value, each transition has a value of its action. The policy of the action selection needs to be considered. The simplest action selection rule is to select the service with the highest estimated state-action value, i.e. the transition corresponding to the maximum $VW_{Cij,i,j}$. This action is called a greedy action. If a greedy action is selected, the learner (agent) exploits the current knowledge. If selecting one of the non-greedy actions instead, agent intends to explore to improve its policy. Exploitation is to do the right thing to maximize the expected reward on the one play; meanwhile exploration may produce the greater total reward in the long run. Here, a method using near-greedy selection rule called ε-greedy method is used in action selection; i.e., the action is randomly selected at a small probability ε and selected the action which has the biggest $VW_{cij,i,j}$ at probability 1−ε. Now, we show the algorithm of LPN which is listed in Table 1.

Algorithm 1. Weight function learning algorithm

Step 1. Initialization: Set all VW_{ij} and r of all input arc's weight function to zero.

Step 2. Initialize the learning Petri net. i.e. make the Petri net state as M_0.

Repeat i) and ii) until system becomes end state.

i. When a place gets a colored Token C_{ij}, there is a choice that which arc weight function is obeyed if the functions include this Token. This choice is according to selection policy which is ε greedy (ε is set according to execution environment by user, usually 0<ε<<1).
A: Select the function which has the biggest $VW_{cij,i,j}$ at probability1-ε;
B: Select the function randomly at probability ε.

ii. The transition which the function correlates fires and reward is observed. Adjust the weight function value using $VW_{Cij,i,j} = VW_{Cij,i,jj} + \alpha[r + \gamma \overline{(VW_{ci+1j,i+1,j})} - VW_{Cij,i,j}$. At the same time. $\alpha[r + \gamma \overline{(VW_{ci+1j,i+1,j})} - VW_{Cij,i,j}]$ is fed back to the weight function with generated C_{ij} as its reward for next time.

Table 1. Weight function learning algorithm in LPN

2.3.2. Continuous parameter learning

The delay time of transition is a continuous variable. So, the delay time learning is a problem of RL in continuous action spaces. Now, there are several methods of RL in continuous spaces: discretization method, function approximation method, and so on [4]. Here, discretization method and function approximation method are used in the delay time learning in LPN.

Discretization method

As shown in Figure 2 (i), the transition tr_1 has a delay time t_1. When p_1 has a token *<token$_n$>*, the system is at a state that p_1 has a Token. This time transition tr_1 is enabled. Because tr_1 has a delay time t_1, tr_1 doesn't fire immediately. After passing time t_1 and tr_1 fires, the token in p_1 is taken out and this state is terminated. Then, during the delay time of tr_1, the state that p_1 has a token continues.

Because the delay time is a continuous variable, the different delay time is discretized for using RL to optimize the delay time. For example, tr_1 in Figure 2 (i) has an undefined delay time t_1. Tr_1 is discretized into several different transitions which have different delay times (shown in Figure 2 (ii)) and every delay time has a value item Q. After Tr_1 fired at delay time t_{1i}, it gets a reward r immediately or after its subsequence gets rewards. The value of Q is updated by formula (3).

$$Q(P,Tr) \leftarrow Q(P,Tr\,) + \alpha[r + \gamma Q(P',Tr'\,) - Q(P,Tr)] \tag{3}$$

where, $Q(P,\ Tr)$ is value of transition Tr at Petri net state P. $Q(P',Tr'\,)$ is value of transition T' at next state P' of P. α is a step-size, γ is a discount rate.

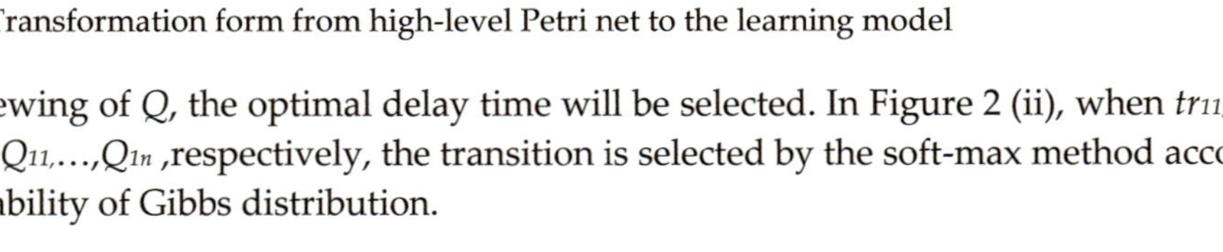

(i) The high-level time Petri net model (ii) The discretization learning model for the delay time

Figure 2. Transformation form from high-level Petri net to the learning model

After renewing of Q, the optimal delay time will be selected. In Figure 2 (ii), when $tr_{11},\ldots,tr_{1n}$ get value $Q_{11},\ldots,Q_{1n}$,respectively, the transition is selected by the soft-max method according to a probability of Gibbs distribution.

$$\Pr\{t_t = t \mid p_t = p\} = \frac{e^{\beta Q(p,t)}}{\sum_{b\in A} e^{\beta Q(p,b)}} \tag{4}$$

where, $\Pr\{t_t = t \mid p_t = p\}$ is a probability selecting of transition t at state p, $\hat{a}$ is a positive inverse temperature constant and A is a set of available transitions.

Now, we found the learning algorithm of delay time of LPN using the discretization method. And it is listed in Table 2.

Transition's delay time learning algorithm 1 (Discretization method):
Step 1. Initialization: discretize the delay time and set $Q(p,t)$ of every transition's delay time to zero.
Step 2. Initialize Petri net, i.e. make the Petri net state as P_1.
Repeat (i) and (ii) until system becomes end state.
i. Select a transition using formula (4).
ii. After transition fired and reward is observed, value of $Q(p,t)$ is adjusted using formula (3).
Step 3. Step 3. Repeat Step2 until t is optimal as required.

Table 2. Delay time learning algorithm using the discretization method

Function approximation method

First, the transition delay time is selected randomly and executed. The value of the delay time is obtained using formula (3). When the system is executed m times, the data $(t_i, Q_i(p,t_i))$ $(i = 1, 2, \ldots, m)$ is yielded. The relation of value of delay time Q and delay time t is supposed as $Q = F(t)$. Using the least squares method, $F(t)$ will be obtained as follows. It is supposed that F is a function class which is constituted by a polynomial. And it is supposed that formula (5) hold.

$$f(t) = \sum_{k=0}^{n} a_k t^k \in F \tag{5}$$

The data $(t_i, Q_i(p,t_i))$ are substituted in formula (5). Then:

$$f(t_i) = \sum_{k=0}^{n} a_k t_i^k \quad (i = 1, 2, \ldots, m\, ;\, m \geq n) \tag{6}$$

Here, the degree m of data $(t_i, Q_i(p,t_i))$ is not less than data number n of formula (5). According to the least squares method, we have (2.7).

$$\|\delta\|^2 = \sum_{i=1}^{m} \delta_i^2 = \sum_{i=1}^{m} [\sum_{k=0}^{n} a_k t_i^k - Q_i]^2 \Rightarrow \min \tag{7}$$

In fact, (7) is a problem which evaluates the minimum solution of function (8).

$$\|\delta\|^2 = \sum_{i=1}^{m} [\sum_{k=0}^{n} a_k t_i^k - Q_i]^2 \tag{8}$$

So, function (9), (10) are gotten from (8).

$$\frac{\partial \|\delta\|^2}{\partial a_j} = 2\sum_{i=1}^{m} \sum_{k=0}^{n} (a_k t_i^k - Q_i) t_i^j = 0 \quad (j = 0, 1, \ldots, n) \tag{9}$$

$$\sum_{i=1}^{m}(\sum_{k=0}^{n} t_i^{j+k})a_k = \sum_{i=1}^{m} t_i^j Q_i \quad (j = 0, 1, \ldots, n). \tag{10}$$

Solution of Equation (10) $a_0, a_1, \ldots, a_n$ can be deduced and $Q = f(t)$ is attained. The solution t^*_{opt} of $Q = f(t)$ which makes maximum Q is the expected optimal delay time.

$$\frac{\partial f(t)}{\partial t} = 0 \tag{11}$$

The multi-solution of (11) $t = t_{opt}$ (opt = 1, 2, …, n-1) is checked by function (5) and a $t^*_{opt} \in t_{opt}$ which makes $f(t^*_{opt})= \max f(t_{opt})$ (opt = 1, 2, …, n-1) is the expected optimal delay time. t^*_{opt} is used as delay time and the system is executed and new $Q(p, t^*_{opt})$ is gotten. This (t^*_{opt}, $Q(p, t^*_{opt})$) is used as the new and the least squares method can be used again to acquire more precise delay time.

After the values of actions are gotten, the soft-max method is selected as the actions selection policy. And then, we found the learning algorithm of delay time of Learning Petri net using the function approximation method. And it is listed in Table 3.

Transition's delay time learning algorithm 2 (Function approximation method):

Step 1. Step 1. Initialization: Set $Q(p, t)$ of every transition's delay time to zero.
Step 2. Step 2. Initialize Petri net, i.e. make the Petri net state as P_1.

Repeat (i) and (ii) until system becomes end state.

i. Randomly select the transition delay time t.
ii. After transition fires and reward is observed, the value of $Q(p, t)$ is adjusted using formula (3).

Step 3. Step 3. Repeat Step 2 until adequacy data are gotten. Then, evaluate the optimal t using the function approximation method.

Table 3. Delay time learning algorithm using the function approximation method

3. Applying LPN to robotic system control

3.1. Application for discrete event dynamic robotic system control

A discrete event dynamic system is a discrete-state, event-driven system in which the state evolution depends entirely on the occurrence of asynchronous discrete events over time [2]. Petri nets have been used to model various kinds of dynamic event-driven systems like computers networks, communication systems, and so on. In this Section, it is used to model Sony AIBO learning control system for the purpose of certification of the effectiveness of the proposed LPN.

AIBO voice command recognition system

AIBO (Artificial Intelligence roBOt) is a type of robotic pets designed and manufactured by Sony Co., Inc. AIBO is able to execute different actions, such as go ahead, move back, sit down, stand up and cry, and so on. And it can "listens" voice via microphone. A command

and control system will be constructed for making AIBO understand several human voice commands by Japanese and English and take corresponding action. The simulation system is developed on Sony AIBO's OPEN-R (Open Architecture for Entertainment Robot) [19]. The architecture of the simulation system is showed in Figure 3. Because there are English and Japanese voice commands for same AIBO action, the partnerships of voice and action are established in part (4). The lasted time of an AIBO action is learning in part (5). After an AIBO action finished, the rewards for correctness of action and action lasted time are given by the touch of different AIBO's sensors.

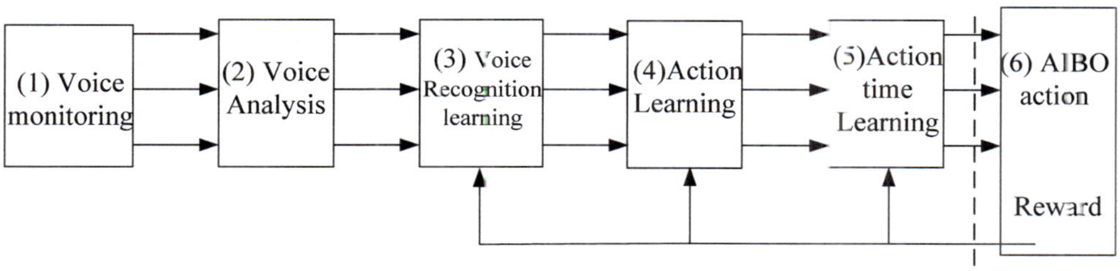

Figure 3. System architecture of voice command recognition

LPN model for AIBO voice command recognition system

In the LPN model for AIBO voice command recognition system, AIBO action change, action time are modeled as transition, transition delay, respectively. The human voice command is modeled by the different color Token. The LPN model is showed in Figure 4. The meaning of every transition is listed below: Tr_{input} changes voice signal as colored Token which describe the voice characteristic. Tr_{11}, Tr_{12} and Tr_{13} can analyze the voice signal. Tr_1 generates 35 different Token $VL_1 .... VL_{35}$ according to the voice length. Tr_2 generates 8 different Token $E2_1 ... E2_8$ according to the front twenty voice sample energy characteristic. Tr_3 generates 8 different Token $E4_1 ... E4_8$ according to the front forty voice sample energy characteristic [8]. These three types of the token are compounded into a compound Token $<VL_l> + <VE2_m> - <VE4_n>$ in p_2 [12].

Tr_{2j} generates the different voice Token. The input arc's weight function is $((<VL_l>+<VE2_m>-<VE4_n>), VW_{Vlmn,2j})$ and the output arc's weight function is different voice Token. And voice Token will generate different action Token through Tr_{3j}. When $Pr_4 - Pr_8$ has Token, AIBO's action will last. Tr_{4j} takes Token out from $p_4 - p_8$, and makes corresponding AIBO action terminates. Tr_{4j} has a delay time DT_{4i}, and every DT_{4i} has a value VT_{4i}. Transition adopts which delay time DT_{4i} according to VT_{4i}.

Results of simulation

When the system begins running, it can't recognize the voice commands. A voice command comes and it is changed into a compound Token in p_2. This compound Token will randomly generate a voice Token and puts into p_3. This voice Token randomly arouses an action Token. A reward for action correctness is gotten, then, VW and VT are updated. For example, a compound colored Token $(<VL_l>+ <VE2_m> + <VE4_n>)$ fired Tr_{21} and colored Token

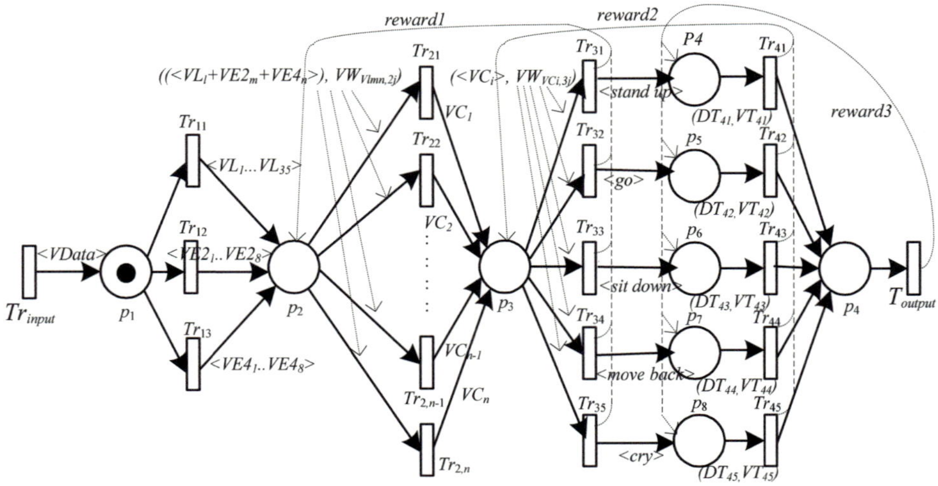

Figure 4. LPN model of voice command recognition

VC_1 is put into p_3. VC_1 fires T_{32} and AIBO acts "go". A reward is gotten according to correctness of action. $VW_{VC1,32}$ is updated by this reward and $VW_{VC1,32}$ updated value is fed back to p_2 as next time reward value of $(<VL_l>+ <VE_{2m}> + <VE_{4n}>)$ fired Tr_{21}. After an action finished, a reward for correctness of action time is gotten and VT is updated.

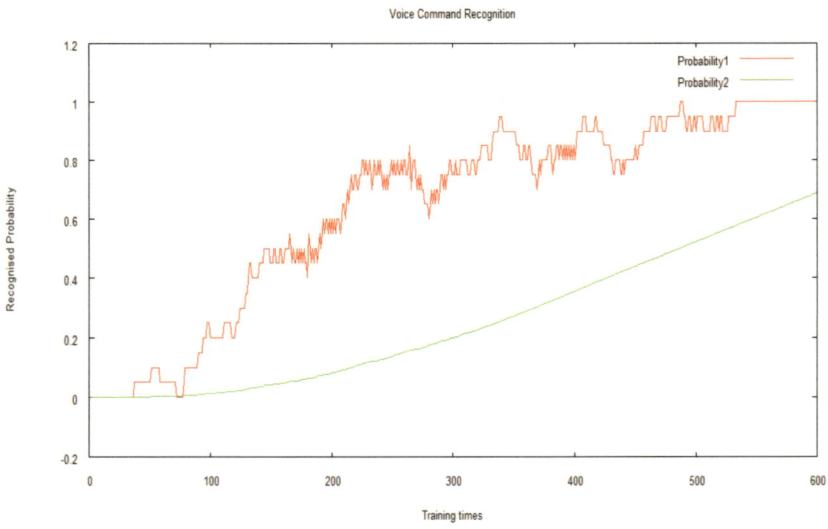

Figure 5. Relation between training times and recognition probability

Figure 5 shows the relation between training times and voice command recognition probability. Probability 1 shows the successful probability of recently 20 times training. Probability 2 shows the successful probability of total training times. From the result of simulation, we confirmed that LPN is correct and effective using the AIBO voice command control system.

3.2. Application for continuous parameter optimization

The proposed system is applied to guide dog robot system which uses RFID (Radio-frequency identification) to construct experiment environment. The RFID is used as navigation equipment for robot motion. The performance of the proposed system is evaluated through computer simulation and real robot experiment.

RFID environment construction

RFID tags are used to construct a blind road which showed in Figure 6. There are forthright roads, corners and traffic light signal areas. The forthright roads have two group tags which have two lines RFID tags. Every tag is stored with the information about the road. The guide dog robot moves, turns or stops on the road according to the information of tags. For example, if the guide dog robot reads corner RFID tag, then it will turn on the corner. If the guide dog robot reads either outer or inner side RFID tags, it implies that the robot will deviate from the path and robot motion direction needs adjusting. If the guide dog robot reads traffic control RFID tags, then it will stop or run unceasingly according to the traffic light signal which is dynamically written to RFID.

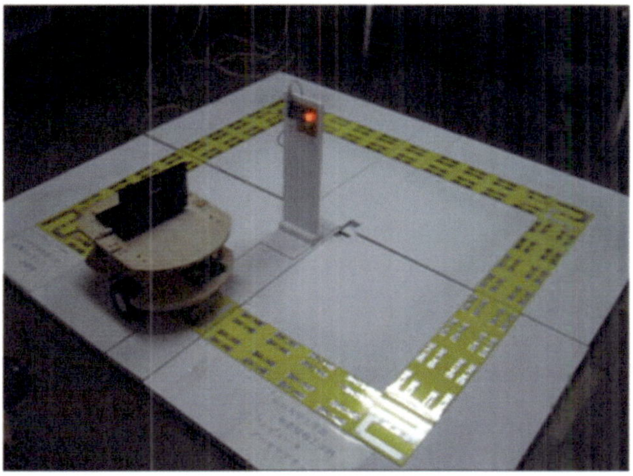

Figure 6. The real experimental environment

LPN model for the guide dog

The extended LPN control model for guide dog robot system is presented in Figure 7. The meaning of place and transition in Figure 7 is listed below:

P1	System starting state	P2	Getting RFID information
P3	Turning corner state	P4	Left adjusting state
P5	Right adjusting state	Tr1	Reading of the RFID environment
Tr2	Stop of the guide dog	Tr3	Guide dog runs
Tr4	Start of the turning corner state	Tr5	Start of left adjusting state
Tr6	Start of the right adjusting state	Tr7	Stop of the turning corner state
Tr8	Stop of the left adjusting state	Tr9	Stop of the right adjusting state

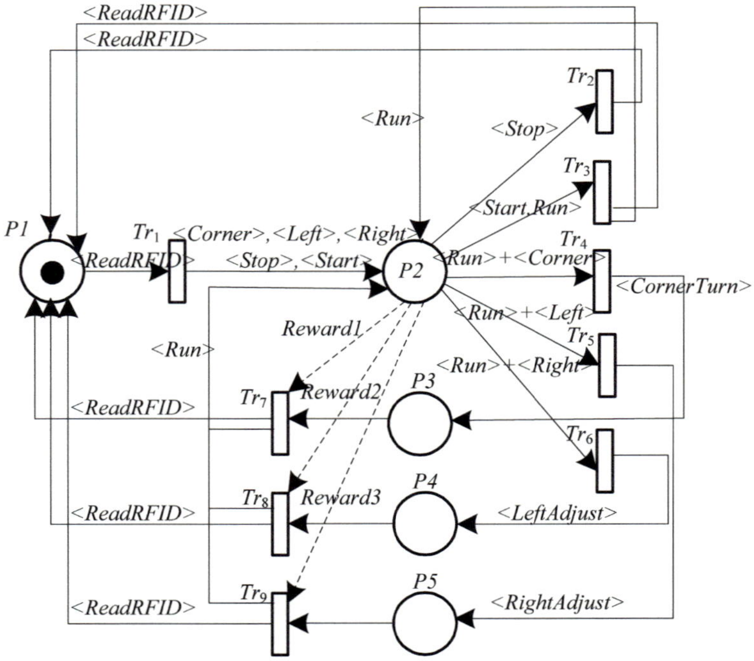

Figure 7. The LPN model for the guide dog robot

When the system begins running, it firstly reads RFID environment and gets the information, Token puts into P_2. These Tokens fire one of transition from Tr_2 to Tr_6 according to weight function on P_2 to Tr_2, ..., Tr_6. Then, the guide dog enters stop, running, turning corner, left adjusting or right adjusting states. Here, at P_3, P_4, P_5 states, the guide dog turns at a specific speed. The delay time of Tr_7-Tr_9 decide the correction of guide dog adjusting its motion direction.

Reward getting from environment

When Tr_7, Tr_8 or Tr_9 fires, it will get reward r as formula (12-b) when the guide dog doesn't get Token <Left> and <Right> until getting Token <corner> i.e. the robot runs according correct direction until arriving corner. It will get reward r as formula (12-a), where t is time from transition fire to get Token <Left> and <Right>. On the contrary, it will get punishment -1 as (12-c) if robot runs out the road.

$$r = \begin{cases} 1/e^t & \text{(a)} \\ 1 \quad . & \text{(b)} \\ -1 & \text{(c)} \end{cases} \tag{12}$$

Computer simulation and real robot experiment

When robot reads the <Left>, <Right> and <corner> information, it must adjust the direction of the motion. The amount of adjusting is decided by the continuing time of the robot at the state of P_3, P_4 and P_5. So, the delay time of Tr_7, Tr_8 and Tr_9 need to learn.

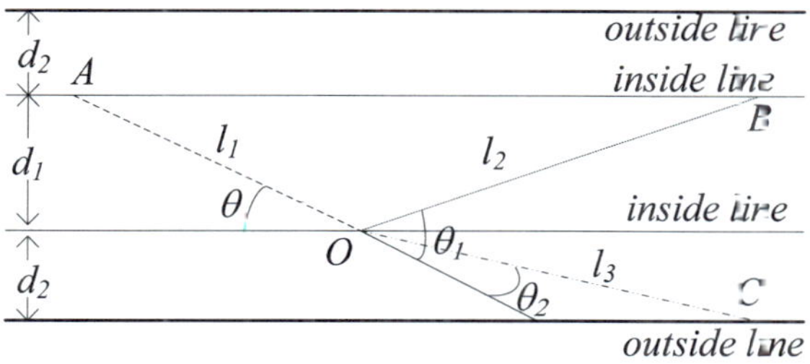

(i) Direction adjustment of the robot motion on the forthright road

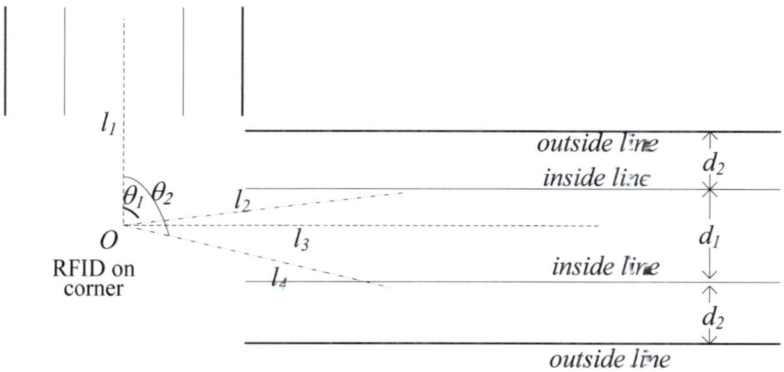

(ii) Direction adjustment of the robot motion at the corner

Figure 8. Direction adjustment of the guide dog robot motion

Before the simulation, some robot motion parameter symbols are given as:

v velocity of the robot
ω angular velocity of the robot
t_{pre} continuous time of the former state
t adjusting time
t_{post} last time of the state after adjusting

v, ω, t_{pre}, t_{post} can be measured by system when the robot is running. The delay time of Tr_7, Tr_8 and Tr_9, i.e. the robot motion adjusting time, is simulated in two cases.

1. As shown in Figure 8 (i), when the robot is running on the forthright road and meets inside RFID line, its deviation angle θ is:

$$\theta = \arcsin(d_1/l_1) = \arcsin(d_1/(t_{pre} \bullet v)). \tag{13}$$

where d_1 and l_1 are width of area between two inside lines and moving distance between two times reading of the RFID, respectively (See Figure 8).

Robot's adjusting time (transition delay time) is t.

If $\omega t - \theta \geq 0$, then

$$t_{post} = \frac{d_1}{v\sin(\omega t - \theta)}, \tag{14}$$

else

$$t_{post} = \frac{d_2}{v\sin(\omega t - \theta)}. \tag{15}$$

Here, t_{post} is used to calculate reward r using formula (12). In the same way, the reward r can be calculated when the robot meets outside RFID line.

When the robot is running on the forthright road and meets the outside RFID line, the deviation angle θ is

$$\theta = \arcsin(d_2/(v \bullet t_{pre})), \tag{16}$$

Robot's adjusting time (transition delay time) is t.

If $\omega t - \theta \geq 0$, then

$$t_{post} = \frac{d_2}{v\sin(\omega t - \theta)}, \tag{17}$$

else the robot will runs out the road. And the reward r is calculated using formula (12).

2. As shown in Figure 8 (ii), when the robot is running at the corner, it must adjust θ=90°. If θ≠90°, the robot will read <Left>, <Right> after it turns corner. Now, the case which the robot will read inner line <Left>, <Right> will be considered. If robot's adjusting time is t. If $\omega t - \theta \geq 0$, then

$$t_{post} = \frac{d_1}{2v\sin(\omega t - \theta)}, \tag{18}$$

else

$$t_{post} = \frac{d_2}{2v\sin(\omega t - \theta)} \tag{19}$$

Same to case (1), t_{post} is used to calculate reward r using formula (12). In the same way, the reward r can calculate when the robot meets outside RFID line. The calculation of reward, which is calculated from t, for other cases of direction adjustment of the robot is considered as the above two cases.

In this simulation, the value of the delay time has only a maximum at optimal delay time point. The graph of relation for the delay time and its value is parabola. So, when transition's delay time learning by function approximation method which states in section 2.2.3, the relation of the delay time and its value is assumed as:

$$Q = a_2 t^2 + a_1 t + a_0 \,. \tag{20}$$

Computer simulations of Transition's delay time learning algorithms were executed in the all cases of the robot direction adjusting. In the simulation of algorithm of discretization, the positive inverse temperature constant β is set as 10.0. After the delay time of different cases was learnt, it is recorded in a delay time table. Then, the real robot experiment was carried out using the delay time table which was obtained by simulation process.

Result of simulation and experiment

The simulation result of transition's delay time learning algorithm in two cases is shown in Figure 9.

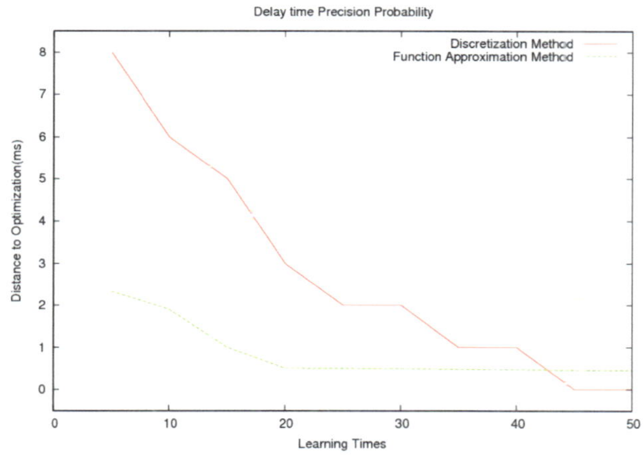

(i) Simulation result of moving adjustment on the forthright road

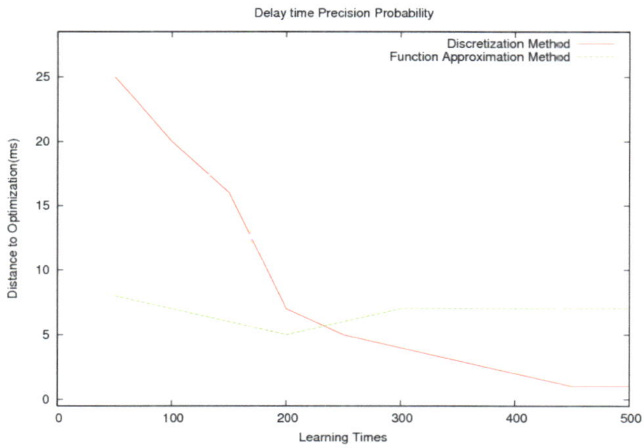

(ii) Simulation result of moving adjustment at the corner

Figure 9. Result of simulation for the guide dog robot

The simulation result of θ=5° for the robot moving adjustment on forthright road is shown in Figure 9 (i). The simulation result of robot moving adjustment at the corner is shown in Figure 9 (ii). From the result, it is found that the function approximation method can quickly approach optimal delay time than the discretization method, but the discretization method can approach more near optimal delay time through long time learning.

4. Construction of the learning fuzzy Petri net model

Petri net (PN) has ability to represent and analyze concurrency and synchronization phenomena in an easy way. PN approach can also be easily combined with other techniques and theories such as object-oriented programming, fuzzy theory, neural networks, etc. These modified PNs are widely used in the fields of manufacturing, robotics, knowledge based systems, process control, as well as other kinds of engineering applications [15]. Fuzzy Petri net (FPN), which combines PN and fuzzy theory, has been used for knowledge representation and reasoning in the presence of inexact data and knowledge based systems. But traditional FPN lacks of learning mechanism, it is the main weakness while modeling uncertain knowledge systems [25]. In this section, we propose a new learning model tool — learning fuzzy Petri net (LFPN) [7]. Contrasting with the existing FPN, there are three extensions in the new model: 1) the place can possess different tokens which represent different propositions; 2) these propositions have different degrees of truth toward different transitions; 3) the truth degree of proposition can be learned through the arc's weight function adjusting. The LFPN model obtains the capability of fuzzy production rules learning through truth degree updating. The artificial neural network is gotten learning ability through weight adjusting. The LFPN learning algorithm which introduces network learning method into Petri net update is proposed and the convergence of algorithm is analyzed.

4.1. The learning fuzzy Petri net model

Petri net is a directed, weighted, bipartite graph consisting of two kinds of nodes, called places and transitions, where arcs are either from a place to a transition or from a transition to a place. Tokens exist at different places. The use of the standard Petri net is inappropriate in situations where systems are difficult to be described precisely. Consequently, fuzzy Petri net is designed to deal with these situations where transitions, places, tokens or arcs are fuzzified.

The definition of fuzzy Petri net

A fuzzy place associates with a predicate or property. A token in the fuzzy place is characterized by a predicate or property belongs to the place, and this predicate or property has a level of belonging to the place. In this way, we may get a fuzzy proposition or conclusion, for example, *speed is low.* A fuzzy transition may correspond to an *if-then* fuzzy production rule for instance and is realized by truth values such as fuzzy inference algorithms [11, 20, 26].

Definition1 *FPN* is a 8-tuple, given by $FPN=<P, Tr, F, D, I, O, \alpha, \beta>$

where:

$P = \{p_1, p_2, \dots, p_n\}$ is a finite set of places;
$Tr = \{tr_1, tr_2, \dots, tr_m\}$ is a finite set of transitions;
$F \subseteq (P\times Tr)\cup(Tr\times P)$ is a finite set of directional arcs;
$D = \{d_1, d_2, \dots, d_n\}$ is a finite set of propositions, where proposition d_i corresponds to place p_i;
$P \cap Tr \cap D = \emptyset$; cardinality of (P) = cardinality of (D);
$I: tr \rightarrow P^{\infty}$ is the input function, representing a mapping from transitions to bags of (their input) places, noting as $*tr$;
$O: tr \rightarrow P^{\infty}$ is the output function, representing a mapping from transitions to bags of (their output) places, noting as $tr*$;
$\alpha: P \rightarrow [0, 1]$ and $\beta: P \rightarrow D$. A token value in place $p_i \in P$ is denoted by $\alpha(p_i) \in [0, 1]$. If $\alpha(p_i)=y_i$, $y_i \in [0, 1]$ and $\beta(p_i)= d_i$, then this states that the degree of truth of proposition d_i is y_i.

A transition tr_k is enabled if for all $p_i \in I(tr_k)$, $\alpha(p_i) \geq th$, where th is a threshold value in the unit interval. If this transition is fired, then tokens are moved from their input place and tokens are deposited to each of its output places. The truth values of the output tokens are $y_i \bullet u_k$, where u_k is the confidence level value of tr_k. FPN has capability of modeling fuzzy production rules. For example, the fuzzy production rule (21) can be modeled as shown in Figure 10.

$$\text{IF } d_i \text{ THEN } d_j \text{ (with Certainty Factor (CF) } u_k) \tag{21}$$

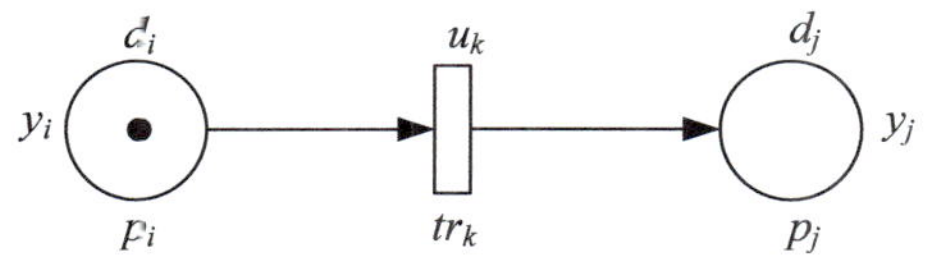

Figure 10. A fuzzy Petri net model (FPN)

The definition of LFPN

In a FPN, a token in a place represents a proposition and a proposition has a degree of truth. Now, three aspects of extension are done at the FPN and learning fuzzy Petri net (LFPN) is constructed. First, a place may have different tokens (Tokens are distinguished with numbers or colors) and the different tokens represent different propositions, i.e. a place has a set of propositions. Second, a place has a special token, i.e. there is a specified proposition. This proposition may have different degrees of truth toward different transitions tr which regard this place as input place $*tr$. Third, the weight of each arc is adjustable and used to record transition's input and output information.

Definition 3 *LFPN* is a 10-tuple, given by $LFPN= <P, Tr, F, D, I, C, Th, W, \alpha, \beta>$ (A LFPN model is shown in Figure 11).

where: Tr, F, I, O are same with definition of FPN.

$P=\{p_1, p_2, \ldots, p_i, \ldots, p_n, \ldots, p'_1, p'_2, \ldots, p'_i, \ldots, p'_r\}$ is a finite set of places, where p_i is input place and p'_i is output places.

$D = \{d_{11}, \ldots, d_{1N}; d_{21}, \ldots, d_{2N}; \ldots, d_{ij}, \ldots; d_{n1}, \ldots, d_{nN}; d'_{11}, \ldots, d'_{1N}; d'_{21}, \ldots, d'_{2N}; \ldots, d'_{ij}, \ldots; d'_{r1}, \ldots, d'_{rN}\}$ is a finite set of propositions, where proposition d_{ij} is j-th proposition for input place p_i and proposition d'_{ij} is j-th proposition for output place p'_i.

$W=\{w_{11}, w_{12}, \ldots, w_{1k}, \ldots, w_{1m}; \ldots; w_{i1}, w_{i2}, \ldots, w_{ik}, \ldots, w_{im}; \ldots; w_{n1}, w_{n2}, \ldots, w_{nm}; w'_{11}, w'_{12}, \ldots, w'_{1r}; \ldots; w'_{k1}, w'_{k2}, \ldots, w'_{kj}, \ldots, w'_{kr}; \ldots; w'_{m1}, w'_{m2}, \ldots, w'_{mr}\}$ is the set of weights on the arcs, where w_{ik} is a weight from i-th input place to k-th transition and w'_{kj} is a weight from k-th transition to j-th output place.

$W=\{w_{11}, w_{12}, \ldots, w_{1k}, \ldots, w_{1m}; \ldots; w_{i1}, w_{i2}, \ldots, w_{ik}, \ldots, w_{im}; \ldots; w_{n1}, w_{n2}, \ldots, w_{nm}; w'_{11}, w'_{12}, \ldots, w'_{1r}; \ldots; w'_{k1}, w'_{k2}, \ldots, w'_{kj}, \ldots, w'_{kr}; \ldots; w'_{m1}, w'_{m2}, \ldots, w'_{mr}\}$ is the set of weights on the arcs, where w_{ik} is a weight from i-th input place to k-th transition and w'_{kj} is a weight from k-th transition to j-th output place.

$\alpha(d_{ij}, tr_k) \rightarrow [0, 1]$ and $\beta: P \rightarrow D$. When $p_i \in P$ has a special $token_{ij}$ and $\beta(token_{ij}, p_i)=d_{ij}$, the degree of truth of proposition d_{ij} in place p_i toward to transition tr_k is denoted by $\alpha(d_{ij}, tr_k) \in [0, 1]$. When tr_k fires, the probability of proposition d_{ij} in p_i is $\alpha(d_{ij}, tr_k)$.

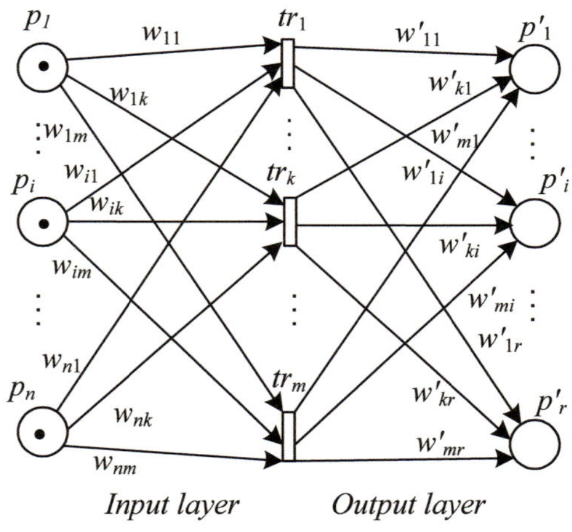

Figure 11. The model of learning fuzzy Petri net (LFPN)

$\alpha(d_{ij}, tr_k) \rightarrow [0, 1]$ and $\beta: P \rightarrow D$. When $p_i \in P$ has a special $token_{ij}$ and $\beta(token_{ij}, p_i)=d_{ij}$, the degree of truth of proposition d_{ij} in place p_i toward to transition tr_k is denoted by $\alpha(d_{ij}, tr_k) \in [0, 1]$. When tr_k fires, the probability of proposition d_{ij} in p_i is $\alpha(d_{ij}, tr_k)$.

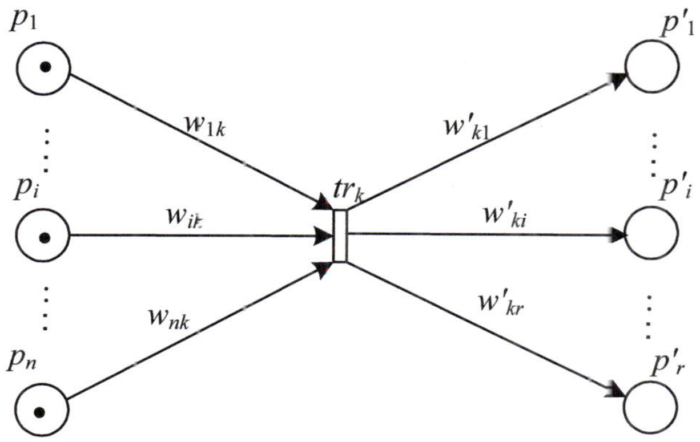

Figure 12. A LFPN model with one transition

$Th = \{th_1, th_2, \ldots, th_k, \ldots, th_m\}$ represents a set of threshold values in the interval [0, 1] associated with transitions (tr_1, tr_2, ..., tr_k, ..., tr_m), respectively; If all $p_i \in I(tr_k)$ and $\alpha(d_{ij}, tr_k) \geq th_k$, tr_k is enable.

As showed in Figure 12, when p_i has a $token_{ij}$, there is proposition d_{ij} in p_i. This proposition d_{ij} has different truth to tr_1, tr_2, ..., tr_k, ..., tr_m. When a transition tr_k fired, tokens are put into p'_1, ..., p'_r according to weight w'_{k1}, ..., w'_{kr} and each of p'_1, ..., p'_r gets a proposition.

Figure 11 shows a LFPN which has n-input places, m-transitions and r-output places. To explain the truth computing, transition fire rule, token transfer rule and fuzzy production rules expression more clearly, a transition and its relation arcs, places are drawn-out from Figure 11 and shown in Figure 12.

Truth computing As shown in Figure 12, w_{ik} is the perfect value for $token_{ij}$ when tr_k fires. When a set of $tokens = (token_{1j}, token_{2j}, \ldots, token_{ij}, \ldots, token_{nj})$ are input to all places of $^*tr_k$, $\beta(token_{1j}, p_1) = d_{1j}$, ..., $\beta(token_{nj}, p_n) = d_{nj}$. $\alpha(d_{ij}, tr_k)$ is computed using the degree of similarity between $token_{ij}$ and w_{ik} and calculation formula is shown in formula (22).

$$\alpha(d_{ij}, tr_k) = 1 - \frac{|w_{ik} - token_{ij}|}{\max(|w_{ik}|, |token_{ij}|)} \tag{22}$$

According to LFPN models for different systems, the token and weight value may have different data types. There are different methods for computing $\alpha(d_{ij}, tr_k)$ according to data type. If value types of token and weight are real number, $\alpha(d_{ij}, tr_k)$ is computed as formula (2). In Section 4, $\alpha(d_{ij}, tr_k)$ will be discussed for a LFPN model which has the textual type token and weight.

Transition fire rule As shown in Figure 12, when a set of $tokens = \{token_{1j}, token_{2j}, \ldots, token_{nj}\}$ are input to all places of $^*tr_k$, and $\beta(token_{1j}, p_1) = d_{1j}$, ..., $\beta(token_{nj}, p_n) = d_{nj}$. If all $\alpha(d_{ij}, tr_k)$ (i=1, 2, ..., n) $\geq th_k$ is held, tr_k is enabled. Maybe, several transitions are enabled at same time. If formula (23) is held, tr_k is fired.

$$\begin{aligned}&\alpha(d_{1j},tr_k)\cdot\alpha(d_{2j},tr_k)\cdot\ldots\cdot\alpha(d_{nj},tr_k)\\&=\max(\alpha(d_{1j},tr_h)\cdot\alpha(d_{2j},tr_h)\cdot\ldots\cdot\alpha(d_{nj},tr_h)_{1\le h\le m})\end{aligned} \tag{23}$$

Token transfer rule As shown in Figure 12, after tr_k fired, token will be taken out from p_1~p_n. The token take rule is:

If $token_{ij} \le w_{ik}$ is held, $token_{ij}$ in p_i will be taken out.
If $token_{ij} \ge w_{ik}$ is held, *token* which equates $token_{ij}-w_{ik}$ will be left in p_i.

Thus, after a transition tr_k fired, maybe the enable transitions still exist in LFPN. An enable transition will be selected and fired according to formula (23) until there isn't any enable transition.

After tr_k fired, the token according w'_{ki} will be put into p'_i. For example, if the weight function of arc tr_k to p'_i is w'_{ki}, then *token* which equates w'_{ki} will be put into p'_i.

Fuzzy production rules expression A LFPN is capable of modeling for fuzzy production rules just as a FPN. For example, as a case which states in **Transition fire rule** and **Token transfer rule**, when tr_k is fired, the below production rule is expressed:

IF d_{1j} AND d_{2j} AND … AND d_{nj} THEN d'_{1k} AND d'_{2k} AND … AND d'_{rk}

$$(CF=\alpha\ (d_{1i},\ tr_k\ )\bullet\alpha(d_{2i},\ tr_k\ )\bullet\ldots\bullet\alpha(d_{ni},\ tr_k\ )) \tag{24}$$

The mathematical model of LFPN

In this section, the mathematical model of LFPN will be elaborated. Firstly, some conceptions are defined. When a $token_{ij}$ is input to a place p_i, it is defined event p_{ij} occurs, i.e. the proposition d_{ij} is generated and probability of event p_{ij} is $Pr(p_{ij})$. The fired tr_k is defined as event tr_k and probability of event tr_k occurrence is $Pr(tr_k)$. Secondly, we assume that each transition tr_1, tr_2, …, tr_k, …, tr_m has the same fire probability in whole event space, then

$$Pr(tr_k)=\frac{1}{m} \tag{25}$$

And when event tr_k occurs, the conditional probability of p_{ij} occurrence is defined as $Pr(p_{ij} \mid tr_k)$, i.e. $á(d_{ij},\ tr_k\ )$ which is the probability of proposition d_{ij} generation when tr_k fires.

When p_1, p_2 , …, p_n have $token_{1j}$, $token_{2j}$…$token_{nj}$ and events p_{1j} , p_{2j} , …, p_{nj} occur. Then, $Pr(tr_k \mid p_{1j}, p_{2j}, \ldots, p_{nj})$ is:

$$Pr(tr_k \mid p_{1j},p_{2j},\ldots,p_{nj})=\frac{Pr(p_{1j},p_{2j},\ldots,p_{nj}\mid tr_k)Pr(tr_k)}{\sum_{h=1}^{m}Pr(tr_h)Pr(p_{1j}p_{2j},\ldots,p_{nj})} \tag{26}$$

When events p_{1j}, p_{2j}, …, p_{nj} occurred, there is one of transitions tr_1, tr_2, …, tr_k, …, tr_m which will be fired, therefore

$$\sum_{h=1}^{m} Pr(tr_h)Pr(p_{1j},p_{2j},...,p_{nj}) = 1 \tag{27}$$

From (25), (26) and (27), (28′) is gotten by the formula of full probability and Bayesian formula.

$$Pr(tr_k \mid p_{1j},p_{2j},...,p_{nj}) = \frac{1}{m} Pr(p_{1j},p_{2j},...,p_{nj} \mid tr_k)$$

$$= \frac{1}{m} Pr(p_{1j} \mid tr_k) \times Pr(p_{2j} \mid tr_k) \times ... \times Pr(p_{nj} \mid tr_k) \tag{28′}$$

$$= \frac{1}{m} \alpha(d_{1j},tr_k) \cdot \alpha(d_{2j},tr_k) \cdot ... \cdot \alpha(d_{nj},tr_k) \tag{28}$$

The transformation from (28′) to (28) is according to definition of $\alpha(d_{ij}, tr_k)$. As shown in Figure 11, when p_1, p_2 , …, p_n have $token_{1j}$, $token_{2j}$…$token_{nj}$, the occurring probability of transition tr_1, …, tr_k, …, tr_m are $\alpha(d_{1j}, tr_1) \bullet \alpha(d_{2j}, tr_1) \bullet ... \bullet \alpha(d_{nj}, tr_1)/m$, …, $\alpha(d_{1j}, tr_k) \bullet \alpha(d_{2j}, tr_k) \bullet ... \bullet \alpha(d_{nj}, tr_k)/m$, …, $\alpha(d_{1j}, tr_m) \bullet \alpha(d_{2j}, tr_m) \bullet ... \bullet \alpha(d_{nj}, tr_m)/m$. Thus, the transition tr_k, which has maximum of $\alpha(d_{1j}, tr_k) \bullet \alpha(d_{2j}, tr_k) \bullet ... \bullet \alpha(d_{nj}, tr_k)$, is selected and fired according to formula (23).

4.2. Learning algorithm for learning fuzzy Petri net

Learning algorithm

The learning fuzzy Petri net (LFPN) can be trained and made it learn fuzzy production rules. When a set of data input LFPN, a set of propositions are produced in each input place. For example, when token vectors ($token_{1j}$, $token_{2j}$, …, $token_{nj}$) (j=1, 2, …, N) input to p_1~p_r, propositions d_{1j}, d_{2j}, …, d_{nj} (j=1, 2, …, N) are produced. To train a fuzzy production rule which is IF d_{1j} AND d_{2j} AND … AND d_{nj} THEN d'_{1k} AND d'_{2k} AND … AND d'_{nk}, there are two tasks:

1. $\alpha(d_{1j}, tr_k) \bullet \alpha(d_{2j}, tr_k) \bullet ... \bullet \alpha(d_{nj}, tr_k)$ ($k \in \{1,2,...m\}$) need to be updated to hold formula (23);
2. 2) The output weight function of tr_k need to be updated for putting correct token to p'_1~p'_r. Then, $\beta(p'_1) = d'_{1k}$, $\beta(p'_2) = d'_{2k}$, …, $\beta(p'_r) = d'_{rk}$.

To accomplish these two tasks, the weights w_{1k}, w_{2k}, …, w_{nk} and w'_{k1}, w'_{k2}, …, w'_{kr} are modified by a learning algorithm of LFPN. Firstly, we define the training data set as {(X_1, Y_1), (X_2, Y_2), …, (X_N, Y_N)}, where X is input token vector, Y is output token vector and X_j, Y_j is defined as X_j=(x_{1j}, x_{2j}, …, x_{nj})^T, Y_j=(y_{1j}, y_{2j}, …, y_{rj})^T, respectively. Thus,

X=(X_1, X_2, …, X_j, …, X_N,), Y=(Y_1, Y_2, …, Y_j, …, Y_N) , i.e.

$$X=\begin{bmatrix} x_{11} & x_{12} & \cdots & x_{1j} & \cdots & x_{1N} \\ x_{21} & x_{22} & \cdots & x_{2j} & \cdots & x_{2N} \\ \vdots & \vdots & \vdots & \vdots & \vdots & \vdots \\ x_{n1} & x_{n2} & \cdots & x_{nj} & \cdots & x_{nN} \end{bmatrix} \quad Y=\begin{bmatrix} y_{11} & y_{12} & \cdots & y_{1j} & \cdots & y_{1N} \\ y_{21} & y_{22} & \cdots & y_{2j} & \cdots & y_{2N} \\ \vdots & \vdots & \vdots & \vdots & \vdots & \vdots \\ y_{r1} & y_{r2} & \cdots & y_{rj} & \cdots & y_{rN} \end{bmatrix}$$

Secondly, the weight $W_k=(w_{1k}, w_{2k}, \ldots, w_{nk})^T$ is the weight on arcs from $^*tr_k$ to tr_k and $W'_k=(w'_{k1}, w'_{k2}, \ldots, w'_{kr})^T$ is the weight on arcs from tr_k to tr_k^*. $W_1, \ldots, W_k, \ldots, W_m$ and $W'_1, \ldots, W'_k, \ldots, W'_m$ are the input and output arcs weight for $tr_1, \ldots, tr_k, \ldots, tr_m$. Thus,

$W=(W_1, W_2, \ldots, W_k, \ldots, W_m)$, $W'=(W'_1, W'_2, \ldots, W'_k, \ldots, W'_m)$, i.e.

$$W=\begin{bmatrix} w_{11} & w_{12} & \cdots & w_{1k} & \cdots & w_{1m} \\ w_{21} & w_{22} & \cdots & w_{2k} & \cdots & w_{2m} \\ \vdots & \vdots & \vdots & \vdots & \vdots & \vdots \\ w_{n1} & w_{n2} & \cdots & w_{nk} & \cdots & w_{nm} \end{bmatrix} \quad W'=\begin{bmatrix} w'_{11} & w'_{21} & \cdots & w'_{k1} & \cdots & w'_{m1} \\ w'_{12} & w'_{22} & \cdots & w'_{k2} & \cdots & w'_{m2} \\ \vdots & \vdots & \vdots & \vdots & \vdots & \vdots \\ w'_{1r} & w'_{2r} & \cdots & w'_{kr} & \cdots & w'_{mr} \end{bmatrix}$$

Lastly, in the learning algorithm, when tr_k is fired, the truth of $d'_{1j}, d'_{2j}, \ldots, d'_{rj}$ to tr_k are defined as $\alpha(d'_{1j}, tr_k)=1-|y_{1j}-w'_{k1}|/\max(|w'_{k1}|, |y_{1j}|)$, $\alpha(d'_{2j}, tr_k)=1-|y_{2j}-w'_{k2}|/\max(|w'_{k2}|, |y_{2j}|)$, ..., $\alpha(d'_{rj}, tr_k)=1-|y_{rj}-w'_{kr}|/\max(|w'_{kr}|, |y_{rj}|)$ according to definition 3.The learning algorithm of learning fuzzy Petri net is shown in Table 4.

Learning Algorithm of LFPN:

Step 1. W and W' are selected randomly.

Step 2. For every training data set $(X_j, Y_j)(j=1, 2, \ldots, N)$, subject propositions $d_{1j}, d_{2j}, \ldots, d_{nj}$ in $p_1 \sim p_n$ and propositions $d'_{1j}, d'_{2j}, \ldots, d'_{rj}$ in $p'_1 \sim p'_r$ are produced. Then do step 3 to step 7;

Step 3. For i=1 to n
  For h=1 to m do
    Compute $\alpha(d_{ij}, tr_h)$ according to formula (2);

Step 4. Compute maximum truth of transition
  4.1 $Max=\alpha(d_{1j}, tr_1) \bullet \alpha(d_{2j}, tr_1) \bullet \ldots \bullet \alpha(d_{nj}, tr_1)$; k=1;
  4.2 For h=1 to m do
    If $\alpha(d_{1j}, tr_h) \bullet \alpha(d_{2j}, tr_h) \bullet \ldots \bullet \alpha(d_{nj}, tr_h) > Max$
      Then { $Max=\alpha(d_{1j}, tr_h) \bullet \alpha(d_{2j}, tr_h) \bullet \ldots \bullet \alpha(d_{nj}, tr_h)$;
        $k=h$; }

Step 5. Fire tr_k;

Step 6. Make $d_{1j}, d_{2j}, \ldots, d_{nj}$ have bigger truth to tr_k,

$$W_k^{(new)} = W_k^{(old)} + \gamma(X_j - W_k^{(old)}) \quad (29)$$

($W_k^{(new)}$ is the vector W_k after update and $W_k^{(old)}$ is the vector W_k before updated. $\gamma \in (0,1)$ is learning rate.)

Step 7. Make $d'_{1j}, d'_{2j}, \ldots, d'_{rj}$ have bigger truth to tr_k,

$$W'^{(new)}_k = W'^{(old)}_k + \gamma(Y_j - W'^{(old)}_k) \quad (30)$$

($W'^{(new)}_k$ is the vector W'_k after update and $W'^{(old)}_k$ is the vector W'_k before updated. $\gamma \in (0,1)$ is learning rate.)

Step 8. Repeat step 2-7, until the truth of $\alpha(d_{1j}, tr_k), \alpha(d_{2j}, tr_k), \ldots, \alpha(d_{nj}, tr_k)$ meet the requirement.

Table 4. Learning algorithm of learning fuzzy Petri net

Some details in the algorithm need to be elaborated further.

1. About the net construction: The number of input and output places can be easily set according to a real problem. It is difficult to decide a number of transitions when the net is initialized. When LFPN is used to solve a special issue, the number of transitions is initially set according to practical situation experientially. Then, transitions can be dynamically appended and deleted during the training. If an input data $\mathbf{X}_j$ has a maximal truth to tr_k but one or several $\alpha(d_{ij}, tr_k)(1 \le i \le n)$ are less than th_k (threshold of tr_k), transition tr_k cannot fire according to definition 3. Thus, data $\mathbf{X}_j$ cannot fire any existed transition. This case means that $\mathbf{W}_1, \mathbf{W}_2, \ldots, \mathbf{W}_k, \ldots, \mathbf{W}_m$ cannot describe the vector characteristic of $\mathbf{X}_j$. Then, a new transition tr_{m+1} and the arcs which connect tr_{m+1} with input and output place are constructed. $\mathbf{X}_j$ can be set as weight $\mathbf{W}_{m+1}$ directly. Second, during a training episode, if there is no data in $\mathbf{X}_1, \mathbf{X}_2, \ldots, \mathbf{X}_N$ that can fire transition tr_d, it means that $\mathbf{W}_d$ cannot describe the vector characteristic of any data $\mathbf{X}_1, \mathbf{X}_2, \ldots, \mathbf{X}_N$. Then, the transition tr_d and the arcs which connect tr_d with input and output place will be deleted.
2. About $\mathbf{W}$ and $\mathbf{W}'$ initialization: for promoting training efficiency at the first stage of training, $\mathbf{W}$ and $\mathbf{W}'$ are set randomly in $[\mathbf{X}_{\min}, \mathbf{X}_{\max}]$, $[\mathbf{Y}_{\min}, \mathbf{Y}_{\max}]$ ($\mathbf{X}_{\min}$ is a vector which every components is minimal component of vector set $\mathbf{X}_1, \mathbf{X}_2, \ldots, \mathbf{X}_N$; $\mathbf{X}_{\max}$ is a vector which every components is maximal component of vector set $\mathbf{X}_1, \mathbf{X}_2, \ldots, \mathbf{X}_N$; $\mathbf{Y}_{\min}$, $\mathbf{Y}_{\max}$ are same meaning with $\mathbf{X}_{\min}$, $\mathbf{X}_{\max}$).
3. Training stop condition of the learning algorithm: According to application case, th_1, $th_2, \ldots, th_k, \ldots th_m$ are generally set a same value th. When training begins, the threshold th is set low (for example 0.2), th increases as training time increasing. A threshold value th_{last} (for example 0.9) is set as training stop condition and algorithm is run until $\alpha(d_{1j}, tr_k) > th_{last}$, $\alpha(d_{2j}, tr_k) > th_{last} \ldots \alpha(d_{nj}, tr_k) > th_{last}$. From transition appending analysis, we understand that number of transitions will near to the number of training data if the threshold of transition sets near to 1. In this case, results will be obtained more correctly but the training time and LFPN running time will increase.

Analysis for convergence of LFPN learning algorithm

In this section, the convergence of the proposed algorithm will be analyzed. In step 6 of the LFPN learning algorithm, the formula (29) is used for making Wk (new) approach Xj than Wk (old) when Xj fired a transition trk. It is proved as follows.

$$
\begin{aligned}
&W_k^{(new)} = W_k^{(old)} + \gamma(X_j - W_k^{(old)}) = W_k^{(old)} + \gamma \mathbf{X}_j - \gamma \mathbf{W}_k^{(old)} \\
&X_j - W_k^{(new)} = X_j - [W_k^{(old)} + \gamma(X_j - W_k^{(old)})] \\
&= X_j - W_k^{(old)} - \gamma \mathbf{X}_j + \gamma \mathbf{W}_k^{(old)} \\
&= (1-\gamma)\ (X_j - W_k^{(old)})
\end{aligned}
\quad (31)
$$

Formula (11′) is rewritten as a scalar type and the scalar type of ($\mathbf{X}_j - \mathbf{W}_k^{(old)}$) is used to divide both sides of formula (11′). We get formula (11).

$$\left(\frac{\boldsymbol{x}_{ij}-\boldsymbol{w}_{kj}{}^{(new)}}{\boldsymbol{x}_{ij}-\boldsymbol{w}_{kj}{}^{(old)}}\right)_{0\le i\le n}=\left(\frac{(1-\gamma)\cdot\left(\boldsymbol{x}_{ij}-\boldsymbol{w}_{kj}{}^{(old)}\right)}{\boldsymbol{x}_{ij}-w_{kj}{}^{(old)}}\right)_{0\le i\le n}=1-\gamma \tag{31}$$

Hence, $\boldsymbol{W}_k$ will converge to $\boldsymbol{X}_j$ after enough training times.

In LFPN learning algorithm, there may be a class of training data $\boldsymbol{X}_j$ which are able to fire same transition tr_k. In this case, $\boldsymbol{W}_k$ approaches to a class of data $\boldsymbol{X}_j$ and converges to a point in the class of data $\boldsymbol{X}_j$ according to formula (31).

Now, we will discuss the point in the class of data $\boldsymbol{X}_j$ where $\boldsymbol{W}_k$ converges to. Supposing, there are b_1 data which are in $\boldsymbol{X}_1, \boldsymbol{X}_2, \ldots, \boldsymbol{X}_j, \ldots, \boldsymbol{X}_N$ and fire a certain transition tr_k at the first training episode. At the second training episode, there are b_2 data which fire tr_k, and so on. If the total training times is ep and the total number of data which fire tr_k is t, $t=\sum_{i=1}^{ep} b_i$. According to the order of the data fired tr_k, these t data are rewritten as $\boldsymbol{X}_{k1}, \boldsymbol{X}_{k2}, \ldots, \boldsymbol{X}_{kt}$. The average of training data $\boldsymbol{X}_{k1}, \boldsymbol{X}_{k2}, \ldots, \boldsymbol{X}_{kt}$ is noted as $\overline{\boldsymbol{X}}_k$. To record the updated process of $\boldsymbol{W}_k$ simply, the updated order of $\boldsymbol{W}_k$ is recorded as $\boldsymbol{W}_{k1}, \boldsymbol{W}_{k2} \ldots . \boldsymbol{W}_{kt}$.

The learning rate γ ($0<\gamma<1$) will decrease according to training time increasing, and it approaches to 0 at last because every training data cannot effect $\boldsymbol{W}_k$ too much in the last stage of training, else $\boldsymbol{W}_k$ will shake at the last stage of training. If learning rate γ is set as $1/(q+1)$ ($q>0$) when training begin, $1/(q+2)$, $1/(q+3)$, …, $1/(q+t)$ are set as learning rate γ when tr_k is fired at 2, 3, …, t time. Here, the initial values of $\boldsymbol{W}_k$ is set as $\boldsymbol{W}_{k0}=\boldsymbol{W}^{(0)}\times 1/q$, every component of $\boldsymbol{W}^{(0)}\times 1/q$ is a random value in $[\boldsymbol{X}_{min}, \boldsymbol{X}_{max}]$. According to formula (29), we get

$$\boldsymbol{W}_{k0}=\frac{1}{q}\boldsymbol{W}^{(0)}$$

$$\boldsymbol{W}_{k1}=\boldsymbol{W}_{k0}+\frac{1}{q+1}(\boldsymbol{X}_{k1}-\boldsymbol{W}_{k0})=\frac{1}{q}\boldsymbol{W}^{(0)}-\frac{1}{q+1}\times\frac{1}{q}\boldsymbol{W}^{(0)}+\frac{1}{q+1}\boldsymbol{X}_{k1}=\frac{1}{q+1}(\boldsymbol{W}^{(0)}+\boldsymbol{X}_{k1})$$

$$\boldsymbol{W}_{k2}=\boldsymbol{W}_{k1}+\frac{1}{q+2}(\boldsymbol{X}_{k2}-\boldsymbol{W}_{k1})=\frac{1}{q+1}\boldsymbol{W}^{(0)}+\frac{1}{q+1}\boldsymbol{X}_{k1}$$

$$-\frac{1}{q+1}\times\frac{1}{q+2}\boldsymbol{W}^{(0)}-\frac{1}{q+1}\times\frac{1}{q+2}\boldsymbol{X}_{k1}+\frac{1}{q+2}\boldsymbol{X}_{k2}$$

$$=\frac{1}{q+2}(\boldsymbol{W}^{(0)}+\boldsymbol{X}_{k1}+\boldsymbol{X}_{k2})$$

$$\boldsymbol{W}_{kt}=\boldsymbol{W}_{k,t-1}+\frac{1}{q+t}(\boldsymbol{X}_{kt}-\boldsymbol{W}_{k,t-1})=\frac{1}{q+t-1}\boldsymbol{W}^{(0)}-\frac{1}{q+t}\times\frac{1}{q+t-1}\boldsymbol{W}^{(0)}+$$

$$\frac{1}{q+t-1}\boldsymbol{X}_{k1}-\frac{1}{q+t}\times\frac{1}{q+t-1}\boldsymbol{X}_{k1}+\ldots+\frac{1}{q+t-1}\boldsymbol{X}_{k,t-1}-\frac{1}{q+t}\times\frac{1}{q+t-1}\boldsymbol{X}_{k,t-1}+\frac{1}{q+t}\boldsymbol{X}_{kt}$$

$$= \frac{1}{q+t}(\boldsymbol{W}^{(0)} + \boldsymbol{X}_{k1} + ... + \boldsymbol{X}_{k,t-1} + \boldsymbol{X}_{kt}) \tag{32}$$

When the training time increases, the training data set $\boldsymbol{X}_{k1}$, $\boldsymbol{X}_{k2}$, …, $\boldsymbol{X}_{kt}$ can be looked as very large, i.e. t is large.

$$\lim_{t\to\infty} \boldsymbol{W}_{kt} = \lim_{t\to\infty} \frac{1}{q+t}(\boldsymbol{W}^{(0)} + \boldsymbol{X}_{k1} + ... + \boldsymbol{X}_{k,t-1} + \boldsymbol{X}_{kt}) \tag{33}$$

Generally, q is a small positive constant and t is large. Then,

$$\lim_{t\to\infty} \boldsymbol{W}_{kt} \approx \lim_{t\to\infty} \frac{1}{t}(\boldsymbol{W}^{(0)} + \boldsymbol{X}_{k1} + ... + \boldsymbol{X}_{k,t-1} + \boldsymbol{X}_{kt})$$

$$= \lim_{t\to\infty} \frac{1}{t}\boldsymbol{W}^{(0)} + \lim_{t\to\infty} \frac{1}{t}(\boldsymbol{X}_{k1} + ... + \boldsymbol{X}_{k,t-1} + \boldsymbol{X}_{kt})$$

$$\approx \lim_{t\to\infty} \frac{1}{t}(\boldsymbol{X}_{k1} + ... + \boldsymbol{X}_{k,t-1} + \boldsymbol{X}_{kt}) = \overline{\boldsymbol{X}_k} \tag{34}$$

From formula (14) will be gotten:

$$\boldsymbol{W}_k \rightarrow \overline{\boldsymbol{X}}_k \tag{35}$$

In the same way, $\boldsymbol{W}_k \rightarrow \overline{\boldsymbol{X}}_k$ (k=1, 2, …, m) and $\boldsymbol{W}'_k \rightarrow \overline{\boldsymbol{Y}}_k$ (k=1, 2, …, m) can be proved. Consequently, the learning algorithm of LFPN converges.

Now, we will analyze the convergence process and signification of convergence.

1. $\boldsymbol{X}_{k1}$, $\boldsymbol{X}_{k2}$, …, $\boldsymbol{X}_{kt}$ fire a certain transition tr_k at training time. As the training time increase, there are almost same data which fire the transition tr_k in every training time. These data belong to a class k. We suppose that these data are $\boldsymbol{X}_{k1}$, $\boldsymbol{X}_{k2}$, …, $\boldsymbol{X}_{ks}$. When training begins, supposing, there is data $\boldsymbol{X}_u$ which does not belong to $\boldsymbol{X}_{k1}$, $\boldsymbol{X}_{k2}$, …, $\boldsymbol{X}_{ks}$ but fires tr_k. But, when training times increase, $\boldsymbol{W}_k$ will approach to $\boldsymbol{X}_{k1}$, $\boldsymbol{X}_{k2}$, …, $\boldsymbol{X}_{ks}$ and the probability which $\boldsymbol{X}_u$ fires tr_k will decrease. Hence, this type data $\boldsymbol{X}_u$ is very small part of $\boldsymbol{X}_{k1}$, $\boldsymbol{X}_{k2}$, …, $\boldsymbol{X}_{kt}$. $\boldsymbol{X}_u$ little affects to $\boldsymbol{W}_k$. On the other hand, when training begins, there is $\boldsymbol{X}_{ke}$ which belongs to $\boldsymbol{X}_{k1}$, $\boldsymbol{X}_{k2}$, …, $\boldsymbol{X}_{ks}$ but doesn't fire transition tr_k. But, when training times increase, the probability which $\boldsymbol{X}_{ke}$ fires tr_k increases, then, $\boldsymbol{X}_{k1}$, $\boldsymbol{X}_{k2}$, …, $\boldsymbol{X}_{ks}$ can be approximately looked firing tr_k according to the training. $\overline{\boldsymbol{X}}_k$ is denoted as the average of training data $\boldsymbol{X}_{k1}$, $\boldsymbol{X}_{k2}$, …, $\boldsymbol{X}_{ks}$.
2. In the convergence demonstration, we use a special series of learning rate γ. Form the analysis in 1), $\boldsymbol{X}_{k1}$, $\boldsymbol{X}_{k2}$, …, $\boldsymbol{X}_{ks}$ can be looked as a class data which fires one transition tr_k. The data series $\boldsymbol{X}_{k1}$, $\boldsymbol{X}_{k2}$, …, $\boldsymbol{X}_{kt}$ can be looked as iterations of $\boldsymbol{X}_{k1}$, $\boldsymbol{X}_{k2}$, …, $\boldsymbol{X}_{ks}$. $\boldsymbol{W}_k$ can converge to a point near $\overline{\boldsymbol{X}}_k$ with any damping learning rate series γ.
3. After training, $\boldsymbol{W}_k$=(w_{1k}, w_{2k}, …, w_{nk}) comes near to the average of data which belong to class k, i.e., $\boldsymbol{W}_k \approx \overline{\boldsymbol{X}}_k$=($\overline{x}_{1k}$, $\overline{x}_{2k}$, …, $\overline{x}_{nk}$). When a data $\boldsymbol{X}_{kj}$ belong to class k comes, $\boldsymbol{X}_{kj}$ will

have same vector characteristic with X_{k1}, X_{k2}, ..., X_{ks}, i.e. $x_{1,kj}$, $x_{2,kj}$, ..., $x_{n,kj}$ are near to w_{1k}, w_{2k}, ..., w_{nk}. Then, each component $x_{i,kj}$ ($1 \le i \le n$) of this data X_{kj} will have bigger similarity to w_{ik} ($1 \le i \le n$) than i-th components of other weight W according to formula (2). X_{kj} will have biggest truth to tr_k according to formula (2). Thus, when data X_{kj} which belongs to class of X_{k1}, X_{k2}, ..., X_{ks} inputs to LFPN, it will fire tr_k correctly and product correct output.

5. Web service discovery based on learning fuzzy Petri net model

Web services are used for developing and integrating highly distributed and heterogeneous systems in various domains. They are described by Web Services Description Language (WSDL). Web services discovery is a key to dynamically locating desired Web services across the Internet [16]. It immediately raises an issue, i.e. to evaluate the accuracy of the mapping in a heterogeneous environment when user wants to invoke a service. There are two aspects which need to evaluate. One is functional evaluation. The service providing function should be completely matched with user's request; another aspect is non-functional evaluation, i.e. Quality of Service (QoS) meets user's requirement. UDDI (Universal Description, Discovery and Integration) is widely used as a kind of discovery approach for functional evaluation. But, as the number of published Web services increases, discovering proper services using the limited description provided by the UDDI standard becomes difficult [17]. And UDDI cannot provide the QoS information of service. To discover the most appropriate service, there are necessary to focus on developing feasible discovery mechanisms from different service description methods and service execution context. Segev proposed a service function selection method [21]. A two-step, context based semantic approach to the problem of matching and ranking Web services for possible service composition is elaborated. The two steps for service function selection are Context extraction and Evaluation for Proximity degree of Service. Cai proposed service performance selection method [3]. The authors used a novel Artificial Neural Network-based service selection algorithm according to the information of the cooperation between the devices and the context information. In this paper, we aim at analyzing different context of services and constructing a services discovery model based on the LFPN. Firstly, different service functional descriptions are used to evaluate service function and an appropriate service is selected. Secondly, context of QoS is used to predict QoS and a more efficient service is selected. Data of QoS is real number and LFPN learning algorithm is directly used. But service function description is literal. Therefore, a Learning Fuzzy Petri Net for service discovery model is proposed for keyword learning based on LFPN.

5.1. Web services discovery model based on LFPN

To map a service's function accurately, free textual service description, WSDL description, Web service's operation and port parameters which are drawn from WSDL are used as input data here. Because the input data type is keyword, the proposed LFPN cannot deal with this type of data. Consequently, a Learning Fuzzy Petri Net for Web Services Discovery model (LFPNSD) is proposed. LFPNSD is a 10-tuple, given by LFPNSD = $<P, Tr, F, W, D, I, O, Th, \alpha, \beta>$ (as shown in Figure 13.)

where: Tr, I, O, Th, β are same with definition of LFPN.
$P=\{P_{input}\} \cup \{P_{output}\}=\{P_{11}, P_{12}, P_{13}\} \cup \{P_{21}, P_{22}, P_{23}, P_{24}\}$
$F \subseteq (P_{input} \times Tr) \cup (Tr \times P_{output})$
$W=F \rightarrow Keywords^{+}$, where weight function on $P_{input} \times Tr$ are different keywords of service description and weight function on $Tr \times P_{output}$ are different service invoking information.
$D = \{d_{11,a}, d_{12,b}, d_{13,c}\} \cup \{d_{21,e}, d_{22,f}, d_{23,g}, d_{24,h}\}$ is a finite set of propositions, where proposition $d_{11,a}$ is that P_{11} has a service description tokens; proposition $d_{12,b}$ is that P_{12} has a free textual description tokens; proposition $d_{13,c}$ is that P_{13} has a service operation and port parameters tokens. And the propositions $d_{21,e}$, $d_{22,f}$, $d_{23,g}$, $d_{24,h}$ are that P_{21}, P_{22}, P_{23}, P_{24} have different invoking information tokens of services.

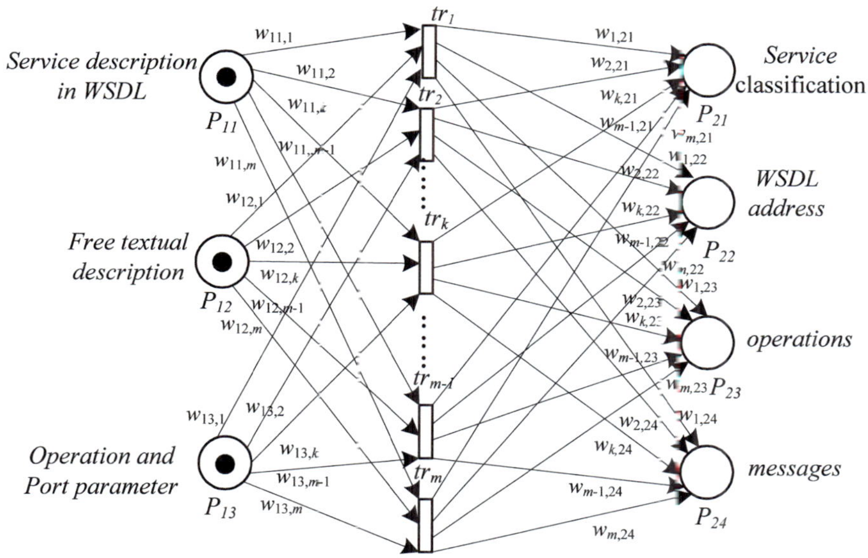

Figure 13. The learning fuzzy Petri net for Web service discovery (LFPNSD)

$\alpha(d_{ij}, tr_k) \rightarrow [0, 1]$. $\alpha(d_{ij}, tr_k)=y_i \in [0, 1]$ is the degree of truth of proposition d_{ij} to tr_k. $\alpha(d_{ij}, tr_k)$ is computed by bellow rules: if input description has n keywords and the w_{ik} on arc P_i to tr_k has s same keywords, the degree of similarity between weight keywords and input description keywords is expressed as:

$$\alpha\left(d_{ij}, tr_k\right) = 1 - \frac{|n-s|}{\max(n,s)} \tag{36}$$

The fire rule of transition: if $\alpha(d_{11,a}, tr_k) \bullet \alpha(d_{12,b}, tr_k) \bullet \alpha(d_{13,c}, tr_k) = \max((\alpha(d_{11,a}, tr_i) \bullet \alpha(d_{12,b}, tr_i) \bullet \alpha(d_{13,c}, tr_i))_{1 \le i \le m})$ and all of $\alpha(d_{11,a}, tr_k)$, $\alpha(d_{12,b}, tr_k)$, $\alpha(d_{13,c}, tr_k)$ are bigger than a threshold value th, then tr_k fires, the tokens in P_{11}~P_{13} are taken out and tokens which according to $w_{k,21}$, $w_{k,22}$, $w_{k,23}$, $w_{k,24}$ are put into P_{21}~P_{24}.

As shown in Figure 13, service free textual description, WSDL description and operation and port information are used as input vector in the learning algorithm. And, service classification, WSDL address, all of service operation names and service SOAP messages are used as output vector. Because the training data type is the keyword, the learning algorithm of LFPN is developed into a learning algorithm of LFPNSD. The learning algorithm of learning fuzzy Petri net for Web service discovery is shown in the table 5.

Learning Algorithm of LFPNSD:

Step 1. Make all weights on arcs be ◎;

Step 2. For every service in training data set,

Repeat:

2.1 Get free textual description; Draw out WSDL description and operation and port name from WSDL;

2.2 Set service textual description, WSDL description, operation and port information as input vector;

2.3 Compare the input with the keywords on the weight of input arc:

If every keyword in weight is in the input data, then compute $\alpha(d_{ij}, tr_k)$ according to formula (16), else set $\alpha(d_{ij}, tr_k)$ =0.

If each of $\alpha(d_{ij}, tr_1)$, $\alpha(d_{ij}, tr_2)$, …, $\alpha(d_{ij}, tr_{m-1})$ equates 0 and the weight of tr_m is ◎, then set $\alpha(d_{ij}, tr_m)$ =1.

If each of $\alpha(d_{ij}, tr_1)$, $\alpha(d_{ij}, tr_2)$, …, $\alpha(d_{ij}, tr_{m-1})$ equates 0◎and tr_m doesn't exist, a new transition tr_m and the arcs which connect tr_m with input and output place are constituted, set weight of arcs to be ◎◎and $\alpha(d_{ij}, tr_m)$ =1.

2.4 If $\alpha(d_{11,a}, tr_k) \bullet \alpha(d_{12,b}, tr_k) \bullet \alpha(d_{13,c}, tr_k) = \max((\alpha(d_{11,a}, tr_i) \bullet \alpha(d_{12,b}, tr_i) \bullet \alpha(d_{13,c}, tr_i))_{1 \le i \le m})$, then tr_k fires.

2.5 If the tr_k fired, get a keyword in service description but not in the weight, and add it into the weight.

If training time is t and the weight is ◎, t keywords in service description are gotten and they are added into the weight.

2.6 If the tr_k fired, compare out training data (service classification, WSDL address, service operation and message) with the weight of $w_{k,21}$, $w_{k,22}$, $w_{k,23}$, $w_{k,24}$, and calculate and record the correct rate of output.

2.7 Update $w_{k,21}$, $w_{k,22}$, $w_{k,23}$, $w_{k,24}$ according to output of training data.

Step 3. Repeat step 2, until each $\alpha(d_{11,a}, tr_k)$, $\alpha(d_{12,b}, tr_k)$, $\alpha(d_{13,c}, tr_k)$ meets the requirement value th_k.

Table 5. Learning algorithm of learning fuzzy Petri net for Web service discovery

Discussion:

1. We discuss about the learning rate γ in the learning algorithm of LFPNSD. In the algorithm, the keyword is learned and added into weights one by one. Hereby, X_j–$W_k^{(new)}$ =1 and X_j–$W^{(old)}$ equates the difference between the number of input data keywords and the number of keywords on arc weight. Because X_j–$W^{(old)}$ is not constant, the learning rate γ is different at each learning episode. For example, when input data has 10 keywords and arc weight has 6 keywords firstly, one keyword is learnt from input data and added into weight. In this case, the learning rate is 1/(10-6)=0.25.
2. If keyword isn't learning one by one, the keywords on W_1, W_2, …, W_k, …, W_m will do not balance at beginning stage of training. Then, the similar but different description

services have unbalance probability to fire transition at beginning stage of training. This makes the similar but different description services improperly fire a transition which has more keywords on its weight. It makes training efficiency lower.

3. In step 2.3 of algorithm, when each of $\alpha(d_{ij}, tr_1)$, $\alpha(d_{ij}, tr_2)$, …, $\alpha(d_{ij}, tr_{m-1})$ equates 0, it means all weights on transition tr_1~ tr_{m-1} cannot describe this service. Therefore, it is a new type service. If there is a transition which has weight arc, it is used to record the new type service; else a new transition needs to be constructed.

5.2. The result of simulation

The two simulations are carried out. One is a more efficient service selection through QoS prediction using LFPN. The other is a service selection for appropriate function using LFPNSD.

Simulation for more efficient Web service selection

During the process of Web services discovery, there are maybe several services which have same function. One service which has the best QoS needs to be select. Hereby, the service performance context is used to predict the QoS value for next execution of service. If the prediction is precise enough, an appropriate service maybe selected.

In this simulation, LFPN is used as learning model for predicting service execution time which is main part of QoS. There are 11 inputs and 1 output in this model. 11 inputs include 10 data which are last 10 times execution time of a service and one data which is reliability of the service. The output is a prediction for execution time of service's next execution. 10 transitions of LFPN is set when initialization.

A Web service performance dataset is employed for simulation. This dataset includes 100 publicly available Web services located in more than 20 countries. 150 service users executed about 100 invocations on each Web service. Each service user recorded execution time and invocation failures in dataset [27]. We selected one use's invocation data as training data. Last 10 times execution time and reliability of each service was set as input and next time execution time was set as output. 20 sets of training data were selected for each of 100 services.

The initial threshold is selected as 0.2 and the threshold is increased 0.001 at every training episode. The initial learning rate is set as 1/1.1 for every transition. The learning rate is $1/(0.1+t)$ when a transition fired t times. Prediction result and training output data are noted as $Output_{predict}$ and $Output_{training}$. Prediction precision probability Pre_{pro} is used to evaluate the precision result. And the precision probability is computed using:

$$Pre_{pro}=1-(|Output_{predict}-Output_{training}|/ Output_{training}).$$

Three different training stop conditions are set as that three threshold values equal to 0.7, 0.8, and 0.9. The simulation result is listed in Table 6. Here, the number of service, which their execution time is precisely predicted, increased with the training threshold value increasing.

In the paper [3], the authors improved the traditional BP algorithm based on three-term method consisting of a learning rate, a momentum factor and a proportional factor for predicting service performance according to service context information. In this paper, this model is used to predict service execution time. The training data is same to LFPN's. And the learning rate is 0.6, momentum factor 0.9, proportional factor 1 and training times is 10,000. We compared the simulation result of the method of [3], i.e. the conventional method, with that of LFPN in Table 7. From Table 7, it is shown that Web service number of high precision in LFPN's prediction is bigger than the number of BP algorithm's prediction and Web service number of low precision in LFPN's prediction is smaller that BP algorithm's prediction. Hereby, the result of LFPN is better than result of three term's BP algorithm.

Precision	0.99~1	0.98~0.99	0.95~0.98	0.9~0.95	0.8~0.9	0.7~0.8	0.6~0.7	0~0.6
Number of Web services (*th*= 0.9)	21	14	17	15	10	8	9	6
Number of Web services (*th*= 0.8)	17	12	14	11	10	12	10	14
Number of Web services (th= 0.7)	10	10	16	8	8	11	19	18

Table 6. Prediction ability of LFPN

Precision	0.99~1	0.98~0.99	0.95~0.98	0.9~0.95	0.8~0.9	0.7~0.8	0.6~0.7	0~0.6
Number of Web services using the LFPN(th=0.9)	21	14	17	15	10	8	9	6
Number of Web services using the conventional method	6	7	15	18	20	12	10	12

Table 7. Prediction ability compares for two methods

Simulation for selection of Web service's function

In this simulation, LFPNSD is used as leaning model. The benchmark Web services which listed at www.xmethods.net are used as training data. Each service of these 260 services has a textual description and its WSDL address. And, we can get WSDL description, operation and port parameters from the WSDL. We want to classify the Web service into four classes: 1) business, 2) finance, 3) nets and 4) life services. After training, Web services are invoked by natural language request [14]. The natural language is decompounded into three inputs of this model. For example, we want to get a short message service (SMS) for sending a message to a mobile phone. The nature language of this discovery is input and decomposed into three parts: 1) WSDL description: send a message to a mobile phone; 2) free textual service description: sending a message to a mobile phone through the Internet; 3) operation and port parameters maybe have operation names: send messages, send message multiple recipients, and so on; port names send service SOAP, and so on.

In this simulation, we firstly set 100 transitions for LFPNSD model. The training stop condition is th_k $(1 \leq k \leq m) \geq 0.6$. The service selection precision is recorded after every time of training. As shown in Figure 14 and 15, using LFPNSD model and its learning algorithm described in Section 5.1, every service class precision probability raised to more than 0.9 when the training time reaches to 10.

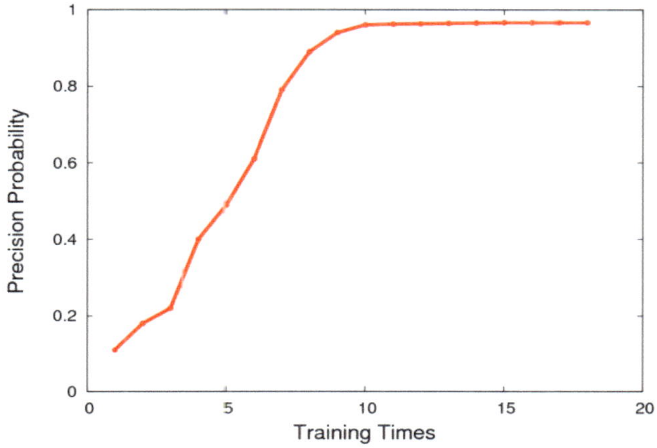

Figure 14. The results of simulation using LFPNSD and its learning algorithm– Discovery Precision Probability for total services

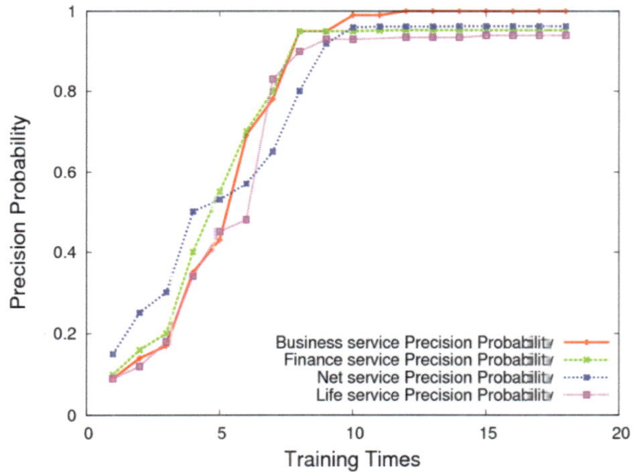

Figure 15. The results of simulation using LFPNSD and its learning algorithm – Discovery Precision Probability for classification services

A method for evaluating the proximity of services is proposed [21]. In the method, WSDL document is represented as $D^{wsdl}=\{t_1, t_2, \ldots, t_{wsdl}\}$ and $D^{desc}=\{t_1, t_2, \ldots, t_{desc}\}$ represents the textual description of the service. Because there is another descriptor of operation and port parameters in LFPNSD model, we add this descriptor as $D^{op\&port}=\{t_1, t_2, \ldots, t_{op\&port}\}$ in order to compare two methods. Here, t_{wsdl}, t_{desc} and $t_{op\&port}$ are last keyword of WSDL, textural description and operation and port parameters. In the proximity of services method, the descriptor of natural language request which is provided by a user is D_{user} and descriptor of invoked service is D_{inv}. The three Context Overlaps (CO) are defined as same keywords between D^{wsdl}_{user}, D^{desc}_{user}, $D^{op\&port}_{user}$ and D^{wadl}_{inv}, D^{desc}_{inv}, $D^{op\&port}_{inv}$. The proximity of user requested service and invoked service is defined as a root of sum of three CO's squares. When a user invoking comes, it is compared with all services in services repository. Then, one service in D_{inv}, which has the biggest proximity value with D_{user}, was selected. We compared the discovery precision probability of this method (conventional method) with the proposed LFPNSD. The simulation results are shown in Figure 16. The LFPNSD method yielded higher precision probabilities than the conventional method proposed in [21]. Especially when the service number of Web services' repository becomes more than 88, the difference is much more significant. Here, a correct service is selected in 14 services, 24 services, 37 services, 54 services, 88 services, 151 services just as they were used in [21].

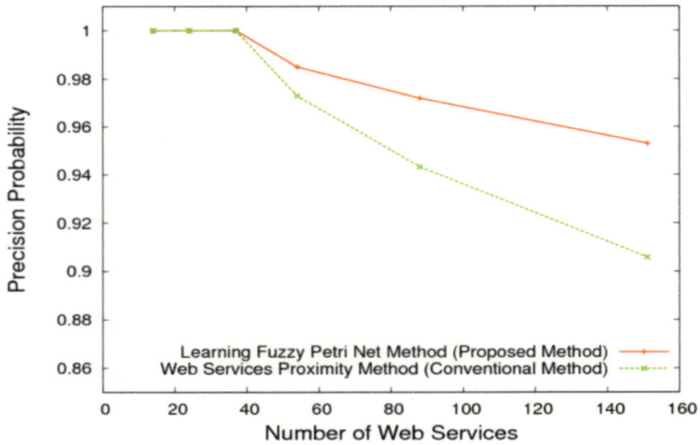

Figure 16. Comparison of two discovery methods

6. Conclusion

In this chapter, Learning Petri net (LPN) was constructed based on High-level Time Petri net and reinforcement learning (RL). The RL was used for adjusting the parameter of Petri net. Two kinds of learning algorithm were proposed for Petri net's discrete and continuous parameter learning. And verification for LPN was shown. LPN model was applied to dynamical system control. We had used the LPN in three robot systems control - the AIBO, Guide Dog. The LPN models were found and controlled for these robot systems. These robot systems could adjust their parameters while system was running. And the correctness and effectiveness of our proposed model were confirmed in these experiments. LPN model was improved to the hierarchical LPN model and this improved hierarchical LPN model was applied to QoS optimization of Web service composition. The hierarchical LPN model was constructed based on stochastic Petri net and RL. When the model was used, the Web service composition was modeled with stochastic Petri net. A Web service dynamical composing framework is proposed for optimizing QoS of web service composition. The neural network learning method was used to Fuzzy Petri net. Learning fuzzy Petri net (LFPN) was proposed. Contrasting with the existing FPN, there are three extensions in the new model: the place can possess different tokens which represent different propositions;

these propositions have different degrees of truth toward different transitions; the truth degree of proposition can be learnt through adjusting of the arc's weight function. The LFPN model obtains the capability of fuzzy production rules learning through truth degree updating. The LFPN learning algorithm which introduced network learning method into Petri net update was proposed and the convergence of the algorithm was analyzed. The LFPN model was used into discovery of Web service. Using the LFPN model, different service functional descriptions are used to evaluate service function and an appropriate service is selected firstly, Secondly, context of QoS is used to predict QoS and a more efficient service is selected.

In the future, the different intelligent computing methods will be used into Petri net for constructing different type of LPN. The efficient different types of LPN used in different special area will be compared and an efficient LPN model for solving various problems will be founded.

Author details

Liangbing Feng, Masanao Obayashi, Takashi Kuremoto and Kunikazu Kobayashi
Division of Computer Science & Design Engineering, Yamaguchi University, Ube, Japan

Liangbing Feng
Shenzhen Institutes of Advanced Technology, Shenzhen, China

7. References

[1] Konar A., Chakraborty U. K. and Wang P. P. Supervised Learning on a Fuzzy Petri Net. Information Sciences 2005; Vol.172, No.3-4, 397-416.

[2] Hrúz B., Zhou M.C. Modeling and Control of Discrete-event Dynamic Systems: with Petri Nets and Other Tools. Springer Press. London, UK, 2007.

[3] Cai H., Hu X., Lu Q. and Cao Q. A Novel Intelligent Service Selection Algorithm and Application for Ubiquitous Web Services Environment. Expert Systems with Applications 2009; Vol. 36, No. 2, 2200-2212.

[4] Doya, K. Reinforcement Learning in Continuous Time and Apace, Neural Computation, 2000; Vol.12, No.1, 219–245.

[5] Feng L. B, Obayashi M., Kuremoto T. and Kobayashi K. A Learning Petri Net Model Based on Reinforcement Learning. Proceedings of the 15th International Symposium on Artificial Life and Robotics (AROB2010); 290-293.

[6] Feng L. B., Obayashi M., Kuremoto T. and Kobayashi K. An Intelligent Control System Construction Using High-Level Time Petri Net and Reinforcement Learning. Proceedings of International Conference on Control, Automation, and Systems (ICCAS 2010); 535 – 539.

[7] Feng L. B., Obayashi M., Kuremoto T. and Kobayashi K. A learning Petri net Model. IEEJ Transactions on Electrical and Electronic Engineering 2012; Volume 7, Issue 3, pages 274–282.

[8] Frederick J. R. Statistical Methods for Speech. The MIT Press. Cambridge, Massachusetts, USA, 1999.

[9] Guangming C., Minghong L., Xianghu W. The Definition of Extended High-level Time Petri Nets. Journal of Computer Science 2006; 2(2):127-143.

[10] Hirasawa K., Ohbayashi M., Sakai S., Hu J. Learning Petri Network and Its Application to Nonlinear System Control. IEEE Transactions on Systems, Man and Cybernetic, Part B: Cybernetics, 1998; 28(6), 781-789.

[11] VIRTANEN H. E. A Study in Fuzzy Petri Nets and the Relationship to Fuzzy Logic Programming, Reports on Computer Science and Mathematics, No. 162, 1995.

[12] Yan H. S., Jian J. Agile concurrent engineering. Integrated Manufacturing Systems 1999; 10(2): 103-113.

[13] Wang J. Petri nets for dynamic event-driven system modeling. Handbook of Dynamic System Modeling 2007; Ed: Paul Fishwick, CRC Press, 1-17.

[14] Lim J. H., Lee. K. H. Constructing Composite Web Services from Natural Language Requests, Web Semantics: Science, Services and Agents on the World Wide Web 2010; Vol. 8, No.1, 1-13.

[15] Li X., Yu W., and Rsano F. L. Dynamic Knowledge Inference and Learning under Adaptive Fuzzy Petri Net Framework, IEEE Transactions on System, Man, and Cybernetics-Part C 2000; Vol. 30, No.4, 442-450.

[16] Papazoglou M.P., Georgakopoulos D. Service-Oriented Computing, Communications of the ACM, 2003; 46(10), 25–65.

[17] Platzer C. and S. Dustdar. A Vector Space Search Engine for Web Services, Proc. Third European Conf. Web Services (ECOWS'05) 2005, 62-71.

[18] Sutton R. S., Batto A. G. Reinforcement learning: An Introduction. The MIT Press, Cambridge, Massachusetts, USA, 1998.

[19] Sony OPEN-R programming group, OPEN-R programming introduction. Sony Corporation, Japan, (2004).

[20] Tzafesta S.G., Rigatos G.G. Stability analysis of an adaptive fuzzy control system using Petri nets and learning automata. Mathematics and computers in Simulation 2000; Vol. 51. No. 3. 315-339.

[21] Segev A. and E. Toch. Context-Based Matching and Ranking of Web Services for Composition, IEEE Transaction on Services computing 2009;, Vol.2, No.3, 210-222.

[22] Baranaushas V., Sarkauskas K. Colored Petri Nets-Tool for control system Learning. Electronics and Electrical Engineering 2006; 4(68):41-46.

[23] Victor R. L. Shen. Reinforcement Learning for High-level Fuzzy Petri Nets, IEEE Transactions on System, Man, and Cybernetics-Part B 2003; Vol.33, No.2, 351-361.

[24] Pedrycz W. and Gomide F. A Generalized Fuzzy Petri Net Model, IEEE Transaction on Fuzzy System 1994; Vol.2, No.4, 295-301.

[25] Xu H., Wang Y., and Jia P. Fuzzy Neural Petri Nets, Proceedings of the 4th International Symposium on Neural Networks: Part II--Advances in Neural Networks, 2007; 328 – 335.

[26] Ding Z. H., Bunke H., Schneider M. and A. Kandel. Fuzzy Time Petri net Definitions, Properties, and Applications, Mathematical and Computer Modeling, 2005, Vol. 41, No. 2-3, 345-360.

[27] Zheng Z. B., Lyu M. R. Collaborative Reliability Prediction for Service -Oriented Systems, Proceedings of the ACM/IEEE 32nd International Conference on Software Engineering (ICSE2010), 35 – 44.

Chapter 8

Control Interpreted Petri Nets – Model Checking and Synthesis

Iwona Grobelna

Additional information is available at the end of the chapter

http://dx.doi.org/10.5772/47797

1. Introduction

The chapter presents a novel approach to formal verification of logic controller programs [2], focusing especially on reconfigurable logic controllers (RLCs). Control Interpreted Petri Nets [8] are used as formal specification of logic controller behavior. The approach proposes to use an abstract rule-based logical model presented at RTL-level. A Control Interpreted Petri Net is written as a logical model, and then processed further. Proposed logical model (Figure 1) is suitable both for formal verification [14] (model checking in the NuSMV tool [19]) and for logical synthesis (using hardware description language VHDL).

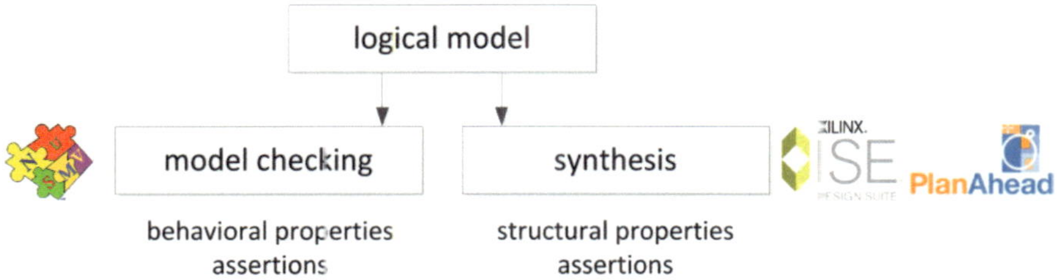

Figure 1. Logical model for model checking and synthesis purposes

Model checking [7, 10] of prepared logical model allows to validate the primary specification of logic controller. It is possible to verify some user-defined properties, which are supposed to be satisfied in designed system.

Logical model derived from a Control Interpreted Petri Nets presented at RTL-level (*Register Transfer Level*) in such a way, that it is easily synthesizable as reconfigurable logic controller or PLC (*Programmable Logic Controller*) without additional changes.

Design methodology at RTL-level allows to convert an algorithm into hardware realization and to use the conception of variables and sequential operation performing. Project description in VHDL language is a specification accepted by synthesis tools at RTL-level [23]. Therefore, logical model is transformed into synthesizable code in VHDL language.

Presented approach to formal verification of reconfigurable logic controllers was tested on several examples of industrial specifications by means of Control Interpreted Petri Nets. Specifications were firstly written as logical models, then transformed into appropriate formats, and finally formally verified (with some properties added) and synthesized.

As a support for testing, a tool has been developed, which allows automatic transformation of logical model into model description in the NuSMV format and into synthesizable code in hardware description language VHDL.

Rules for definition of rule-based logical model and model description in the NuSMV tool are described in section 3, while rules for synthesizable model definition in VHDL are given in section 4.

2. Description and illustration of proposed RLCs design system

Logic controller development process usually starts with specification, further goes through verification [16] and simulation, finally ending with implementation. Schema of proposed system for designing of logic controllers is presented in Figure 2.

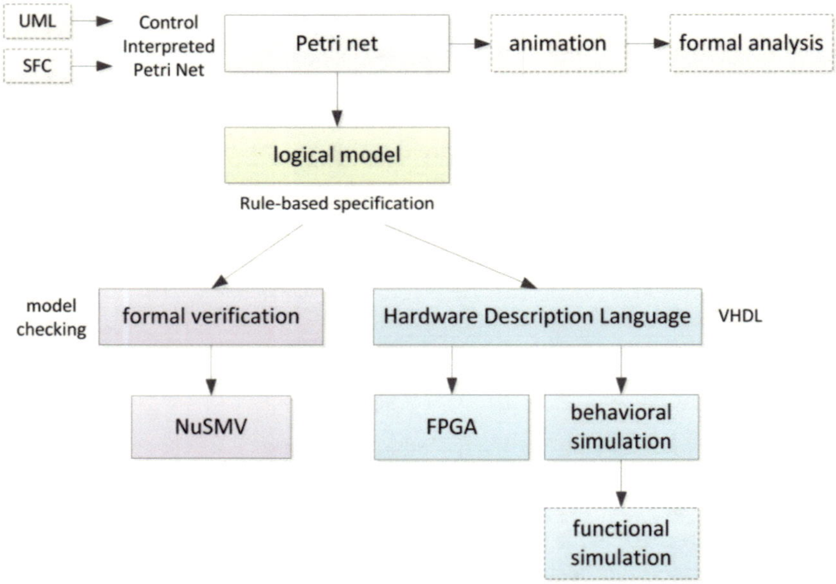

Figure 2. Schema of proposed system for designing of logic controllers

Formal specification is prepared by means of Control Interpreted Petri Nets [8]. They specify and model the behaviour of concurrent logic controllers and take into account properties of controlled objects. Local states, as in typical P/T Petri nets, may change after firing of transitions, if some events occur. Additionally, transition guards are associated with input signals of controller, while places are associated with its output signals.

Formally, a Control Interpreted Petri Net can be defined as a six-tuple:

$$CIPN = (PN, X, Y, \varrho, \lambda, \gamma) \tag{1}$$

where:

- PN is an alive and safe Petri net,
- X is a set of input states,
- Y is a set of output states,
- ρ is a function $T \rightarrow 2^X$, that each transition assigns the subset of input states $X(T)$; 2^X states for the set of all possible subsets of X,
- λ is a function of Moore outputs $M \rightarrow Y$, that each marking M assigns the subset of output states $Y(M)$,
- γ is a function of Mealy outputs $(M \times X) \rightarrow Y$, that each marking M and input states X assigns the subset of output states Y.

3. Novel approach to formal verification of logic controller specification

Control Interpreted Petri Net is first written as an abstract rule-based logical model. Then, basing on that model two other models are built – a verifiable model for the NuSMV model checker (described in details in section 3.2, together with requirements list definition expressed in temporal logic) and a synthesizable model in VHDL (for reconfigurable logic controllers, discussed in section 4). Thanks to proposed methodology, synthesized model is formally verified before the implementation and the two models are fully consistent with each other.

3.1. Rule-based logical model of a Control Interpreted Petri Net

Proposed rule-based logical model used for synthesis and verification purposes is an intermediate format describing desired behaviour of designed logic controller [13, 14]. Model includes variables definition and their initial values, rules describing net functionality, changes of logic controller output and input signal values.

Proposed logical model reflects the behaviour of Moore digital automaton with inputs register (optionally) and outputs register (Figure 3). Combinational circuit (CC) controls system behaviour and operates on internal system states.

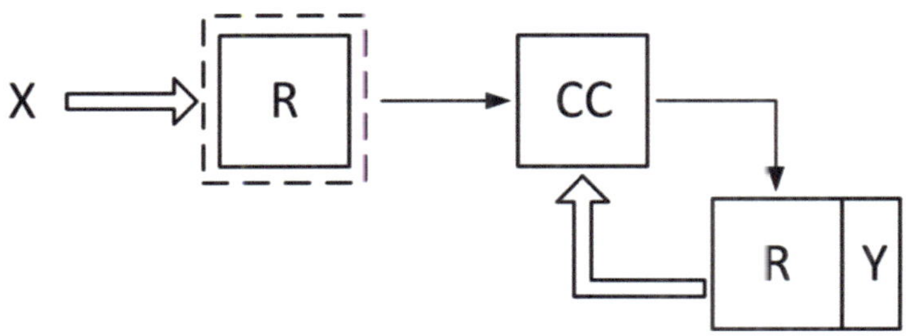

Figure 3. Moore digital automaton with inputs and outputs register

Formally, rule-based logical model can be defined as a seven-tuple:

$$LM = \{P, X, Y, S, T, O, I\} \quad (2)$$

where:

- *P* stands for places of a Control Interpreted Petri Net (internal local states),
- *X* stands for inputs of a Control Interpreted Petri Net (input signals to logic controller),
- *Y* stands for outputs of a Control Interpreted Petri Net (output signals to logic controller),
- *S* stands for initial values of places, inputs and outputs,
- *T* stands for rules describing transitions (indicating changes of local states),
- *O* stands for active outputs corresponding to appropriate places,
- *I* stands for inputs supposed to be active in appropriate places (for formal verification simplification).

As an example to demonstrate proposed solution a sample control process was chosen, described by means of Control Interpreted Petri Nets, then formally verified for behavioral properties and synthesized. Control process example was taken from. It was verified using CTL temporal logic and the NuSMV model checker in 2.5.2 version [19].

A simple embedded system for drink production is considered (Figure 4).

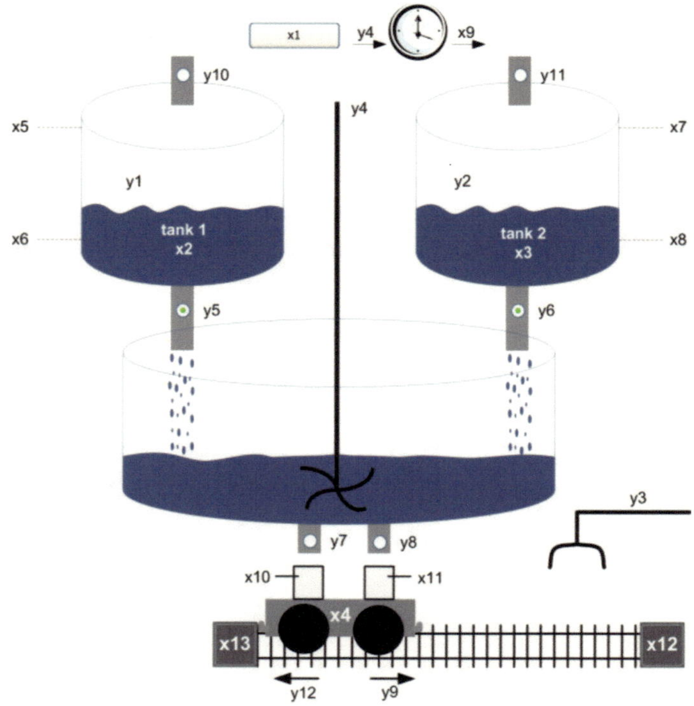

Figure 4. Real model of process for drink production

Logic controller schema with input and output signals (Table 1) is presented in Figure 5. A Control Interpreted Petri Net for drink production process is presented in Figure 6. It has 20 local states and initial marking involves two places – *P1* and *P14*.

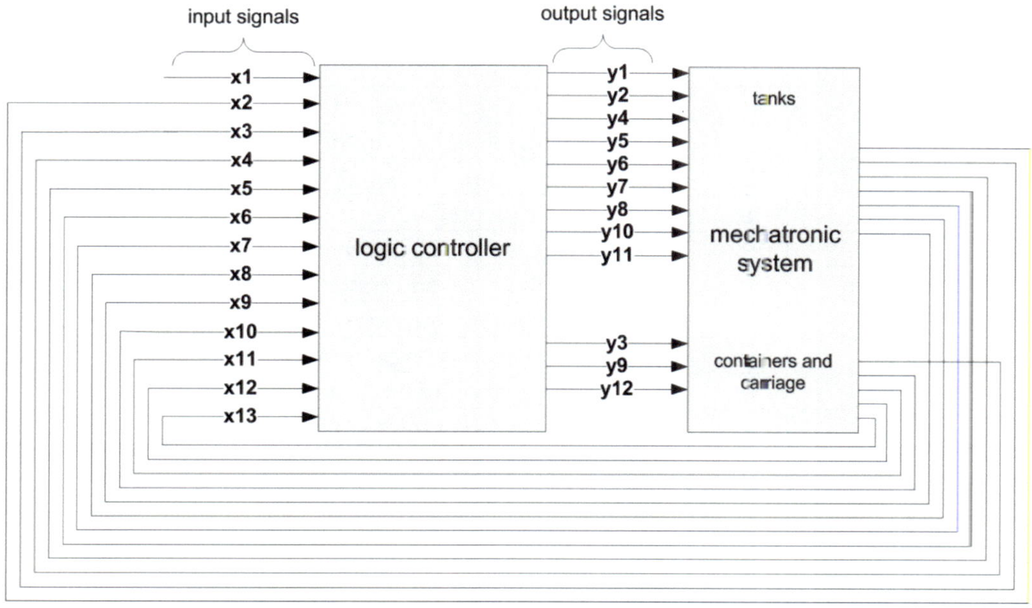

Figure 5. Logic controller schema

Initially, both tanks are empty and process can be started. After pressing the *x1* button, drink production process starts. Valves *y10* and *y11* are opened and target containers are loaded on the carriage (*y3*). Filling tanks process (active signals *y1* and *y2*) is a concurrent process. When a tank is already full (signalized by sensor *x5* or *x7* respectively), the appropriate valve for filling tank is closed. Meanwhile, loaded containers and transported (*y12*) to a proper location (sensor *x13*). When the ingredients are ready, it is signalized by sensors *x2*, *x3* and *x4*. Then, ingredients from both tanks are dropped into the main tank (signals *y5* and *y6*), where they are mixed (signal *y4*). Emptying of small tanks is signalized by sensors *x6* and *x8*. When the drink is well mixed, it is indicated by sensor *x9*. Then, ready drink is filled into containers (*y7*, *y8*). When containers filling process ends (sensors *x10*, *x11*), they are transported (signal *y9*) to their starting location (sensor *x12*).

A Control Interpreted Petri Net is written formally using temporal logic [15]. Logic representation well corresponds to net structure and behavior, and at the same time is easy to formally verify and to synthesize.

Logical model includes variables definition and their initial values. The following elements of Control Interpreted Petri Net are interpreted as model variables: places, input and output signals. Logical model involves also set of rules, which describe how defined variables change over time. Set of rules influences the system behaviour. Each rule (transition) is presented in a separate row and starts with transition name (a label for particular rule).

	Signal	Description
Inputs	*x1*	Signal to start the process
	x2	Ingredients preparation in the first tank is finished
	x3	Ingredients preparation in the second tank is finished
	x4	Containers preparation is finished
	x5	Maximal fluid level in the first tank
	x6	Minimal fluid level in the first tank
	x7	Maximal fluid level in the second tank
	x8	Minimal fluid level in the second tank
	x9	Drink preparation is finished
	x10	Filling of the first container is finished
	x11	Filling of the second container is finished
	x12	The carriage is in its starting location (the right side)
	x13	The carriage is in its target location (the left side)
Outputs	*y1*	Preparation of the first ingredient
	y2	Preparation of the second ingredient
	y3	Loading containers
	y4	Mixing ingredients
	y5	Valve for emptying the first tank
	y6	Valve for emptying the second tank
	y7	Valve for filling the first container
	y8	Valve for filling the second container
	y9	Carriage movement to the right
	y10	Valve for filling the first tank
	y11	Valve for filling the second tank
	y12	Carriage movement to the left

Table 1. Logic controller input and output signals

A rule consists of two separated parts. The first part contains conditions for transition firing, namely names of active places and input signals (if required) needed to fire the transition. If the condition involves more than one variable, variables are usually connected with a logical operator *and* (written as &). It is also possible to connect the variables with logical operator *or* (written as |), what can be used by transition activation with one of many input signals. Similar as by initial values of variables, a variable can take the *TRUE* value (active place / input signal) or the *FALSE* value (inactive input signal). The second part describes marking changing of Petri net places. Usage of a temporal logic operator *X* indicates that marking changing will take place in the next system state. Analogously to previous possible variable values, after transition firing some places can become active (transition output places) or inactive (transition input places, names of these variables are preceded by an exclamation mark). Proposed solution is focused on transitions. Here, transition input places, firing conditions (corresponding to appropriate combinations of input signals) and transition output places are taken into account.

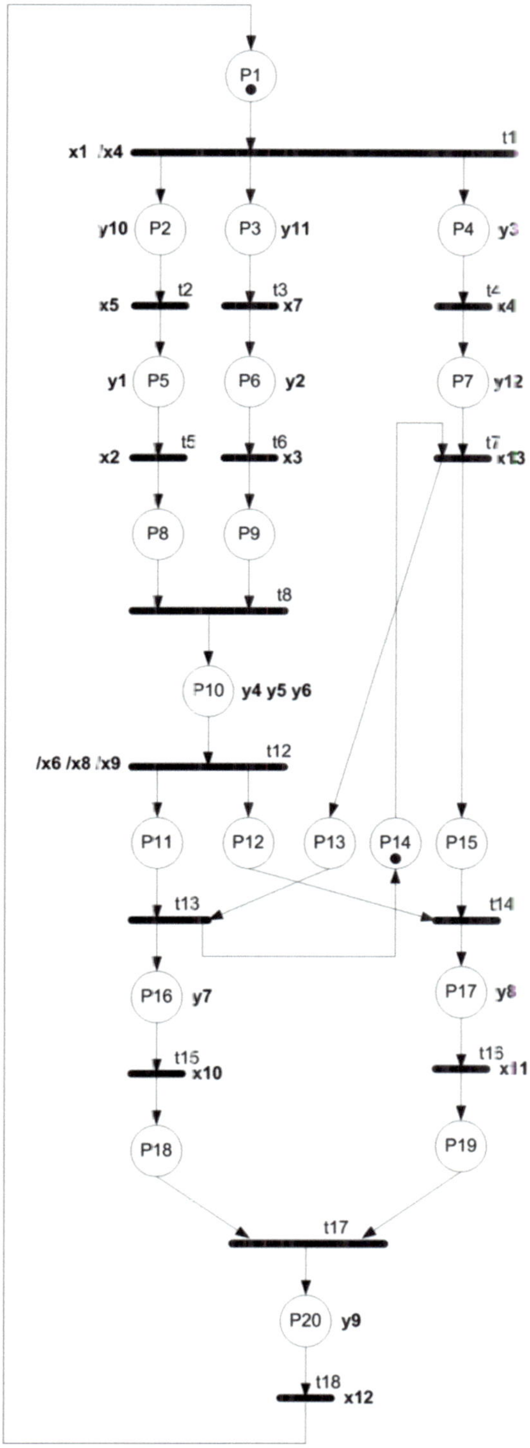

Figure 6. Control Interpreted Petri Net

Transitions from net from Figure 6 are described as separate rules (Figure 7). Firing of each transition changes marking of its input and output places. For example, firing of the *t1* transition removes token from the *p1* place (expressed by *!p1*) and adds a token into three places staring three concurrent processes: *p2, p3* and *p4* (expressed by *p2 & p3 & p4*).

```
t1: p1 & x1 & !x4 -> X (!p1 & p2 & p3 & p4);
t2: p2 & x5 -> X (!p2 & p5);
t3: p3 & x7 -> X (!p3 & p6);
...
```

Figure 7. Set of rules in logical model

Places not mentioned in particular rule do not change marking after firing of the (considered) transition. It means that the particular rule does not change marking of not mentioned places. Rules correspond therefore to Petri net transitions firings, and ipso facto marking changing of places. Situations, when a transition cannot be realized are not considered, supposing that active places hold then their marking. Proposed approach is an inertial description oriented on transitions (based on publications [1]. In the paper [11], because of the presence of Mealy outputs (where output signals values depend on input signal values and current internal system state), additionally output signals connected with particular transition firing are taken into account, besides places and input signals.

Output signals are considered for successive Petri net places. If the activity of particular output signal is connected with more than one place, this signal occurs multiple times on the right side of an arrow, by different places. Proposed notation concerns Moore outputs, where output state depends only from internal state of the system.

Output signals from the net in Figure 6 are therefore assigned to places, in which they are active (Figure 8). For example, the *y10* output signal is active only by active marking of the *p2* place, and active marking of the *p10* place implies the activity of output signals *y4, y5* and *y6*. The other output signals, which are not present on the right side of particular rule (for particular places) remain default inactive. It is also possible to evidently indicate the activity or inactivity of output signal, as in [1], proposed solutions seems however to be intuitive and does not enforce additional information, which could negative influence its readability.

```
p2 -> y10;
p3 -> y11;
p4 -> y3;
...
p10 -> y4 & y5 & y6;
...
```

Figure 8. Output signals in logical model

Input signals changes are also defined in logical model. However, the definition is only used by model checking process (model description preparation). In the HDL (*Hardware Description Language*) file, input signals are not concerned as they are inputs to the logic controller. Input signals coming from different objects, supervising system or system operator are considered analogously like output signals for successive Petri net places.

Input signals from the net in Figure 6 are assigned to places, where they are essential and may become active (Figure 9). In each other state, the signals remains by default inactive. For example, input signal *x5* can be activated, when Petri net marking involves the place *p2*.

```
p1 -> (!x1 | x1) & (!x4 | x4);
p2 -> !x5 | x5;
p3 -> !x7 | x7;
...
```

Figure 9. Input signals in logical model

3.2. Model checking of rule-based logical model

Model checking technique [7, 10] is one of formal verification methods among others like e.g. *theorem proving* or *equivalence checking* and is currently used in the industry in software and hardware production [12]. System model is compared with defined properties and an answer whether they are satisfied or not is given. In case of any detected errors, appropriate counterexamples are generated which allow to localize error source.

Model checking process can be performed on the whole system or just on a part of it (so-called *partial verification*), what has an important meaning especially by complex systems which can be divided into subsystems.

Logical model derived from Control Interpreted Petri Net is transformed into format of the NuSMV model checker according to some strictly specified rules [13, 14]:

a. Each place $p \in P$ is a variable of Boolean type,
b. Each input signal $x \in X$ is a variable of Boolean type,
c. Each output signal $y \in Y$ is a variable of Boolean type,
d. Defined variable take some initial values. Each variable takes any of two values (*TRUE* or *FALSE*),
e. Each place changes according to the rules defined in the transitions T and the function $\rho: T \rightarrow 2^X$; conditions of changes between places (token flow) occur in pairs (groups) – in the previous place(s) and in the next place(s),
f. Each output signal changes according to the rules defined in the function $\lambda: M \rightarrow Y$,
g. Each input signal changes randomly, but can take the expected values connected with Petri net places or change adequately to the situation.

Logical model into NuSMV model description translation is done automatically using implemented software application.

Similar like in logical model, model description for verification starts with variables definition, which correspond to places, input and output signals. Then, initial values are assigned to the variables. Rules describing net behaviour and token flow correspond to values changes of appropriate places (active/inactive marking of places, Figure 10). Input signals change their value only in expected situations (Figure 11). Output signals are in turn active when appropriate places include token (Figure 12).

```
next(p1) := case
   p1 & x1 & !x4   : FALSE;
   p20 & x12       : TRUE;
   TRUE            : p1;
esac;
next(p2) := case
   p2 & x5         : FALSE;
   p1 & x1 & !x4   : TRUE;
   TRUE            : p2;
esac;
...
```

Figure 10. Rules in verifiable model (assignment of next values to places)

```
next(x1) := case
   p1    : {FALSE, TRUE};
   TRUE  : FALSE;
esac;
next(x2) := case
   p5    : {FALSE, TRUE};
   TRUE  : FALSE;
esac;
...
```

Figure 11. Assignment of next values to input signals in verifiable model

```
next(y1) := case
   p5    : TRUE;
   TRUE  : FALSE;
esac;
next(y2) := case
   p6    : TRUE;
   TRUE  : FALSE;
esac;
...
```

Figure 12. Assignment of next values to output signals in verifiable model

Model description is the first part needed for model checking. Additionally, it is necessary to specify some requirements, which are supposed (expected) to be true in defined model. Structural properties can also be checked on the Petri net level (and do not require model checking technique). However, the most important are here behavioural properties, which describe system functionality, impact of input signals and output signals activity.

Properties to be checked are defined using temporal logic [6, 15, 20] – either LTL (*Linear Temporal Logic*) or CTL (*Computation Tree Logic*). Properties describe safety requirements (*something bad will never happen*), as well as liveness requirements (*something good will eventually happen*). Safety and liveness requirements are the most frequently specified requirements to be verified.

The requirements list should include as much desired properties as possible, as only they will be checked. It is often written basing on an informal specification. In the best practices, it is specified by customer (in textual form) or by engineers not involved in design process (in more or less formalized way).

Using CTL temporal logic the requirements list for considered case study was defined (properties are listed in Figure 13 and described in details in Table 2). All specified requirements are satisfied in the corresponding model description. Some properties concern Petri net structure itself (properties 1 – 20). It is checked, whether particular places are reachable. Next properties describe output signals, which cannot be active at the same time (properties 21 – 23). The last part of properties regards the correlation of input and output signals.

```
CTLSPEC EF p1;                      --1
...                                 ...
CTLSPEC EF p20;                     --20
CTLSPEC AG !(y5 & y10);             --21
CTLSPEC AG !(y6 & y11);             --22
CTLSPEC AG !(y9 & y12);             --23
CTLSPEC AG (x5 -> AF !y10);         --24
CTLSPEC AG (x7 -> AF !y11);         --25
CTLSPEC AG (x13 -> AF !y12);        --26
CTLSPEC AG (x12 -> AF !y9);         --27
```

Figure 13. Requirements list

Property	Description
1	It is possible to reach the *p1* place
...	...
20	It is possible to reach the *p20* place
21	The *y5* and *y10* output signals can never be active at the same time
22	The *y6* and *y11* output signals can never be active at the same time
23	The *y9* and *y12* output signals can never be active at the same time
24	Always, when the *x5* input signal is active (maximal fluid level in the first tank), finally the *y10* output signal (controlling valve for filling the first tank) becomes inactive
25	Always, when the *x7* input signal is active (maximal fluid level in the second tank), finally the *y11* output signal (controlling valve for filling the second tank) becomes inactive
26	Always, when the *x13* input signal is active (carriage location on the left), finally the *y12* output signal (carriage movement to the left) becomes inactive
27	Always, when the *x12* input signal is active (carriage location on the right), finally the *y9* output signal (carriage movement to the right) becomes inactive

Table 2. Requirements list description

By introducing a subtle modification into Control Interpreted Petri Net, which regards initial marking removing from place *p14* (initial marking involves then only the *p1* place), the corresponding part of logical model and NuSMV model description is also changed. However, such a subtle change dramatically changes net behavior, and thereby designed logic controller behavior. Model checking of the same properties shows now another results. User receives multiple generated counterexamples indicating unsatisfied requirements. Places *p1* to *p12* are reachable, but it is not possible to reach active marking of further places. Next to last requirement is also not satisfied (*CTLSPEC AG (x13 -> AF !y12)*). Summarizing the report – an error occurs starting from transitions *t7* and t*13*, what confirms the fact, that it is indeed correlated with additional initial marking (and actually the lack of it) of Control Interpreted Petri Net.

When model checking process does not indicate any errors, it is then possible and advisable to focus on synthesizable code. Basing on logical model, model in hardware description language VHDL is built. The model is fully synthesizable and may be then implemented in FPGA for a reconfigurable logic controller.

4. Synthesis of rule-based logical model

Combining FPGA [18] as a target hardware platform with hardware description language VHDL ensures high reliability, speed and safety. Additionally, it is possible to modify anytime the already running system, what has a practical sense. Direct implementation of concurrent logic controllers in FPGA is similar to rule-based realization based on classical sequence diagrams. Transition firings are synchronized with clock rising edge.

Control Interpreted Petri Net, which is the core for logical model, is a safe net. Places can be then implemented using simple flip-flops, as their marking is expressed by a binary value. Flip-flops amount (for places) using one-hot encoding is equal to the amount of places (and so to the amount of local states).

Logical model can be easy synthesized as reconfigurable logic controller. Logical model, derived from Control Interpreted Petri Net, is transformed into VHDL language according to some strictly defined rules [13]:

a. Each place is an internal signal of *std_logic* type,
b. Each input signal is an input port of *std_logic* type,
c. Each output signal is an output port of *std_logic* type,
d. Each defined internal signal (Petri net place) takes an initial value, set by clock rising edge and active reset signal,
e. Each place changes its marking according to defined rules; fired transition changes marking of its input and output places,
f. Input signals are not considered, as they are inputs to the logic controller,
g. Each output signal changes its value according to active places; output signals are active by active marking of corresponding places.

Model in VHDL is oriented on places and transitions. It can be simulated and synthesized. Synthesis is performed in form of rapid prototyping [5], what in modern methodology for digital circuits design allows for frequent verification (simulation, analysis) of developed system. Its main goal is to check, whether designed system works at all, but the circuit might be not optimized. Circuit optimization and minimization of resources usage are here out of scope, however they may be important in some fields [9, 18].

Logical model into VHDL model translation is done automatically using implemented software application. Generated VHDL file for considered drink production process is fully synthesizable.

Model for synthesis starts with input and output signals definition. Petri net places are defined as internal signals. By clock rising edge and active reset signal, some initial values are assigned to places, which correspond to initial marking of a Control Interpreted Petri Net. Additionally, by each clock rising edge places hold their heretofore marking.

For places the one-hot encoding was used (called also *isomorphic places encoding*), which is the most accurate (and the simplest) representation of logical model, however it can cause bigger resources usage. For each place one flip-flop is generated, which label corresponds to particular place etiquette. Flip-flop sets the *1* value, if a place contains token, otherwise it holds the *0* value. Additionally, one-hot encoding is recommended by implementation in FPGA circuits, and even seen as the most effective method for states encoding [23], i.e. in FPGA circuits of Xilinx [21], especially for small automata. It is also possible to extend the work to any other encoding.

Places marking can change after transitions firing. Conditions connected with transitions correspond to values of input signals and active marking of particular places. If a condition is satisfied, Petri net transition is realized, and thereby its input and output places change their marking (Figure 14).

```
if p1 = '1' and x1 = '1' and x4 = '0' then
   p1 <= '0';
   p2 <= '1';
   p3 <= '1';
   p4 <= '1';
end if;
```

Figure 14. The *t1* transition firing in VHDL model

Output signals are active by active marking of appropriate places, what is denoted as shown in Figure 15.

```
y1 <= p5;
y2 <= p6;
y3 <= p4;
...
```

Figure 15. Outputs assignment in VHDL model

Input signals value changes come from outside and are not modified inside VHDL model file. Their values are just read out by conditions related to transition firings.

VHDL file can also be simulated i.e. in *Active-HDL* environment [4]. Simulation confirms the proper functionality of designed logic controller (simulation results are presented in Figure 16).

It is then possible to perform logic synthesis and implementation, i.e. in *Xilinx PlanAhead* environment, in version *13.1* [21]. Sample resources usage for the *xa6slx4csg225-2* circuit from *Spartan6* family of *XILINX* [22] is listed in Table 3.

Resource	Utilization	Available	Utilization
Register	18	4800	1%
LUT	18	2400	1%
Slice	6	600	1%
IO	27	132	20%
Global Clock Buffer	1	16	6%

Table 3. Resources usage

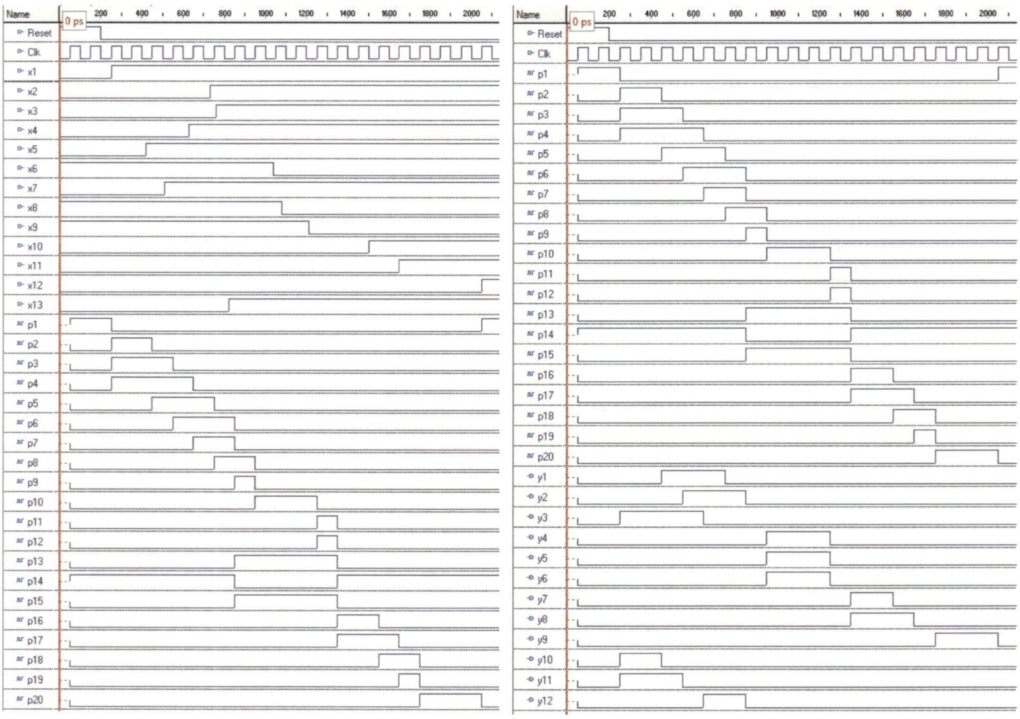

Figure 16. Simulation results in *Active-HDL*

It is also possible to transform logical model into synthesizable code in Verilog language [9, 17], this aspect is however not discussed further in this chapter.

5. Summary and conclusions

Proposed novel approach to verification of reconfigurable logic controller programs and specification by means of Control Interpreted Petri Nets allows to detect even subtle errors on an early stage of system development. Rule-based representation of Control Interpreted Petri Nets in temporal logic is presented at RTL-level and is easy to formally verify using model checking technique and to synthesize using hardware description languages.

Results of the work include the assurance that verified behavioural specification in temporal logic will be an abstract program of matrix reconfigurable logic controller. Hence, logic controller program (its implementation) will be valid according to its primary specification. This may shorten the duration time of logic controllers development process (as early discovered errors are faster corrected) and, consequently, save money (as project budgets will not be exceeded).

Furthermore, formal verification can improve the quality of final products, making them work more reliable. And even if a logic controller, already delivered to customer, will not work properly (it can always happen that some subtle error was overseen or that the specification was incomplete), it is possible to find error source using available techniques (verification, simulation, etc.). Then, some part of corrected system (or the whole system) may be one more time formally verified using extended requirements list and modified logical model.

Future research directions include i.e. (but are not limited to) model checking of other forms of logic controllers specification and mechanisms for behavioural properties specification.

Author details

Iwona Grobelna
University of Zielona Góra, Poland

6. Acknowledgement

The author is a scholar within Sub-measure 8.2.2 Regional Innovation Strategies, Measure 8.2 Transfer of knowledge, Priority VIII Regional human resources for the economy Human Capital Operational Programme co-financed by European Social Fund and state budget.

7. References

[1] Adamski, M & Monteiro, J. L., From Interpreted Petri net specification to Reprogrammable Logic Controller Design, In: *Proceedings of the IEEE International Symposium on Industrial Electronics*, 2000, Vol. 1, pp. 13 – 19.

[2] Adamski, M.A.; Karatkevich, A. & Węgrzyn, M.. *Design of embedded control systems*, Springer Verlag ; 2005.

[3] Adamski, M.; Kołopieńczyk, M. & Mielcarek, K.. Perfect Petri Net in parallel control circuits (in Polish), *Measurement Automation and Monitoring*, 2011, Vol. 57, No. 6, pp. 656 – 660.

[4] Aldec home page. The producer of Active-HLD environment. http://www.aldec.com/ (access 15.04.2012)

[5] Andreu, D.; Souquet, G. & Gil, T.. Petri Net based rapid prototyping of digital complex system, *IEEE Computer Society Annual Symposium on VLSI 2008*, pp. 405 – 410.

[6] Ben-Ari, M., *Mathematical logic for computer science*, Springer Verlag ; 2001.

[7] Clarke, E.M.; Grumberg, O. &Peled, D.A., Model checking, The MIT Press ; 1999.

[8] David, R. & Alla, H., *Discrete, Continuous, and Hybrid Petri Nets*, Springer Verlag ; 2010.

[9] De Micheli, G., *Synthesis and Optimization of Digital Circuits*, McGraw-Hill Higher Education; 1994.

[10] Emerson, E.A., The Beginning of Model Checking: A Personal Perspective, In: *25 Years of Model Checking: History, Achievements, Perspectives*, O. Grumberg, H. Veith (Ed.), Springer Verlag ; 2008, pp. 27 – 45.

[11] Fernandes, J.M. ; Adamski, M. & Proenca, A.J., VHDL generation from hierarchical Petri net specifications of parallel controllers, *IEE Proceedings – Computers and Digital Techniques*, 1997, Vol. 144, No. 2, pp. 127 – 137.

[12] Fix, L., Fifteen years of formal property verification in Intel, In: O. Grumberg, H. Veith (Ed.), *25 Years of Model Checking: History, Achievements, Perspectives*, Springer Verlag ; 2008, pp. 139 – 144.

[13] Grobelna, I., Formal verification of embedded logic controller specification with computer deduction in temporal logic, Electrical Review, 2011, nr 12a, 2011, pp. 47 – 50.

[14] Grobelna, I. & Adamski, M., Model Checking of Control Interpreted Petri Nets, *Proceedings of the 18th International Conference Mixed Design of Integrated Circuits and Systems 2011*, pp. 621 – 626 (available in IEEE Xplore).

[15] Huth, M. & Ryan, M., *Logic in Computer Science. Modelling and Reasoning about Systems*, Cambridge University Press ; 2004.

[16] Kropf, T., *Introduction to Formal Hardware Verification*, Springer Verlag ; 1999.

[17] Minns, P. & Elliott, I., *FSM based Digital Design using Verilog HDL*, Wiley ; 2008.

[18] Nemec, J., Stoke the fires of FPGA design, *Electronic design*, 1994, Vol. 42, Issue 22, pp. 97 – 105.

[19] NuSMV model checker homepage: http://nusmv.fbk.eu/ (access 15.04.2012)

[20] Rice, M.V. & Vardi, M.Y., *Branching vs. Linear Time: Final Showdown*, Proceedings of the 2001 Conference on Tools and Algorithms for the Construction and Analysis of Systems, Lecture Notes in Computer Science, Vol. 2031, Springer Verlag; 2001, pp. 1 – 22.

[21] Xilinx homepage. The producer of XILINX ISE and XILINX PlanAhead software. http://www.xilinx.com (access 15.04.2012)

[22] Xilinx FPGA Spartan6 family home page. http://www.xilinx.com/products/silicon-devices/fpga/spartan-6/index.htm(access 15.04.2012)

[23] Zwoliński, M., *Digital System Design with VHDL*, Prentice Hall; 2004.

Section 2

Computer Science

Sequential Object Petri Nets and the Modeling of Multithreading Object-Oriented Programming Systems

Ivo Martiník

Additional information is available at the end of the chapter

http://dx.doi.org/10.5772/48470

1. Introduction

Sequential object Petri nets are the newly introduced class of Petri nets, whose definition is the main topics of this article; they feature certain original concepts and can be successfully used at a design, modeling and verification of multithreading object-oriented programming systems executing in highly-parallel or distributed environment. In this article basic characteristics of sequential object Petri nets are very briefly presented including possibilities in their definition of newly introduced tokens as non-empty finite recursive sequences over the set of non-negative integer numbers, functionalities of multiarcs and the mechanism of the firing of transitions. These properties significantly increase modeling capabilities of this class of Petri nets at the modeling of multithreading object-oriented programming systems. Sequential object Petri nets can be used also in the area of recursive algorithms modeling and they are also the initial step to explicitly represent paradigms of functional programming. The fusion of object-oriented and functional programming enables to express new kinds of programming patterns and component abstractions.

The theory of sequential object Petri nets proceeds from the theories of various types of Petri nets, starting with Place/Transition nets (Diaz, 2009) and their sub-classes, followed by High-Level nets (Jensen & Rozenberg, 1991), (Reisig, 2009) such as Predicate-Transition nets and Coloured nets (Jensen & Kristensen, 2009), enabling to model apart from the management structure of the system even data processing, and in connection with modeling of object-oriented programming systems it is Object nets (Agha et. al., 2001), (Köhler & Rölke, 2007), which are being studied lately. But practical usability of Petri nets (in their original form) in the role of the parallel programming language is mainly impeded by the static nature of their structure. They are missing standard mechanisms for description of methods alone, programming modules, classes, data types, hierarchical structures, etc.

Positive characteristics of Petri nets demonstrate only in not too much large-scale modules at high abstraction level. That is why Petri nets are often understood as the theoretical abstract module only, whose applicability for design, analysis and verification of extensive programming systems is limited. Therefore, this article briefly describes a special class of sequential object Petri nets and its possibilities of multithreading object-oriented programming systems modeling, which eliminates the stated shortcomings required for design, analysis and verification of these systems in several directions.

This chapter is arranged into the following sections: in the section 2 is described the term of the sequence over the finite set and its properties which denominates the class of the sequential object Petri nets; section 3 explains the base term of this chapter, ie. sequential object Petri net and its properties; section 4 explains in details implementation of the mechanism of firing of transitions in a sequential object Petri net; section 5 then discusses the area of object-oriented programming systems and their representation by the sequential object Petri nets; section 6 explains the example of simple class hierarchy represented by the sequential object Petri net and it is inspired by the several base classes of the Java programming language class hierarchy. Finally, the section 7 gives the conclusions of the research to conclude the chapter.

2. Sequences and their properties

Prior to the formal introduction of the term of sequential object Petri net, we present the definition of sequence over the finite set from which the denomination of this class of Petri nets has been derived. $\mathbf{N}$ denotes the set of all natural numbers, $\mathbf{N}_0$ the set of all non-negative integer numbers, $P(A)$ denotes the family of all the subsets of given set A.

Let A be a non-empty set. By the (non-empty finite) **sequence** σ over the set A we understand a mapping σ: $\{1, 2, \ldots, n\} \rightarrow A$, where $n \in \mathbf{N}$. Mapping ε: $\varnothing \rightarrow A$ is called the **empty sequence** over the set A. We usually represent the sequence σ: $\{1, 2, \ldots, n\} \rightarrow A$ by the notation $\sigma = \langle a_1, a_2, \ldots, a_n \rangle$ of the elements of the set A, where $a_i = \sigma(i)$ for $1 \leq i \leq n$. We also consider any element of the set A as the sequence over the set A, ie. mapping σ:$\{1\} \rightarrow A$. Empty sequence ε: $\varnothing \rightarrow A$ over the set A we usually represent by the notation $\varepsilon = \langle\rangle$. We denote the set of all **finite non-empty** sequences over the set A by the notation A_{SQ}, the set of all **finite** (and possible empty) sequences over the set A by the notation A_{ESQ}.

Note also, that the set A can be any non-empty set, which means that it can be also the non-empty set of sequences over some non-empty set B, ie. $A = B_{ESQ}$. Thus member of the sequence over the set B_{ESQ} can be then another sequence over the set B. This fact thus also similarly allows sequences over the sets $(B_{ESQ})_{ESQ}$, $((B_{ESQ})_{ESQ})_{ESQ}$, etc. The term of sequence over some non-empty set has thus **recursive character** and every such sequence can consists from **subsequences** consisting from subsequences etc. We denote the set of all **finite non-empty** sequences without the empty subsequences over the union of sets A, A_{SQ}, $(A_{SQ})_{SQ}$, $((A_{SQ})_{SQ})_{SQ}$, … by the notation A_{RQ}, the set of all **finite** (and possible empty or with empty subsequences) sequences over the union of sets A, A_{ESQ}, $(A_{ESQ})_{ESQ}$, $((A_{ESQ})_{ESQ})_{ESQ}$, … by the notation A_{ERQ}.

The **length of the sequence** $\sigma = \langle a_1, a_2, \ldots, a_n \rangle$, where $\sigma \in A_{ERQ}$, $n \in N$, is equal to the natural number n, the length of the empty sequence ε is equal to the number 0. The length of the sequence σ we represent by the notation $length(\sigma)$, or $@\sigma$, the set of all the elements of the sequence σ we represent by the notation $elem(\sigma)$, ie. $elem(\sigma) = \{a_i \mid a_i = \sigma(i) \text{ for } 1 \le i \le n\}$, $elem(\varepsilon) = \emptyset$. The **subsequences of the sequence** σ is the mapping $subsq$: $A_{ERQ} \to P(A_{ERQ})$, such that for $\forall i, 1 \le i \le n$: $((\sigma \in subsq(\sigma)) \vee (((a_i == \varepsilon) \vee (a_i \in A)) \Rightarrow a_i \in subsq(\sigma)) \vee (((a_i \,!= \varepsilon) \wedge (a_i \notin A)) \Rightarrow ((a_i \in subsq(\sigma)) \wedge (subsq(a_i) \in subsq(\sigma)))$. The **members of the sequence** σ is the mapping $memb$: $A_{ERQ} \to P(A)$, so that $memb(\sigma) = \{a \mid (a \in subsq(\sigma)) \wedge (a \in A)\}$, $memb(\varepsilon) = \emptyset$.

If $\sigma = \langle a_1, a_2, \ldots, a_n \rangle$ and $\tau = \langle b_1, b_2, \ldots, b_m \rangle$ are the finite sequences, where $\sigma \in A_{ERQ}$, $\tau \in A_{ERQ}$, $n \in \mathbf{N}$, $m \in \mathbf{N}$, then by the **concatenation of the sequences** σ and τ, denoted by $\sigma\tau$, we understand the finite sequence $\sigma\tau = \langle a_1, a_2, \ldots, a_n, b_1, b_2, \ldots, b_m \rangle$ and its length is equal to $n + m$. We say, that the sequences σ and τ are **equal**, denoted by $\sigma == \tau$, if the following is simultaneously true: $(n = m) \wedge (\forall i, 1 \le i \le n$: $(((a_i = \varepsilon) \wedge (b_i = \varepsilon)) \vee ((a_i \in A) \wedge (b_i \in A) \wedge (a_i = b_i)) \vee ((a_i \ne \varepsilon) \wedge (b_i \ne \varepsilon) \wedge (a_i \notin A) \wedge (b_i \notin A) \wedge (a_i == b_i))))$.

If, for instance, $\tau \in A_{ERQ}$, $\tau = \langle\langle a, \langle a, b\rangle\rangle, \langle a, \langle c\rangle, b\rangle, \langle\rangle\rangle$, then $length(\tau) = 3$, $elem(\tau) = \{\langle a, \langle a, b\rangle\rangle, \langle a, \langle c\rangle, b\rangle, \langle\rangle\}$, $subsq(\tau) = \{\langle\langle a, \langle a, b\rangle\rangle, \langle a, \langle c\rangle, b\rangle, \langle\rangle\rangle, \langle a, \langle a, b\rangle\rangle, \langle a, \langle c\rangle, b\rangle, \langle a, b\rangle, \langle a\rangle, \langle b\rangle, \langle c\rangle, \langle\rangle\}$ and $memb(\tau) = \{a, b, c\}$.

When operating with sequences, notation in the form of $n^*(\sigma)$ can be utilized, where $\sigma \in A_{ERQ}$, $n \in \mathbf{N}$. Informally, that notation expresses sequence consisting of n concatenations of the sequence σ. If, for example $A = \mathbf{N}_0$, $\sigma = \langle 1, 2\rangle$, then notation $3^*(\sigma)$ represents the sequence $3^*(\langle 1, 2\rangle) == \langle 1, 2\rangle\langle 1, 2\rangle\langle 1, 2\rangle == \langle 1, 2, 1, 2, 1, 2\rangle$.

Multiset M over a non-empty set S is a function m: $S \to \mathbf{N}_0$. By the non-negative number $m(a) \in \mathbf{N}_0$, $a \in S$, we denote the number of occurrences of the element a in the multiset m. We usually represent the multiset m by the formal sum $\sum_{a \in S} m(a)`a$. By S_{MS} we denote the set of all non-empty multisets over the set S, by S_{EMS} we denote the set of all multisets over the set S.

IDENT denotes the set of all **identifiers** and it is understood to be a set of non-empty finite sequences over the set of all letters of the selected national alphabet and the set of all decadic digits that starts with a letter. Identifiers are recorded in a way usual for standard programming languages. Examples of correctly formed identifiers for example involve the *thread, var22, $\alpha\beta\chi\delta$*, etc. On the contrary, for example sequences *2main, first goal, _input*, are not identifiers. Moreover is it true, that if $ID_1, ID_2, \ldots, ID_n \in$ ***IDENT***, where $n \in \mathbf{N}$, $n > 1$, then we call the sequence in the form $ID_1.ID_2. \ldots .ID_n$ **compound identifier** (i.e. for example the sequence *Main.Thread.Variable1* is a compound identifier). ***#IDENT*** set is understood to be the set of all non-empty finite sequences in the form #A, where A $\in$ ***IDENT***. Then, elements of ***#IDENT*** set for example include sequences *#thread, #var22, #$\alpha\beta\chi\delta$*, etc.

The set $(\mathbf{N}_0)_{RQ}$ we will denote by the symbol ***Tokens***. The set ***ArcSeq*** (*arc sequences*) is defined by the following:

i. if $x \in$ (***IDENT*** $\cup$ ***#IDENT***), then $\langle x\rangle \in$ ***ArcSeq***,
ii. if $x \in$ ***Tokens***, then $x \in$ ***ArcSeq***,

iii. if $x \in \boldsymbol{ArcSeq}$, then $<x> \in \boldsymbol{ArcSeq}$ and also $<length(x)> \in \boldsymbol{ArcSeq}$,
iv. if $x \in \boldsymbol{ArcSeq}$ and $y \in \boldsymbol{ArcSeq}$, then $xy \in \boldsymbol{ArcSeq}$,
v. if $n \in (\boldsymbol{IDENT} \cup \boldsymbol{N})$ and $x \in \boldsymbol{ArcSeq}$, then $n^*(x) \in \boldsymbol{ArcSeq}$.

The elements of ***Tokens*** set for example involve sequences <1>, <22, <0, 0>>, <<3, 2>, <4, <7, 8>>>, etc.). The set of arc sequences ***ArcSeq*** is, informally said, the set of **non-empty final recursive sequences** over the set (***IDENT*** ∪ ***#IDENT*** ∪ ***Tokens***) which do not contain empty subsequences and which can contain as their members even selected operations over those recursive sequences, between which is the determination of the recursive sequence length and concatenation of recursive sequences. So examples of elements of the set ***ArcSeq*** can be sequences <a, b, 1>, <#s, @(s), <1, <2, 3>>>, <a, thread, a*(<thread>), <1, 0>>, etc.

Let $AS \in \boldsymbol{ArcSeq}$, $AS = <a_1, a_2, \ldots, a_n>$, where $n \in \boldsymbol{N}$. Then the mapping *variables*: ***ArcSeq*** → $P(\boldsymbol{IDENT} \cup \boldsymbol{\#IDENT} \cup \boldsymbol{N_0})$ is defined so that for $\forall AS \in \boldsymbol{ArcSeq}\ \forall i, 1 \le i \le n$:

i. if $a_i \in (\boldsymbol{IDENT} \cup \boldsymbol{\#IDENT})$, then $a_i \in variables(AS)$,
ii. if $a_i \in \boldsymbol{Tokens}$, then $memb(a_i) \subseteq variables(AS)$,
iii. if $a_i = <x>$, where $x \in \boldsymbol{ArcSeq}$, then $variables(x) \subseteq variables(AS)$,
iv. if $a_i = length(x)$, where $x \in \boldsymbol{ArcSeq}$, then $variables(x) \subseteq variables(AS)$,
v. if $a_i = xy$, where $x \in \boldsymbol{ArcSeq}$ and $y \in \boldsymbol{ArcSeq}$, then $(variables(x) \subseteq variables(AS)) \wedge (variables(y) \subseteq variables(AS))$,
vi. if $a_i = n^*(x)$, where $n \in (\boldsymbol{IDENT} \cup \boldsymbol{N})$ and $x \in \boldsymbol{ArcSeq}$, then $(n \in variables(AS)) \wedge (variables(x) \subseteq variables(AS))$.

Thus mapping *variables* assigns to each arc sequence $AS \in \boldsymbol{ArcSeq}$, $AS = <a_1, a_2, \ldots, a_n>$, where $n \in \boldsymbol{N}$, the set of members from the sets ***IDENT***, ***#IDENT*** a $\boldsymbol{N_0}$ contained in it. The set of *variables*(*AS*) associated with a particular arc *AS* will be identified in the text by the term **variables of the arc sequence *AS***. So if for example *AS* = <a, thread, a*(<thread>), <1, 0>>, then *variables*(*AS*) = {a, thread, 1, 0}.

3. Sequential object Petri nets and their properties

Sequential Object Petri Net is an ordered pair $SOPN = (\Sigma, PN)$, where

i. Σ is a finite non-empty set of **pages,**
ii. *PN* is a **page number function**, $PN: \Sigma \to \boldsymbol{N}$, that is injective.

By elements of the finite non-empty set Σ of pages we routinely mark identifiers from the set ***IDENT***. Injective function *PN* of numbering of pages of the net assigns to each page of sequential object Petri net *SOPN* the unique natural number within the net.

Let $SOPN = (\Sigma, PN)$ is a sequential object Petri net. **Page** of the sequential object Petri net *SOPN* is an ordered touple $PG = (P, IP, OP, T, A, MA, IOPN, AF, MAF, TP, IPF, OPF, SP, IF)$, $PG \in \Sigma$, where:

i. *P* is a finite set of **places**,
ii. *IP* is a finite set of **input places**, $P \cap IP = \emptyset$,

iii. OP is a finite set of **output places**, $P \cap OP = \emptyset$,
iv. T is a finite set of **transitions**, $(P \cup IP \cup OP) \cap T = \emptyset$,
v. A is a finite set of **arcs**, $A \subseteq ((P \cup IP) \times T) \cup (T \times (P \cup OP))$,
vi. MA is a finite set of **multiarcs**, $MA \subseteq ((P \cup IP) \times T) \cup (T \times (P \cup OP))$, $A \cap MA = \emptyset$,
vii. $IOPN$ is a function of **input and output place numbers**, $IOPN$: $(IP \cup OP) \rightarrow \mathbf{N}$, that is injective,
viii. AF is an **arc function**, AF: $(A \cup MA) \rightarrow \boldsymbol{ArcSeq}$,
ix. MAF is a **multiarc function**, MAF: $MA \rightarrow \boldsymbol{ArcSeq}$,
x. TP is a function of **transition priorities**, TP: $T \rightarrow \mathbf{N}$,
xi. IPF is an **input place function** of multiarcs, IPF: $(T \times (P \cup OP)) \rightarrow AIP$, where $(T \times (P \cup OP)) \subseteq MA$, $AIP = \{p \mid \exists \gamma \in \Sigma : p \in IP \in \gamma\}$,
xii. OPF is an **output place function** of multiarcs, OPF: $((P \cup IP) \times T) \rightarrow AOP$, where $((P \cup IP) \times T) \subseteq MA$, $AOP = \{p \mid \exists \gamma \in \Sigma : p \in OP \in \gamma\}$,
xiii. SP is a finite set of **subpages**, $SP \subseteq \Sigma$
xiv. IF is an **initialization function**, IF: $(P \cup IP \cup OP) \rightarrow \boldsymbol{Tokens}_{EMS}$

The finite set of places P is used for expressing of conditions of a modeled programming system and in the net layout we notate them with circles. IP is a finite set of input places of the net page representing its input interface. Additionally, no input place of the net page can be identical with any of its places. Input places are represented in the page layout with circles of highlighted upper semicircle. Then, OP is a finite set of output places of the net page representing its output interface. Additionally, no output place of the net page can be identical with any of its places. The definition admits even such possibility that the selected input place is identical with any of output places of the given net page. Output places are represented in the net page layout with circles of highlighted lower semicircle.

Likewise the finite set of transitions T is used for describing events in the programming system and we notate them with rectangles. That set is disjoint with the set of places P of the given net page. A is the finite set of arcs being principally oriented while connecting the place with transition or transition with place and in the layout of net we represent them by oriented arrows drawn in full line. It is worth considering that none of output arcs of any transition can be associated with any input place of the net page, and none of input arcs of any transition can be associated with any output place of the net page. MA is finite set of multiarcs, newly introduced type of arc in sequential object Petri nets. Functionalities of multiarc are used for the modeling of synchronous and asynchronous calling of methods in the given programming system and they follow the principles of the multiarcs in the bi-relational P/T Petri nets (Martiník, 2011). Multiarcs are represented in layouts of the net with oriented arrows drawn with dash line. The set of arcs of the given page is disjoint with the set of its multiarcs, hence it is not allowed the existence of the ordered pair (*place, transition*) or (*transition, place*) connected by both types of oriented arcs.

$IOPN$ function of the identification of input and output places of the net page assigns to each input and output place of the particular net page **unique** natural number which is used at the implementation of mechanism of execution of transitions associated with multiarcs of the net page. With each arc or multiarc of the net page is associated the value of its arc function *AF*, which assigns to each arc or multiarc (one) **arc sequence**, i.e. the element of ***ArcSeq*** set. With each multiarc of the net page is additionally associated the value of its multiarc function *MAF*, which assigns to each such multiarc (one) **arc sequence**, i.e. the element of ***ArcSeq*** set. The layout of the net page shows values of *AF* and *MAF* functions associated with particular multiarc in the form *AF* I *MAF*. With all transitions of the net page are associated values of their functions of transition priorities *TP* assigning each transition with (the only) value of such transition priority, which is the value of a certain natural number. If the value of function of transition priorities is not explicitly indicated in the net layout with the particular transition, we assign it to the value of natural number 1.

The input place function of multiarcs *IPF* assigns each multiarc of the net page connecting ordered pair (*transition, place*) a certain **input place of the selected net page**. The definition admits even the possibility of assigning the selected multiarc of the particular net page with some of the input places of the same net page (ie. it is allowed to model recursive methods). The particular input place p of the selected net page γ ($\gamma \in \Sigma$) is in the layout of network identified by ordered pair of natural numbers ($PN(\gamma)$, $IOPN(\gamma.p)$), where the first member of the pair indicates the value of page number function *PN* and the second member of the pair identifies the selected input place p on the net page γ with the particular value of function *IOPN*. We present this ordered pair in layouts of net pages usually in the form $PN(\gamma).IOPN(\gamma.p)$. The output place function of multiarcs *OPF* assigns each multiarc of the net page connecting the ordered pair (*place, transition*) with a certain **output place of the selected net page.** The definition again admits the possibility of assigning to the selected multiarc of the given net page some of the output places of the same net page. The particular output place p of the selected net page γ is marked in a similar way as in case of the function *IPF*.

A part of each net page can be the finite set *SP* of its subpages, which are by themselves the net pages (i.e. elements of the set Σ). Initialization function *IF* assigns each place including input and output places of the net page with a **multiset of tokens.** That function is also identified in literature as M_0. We routinely mark identifiers from the set ***IDENT*** by elements of the set of places, input places, output places and transitions.

Figure 1 shows the sequential object Petri net *SOPN* = (Σ, *PN*), where Σ = {**Main, Sub**}, *PN* = {(**Main,** 1), (**Sub,** 2)}. Net page of this sequential object Petri net **Main** = (*P, IP, OP, T, A, MA, IOPN, AF, MAF, AP, IPF, OPF, SP, IF*), where *P* = {**P1, P2**}, *IP* = {**in**}, *OP* = {**In**}, *T* = {**T1, T2**}, *A* = {(**in, T1**), (**P1, T1**), (**T2, In**)}, *MA* = {(**T1, P2**), (**P2, T2**)}, *IOPN* = {(**in**, 1), (**In**, 2)}, *AF* = {((**in, T1**), <a>), ((**P1, T1**), <b, 1>), ((**T1, P2**), <a>), ((**P2, T2**), <a>), ((**T2, In**), <b>)}, *MAF* = {((**P2, T2**), <b>), ((**T1, P2**), <b,1>)}, *TP* = {(**T1**, 1), (**T2**, 1)}, *IPF* = {((**T1, P2**), (2.1))}, *OPF* = {((**P2, T2**), (2.2))}, *SP* = $\emptyset$, *IF* = {(**in**, 1`<1>), (**P1**, $\emptyset$), (**P2**, $\emptyset$), (**In**, $\emptyset$)}. Net page **Sub** = (*P, IP, OP, T, A, MA, IOPN, AF, MAF, AP, IPF, OPF, SP, IF*), where *P* = $\emptyset$, *IP* = {**start**}, *OP* = {**Start**}, *T* = {**T1**}, *A* = {(**start, T1**), (**T1, Start**)}, *MA* = $\emptyset$, *IOPN* = {(**start**, 1), (**Start**, 2)}, *AF* = {((**start, T1**), <c, 1>), ((**T1, Start**), <c>)}, *MAF* = $\emptyset$, *TP* = {(**T1**, 1)}, *IPF* = $\emptyset$, *OPF* = $\emptyset$, *SP* = $\emptyset$, *IF* = {(**start**, $\emptyset$), (**Start**, 1`<3>)}.

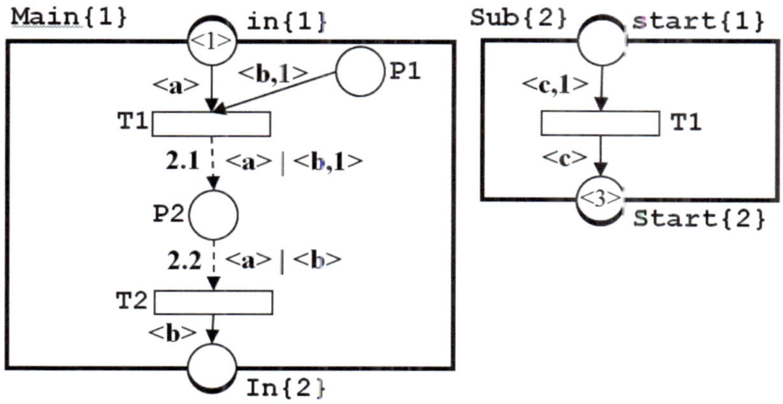

Figure 1. Sequential object Petri net

If **page_identifier** is the identifier of the selected net page and **element_identifier** is the identifier of a place, input place, output place or transition of the net page, we call the compound identifier in the form **page_identifier.element_identifier** so called **distinguished identifier of the element of net page**, which uniquely identifies it within the given sequential object Petri net. Designs of distinguished identifiers of subpages of the net and of its elements can be also executed for cases of sub subpages of the net pages, etc.

For the sake of better transparency we will not indicate in layouts of nets explicit values of page number function *PN*, and explicit values of function of input and output place numbers *IOPN* of identification of input and output places of individual net pages any more. Moreover, we will not indicate values of functions *IPF* and *OPF* of particular multiarcs in the form of **a.b** pair of natural numbers, but in the form of the pair of identifiers **page.ioplace**, where **page** $\in \Sigma$ is the net page and **ioplace** $\in$ *IP* $\in$ **page**, perhaps **ioplace** $\in$ *OP* $\in$ **page** is particular input, or output place of the net page while it holds that **a** = *PN*(**page**) and **b** = *IOPN*(**page.ioplace**).

Layouts of sequential object Petri nets are usually further adjusted in the sense of notations of declarations of headings of methods and their calling within the text of the program, similarly as shown in Figure 2. Here, identifiers of input and output places of the net pages are complemented by (informative) notation of the shape of tokens, which are accepted by those input and output places (see the notation of the input places **Main.in<a>, Sub.start<c, 1>** and of the output places **Main.In<b>, Sub.Start<c>**). We will not record values of functions *AF* and *MAF* in the form of the ordered pair separated by | line any more. The value of the arc function *AF* is indicated separately and the value of the multiarc function *MAF* is indicated behind the value of the input place function *IPF* on the net page, perhaps with a value of the output place function *OPF* of particular multiarc (see notation **Sub.start<b, 1>** and **Sub.Start<b>** of the net page **Main**) in the sense of declaration of calling of methods with the entry of values of input parameters or output values of these methods.

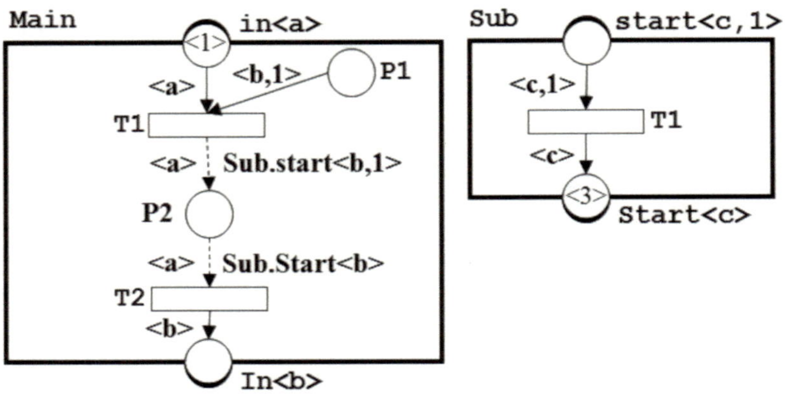

Figure 2. Sequential object Petri net

Let $SOPN = (\Sigma, PN)$ is a sequential object Petri net, $PG \in \Sigma$ is its net page. By the marking M of the net page PG we understand the mapping M: $(P \cup IP \cup OP) \rightarrow$ ***Tokens***$_{EMS}$, where $P \in PG$, $IP \in PG$, $OP \in PG$. By the marking of the net $SOPN$ we understand the marking of all its net pages.

Let $SOPN = (\Sigma, PN)$ is a sequential object Petri net, $PG \in \Sigma$ is its page. Then:

i. by *InputArcs*(x) we denote the set of all input arcs of selected place, output place or transition x, ie. $\forall\, x \in (P \cup OP \cup T) \in PG$: $InputArcs(x) = \{a \in A \mid \exists\, y \in (P \cup IP \cup T): a = (y, x)\}$.
ii. by *InputMultiArcs*(x) we denote the set of all input multiarcs of selected place, output place or transition x, ie. $\forall\, x \in (P \cup OP \cup T) \in PG$: $InputMultiArcs(x) = \{a \in MA \mid \exists\, y \in (P \cup IP \cup T): a = (y, x)\}$.
iii. by *InputNodes*(x) we denote the set of all input nodes of selected place, output place or transition x, ie. $\forall\, x \in (P \cup OP \cup T) \in PG$: $InputNodes(x) = \{y \in (P \cup IP \cup T) \mid \exists\, a \in (A \cup MA): a = (y, x)\}$. We denote the set *InputNodes*(x) by $\bullet x$.
iv. by *OutputNodes*(x) we denote the set of all output nodes of selected place, input place or transition x, ie. $\forall\, x \in (P \cup IP \cup T) \in PG$: $OutputNodes(x) = \{y \in (P \cup OP \cup T) \mid \exists\, a \in (A \cup MA): a = (x, y)\}$. We denote the set *OutputNodes*(x) by $x\bullet$.
v. by *TransitionInputVariables*(x) we denote the set of all variables included in the values of arc functions AF (resp. multiarc functions MAF) of all the input arcs and multiarcs of the transition x, ie. $\forall\, x \in T \in PG$: $TransitionInputVariables(x) = \{v \mid ((v \in variables(AF(y)) \vee (v \in variables(MAF(y))) \wedge ((y \in InputArcs(x)) \vee (y \in InputMultiArcs(x)))\}$.

4. Firing of transitions in sequential object Petri nets

An important term used at the implementation of the mechanism of firing of transitions in a sequential object Petri net is the term of **binding of the arc sequence** contained in the value of AF, or MAF, function of the particular arc, or multiarc, to the token found at a certain marking of the net page in the place associated with this arc (for short, we will refer to that in the text also as **binding of token**).

Let $T \in$ ***Tokens***, $T = <t_1, t_2, \dots, t_n>$, where $n \in$ **N**, $AS \in$ ***ArcSeq***. We denote, that there exists **input binding of the arc sequence** *AS* to the token *T*, if there exists mapping *InputBind*: $AS \to T$ that satifies the following:

i. If $AS = <a_1, a_2, \dots, a_n>$, where $a_1, a_2, \dots, a_n \in (\textbf{IDENT} \cup \textbf{\#IDENT} \cup \textbf{N}_0)$, then:
a. if $a_i \in (\textbf{IDENT} \cup \textbf{\#IDENT})$ for $1 \le i \le n$, then $InputBind(a_i) = t_i$,
b. if $a_i \in \textbf{N}_0$ for $1 \le i \le n$, then $(InputBind(a_i) = t_i) \wedge (a_i = t_i)$,
c. $\forall$ u $\in variables(AS)\ \forall\ v \in variables(AS)$: $((u = v) \Rightarrow (InputBind(u) == InputBind(v)))$.
ii. If $AS = <a_1, a_2, \dots, a_{k-1}, a_k, a_{k+1}, \dots, a_m>$, where $m < n$, $1 \le k \le m$, $a_k \in$ ***#IDENT***, $a_1, \dots, a_{k-1}, a_{k+1}, \dots, a_m \in (\textbf{IDENT} \cup \textbf{N}_0)$, $m \in$ **N**, then:
a. $InputBind(a_k) = <t_k, t_{k+1}, \dots, t_{k+n-m}>$,
b. if $a_i \in$ ***IDENT*** for $1 \le i \le k\text{-}1$, then $InputBind(a_i) = t_i$,
c. if $a_i \in$ ***IDENT*** for $k+1 \le i \le m$, then $InputBind(a_i) = t_{n-m+i}$,
d. if $a_i \in \textbf{N}_0$ for $1 \le i \le k\text{-}1$, then $(InputBind(a_i) = t_i) \wedge (a_i = t_i)$,
e. if $a_i \in \textbf{N}_0$ for $k+1 \le i \le m$, then $(InputBind(a_i) = t_{n-m+i}) \wedge (a_i = t_{n-m+i})$,
f. $\forall\ u \in variables(AS)\ \forall\ v \in variables(AS)$: $((u = v) \Rightarrow (InputBind(u) == InputBind(v)))$.
iii. In other case the mapping *InputBind* is not defined.

Then, input binding of the arc sequence *AS* to the token *T* via mapping *InputBind*: $AS \to T$ can be successfully realized in the following two cases:

i. Arc sequence is in the form $AS = <a_1, a_2, \dots, a_n>$, where $n \in$ **N**, i.e. it holds that ***length(AS) = length(T) = n***, while generally **more than one** of elements $a_1, a_2, \dots, a_n$ of that sequence can be the element of the set ***#IDENT***. Then, at the input binding of the arc sequence *AS* to the token *T* we execute, informally said, binding of mutually corresponding elements of sequences according to their order. If an element a_i of the arc sequence *AS* is a nonnegative integer, then such element must be bound to single-element t_i of token *T*, where $1 \le i \le n$, which is also nonnegative integer and the value of both those numbers must be identical. If *u* and *v* are two identical variables of the arc sequence *AS*, then the values of elements of the token *T* bound to them must be identical. Figure 3 shows a very simple example of input binding of the arc sequence *AS* = <1, a, a, #c, 3> to the token *T* = <1, 10, 10, 2, 3>:

```
T:  <1, 10, 10, 25, 3>
      ↑   ↑   ↑   ↑   ↑
AS: <1,  a,  a,  #c, 3>
```

Figure 3. Binding of arc sequence to token

ii. Arc sequence is in the form $AS = <a_1, a_2, \dots, a_{k-1}, a_k, a_{k+1}, \dots, a_m>$, where $m \in$ **N**, holds that ***length*(*AS*) < *length*(*T*)**, i.e. $m < n$, and at the same time just a single element $a_k \in$ ***#IDENT***, where $1 \le k \le m$. Then, that only element a_k is bound to the **sequence** $<t_k, t_{k+1}, \dots, t_{k+n-m}>$ of elements of the token *T*. In binding of other elements of the sequence *AS* the same rules hold as it was in the case of (i). An example of that type of binding of the arc sequence *AS* = <x, #y, 5, z> (and thus element $a_2 \in$ ***#IDENT***) to the token *T* = <4, 8, 10, 2, 5, 19> is shown in Figure 4.

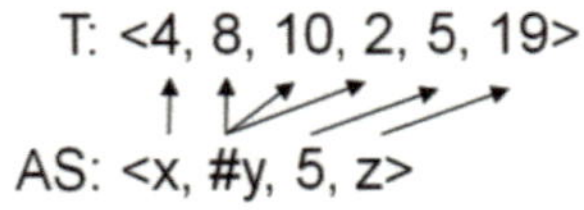

Figure 4. Binding of arc sequence to token

Next examples of the arc sequences binding to tokens in a sequential object Petri net involve:

- arc sequence <a, a, 1> can be successfully bound to token <2, 2, 1>, where *InputBind*(a) = 2, *InputBind*(1) = 1,
- arc sequence <a, a, 1> cannot be successfully bound to token <1, 2, 3> (it would hold that *InputBind*(a) = 1 and *InputBind*(a) = 2),
- arc sequence <#x> can be successfully bound to token <1, 2, 3>, where *InputBind*(#x) = <1, 2, 3>,
- arc sequence <x, #y> can be successfully bound to token <1, 2, 3>, where *InputBind*(x) = 1, *InputBind*(#y) = <2, 3>,
- arc sequence <x, y> can be successfully bound to token <<1, 2>, <3, 3>>, where *InputBind*(x) = <1, 2>, *InputBind*(y) = <3, 3>,
- arc sequence <x, #y> can be successfully bound to token <<1, 2>, <3, 3>, 4>, where *InputBind*(x) = <1, 2>, *InputBind*(#y) = <<3, 3>, 4>.

Let $SOPN = (\Sigma, PN)$ is a sequential object Petri net, $PG \in \Sigma$ is a net page, $t \in T$ is a transition of the net page PG, $p \in \bullet t \in (P \cup IP)$ is a place or input place of the net page PG, $q \in t\bullet \in (P \cup OP)$ is a place or output place of the net page PG, M is a marking of the net $SOPN$. Transition t is ***enabled*** in the marking M of the net $SOPN$, if:

i. $\forall\ (p, t) \in (InputArcs(t) \cup InputMultiArcs(t))\ \exists\ InputBind\text{: } AF(p, t) \rightarrow e$, where $e \in M(p)$,
ii. $\forall\ (p, t) \in InputMultiArcs(t)\ \exists\ InputBind\text{: } MAF(p, t) \rightarrow e$, where $e \in M(OPF(p, t))$,
iii. $\forall\ u \in TransitionInputVariables(t)\ \forall\ v \in TransitionInputVariables(t)$:

$$((u = v) \Rightarrow (InputBind(u) == InputBind(v))).$$

If transition t is enabled in the marking M of the net $SOPN$, we record that fact symbolically in the form of t ***en*** M.

Let $AS = \langle a_1, a_2, \ldots, a_n\rangle \in$ ***ArcSeq***, $n \in$ **N**. If transition t is ***enabled*** in the marking M of the net $SOPN$, then we say, that there exists partial mapping *OutputBind*: ***ArcSeq*** $\rightarrow$ ***Tokens***, if

$$OutputBind(AS) = OB(a_1)\ OB(a_2)\ \ldots\ OB(a_n)$$

where *OB*: ***ArcSeq*** $\rightarrow$ ***Tokens*** and $\forall i,\ 1 \le i \le n$:

a. $OB(a_i) = \langle InputBind(a_i)\rangle$, if $a_i \in$ ***IDENT***,
b. $OB(a_i) = InputBind(a_i)$, if $a_i \in$ ***#IDENT***,
c. $OB(a_i) = a_i$, if $a_i \in$ **Tokens**,
d. $OB(a_i) = \langle OB(x)\rangle$, if $a_i = \langle x\rangle$, where $x \in$ ***ArcSeq***,
e. $OB(a_i) = \langle @(OB(x))\rangle$, if $a_i = @(x)$, where $x \in$ ***ArcSeq***,
f. $OB(a_i) = OB(b_1)\ OB(b_2)\ \ldots\ OB(b_k)$, if $a_i = b_1 b_2 \ldots b_k$, where $b_1, b_2, \ldots, b_k \in$ ***ArcSeq***, $k \in$ **N**,
g. $OB(a_i) = OB(b)^*(OB(x))$, if $a_i = b^*(x)$, where $b \in$ (***IDENT*** $\cup$ $\mathbf{N_0}$), $x \in$ ***ArcSeq***.

Thus transition t on the net page PG of the net $SOPN$ is ***enabled***, if the following is satisfied:

i. for all the input arcs (p, t), resp. input multiarcs (p, t), of the transition t there exists input binding of the value of the arc function $AF(p, t)$ to some token e in the place p of the marking M,
ii. for all the input multiarcs (p, t) of the transition t there exists input binding of the value of the multiarc function $MAF(p, t)$ to some token e in the output place of the net page that is given by the value of the output place function OPF of the multiarc (p, t) in the net marking M,
iii. if u and v are two equal variables of the set *TransitionInputVariables*(t), then the values of elements (resp. subsequences) bound by them in the frame of mapping *InputBind* must be equal.

Figure 5 shows the fragment of sequential object Petri net in its marking M and the construction of the mapping *InputBind*: *AF*(**P1**, **T1**) → <2, 0>, where <2, 0> ∈ *M*(**P1**) and *InputBind*: *AF*(**P2**, **T1**) → <1, 1, 1>, where <1, 1, 1> ∈ *M*(**P2**). It is easily to find that transition **T1** is enabled.

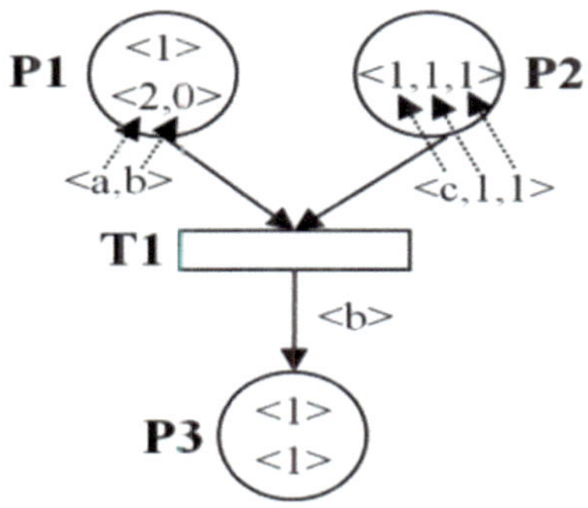

Figure 5. Mapping *InputBind* in sequential object Petri net

Partial mapping *OutputBind*: ***ArcSeq*** → ***Tokens*** is for the given transition t of the net page realized only in case that the transition t is enabled in the marking M of the net. Hence, partial mapping *OutputBind* assigns the selected arc sequence AS the **token**, being the element of the set of all ***Tokens*** (i.e. that token is not generally located in any of places of the net $SOPN$ in its current marking M). The definition assumes that arc sequence AS is generally in the form $AS = \langle a_1, a_2, \ldots, a_n \rangle$, $n \in \mathbf{N}$. The value $OutputBind(\langle a_1, a_2, \ldots, a_n \rangle)$, which is generally the element of the set ***Tokens***, is given by concatenation of sequences in the form $OB(a_1)\ OB(a_2) \ldots OB(a_n)$, while individual values $OB(a_i)$ are for $1 \leq i \leq n$ determined according to specified rules.

Regarding recursive nature of the partial mapping *OutputBind* we will include several examples of binding of the arc sequences to elements of the set ***Tokens***. Let us assume in all cases that a certain sequential object Petri net $SOPN$ is given containing the transition **T**, whose set of input variables *TransitionInputVariables*(**T**) = {a, b, c, x, #x} and in certain marking *M* of the net *SOPN* there exists binding of those input variables given as follows: *InputBind*(a) = 10, *InputBind*(b) = 2, *InputBind*(c) = <<1, 1>, 3>, *InputBind*(x) = <1, 2, 3>, *InputBind*(#x) = <1, 2, 3>. In the following examples we will investigate values of partial mapping *OutputBind* applied to various values of the arc sequence *AS*.

- if *AS* = <a>, then *OutputBind*(<a>) = *OB*(a) = <*InputBind*(a)> = <10>.
- if *AS* = <c, 1>, then *OutputBind*(<c, 1>) = *OB*(c) *OB*(1) = <*InputBind*(c)><1> = <<<1, 1>, 3>><1> = <<<1, 1>, 3>, 1>.
- if *AS* = <x, a, 5>, then *OutputBind*(<x, a, 5>) = *OB*(x) *OB*(a) *OB*(5) = <*InputBind*(x)><*InputBind*(a)><5> = <<1, 2, 3>><10><5> = <<1, 2, 3>, 10, 5>.
- if *AS* = <#x, a, 5>, then *OutputBind*(<#x, a, 5>) = *OB*(#x) *OB*(a) *OB*(5) = *InputBind*(#x)<*InputBind*(a)><5> = <1, 2, 3><10><5> = <1, 2, 3, 10, 5>.
- if *AS* = <b*(#x)>, then *OutputBind*(<b*(#x)>) = *OB*(b*(#x)) = *OB*(b)*(*OB*(#x)) = *InputBind*(b)*(*InputBind*(#x)) = 2*(<1, 2, 3>) = <1, 2, 3><1, 2, 3> = <1, 2, 3, 1, 2, 3>.
- if *AS* = <@(<x, a, 5>)>, then *OutputBind*(<@(<x, a, 5>)>) = <*OB*(@(<x, a, 5>))> = <@(*OB*(x) *OB*(a) *OB*(5))> = <@(<*InputBind*(x)><*InputBind*(a)>*OB*(5))> = <@(<<1, 2, 3>><10><5>)> = <@(<<1, 2, 3>, 10, 5>)> = <3>.

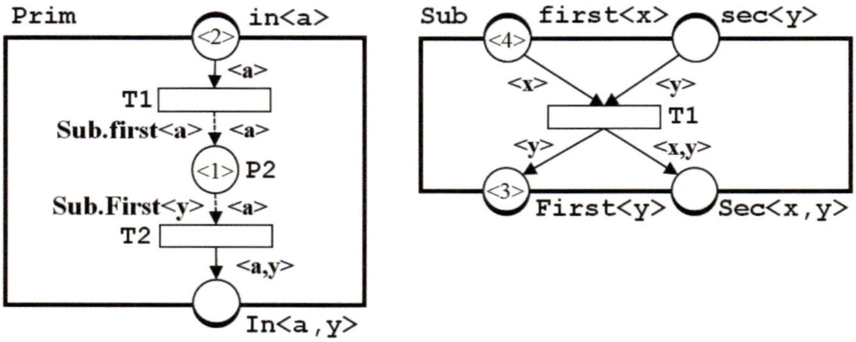

Figure 6. Marking of sequential object Petri net

Figure 6 shows the net pages **Prim** and **Sub** of a certain sequential object Petri net in their marking *M* and we are interested, if there exists input binding of transition variables associated with the transitions **Prim.T1** and **Prim.T2**. With the transition **Prim.T1** is associated one input arc (**Prim.in, Prim.T1**) whose value of the arc function *AF*(**Prim.in, Prim.T1**) = <a>, and thus the set *TransitionInputVariables*(**Prim.T1**) = {a}. We can easily determine that for the input arc (**Prim.in, Prim.T1**) there exists mapping *InputBind*: <a> → <2>, and thus holds that *InputBind*(a) = 2. With the transition **Prim.T2** is associated one input multiarc (**Prim.P2, Prim.T2**) whose value of arc function *AF*(**Prim.P2, Prim.T2**) = <a>, the value of multiarc function *MAF*(**Prim.P2, Prim.T2**) = <y> and thus the set *TransitionInputVariables*(**Prim.T2**) = {a, y}. And again, we can easily determine that for the input multiarc (**Prim.P2, Prim.T2**) there exists mapping *InputBind*: <a> → <1>, and thus holds that *InputBind*(a) = 1. With that input multiarc it is also necessary to determine the mapping *InputBind*: *MAF*(**Prim.P2, Prim.T2**) → e, where *e* ∈ *M*(*OPF*(**Prim.P2, Prim.T2**)). The value of the output place function *OPF*(**Prim.P2**, **Prim.T2**) = **Sub.First**, whose marking *M*(**Sub.First**) = 1`<3>. So we investigate, if there exists mapping *InputBind*: <y> → <3>. We can easily determine that the mapping exists and it holds that *InputBind*(y) = 3. Generally, for the transition **Prim.T2** holds that *InputBind*(a) = 1 and *InputBind*(y) = 3.

So it can be stated that for both transitions **Prim.T1** a **Prim.T2** exist particular input bindings of all the transition input variables associated with their input arcs and thus, both transitions are enabled. We are further interested, if there exists the mapping *OutputBind* of the values of functions *AF* and *MAF* associated with output arcs (or multiarcs) of both transitions. With transition **Prim.T1** is associated the only output multiarc (**Prim.T1**, **Prim.P2**) whose value of the arc function *AF*(**Prim.T1, Prim.P2**) = <a> and the value of the multiarc function *MAF*(**Prim.T1, Prim.P2**) = <a>. So we can easily find out that *OutputBind*(<a>) = <2>. With the transition **Prim.T2** is associated the only output arc (**Prim.T2, Prim.In**) whose value of the arc function *AF*(**Prim.T2, Prim.In**) = <a, y>. So again, we can easily find out that *OutputBind*(<a, y>) = <1, 3>.

Let $SOPN = (\Sigma, PN)$ is a sequential object Petri net, $PG \in \Sigma$ is a net page, $t \in T$ is a transition of the net page PG, M is a marking of the net $SOPN$.

i. If the transition t is enabled in the marking M, then we obtain by its **firing** marking M' of the net $SOPN$, defined as follows:

$$
\begin{array}{ll}
M'(p) = M(p) \setminus InputBind(AF(p, t)), & \text{if } (p \in \bullet t) \wedge ((p, t) \in (A \cup MA)) \wedge \\
 & (\exists\, InputBind: AF(p, t) \rightarrow e,\ e \in M(p)), \\
M'(p) = M(p) \cup OutputBind(AF(t, p)), & \text{if } (p \in t\bullet) \wedge ((t, p) \in (A \cup MA)), \\
M'(q) = M(q) \setminus InputBind(MAF(p, t)), & \text{if } (p \in \bullet t) \wedge ((p, t) \in MA) \wedge (q = OPF(p, t)) \wedge \\
 & (\exists\, InputBind: MAF(p, t) \rightarrow e,\ e \in M(OPF(p, t))), \\
M'(q) = M(q) \cup OutputBind(MAF(t, p)), & \text{if } (p \in t\bullet) \wedge ((t, p) \in MA) \wedge (q = IPF(t, p)). \\
M'(p) = M(p), & \text{otherwise.}
\end{array}
$$

ii. Firing of transition $t \in T$, which will change the marking M of the sequential object Petri net $SOPN$ into the marking M', is symbolically denoted as $M\ [\,t\,\rangle\, M'$.

iii. Step is understood as firing of non-empty subset from the set of enabled transitions in the given marking M of the sequential object Petri net $SOPN$. Step Y which will the marking M into the marking M' is symbolically denoted as $M\ [\ Y\ \rangle\ M'$.

iv. Let step Y be enabled at the marking M of the net $SOPN$. If $t_1, t_2 \in Y$ and $t_1 \neq t_2$, we say then that transitions t_1 a t_2 are **concurrently enabled** and that fact is symbolically denoted in the form of $\{t_1, t_2\}$ ***en*** M.

Firing of transition will result in the new marking of given sequential object Petri net, which we will obtain as follows:

- from each input place p of the fired transition t we will remove the (unique) token in the marking M, which is bound to the value of the arc function $AF(p, t)$,
- to each output place p of the fired transition t we will add up the (unique) token which is the value of partial function $OutputBind(AF(t, p))$,

- from each output place of page *q*, being the value of function *OPF* of the input multiarc (*p*, *t*) of the fired transition *t*, we will remove the (unique) token in the marking *M*, bound to the value of the multiarc function *MAF*(*p*, *t*),
- to each input place of page *q*, being the value of function *IPF* of the output multiarc (*t*, *p*) of fired transition *t*, we will add up the (unique) token being the value of partial function *OutputBind*(*MAF*(*t*, *p*)),
- in all the remaining places of the net we will leave their original marking.

Figure 6 shows the net pages **Prim** and **Sub** of a certain sequential object Petri net in its marking *M*. From previous text we know that transitions **Prim.T1** and **Prim.T2** are **concurrently enabled.** Hence, firing of transition **Prim.T1** consists in:

- removing token <2> from the input place **Prim.in**,
- adding token <2> to the place **Prim.P2**,
- adding token <2> to the input place **Sub.first**.

Hence, firing of transition **Prim.T2** consists in:

- removing token <1> from the place **Prim.P2**,
- removing token <3> from the output place **Sub.First**,
- adding token <1, 3> to the output place **Prim.In**.

Marking M′ of the net after concurrent firing of transitions **Prim.T1** and **Prim.T2** is shown in Figure 7.

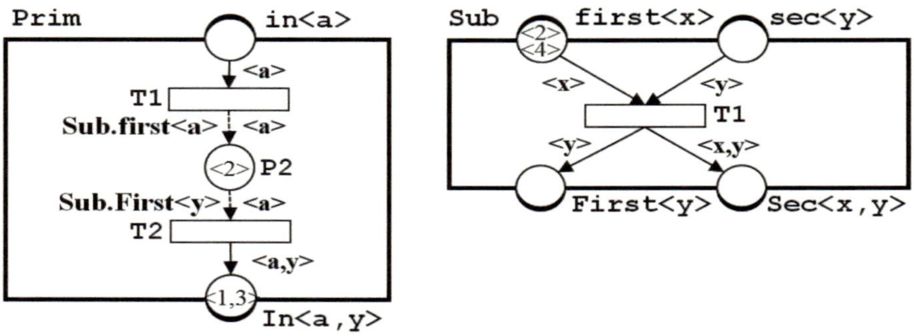

Figure 7. Firing of transitions in sequential object Petri net

Relatively complicated mechanism of firing of transitions in sequential object Petri nets can be better explained by notional substituting of all the multiarcs of the net by standard arcs, which can be realized as follows:

- if *p* is place and *t* transition of the given net page and (*p*, *t*) its multiarc whose value of arc function equals to *AF*(*p*, *t*), the value of output place function equals to *OPF*(*p*, *t*) and the value of multiarc function equals to *MAF*(*p*, *t*), we substitute this multiarc by notional pair of the following standard arcs:
  - by the arc (*p*, *t*) with the value of the arc function equal to *AF*(*p*, *t*),
  - by the arc (*OPF*(*p*, *t*), *t*) with the value of the arc function equal to *MAF*(*p*, *t*).

- if p is place and t transition of the given net page and (t, p) its multiarc whose value of arc function equals to $AF(t, p)$, the value of input place function equals to $IPF(t, p)$ and the value of multiarc function equals to $MAF(t, p)$, we substitute that multiarc with notional pair of the following standard arcs:
  - by the arc (t, p) with the value of the arc function equal to $AF(t, p)$,
  - by the arc $(t, IPF(t, p))$ with the value of the arc function equal to $MAF(t, p)$.

That notional substitution of multiarcs in the previous net is shown in Figure 8 where:

- multiarc (**Prim.T1, Prim.P2**) was substituted by the following pair of arcs:
  - the arc (**Prim.T1, Prim.P2**) with the value of the arc function *AF* equal to <a>,
  - the arc (**Prim.T1, Sub.first**) with the value of the arc function *AF* equal to <a>,
- multiarc (**Prim.P2, Prim.T2**) was substituted by the following pair of arcs:
  - the arc (**Prim.P2, Prim.T2**) with the value of the arc function *AF* equal to <a>,
  - the arc (**Sub.First, Prim.T2**) with the value of the arc function *AF* equal to <y>.

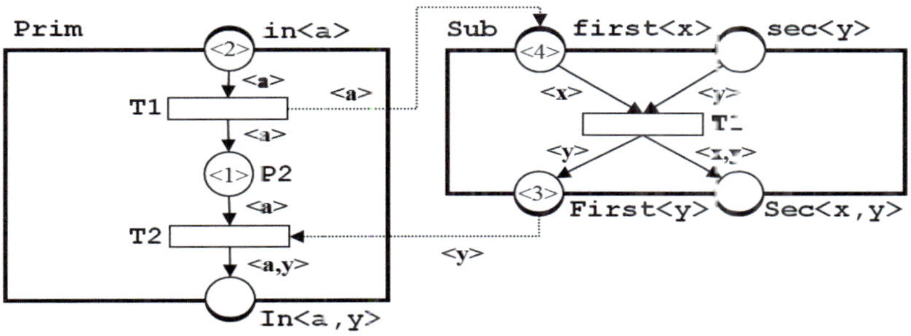

Figure 8. Substitution of multiarcs in sequential object Petri net

When enabling individual steps of the sequential object Petri net, so called *conflicts* can originate in certain markings of the net (or *conflict transitions*). At the enabling of transitions t_1 and t_2 of the given net and its marking M the conflict occurs, if both transitions t_1 and t_2 have at least one input place, each of t_1 and t_2 transitions is individually enabled in the marking M of the net, but t_1 and t_2 transitions are not in that marking M concurrently enabled, i.e. enabling of one of them will prevent enabling the other. The term of conflict transitions can be obviously easily generalized for the case of finite set $t_1, t_2, \ldots, t_n$ $(n \in N)$ of transitions of the given net.

A typical example of the conflict at enabling transitions in the particular marking of the net is shown in Figure 9, where transitions **T1** and **T2** of the net have a common input place **P1**, both are enabled (particular binding of tokens can be easily found), but not concurrently enabled, i.e. enabling of the transition **T1** will disable enabling of the transition **T2** and vice versa. When solving conflicts at enabling of transitions in sequential Petri nets we will therefore follow the rule which determines, informally said, that from the set of conflict transitions at the given binding of tokens the one will be enabled, whose value of transition priority function *TP* is the highest. If such transition from the set of conflict transitions does not exist, the given conflict would have to be solved by other means. In our studied example will be then on the basis of that rule the transition **T2** enabled (because *TP*(**T1**) = 1 and *TP*(**T2**) = 2).

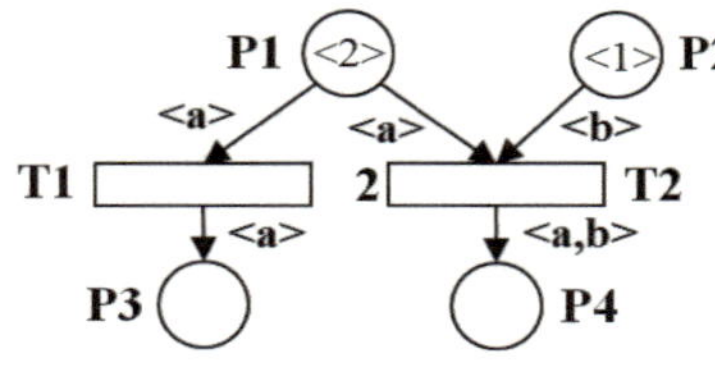

Figure 9. Conflict transitions in sequential object Petri net

5. Object-oriented programming systems and their representation by the sequential object Petri nets

This section deals with main principles applied at modeling of multithreading object-oriented programming systems with the sequential object Petri nets. All program listings are developed in the Java programming language (Goetz et. al, 2006), (Lea, 1999), (Subramaniam, 2011).

Each declared class of the object–oriented programming system is in the sequential object Petri net represented by a net page containing declared data items and methods. Their declarations are made by using elements of the net page. Individual input places of the net page then represent input points of static and non-static methods as a part of the class declaration, and output places of the net page then represent their output points. Input and output places of the net page are associated with identifiers of the particular method whose input and output point they represent while each method has one input and output place. In so doing, we abide to the convention whereby input place identifier of the particular method starts with a small letter and identifier of the output place of the same method with a capital letter. In order to differentiate graphically in layouts of the net declaration of static methods from non-static methods on a given net page, we demarcate identifiers of input and output places of the net page representing input and output points of static methods with the square brackets. Moreover, it is possible on the net page via a position of input and output places in its layout represent visibility of *public, protected* and *private* type of individual declared methods thus implementing the characteristic of encapsulation of the object-oriented programming.

Figure 10 illustrates the net page representing the following declaration of the class **Sys**:

```
public class Sys {
  public static void compute() { ... }
  protected void run() { ... }
  private void init() { ... }
}
```

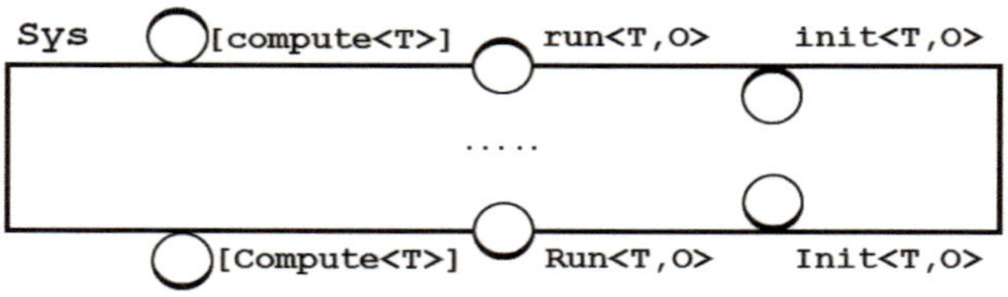

Figure 10. Net page representing declaration of class **Sys**

Static and non-static data items are on the net pages represented in the form of **tokens** in the given net marking, i.e. by elements of the set ***Tokens***. When representing values of static and non-static data items being the elements of particular tokens of the net, it is for example possible to proceed as follows:

- If the data type of the particular data item is a non-negative integer (*int*), its actual value equals to that non-negative integer.
- If the data type of the particular data item is *boolean*, we represent the truth value *false* most frequently with constant 0 and the truth value *true* with constant 1, while in layouts of the net we are also using symbolic values *false* and *true*.
- If the data type of the particular data item is *char*, whose value is the element of the set contained in the code table given by the Unicode standard, we represent its value corresponding to the value of the symbol code given in the Unicode Standard, i.e. the letter 'A' can be represented by the value 65. In order to make again layouts of nets more readable, the element of token can be entered as the particular symbol bounded by apostrophes, i.e. instead of token <65> we will indicate in layouts of nets token <'A'>.
- If the data type of the particular data item is *string*, whose value is text string, the values can be represented by sequences of codes of symbols according to the Unicode standard. Again, for better transparency of notations, it is possible to use instead of codes of symbols directly the sequence of symbols bounded by apostrophes, i.e. in layouts of nets represent data items of the data type *string* with the tokens of <'H', 'e', 'l', 'l', 'o'> shape, or to bound sequence of symbols of the string with quotation marks, i.e. to note the tokens in the form of <"Hello">.
- Data items whose data type are numbers with floating decimal point (*float*, *double*), or other numerical data type being the superset of the set of non-negative integer numbers, it is not possible to declare it directly on the basis of the stated definition of the sequential object Petri net. If a need emerges to operate with those numerical sets during simulation of multithreading object-oriented programming system, it is always easy to extend in this sense the definition of the token, arc sequence and other particular definitions, in order to ensure the support of those numerical sets (e.g. it is possible to define the token of sequential object Petri net as the finite non-empty sequence over the set of real numbers ***R***, etc.).
- In the case of data items whose data type is the pointer to instance of class, we represent their values with natural numbers. Each instance of the class has at its creation allocated unique natural number expressing its address within the programming heap. Number 0 than represents the value of pointer *null*.

Static data items are usually represented in layouts of nets with the tokens containing only their actual values. Non-static data items are usually represented by tokens containing both the value of pointer to a given instance of the class in which the particular data item is declared, and its actual value according to particular data type. So if within the declaration of the class First for example the following data items are declared:

```
public class First {
  private static boolean  indicator = true;
  private char status = 'a';
}
```

then, the static data item **indicator** can be represented by the token **<true>** and the non-static data item **status** by the token **<11, 'a'>**, where numerical value **11** represents the value of the pointer to the particular instance of class.

The dynamic creation of the instance of the class is not in the sequential object Petri net realized by the creation of a new instance of the particular net page representing declaration of the given class, but by creation of all the tokens representing non-static data items of the declared class. At the same time, each such token contains (usually as its first element) the value of the pointer to the newly created class instance. The fact, that during dynamic creation of instances of classes it is not necessary to create instances of net pages, dramatically simplifies its analysis.

All methods represented by elements of the net pages are executed by the programming threads. Each such programming thread is represented by the particular instance of class (usually by the class **Thread**). Thus, the token accepted by the input place of the net page must contain the pointer for particular programming thread realizing execution of the given method, while that pointer is within arc sequences of the net represented by default by some of the identifiers **T**, **U**, **V**, etc. By the element of the token accepted by the input place of the page representing the input point of some of the non-static methods must be then the pointer of the particular instance of class whose non-static method is (i.e. pointer **this**). That pointer is then within the arc sequences of the net standardly represented by the identifier **O** (while indeed, within representation of static methods that pointer cannot be used). When entering identifiers of static and non-static data items, parameters and local variables of methods, we use by default in layouts of the net so called Hungarian notations, where the first letter (or the first part) of identifier expresses its data type. For identification of standard data types we use the acronym **i** even for data type *int*, **b** for *boolean*, **c** for *char*, **s** for *string* and **p** for *pointer*. Hence for example the identifier **sName** within the arc sequence represents the variable of the data type *string* with the identifier **name**.

Figure 11 shows the net page representing the declaration of the following class **Obj** in its marking *M*:

```
public class Obj {
  private char val = 'a';
  public synchronized char getVal() { return value; }
  public synchronized void setVal(char value) { this.val = value; }
}
```

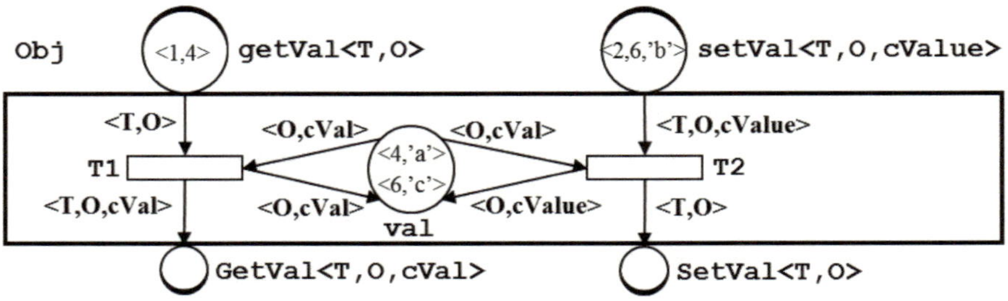

Figure 11. Net page representing declaration of class **Obj**

The current notation of that net page suggests, that within the program execution modeled by that net two instances of the class **Obj** have been already created, as in the place **Obj.val** appear tokens **<4, 'a'>** a **<6, 'c'>**, where the first element of each of those tokens is the pointer to the instance of the class **Obj** and second the actual value of the non-static data item **val** of the data type *char*. The non-static method **getVal** will be executed above the instance of class with the pointer **4** by the programming thread with the pointer equal to the value **1**, the non-static method **setVal** will be executed above the instance of the class with the pointer **6** by the programming thread with the pointer equal to the value **2**, while the value of method parameter **value** equals to character **'b'**. The shape of the net demonstrates, that over the selected instance of the class can be concurrently executed with any programming thread maximum one of **getVal** or **setVal** methods.

Additionally, in layouts of nets can be simply represented the relation of a simple inheritance between two declared classes. The identifier of the net page representing the class declaration being superclass of the given class, we indicate in the layout of the given net page of the class in its left bottom corner. If that identifier of the net page of the superclass is not explicitly indicated in the layout of the net, we consider the given class to be implicitly subclass of the top class in the hierarchy of classes created on the basis of relation of simple inheritance of classes (e.g. within the hierarchy of classes of the Java programming language it is the class **java.lang.Object**).

With the inheritance relation of classes is organically connected even the term of polymorphism of the object-oriented programming and the possibility of declaration of so called virtual methods. Figure 12 shows two net pages out of which the first represents declaration of the class **Object** and the second declaration of the class **System**, being subclass of the class **Object**. Within the class **Object** is also declared virtual method with the head **public int hashCode()**, which is in the declaration of the class **System** overwritten with the virtual method of identical method head. Input and output places of net pages **Object** and **System**, which appertain to input and output points of both virtual methods are indicated in the net layout by default while in the case of declaration of the virtual methods it is necessary that **all input places representing the input point of the given virtual method had assigned on all the net pages containing the declaration of this method the identical value of *IOPN* function and all output places representing the output point of the given virtual method had assigned on all relevant net pages the identical value of *IOPN* function** (see Figure 12).

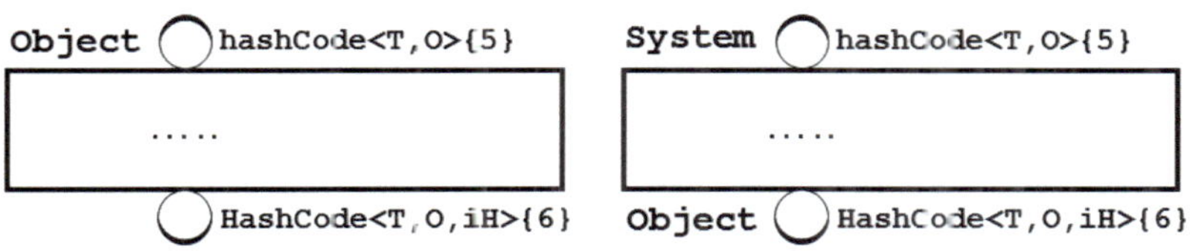

Figure 12. Virtual methods representation in sequential object Petri net

Next example demonstrates representation of classes containing declaration of virtual and abstract methods. **Virt** and **Add** classes are declared as follows:

```
public abstract class Virt {
  public abstract int compute(int a, int b);
  public int make(int a, int b)  { return compute(a, b); }
}

public class Add extends Virt {
  public int compute(int a, int b) { return (a + b); }
}
```

The **Virt** class is an abstract class with the declared abstract method **compute**. That method is called as a part of the declared method **make** of the **Virt** class. The method **compute** is then overwritten at the level of declaration of the class **Add**, being the subclass of the class **Virt**. The net page representing the declaration of the class **Virt** is shown in Figure 13. Abstract method **compute** is represented only by a pair of the input place **Virt.compute** and the output place **Virt.Compute**. Regarding the fact that it is also declaration of the virtual method, the selection of function *IOPN* values is important (i.e. in our case *IOPN*(**Virt.compute**) = 1 and *IOPN*(**Virt.Compute**) = 2). The key element of the net page is the manner of calling of the virtual method **compute** represented by the multiarc (**Virt.T1**, **Virt.P1**) and its value of input place function *IPF*, the multiarc (**Virt.P1**, **Virt.T2**) and its value of output place function *OPF*. The value of input place function *IPF* of the multiarc (**Virt.T1**, **Virt.P1**) is in the form of **O.compute** (more precisely in the **O.1** form), where identifier **O** represents the pointer of particular instance of non-abstract subclass of class **Virt**, whose non-static method **compute** is executed. The value of identifier **O** is in our case non-constant, ie. generalized at the realization of steps, and depends on binding of the specific token to the arc sequence in the form **<T, O, iA, iB>**, which shares in the given identification of the net execution of transition **Virt.T1**. According to the numerical value bound to identifier **O** the particular net page net will be determined whose value of the function *PN* of numbering net pages is identical with the numerical value bound to the identifier **O**. Then on this net page the input place with the value of *IOPN* function equal to number **1** will be selected (representing the input point of the virtual method **compute**), into which the particular token in the form **<T, O, iA, iB>** will be placed.

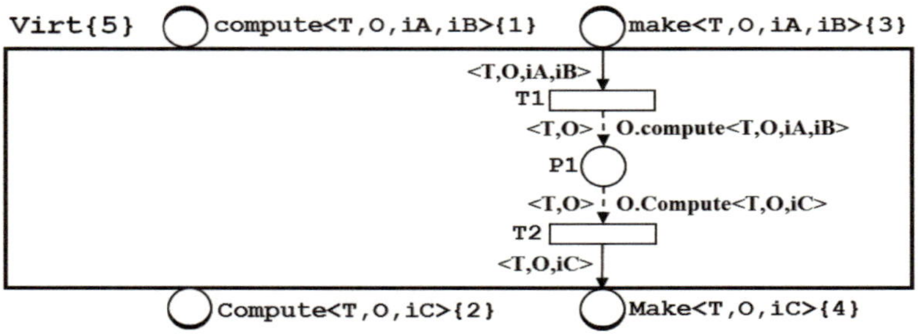

Figure 13. Polymorphism representation in sequential object Petri net

Net page representing the declaration of the class **Add**, being the subclass of the class **Virt**, is shown in Figure 14. In the class **Add** is declared the only non-static virtual method

compute, which overwrites the abstract method **compute** declared in the body of the class **Virt**. Thus, on the grounds of that fact it is necessary to correctly assign values of *IOPN* function (in our case *IOPN*(**Add.compute**) = 1 and *IOPN*(**Add.Compute**) = 2). An interesting detail of this net page is the way of determination of the addition of integral values bound to variables **iA** and **iB** of the arc sequence of the arc (**Add.compute**, **Add.T1**). The expression in the form **@(iA*<0>iB*<0>)** represents length of the sequence formed by concatenation of two sequences: first sequence containing in total **iA** of numbers **0** and the second sequence containing in total **iB** numbers **0** (in this case, it is worth mentioning, that e.g. via the expression in the form **@(iA*(iB*<0>))** product of integral values of variables **iA** a **iB** can be determined).

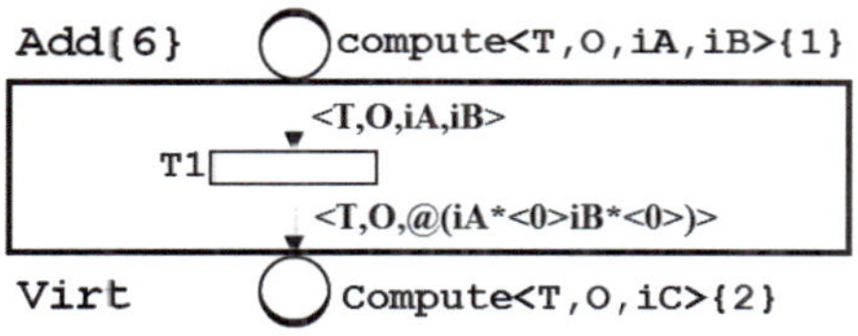

Figure 14. Polymorphism representation in sequential object Petri net

Next generalization of the form of functions *IPF* and *OPF* associated with multiarcs is possible within the sequential object Petri nets to implement the explicit support of the mechanism of **first order and higher order functions** known from functional programming (ie. given method can take another methods as parameters and return the method as the return value). Figure 15 shows the net page of the class **Func** containing declaration of method **call**. Arc sequence of the token accepted by the input place of that method contains a variable **mO**, the value of which is the value of the function *PN* for the net page with the input place **make** and output place **Make**, which are represented by particular integral values of the function *IOPN*. Values of functions *MAF* of multiarcs of the net in the form **mO.make** and **mO.Make**, whose all components are variables and whose values are not determined until particular arc sequence is bound to token of the net, provide general mechanism for the possibility of declaration of first order and higher order functions.

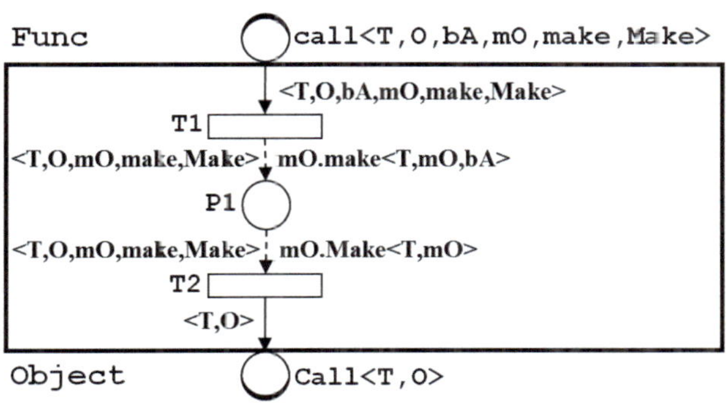

Figure 15. Higher order function representation in sequential object Petri net

Example of recursive method represented by the net page can be seen on Figure 16. This static recursive method **fact** of the class **Integer** implements calculation of the value of factorial function whose parameter is a certain natural number **n**. Recursive algorithm for calculation of factorial of the integer value **n** in the Java programming language is represented by the following listing:

```
public class Integer {
  public static int fact(int n) {
    if (n == 1) return 1;
    else return (n * fact(n – 1));
}
```

If the value of the parameter **iN** equals to number 1, the transition **Integer.T4** is enabled and in the output place **Integer.Fact** the token **<T, 1>** is stored, whose first element **T** represents the programming thread and the second element the value of factorial of number 1. If the value of number **iN** is greater than number 1, by enabling the transition **Integer.T2** that number **iN** is substituted by the sequence consisting of **iN** numbers 0, which is then used at recursive call modeled by the multiarc (**Integer.T3**, **Integer.P2**), whose enabling will always result in elimination of one element of that sequence. The programming stack which is used at realization of recursive procedure of the algorithm is represented by the token in the place **Integer.P3** in the form of the sequence **<T, ..., iN-2, iN-1, iN>**. At the moment where the sequence composed from 0 numerals contains after the series of recursive calls of algorithm one element (i.e. it is necessary to determine the value of factorial of number 1 within the stop condition of algorithm), the transition **Integer.T4** is enabled and the value of factorial of number 1 is represented in token **<T, 1>** located in the output place **Integer.Fact**. Then, by repeatedly enabling the transition **Integer.T5** and finally the transition **Integer.T6** the return from recursion is implemented with the gradual calculation of the value of factorial function, which is represented in the token of the form **<T, @(iM*(iF*0))>**. Following completion of the process of reverse return of recursion in the output place **Integer.Fact** the token in the form **<T, iF>** is stored, whose second element represents the value of factorial of the natural number **iN**.

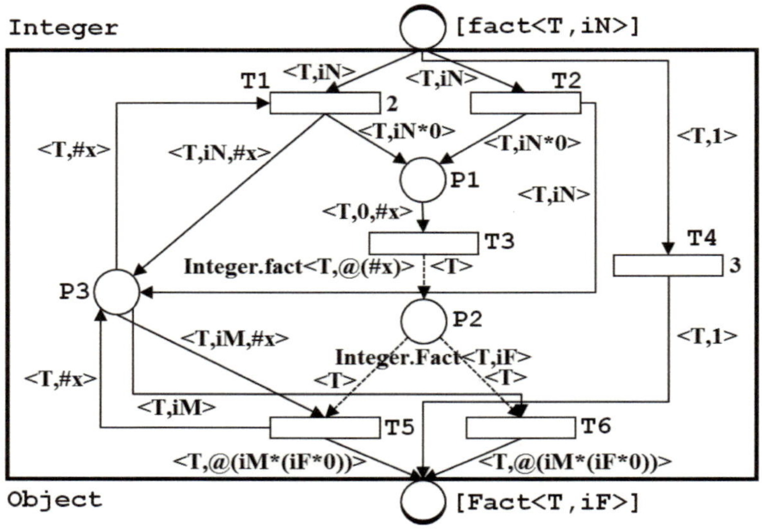

Figure 16. Recursive function representation in sequential object Petri net

Moreover, in the sequential object Petri nets can be simply represented declarations of inner classes of the selected class via subpages of the net page. So if for example the class **Obj** which within its declaration contains declaration of its own inner class **InnerObj**, that declaration can be represented by the subpage **InnerObj** of the page **Obj** (see Figure 17)

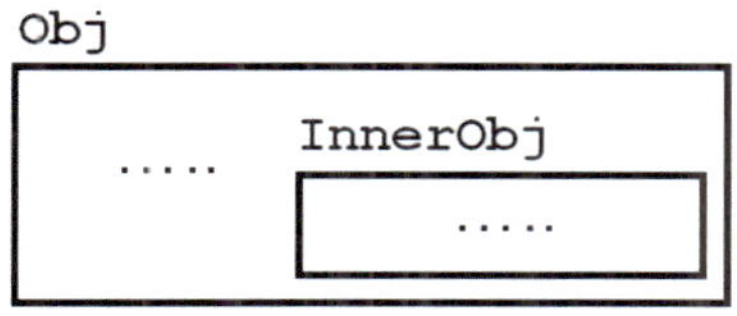

Figure 17. Inner class declaration representation in sequential object Petri net

The representation of declared interfaces, which can contain only declarations of headings of publicly accessible abstract methods, is also easy. Figure 18 shows the representation of interface ***Runnable*** (identifiers of interface we indicate in layouts of the net with spaced letters) containing declaration of the method with the head **public abstract void run()**.

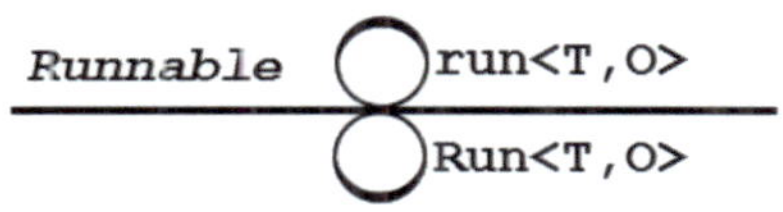

Figure 18. Interface declaration in sequential object Petri net

6. Example of simple class hierarchy represented by sequential object Petri net

In this section we will demonstrate how simple hierarchy of the classes via sequential object Petri nets is built. The model of those examples involve selected classes contained in standard library of classes of the Java programming language. (e.g. classes **java.lang.Object**, **java.lang.Thread**, etc.). For better visibility of layouts we usually present individual declared methods in separate figures representing individual parts of the particular net page (while naturally places and transitions of the net which appear in individual parts of the net page and have identical identifiers, always represent the same place or transition of the total page of the net). Thus, top of our hierarchy of classes will be the class **Object** whose declaration made in the Java programming language is the following:

```
public class Object {
  private Object monitor;
  private Thread thread;
  private Vector<Thread> = new Vector<Thread>;
  private synchronized static int getPointer() { … }
  public Object() { … }
  protected void finalize() { … }
  public void lock() { … }
  public void unlock() { … }
```

```
  public void wait() { ... }
  public void notify() { ... }
}
```

The static method **getPointer** (see Figure 19) can be executed by the only one programming thread only and it is determined for assigning unique integral values of pointers to individual instances of the classes. At the first execution of the method the integral value 1 is returned in variable **P** (because *InputBind*(#p) = 0 a @(#p) = @(<0>) = 1), in the place **Object.P1** is then stored the token **<0, 0>**, and at next execution of the method is in the variable **P** returned the value 2, etc.

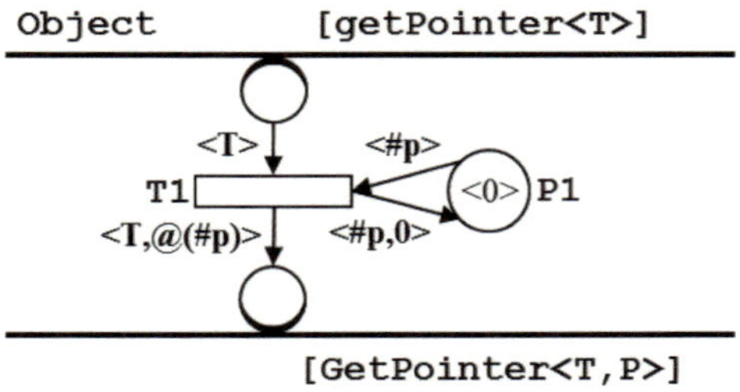

Figure 19. Declaration of class **Object** in sequential object Petri net

Within the declaration of the constructor of the object of the class **Object** (see Figure 20) is by the programming thread firstly obtained the value of the pointer for a newly created object by calling the method **getPointer**, that value is then stored to the variable **O** and the value of non-static data item **monitor** representing the monitor of particular instance of the class is then stored in the form of the token **<O>** in the place **Object.monitor**. The destructor of the object represented by the method **finalize** will then mainly ensure cancellation of the monitor of the object represented by the token **<O>** in the place **Object.monitor**.

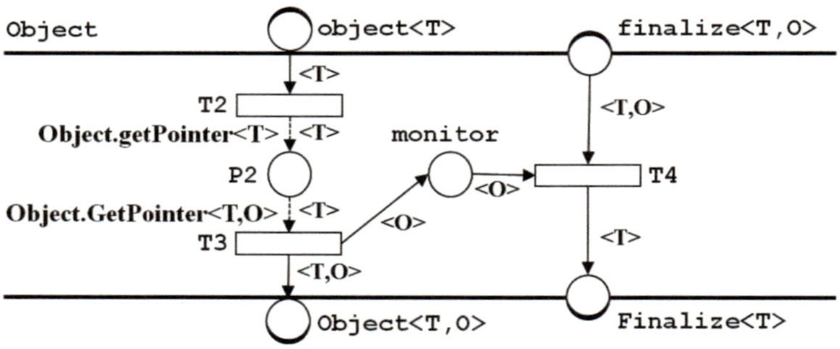

Figure 20. Declaration of class **Object** in sequential object Petri net

Entry into the critical section of the object (i.e. execution of the non-static method with the modifier **synchronized**) is conditioned by getting the object monitor with the particular programming thread. As a part of the execution of the method **lock** the programming thread **T** can respectively allocate the object monitor with the value of the pointer **O**, (i.e. the token **<O>** in the place **Object.monitor**) and then enter into the critical section of the object while the programming thread is permitted to enter the critical section of the same object several times in sequence. First entry of the programming thread **T** into the critical section of the object **O** is realized by execution of the transition **Object.T5**. Pointer to the programming thread, which successfully obtained the object monitor, is then stored in the variable **thread** (i.e. the token **<T, O, 1>** is located in the place **Object.thread**). At repeated entry of the programming thread into the critical sections of the object **O** the transition **Object.T6** is executed and particular token in the place **Object.thread** is added with the next element which is the number **1** (i.e. at second entry of the thread **T** into the critical section of the object **O** is in the place **Object.thread** stored the token **<T, O, 1, 1>**, at the third entry the token **<T, O, 1, 1, 1>**, etc). Deal location of the object monitor and initialization of its critical section is then realized by execution of the non-static method **unlock**, whose functionalities are inverse to functionalities of the method **lock** (see Figure 21).

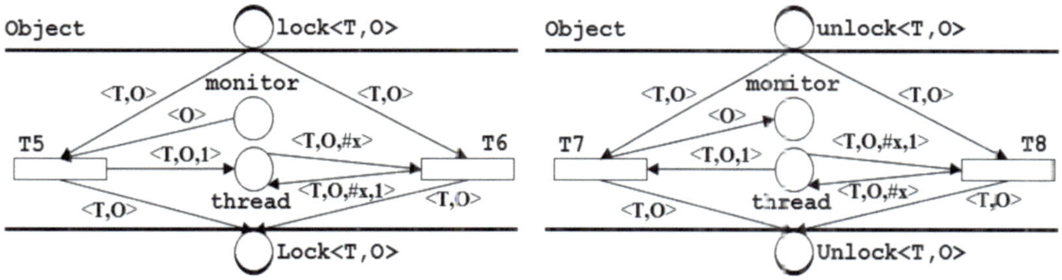

Figure 21. Declaration of class **Object** in sequential object Petri net

Method **wait** causes the current thread **T** to wait until another thread invokes the **notify** method for the object **O**. The current thread **T** must own the monitor of the object **O**. The thread releases ownership of this monitor and waits in the place **Object.pool** until another thread notifies threads waiting on the object's monitor to wake up through a call to the notify method. The thread **T** then waits in the place **Object.P3** until it can re-obtain ownership of the object monitor and resumes execution (see Figure 22).

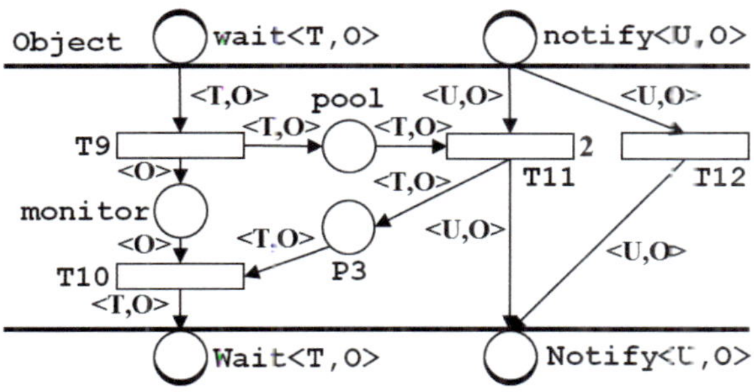

Figure 22. Declaration of class **Object** in sequential object Petri net

Next declared class in our hierarchy will be the class **Thread** representing the programming thread, which is the subclass of the class **Object** and it also implements the interface ***Runnable*** (see Figure 23). Its declaration in the Java programming language is as follows:

```
public class Thread extends Object implements Runnable {
  private Runnable runnable;
  public Thread(Runnable run) { ... }
  protected void finalize() { ... }
  public void start() { ... }
  public void run() { ... }
}
```

The method **Thread** is the constructor of the object which during its execution firstly invokes the construction of the instance of the class **Object**, that is the superclass of the class **Thread**, which in the variable value **U** returns the pointer to the newly created programming thread. In the place **Thread.runnable** (i.e. in the value of the variable **runnable**) is then stored the token **<U, pRun>**, where the value of the variable **pRun** contains the pointer to the class instance implementing the interface ***Runnable*** (see Figure 18) whose method **run** will be then executed by the newly created programming thread. That will be implemented through execution of the method **start** with programming thread **T**. The token **<U, pRun, 0>** is then located into the place **Thread.runnable** representing the fact that the execution of the method **pRun.run** was initiated. Its invocation itself is realized by asynchronous method call by the firing of the transition **Thread.T3** and by the mechanism of multiarc (**Thread.T3**, **Thread.Start**). The class **Thread** itself has the method **run** implemented the easiest possible way.

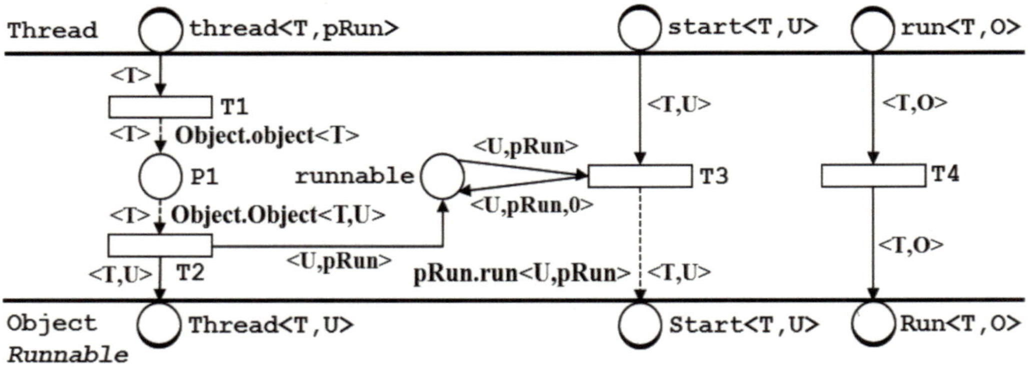

Figure 23. Declaration of class **Thread** in sequential object Petri net

As a part of execution of the destructor of the instance of the class **Thread**, i.e. the method **finalize** (see Figure 24), the particular token is removed from the place **Thread.runnable** and the destructor of the superclass **Object** is then executed. If in the place **Thread.runnable** is the token of the form **<U, pRun>**, the programming thread is not active to obeyed destruction and the transition **Thread.T7** can be fired. If, on the contrary, in the place **Thread.runnable** is the token in the form **<U, pRun, 0>**, the programming thread is active and the execution of the destructor must be delayed until the completion of the activities of this thread (i.e. returning of the thread **U** after executing the method **pRun.run** ensured by the mechanism of the multiarc (**Thread.finalize**, **Thread.T8**)).

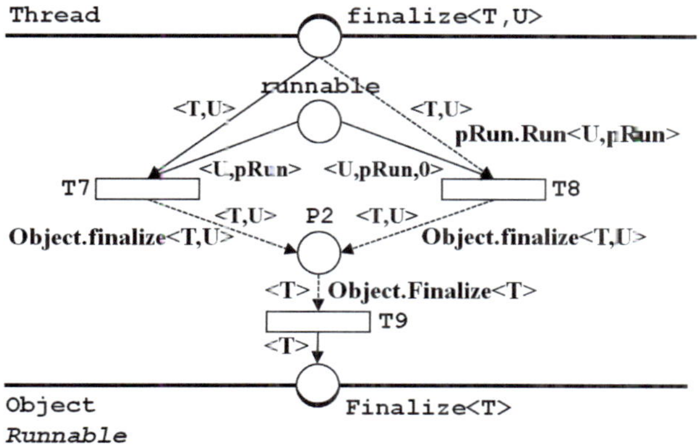

Figure 24. Declaration of class **Thread** in sequential object Petri net

Next declared class in our hierarchy will be the class **Semaphore** representing a counting semaphore. Conceptually, a semaphore maintains a set of permits. Method **down** blocks if necessary until a permit is available, and then takes it. Method **up** adds a permit, potentially releasing a blocking acquirer. However, no actual permit objects are used and the **Semaphore** just keeps a count of the number available and acts accordingly. Declaration of the class in the Java programming language is the following:

```
public class Semaphore extends Object {
  private int value = 1;
  public Semaphore() { … }
  protected void finalize() { … }
  public synchronized void down() { … }
  public synchronized void up() { … }
}
```

The constructor of the object, i.e. the method **Semaphore**, following execution of the constructor of the instance of the superclass **Object** will store in the place **Semaphore.value** the token **<O, 1>** representing the initial value of the data item value of the class instance **O**. As a part of the execution of the destructor of the instance of the class **Semaphore**, i.e. of the method **finalize**, that token is removed from the place **Semaphore.value** and then the destructor of the superclass **Object** is executed (see Figure 25).

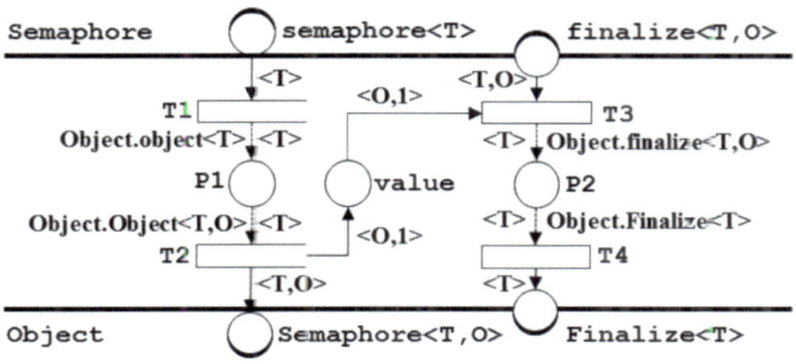

Figure 25. Declaration of class **Semaphore** in sequential object Petri net

Method **down** acquires a permit from this semaphore, blocking until one is available. Following entry into the critical section of the object instance the programming thread acquires a permit from this semaphore (ie. token in the place **Semaphore.value** can be bound to the arc sequence **<O, 1, #x>** after at least one execution of the method **up**) and will leave the critical section of the object. If no permit is available then the current thread becomes disabled for thread scheduling purposes and waits (i.e. the transition **Semaphore.T7** is executed and the method **Object.wait** is invoked, the programming thread will release the monitor of the object in order to enable execution of the method **up** by other programming thread) until some other thread invokes the **up** method for this semaphore and the current thread is next to be assigned a permit (see Figure 26).

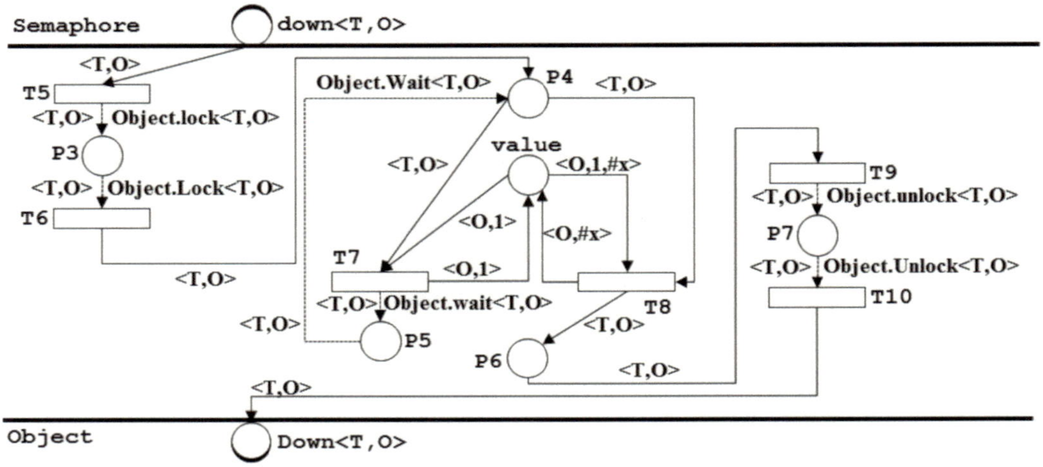

Figure 26. Declaration of class **Semaphore** in sequential object Petri net

Method **up** releases a permit, increasing the number of available permits by one. If any threads are trying to acquire a permit, then one is selected and given the permit that was just released. That thread is (re)enabled for thread scheduling purposes (see Figure 27).

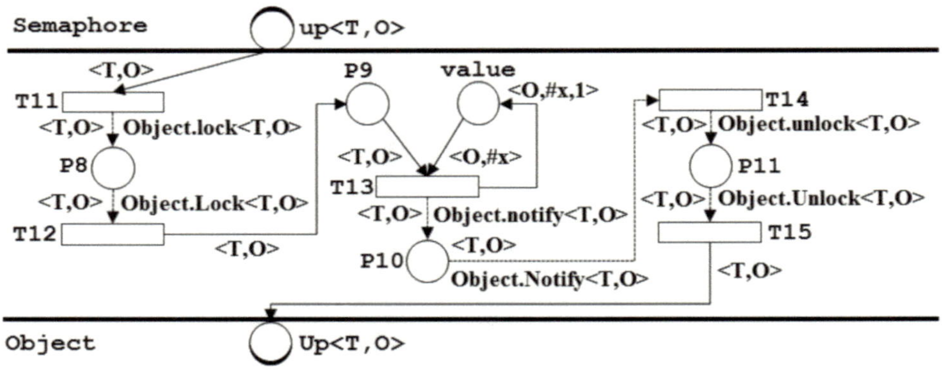

Figure 27. Declaration of class **Semaphore** in sequential object Petri net

7. Conclusion

Sequential object Petri nets represent an interesting class in the area of object Petri net classes, which can be applied at design, modeling, analysis and verification of generally distributed multithreading object-oriented programming systems. A newly introduced term of token as finite non-empty recursive sequence over the set of non-negative integer numbers, functionalities of multiarcs and the mechanism of the firing of transitions do not increase demands on performance of analysis of characteristics, as seen in other classes of high-level or colored Petri Nets.

Functional programming is one of the most important paradigms of programming that looks back on a long history. The recent interest in functional programming started as a response to the growing pervasiveness of concurrency as a way of scaling horizontally. Multithreaded programming is difficult to do well in practice and functional programming offers (in many ways) better strategies than object-oriented programming for writing robust, concurrent software. Functional programming is generally regarded a paradigm of programming that can be applied in many languages - even those that were not originally intended to be used with that paradigm. Like the name implies, it focuses on the application of functions. Functional programmers use functions as building blocks to create new functions and the function is the main construct that architecture is built from. Several programming languages (like Scala, C#, Java, Delphi, etc) are a blend of object-oriented and functional programming concepts in a statically typed language in the present time. The fusion of object-oriented and functional programming makes it possible to express new kinds of programming patterns and component abstractions. It also leads to a legible and concise programming style. Sequential object Petri nets then also fully support design, modeling, analysis and verification of programming systems based on this fusion of object-oriented and functional programming paradigms.

Author details

Ivo Martiník
VŠB-Technical University of Ostrava, Czech Republic

Acknowledgement

This paper has been elaborated in the framework of the IT4Innovations Centre of Excellence project, reg. no. CZ.1.05/1.1.00/02.0070 supported by Operational Programme 'Research and Development for Innovations' funded by Structural Funds of the European Union and state budget of the Czech Republic.

8. References

Agha, G. A.; Cinindio, F. & Rozenberg, G. (2001). *Concurrent Object-Oriented Programming and Petri Nets: Advances in Petri Nets*. Springer, ISBN 978-3-540-41942-6, Berlin, Germany

Diaz, M. (2009). *Petri Nets: Fundamental Models, Verification and Applications*, John Willey & Sons, ISTE Ltd., ISBN: 978-0-470-39430-4, London, United Kingdom

Goetz, B.; Peierls, T., Bloch, J.; Bowbeer, J.; Holmes, D. & Lea, D. (2006). *Java Concurrency in Practice*, Addison-Wesley, ISBN 978-0321349606, Reading, United Kingdom

Jensen, K.; Kristensen, L. M. (2009). *Coloured Petri Nets: Modelling and Validation of Concurrent Systems*, Springer, ISBN 978-3-642-00283-0, Berlin, Germany

Jensen, K.; Rozenberg, G. (1991). *High-Level Petri Nets: Theory and Application*, Springer, ISBN 3-540-54125-x, London, United Kingdom

Köhler, M.; Rölke, H. (2007). Web Services Orchestration with Super-Dual Object Nets, *ICATPN 2007, Lecture Notes in Computer Science 4546*, Springer-Verlag, pp. 263–280, ISBN 978-3-540-73093-4

Lea, D. (1999). *Concurrent Programming in Java, Second Edition*, Addison-Wesley, ISBN 0-201-31009-0, Reading, United Kingdom

Martiník, I. Bi-relational P/T Petri Nets and the Modeling of Multithreading Object-oriented Programming Systems, *Communications in Computer and Information Science.* 188 CCIS (Part 1), (July 2011), pp. 222-236. ISSN 1865-0929

Reisig, W. (2009). *Elements of Distributed Algorithms*, Springer, ISBN 3-540-62752-9, Berlin, Germany

Subramaniam, V. (2011). *Programming Concurrency on the JVM: Mastering Synchronization, STM and Actors*, Pragmatic Bookshelf, ISBN 978-1934356760, Dallas, USA

Chapter 10

Fluid Stochastic Petri Nets: From Fluid Atoms in ILP Processor Pipelines to Fluid Atoms in P2P Streaming Networks

Pece Mitrevski and Zoran Kotevski

Additional information is available at the end of the chapter

http://dx.doi.org/10.5772/50615

1. Introduction

Fluid models have been used and investigated in queuing theory [1]. Recently, the concept of fluid models was used in the context of Stochastic Petri Nets, referred to as *Fluid Stochastic Petri Nets* (FSPNs) [2-6]. In FSPNs, the fluid variables are represented by fluid places, which can hold fluid rather than discrete tokens. Transition firings are determined by both discrete and fluid places, and fluid flow is permitted through the enabled timed transitions in the Petri Net. By associating exponentially distributed or zero firing time with transitions, the differential equations for the underlying stochastic process can be derived. The dynamics of an FSPN are described by a system of first-order hyperbolic *partial differential equations* (PDEs) combined with initial and boundary equations. The general system of PDEs may be solved by a standard discretization approach. In [6], the problem of immediate transitions has also been addressed in relation to the fluid levels, by allowing fluid places to be connected to immediate transitions. The transportation of fluid in zero time is described by appropriately chosen boundary conditions.

In a typical multiple-issue processor, instructions flow through pipeline and pass through separate pipeline stages connected by buffers. An open multi-chain queuing network can present this organization, with each stage being a service center with a limited buffer size. Considering a machine that employs multiple execution units capable to execute large number of instructions in parallel, the service and storage requirements of each individual instruction are small compared to the total volume of the instruction stream. Individual instructions may then be regarded as *atoms of a fluid* flowing through the pipeline. The objective of this approach is to approximate large buffer levels by continuous fluid levels and decrease state-space complexity. Thus, in the first part of this chapter, we employ an analytical model based on FSPNs, derive the state equations for the underlying stochastic process and present performance evaluation results to illustrate its usage in deriving measures of interest. The attempt to capture the dynamic behavior of an ILP processor with aggressive use of prediction techniques and speculative execution is a rare example that demonstrates the usage of this recently introduced formalism in modeling actual systems. Moreover, we take into consideration numerical transient analysis and present numerical solution of a FSPN with more than three fluid places. Both the application of finite-difference approximations for the partial derivatives [7,8], as well as the discrete-event simulation of the proposed FSPN model [9,10], allow for the evaluation of a number of performance measures and lead to numerous conclusions regarding the performance impact of predictions and speculative execution with varying parameters of both the microarchitecture and the operational environment. The numerical solution makes possible the probabilistic analysis of the dynamic behavior, whereas the advantage of the discrete-event simulation is the much faster generation of performance evaluation results. Since the modeling framework is implementation-independent, it can be used to estimate the performance potential of branch and value prediction, as well as to assess the operational environment influence on the performance of ILP processors with much more aggressive, wider instruction issue.

Another challenging task in the application of FSPNs is the modeling and performance analysis of *Peer-to-Peer* (P2P) live video streaming systems. Web locations offering live video content increasingly attract more and more visitors, which, if the system is based on the client/server architecture, leads to sustainability issues when clients rise above the upload capabilities of the streaming servers. Since IP Multicast failed to satisfy the requirements of an affordable, large scale live video streaming, in the last decade the science community intensively works in the field of P2P networking technologies for live video broadcast. P2P live video streaming is a relatively new paradigm that aims for streaming live video content to a large number of clients with low cost. Even though many such applications already exist, these systems are still in their early stages and prior to creation of such a system it is necessary to analyze performance via representative model that provides significant insight into the system's behavior. Nevertheless, modeling and performance analysis of P2P live video streaming systems is a complex combinatorial problem, which requires addressing many properties and issues of such systems. Inspired by several research articles concerned with modeling of their behavior, in the second part of this chapter, we present how FSPNs can be used for modeling and performance analysis of a mesh based P2P live video streaming system. We adopt fluid flow to represent bits as *atoms of a fluid* that travel through fluid pipes (network infrastructure). If we represent peers with discrete tokens and video bits as fluid, then we have numerous possibilities to evaluate the performance of the system. The developed model is simple and quite flexible, providing performance evaluation of a system that accounts for a number of system features, such as: network topology, peer churn, scalability, peer average group size, peer upload bandwidth heterogeneity, video buffering, control traffic overhead and admission control for lesser contributing peers. In this particular case, discrete-event simulation (DES) is carried out using SimPy (http://simpy.sourceforge.net) – an object-oriented, process-based discrete-event simulation language based on standard Python (http://www.python.org), which provides the modeler with components of a simulation model including processes (for active components) and resources (for passive components) and provides monitor variables to aid in gathering statistics.

2. Part A: Fluid atoms in ILP processor pipelines

Most of the recent microprocessor architectures assume *sequential programs* as input and use a *parallel execution* model. The hardware is expected to extract the parallelism out of the instruction stream at run-time. The efficiency is highly dependent on both the hardware mechanisms and the program characteristics, i.e. the *instruction-level parallelism* (ILP) the programs exhibit. Many ILP processors *speculatively* execute control-dependent instructions before resolving the branch outcome. They rely upon *branch prediction* in order to tolerate the effect of *control dependences*. A branch predictor uses the current fetch address to predict whether a branch will be fetched in the current cycle, whether that branch will be taken or not, and what the target address of the branch is. The predictor uses this information to decide where to fetch from in the next cycle. Since the branch execution penalty is only seen if the branch was mispredicted, a highly accurate branch predictor is a very important mechanism for reducing the branch penalty in a high performance ILP processor.

A variety of branch prediction schemes have been explored [11] – they range between *fixed, static displacement-based, static with profiling,* and various dynamic schemes, like *Branch History Table with n-bit counters, Branch Target Address Cache, Branch Target Instruction Cache, mixed, two-level adaptive, hybrid,* etc. Some research studies have also proposed concepts to implement high-bandwidth instruction fetch engines based on *multiple branch prediction*. Such concepts include *trace cache* [12] or the more conventional *multiple-block fetching* [13].

On the other hand, given that a majority of static instructions exhibit very little variations in values that they produce/consume during the course of a program's execution [14], *data dependences* can be eliminated at run-time by predicting the outcome values of instructions (*value prediction*) and by executing the true data dependent instructions. In general, the outcome value of an instruction can be assigned to registers, memory locations, condition codes, etc. The execution is *speculative*, as it is not assured that instructions were fed with correct input values. Since the correctness of execution must be maintained, speculatively executed instructions retire only if the prediction was proven correct – otherwise, they are discarded.

Several architectures have been proposed for value prediction [15] – *last value predictor, stride predictor, context predictors* and *hybrid approaches* in order to get good accuracy over a set of programs due to the different data value locality characteristics that can be exploited only by different schemes. Based on instruction type, value prediction is sometimes identified as prediction of the outcome of *arithmetic instructions* only, and the prediction of the outcome of *memory access instructions* as a different class, referred to as *memory prediction*.

2.1. Model definition

A model should always have a form that is more concise and closer to a designer's intuition about what a model should look like. In the case of a processor pipeline, the simplest description would be that the instructions flow and pass through separate pipeline stages connected by buffers. Control dependences stall the inflow of useful instructions (fluid) into the pipeline, whereas true data dependences decrease the aperture of the pipeline and the outflow rate. The buffer levels always vary and affect both the inflow and outflow rates. Branch prediction techniques tend to eliminate stalls in the inflow, while value prediction techniques help keeping outflow rate as high as possible.

Representing the dynamic behavior of systems subject to randomness or variability is the main concern of *stochastic modeling*. It relies on the use of random variables and their distribution functions [16]. We assume that the distribution of the time between two consecutive occurrences of branch instructions in the fluid stream is exponential with rate λ. The rate depends on the instruction fetch bandwidth, as well as the program's average *basic block size*. Branches vary widely in their dynamic behavior, and predictors that work well on one type of branches may not work as well on others. A set of hard-to-predict branches that comprise a fundamental limit to traditional branch predictors can always be identified [17]. We assume that there are two classes: *easy-to-predict* and *hard-to-predict branches*, and the expected branch prediction accuracy is higher for the first, and lower for the second. The probabilities to classify a branch as either easy- or hard-to-predict depend on the program characteristics.

When the instruction fetch rate is low, a significant portion of data dependences span across instructions that are fetched consecutively [18]. As a result, these instructions (a producer-consumer pair) will eventually initiate their execution in a sequential manner. In this case, the prediction becomes useless due to the availability of the consumer's input value. Hence, in each cycle, an important factor is the number of instructions that consume results of *simultaneously* initiated producer instructions. We assume that the distribution of the time between two consecutive occurrences of consuming instructions in the fluid stream is exponential with rate μ. The rate depends on the number of instructions that simultaneously initiate execution at a functional unit, as well as the program's average *dynamic instruction distance*. We assume that there are two classes of consuming instructions: (1) instructions that consume *easy-to-predict values* and (2) instructions that consume *hard-to-predict values*. The expected value prediction accuracy is higher for the first and lower for the second. The probability to classify a value as either easy- or hard-to-predict depends on the program's characteristics, similarly to the branch classification.

The set of programs executed on the machine represent the *input space*. Programs with different characteristics are executed randomly and independently according to the *operational profile*. We partition the input space by grouping programs that exhibit as nearly as possible homogenous behavior into *program classes*. Since there are a finite number of partitions (classes), the upper limits of λ and μ, as well as the probabilities to classify a branch/value as either easy- or hard-to-predict are considered to be discrete random variables and have different values for different program classes.

2.2. FSPN representation

We assume that the pipeline is organized in four stages: Fetch, Decode/Issue, Execute and Commit. Fluid places P_{IC}, P_{IB}, $P_{RS/LSQ}$, P_{ROB}, P_{RR}, P_{EX} and P_{REG}, depicted by means of two concentric circles (Figure 1), represent buffers between pipeline stages: *instruction cache, instruction buffer, reservation stations and load/store queue, reorder buffer, rename registers, instructions that have completed execution* and *architectural registers*. Five of them have limited capacities: Z_{IBmax}, $Z_{RS/LSQmax}$, Z_{RRmax}, Z_{ROBmax} and Z_{EXmax}. We prohibit both an overflow and a negative level in a fluid place. The fluid place P_{TIME} has the function of an hourglass: it is constantly filled at rate 1 up to the level 1 and then flushed out, which corresponds to the machine clock cycle. $Z_{TIME}(t)$ denotes the fluid level in P_{TIME} at time t. Fluid arcs are drawn as double arrows to suggest a pipe. Flow rates are piecewise constant, i.e. take different values at the beginning of each cycle and are limited by the fetch/issue width of the machine (W). Rates depend on the vector of fluid levels $\mathbf{Z}(t)$ and change when T_{CLOCK} fires and the fluid in P_{TIME} is flushed out. The flush out arc is drawn as thick single arrow.

Let $Z_{IC_0}, Z_{IB_0}, Z_{RS/LSQ_0}, Z_{RR_0}, Z_{ROB_0}$ and Z_{EX_0} be the fluid levels at the beginning of the clock cycle, i.e. $Z_{IC_0} = Z_{IC}(t_0)$, $Z_{IB_0} = Z_{IB}(t_0)$, $Z_{RS/LSQ_0} = Z_{RS/LSQ}(t_0)$, $Z_{RR_0} = Z_{RR}(t_0)$, $Z_{ROB_0} = Z_{ROB}(t_0)$ and $Z_{EX_0} = Z_{EX}(t_0)$, where $t_0 = \lfloor t \rfloor$ and $Z_{TIME}(t_0) = 0$.

A high-bandwidth instruction fetch mechanism fetches up to W instructions per cycle and places them in the instruction buffer. The fetch rate is given by:

$$r_{FETCH} = \min(Z_{IB_{\max}} - Z_{IB_0} + r_{ISSUE}, Z_{IC_0}, W) \quad (1)$$

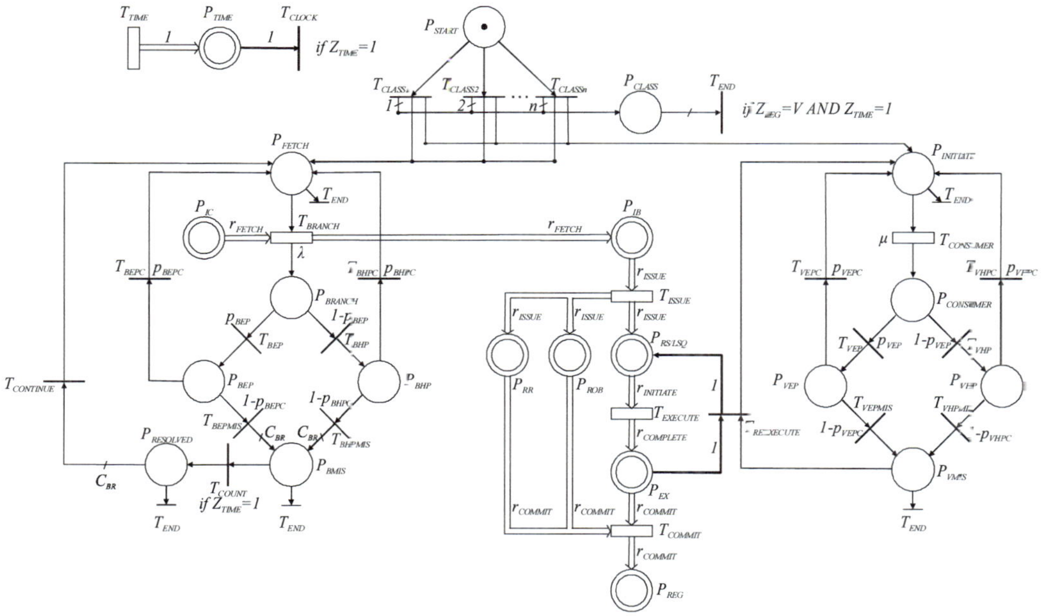

Figure 1. A Fluid Stochastic Petri Net model of an ILP processor

In the case of a branch misprediction, the fetch unit is effectively stalled and no useful instructions are added to the buffer. Instruction cache misses are ignored.

Instruction issue tries to send W instructions to the appropriate reservation stations or the load/store queue on every clock cycle. Rename registers are allocated to hold the results of the instructions and reorder buffer entries are allocated to ensure in-order completion. Among the instructions that initiate execution in the same cycle, speculatively executed consuming instructions are forced to retain their reservation stations. As a result, the issue rate is given by:

$$r_{ISSUE} = \min(Z_{RR\max} - Z_{RR0} + r_{COMMIT}, Z_{ROB\max} - Z_{ROB0} + r_{COMMIT}, Z_{RS/LSQ\max} - Z_{RS/LSQ0}, Z_{IB0}, W) \quad (2)$$

Up to W instructions are *in execution* at the same time. With the assumptions that functional units are always available and out-of-order execution is allowed, the instructions *initiate* and *complete* execution with rate:

$$r_{INITIATE} = r_{COMPLETE} = \min(Z_{RS/LSQ_0}, W) \quad (3)$$

During the execute stage, the instructions first check to see if their source operands are available (predicted or computed). For simplicity, we assume that the execution latency of each instruction is a single cycle. Instructions execute and forward their own results back to subsequent instructions that might be waiting for them (no result forwarding delay). Every reference to memory is present in the first-level cache. With the last assumption, we eliminate the effect of the memory hierarchy.

The instructions that have completed execution are ready to move to the last stage. Up to W instructions may commit per cycle. The results in the rename registers are written into the register file and the rename registers and reorder buffer entries freed. Hence:

$$r_{COMMIT} = \min(Z_{EX_0}, W) \quad (4)$$

In order to capture the relative occurrence frequencies of different program classes, we introduce a set of weighted immediate transitions in the Petri Net. Each program class is assigned an immediate transition T_{CLASS_i} with weight w_{CLASS_i}. The operational profile is a set of weights. The probability of firing the immediate transition T_{CLASS_i} represents the probability of occurrence of a class i program, given by:

$$\hat{w}_{T_{CLASS_i}} = \frac{w_{T_{CLASS_i}}}{\sum_{k=1}^{n} w_{T_{CLASS_k}}} \quad (5)$$

A token in P_{START} denotes that a new execution is about to begin. The process of firing one of the immediate transitions randomly chooses a program from one of the classes. The firing of transition T_{CLASS_i} puts i tokens in place P_{CLASS}, which identify the class. At the same time instant, tokens occur in places P_{FETCH} and $P_{INITIATE}$, while the fluid place P_{IC} is filled with fluid with volume V_i equivalent to the total number of useful instructions (*program volume*).

Firing of exponential transition T_{BRANCH} corresponds to a branch instruction occurrence. The parameter λ changes at the beginning of each clock cycle and formally depends on both the number of tokens in P_{CLASS} and the fetch rate:

$$\lambda = \mathrm{f}\left(\# P_{CLASS}\right)\frac{r_{FETCH}}{W} = \mathrm{f}\left(i\right)\frac{r_{FETCH}}{W} = \lambda_i \frac{r_{FETCH}}{W} \tag{6}$$

where λ_i is its upper limit for a given program class i at maximum fetch rate ($r_{FETCH}=W$). The branch is classified as easy-to-predict with probability p_{BEP}, or hard-to-predict with probability $1-p_{BEP}$. In either case, it is correctly predicted with probability p_{BEPC} (p_{BHPC}), or mispredicted with probability $1-p_{BEPC}$ ($1-p_{BHPC}$). These probabilities are included in the FSPN model as weights assigned to immediate transitions T_{BEP}, T_{BHP}, T_{BEPC}, T_{BHPC}, T_{BEPMIS} and T_{BHPMIS}, respectively. This approach is known as *synthetic branch prediction*. Branch mispredictions stall the fluid inflow for as many cycles as necessary to resolve the branch (C_{BR} tokens in place P_{BMIS}). Usually, a branch is not resolved until its execution stage ($C_{BR}=3$). With several consecutive firings of T_{CLOCK}, these tokens are consumed one at a time and moved to $P_{RESOLVED}$. As soon as the branch is resolved, transition $T_{CONTINUE}$ fires, a token appears in place P_{FETCH} and the inflow resumes.

Similar to this, firing of exponential transition $T_{CONSUMER}$ corresponds to the occurrence of a consuming instruction among the instructions that initiated execution. The parameter μ changes at the beginning of each clock cycle and formally depends on both the number of tokens in P_{CLASS} and the initiation rate:

$$\mu = \mathrm{g}\left(\# P_{CLASS}\right)\frac{r_{INITIATE}}{W} = \mathrm{g}\left(i\right)\frac{r_{INITIATE}}{W} = \mu_i \frac{r_{INITIATE}}{W} \tag{7}$$

where μ_i is its upper limit for a given program class i when maximum possible number of instructions simultaneously initiate execution ($r_{INITIATE}=W$). The consumed value is classified as easy-to-predict with probability p_{VEP}, or hard-to-predict with probability $1-p_{VEP}$. In either case, it is correctly predicted with probability p_{VEPC} (p_{VHPC}), or mispredicted with probability $1-p_{VEPC}$ ($1-p_{VHPC}$). These probabilities are included in the FSPN model as weights assigned to immediate transitions T_{VEP}, T_{VHP}, T_{VEPC}, T_{VHPC}, T_{VEPMIS} and T_{VHPMIS}, respectively. Whenever a misprediction occurs (token in place P_{VMIS}), the consuming instruction has to be *rescheduled* for execution. The firing of immediate transition $T_{REEXECUTE}$ causes transportation of fluid in zero time. Fluid jumps have deterministic height of 1 (one instruction) and take place when the fluid levels in P_{RS} and P_{EX} satisfy the condition $Z_{RS}(t) \le Z_{RS_{\max}} - 1$ and $Z_{EX}(t) \ge 1$. Jumps that would go beyond the boundaries cannot be carried out. The arcs connecting fluid places and immediate transitions are drawn as thick single arrows. The fluid flow terminates at the end of the cycle when all the fluid places except P_{REG} are empty and T_{END} fires.

2.3. Derivation of state equations

When executing a class i program, the nodes m_i of the reachability graph (Figure 2) consist of all the tangible discrete markings, as well as those in which the enabling of immediate transitions depends on fluid levels and cannot be eliminated, since they are of mixed tangible/vanishing type (Table 1). It is important to note that the number of discrete markings does not depend on the machine width in any way.

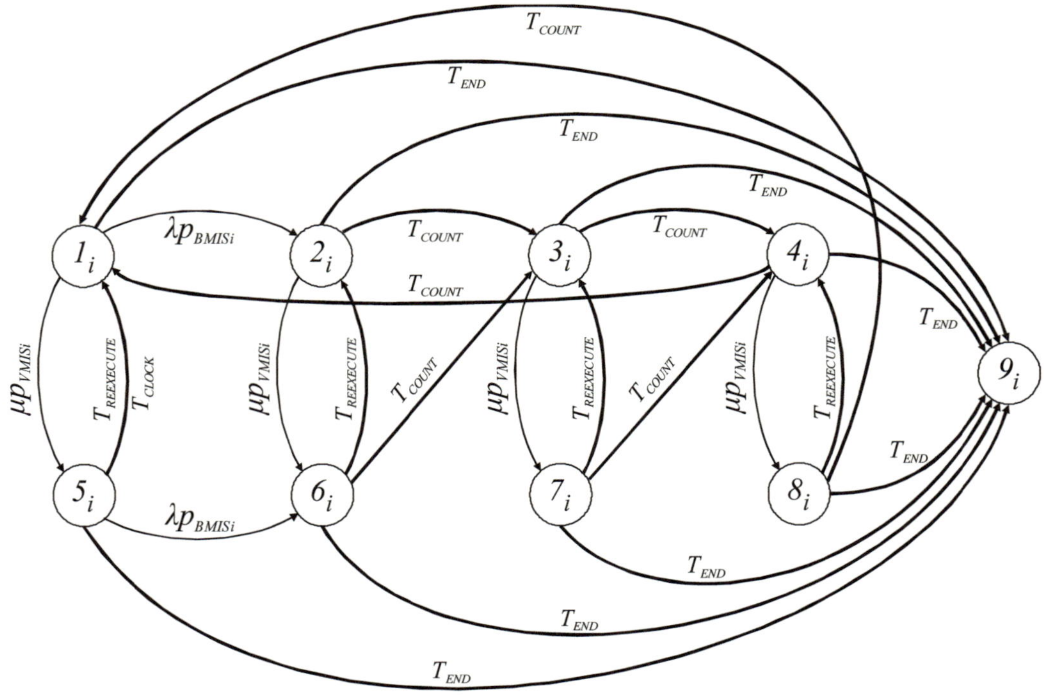

Figure 2. Reachability graph of the FSPN model

Number of tokens / Marking (m_i)	$\#P_{FETCH}$	$\#P_{BMIS}$	$\#P_{INITIATE}$	$\#P_{VMIS}$
1_i	1	0	1	0
2_i	0	3	1	0
3_i	0	2	1	0
4_i	0	1	1	0
5_i	1	0	0	1
6_i	0	3	0	1
7_i	0	2	0	1
8_i	0	1	0	1
9_i	0	0	0	0

Table 1. Discrete markings of the FSPN model (C_{BR}=3)

A vector of fluid levels supplements discrete markings. It gives rise to a stochastic process in continuous time with continuous state space. The total amount of fluid contained in P_{IC}, P_{IB}, $P_{RS/LSQ}$, P_{EX} and P_{REG} is always equal to V_i, and the amount of fluid contained in P_{RR} (as well as

P_{ROB}) is equal to the total amount of fluid in $P_{RS/LSQ}$ and P_{EX}. Therefore, only the fluid levels Z_{IB}(t), $Z_{RS/LSQ}$(t), Z_{EX}(t) and Z_{REG}(t) are identified as four supplementary variables (components of the fluid vector $\mathbf{Z}(t)$), which provide a full description of each state.

The instantaneous rates at which fluid builds in each fluid place are collected in diagonal matrices:

$$\begin{aligned}
&\mathbf{R}_{IB} = \mathbf{diag}\left(r_{FETCH} - r_{ISSUE}, -r_{ISSUE}, -r_{ISSUE}, -r_{ISSUE}, r_{FETCH} - r_{ISSUE}, -r_{ISSUE}, -r_{ISSUE}, -r_{ISSUE}, 0\right) \\
&\mathbf{R}_{RS/LSQ} = \mathbf{diag}\left(r_{ISSUE} - r_{INITIATE}, \ldots, r_{ISSUE} - r_{INITIATE}, 0\right) \\
&\mathbf{R}_{EX} = \mathbf{diag}\left(r_{COMPLETE} - r_{COMMIT}, \ldots, r_{COMPLETE} - r_{COMMIT}, 0\right) \\
&\mathbf{R}_{REG} = \mathbf{diag}\left(r_{COMMIT}, \ldots, r_{COMMIT}, 0\right)
\end{aligned} \tag{8}$$

The matrix of *transition rates* of exponential transitions causing the state changes is:

$$\mathbf{Q}_i = \begin{bmatrix}
-(\lambda p_{BMIS_i} + \mu p_{VMIS_i}) & \lambda p_{BMIS_i} & 0 & 0 & \mu p_{VMIS_i} & 0 & 0 & 0 & 0 \\
0 & -\mu p_{VMIS_i} & 0 & 0 & 0 & \mu p_{VMIS_i} & 0 & 0 & 0 \\
0 & 0 & -\mu p_{VMIS_i} & 0 & 0 & 0 & \mu p_{VMIS_i} & 0 & 0 \\
0 & 0 & 0 & -\mu p_{VMIS_i} & 0 & 0 & 0 & \mu p_{VMIS_i} & 0 \\
0 & 0 & 0 & 0 & -\lambda p_{BMIS_i} & \lambda p_{BMIS_i} & 0 & 0 & 0 \\
0 & 0 & 0 & 0 & 0 & 0 & 0 & 0 & 0 \\
0 & 0 & 0 & 0 & 0 & 0 & 0 & 0 & 0 \\
0 & 0 & 0 & 0 & 0 & 0 & 0 & 0 & 0 \\
0 & 0 & 0 & 0 & 0 & 0 & 0 & 0 & 0
\end{bmatrix}$$

where:

$$\begin{aligned}
&p_{BMIS_i} = p_{BEP_i}\left(1 - p_{BEPC}\right) + \left(1 - p_{BEP_i}\right)\left(1 - p_{BHPC}\right) \\
&\text{and} \\
&p_{VMIS_i} = p_{VEP_i}\left(1 - p_{VEPC}\right) + \left(1 - p_{VEP_i}\right)\left(1 - p_{VHPC}\right)
\end{aligned} \tag{9}$$

Let π_{m_i} be an abbreviation for the *volume density* $\pi_{m_i}(t, z_{IB}, z_{RS/LSQ}, z_{EX}, z_{REG})$ that is the transient probability of being in discrete marking m_i at time t, with fluid levels in an infinitesimal environment around $\mathbf{z} = [z_{IB} \quad z_{RS/LSQ} \quad z_{EX} \quad z_{REG}]$. If $\boldsymbol{\pi}_i = [\pi_{1_i} \quad \pi_{2_i} \quad \ldots \quad \pi_{9_i}]$, according to [4-6] the evolution of the process is described by a coupled system of nine *partial differential equations* in four continuous dimensions plus time:

$$\frac{\partial \boldsymbol{\pi}_i}{\partial t} + \frac{\partial(\boldsymbol{\pi}_i \cdot \mathbf{R}_{IB})}{\partial z_{IB}} + \frac{\partial(\boldsymbol{\pi}_i \cdot \mathbf{R}_{RS/LSQ})}{\partial z_{RS/LSQ}} + \frac{\partial(\boldsymbol{\pi}_i \cdot \mathbf{R}_{EX})}{\partial z_{EX}} + \frac{\partial(\boldsymbol{\pi}_i \cdot \mathbf{R}_{REG})}{\partial z_{REG}} = \boldsymbol{\pi}_i \cdot \mathbf{Q}_i \tag{10}$$

If $\mathbf{z_0} = \begin{bmatrix} 0 & 0 & 0 & 0 \end{bmatrix}$ is the vector of initial fluid levels, the *initial conditions* are:

$$\begin{aligned}
&\pi_{1_i}(0, \mathbf{z}) = \delta(\mathbf{z} - \mathbf{z_0}) \\
&\pi_{m_i}(0, \mathbf{z}) = 0 \quad (2 \le m \le 9)
\end{aligned} \tag{11}$$

Since fluid jumps shift probability mass along the continuous axes (in addition to discrete state change), firing of transition $T_{REEXECUTE}$ at time t can be seen as a *jump* to another location in the four-dimensional hypercube defined by the components of the fluid vector. It can be described by the following *boundary conditions*:

$$\begin{aligned}
&\pi_{1_i}(t^+, z_{IB}, z_{RS/LSQ}+1, z_{EX}-1, z_{REG}) = \pi_{1_i}(t^-, z_{IB}, z_{RS/LSQ}+1, z_{EX}-1, z_{REG}) + \pi_{5_i}(t^-, z_{IB}, z_{RS/LSQ}, z_{EX}, z_{REG}) \\
&\pi_{2_i}(t^+, z_{IB}, z_{RS/LSQ}+1, z_{EX}-1, z_{REG}) = \pi_{2_i}(t^-, z_{IB}, z_{RS/LSQ}+1, z_{EX}-1, z_{REG}) + \pi_{6_i}(t^-, z_{IB}, z_{RS/LSQ}, z_{EX}, z_{REG}) \\
&\pi_{3_i}(t^+, z_{IB}, z_{RS/LSQ}+1, z_{EX}-1, z_{REG}) = \pi_{3_i}(t^-, z_{IB}, z_{RS/LSQ}+1, z_{EX}-1, z_{REG}) + \pi_{7_i}(t^-, z_{IB}, z_{RS/LSQ}, z_{EX}, z_{REG}) \\
&\pi_{4_i}(t^+, z_{IB}, z_{RS/LSQ}+1, z_{EX}-1, z_{REG}) = \pi_{4_i}(t^-, z_{IB}, z_{RS/LSQ}+1, z_{EX}-1, z_{REG}) + \pi_{8_i}(t^-, z_{IB}, z_{RS/LSQ}, z_{EX}, z_{REG}) \\
&\pi_{m_i}(t^+, z_{IB}, z_{RS/LSQ}, z_{EX}, z_{REG}) = 0 \quad (\text{if } z_{RS/LSQ} \le Z_{RS/LSQ_{\max}} - 1,\ z_{EX} \ge 1,\ 5 \le m \le 8)
\end{aligned} \tag{12}$$

The firing of transitions T_{CLOCK} and T_{COUNT} at time t_0 causes switching from one discrete marking to another. Therefore:

$$\begin{aligned}
&\pi_{1_i}(t_0^+, z_{IB}, z_{RS/LSQ}, z_{EX}, z_{REG}) = \pi_{1_i}(t_0^-, z_{IB}, z_{RS/LSQ}, z_{EX}, z_{REG}) + \pi_{4_i}(t_0^-, z_{IB}, z_{RS/LSQ}, z_{EX}, z_{REG}) + \\
&\qquad + \pi_{5_i}(t_0^-, z_{IB}, z_{RS/LSQ}, z_{EX}, z_{REG}) + \pi_{8_i}(t_0^-, z_{IB}, z_{RS/LSQ}, z_{EX}, z_{REG}) \\
&\pi_{4_i}(t_0^+, z_{IB}, z_{RS/LSQ}, z_{EX}, z_{REG}) = \pi_{3_i}(t_0^-, z_{IB}, z_{RS/LSQ}, z_{EX}, z_{REG}) + \pi_{7_i}(t_0^-, z_{IB}, z_{RS/LSQ}, z_{EX}, z_{REG}) \\
&\pi_{3_i}(t_0^+, z_{IB}, z_{RS/LSQ}, z_{EX}, z_{REG}) = \pi_{2_i}(t_0^-, z_{IB}, z_{RS/LSQ}, z_{EX}, z_{REG}) + \pi_{6_i}(t_0^-, z_{IB}, z_{RS/LSQ}, z_{EX}, z_{REG}) \\
&\pi_{m_i}(t_0^+, z_{IB}, z_{RS/LSQ}, z_{EX}, z_{REG}) = 0 \quad (m \in \{2,5,6,7,8\})
\end{aligned} \tag{13}$$

Similarly, the firing of transition T_{END} when all the fluid places except P_{REG} are empty, causes switching from any discrete marking to 9_i:

$$\pi_{9_i}(t_0^+, 0,0,0, V_i) = \sum_{m=1}^{9} \pi_{m_i}(t_0^-, 0,0,0, V_i) \qquad \pi_{m_i}(t_0^+, 0,0,0, V_i) = 0 \quad (m \le 8) \tag{14}$$

The *probability mass conservation law* is used as a normalization condition. It corresponds to the condition that the sum of all state probabilities must equal one. Since no particle can pass beyond barriers, the sum of integrals of the volume densities over the definition range evaluates to one:

$$\sum_{m=1}^{9} \int_0^{Z_{IB_{\max}}} \int_0^{Z_{RS/LSQ_{\max}}} \int_0^{Z_{EX_{\max}}} \int_0^{V_i} \pi_{m_i}\left(t, z_{IB}, z_{RS/LSQ}, z_{EX}, z_{REG}\right) dz_{IB} dz_{RS/LSQ} dz_{EX} dz_{REG} = 1 \tag{15}$$

Let $M_i(t)$ be the state of the discrete marking process at time t. The *probabilities of the discrete markings* are obtained by integrating volume densities:

$$\Pr\{M_i(t) = m_i\} = \int_0^{Z_{IB_{MAX}}} \int_0^{Z_{RS/LSQ_{MAX}}} \int_0^{Z_{EX_{MAX}}} \int_0^{V_i} \pi_{m_i}\left(t, z_{IB}, z_{RS/LSQ}, z_{EX}, z_{REG}\right) dz_{IB} dz_{RS/LSQ} dz_{EX} dz_{REG} \quad (m \le 9) \tag{16}$$

The *fluid levels* at the beginning of each clock cycle are computed as follows:

$$Z_{IB_0} = E(Z_{IB}(t_0)) = \int_0^{Z_{IB_{\max}}} z_{IB} \underbrace{\left(\int_0^{Z_{RS/LSQ\max}} \int_0^{Z_{EX_{\max}}} \int_0^{V_i} \left(\sum_{m=1}^{9} \pi_{m_i}(t_0, z_{IB}, z_{RS/LSQ}, z_{EX}, z_{REG}) \right) dz_{RS/LSQ} dz_{EX} dz_{REG} \right)}_{\text{marginal density for } Z_{IB}} dz_{IB}$$

$$Z_{RS/LSQ_0} = E(Z_{RS/LSQ}(t_0)) = \int_0^{Z_{RS/LSQ\max}} z_{RS/LSQ} \underbrace{\left(\int_0^{Z_{IB_{\max}}} \int_0^{Z_{EX_{\max}}} \int_0^{V_i} \left(\sum_{m=1}^{9} \pi_{m_i}(t_0, z_{IB}, z_{RS/LSQ}, z_{EX}, z_{REG}) \right) dz_{IB} dz_{EX} dz_{REG} \right)}_{\text{marginal density for } Z_{RS/LSQ}} dz_{RS/LSQ} \quad (17)$$

$$Z_{EX_0} = E(Z_{EX}(t_0)) = \int_0^{Z_{EX_{\max}}} z_{EX} \underbrace{\left(\int_0^{Z_{IB_{\max}}} \int_0^{Z_{RS/LSQ\max}} \int_0^{V_i} \left(\sum_{m=1}^{9} \pi_{m_i}(t_0, z_{IB}, z_{RS/LSQ}, z_{EX}, z_{REG}) \right) dz_{IB} dz_{RS/LSQ} dz_{REG} \right)}_{\text{marginal density for } Z_{EX}} dz_{EX}$$

$$Z_{REG_0} = E(Z_{REG}(t_0)) = \int_0^{V_i} z_{REG} \underbrace{\left(\int_0^{Z_{IB_{\max}}} \int_0^{Z_{RS/LSQ\max}} \int_0^{Z_{EX_{\max}}} \left(\sum_{m=1}^{9} \pi_{m_i}(t_0, z_{IB}, z_{RS/LSQ}, z_{EX}, z_{REG}) \right) dz_{IB} dz_{RS/LSQ} dz_{EX} \right)}_{\text{marginal density for } Z_{REG}} dz_{REG}$$

$$Z_{IC_0} = V_i - (Z_{IB_0} + Z_{RS/LSQ_0} + Z_{EX_0} + Z_{REG_0}) \text{ and } Z_{RR_0} = Z_{ROB_0} = Z_{RS/LSQ_0} + Z_{EX_0}.$$

Finally, the flow rates and the parameters λ and μ are computed as indicated by Eqs. 1-4, 6 and 7, respectively.

2.4. Performance measures

Let τ be a random variable representing the time to absorb into $A = \{m_i \mid \pi_{m_i}(t,0,0,0,V_i) = 1\}$. The *distribution of the execution time* of a program with volume V_i is:

$$F_{t_{EX_i}}(t) = \Pr\{\tau \le t \wedge M_i(t) \in A\} = \Pr\{M_i(t) = 9_i\} =$$
$$= \int_0^{Z_{IB_{MAX}}} \int_0^{Z_{RS/LSQ_{MAX}}} \int_0^{Z_{EX_{MAX}}} \int_0^{V_i} \pi_{9_i}(t, z_{IB}, z_{RS/LSQ}, z_{EX}, z_{REG}) dz_{IB} dz_{RS/LSQ} dz_{EX} dz_{REG} = \pi_{9_i}(t,0,0,0,V_i) \quad (18)$$

with *mean execution time*:

$$t_{EX_i} = \int_0^{\infty} \left(1 - F_{t_{EX_i}}(t)\right) dt \quad (19)$$

Consequently, the *sustained number of instructions per cycle* (*IPC*) is given by:

$$IPC_i = V_i / t_{EX_i} \quad (20)$$

When the input space is partitioned, *IPC* is the ratio between the average volume and the average execution time of all the programs of different classes, as indicated by the operational profile:

$$IPC = \sum_{k=1}^{n} V_k \widehat{w}_{T_{CLASS_k}} \Big/ \sum_{k=1}^{n} t_{EX_k} \widehat{w}_{T_{CLASS_k}} \quad (21)$$

The sum of probabilities of the discrete markings that do not carry a token in place P_{FETCH} gives the *probability of a stall* in the instruction fetch unit at time *t*:

$$P_{STALL_i}(t) = \Pr\{M_i(t) \neq 1_i \wedge M_i(t) \neq 5_i\} = \\ = \sum_{\substack{m\neq 1\\ m\neq 5}} \int_0^{Z_{IB_{MAX}}} \int_0^{Z_{RS/LSQ_{MAX}}} \int_0^{Z_{EX_{MAX}}} \int_0^{V_i} \pi_{m_i}\left(t, z_{IB}, z_{RS/LSQ}, z_{EX}, z_{REG}\right) dz_{IB} dz_{RS/LSQ} dz_{EX} dz_{REG} \tag{22}$$

Because of the discrete nature of pipelining, additional attention should be given to the probability that no useful instructions will be added to the instruction buffer in the cycle beginning at time t_0 (complete stall in the instruction fetch unit that can lead to an effectively empty instruction buffer) due to branch misprediction. It can be obtained by summing up the probabilities of the discrete markings that still carry one or more tokens in place P_{BMIS} immediately after firing of T_{CLOCK}:

$$P_{NO\_FETCH_i}(t_0) = \Pr\{M_i(t_0) = 3_i \vee M_i(t_0) = 4_i\} = \\ = \sum_{m=3}^{4} \int_0^{Z_{IB_{MAX}}} \int_0^{Z_{RS/LSQ_{MAX}}} \int_0^{Z_{EX_{MAX}}} \int_0^{V_i} \pi_{m_i}\left(t_0, z_{IB}, z_{RS/LSQ}, z_{EX}, z_{REG}\right) dz_{IB} dz_{RS/LSQ} dz_{EX} dz_{REG} \tag{23}$$

In addition, the *execution efficiency* is introduced, taken as a ratio between the number of useful instructions and the total number of instructions executed during the course of a program's execution:

$$\eta_{EX_i} = \frac{V_i}{V_i + \begin{pmatrix}\text{instructions reexecuted}\\ \text{due to value misprediction}\end{pmatrix}} \approx \frac{V_i}{V_i + \bar{\mu} \cdot p_{VMIS_i} \cdot t_{EX_i}} = \frac{1}{1 + \dfrac{\mu_i \cdot \bar{r}_{INITIATE_i} \cdot p_{VMIS_i}}{W \cdot IPC_i}} \tag{24}$$

where $\bar{r}_{INITIATE}$ is the *average initiation rate*.

2.5. Numerical experiments and performance evaluation results

We have used *finite difference approximations* to replace the derivatives that appear in the PDEs: *forward* difference approximation for the time derivative and first-order *upwind* differencing for the space derivatives, in order to improve the stability of the method [7,8]:

$$\frac{\partial \pi_{m_i}(t, z_1, \ldots, z_n)}{\partial t} \approx \frac{\pi_{m_i}(t + \Delta t, z_1, \ldots, z_n) - \pi_{m_i}(t, z_1, \ldots, z_n)}{\Delta t} \\ r \frac{\partial \pi_{m_i}(t, z_1, \ldots, z_k, \ldots, z_n)}{\partial z_k} \approx r \cdot \text{sgn}(r) \cdot \frac{\pi_{m_i}(t, z_1, \ldots, z_k, \ldots, z_n) - \pi_{m_i}(t, z_1, \ldots, z_k - \text{sgn}(r)\Delta z_k, \ldots, z_n)}{\Delta z_k} \tag{25}$$

The explicit discretization of the right-hand-side coupling term allows the equations for each discrete state to be solved separately before going on to the next time step. The discretization is carried out on a hypercube of size $Z_{IB_{max}} \times Z_{RS/LSQ_{max}} \times Z_{EX_{max}} \times V_i$ with step size Δz in direction of z_{IB}, z_{RS}, z_{EX} and z_{REG}, and step size Δt in time. The computational complexity for the solution is

$$O\left(8 \cdot \frac{t}{\Delta t} \cdot \frac{Z_{IB_{\max}} \cdot Z_{RS/LSQ_{\max}} \cdot Z_{EX_{\max}} \cdot V_i}{\Delta z^4}\right) \text{ floating-point operations,}$$

since for each of $t/\Delta t$ time steps we must increment each solution value in the four-dimensional grid for eight of the nine discrete markings. The storage requirements of the algorithm are at least

$$8 \cdot \frac{Z_{IB_{\max}} \cdot Z_{RS/LSQ_{\max}} \cdot Z_{EX_{\max}} \cdot V}{\Delta z^4} \cdot 4 \text{ bytes,}$$

since for eight of nine discrete markings we must store a four-dimensional grid of floating-point numbers (solutions at successive time steps can be overwritten).

Unless indicated otherwise, $Z_{IB_{\max}} = W$, $Z_{RS/LSQ_{\max}} = Z_{RR_{\max}} = Z_{ROB_{\max}} = Z_{EX_{\max}} = 2W$ and $\Delta t = \Delta z/(n \cdot W)$, where n=4 is the number of continuous dimensions. With these capacities of fluid places, virtually all name dependences and structural conflicts are eliminated. Step size Δz is varied between $\Delta z = 1/2$ (coarser grid, usually when the prediction accuracy is high) and $\Delta z = 1/6$ (finer grid, usually when the prediction accuracy is low).

Considering a low-volume program (V_i=50 instructions) executed on a four-wide machine (W=4), we investigate:

- The influence of branch prediction accuracy on the distribution of the program's execution time, when value prediction is not involved (Figure 3a),
- The influence of branch prediction accuracy on the probability of a complete stall in the instruction fetch unit (Figure 3b), and
- The influence of value prediction accuracy on the distribution of the program's execution time, when *perfect* branch prediction is involved (Figure 4).

It is indisputably clear that both branch and value prediction accuracy improvements reduce the mean execution time of a program and increase performance. As an illustration, the size of the shaded area in Figure 3a is equal to the mean execution time when perfect branch prediction is involved, and IPC is computed as indicated by Eq. (20). In addition, looking at Figure 3b one can see that the probability of a complete stall in the instruction fetch unit, which can lead to an empty instruction buffer in the subsequent cycle, decreases with branch prediction accuracy improvement. As a result, both the utilization of the processor and the size of dynamic scheduling window increase as branch prediction accuracy increases.

The correctness of the discretization method is verified by comparing the numerical transient analysis results with the results obtained by discrete-event simulation, which is specifically implemented for this model and not for a general FSPN. The types of events that need to be scheduled in the event queue are either *transition firings* or the *hitting of a threshold* dependent on fluid levels. We have used a *Unif[0,1]* pseudo-random number generator to generate samples from the respective cumulative distribution functions and determine transition firing times via inversion of the *cdf* ("Golden Rule for Sampling"). Discrete-event simulation alone has been used to obtain performance evaluation results for wide machines with much more aggressive instruction issue (*W*>>1).

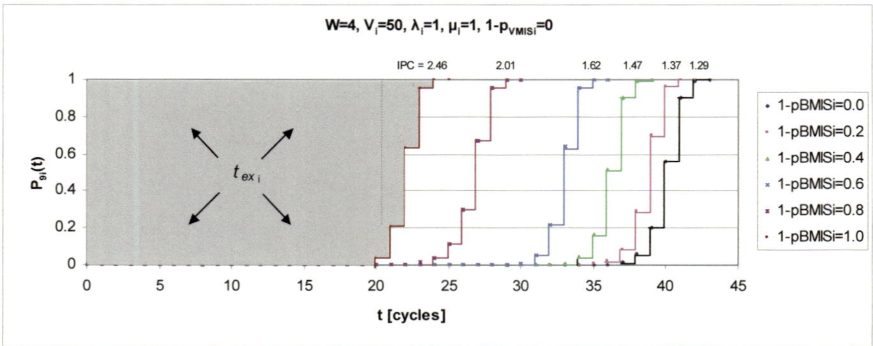

(a)

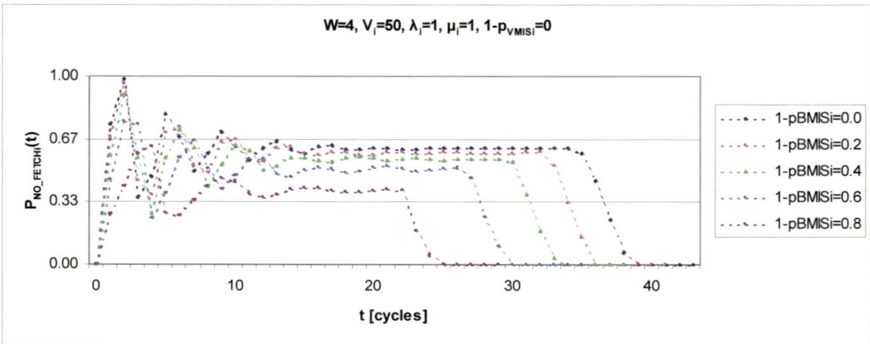

(b)

Figure 3. Influence of branch prediction accuracy on (a) the distribution of the program's execution time and (b) the probability of a complete stall in the instruction fetch unit

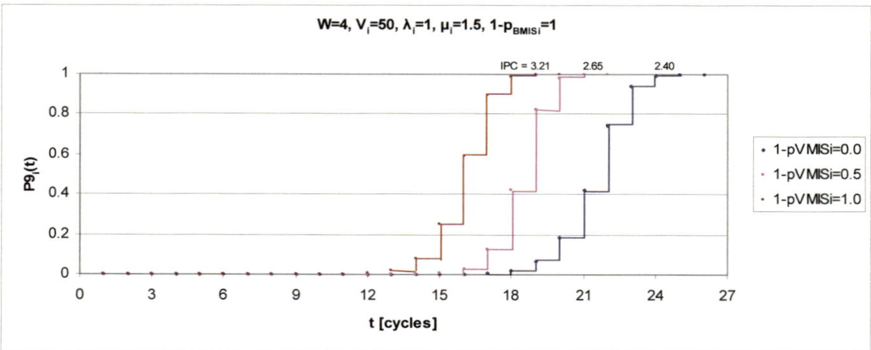

Figure 4. Influence of value prediction accuracy on the distribution of the program's execution time

It takes quite some effort to tune the numerical algorithm parameters appropriately, so that a sufficiently accurate approximation is obtained. Various discretization and convergence errors may cancel each other, so that sometimes a solution obtained on a coarse grid may agree better with the discrete-event simulation than a solution on a finer grid – which, by definition, should be more accurate. In Figures 5a-b, a comparison of discretization results and results obtained using discrete-event simulation for a four-wide machine is given. Furthermore, Figure 5c shows the performance of several machines with realistic predictors executing a program with an average basic block size of eight instructions, given that about 25% of the instructions that initiate execution in the same clock cycle are consuming instructions.

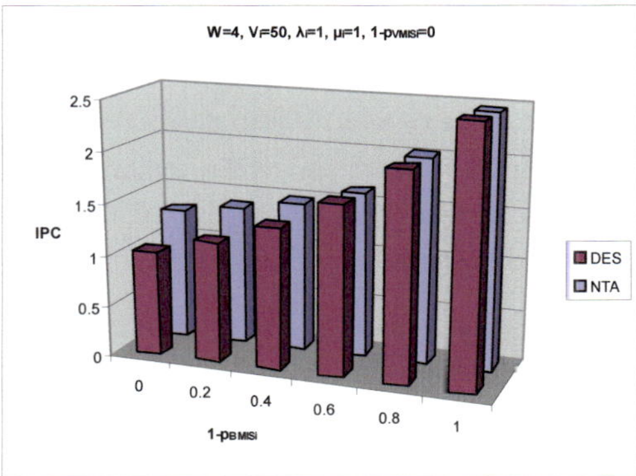

(a)

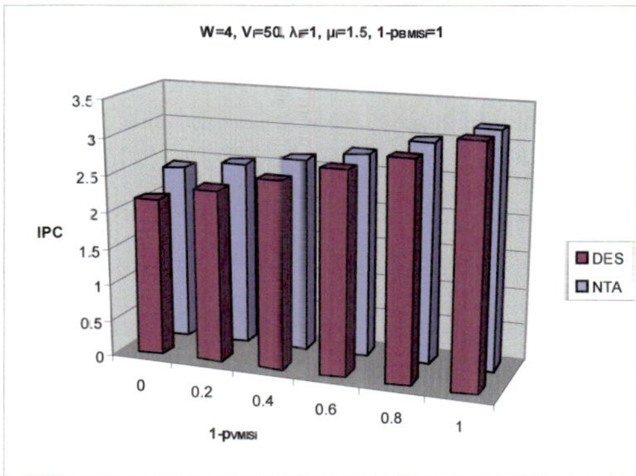

(b)

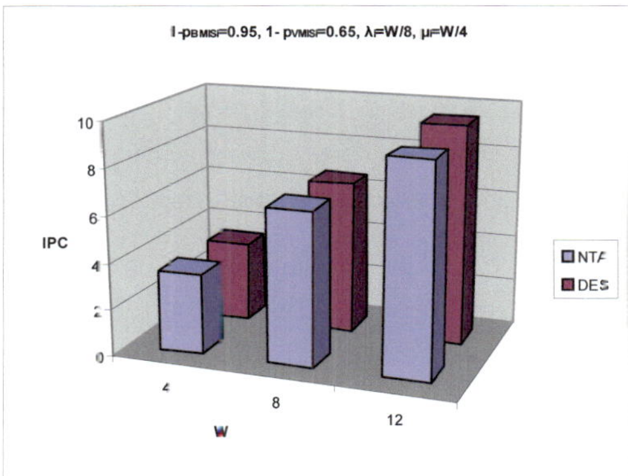

(c)

Figure 5. Comparison of numerical transient analysis results (NTA) and results given by discrete-event simulation (DES)

Since the conservation of probability mass is enforced, the differences between the numerical transient analysis and the discrete-event simulation results arise only from the improper distribution of the probability mass over the solution domain. Due to the inherent dissipation error of the first-order accurate numerical methods, the solution at successive time steps is more or less dissipated to neighboring grid nodes. The phenomenon is emphasized when the number of discrete state changes is increased owing to the larger number of mispredictions.

The results are satisfactorily close to each other, especially when the prediction accuracy is high, which is common in recent architectures. Yet, we believe that much work is still uncompleted and many questions are still open for further research in the field of development of strategies for reducing the amount of memory needed to represent the volume densities, as well as efficient discretization schemes for numerical transient analysis of general FSPNs. *Alternating direction implicit* (ADI) methods [19] in order to save memory, and parallelization of the numerical algorithms to reduce runtime have been suggested.

In the remainder of this part, we do not distinguish the numerical transient analysis results from the results given by discrete-event simulation of the FSPN model. Initially we analyze the efficiency of branch prediction by varying branch prediction accuracy. Value prediction is not involved at all. The speedup is computed by dividing the IPC achieved with certain branch prediction accuracy over the IPC achieved without branch prediction ($1-p_{BMIS_i}=0$). For the moment, the input space is not partitioned and program volume is set to $V_i=10^6$ instructions.

It is observed that, looking at Figures 6a-b, branch prediction curves have an exponential shape. Therefore, building branch predictors that improve the accuracy just a little bit may be reflected in a significant performance increase. The impact of a given increment in accuracy is more noticeable when it experiences a slight improvement beyond the 90%. Another conclusion drawn from these figures is that one can benefit most from branch prediction in programs with relatively short basic blocks (high λ_i / W) and which do not suffer excessively from true data dependences (low μ_i / W). When the ratio μ_i / W is high, true data dependences overshadow control dependences. As a result, the amount of ILP that is expected without value prediction in a machine with extremely aggressive instruction issue is far below the maximum possible value, even with perfect branch prediction. Value prediction has to be involved to go beyond the limits imposed by true data dependences.

Next, we analyze the efficiency of value prediction by varying value prediction accuracy (Figures 7a-b). The speedup is computed by dividing the IPC achieved with certain value prediction accuracy over the IPC achieved without value prediction ($1-p_{VMIS_i}=0$). With perfect branch prediction, it seems clear that the value prediction curves have a linear behavior. Therefore, it is worthwhile to build a predictor that significantly improves the accuracy. Only a small improvement on the value predictor accuracy has a little impact on ILP processor performance, regardless of the accuracy range. Another conclusion drawn from these figures is that the effect of value prediction is more noticeable when a significant number of instructions consume results of simultaneously initiated producer-instructions during execution (high μ_i / W), i.e. when true data dependences have a much higher influence on the program's total execution time.

Branch prediction has a very important influence on the benefits of value prediction. One can see that the performance increase is less significant when branch prediction is realistic.

Because mispredicted branches limit the number of useful instructions that enter the instruction window, the processor is able to provide almost the same number of instructions to leave the instruction window, even with lower value prediction accuracy. As a result, graphs tend to flatten out. Correct value predictions can only be exploited when the fetch rate is quite high, i.e. when mispredicted branches are infrequent. Branch misprediction becomes a more significant performance limitation with wider processors (Figure 7b).

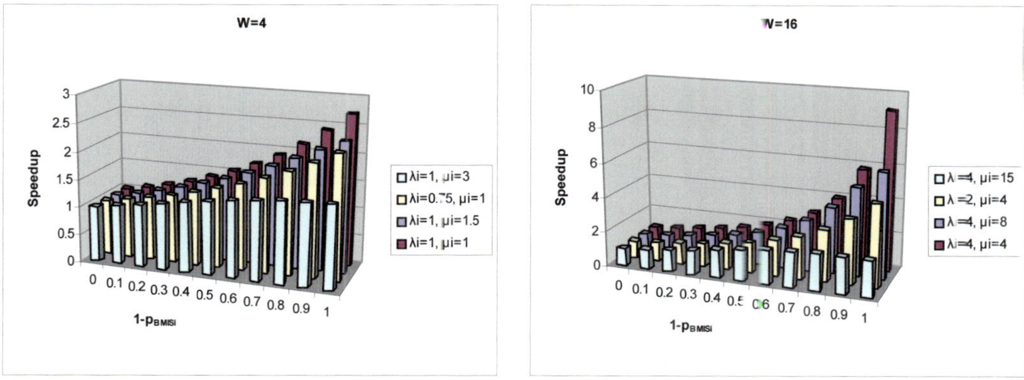

(a) (b)

Figure 6. Speedup achieved by branch prediction with varying accuracy

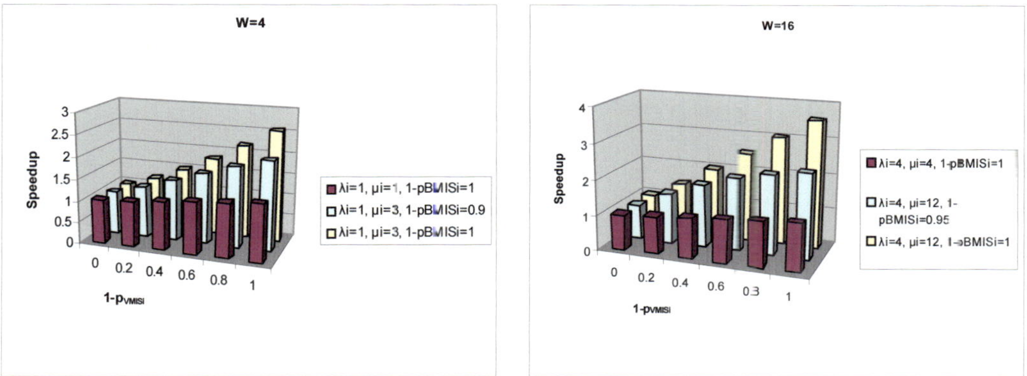

(a) (b)

Figure 7. Speedup achieved by value prediction with varying accuracy

In addition, we investigate branch and value prediction efficiency with varying machine width (Figures 8a-c). The speedup in this case is computed by dividing the IPC achieved in a machine over the IPC achieved in a *scalar* counterpart (W=1, μ_i=0). The speedup due to branch prediction is obviously higher in wider machines. With perfect branch prediction, the speedup unconditionally increases with the machine width. For a given width, the speedup is higher when there are a smaller number of consuming instructions (low μ_i / W). With realistic branch prediction, there is a threshold effect on the machine width: below the threshold the speedup increases with the machine width, whereas above the threshold the speedup is close to a limit – machine width is by far larger than the average number of instructions provided by the fetch unit. The threshold decreases with increasing the number of mispredicted branches.

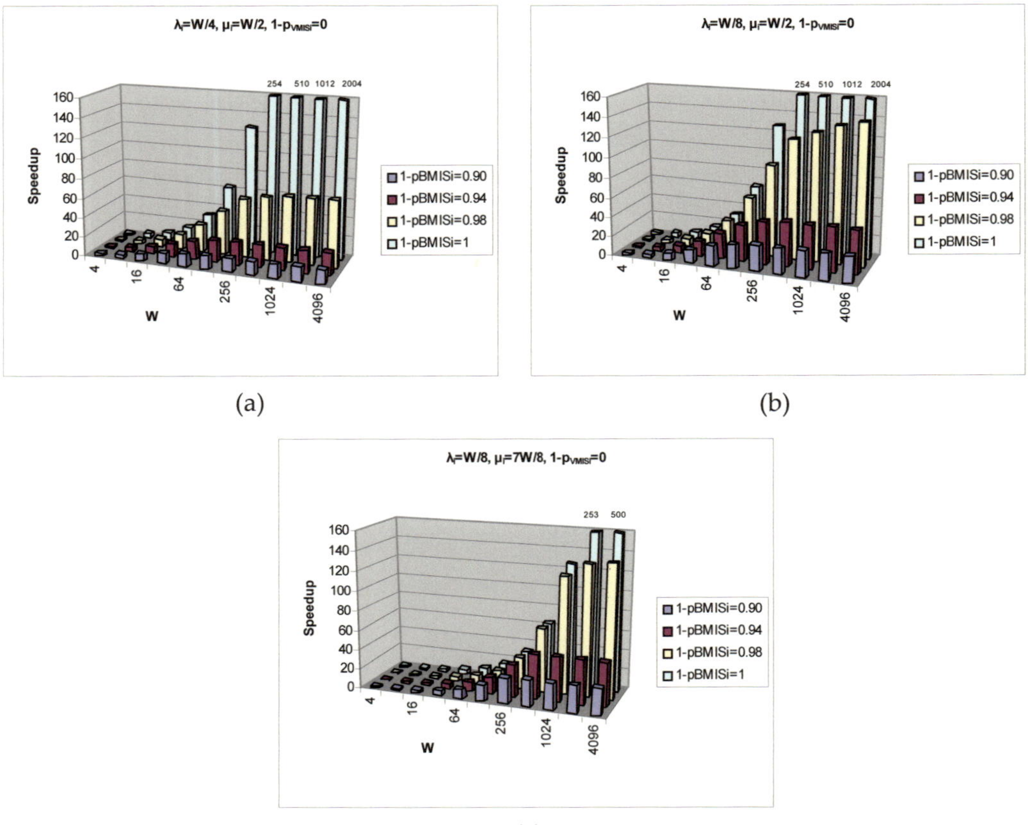

Figure 8. Speedup achieved by branch prediction with varying machine width

The maximum *additional speedup* that value prediction can provide is computed by dividing the IPC achieved with perfect value prediction over the IPC achieved without value prediction (Figures 9a-c). With perfect branch prediction, some true data dependences can always be eliminated, regardless of the machine width. Actually, the maximum additional speedup is predetermined by the ratio $W/(W-\mu_i)$. However, with realistic branch prediction, the additional speedup diminishes when the machine width is above a threshold value. It happens earlier when there are a smaller number of consuming instructions and/or a larger number of mispredicted branches. In either case, the number of independent instructions examined for simultaneous execution is sufficiently higher than the number of fetched instructions that enter the instruction window. Again, branch prediction becomes more important with wider processors.

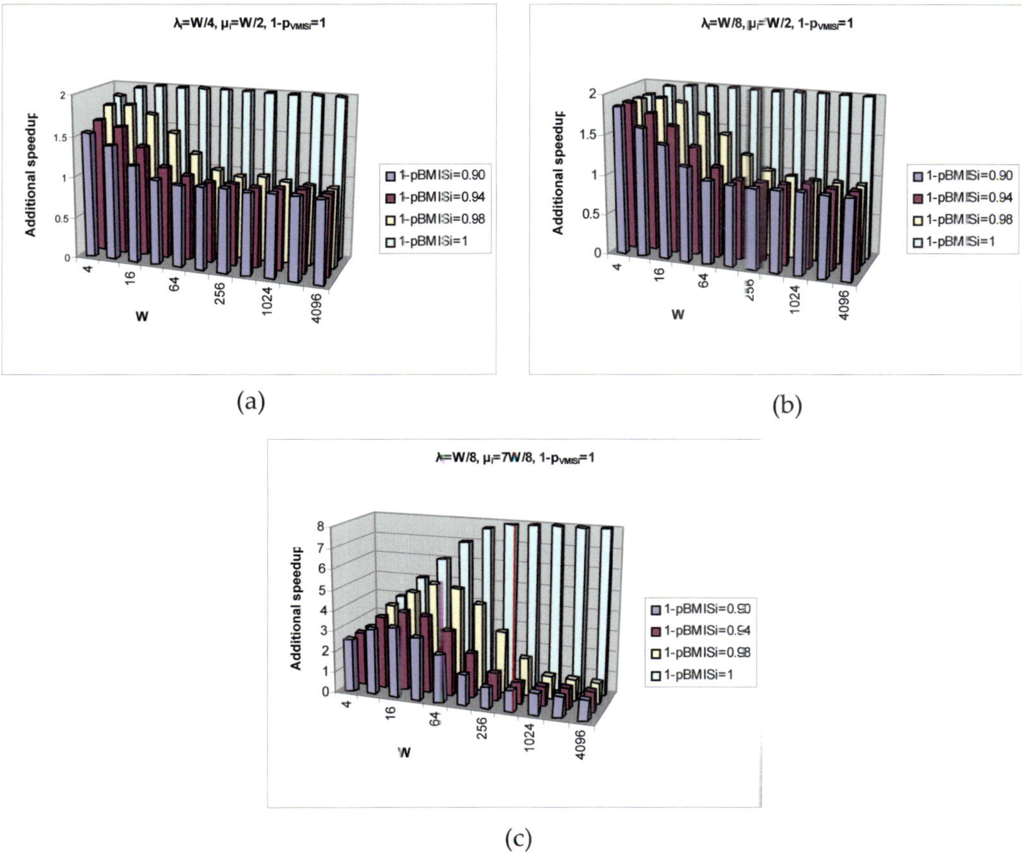

Figure 9. Additional speedup achieved by perfect value prediction with varying machine width

The rate at which consuming instructions occur depends on the initiation rate. Therefore, we also investigate the value prediction efficiency with varying instruction window size (varying capacity $Z_{RS/LSQ_{MAX}}$ of the fluid place $P_{RS/LSQ}$) (Figures 10a-b). The speedup is computed in the same way as in the previous instance. It increases with the instruction window size in [*W*, 2*W*], but the increase is more moderate when there are a smaller number of consuming instructions (low μ_i / W) and/or branch prediction is not perfect. As the instruction window grows larger, performance without value prediction saturates, as does the performance with perfect value prediction. The upper limit value emerges from the fact that in each cycle up to *W* new instructions may enter the fluid place $Z_{RS/LSQ_{MAX}}$ and up to *W* consuming instructions may be forced to retain their reservation stations. One should also note that the speedup for *W*>>1 and realistic branch prediction is almost constant with increasing instruction window size. Two scenarios arise in this case: (1) the number of consuming instructions is large – the speedup is constant but still noticeable as there are not enough independent instructions in the window without value prediction, and (2) the number of consuming instructions is small – there is no speedup as there are enough independent instructions in the window even without value prediction, regardless of the window size. Again, the main reasons for this behavior are the small number of consuming instructions and the large number of mispredicted branches.

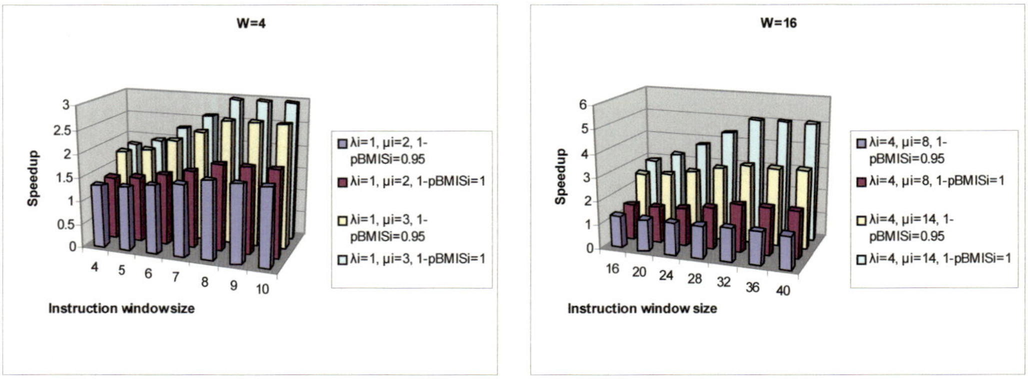

(a) (b)

Figure 10. Speedup achieved by perfect value prediction with varying instruction window size

In order to investigate the operational environment influence, we partitioned the input space into several program classes, each of them with at least one different aspect: branch rate, consuming instruction rate, probability to classify a branch as easy-to-predict or probability to classify a value as easy-to-predict. We concluded that the set of programs executed on a machine have a considerable influence on the *perceived IPC*. Since the term *program* may be interchangeably used with the term *instruction stream*, these observations give good reason for the analysis of the time varying behavior of programs in order to find simulation points in applications to achieve results representative of the program as a whole. From a user perspective, a machine with more sophisticated prediction mechanisms will not always lead to a higher *perceived performance* as compared to a machine with more modest prediction mechanisms but more favorable operational profile [20,21].

3. Part B: fluid atoms in P2P streaming networks

In P2P live streaming systems every user (peer) maintains connections with other peers and forms an application level *logical network* on top of the *physical network*. The video stream is divided in small pieces called *chunks* which are streamed from the source to the peers and every peer acts as a client as well as a server, forwarding the received video chunks to the next peer after some short buffering. The peers are usually organized in one of the two basic types of logical topologies: *tree* or *mesh*. Hence, the tree topology forms structured network of a single tree as in [22], or multiple multicast trees as in [23], while mesh topology is unstructured and does not form any firm logical construction, but organizes peers in *swarming* or gossiping-like environments, as in [24]. To make greater use of their complementary strengths, some protocols use combination of these two aspects, forming a hybrid network topology, such as [25]. Hence, members are free to join or leave the system at their own free will (*churn*), which leads to a certain user driven dynamics resulting in constant disruptions of the streaming data delivery. This peer churn has high influence on the quality of offered services, especially for P2P systems that offer live video broadcast. Also, P2P network members are heterogeneous in their upload bandwidth capabilities and provide quite different contribution to the overall system performance. Efficient construction of P2P live video streaming network requires data latency reduction as much as possible, in order to disseminate the content in a live manner. This latency is firstly introduced by network infrastructure latency presented as a sum of serialization latency, propagation delay, router processing delay and router queuing delay. The second type of delay is the initial start-up delay required for filling the peer's buffer prior to the start of the video play. The buffer is used for short term storage of video chunks which often arrive out of sequence in manner of order and/or time, and resolving this latency issue requires careful buffer modeling and management. Thus, buffer size requires precise dimensioning because even though larger buffers offer better sequence order or latency compensation, they introduce larger video playback delay. Contrary, small buffers offer smaller playback delay, but the system becomes more error prone. Also, since the connections between participating peers in these P2P logical networks are maintained by the means of control messages exchange, the buffer content (buffer map) is incorporated in these control messages and it is used for missing chunks acquisition. Chunk requesting and forwarding is controlled by a chunk scheduling algorithm, which is responsible for on-time chunk acquisition and delivery among the neighboring peers, which is usually based on the available content and bandwidth of the neighboring peers. A lot of research activities are strictly focused on designing better chunk scheduling algorithms [26,27] that present the great importance of carefully composed scheduling algorithm which can significantly compensate for churn or bandwidth/latency disruptions. Beside the basic coding schemes, in latest years an increasing number of P2P live streaming protocols use *Scalable Video Coding* (SVC) technologies. SVC is an emerging paradigm where the video stream is split in several sub-streams and each sub-stream contributes to one or more characteristics of video content in terms of temporal, spatial and SNR/quality scalability. Mainly, two different concepts of SVC are in greater use: *Layered Video Coding* (LVC) where the video stream is split in several dependently decodable sub-stream called *Layers*, and *Multiple Description Coding* (MDC) where the video stream is split in several independently decodable sub-stream called *Descriptions*. A number of P2P video streaming models use LVC [27] or MDC [23,28] and report promising results.

3.1. Model definition

As a base for our modeling we use the work in [29,30], where several important terms are defined. One of them is the maximum achievable rate that can be streamed to any individual peer at a given time, which is presented in Eq. (26).

$$r_{MAX} = \min\left\{ r_{SERVER}, \frac{r_{SERVER} + \sum_{i=1}^{n} r_{Pi}}{n} \right\} \tag{26}$$

where:
r_{MAX} – maximum achievable streaming rate
r_{SERVER} – upload rate of the server
r_{Pi} – upload rate of the ith peer
n – number of participating peers.

Clearly, r_{MAX} is a function of r_{SERVER}, r_{Pi} and n, i.e. $r_{MAX} = \phi(r_{SERVER}, r_P, n)$. This maximum achievable rate to a single peer is further referred to as the *fluid function*, or $\phi()$. The second important definition is of the term *Universal Streaming*. Universal Streaming refers to the streaming situations when each participating peer receives the video stream with bitrate no less than the video rate, and in [29] it is achievable if and only if:

$$\varphi() \geq r_{VIDEO} \tag{27}$$

where r_{VIDEO} is the rate of the streamed video content.

Hence, the performance measures of the system are easily obtained by calculating the *Probability for Universal Streaming* (P_{US}).

Now, we add one more parameter to the previously mentioned to fulfill the requirements of our model. We define the *stream function* $\psi()$ which, instead of the maximum, represents the *actual* streaming rate to any individual peer at any given time, and $\psi()$ satisfies:

$$\psi() \leq \varphi() \tag{28}$$

3.2. FSPN representation

The FSPN representation of the P2P live streaming system model that accounts for: network topology, peer churn, scalability, peer average group size, peer upload bandwidth heterogeneity, video buffering, control traffic overhead and admission control for lesser contributing peers, is given in Figure 11. We assume asymmetric network settings where peers have infinite download bandwidths, while stream delay, peer selection strategies and chunk size are not taken into account.

Similar as in [29] we assume two types of peers: high contributing peers (HP) with upload bitrate higher than the video rate, and low contributing peers (LP) with upload bitrate lower than the video rate. Different from the fluid function $\phi()$, beside the dependency to r_{SERVER}, r_P, and n, the stream function $\psi()$ depends on the level of fluid in the unique fluid place P_B as well:

$$\psi() = f\left(r_{SERVER}, \# P_{HP}, \# P_{LP}, r_{HP}, r_{LP}, Z_B\right) \tag{29}$$

where Z_B represents the level of fluid in P_B.

The FSPN model in Figure 11 comprises two main parts: the discrete part and the continuous (fluid) part of the net. Single line circles represent discrete places that can contain discrete tokens. The tokens, which represent peers, move via single line arcs to and

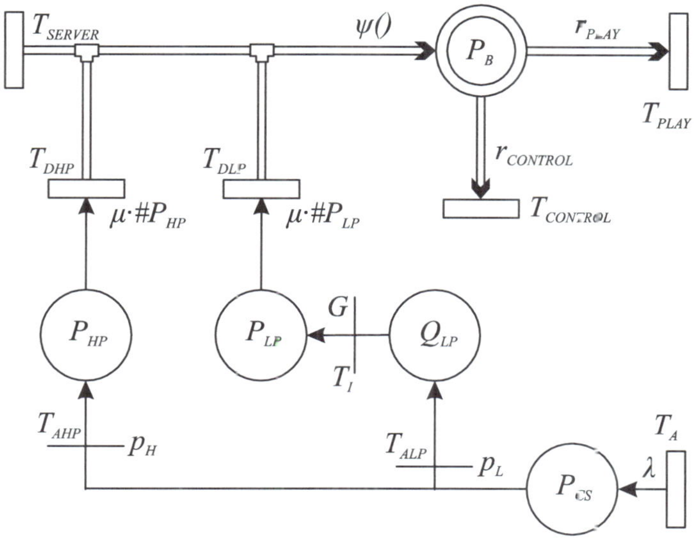

Figure 11. FSPN model of a P2P live video streaming system

out of the discrete places. Fluid arcs, through which fluid is pumped, are drawn as double lines to suggest a pipe. The fluid is pumped through fluid arcs and is streamed to and out of the unique fluid place P_B which represents a single peer buffer. The rectangles represent timed transitions with exponentially distributed firing times, and the thin short lines are immediate transitions. Peer arrival, in general, is described as a stochastic process with exponentially distributed interarrival times, with mean $1/\lambda$, where λ represents the arrival rate. We make another assumption that after joining the system peers' sojourn times (T) are also exponentially distributed. Clearly, since each peer is immediately served after joining the system, we have a queuing network model with an infinite number of servers and exponentially distributed joining and leaving rates. Hence, the mean service time T is equal to $1/\mu$, which transferred to FSPN notation leads to the definition of the departure rate as μ multiplied by the number of peers that are concurrently being served. Now, λ represents peer arrival in general, but the different types of peers do not share the same occurrence probability (p_H and p_L). This occurrence distribution is defined by immediate transitions T_{AHP} and T_{ALP} and their weight functions p_H and p_L. Hence, HP arrive with rate $\lambda_H = p_H * \lambda$, and LP arrive with rate $\lambda_L = p_L * \lambda$, where $p_H + p_L = 1$. In this particular case $p_H = p_L = 0.5$, but, if needed, these occurrence probabilities can be altered. This way the model with peer churn is represented by two independent $M/M/\infty$ Poisson processes, one for each of the different types of peers. The average number of peers that are concurrently being served defines the size of the system as a whole (S_{SIZE}) and is derived from the queuing theory:

$$S_{SIZE} = \lambda/\mu \tag{30}$$

T_A is a timed transition with exponentially distributed firing times that represents peer arrival, and upon firing (with rate λ) puts a token in P_{CS}. P_{CS} (representing the control server) checks the type of the token and immediately forwards it to one of the discrete places P_{HP} or Q_{LP} (P_{LP}). Places P_{HP} and P_{LP} accommodate the different types of peers in our P2P live streaming system model. Q_{LP} on the other hand, represents queuing station for the LP, which is connected to the place P_{LP} with the immediate transition T_I that is guarded by a *Guard function* G.

The Guard function G is a Boolean function whose values are based on a given condition. The expression of a given condition is the argument of the Guard function and serves as enabling condition for the transition T_I. If the argument of G evaluates to true, T_I is enabled. Otherwise, if the argument of G evaluates to false, T_I is disabled. For the model that does not take admission control into account G is always enabled, but when we want to evaluate the performance of a system that incorporates admission control we set the argument of the guard function as in Eq. (31):

$$G\left\{\frac{r_{SERVER} + \# P_{HP} \cdot r_{HP} + (\# P_{LP} + 1) \cdot r_{LP}}{\# P_{HP} + \# P_{LP}} \geq r_{VIDEO} + r_{CONTROL}\right\} \tag{31}$$

Transitions T_{DHP} and T_{DLP} are enabled only when there are tokens in discrete places P_{HP} and P_{LP}. These are marking dependent transitions, which, when enabled, have exponentially distributed firing times with rate $\mu \cdot \# P_{HP}$ and $\mu \cdot \# P_{LP}$ respectively, where $\# P_{HP}$ and $\# P_{LP}$ represent the number of tokens in each discrete place. Upon firing they take one token out of the discrete place to which they are connected.

Concerning the fluid part of the model, we represent bits as atoms of fluid that travel through fluid pipes (network infrastructure) with rate dependent on the system's state (marking). Beside the stream function as a derivative of several parameters, we identify three separate fluid flows (streams) that travel through the network with different bitrates. The main video stream represents the video data that is streamed from the source to the peers that we refer to as the *video rate* (r_{VIDEO}). The second stream is the play stream which is the stream at which each peer plays the streamed video data, referred to as the *play rate* (r_{PLAY}), and the third stream is the control traffic overhead, referred to as *control rate* ($r_{CONTROL}$), which describes the exchange of control messages needed for the logical network construction and management. As mentioned earlier, transitions T_{DHP} and T_{DLP} are enabled only when there are tokens in discrete places P_{HP} and P_{LP} respectively and beside the fact that they consume tokens when firing, when enabled, they constantly pump fluid through the fluid arc to the fluid place. Flow rates of $\psi()$ are piecewise constant and depend on the number of tokens in the discrete places and their upload capabilities. Continuous place P_B represents single peer's buffer, which is constantly filled with rate $\psi()$ and drained with rate (r_{PLAY} + $r_{CONTROL}$). Z_B is the amount of fluid in P_B and Z_{BMAX} is the buffer's maximum capacity. Transition T_{SERVER} represents the functioning of the server, which is always enabled (except when there are no tokens in any of the discrete places) and constantly pumps fluid toward the continuous place P_B with maximum upload rate of r_{SERVER}. Transition T_{PLAY} represents the video play rate, which is also always enabled and constantly drains fluid from the continuous place P_B, with rate r_{PLAY}. $T_{CONTROL}$, that represents the exchange of control messages among neighboring peers, is the third transition that is always enabled, has the priority over T_{PLAY}, and constantly drains fluid from P_B with rate $r_{CONTROL}$. For further analysis we derived the rate of $r_{CONTROL}$ from [31] where it is declared that it *linearly* depends on the number of peers in the neighborhood, and for r_{VIDEO} of 128 kbps, the protocol overhead is 2% for a group of 64 users, which leads to a bitrate of 2.56 kbps. Thus, for our performance analysis we assume that peers are organized in neighborhoods with an average size of 60 members where $r_{CONTROL}$ is 2.4 kbps. For the sake of convenience and chart plotting we also define the average upload rate of the participating peers as $r_{AVERAGE}$, which is given in Eq. (32):

$$r_{AVERAGE} = \frac{\# P_{HP} * r_{HP} + \# P_{LP} * r_{LP}}{\# P_{HP} + \# P_{LP}} \tag{32}$$

Since in our model of a P2P live video streaming system we take in consideration $r_{CONTROL}$ as well, Universal Streaming is achievable if and only if:

$$\psi() \geq r_{VIDEO} + r_{CONTROL} \tag{33}$$

3.3. Discrete-event simulation

The FSPN model of a P2P live video streaming system accurately describes the behavior of the system, but suffers from state space explosion and therefore analytic/numeric solution is infeasible. Hence, we provide a solution to the presented model using *process-based discrete-event simulation* (DES) language. The simulations are performed using SimPy which is a DES package based on standard Python programming language. It is quite simple, but yet extremely powerful DES package that provides the modeler with simulation processes that can be used for active model components (such as customers, messages or vehicles), and resource facilities (resources, levels and stores) which are used for passive simulation components that form limited capacity congestion points like servers, counters, and tunnels. SimPy also provides monitor variables that help in gathering statistics, and the random variables are provided by the standard Python random module.

Now, although we deal with vast state space, we provide the solution by identifying four distinct cases of state types. These cases of state types are combination of states of the discrete part and the continuous part of the FSPN, and are presented in Table 2. Hence, the rates at which fluid builds up in the fluid place P_B, in each of these four cases, can be described with linear differential equations that are given in Eq. (34)

case 1	if	$Z_B = Z_{BMAX}$ and $\phi() \geq r_{VIDEO}+r_{CONTROL}$	then	$\psi() = r_{VIDEO}+r_{CONTROL}$ and $r_{PLAY} = r_{VIDEO}$
case 2	if	$0 < Z_B \leq Z_{BMAX}$ *and* $\phi() < r_{VIDEO}+r_{CONTROL}$	then	$\psi() = \phi()$ and $r_{PLAY} = r_{VIDEO}$
case 3	if	$0 \leq Z_{BUF} < Z_{BUFMAX}$ *and* $\phi() \geq r_{VIDEO}+r_{CONTROL}$	then	$\psi() = \phi()$ and $r_{PLAY} = r_{VIDEO}$
case 4	if	$Z_{BUF} = 0$ *and* $\phi() < r_{VIDEO}+r_{CONTROL}$	then	$\psi() = \phi()$ and $r_{PLAY} < r_{VIDEO}$

Table 2. Cases of state types

$$\frac{dZ_B(t)}{dt} = \begin{cases} 0 & case1, \\ \psi() - V_R - C_R & case2, \\ \psi() - V_R - C_R & case3, \\ 0 & case4. \end{cases} \tag{34}$$

In the next few lines (Table 3a-d) we briefly present the definitions of some of the the FSPN model components in SimPy syntax. Algorithm 1 presents the definition of SimPy processes for the different types of tokens. All the FSPN places (as well as r_{PLAY}) are defined as *resource facilities* of the type "Level" and are given in Algorithm 2. The formulation of a "Level" for representing the r_{PLAY} was enforced by the requirement for monitoring and modifying the r_{PLAY} at each instant of time. Algorithm 3 presents T_A combined with T_{AHP} and T_{ALP} where it is defined as two separate SimPy Proceses that independently generate two different types of token processes. Algorithm 4 represents the definition of transitions T_{DHP} and T_{DLP}.

Definition of HP token

```
class tokenHP (Process):
    def join (self):
        yield put, self, Php, 1
```

Definition of LP token with integrated Guard for T_I

```
class tokenLP (Process):
    def join (self):
        if (Php.amount + Plp.amount) == 0:
            yield put, self, Plp, 1
        else:
            yield put, self, Qlp, 1
            def GuardOFF():
                    return (((Rserver + (Plp.amount + 1)*Rlp + Php.amount*Rhp)/((Plp.amount +
                        1) + Php.amount)) >= Rvideo + Rcontrol)
            while True:
                yield waituntil, self, GuardOFF
                yield get, self, Qlp, 1
                yield put, self, Plp, 1
                yield passivate, self
```

(a) Algorithm 1: Definition of tokens in SimPy

Pcs = Level (name = 'Control Server', initialBuffered=0, monitored = True)
Php = Level (name = 'Discrete Place Php', initialBuffered=0, monitored = True)
Plp = Level (name = 'Discrete Place Plp', initialBuffered=0, monitored = True)

```
Qlp = Level (name = 'Queuing Station', initialBuffered=0, monitored = True)
Pb = Level (name = 'Peer Buffer', initialBuffered=Zbmax, monitored = True)
Pplay = Level (name = 'Play rate', initialBuffered=Rvideo, monitored = True)
```

(b) Algorithm 2: Definition of FSPN places in SimPy

Transition T_A combined with T_{AHP}	class HPgenerator (Process):
	  def generate (self, end):
	    while now() < end:
	      yield peerHP = tokenHP ()
	      activate (peerHP, peerHP.join())
	      yield hold, self, expovariate (p_H * Lamda)

Transition T_A combined with T_{ALP}	class LPgenerator (Process):
	  def generate (self, end):
	    while now() < end:
	      peerLP = tokenLP ()
	      activate (peerLP, peerLP.join())
	      yield hold, self, expovariate (p_L * Lamda)

(c) Algorithm 3: Definition of transition T_A combined with T_{AHP} and T_{ALP}

Transition T_{DHP}	class HPdeparture (Process):
	  def depart (self, end):
	    def Condition():
	        return (Php.amount > 0)
	      while True:
	        yield waituntil, self, Condition
	        yield hold, self, expovariate (Mi * Php.amount)
	        yield get, self, Php, 1

Transition T_{DLP}	class LPdeparture (Process):
	  def depart (self, end):
	    def Condition():
	        return (Plp.amount > 0)
	      while True:
	        yield waituntil, self, Condition
	        yield hold, self, expovariate (Mi * Plp.amount)
	        yield get, self, Plp, 1

(d) Algorithm 4: Definition of transitions T_{DHP} and T_{DLP}

Table 3. Definitions of FSPN model components in SimPy

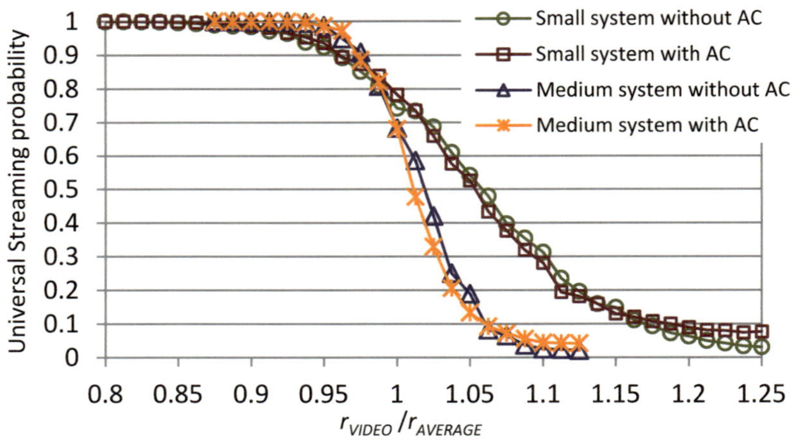

Figure 12. Performance of small and medium systems with and without AC

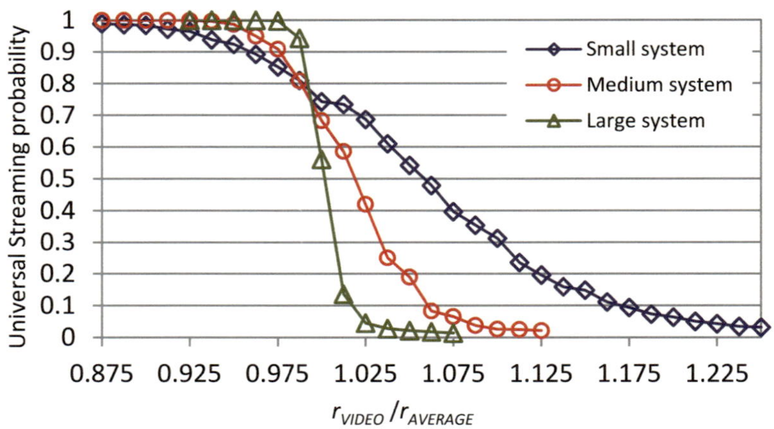

Figure 13. Performance in respect to system scaling

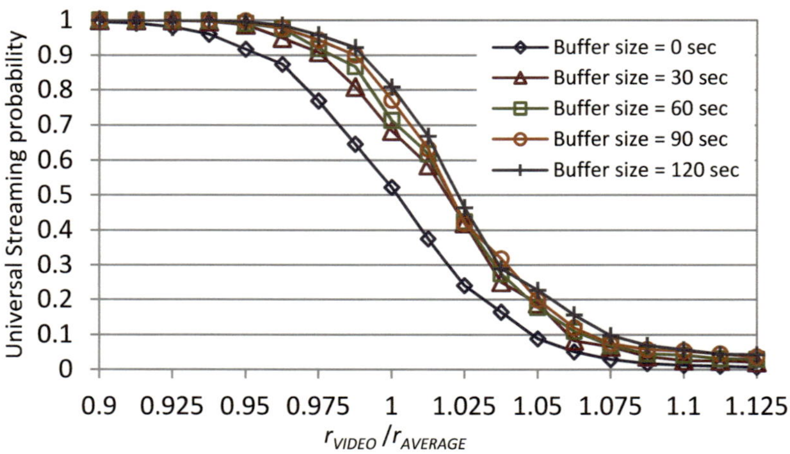

Figure 14. Buffer analysis of medium system without admission control

For simulating the fluid part of the FSPN, time discretization is applied where a SimPy "Stream Processs" checks the system state in small time intervals and consequently makes changes to the level of fluid in the fluid place P_B and r_{PLAY} according to Eq. (34). For gathering the results we use the frequency theory of probability where the probability for Universal Streaming is computed as the amount of time the system spends in Universal Streaming mode against the total simulation time.

3.4. Performance evaluation results and analysis

In this section we make a brief evaluation of three system sizes:

1. Small system with an average of 100 concurrent participating peers
2. Medium system with an average of 500 concurrent participating peers
3. Large system with an average of 5000 concurrent participating peers

The simulation scenario is as follows: $r_{SERVER} = (r_{VIDEO} + r_{CONTROL})*3$, upload bandwidth of HP is r_{HP} = 700kbps, upload bandwidth of LP is r_{LP} = 100kbps, and sojourn time T = 45 minutes. For gathering the performance results we vary the r_{VIDEO} and we plot the P_{US} against the quotient of $r_{VIDEO}/r_{AVERAGE}$, where $r_{AVERAGE}$ for this case is 400kbps. For calculating the P_{US} of a single scenario we calculate the average of 150 simulations for the small system, and an average of 75 simulations for the medium and large system, while each single simulation simulates 10 hours of system activity. Initial conditions are: $Z_{B0} = Z_{BMAX}$, where Z_{B0} is the amount of fluid in P_B in time $t_0 = 0$ and all discrete places are empty.

Comparison of performance of small and medium systems with and without AC is presented in Figure 12, from which an obvious conclusion is inferred that AC almost does not have any direct influence on the performance, but considering the incremented initial delay, incorporation of AC would only have a negative effect on the quality of offered services. Regarding the performance of the system in respect to system scaling, presented in Figure 13, it is obvious that scaling causes increase in performance, but only to a certain point after which performance steeply decreases. Fortunately, the performance decrease is in the region of under capacity which is usually avoided, so it can be concluded that larger systems perform better than smaller ones. Finally, Figure 14 shows that optimal buffer size is about 30 seconds of stored material, and larger buffers only slightly improve performance, but introduce quite large play out delay which leads to diminished quality of user experience.

4. Conclusion

In the first part of this chapter, we have introduced an implementation-independent analytical modeling approach to evaluate the performance impact of branch and value prediction in modern ILP processors, by varying several parameters of both the microarchitecture and the operational environment, like branch and value prediction accuracy, machine width, instruction window size and operational profile. The proposed analytical model is based on recently introduced Fluid Stochastic Petri Nets (FSPNs). We have also presented performance evaluation results in order to illustrate its usage in deriving measures of interest. Since the equations characterizing the evolution of FSPNs are a coupled system of partial differential equations, the numerical transient analysis poses some interesting challenges. Because of a mixed, discrete and continuous state space, another important avenue for the solution is the discrete-event simulation of the FSPN model. We believe that our stochastic modeling framework reveals considerable potential for further research in this area, needed to better understand speculation techniques in ILP processors and their performance potential under different scenarios.

In the second part of this chapter, we have shown how the FSPN formalism can be used to model P2P live video streaming systems. We have also presented a simulation solution method using process-based discrete-event simulation language whenever analytic/numeric solution becomes infeasible, that is usually a result of state space explosion. We managed to create a model that accounts for numerous features of such complex systems including: network topology, peer churn, scalability, average size of peers' neighborhoods, peer upload bandwidth heterogeneity and video buffering, among which control traffic overhead and admission control for lesser contributing peers are introduced for the first time.

Author details

Pece Mitrevski* and Zoran Kotevski
Faculty of Technical Sciences, University of St. Clement Ohridski, Bitola, Republic of Macedonia

5. References

[1] Rajan R (1995) General Fluid Models for Queuing Networks. PhD Thesis. University of Wisconsin - Madison.
[2] Gribaudo M, Sereno M, Bobbio A (1999) Fluid Stochastic Petri Nets: An extended Formalism to Include non-Markovian Models. Proc. 8th Int. Workshop on Petri Nets and Performance Models. Zaragoza.
[3] Gribaudo M, Sereno M, Horvath A, Bobbio A (2001) Fluid Stochastic Petri Nets Augmented with Flush-out Arcs: Modeling and Analysis. Kluwer Academic Publishers: Discrete Event Dynamic Systems. 11(1/2): 97-117.
[4] Horton G, Kulkarni V, Nicol D, Trivedi K (1998) Fluid Stochastic Petri Nets: Theory, Applications, and Solution. European Journal of Operations Research. 105(1): 184-201.
[5] Trivedi K, Kulkarni V (1993) FSPNs: Fluid Stochastic Petri Nets. In: M. Ajmone Marsan, editor. Lecture Notes in Computer Science: Proc. 14th Int. Conf. on Applications and Theory of Petri Nets. 691: 24-31.
[6] Wolter K, Horton G, German R (1996) Non-Markovian Fluid Stochastic Petri Nets. TU Berlin: TR 1996-13.
[7] Ferziger JH, Perić M (1997) Computational Methods for Fluid Dynamics. Springer-Verlag.

---

* Corresponding Author

[8] Hoffmann KA, Chiang ST (1993) Computational Fluid Dynamics for Engineers: Volume I & II. Engineering Education System.

[9] Ciardo G, Nicol D, Trivedi K (1997) Discrete-Event Simulation of FSPNs. Proc. 7th Int. Workshop on Petri Nets and performance Models (PNPM'97). Saint Malo. pp. 217-225.

[10] Gribaudo M, Sereno M (2000) Simulation of Fluid Stochastic Petri Nets. Proc. 8th Int. Symposium on Modeling, Analysis and Simulation of Computer and Telecommunication Systems. San Francisco. pp. 231-239.

[11] Chang PY, Hao E, Patt Y (1995) Alternative Implementations of Hybrid Branch Predictors. Proc. 28th Annual Int. Symposium on Microarchitecture. Ann Arbor. pp. 252-263.

[12] Rotenberg E, Bennett S, Smith J (1996) Trace Cache: a Low Latency Approach to High Bandwidt Instruction Fetching. Proc. 29th Annual Int. Symposium on Microarchitecture. Paris. pp. 24-35.

[13] Yeh TY, Marr D, Patt Y (1993) Increasing the Instruction Fetch Rate via Multiple Branch Prediction and a Branch Address Cache. Proc. Int. Conf. on Supercomputing. Tokyo. pp. 67-76.

[14] Lipasti M, Wilkerson C, Shen JP (1996) Value Locality and Load Value Prediction. Proc. 7th Int. Conf. on Architectural Support for Programming Languages and Operating Systems. Cambridge. pp. 138-147.

[15] Wang K, Franklin M (1997) Highly Accurate Data Value Prediction using Hybrid Predictors. Proc. 30th Annual Int. Symposium on Microarchitecture. Research Triangle Pk. pp. 281-290.

[16] Milton JS, Arnold JC (1990) Introduction to Probability and Statistics: Principles and Applications for Engineering and the Computing Sciences (2nd Edition). McGraw-Hill.

[17] Chang PY, Hao E, Yeh TY, Patt Y (1994) Branch Classificaion a New Mechanism for Improving Branch Predictor Performance. Proc. 27th Annual Int. Symposium on Microarchitecture. San Jose. pp. 22-31.

[18] Gabbay F, Mendelson A (1998) The Effect of Instruction Fetch Bandwidth on Value Prediction. Proc. 25th Int. Symposium on Computer Architecture. Barcelona. pp. 272-281.

[19] Wolter K (1999) Performance and Dependability Modelling with Second Order Fluid Stochastic Petri Nets. PhD Thesis. TU Berlin.

[20] Mitrevski P, Gušev M (2003) On the Performance Potential of Speculative Execution Based on Branch and Value Prediction. Int. Scientific Journal Facta Universitatis. Series: Electronics and Energetics. 16(1): 83-91.

[21] Gušev M, Mitrevski P (2003) Modeling and Performance Evaluation of Branch and Value Prediction in ILP Processors. International Journal of Computer Mathematics. 80(1): 19-46.

[22] Tu X, Jin H, Liao X (2008) Nearcast: A Locality-Aware P2P Live Streaming Approach for Distance Education. ACM Transactions on Internet Technology. 8(2): Article No. 2.

[23] Zezza, S., Magli E, Olmo G, Grangetto M (2009) Seacast: A Protocol for Peer to Peer Video Streaming Supporting Multiple Description Coding. IEEE Int. Conf. on Multimedia and Expo. pp. 1586-1587.

[24] Covino F, Mecella M (2008) Design and Evaluation of a System for Mesh-based P2P Live Video Streaming. ACM Int. Conf. on Advances in Mobile Computing and Multimedia. pp. 287-290.

[25] Lu Z, Li Y, Wu J, Zhang SY, Zhong YP (2008) MultiPeerCast: A Tree-mesh-hybrid P2P Live Streaming Scheme Design and Implementation based on PeerCast. 10th IEEE Int. Conf. on High Performance Computing and Communications. pp. 714-719.

[26] Chen Z, Xue K, Hong P (2008) A Study on Reducing Chunk Scheduling Delay for Mesh-Based P2P Live Streaming. In: 7th IEEE Int. Conf. on Grid and Cooperative Computing, pp. 356-361.

[27] Xiao X, Shi Y, Gao Y (2008) On Optimal Scheduling for Layered Video Streaming in Heterogeneous Peer-to-Peer Networks. ACM Int. Conf. on Multimedia. pp. 785-788.

[28] Guo H, Lo KT (2008) Cooperative Media Data Streaming with Scalable Video Coding. IEEE Transactions on Knowledge and Data Engineering. 20(9): 1273-1281.

[29] Kumar R, Liu Y, Ross K (2007) Stochastic Fluid Theory for P2P Streaming Systems. IEEE INFOCOM. pp. 919–927.

[30] Kotevski Z, Mitrevski P (2011) A Modeling Framework for Performance Analysis of P2P Live Video Streaming Systems. In: Gušev M, Mitrevski P, editors. ICT Innovations 2010. Berlin Heidelberg: Springer Verlag. pp. 215-225.

[31] Chu Y, Rao SG, Seshan S, Zhang H (2000) A Case for End System Multicast. IEEE Journal on Selected Areas in Communications. 20(8): 1456–1471.

Chapter 11

Performance Evaluation of Distributed System Using SPN

Razib Hayat Khan, Poul E. Heegaard and Kazi Wali Ullah

Additional information is available at the end of the chapter

http://dx.doi.org/10.5772/48813

1. Introduction

Distributed system poses one of the main streams of information and communication technology arena with immense complexity. Designing and implementation of such complex systems are always an intricate endeavour. Likewise, performance evaluation is also a great concern of such complex system to evaluate whether the system meets the performance related system requirements. Hence, modeling plays an important role in the whole design process of the system for qualitative and quantitative analysis. However, in a distributed system, system functional behavior is normally distributed among several objects. The overall behavior of the system is composed of the partial behavior of the distributed objects of the system. So it is indispensable to capture the functional behavior of the distributed objects for appropriate analysis to evaluate the performance related factors of the overall system. We therefore adopt UML collaboration and activity oriented approach as UML is the most widely used modeling language which models both the system requirements and qualitative behavior through different notations. Collaboration and activity diagram are utilized to demonstrate the overall system behavior by defining both the structure of the partial object behavior as well as the interaction between them as reusable specification building blocks and later on, this UML specification style is applied to generate the SPN model by our performance modeling framework. UML collaboration and activity provides a tremendous modeling framework containing several interesting properties. Firstly, collaborations and activity model the concept of service provided by the system very nicely. They define structure of partial object behavior, the collaboration roles and enable a precise definition of the overall system behavior. They also delineate the way to compose the services by means of collaboration and role bindings [12].

Considering system execution architecture to specify the deployment of the service components is realized by the UML deployment diagram. Abstract view of the system execution architecture captured by the UML deployment diagram defines the execution architecture of the system by identifying the system components and the assignment of software artifacts to those identified system components. Considering the system architecture to generate the performance model resolves the bottleneck of system performance by finding a better allocation of service components to the physical nodes. This needs for an efficient approach to deploy the service components on the available hosts of distributed environment to achieve preferably high performance and low cost levels. The most basic example in this regard is to choose better deployment architectures by considering only the latency of the service. The easiest way to satisfy the latency requirements is to identify and deploy the service components that require the highest volume of interaction onto the same resource or to choose resources that are connected by the links with sufficiently high capacity [12].

It is indispensable to extend the UML model to incorporate the performance-related quality of service (QoS) information to allow modeling and evaluating the properties of a system like throughput, utilization and mean response time. So the UML models are annotated according to the *UML profile for MARTE: Modeling & Analysis of Real-Time Embedded Systems* to include quantitative system parameters [1]. Thus, it helps to maintain consistency between system design and implementation with respect to requirement specifications.

Markov models, stochastic process algebras, SPN (Stochastic Petri Net) are popular and much studied analytical approaches to conduct performance modeling and evaluation. Among all of them, we will focus on the SPN as the performance model generated by our framework due to its increasingly popular formalisms for describing and analyzing systems, its modeling generality, its ability to capture complex system behavior concisely, its ability to preserve the original architecture of the system, to allow marking dependency firing rates & reward rates defined at the net level, to facilitate any modification according to the feedback from performance evaluation and above all, the existence of analysis tools.

Several approaches have been followed to generate the performance model from system design specification. Lopez-Grao *et al.*, described a conversion method from annotated UML activity diagram to stochastic petrinet model [2]. Distefano *et al.*, proposed a possible solution to address software performance engineering that evolves through system specification using an augmented UML notation, creation of an intermediate performance context model, generation of an equivalent stochastic petri net model whose analytical solution provides the required performance measures [3]. D'Ambrogio proposed a framework for transforming source software models into target performance models by the use of meta-modeling techniques for defining the abstract syntax of models, the interrelationships between model elements and the model transformation rules [4]. Trowitzsch and Zimmermann proposed the modeling of technical systems and their behavior by means of UML and for the resulting models, a transformation into a Stochastic Petri Net was established [13]. Abdullatif and Pooly presented a method for providing computer support for extracting Markov chains from a performance annotated UML sequence diagram [14]. However, most existing approaches do not highlight more on the issue of how to optimally conduct the system modeling and performance evaluation. The approach presented here is the first known attempt that introduces a new specification style utilizing UML behavioral diagrams as reusable specification building block which is later on used for generating performance model to produce performance prediction result at early stage of the system development process. Building blocks describe the local behavior of several components and the interaction between them. This provides the advantage of reusability of building blocks, since solution that requires the cooperation of several components may be reused within one self-contained, encapsulated building block. In addition, the resulting deployment mapping provided by our approach has great impact with respect to QoS provided by the system. Our aim here is to deal with vector of QoS properties rather than restricting it in one dimension. Our presented deployment logic is surely able to handle any properties of the service, as long as we can provide a cost function for the specific property. The cost function defined here is flexible enough to keep pace with the changing size of search space of available host in the execution environment to ensure an efficient deployment of service components. Furthermore, we aim to be able to aid the deployment of several different services at the same time using the same framework. The novelty of our approach also reflected in showing the optimality of our solution with respect to both deployment logic and evaluation of performance metrics.

The objective of the chapter is to provide an extensive performance modeling framework that provides a translation process to generate SPN performance model from system design specification captured by the UML behavioral diagram and solves the model for relevant performance metrics to demonstrate performance prediction results at early stage of the system development life cycle. To incorporate the cost function to draw relation between service component and available physical resources permit us to identify an efficient deployment mapping in a fully distributed manner. The work presented here is the extension of our previous work described in [5, 6, 7, 12] where we present our framework with respect to the execution of single and multiple collaborative sessions and to consider alternatives system architecture candidates to describe system functional behavior and later on to evaluate the performance factors. The chapter is organized as follows: section 2 describes the performance evaluation of distributed system where the requirements of the successful performance evaluation are mentioned, section 3 introduces our performance modeling framework in details by considering the requirements outlined in the previous section, section 4 shows the applicability of our performance modeling framework with respect to performance modeling of a distributed system, and section 5 mentions the concluding remarks with future directions.

2. Performance evaluation of distributed software system

Performance evaluation is an integral part of any distributed software system which gives an indication of whether the system will meet non functional properties, once system built. The evaluation can be done in one of the two stages of the software development process:

1. Evaluation can be conducted at the early stage of the software development process
2. Evaluation can be done when the development process is completed.

Conducting the performance evaluation in any of the two stages has some merits and demerits. Early assessment of performance evaluation allows system designer predicting the system response in order to meet the non functional requirements before the system being built. This in turn guides the system designer about the system development process in right manner which thus increases the productivity and quality in accordance with the reduction in cost. But conducting performance evaluation in the early stage of the software development process is challenging because of the absence of the real system in hand. So predication in advance not always guides the system designer in right way. Modeling system functional behavior perfectly works as a catalyst to successfully conduct the system performance evaluation. System functional behavior is disseminated across several components that are physically distributed which increases the complexity in developing distributed software systems. Perfect modeling of distributed system functional behavior is realized by capturing the local behavior of the system components and also the interaction among them. It is very difficult to achieve these tasks in correct way when development of system is limited in the laboratory where modeling will be done by generating case study or scenario.

Conducting performance evaluation after the system development process being completed is less challenging than the former case. It is possible to retrieve the real system response in order to meet the system non functional requirements as the real system is already implemented. So the designer can get a real understanding about the correct status of the development process to know whether the system can meet the non functional requirements and end user's expectation. If the system fails to satisfy non functional requirements and can't meet the end user expectation, the only alternative is to rethink about the system design process. Any change in the system design process can cause the modification in the system development process. In worst case the development process might start from the beginning which in turn costs a lot.

In order to conduct the performance evaluation of distributed software system, the decision is not only influenced by when the evaluation should be performed but also other factors like which evaluation technique is appropriate and reasonable. There are mainly two evaluation techniques:

1. Simulation based evaluation
2. Analytic solution

Simulation based solution of the actual implementation gives a better assessment of the performance evaluation of the system. Simulation based solution gives the freedom to build the system arbitrary detailed and there is no restriction on building the simulation model of the real system [8]. Thus, it allows modeling and evaluating the system performance in a flexible way. But to develop the simulation model is not an easy task and sometimes it is error-prone. Implementing a complex system is usually a time-consuming, expensive task and needs experience [8]; mastering to handle this complexity is driven by the gaining vast knowledge in simulation language and how to apply this language to build and present the logic behind the complex distributed system to capture system functional behavior properly for conducting performance evaluation.

Analytical solution is another way to conduct the performance evaluation of the complex distributed software system. Presence of well established mathematical formula for analytical methods makes it popular to the scientific community to obtain the performance evaluation of the systems. This method of finding solution is more acceptable than simulation based evaluation because of the direct applicability of the mathematical formula and the availability of evaluation tools. Another advantage of using analytic model is the rapid development of model for performance evaluation of large and multifaceted system using the formalisms of analytical methods. However, sometimes such analytical models can usually be constructed by placing some structural restrictions and assumptions on the original system model based on the explicit modeling formalism which has been selected; the reason is that analytical models have a limited expressiveness in some cases to capture the complex system behavior. While it is sometimes doable to simplify the model of the system in order to make it analytically tractable, there are many cases in which the significant aspects of the system can not be effectively represented into the analytical model for performance evaluation [8].

In this chapter we particularly focus on the performance evaluation of the distributed software system at the early stage of the system development process using analytical models. The requirements for performance evaluation of distributed software system are not only influenced by the question of when to conduct the evaluation and which method is appropriate for the obtaining performance results but also driven by the other requirements such as:

1. Need for an efficient approach that will help to model the system functional behavior in a way that can reflect real system behavior so that performance evaluation can be meaningful afterwards.
2. Deployment mapping is an integral part of the distributed software system development process which is defined by the assignment of software components in the physical resources that are distributed. For large and complex system it requires an efficient approach for handling the deployment mapping so that it can also ensure the efficiency with respect to performance evaluation.
3. Model that captures the system functional behavior will be used as an input model for developing the analytical model. So we need a mechanism that can also include the performance parameters to the input models for conducting the successful evaluation.
4. Need for a scalable and efficient approach to establish the correspondence between the input model that will be utilized to capture the system functional behavior and the output model that will be used to conduct the performance evaluation of the distributed software system.
5. At last, developing a tool based support for the whole process of performance evaluation considering above requirements which can ensure the rapid development, evaluation and user friendliness.

The following Figure 1 mentions the requirements or factors that we need to consider for the successful performance evaluation of the distributed software systems. In order to capture all the above mentioned factors, it needs an efficient approach or developing a framework that will allow rapid and successful performance evaluation of distributed software system which at the end reflects the aim of this chapter.

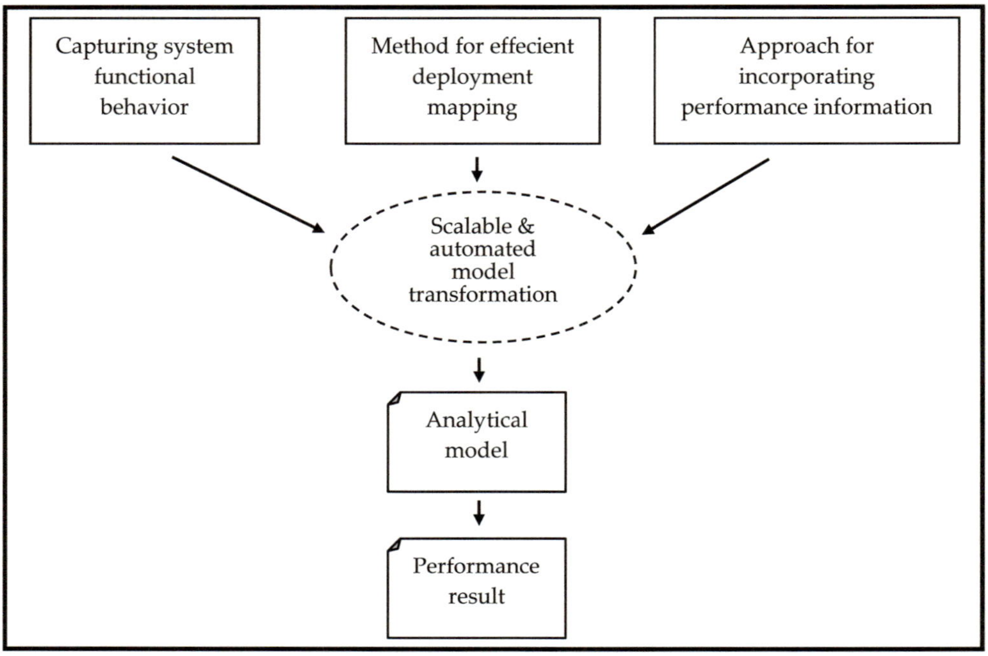

Figure 1. Performance modeling framework

3. Performance modeling framework

We already mentioned our main objective in the previous section that will be presented broadly in this section. In order to achieve the main objective, we need to follow an engineering approach that will accelerate the distributed software system development process. We also need to define the method that will be accounted for evaluating the system performance. We limit ourselves to methods targeting system development process using the standards of UML (Unified Modeling Languages) [9]. In the evaluation side we limit ourselves to methods that will analytically solve our problem using the technique SPN (Stochastic Petri Nets). This section mainly presents these two main techniques and also focuses on their properties that will be utilized to design our performance modeling framework.

3.1. Capturing system functional behavior

We use UML collaboration as main specification unit to specify system functional behavior. The UML standard focuses in particular on the structural aspects of UML collaborations. UML does not, however, elaborate detailed semantics of the behavioral implications of the structural composition. Collaborations are intended as a context in which behaviors may be defined. Compared to the other uses of collaborations, and what we need, this is an obvious shortcoming. We will later see how a combination of collaborations with activities may solve this problem [9].

Collaboration is an illustration of the relationship and interaction among software objects in the UML. Objects are shown as rectangles with naming label inside. The relationships between the objects are shown as line connecting the rectangles [11]. As a representative example, we introduce a scenario description utilizing UML collaboration 2. Several users equipped with cell phone or smart phone want to receive weather information of their current location using his/her hand held device. The user request is first transferred to authentication server through base transceiver station to ensure the authenticity of the user. Thereafter, the request of the legitimate user is transferred to the location server to retrieve the location information of the user. The location information is then transferred to weather server for retrieving the weather information according to the location of the user. Figure 2 defines this scenario as UML 2 collaboration. Participants in the system are users, mobile terminals, base transceiver stations, authentication servers, location servers, weather servers which are represented by the collaboration roles user, MT, BTS, AuS, LS, and WS. The users are the part of the environment and therefore labeled as <<external>>.The default multiplicity of the users, mobile terminals, base transceiver stations, authentication servers, location servers, weather servers are one to many, which are denoted by (1..*). The interactions between the collaboration roles are represented by the collaboration such as mobile terminal and BTS interact through *t: transfer*, BTS and authentication server, location server, weather server interact successively through *a: authenticate*, *l: request location info*, *w: request weather info,* while the user interacts with the mobile terminal by collaboration *g: generate request* [6].

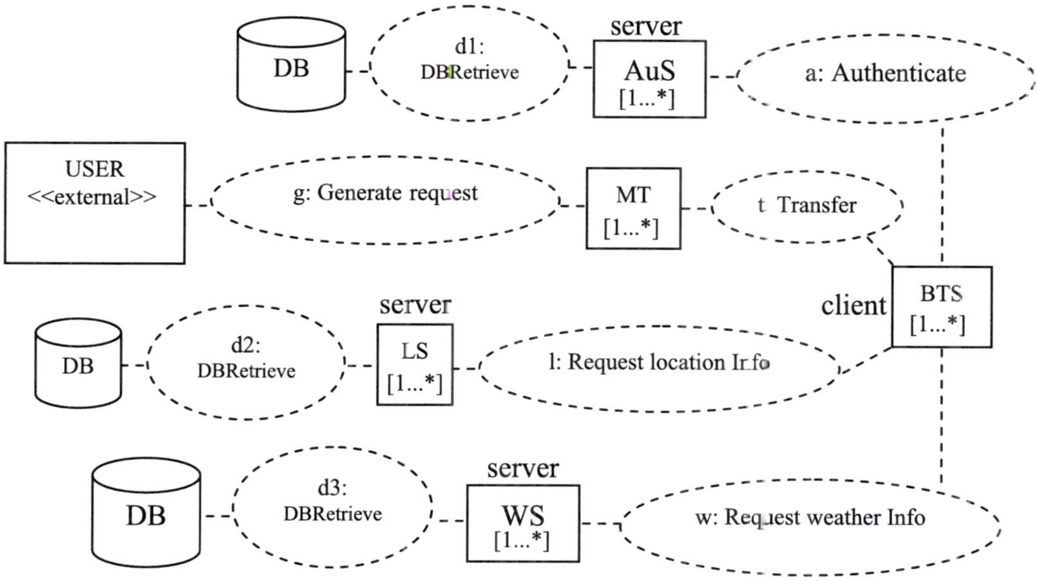

Figure 2. Collaboration diagram

The specifications for collaborations are given as coherent, self-contained reusable building blocks. The internal behavior of building block is described by the UML activity. It is declared as the classifier behavior of the collaboration and has one activity partition for each collaboration role in the structural description [6]. For each collaboration, the activity declares a corresponding call behavior action refereeing to the activities of the employed building blocks. Depending on the number of participants, connectivity to other blocks and level of decomposition, we distinguish three different kinds of building blocks [10]:

1. The most general building block is collaboration with two participants providing functionality that is intended to be composed with other functionality. We refer to such a building block as service collaboration.
2. Building blocks that involve only local behavior of one participant are referred to as activity blocks. They are represented by activities.
3. A special building block is system collaboration, which is collaboration on the highest composition level. In contrast to a service, a system is closed and cannot be composed with other building blocks.

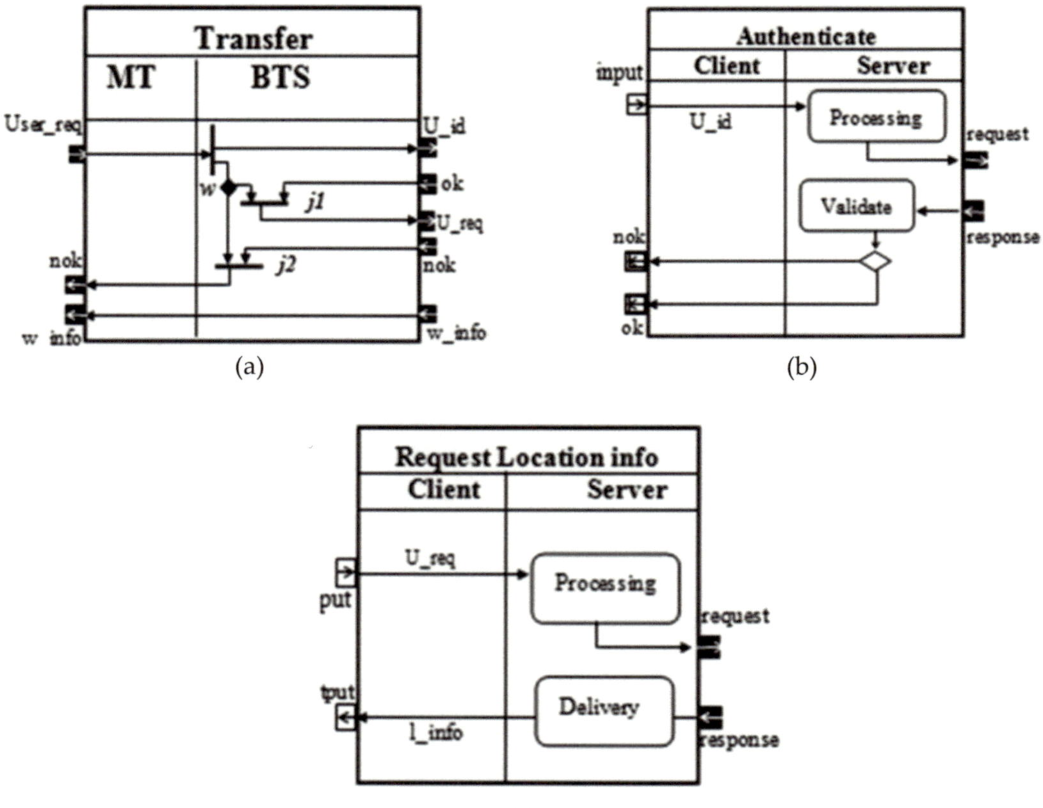

Figure 3. Activity diagram for expressing the internal behavior of collaboration

Hereby collaborations of Figure 2 are modeled by a call behavior action referring to the activity describing the behavior of the corresponding collaboration [10]. Activity diagram presents complete behavior in a quite compact form and may define connections to other behaviors via input and output pins [6]. Here we specify the behavior of one user request to show how the request is generated from his/her mobile terminal and served by the BTS, authentication server, location server and weather server and later on, compose this behavior to show how the requests will be processed by the BTS, authentication servers, location servers and weather servers so that the overall system behavior can be delineated. The activity *transfer* describes the behavior of the corresponding collaboration shown in Figure 3 (a). It has one partition for each collaboration role: mobile terminal (MT) and base transceiver station (BTS). Activities base their semantics on token flow [1]. The system starts by placing a token in the initial node of the mobile terminal when one request is generated by the user through his/her mobile terminal. The token is then transferred to the BTS where it moves through the fork node generating two flows. One flow places a token in the waiting decision node *w* which is the extension of a decision node with the difference that it may hold a token similar to an initial node, as defined in [1]. *w* is used in combination with join nodes *j1* and *j2* to explicitly model the acceptance or rejection of the user request based on the user authenticity. The other flow is forwarded as input to the authentication server to check whether the user is legitimate to generate service request. If the user is legitimate to generate the request a token is offered to the join node *j1*. If *w* still has its token *j1* can fire which emits a token which then forwarded to the location server for further processing. If the user is not legitimate to generate the request, a token is offered to the join node *j2*. If *w* still has its token *j2* can fire notifying the user upon the cancellation of request and then terminates the activity.

In order to validate the user identity (mobile number in this case) provided by a user who requests for service, BTS participates in the collaboration *authenticate* together with the authentication server. This is specified by collaboration *a: authenticate* where BTS plays the role of client and the authentication server plays the role of server. The behavior of the collaboration defined by the UML activity which is divided into two partitions, one for each collaboration role: client & server shown in Figure 3(b). The activity is started on the client side, when user id is provided as parameter *u_id* at the input pin. The input is then directly sent to the server, where it is converted into a database request in the call behavior action *processing*. Thereafter, it is the task of the collaboration between the server and the database to provide the stored user information. In order to get the information, the request leaves the activity *authenticate* and the server waits for the reception of the response. This is modeled with the input and output pins *request* and *response*. Depending on the validity of the user id, the server may decide to report *ok* or *nok* (not ok) to the client by the call behavior action *validate*. The result is then forwarded to the corresponding output pin in the client side and the activity is terminated. The semantics of all the pins are given in [12]. Likewise, we can describe the behavior of collaboration *l: Request Location info* (shown in Figure 3(c)) and w: *Request Weather info* through activity partition of client and server where BTS plays the role of client and location server and weather server play the role of server to deliver the requested information to the user through his/her mobile terminal.

The collaborative building blocks with help of activities specify overall system functional behavior which is introduced in Figure 4 for our scenario. For specifying detail behavior, UML collaborations and activities are used complementary to each other; UML collaborations focus on the role binding and structural aspect, while UML activities complement this by covering also the behavioral aspect for composition. For this purpose, call behavior actions are used. Each sub-service is represented by a call behavior action referring to the respective activity of the building blocks. Each call behavior action represents an instance of a building block. For each activity parameter node of the referred activity, a call behavior action declares a corresponding pin. Pins have the same symbol as activity parameter nodes to represent them on the frame of a call behavior action. Arbitrary logic between pins may be used to synchronize the building block events and transfer data between them. By connecting the individual input and output pins of the call behavior actions, the events occurring in different collaborations can be coupled with each other. There are different kinds of pins described as follows [10]:

1. Starting pins activate the building block, which is the precondition of any internal behavior.
2. Streaming pin may pass tokens throughout the active phase of the building block.
3. Terminating pins mark the end of the block's behavior. If collaboration is started and terminated via several alternative pins, they must belong to different parameter sets. This is visualized in UML diagram by an additional box around the corresponding node.

Figure 4 shows the activity diagram for our system to highlight the overall behavior of the system by composing all the building blocks. The initial node (·) marks the starting of the activity. The activity is started on the client side. When a user service request is generated via mobile terminal, *g: Generate request* will transfer the user service request as parameter *u_req* to the BTS via collaboration *t: Transfer*. Once the request arrived at the BTS the user id as parameter *u_id* is transferred to the authentication server to check whether the user is authentic to accept the service and the activity is represented by *a: authenticate*. The activity *authenticate* initiates a database request, modeled by collaboration *d1: DBRetrieve* and terminates with one of the alternative results *ok* or *nok*. After arriving the positive response at the BTS, request for location information is forwarded to the location server represented by activity *Request location info*. Location server makes a database request which is modeled by *d1: DBRetrieve* and terminates with result *l_info* (Location information). After getting the location information, request for weather information according to user current location is forwarded by the BTS to the weather server represented by activity *Request weather info.* Weather server makes a database request which is modeled by *d2: DBRetrieve* and terminates with result *w_info* (Weather information). After that, the final result is transferred to the user hand held device by BTS via activity *t: Transfer*. But if the user is failed to prove his/her identity then immediately a *nok* is sent to the user's hand held device.

So far, we introduced the system functional behavior with respect to specific example. Now we would like to introduce the specification in more generalized way. For example, the

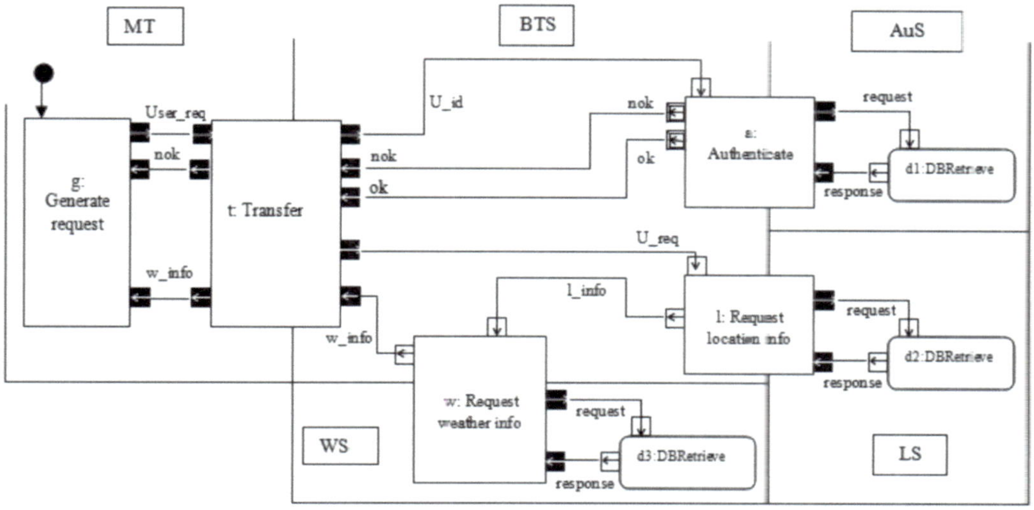

Figure 4. Activity diagram for detail system behavior

general structure of the building block *t* is given in Figure 5 where it only declares the participants A and B as collaboration roles and the connection between them is defined as collaboration use t_x (x=1…n_{AB} (number of collaborations between collaboration roles A and B)). The internal behavior of the same building block is shown in Figure 6(b). The activity *transfer*$_{ij}$ (*where ij = AB*) describes the behavior of the corresponding collaboration. It has one activity partition for each collaboration role: A and B. Activities base their semantics on token flow [1]. The activity starts by placing a token when there is a response (indicated by the streaming pin *res*) to transfer by either participant A or B. After completion of the processing by the collaboration role A and B the token is transferred from the participant A to participant B and from participant B to Participant A which is represented by the call behavior action *forward.*

Figure 5. Collaboration diagram in generalized way

The detailed behavior of collaboration is given in following Figure 6(a). The initial node ( ) indicates the starting of the activity. The activity is started at the same time from each participant A and B. After being activated, each participant starts its processing of the request which is mentioned by call behavior action P_i (Processing$_i$, where i = A, B). Completions of the processing by the participants are mentioned by the call behavior action d_i (Processing_done$_i$, i = A, B). After completion of the processing, the responses are delivered to the corresponding participants indicated by the streaming pin *res*. The response of the collaboration role A will be forwarded to B and vice versa which is mentioned by collaboration *t: transfer*$_{ij}$ (where ij = AB).

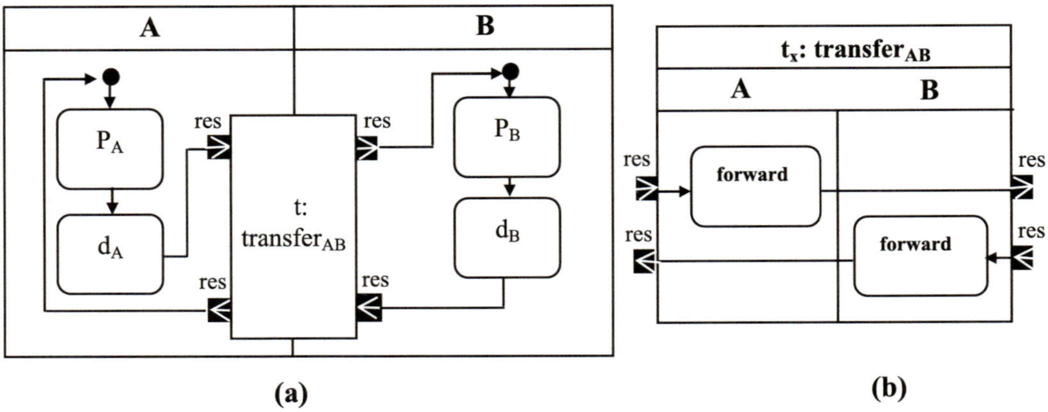

Figure 6. (a) Detail behavior of collaborative building block (b). Internal behavior of collaboration

3.2. Method for efficient Deployment mapping

Deployment diagram can be used to define the execution architecture of the system by identifying the system physical components and the assignment of software artifacts to those identified physical components [11]. After designing the deployment diagram the relation between system component and collaboration will be delineated to describe the service delivered by the system. The service is delivered by the joint behavior of the system components which may be physically distributed. The necessary partial behavior of the component used to realize the collaboration is represented by the collaboration role. In this way, it is possible to expose direct mapping between the collaboration roles to the system components to show the probable deployment of service components to the physical nodes of the system [6].

We consider two design alternatives of system architecture captured by UML deployment diagram to demonstrate the relationship between collaboration and system component for the scenario mentioned in Figure 2. For our defined scenario the identified system components by the 1st variation of deployment diagram are Mobile terminal, Base transceiver station, Authentication server, Location server and Weather server. After designing the deployment diagram the relationship between system component and collaboration will be delineated to describe the service delivered by the system. The service is delivered by the joint behavior of system components which may be physically distributed. The necessary partial behavior of the components used to realize the collaboration is represented by the collaboration role. Behavior of the components Mobile terminal, Base transceiver station, Authentication server, Location server, Weather server are represented by the collaboration roles MT, BTS, AuS, LS & WS to utilize the collaboration *t: transfer, a: authenticate, l: request location info, w: request weather info*. Here it is one to one mapping between system component & collaboration role shown in Figure 7(a).

We consider other variation of deployment diagram for mentioned scenario. In this variation of deployment diagram the identified system components are mobile terminal,

Base transceiver station, application server. In this case, the behavior of the components Mobile terminal and Base transceiver station is represented by the collaboration roles MT and BTS to utilize the collaboration *t: transfer* and the behavior of the component application behavior is represented jointly by the collaboration role AuS, LS and WS to utilize the collaboration *a: authenticate, l: request location info, w: request weather info*. In second case, the mapping between system component & collaboration role is generalized into one to many relations mentioned in Figure 7(b).

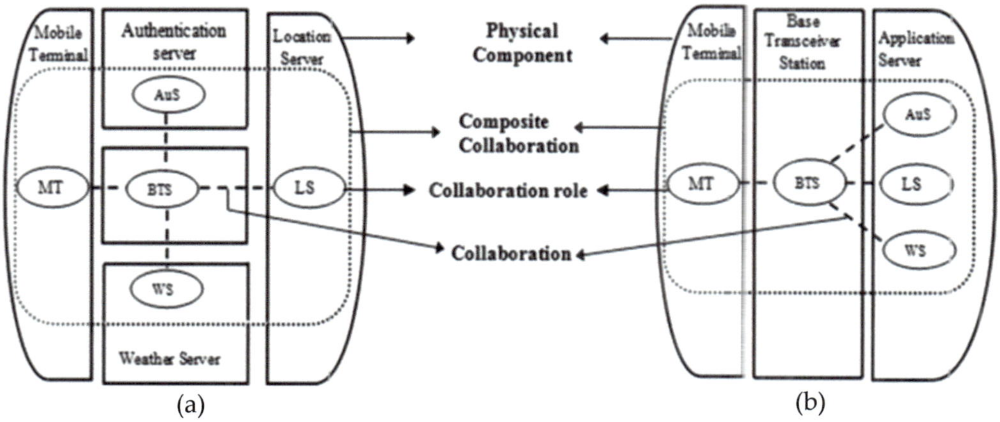

Figure 7. UML deployment diagram with service components deployment mapping

For large and complex system, conducting the deployment mapping is not straight forward like the previous cases. The deployment mapping has implication with respect to satisfying the non functional properties of the system. So we need for an approach that will be apposite for conducting the deployment mapping for complex system considering constraints and capabilities of the system components. We introduce our approach by considering the system as collection of N interconnected nodes. Our objective is to find a deployment mapping for this execution environment for a set of service components C available for deployment that comprises the service. Deployment mapping M can be defined as $(M : C \rightarrow N)$ between a numbers of service components instances c, onto nodes n mentioned in Figure 8. A components $c_i \in C$ can be a client process or a service process, while a node, $n \in N$ is a physical resource. Generally, nodes can have different responsibilities, such as providing services (*S1*), relaying traffic (*R1*), accommodating clients (*C1*), or a mixture of these (*SC1*). Components can communicate via a set of collaborations. We consider 3 types of requirements in the deployment problem where the term cost is introduced to capture several non-functional requirements those are later on utilized to conduct performance evaluation of the systems:

1. Components have execution costs
2. Collaborations have communication costs and costs for running of background process known as overhead cost
3. Some of the components can be restricted in the deployment mapping to specific nodes which are called bound components.

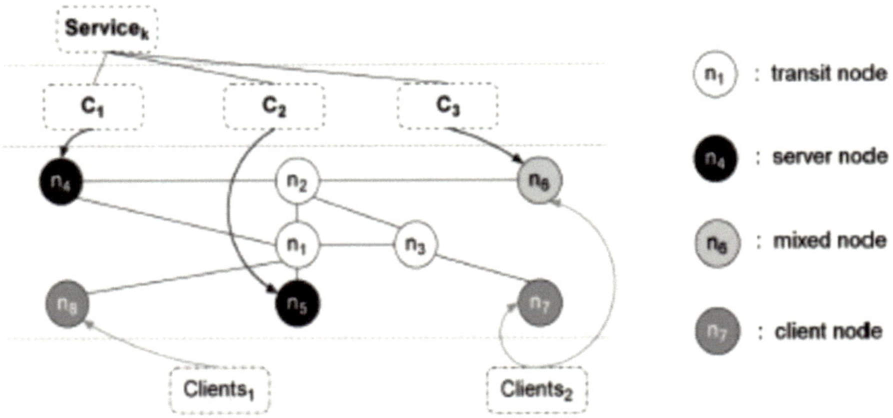

Figure 8. Service component mapping example

Furthermore, we consider identical nodes that are interconnected each other and are capable of hosting components with unlimited processing demand. We observe the processing cost that nodes impose while host the components and also the target balancing of cost among the nodes available in the network. Communication costs are considered if collaboration between two components happens remotely, i.e. it happens between two nodes [15]. In other words, if two components are placed onto the same node the communication cost between them will not be considered. The cost for executing the background process for conducting the communication between the collaboration roles is always considerable no matter whether the collaboration roles deploy on the same or different nodes. Using the above specified input, the deployment logic provides an optimal deployment architecture taking into account the QoS requirements for the components providing the specified services. We then define the objective of the deployment logic as obtaining an efficient (low-cost, if possible optimum) mapping of components onto the nodes that satisfies the requirements in reasonable time. The deployment logic providing optimal deployment architecture is guided by the cost function F(M). The cost function is designed here to reflect the goal of balancing the execution cost and minimizing the communications cost. This is in turn utilized to achieve reduced task turnaround time by maximizing the utilization of resources while minimizing any communication between processing nodes. That will offer a high system throughput, taking into account the expected execution and inter-node communication requirements of the service components on the given hardware architecture. The evaluation of cost function F(M) is mainly influenced by our way of service definition. Service is defined in our approach as a collaboration of total E components labeled as c_i (where i = 1…. E) to be deployed and total K collaborations between them labeled as k_j, (where j = 1 … K). The execution cost of each service component can be labeled as f_{ci}; the communication cost between the service components is labeled as f_{kj} and the cost for executing the background process for conducting the communication between the service components is labeled as f_{Bj}. Accordingly, we only observe the total cost ($\hat{l}_n$, n = 1… X) ofa given deployment mapping at each node where X defines the total number of physical nodes available in the execution environment. We will strive for an optimal solution of equally distributed cost among the processing nodes and the lowest cost possible, while taking into account the execution cost f_{c_i}, i = 1….E, communication cost f_{k_j}, j = 1….K and cost for executing the background process f_{B_j}, j = 1….k. f_{c_i}, f_{k_j} and f_{B_j} are derived from the service specification, thus the offered execution cost can be calculated as $\sum_{i=1}^{|E|} fc_i$. This way, the logic can be aware of the target cost T [15]:

$$T = \frac{1}{|X|} \sum_{i=1}^{|E|} fc_i \quad (1)$$

To cater for the communication cost f_{k_j} of the collaboration k_j in the service, the function $q_0(M, c)$ is defined first [15]:

$$q_0(M,c) = \{n \in N \mid \exists (c \to n) \in M\} \quad (2)$$

This means that $q_0(M,c)$ returns the node n that hosts components in the list mapping M. Let collaboration $k_j = (c_1, c_2)$. The communication cost of k_j is 0 if components c_1 and c_2 are collocated, i.e. $q_0(M,c_1) = q_0(M,c_2)$, and the cost is f_{k_j} if components are otherwise (i.e. the collaboration is remote). Using an indicator function I(x), which is 1 if x is true and 0 otherwise, this expressed as $I(q_0(M,c_1) \neq q_0(M,c_2)) = 1$, if the collaboration is remote and 0 otherwise. In order to determine which collaboration k_j is remote, the set of mapping M is used. Given the indicator function, the overall communication cost of service, $F_k(M)$, is the sum [15]:

$$F_k(M) = \sum_{j=1}^{|k|} I\left(q_0(M, K_{j,1}) \neq q_0(M, K_{j,2})\right) \cdot f_{k_j} \quad (3)$$

Given a mapping M = {m_n} (where m_n is the set of components at node n & $n \in$ N) the total load can be obtained as $\hat{l}_n = \sum_{c_i \in m_n} fc_i$. Furthermore the overall cost function F(M) becomes (where I_j = 1, if k_j external or 0 if k_j internal to a node) [15]:

$$F(M) = \sum_{n=1}^{|N|} |\hat{l}_n - T| + F_k(M) + \sum_{j=1}^{|k|} f_{B_j} \quad (4)$$

3.3. Approach for incorporating performance information

UML is no doubt a well established language for modeling system functional behavior. But UML has lacking of incorporating non functional parameters in the model while specifying the functional behavior of any system. This needs for an approach or specification to incorporate the performance parameters in the UML for quantitative analysis. That's why we use a specification called the *UML profile for MARTE* for Modeling and Analysis of Real-Time and Embedded systems, provides support for specification, design, and verification/validation stages [1]. This new profile is intended to replace the existing UML Profile for Schedulability, Performance and Time. This specification of a UML profile adds capabilities to UML for model-driven development of Real Time and Embedded Systems (RTES) [1].

MARTE defines foundations for model-based descriptions of real time and embedded systems. These core concepts are then refined for both modeling and analyzing concerns. Modeling parts provides support required from specification to detailed design of real-time and embedded characteristics of systems. MARTE concerns also model-based analysis. In this sense, the intent is not to define new techniques for analyzing real-time and embedded systems, but to support them. Hence, it provides facilities to annotate models with information required to perform specific analysis. Especially, MARTE focuses on performance and schedulability analysis. But it defines also a general analysis framework that intends to refine/specialize any other kind of analysis. Among others, the benefits of using this profile are thus [1]:

1. Providing a common way of modeling both hardware and software aspects of an RTES in order to improve communication between developers.
2. Enabling interoperability between development tools used for specification, design, verification, code generation, etc.
3. Fostering the construction of models that may be used to make quantitative predictions regarding real-time and embedded features of systems taking into account both hardware and software characteristics.

We apply several stereotypes of MARTE that permit us to map model elements into the semantics of an analysis domain such as schedulability, and give values for properties that are needed in order to carry out the analysis [1]. Specific tagged values are also applied. Tagged values are a kind of value slots associated with attributes of specific UML stereotypes [1]. In order to annotate the UML diagram we use several stereotypes and tag values according to the UML profile for MARTE. The stereotypes are the following [1]:

1. *saStep* is a kind of step that begins and ends when decisions about the allocation of system resources are made.
2. *ComputingResource* represents either virtual or physical processing devices capable of storing and executing program code. Hence its fundamental service is to compute.
3. *Scheduler* is defined a kind of ResourceBroker that brings access to its brokered ProcessingResource or resources following a certain scheduling policy mentioned by tag value *schedPolicy*. The ResourceBroker is a kind of resource that is responsible for allocation and de-allocation of a set of resource instances (or their services) to clients according to a specific access control policy [1].

The tagged values are the following [1]:

1. *execTime*: The duration of the execution time is mentioned by the tagged value *execTime* which is the average time in our case. The execution cost of service component is expressed by this tagged value in the annotated UML model that is later on used by the performance model to conduct the performance evaluation.

2. *deadline* defines the maximum time bound on the completion of the particular execution segment that must be met. The overhead cost and communication cost between the service components are specified by this tagged value in the annotated UML model that is later on used as well by the performance model to conduct the performance evaluation.

3.4. Scalable and automated model transformation

We already mentioned that SPN model will be generated as analytical model from the UML specification style to conduct the performance evaluation. This needs for an efficient, scalable and automated approach to conduct the model transformation for large, complex and multifaceted distributed system. In this literature, the approach for efficient model transformation is realized by producing model transformation rules that can be applied in generalized way for various application domains. As we generate SPN model as analytical model we will give a brief introduction about SPN model. SPN model has the following elements: Finite set of the places (drawn as circles), finite set of the transition defined as either timed transition (drawn as thick transparent bar) or immediate transition (drawn as thin black bar), set of arcs connecting places and transition, multiplicity associated with the arcs, marking that denotes the number of token in each place. SPN model is mentioned formally by the 6-tuple $\{\mathbf{\Phi}, \mathbf{T}, \mathbf{A}, \mathbf{K}, \mathbf{N}, \mathbf{m_0}\}$:

$\mathbf{\Phi}$ = Finite set of the places

$\mathbf{T}$ = Finite set of the transition

$\mathbf{A} \subseteq \{\Phi \times T\} \cup \{T \times \Phi\}$ is a set of arcs connecting Φ and T

$\mathbf{K}$: T $\rightarrow$ {Timed (time>0), Immediate (time = 0)} specifies the type of the each transition

$\mathbf{N}$: A $\rightarrow$ {1, 2, 3…} is the multiplicity associated with the arcs in A

$\mathbf{m}$: $\Phi \rightarrow$ {0, 1, 2...} is the marking that denotes the number of tokens for each place in Φ. The initial marking is denoted as $\mathbf{m_0}$.

By utilizing the above formal representation of the SPN model, we initiate the model transformation rules that will generate SPN model from UML collaboration and activity oriented approach that captures the system functional behavior. The model transformation rules are the following:

Rule 1: The SPN model of a collaboration role is represented by the 6-tuple in the following way:

$\mathbf{\Phi} = \{P_i, d_i\}$

$\mathbf{T} = \{do, exit\}$

$\mathbf{A} = \{\{(P_i \times do) \cup (do \times d_i)\}, \{(d_i \times exit) \cup (exit \times P_i)\}\}$

$\mathbf{K} = (do \rightarrow Timed, exit \rightarrow Immediate)$

$\mathbf{N} = \{(P_i \times do) \rightarrow 1, (do \times d_i) \rightarrow 1, (d_i \times exit) \rightarrow 1, (exit \times P_i) \rightarrow 1\}$

$\mathbf{m_0} = \{(P_i \rightarrow 1\}, (d_i \rightarrow 0)\}$

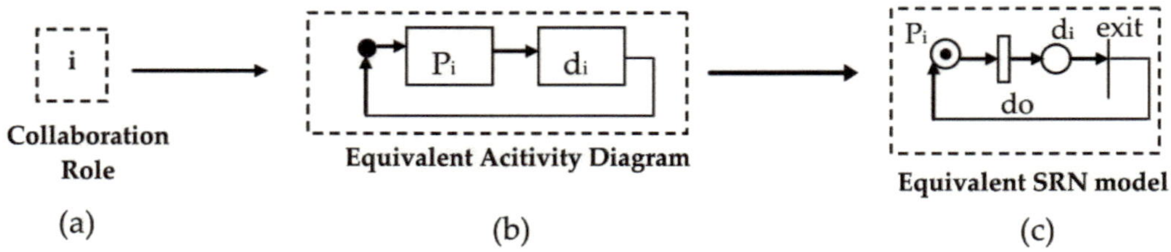

Figure 9. Model transformation rule 1

SPN model of a collaboration role is mentioned in Figure 9 (where P_i = Processing of ith collaboration role and d_i = Processing done of the ith collaboration role).

Rule 2: When the collaboration role of a building block deploys onto a physical node the equivalent SPN model is represented by 6-tuple in following way:

$\mathbf{\Phi} = \{P_i, d_i, PP_n\}$

$\mathbf{T} = \{do, exit\}$

$\mathbf{A} = \{\{(P_i \times do) \cup (do \times d_i)\}, \{(PP_n \times do) \cup (do \times PP_n)\}, \{(d_i \times exit) \cup (exit \times P_i)\}\}$

$\mathbf{K} = (do \rightarrow Timed, exit \rightarrow Immediate)$

$\mathbf{N} = \{(P_i \times do) \rightarrow 1, (do \times d_i) \rightarrow 1, (PP_n \times do) \rightarrow 1, (do \times PP_n) \rightarrow 1 (d_i \times exit) \rightarrow 1, (exit \times P_i) \rightarrow 1\}$

$\mathbf{m_o} = \{(P_i \rightarrow 1\}, (d_i \rightarrow 0), (PP_n \rightarrow q)\}$

Initially place PP_n contains **q** (where integer **q** > 0) tokens which define the upper bound of the execution of the process in parallel by a physical node *n* and the timed transition *do* will fire only when there is a token available in both the place P_i and PP_n. The place PP_n will again get back it's token after firing of the timed transition *do* indicating that the node is ready to execute other processes deployed on that physical node. The equivalent SPN model when a collaboration role deploy on a physical node is mentioned in Figure 10:

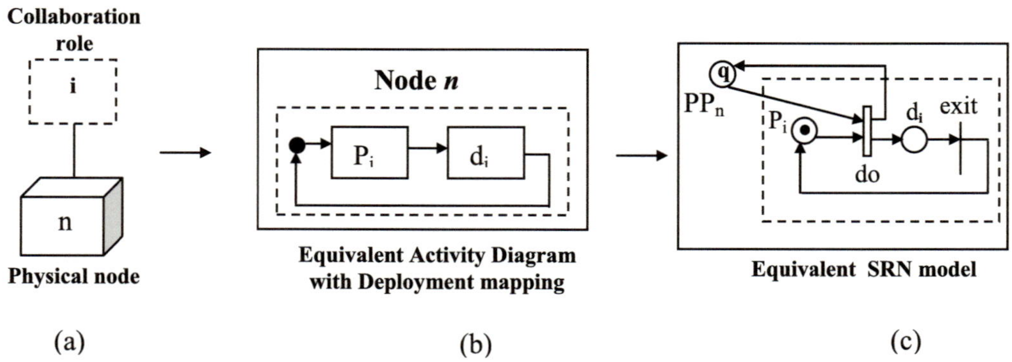

Figure 10. Model transformation rule 2

Rule 3: The SPN model of a collaboration where collaboration connects only two collaboration roles those deploy on the same physical node can be represented by the 6-tuple in the following way in Figure 11:

$\mathbf{\Phi} = \{P_i, d_i, P_j, d_j\ PP_n\}$

$\mathbf{T} = \{do_i, do_j, t_{ij}\}$

$\mathbf{A} = \{(P_i \times do_i) \cup (do_i \times d_i), (PP_n \times do_i) \cup (do_i \times PP_n), (d_i \times t_{ij}) \cup (t_{ij} \times P_i), (P_j \times do_j) \cup (do_j \times d_j), (PP_n \times do_j) \cup (do_j \times PP_n), (d_j \times t_{ij}) \cup (t_{ij} \times P_j)\}$

$\mathbf{K} = \{(do_i, do_j, t_{ij}) \rightarrow \text{Timed}\}$

$\mathbf{N} = \{((P_i \times do_i), (do_i \times d_i), (PP_n \times do_i), (do_i \times PP_n), (d_i \times t_{ij}), (t_{ij} \times P_i), (P_j \times do_j), (do_{ij} \times d_j), (PP_n \times do_j), (do_j \times PP_n), (d_j \times t_{ij}), (t_{ij} \times P_j)) \rightarrow 1\}$

$\mathbf{m_o} = \{(P_i \rightarrow 1), (d_i \rightarrow 0), (P_j \rightarrow 1)\ (d_j \rightarrow 0), (PP_n \rightarrow q)\}$

Here timed transition t_{ij} in the SPN model is only realized by the overhead cost as service components *i* and *j* deploy on the same physical node which makes the communication cost = 0.

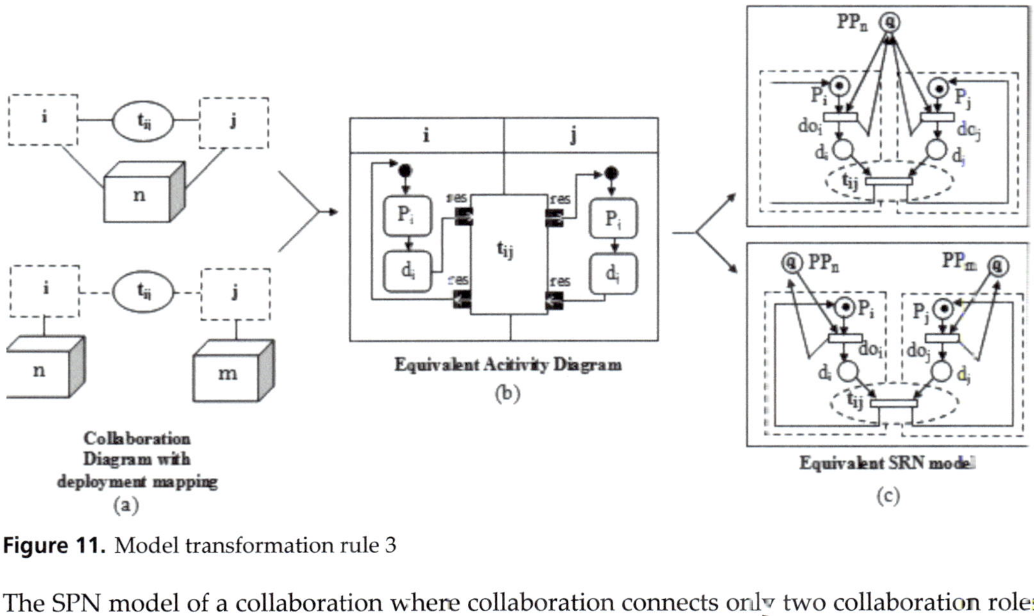

Figure 11. Model transformation rule 3

The SPN model of a collaboration where collaboration connects only two collaboration roles those deploy on the different physical node can be represented by the 6-tuple in the following way in Figure 11:

$\mathbf{\Phi} = \{P_i, d_i, P_j, d_j\ PP_n, PP_m\}$

$\mathbf{T} = \{do_i, do_j, t_{ij}\}$

$\mathbf{A} = \{(P_i \times do_i) \cup (do_i \times d_i), (PP_n \times do_i) \cup (do_i \times PP_n), (d_i \times t_{ij}) \cup (t_{ij} \times P_i), (P_j \times do_j) \cup (do_j \times d_j), (PP_m \times do_j) \cup (do_j \times PP_m), (d_j \times t_{ij}) \cup (t_{ij} \times P_j)\}$

K = {(do_i, do_j, t_{ij}) $\rightarrow$ Timed}

N= {(($P_i \times do_i$), ($do_i \times d_i$), ($PP_n \times do_i$), ($do_i \times PP_n$), ($d_i \times t_{ij}$), ($t_{ij} \times P_i$), ($P_j \times do_j$), ($do_{ij} \times d_j$), ($PP_m \times do_j$), ($do_j \times PP_m$), ($d_j \times t_{ij}$), ($t_{ij} \times P_j$)) $\rightarrow$ 1}

$\mathbf{m_0}$ = {($P_i \rightarrow 1$), ($d_i \rightarrow 0$), ($P_j \rightarrow 1$), ($d_j \rightarrow 0$), ($PP_n \rightarrow q$), ($PP_m \rightarrow q$)}

Here timed transition $\mathbf{t_{ij}}$ in the SPN model is realized by both the overhead cost and communication cost as service components *i* and *j* deploy on the different physical node.

3.5. Performance model Evaluation

We focus on measuring the throughput of the system from the developed SPN model. We are interested in throughput calculation as a measure of job that a system can process in a given time period which in turn justify the efficiency of our deployment logic mentioned in section 3.2 in accordance with system performance evaluation. Before deriving formula for throughput estimation, we consider several assumptions that will allow us to determine the parameters necessary for the throughput calculation of our system.

1. Executions of the processes occur independently each other.
2. All the communications occur in parallel.
3. Finally the communications between interconnected nodes will be started following the completion of all the processing and communication inside each physical node.

The above assumption is important for retrieving the parameters necessary for the throughput calculation from our system specification. We define the throughput as function of expected number of jobs in the system, E(N) and cost of the network, C_Net which defines the time required to complete the expected number of jobs in the system. The value of E(N) is calculated by solving the SPN model using SHARPE [16]. Cost of the network, C_Net is defined in the following: First the cost of a subnet (Csn) will be calculated as follows:

$$Csn_x = \sum_{i=1}^{|m|} fc_i + \max\left\{ f_{B_j} \right\} + F_k(M)$$

$$= \sum_{i=1}^{|m|} fc_i + \max\left\{ f_{B_j} \right\} \qquad (5)$$

Here:

- Csn_x = cost of the xth subnet (where x = 1….n; n is the total number of subnet that comprises the network)
- fc_i = execution cost of the ith process of the xth subnet
- m = total number of service components deployed on the xth subnet
- f_{Bj} = overhead cost of collaboration j (where j =1….n; n is the total number of collaboration in the xth subnet)
- f_{kj} = communication cost of collaboration j (where j =1….n; n is the total number of collaboration in the xth subnet)

- $F_k(M) = 0$ (defined in section 3.2.); as in this case processes connected by the collaboration deploy on the same physical node

Now we evaluate the cost between each pair of subnet with respect to the subnet's own processing cost, overhead cost and the cost associated with the communication with other subnet in the network.

$$Csnp_x = \left\{ \max\left(Csn_i , Csn_j \right) \right\} + f_{B_j} + F_k(M) \} \qquad (6)$$

Here:

- $Csnp_y$ = cost of the yth subnet pair (y = 1….n; n is the total number of subnet pair in the network where each subnet pair corresponds between two subnets)
- Csn_i, Csn_i = cost of the ith and j^{th} subnet (where (i, j) ϵ x and i≠j)
- $F_k(M) = 1$ (defined in section 3.2.2); as in this case processes connected by the collaboration deploy on the different physical nodes

$$C\_Net = \max\left\{ Csnp_1, ..., ..., Csnp_n \right\} \qquad (7)$$

$$Throughput = \frac{E(N)}{C\_Net} \qquad (8)$$

4. Case study

As a representative example, we consider the scenario dealing with heuristically clustering of modules and assignment of clusters to nodes [15, 17]. This scenario is sufficiently complex to show the applicability of our performance modeling framework. The problem is defined in our approach as a service of collaboration of $E = 10$ components or collaboration roles (labeled $C_1 \ldots C_{10}$) to be deployed and $K = 14$ collaborations between them depicted in Figure 12. We consider three types of requirements in this specification. Besides the execution cost, communication cost and overhead cost, we have a restriction on components C_2, C_7, C_9 regarding their location. They must be bound to nodes n_2, n_1, n_3, respectively. The internal behavior of the collaboration K_i of our example scenario is realized by the call behavior action through same UML activity diagram mentioned in Figure 6(b). The detail behavior of the collaboration role C is realized through same UML activity diagram already illustrated in Figure 6(a). However, there is no behavior modeled in detail, only that collaboration between processes deployed on different physical nodes. The UML collaboration diagram can be modeled by the activity that may model the detail behavior but the level of details must be selected with care in order for the model to scale while generating the performance model.

In this example, the target environment consists only of $N = 3$ identical, interconnected nodes with a single provided property, namely processing power and with infinite communication capacities depicted in Figure 13. The optimal deployment mapping can be observed in Table. 1. The lowest possible deployment cost, according to equation (4) is 17 + 100 + 70 = 187 [15, 17].

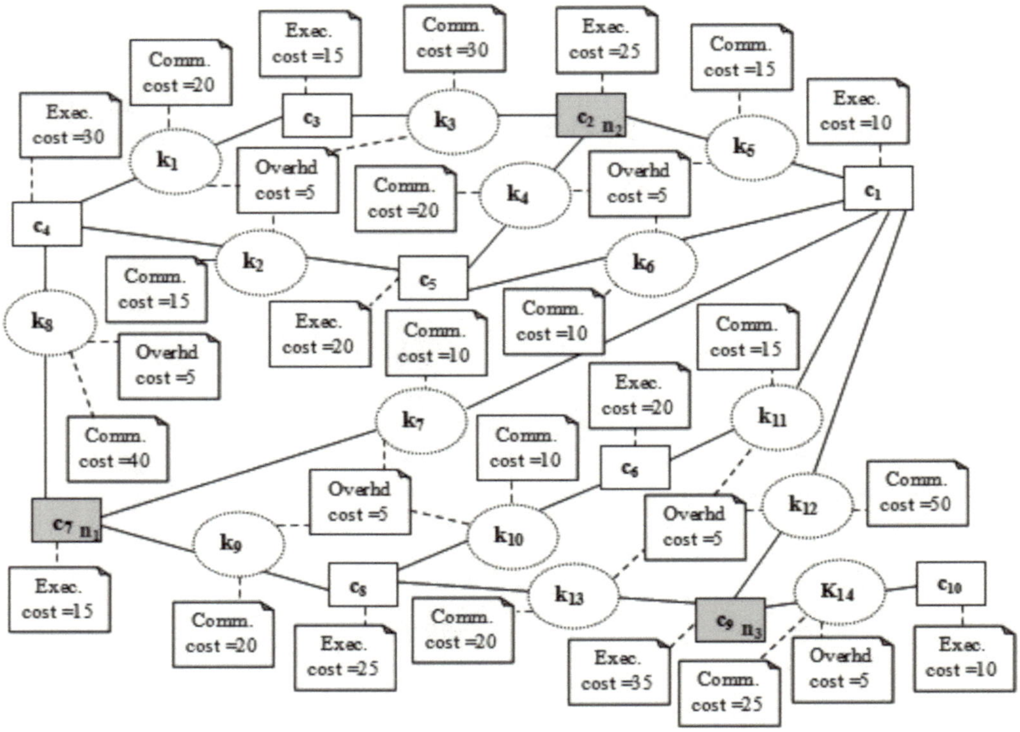

Figure 12. Collaborations and components in the example scenario

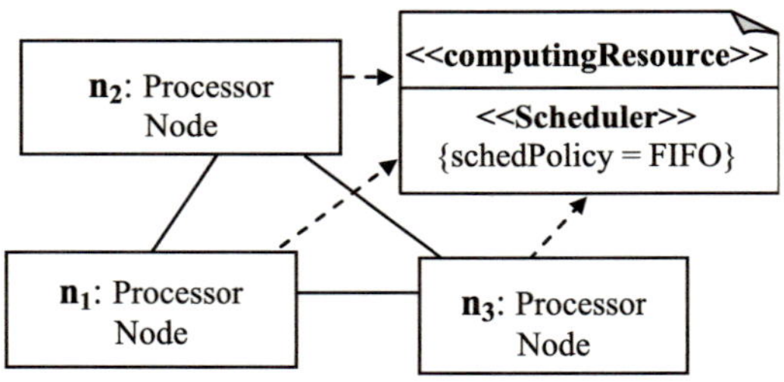

Figure 13. The target network of hosts

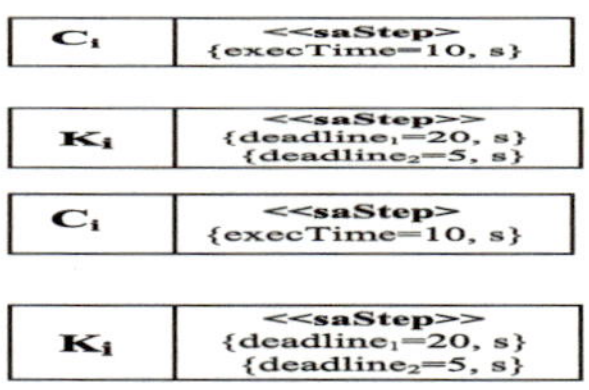

Figure 14. Annotated UML model

In order to annotate the UML diagram in Figure 12 and 13 we use the stereotypes *saStep, computingResource, scheduler* and the tag values *execTime, deadline* and *schedPolicy* which are already described in section 3.3. Collaboration K_i is associated with two instances of *deadline*

(Figure 14) as collaborations in example scenario are associated with two kinds of cost: communication cost and overhead cost.

Node	Components	$\hat{l}_n$	$\mid \hat{l}_n - T \mid$	Internal collaborations
n_1	c_4, c_7, c_8	70	2	k_8, k_9
n_2	c_2, c_3, c_5	60	8	k_3, k_4
n_3	c_1, c_6, c_9, c_{10}	75	7	k_{11}, k_{12}, k_{14}
			17	100
$\sum$ cost			117	

Table 1. Optimal deployment mapping in the example scenario [15, 17]

By considering the above deployment mapping and the transformation rules, the corresponding SPN model of our example scenario is depicted in Figure 15. Figure 15 sketches the resulting SPN model by illustrating details of all the places and transitions. According to the transformation rule 1, each collaboration role is defined by the two places P_i and d_i and the passing of token from place P_i to d_i is realized by the timed transition t_i

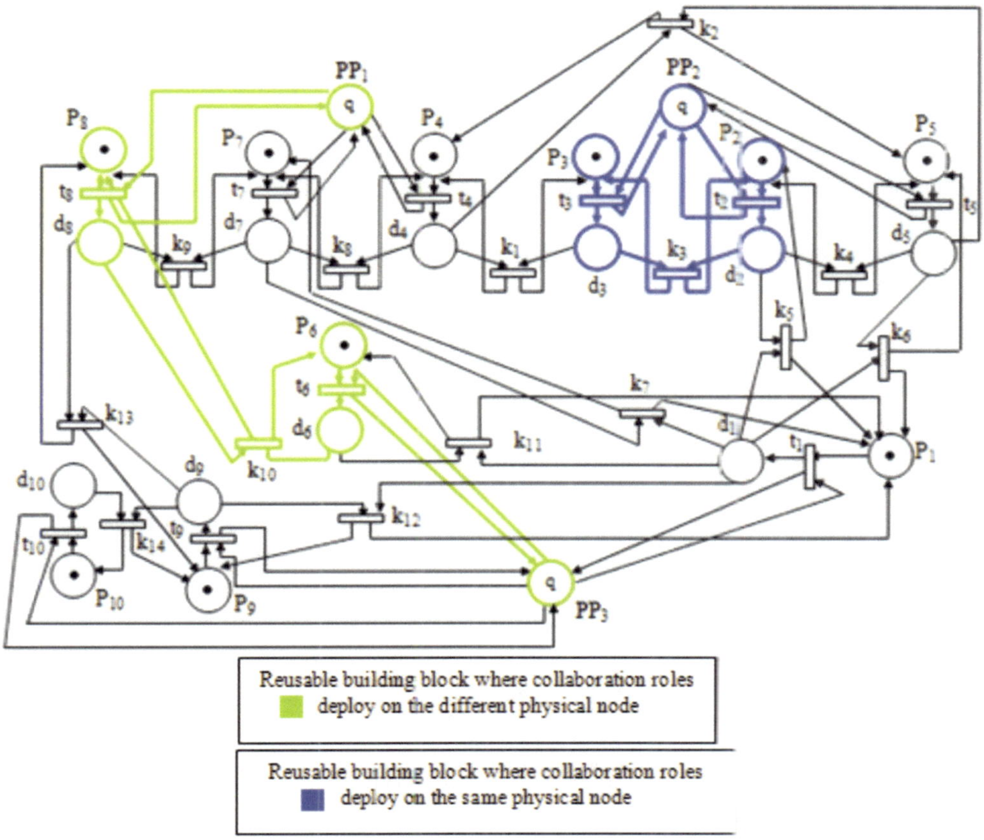

Figure 15. SPN model of our example scenario

which is derived from the annotated UML model. Initially, there will be a token from place P_1 to P_{10}. According to rule 2, in order to define the upper bound of the execution of parallel processes by a network node, we introduce three places PP_1, PP_2 and PP_3 in the SPN model for the corresponding three physical nodes and initially, these three places will contain q ($q > 0$) tokens where q will define the maximum number of the process that will be handled in parallel by a physical node at certain time. In order to ensure the upper bound of the parallel processing of a network node n_1, we introduce arcs from place PP_1 to transition t_4, t_7 and t_8. That means, components C_4, C_7 and C_8 can start their processing if there is token available in place PP_1 as the firing of transitions t_4, t_7 and t_8 not only depend on the availability of the token in the place P_4, P_7 and P_8 but also depend on the availability of the token in the place PP_1. Likewise, to ensure the upper bound of the parallel processing of a network node n_2 and n_3, we introduce arcs from place PP_2 to transition t_2, t_3 and t_5 and from place PP_3 to transition t_1, t_6, t_9, t_{10}.

For generating the SPN model from annotated UML model, firstly, we will consider the collaboration roles deploy on the processor node n_1 which are C_4, C_7 and C_8. Here components C_7 connects to C_4 and C_8. The communication cost between the components is zero but there is still cost for execution of the background process. So according to rule 3, after the completion of the transition from place P_7 to d_7 (places of component C_7), from P_4 to d_4 (places of component C_4) and from P_8 to d_8 (places of component C_8) the places d_7, d_4 and d_7, d_8 are connected by the timed transition k_8 and k_9 to generate the SPN model. Collaboration roles C_2, C_3 and C_5 deploy on the processor node n_2. Likewise, after the completion of the transition from place P_2 to d_2 (places of component C_2), from P_3 to d_3 (places of component C_3) and from P_5 to d_5 (places of component C_5) the places d_2, d_3 and d_2, d_5 are connected by the timed transition k_3 and k_4 to generate the SPN model according to rule 3. Collaboration roles C_6, C_1, C_9 and C_{10} deploy on the processor node n_3. In the same way, after the completion of the transition from place P_1 to d_1 (places of component C_1), from P_6 to d_6 (places of component C_6), P_9 to d_9 (places of component C_9) and from P_{10} to d_{10} (places of component C_{10}) the places d_1, d_6; d_1, d_9 and d_9, d_{10} are connected by the timed transition k_{11}, k_{12} and K_{14} to generate the SPN model following rule 3. In order to generate the system level SPN model we need to combine the entire three SPN model generated for three processor nodes by considering the interconnection among them. In order to compose the SPN models of processor node n_1 and n_2, places d_4 and d_3 are connected by the timed transition k_1 and places d_4 and d_5 are connected by the timed transition k_2 according to rule 3. Likewise, to compose the SPN models of processor node n_2 and n_3, places d_2 and d_1 are connected by the timed transition k_5 and places d_5 and d_1 are connected by the timed transition k_6 according to rule 3. In order to compose the SPN models of processor node n_1 and n_3, places d_7 and d_1 are connected by the timed transition k_7, places d_8 and d_6 are connected by the timed transition k_{10} and places d_8 and d_9 are connected by the timed transition k_{13} according to rule 3. By the above way, the system level SPN model is derived and all these are done automatically. The algorithm for automatic generation of SPN model from the annotated UML model is beyond the scope of this chapter.

The throughput calculation according to equation (8) for the different deployment mapping including the optimal deployment mapping is shown in Table 2. The optimal deployment mapping presented in Table 1 (first entry) also ensures the optimality in case of throughput calculation though we present here the throughput calculation of some of the deployment mappings of the software artifacts but obviously, the approach presented here confirms the optimality.

Deployment Mapping			Possible total cost	Throughput
n_1	n_2	n_3		
{c4, c7, c8}	*{c2, c3, c5}*	*{c1, c6, c9, c10}*	*187 (min)*	*0.0663 (max)*
{ c4, c7},	{c2, c3, c5, c6,}	{c1, c8, c9, c10}	232	0.0603
{c4, c6, c7, c8}	{c2, c3, c5}	{c1, c9, c10}	218	0.0575
{c5, c7, c8}	{c2, c3, c4}	{ c1, c6, c9, c10}	227	0.0574
{c1, c6, c7, c8}	{c2, c3, c4}	{c5, c9, c10}	247	0.0545
{ c3, c7, c8}	{c2, c4, c5}	{c1, c6, c9, c10}	252	0.0538
{c4, c7, c8}	{ c1, c2, c3, c5}	{ c6, c9, c10}	217	0.0532
{ c1, c6, c7, c8}	{c2, c3, c5}	{ c4, c9, c10}}	257	0.052
{c3, c6, c7, c8}	{c1, c2, c4, c5},	{c9, c10}	302	0.0469
{c6, c7, c8}	{ c1, c2, c4, c5}	{c3, c9, c10}}	288	0.0464

Table 2. Deployment mapping in the example scenario along with throughput

5. Conclusion

The contribution of this chapter is to develop a framework that focuses on the performance evaluation of the distributed system using SPN model. The developed framework recognizes the fact of rapid and efficient way of capturing the system dynamics utilizing reusable specification of software components that has been utilized to generate SPN performance model. The deployment logic presented here, is applied to provide the optimal, initial mapping of components to hosts, i.e. the network is considered rather static. Performance related QoS information is taken into account and included in the SPN model with equivalent timing and probabilistic assumption for enabling the evaluation of performance prediction result of the system at the early stage of the system development process. However, our eventual goal is to develop support for run-time redeployment of components, this way keeping the service within an allowed region of parameters defined by the requirements. Our modeling framework support that, our logic will be a prominent candidate for a robust and adaptive service execution platform for assessing a deployment of service components on an existing physical topology. Future work includes providing a tool based support of the developed performance modeling framework.

Author details

Razib Hayat Khan and Poul E. Heegaard
Norwegian University of Science & Technology, Trondheim, Norway

Kazi Wali Ullah
Aalto University, Helsinki, Finland

6. References

[1] OMG 2009, "UML Profile for MARTE: Modeling & Analysis of Real-Time Embedded Systems", V – 1.0

[2] J. P. Lopez, J. Merseguer, and J. Campos, "From UML Activity Diagrams to SPN: Application to Software Performance Engineering", Workshop on Software & Performance, ACM SIGSOFT software engineering notes, pp. 25-36, NY, 2004

[3] S. Distefano,M. Scarpa, and A. Puliafito, "Software Performance Analysis in UML Models", Workshop on Techniques Methodologies and Tools for Performance Evaluation of Complex Systems, Vol. 2005, pp. 115-125, 2005

[4] A. D'Ambrogio, "A Model Transformation Framework for the Automated Building of Performance Models from UML Models", Workshop on Software & Performance, ACM SIGSOFT software engineering notes, NY, 2005

[5] R H Khan, P E Heegaard, "Translation from UML to SPN model: A Performance Modeling Framework", EUNICE, pp. 270-271, LNCS, Springer, 2010

[6] R H Khan, P E Heegaard, "Translation from UML to SPN model: A Performance Modeling Framework for Managing Behavior of Multiple Collaborative Sessions & Instances" ICCDA, pp. V5-72-V5-80, IEEE computer Society, China, 2010

[7] R H Khan, P E Heegaard, " A Performance Modeling Framework Incorporating Cost Efficient Deployment of Collaborating Components" ICSTE, pp. V1-340-V1-349, IEEE computer Society, San Juan, USA, 2010

[8] Moreno Marzolla, "Simulation-based Performance Modeling of UML Software Architectures", PhD thesis, Universit`a Ca' Foscari di Venezia, 2004

[9] Frank Kræmer, "Engineering System: A Compositional and Mode-Driven Method Based on Collaborative Building block", PhD Thesis, NTNU, Trondheim, Norway, 2008

[10] F. A. Kramer, R. Bræk, P. Herrmann, "Synthesizes Components with Sessions from Collaboration-oriented Service Specifications", Proceedings of SDL, V-4745, LNCS, Springer, 2007.

[11] OMG UML Superstructure, Version-2.2

[12] R H Khan, P E Heegaard, "A Performance Modeling Framework Incorporating Cost Efficient Deployment of Multiple Collaborating Instances" ICSECS, pp. 31-45, Springer, 2011

[13] J. Trowitzsch, A. Zimmermann, "Using UML State Machines and Petri Nets for the Quantitative Investigation of ETCS", Valuetools, 2006

[14] Abdullatif, R. Pooly, "A Computer Assisted State Marking Method for Extracting Performance Models from Design Models", International Journal of Simulation, Vol. 8, No. 3, pp. 36-46, 2008

[15] Mate J Csorba, "Cost Efficient Deployment of Distributed Software Services", PhD Thesis, NTNU, Norway, 2011

[16] K. S. Trivedi and R Sahner, "Symbolic Hierarchical Automated Reliability / Performance Evaluator (SHARPE)", Duke University, NC, 2002

[17] Efe, K., "Heuristic Models of Task Assignment Scheduling in Distributed Systems", Computer, 1982

Chapter 12

State of the Art in Interactive Storytelling Technology: An Approach Based on Petri Nets

Hussein Karam Hussein Abd El-Sattar

Additional information is available at the end of the chapter

http://dx.doi.org/10.5772/48549

1. Introduction

Interactive Storytelling is one of most promising technologies for the development of new media and new forms of digital entertainment. Interactive Storytelling can be defined as the endeavour to develop new media in which the presentation of a narrative, and its evolution can be influenced, in real-time, by the user. In traditional forms of storytelling, a storyteller would present the scenario of a story to the audiences in a predefined way (also known as a plot), which limited the variation in character interactions and context. The story refers to the succession of actions that happen in the world represented by the narrative. The origin of computerized storytellers can be traced to the "story-generation system TALE-SPIN" (Meehan, J., 1981) which is the most popular generator of short tales A scene of the storyline is composed of beats, where the term beat refers to the smallest unit of action that has its own complete shape. A beat is a dramatic action that occurs in a scene to achieve a narrative goal. It consists of

i. Pre-conditions, a list of predicates that need to be true for the beat to be selected;
ii. Post-conditions; a list of predicates that will be true as a consequence of firing the beat;
iii. Success and failure conditions, and
iv. A joint plan to be executed by the actors.

The growing interest in Interactive Storytelling as a Research topic and as a potential technology derives from the current competition between traditional and interactive digital media. Interactive Storytelling is of interest to broadcasters and computer game producers alike. In the former case, Interactive Storytelling will bring interactivity into traditional media, potentially revolutionizing the entertainment experience. In the latter, it would improve the narrative and "aesthetic" value of computer games, with the potential to develop new game genres and attract a wider audience. The term Interactive Storytelling is sometimes used in a broader sense in the field of new media, to reflect the fact that some interactive systems, like computer games, can be designed to reflect an underlying narrative, which is conveyed via the gameplay, often enhanced by animation cut scenes.

On the other hand, several years of research are establishing Petri nets (PN) (Tado, M., 1990; Peterson, J. L., 1997) and its extension High-level PN as a process modelling formalism for a variety of application domains. A high level PN is a Petri net extended with colour, time, and hierarchy (Jenson, K., 1997). The power of Petri nets lies in its formal semantics and non semantics properties. This chapter addresses a new application domain of PN for modeling game systems and game workflow control in the context of workflow management concept and game rules principles. It presents state-of-the-art results with respect to interactive storytelling and PN, and highlights some petri-net-based workflow tools for game design. This is done by proposing an integrated framework for deeply combining interactivity and narrative in computer games which is achieved by:

i. composing the game rules in the game's workflow environment by different triggers and effects, and
ii. separating the rules of the game environment into two parts: controllable rules, and uncontrollable rules. The controllable rules are the rules in which its template is directly related to the goal of the game, mainly as a feedback within the rule effects. The uncontrollable rules are the rules in which its template is independent from the game goal. The rule is then characterized by a trigger based on the computer game's input, and an effect targeting only the game elements.

Evaluation and performance results supported by some case study called crazy ball 2 are also demonstrated. Crazy ball 2 is a platform-type genre, much like the worldwide-known game Mario and the Konami's Castlevania series.

In the reminder of this chapter we will offer insights into how workflow management concepts can be jointly utilized with Petri nets (PN) for modeling game systems and game workflow control. To do this, we first introduces the problem statatment, prior research and objectives in section 2. Section 3, briefly summarizes the background and the basic terminology and notions that will be used throughout this chapter. Section 4 introduces the methodology used. Evaluation and practical performance results are discussed in Section 5. Sections 6 concludes this chapter and outlines some directions for future work.

2. Prior research, problem statement, and objectives

2.1. Prior research

Building interactive storytelling systems is gained a growing attention among a growing number of researchers from a huge diversity of discipline and orgins of expertise. As a result, many different approaches which differ on various dimensions and sometimes overlap are developed under the following four and some other research directions:

i. Generative computer graphics, animated storytelling for film production;
ii. Human-computer interaction (HCI);

iii. Computer game design, and
iv. Artificial intelligence.

Story plot and character(s) are the two most important element of a story. As a consequence, several approaches, at different levels of complexity, have been developed for representing plots in games, monitoring the course of the story and controlling stories in games and storytelling applications. These techniques are summarized as follows:

i. Planning techniques (Riedl, M. & Stern, A., 2006);
ii. Beat approach (Brom, et. al., 2007);
iii. Finite-state machines (Sheldon, L., 2004), and
iv. Petri nets (PN) (Delmas, G. et. al, 2007; Brom, C. & Abonyi, A. 2006; Karam, H., 2010).

Several years of research are establishing Petri nets (PN) and its extension High-level PN as a process modelling formalism for a variety of application domains, for instance: network protocols, logistics, scientific workflows and gaming theory. Their power lies in their formal semantics and non semantics properties. The main contribution of this chapter is to show how workflow management concepts can be jointly utilized with Petri nets (PN) for modeling game systems and game workflow control. This is done by composing the game rules in the game's workflow environment by different triggers and effects. The idea is derived from the study of PN, game theory, workflow management, story writting, AI, and cinematography in interactive storytelling. In this contribution, interactive storytelling is viewed as a hybrid form of game design and cinematic storytelling for entertainment applications among two skills: artistic and technical. Evaluation and performance results in terms of some case study called crazy ball 2 are also demonstrated. Crazy ball 2 is a platform-type genre, much like the worldwide-known game Mario and the Konami's Castlevania series.

2.2. Problem statement and objectives

Recently, interactive storytelling has become a major issue in video games development. Several categories of video games arose to either historical, editorial or narrative criteria. Within the field of Interactive Storytelling, interactive drama is a computer-based fiction where a user chooses most of the actions for the main character in a story. Interactive drama is the ultimate challenge of digital entertainment because it involves both the dynamic generation of narrative events and the integration of user inputs within the generation. This is a hard challenge, because it involves both the dynamic generation of narrative events and the integration of user inputs within the generation. Moreover, both Storytelling unfolding and player's interaction can't take place at the same time. The first relates to game designer's control of the game he/she has created as the second relates to player's control on the game he/she has bought. Each interactive drama needs a model of narrative. The challenge of interactive drama is to find a model suited to the interactive nature of computers. Interactive drama architecture has several key components: the environment, the player, the user, the writer, and the director. For successful interactive drama architecture, three requirements are necessary (Magerko, B. & Laird, J. 2003):

i. the balance between writer flexibility vs. user flexibility;
ii. temporal variability (i.e. allowing time to be the key variable for the flexibility in an interactive experience), and
iii. transparency (How do we encourage the User to follow a particular destiny without having him feel forced into it?).

Moreover, it is necessary to overcome two obstacles (Szilas, N., 2005): technical problem and conceptual problem. This chapter attempts to solve these problems by proposing an integrated framework for deeply combining interactivity and narrative in computer games. The approach is based on separating the actions of the system into two parts, the controllable and the controllable actions. The controllable actions are controllable by the system we model. The system can choose which and when to execute controllable actions. The controllable actions are not controllable by the system, but can occur whenever they are enabled. In this contribution, interactive drama is viewed as a hybrid form of game design and cinematic storytelling for entertainment applications among two skills: artistic and technical. The idea is derived from the study of interactive drama, Petri nets (PN), narrative structures in computer games and game workflow activity process. The main advantages of using PN are that it copes well with branching stories and can evolve in parallel in large virtual world. The proposed idea is supported by some case study called Crazy ball 2. Crazy ball 2 is a platform-type genre, much like the worldwide-known game Mario and the Konami's Castlevania series. It possesses many universally-shared game features such as Hit Points (HP), Game Over, Enemies, and Bosses. One of the advantages of the proposed computer game is the inclusion of the "Freestyle combat system", which allows the user to completely control the attacks of the player using a mouse. Moreover, it possesses a feature which is called an "even game", in which the game challenge level matches the skill of the human player.

3. Fundamentals and basic notions

3.1. Petri Nets

Petri nets are a "pinball game" for mathematicians (Tado, M., 1990; Peterson, J. L., 1997). It is a particular kind of directed graph, together with an initial state called the initial marking M_0. The underlying graph G of a PN is a directed, weighted, bipartite graph consisting of two kinds of nodes, called places (P) and transitions (T), where arcs are either from a place to a transition or from a transition to a place. N=(T,P,F) is called a net, iff

$$\begin{cases} (i) P \cap T = \emptyset, \textit{and} \\ (ii) F \subseteq (P \times T) \cup (T \times P) \textit{ is a binary relation} \end{cases} \quad (1)$$

Let N be a net and let $x \in (P \cup T)$, then

$$\begin{cases} {}^{\cdot}x = \{y|yFx\} \textit{ is called the set of pre-conditions} \\ x^{\cdot} = \{y|xFy\} \textit{is called the set of post-conditions} \end{cases} \quad (2)$$

Formally, a Petri nets $PN = (N, M_0)$ consists of a structure N and an initial marking M_0, where:

i. N=(P,T,F,W) is a Petri nets structure,
ii. $P = \{p_1, p_2, \cdots, p_m\}$ is a finite set of m places,
iii. $T = \{t_1, t_2, \cdots, t_n\}$ is a finite set of n transitions,
iv. $F \subseteq (P \times T) \cup (T \times P)$ is a set of arcs with $P \cap T = \phi, P \cup T \neq \phi$.

Arcs are labeled with their weights (positive integers), where a k-weighted arc is interpreted as a set of k parallel arcs. Labels for unitary weight are usually omitted.

$$W : F \rightarrow \{1,2,3,\cdots\}$$

is a mapping which associates to each arc of the net its weight,

$$M_0 : P \rightarrow \{1,2,3,\cdots\}$$

is the initial marking representing the initial state of PN. The state of PN is described by means of the concepts of marking. A marking is a transition function that assigns to each place a nonnegative integer called a token. A token is the main information unit and a primitive concept of PN like places and transitions. If a sufficient number of tokens are contained in specific places, an action is triggered. After firing an action, the tokens that helped to fire this action are removed, and some new tokens are generated. Which tokens fire which action and which action generates tokens to which places is specified by the transition function. In graphical representation, places, transitions, tokens and transition function are represented by circles, rectangles or bars, pellets and arrows respectively. Table 1, illustrates such representations and its interpretations of a PN model. Figure 1 presents an example of a PN model with graphical and mathematical notations.

In modeling using PN, we regard the places as conditions, the transitions as events or actions, and a marking as triggers. A trigger can be associated with an action (action trigger) or a place (place trigger). A transition has a certain number of input and output places representing the pre-conditions and post-conditions of the event, respectively. The presence of a token in a place is interpreted as holding the truth of the condition associated with the place. In another interpretation, "k" tokens are put in a place to indicate that "k" data items or resources are available. Some typical interpretations of transitions and their inputs and outputs places are shown in Table 2.

PN Model	Graphical representations	Interpretations
Places	○	States/conditions
Transitions	▭	Events/actions
Tokens	●	Marks/States
Transition function	→	Triggers

Table 1. Graphical Representations and Interpretations of a PN Model.

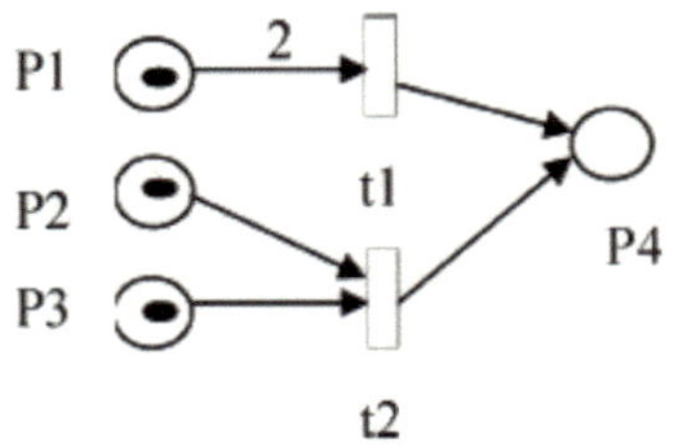

$P=\{P1,P2,P3,P4\}$,
$T=\{t1,t2\}$,
$F=\{(P1,t1), (P2,t2), (P3,t2), (t1,P4),(t2,P4)\}$,
$W(P1,t1)=2$,
$W(P2,t2)= W(P3,t2)= W(t1,P4)=W(t2,P4)=1$,
$M_0 = [1 \;\; 1 \;\; 1 \;\; 0]^T$.

Figure 1. An illustration example of a PN model with graphical notation (left), and mathematical notation (right).

Input Places	Transition	Output Places
Pre-conditions	Event	Post-conditions
Input data	Computation step	Output data
Conditions	Clause in logic	Conclusion(s)
Resources needed	Task/job/behavior	Resources released

Table 2. Some typical interpretations of transitions and places.

The dynamics of the net is described by moving tokens among places according to the transition firing rules or enabling test in marking. A transition t is said to be enabled if each input place P of t is marked with at least W (P, t) tokens, where W (P, t) is the weight of the arc from P to t. Once enabled, a transition will fire when its associated event occurs. A firing of an enabled transition t removes W (P, t) tokens from each input place P of t, and adds W (t, P) tokens to each output place P of t, where W (t, P) is the weight of the arc from t to P. Figure 2 demonstrates an example for the transition firing rules of a PN model shown in Figure 1. In the PN of Figure 2, only transition t2 is enabled; t1 is not enabled because it would require two tokens in P1 to fire, since W (P1, t1) =2. When t2 is fired, the tokens in P2 and P3 are removed and P4 receives one token (see Figure 2).

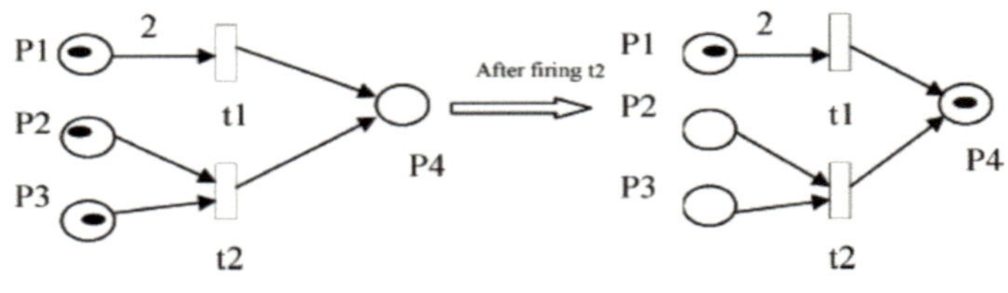

Figure 2. PN marking example before and after firing the enabled transition t2.

3.2. Workflow management concept

Workflows are gaining a lot of interest both in the business and scientific environments for automating the execution of complex IT processes. The term workflow management (WM) refers to the domain which focuses on the logistics of business processes (Van der Aalst, W., 1998). The goal of workflow management is to handle cases as efficiently and effectively as possible by the right resource (e.g. actor, person, participant, or application) at the right time. Workflows are case-based, i.e. every piece of work is executed for a specific case. The key concept of WM is task. A task is a piece of work to be done by one or more resources in a pre-determined time interval. A task item is a task that needs to be executed to handle a specific case. Task items are executed by resources. Synonyms for resource are actor or participant. A work item which is being executed by a specific resource is called an activity, which is an actual performance of a work item. The activity contains the rule entities to describe the conditions under which the activity may be fired. A workflow procedure defines a partial ordering of tasks to handle cases of a specific type. A workflow process definition comprises a workflow procedure, a set of resources and a strategy to map task items to resources. Figure 3 shows that a workflow has three dimensions: case, resource and process definition dimension. A number of dots shown represent either a work item (case+task) or an activity (case+task+resource). Note that, work items link cases and tasks. Activities link cases, tasks, and resources

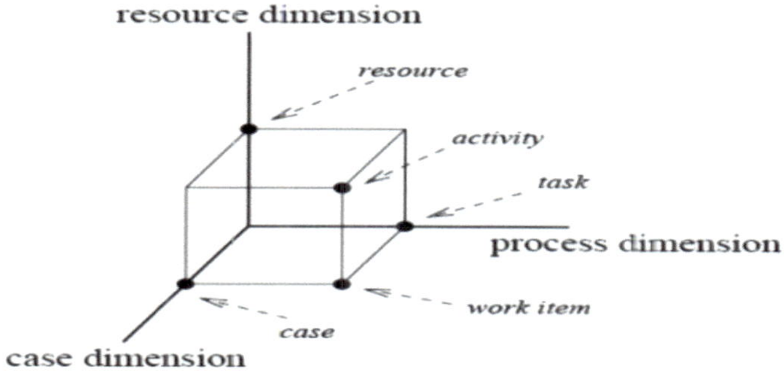

Figure 3. A three dimensional view of a workflow

A "workflow process definition" dimension specifies how the cases are routed along the tasks that need to be executed. Routing of cases describes the lifecycle of a case, i.e., which tasks need to be performed and in which order. Four types of routed are identified as shown in Figure 4: sequential (tasks are executed sequentially), parallel (task B and C are executed in parallel), conditional (either task B or C is executed), and iteration (multiple B's). These four routed types outlined the currently accepted narrative structures used in the creation of computer games (Mark Reidl, O., Michael R., 2005). For instance, linear narrative which corresponds to the sequential routing is a traditional form of narrative in which a sequence

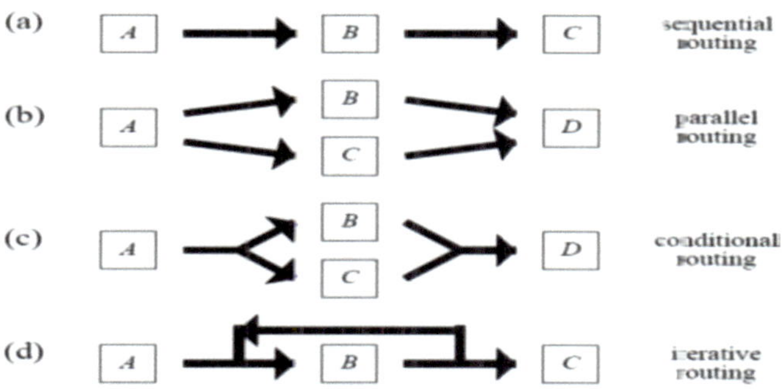

Figure 4. Four routing constructions demonstration.

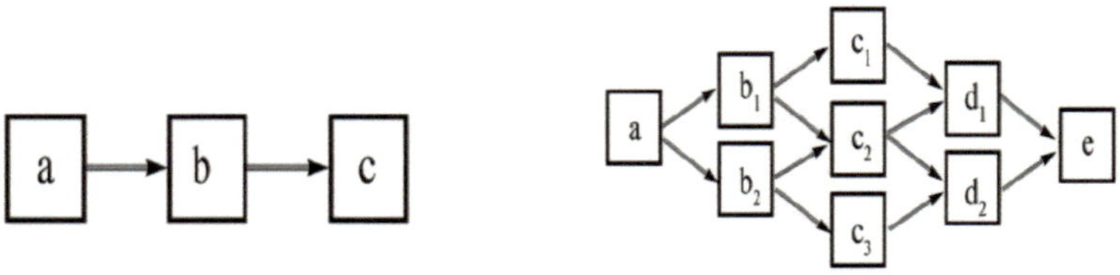

(a) Linear Narrative Progression (b) Branching Narrative Progression

Figure 5. An illustration for both linear and branching narrative progressions.

of events is narrated from beginning to ending without variation or possibility of a user altering the way in which the story unfolds or ends. Some computer games use branching narrative in which there are many points in the story at where some action or decision made by the user alters the way in which a narrative unfolds or ends. Both narratives are shown in Figures 5(a)-(b).

Since Petri Nets (PN) are a process modeling technique, then modeling a "workflow process definition" onto PN is straightforward: tasks, conditions, and cases are modeled by transitions, conditions and tokens respectively. Figure 6 shows how all these concepts can be mapped onto the Petri net. Table 3 shows the mapping between the workflow process definitions and PN terms.

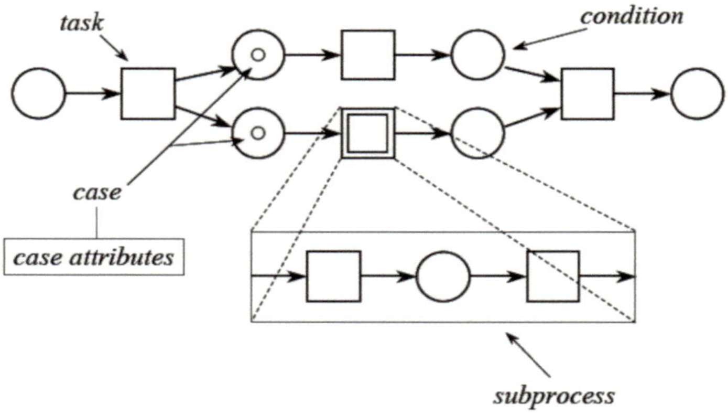

Figure 6. Mapping a process definition onto Petri nets.

Workflow Perspective	PN terms
Task execution	One or more transition
Work item	Transition being enabled
Activity	Firing of a transition
Data that flows between tasks/case attributes	Tokens
Conditions	Places

Table 3. Mapping Workflow process onto Petri nets (PN) terms.

4. Methodology

Computer games are defined as an activity with some rules engaged in for an outcome. Key components of games are goals, rules, challenge, and interactivity. Games are regarded in terms of three levels of temporal design, from simulation at the lowest time scale, through the design of game moves above the simulation level, to the structure of specific narrative patterns at the highest level. The methodology in our approach is based on the study of workflow process under these levels for the structural parts of a computer games and is shown in Figure 7.

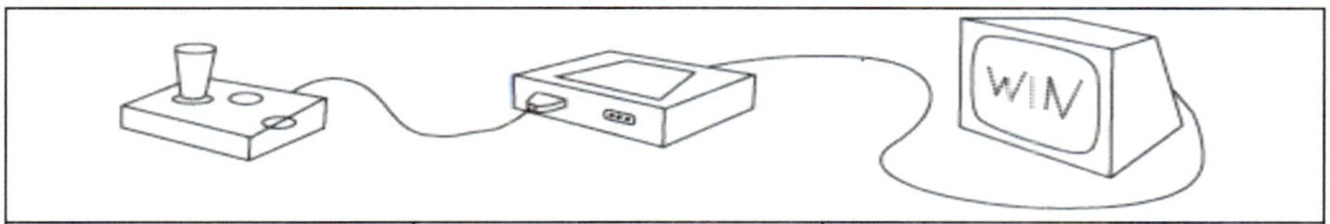

Input: Player pushes any buttons	Computing: the computer is thinking	Output: A "result" is displayed on the screen

Figure 7. The structural parts of computer games.

The diagram in Figure 7 is composed of three parts: the "Input" peripheral devices allowing the user to enter choices. These choices are then evaluated by the rules of the "Computing" part, in order to produce a "result". This result is finally communicated to the player through the "Output" device. Computer game development is a tremendous task that requires different roles for the storyteller and audience, and a lot of resources including: storytelling elements and elemental interplay. Storytelling elements includes: narrative, plot, and story. The interplay of elements in the game environment consists of: structure, theme and metaphor. The structure describes the influence of plot on narrative. Theme is the expression of the story within the plot. Metaphor is the means by which story is encoded within the narrative. From the technical point of view, game can be seen as a client-server application connected with some data. From the conceptual point of view for game representation and according to (Salen, K., Zimmerman, E., 2003), computer games are defined as an activity with some rules engaged in for an outcome. Therefore, there is a need to develop an integrated framework for deeply combining interactivity and narrative. As a sort for achieving this goal and under the study of workflow management concept, Figure 8 shows a design of a workflow activity process for the conceptual representation of computer games.

Figure 8 shows how the conceptual representation of a game can be modeled as a series of processes, where each process consists of some activities. Activity is a description of a piece of work that forms one logical step within a process. An activity has one or multiple roles, zero or multiple rules, zero or multiple event and one or more multiple data. Partial order relationships between activities (e.g. sequential, parallel, alternative and looped) are notated with the arc, which links the activity entity to itself. The activity also contains the rule entities to describe the conditions under which the activity may be fired. The rule is used to

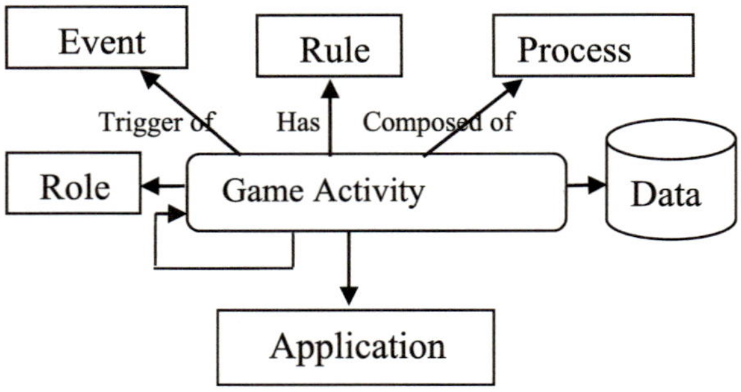

Figure 8. Game workflow activity process

describe logic conditions for executing activity and always related to case "data". The "application" entity extracts software tools, by which the role completes the activity, and the "data" depicts the input and output data of the activity. Since the game engine we are going to propose in this paper executes workflows represented in terms of PN. The classical structure of a PN model is formally defined by a set of places, a set of transitions and a set of arcs connecting places to transitions and vice versa. For the purpose of this chapter we extend the classical PN with features that make them more suitable for workflow representation given in terms of High level Petri nets (HLPN) workflow (Jenson, K., 1997). An HLPN is normally represented using a graphical form which allows visualization of system dynamics (flows of data and control). By using HLPN formalism it is possible to

i. formally represent the workflow state (and its evolution);
ii. formally describe both the control and the data flow, and
iii. deal with dynamic workflows.

An HLPN can be defined by the tuple: HLPN= (P, T, Type, Pre, Post, E, G, M_0), where

- P is a finite set of elements called places
- T is a finite set of elements called transitions
- "Type" is a function that assigns a type to places and expressions;
- $Pre \subseteq (P \times T)$ is the subset of arcs from places to transitions and $Post \subseteq (T \times P)$ is the set of arcs from transition to places
- E is an expression. It is defined from $(Pre \cup Post)$ into expressions. Expressions may comprise constants, variables (e.g. m,n) and functions (e.g. g(x)) which are types;
- G is the guard function, a Boolean expression inscribing a transition $(t \in T)$ (where Type(G(t))=Boolean);
- M_0 is the initial marking: a multi-set of tokens associated with the places

Now let us analyze the game workflow activity shown in Figure 8 in terms of HLPN and game components. Key components of games are goals, rules, challenge, and interactivity. Games takes place in a virtual universe and it is composed by several elements, where these elements are submitted to "rules", in accordance to the game. Since a workflow system is a reactive system, i.e. it is triggered by the environment. This means that, enabling of a task doesn't imply that the task will be directly executed. Therefore, the objective is to analyze the workflow management process of games rules and an attempt to classify them in terms of the game elements constitutes the game environment. By focusing on games as rules we means looking at games as reactive systems, both in the sense that the rules are inner structures that constitute the games and also in the sense that the rules schemas are analytic tools that mathematically dissects games. As a result, we found it is necessary for game developers to distinguish between the enabling of a task and the execution of a task. Since the enabling of a task does not imply that the task will be executed immediately, it is important to have this distinction. In order to have this distinction, we should consider triggering of tasks in the game's flow environment. A trigger is an external condition which leads to the execution of an enabled task. One way to perform this is to separate the rules of the game environment based on whether its template is direct or indirect related to the goal of the game into two parts: controllable rules, and uncontrollable rules. Controllable rules are the rules in which its template is directly related to the goal of the game, mainly as a feedback within the rule effects. In this case, the rule is characterized by a trigger based on the state of the game elements, and an effect linked to the computer game's output. The uncontrollable rules are the rules in which its template is independent from the game goal. The rule is then characterized by a trigger based on the computer game's input, and an effect targeting only the game elements. An example for the template is the one given by: "if player element collides with a hostile element, then there is a negative feedback towards the player element". The real power of separating these rules illustrates how the separation of them allow us to explicitly specify what parts of the model comprise the system and what parts comprise the environment. For this purpose we used four types of tasks:

i. automatic: a task is triggered the moment it is enabled (i.e. No trigger is required);
ii. user: a task is triggered by participant/actor;
iii. Message: an external event is required, and
iv. time: the task requires a time trigger.

An awareness of a narrative's time line is an important element to focus on when creating the environment for an audience's imagination. The triggering concept can be modeled in terms of HLPN for user task "A" as shown in Figure 9.

Figure 9. The triggering concept for user task called "A" workflow activity process

Since game is defined as an activity with some rules engaged in for an outcome. So, game activity can be represented now as: activity = task + case + (resource) + (trigger), where trigger is one of the previous mentioned tasks. This activity represents the actual execution of a task for a specific case. Now let us analyze the effects of trigger concept and game rules (controllable/uncontrollable) applied to the proposed case study game "crazy ball 2". Games takes place in a virtual universe and it is composed by several elements, where these elements are submitted to "rules", in accordance to the game. For example, table 4, shows some of the universe "elements" applied for the case study game "crazy ball 2" and its uses. These elements are submitted to different rules, for instance, "if the red ball element jumps towards the player, then it explodes on touch". By analyzing this rule, we realized that it is composed of two parts: (i) the "trigger": "if the red ball element jumps towards the player,", and (ii) the "effect(s)": "then it explodes on touch". In the same logic, the goal of a game can also be described and controlled by its rules.

Game Elements	Uses
	Used in the combat system to control the player using mouse and also used for the render that made the Game Over screen
	Used as a model for Bad Ball and Red Ball enemies.
	Used as the door object in the game's stage, it has an animation that allows the grey stone part to slide open upwards.
	Used as the model for the player's hit points (HP). Eight heart graphics models are used to display player's HP on the screen.
	Used as the Information Signs' object. The question mark has a rotation animation that is constantly active in the game.
	Used for setting the sword swing power (force) display
	Player control
	Game envirnoment

Table 4. Some game elements for the Crazy ball 2 game and its uses.

Now, the question is how can we construct game rules that include game goals? The answer to this question is derived from the study of both HLPN and game workflow activity process previously mentioned. As a result, we defined the "game elements" as "a canvas of rules", a diagram to follow in order to build a rule or a group of rules in a computer games. This is done by composing the game rules by different triggers and effects as shown in Figure 10. The game workflow activity engine forr crazy ball 2 is shown in Figure 11.

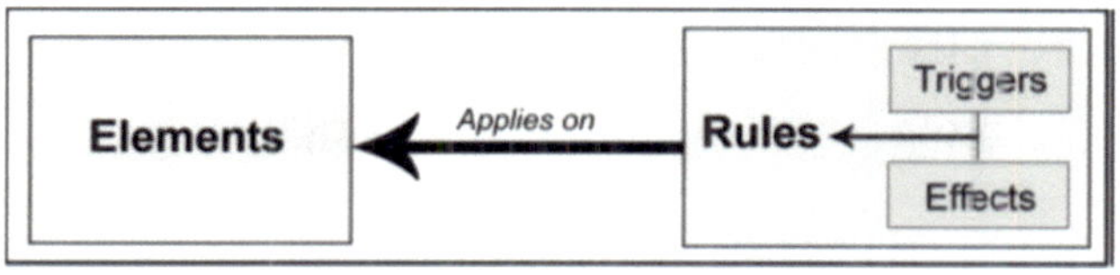

Figure 10. Game rules as a triggers and effects.

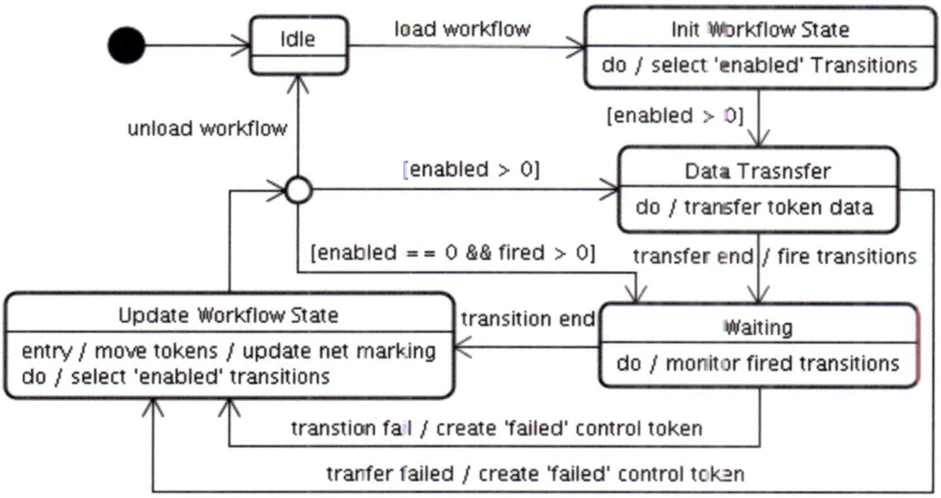

Figure 11. Game workflow activity engine

The following flowchart summarizes the idea, where T is a set of transition instances in the given HLPN, $T_{disabled}$ is a subset of T with elements having status disabled, and $T_{unknowns}$ is a subset of T with elements having status unknown

Step 1. (Initialization)

- $T_{disabled} \leftarrow \phi$
- $T_{unknowns} \leftarrow T$ and $count \leftarrow 0$

Step 2. (Loop)

- While ($T_{unknowns} \neq \phi$) do
  - $t_{candidate} \leftarrow$ (random element from $T_{unknowns}$)
  - Status $\leftarrow$ (try finding an enabled binding for $t_{candidate}$, make it occur and return occurred. Otherwise return enabling status)
- if (status = disabled) Then (move $T_{candidate}$ from $T_{unknowns}$ to $T_{disabled}$)
- else if status=occurred Then ($count \leftarrow count + 1$)
- $T_{dependents} \leftarrow (\{T_{candidate}\}^{\bullet})^{\bullet}$
- Move $(T_{dependents} \cap T_{disabled})$ from $T_{disabled}$ to $T_{unknowns}$
- End if ;
- End while

5. Experimental results and discussion

In the implementation of the Crazy ball 2 case study game, five game rules in terms of five modules are used namely: "Enemy Create", "Enemy Active", "Enemy Move", "Enemy effect", and "Enemy Attack". The "Enemy Create" module is basically used to create the desired enemy with some collection of predefined attributes and values. The "Enemy Move" module is used to move the enemy object based on its Move ID parameter. For instance, in the case of the "Bad Ball", enemy model, "Enemy Move" module will make it gain positive or negative speed based on the position of the player object. The "Enemy effect" module is used to make the object emit special effects or change colors based on its Effect ID parameter. The "Enemy Attack" module will make the enemy engages or do damage based on its Attack ID parameter. Finally, the "Enemy Active" module enables the enemy to receive collision and physics calculations. Figure 12 shows some screen shoots for the crazy ball 2 game environment with some enemies challenging modules.

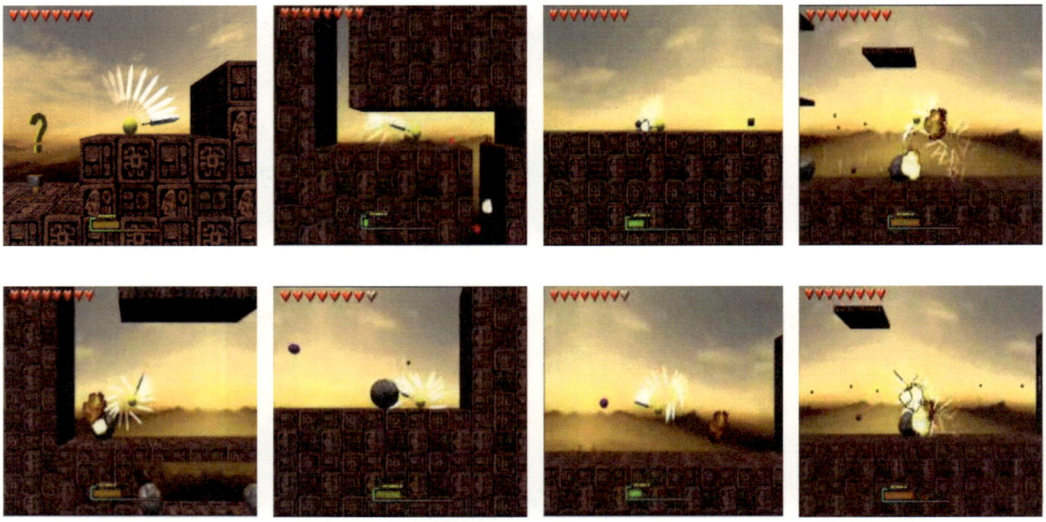

Figure 12. Screenshots for Crazy ball 2 game environment with some enemies challenging modules.

6. Conclusion and future work

This chapter attempts to overcome some problems which are encountered in the interactive drama systems as well as storytelling applications. This is achieved by proposing an integrated framework for deeply combining interactivity and narrative in computer games workflow. The idea is derived from the study of interactive drama, Petri nets (PN), narrative structures in computer games and game workflow activity process. The main contribution of this paper is to show how workflow management concepts can be jointly utilized with Petri nets (PN) for modeling game systems and game workflow control. The main advantages of using PN are that it copes well with branching stories and can evolve in parallel in large virtual world. The proposed idea is supported by some case study called Crazy ball 2. Further research effort is still needed for establishing more relationship between the game workflow activity process and other entertainment game applications with different graphics aspects, interfaces and contents.

Author details

Hussein Karam Hussein Abd El-Sattar
Ain Shams University, Faculty of Science, Mathematics & Computer Science Dept., Abbassia, Cairo, Egypt
Al-Yamamah University, CCIS, Riyadh, KSA

7. References

Brom, C.; Abonyi, A. (2006). Petri nets for game plot, *In Proc. of AISB*, Vol. 3, pp. 3-13, AISB press, 2006

Brom, C.; Sisler, V.; and Holan, T. (2007). Story manager in Europe 2045 uses Petri nets, Proceedings of the 4th International Conf. on Virtual Storytelling, LNCS 4871, pp. 38-50, Springer-verlag, 2007

Delmas, G.; Champagnat, R.; and Augeraud, M., (2007). Plot monitoring for interactive narrative games, *Proc. of ACE07,* Austria, pp. 17-20, 2007

Jenson, K. (1997). *Coloured Petri nets-based concepts, analysis methods and practical use* (2nd Edition), Springer-Verlage, New York, 1997

Karam, H., (2010). A new plot/character-based interactive system for story-based virtual reality applications, *International Journal of image and graphics*, Vol. 10, No. 1, 2010

Magerko, B.; Laird, J. (2003). Building interactive drama architecture, ACM SIGCHI International Conf. on Advances in Computer Entertainment technology, ACE 2003

Mark Reidl, O., Michael R. (2005). From linear story generation to branching story graphs, *American Association for AI,* 2005

Meehan, J. (1981). TALE_SPIN, Shank, R. C. and Riesbeck C. K. (Eds.), *Inside Computer Understanding: Five programs plus Miniatures* (Erlbaum, Hillsdale NJ), pp.197

Peterson, J. L. (1997). Petri Nets. ACM Computing Sueveys, Vol 9, No. 3, 1977

Riedl , M.; Stern, A., (2006). Believable agent and intelligent story adaptation for interactive storytelling, In Proc. of TIDSE, LNCS 4326, Springer-verlage, pp. 1-12, 2006

Salen, K., Zimmerman, E. (2003). *The rules of play,* MIT Press, 2003

Sheldon, L., (2004). *Character development and storytelling, Thompson course Technology, 2004.*

Szilas, N. (2005). The future of interactive drama, Proc. of IE2005, the Second Australian Conference on Interactive Entertainment, ISBN: 0-9751533-2-3, 2005

Tado, M. (1990). Petri Nets: Properties, Analysis and Applications. Proc. IEEE, 77, 1990

Van der Aalst, W. (1998). The application of petri nets to workflow management, the journal of Circuits, Systems and Computers 8, (1), pp. 21-66, 1998.

Chapter 13

Timed Petri Nets in Performance Exploration of Simultaneous Multithreading

Wlodek M. Zuberek

Additional information is available at the end of the chapter

http://dx.doi.org/10.5772/48601

1. Introduction

In modern computer systems, the performance of the whole system is increasingly often limited by the performance of its memory subsystem [1]. Due to continuous progress in manufacturing technologies, the performance of processors has been doubling every 18 months (the so–called Moore's law [2]), but the performance of memory chips has been improving only by 10% per year [1], creating a "performance gap" in matching processor's performance with the required memory bandwidth [3]. More detailed studies have shown that the number of processor cycles required to access main memory doubles approximately every six years [4]. In effect, it is becoming more and more often the case that the performance of applications depends on the performance of the system's memory hierarchy and it is not unusual that as much as 60% of time processors spend waiting for the completion of memory operations [4].

Memory hierarchies, and in particular multi–level cache memories, have been introduced to reduce the effective latency of memory accesses [5]. Cache memories provide efficient access to information when the information is available at lower levels of memory hierarchy; occasionally, however, long–latency memory operations are needed to transfer the information from the higher levels of memory hierarchy to the lower ones. Extensive research has focused on reducing and tolerating these large memory access latencies.

Techniques which tolerate long–latency memory accesses include out–of–order execution of instructions and instruction–level multithreading. The idea of out–of–order execution [1] is to execute, instead of waiting for the completion of a long–latency operation, instructions which (logically) follow the long–latency one, but which do not depend upon the result of this long–latency operation. Since out–of–order execution exploits instruction–level concurrency in the executed sequential instruction stream, it conveniently maintains code–base compatibility [6]. In effect, the instruction stream is dynamically decomposed into micro-threads, which are scheduled and synchronized at no cost in terms of executing additional instructions. Although this is desirable, speedups using out–of–order execution on superscalar pipelines are not so impressive, and it is difficult to obtain a speedup greater than 2 using 4 or 8-way superscalar issue [7]. Moreover, in modern processors, memory latencies are so long that out–of–order processors require very large instruction windows to tolerate them.

Although ultra–wide out-of-order superscalar processors were predicted as the architecture of one-billion-transistor chips, with a single 16 or 32-wide-issue processing core and huge branch predictors to sustain good instruction level parallelism, the industry has not been moving toward the wide–issue superscalar model [8]. Design complexity and power efficiency direct the industry toward narrow–issue, high–frequency cores and multithreaded processors. According to [6]: "Clearly something is very wrong with the out–of–order approach to concurrency if this extravagant consumption of on–chip resources is only providing a practical limit on speedup of about 2."

Instruction–level multithreading [9], [10], [1] is a technique of tolerating long–latency memory accesses by switching to another thread (if it is available for execution) rather than waiting for the completion of the long–latency operation. If different threads are associated with different sets of processor registers, switching from one thread to another (called "context switching") can be done very efficiently [11], in one or just a few processor cycles.

In simultaneous multithreading [12], [6] several threads can issue instructions at the same time. If a processor contains several functional units or it contains more than one instruction execution pipeline, the instructions can be issued simultaneously; if there is only one pipeline, only one instruction can be issued in each processor cycle, but the (simultaneous) threads complement each other in the sense that whenever one thread cannot issue an instruction (because of pipeline stalls or context switching), an instruction is issued from another thread, eliminating 'empty' instruction slots and increasing the overall performance of the processor.

Simultaneous multithreading combines hardware features of wide-issue superscalar processors and multithreaded processors [12]. From superscalar processors it inherits the ability to issue multiple instructions in each cycle; from multithreaded processors it takes hardware state for several threads. The result is a processor that can issue multiple instructions from multiple threads in each processor cycle, achieving better performance for a variety of workloads.

The main objective of this work is to study the performance of simultaneously multithreaded processors in order to determine how effective simultaneous multithreading can be. In particular, an indication is sought if simultaneous multithreading can overcome the out–of–order's "barrier" of the speedup (equal to 2 [13]). A timed Petri net [14] model of multithreaded processors at the instruction execution level is developed, and performance results for this model are obtained by event–driven simulation of the developed model. Since the model is rather simple, simulation results are verified (with respect to accuracy) by state–space–based performance analysis (for those combinations of modeling parameters for which the state space remains reasonably small).

Section 2 recalls basic concepts of timed Petri nets which are used in this study. A model of simultaneous multithreading, used for performance exploration, is presented in Section 3. Section 4 discusses the results obtained by event–driven simulation of the model introduced in Section 3. Section 5 contains concluding remarks including a short comparison of simulation and analytical results.

2. Timed Petri nets

A marked place/transition Petri net $\mathcal{M}$ is typically defined [15] [16] as $\mathcal{M} = (\mathcal{N}, m_0)$, where the structure $\mathcal{N}$ is a bipartite directed graph, $\mathcal{N} = (P, T, A)$, with a set of places P, a set of transitions T, a set of directed arcs A connecting places with transitions and transitions with places, $A \subseteq T \times P \cup P \times T$, and the initial marking function m_0 which assigns nonnegative numbers of tokens to places of the net, $m_0 : P \rightarrow \{0, 1, ...\}$. Marked nets can be equivalently defined as $\mathcal{M} = (P, T, A, m_0)$.

A place p is an input place of a transition t if the (directed) arc (p, t) is in the set A. A place is shared if it is an input place to more than one transition. If a net does not contain shared places, the net is (structurally) conflict–free, otherwise the net contains conflicts. The simplest case of conflicts is known as a free–choice (or generalized free–choice) structure; a shared place is (generalized) free–choice if all transitions sharing it have identical sets of input places. A net is free–choice if all its shared places are free–choice. The transitions sharing a free–choice place constitute a free–choice class of transitions. For each marking function, and each free–choice class of transitions, either all transitions in this class are enabled or none of them is. It is assumed that the selection of transitions for firing within each free–choice class is a random process which can be described by "choice probabilities" assigned to (free–choice) transitions. Moreover, it is usually assumed that the random variables describing choice probabilities in different free–choice classes are independent.

All places which are not conflict–free and not free–choice, are conflict places. Transitions sharing conflict places are (directly or indirectly) potentially in conflict (i.e., they are in conflict or not depending upon a marking function; for different marking functions the sets of transitions which are in conflict can be different). All transitions which are potentially is conflict constitute a conflict class. All conflict classes are disjoint. It is assumed that conflicts are resolved by random choices of occurrences among the conflicting transitions. These random choice are independent in different conflict classes.

In timed nets [14], occurrence times are associated with transitions, and transition occurrences are real–time events, i.e., tokens are removed from input places at the beginning of the occurrence period, and they are deposited to the output places at the end of this period. All occurrences of enabled transitions are initiated in the same instants of time in which the transitions become enabled (although some enabled transitions may not initiate their occurrences). If, during the occurrence period of a transition, the transition becomes enabled again, a new, independent occurrence can be initiated, which will overlap with the other occurrence(s). There is no limit on the number of simultaneous occurrences of the same transition (sometimes this is called infinite occurrence semantics). Similarly, if a transition is enabled "several times" (i.e., it remains enabled after initiating an occurrence), it may start several independent occurrences in the same time instant.

More formally, a timed Petri net is a triple, $\mathcal{T} = (\mathcal{M}, c, f)$, where $\mathcal{M}$ is a marked net, c is a choice function which assigns choice probabilities to free–choice classes of transitions or relative frequencies of occurrences to conflicting transitions (for non–conflict transitions c simply assigns 1.0), $c : T \rightarrow \mathbf{R}^{0,1}$, where $\mathbf{R}^{0,1}$ is the set of real numbers in the interval [0,1], and f is a timing function which assigns an (average) occurrence time to each transition of the net, $f : T \rightarrow \mathbf{R}^{+}$, where $\mathbf{R}^{+}$ is the set of nonnegative real numbers.

The occurrence times of transitions can be either deterministic or stochastic (i.e., described by some probability distribution function); in the first case, the corresponding timed nets are referred to as D–timed nets [18], in the second, for the (negative) exponential distribution of firing times, the nets are called M–timed nets (Markovian nets [17]). In both cases, the concepts of state and state transitions have been formally defined and used in the derivation of different performance characteristics of the model [14]. Only D–timed Petri nets are used in this paper.

The firing times of some transitions may be equal to zero, which means that the firings are instantaneous; all such transitions are called *immediate* while the other are called *timed*. Since the immediate transitions have no tangible effects on the (timed) behavior of the model, it is convenient to split the set of transitions into two parts, the set of immediate and the set of timed transitions, and to fire first the (enabled) immediate transitions; only when no more immediate transitions are enabled, the firings of (enabled) timed transitions are initiated (still in the same instant of time). It should be noted that such a convention effectively introduces the priority of immediate transitions over the timed ones, so the conflicts of immediate and timed transitions should be avoided. Consequently, the free–choice and conflict classes of transitions must be "uniform", i.e., all transitions in each such class must be either immediate or timed, but not both.

Performance analysis of net models can be based on their behavior (i.e., the set of reachable states) or on the structure of the net; the former is called *reachability analysis* and the latter – *structural analysis*. For reachability analysis, the state space of the analyzed model must be finite and reasonably small while for structural analysis the model must satisfy a number of structural conditions. However, since timed Petri net models are discrete–event systems, their analysis can also be based on discrete–event simulation, which imposes very few restrictions on the class of analyzed models. All performance characteristics of simultaneous multithreading presented in Section 4 are obtained by event–driven simulation [19] of timed Petri net models shown in the next section.

3. Models of simultaneous multithreading

A timed Petri net model of a simple multithreaded processor is shown in Fig.1 (as usually, timed transitions are represented by solid bars, and immediate ones, by thin bars).

For simplicity, Fig.1 shows only one level of memory; this simplification is removed further in this section.

Ready is a pool of available threads; it is assumed that the number of of threads is constant and does not change during program execution (this assumption is motivated by steady–state considerations). If the processor is idle (place *Next* is marked), one of available threads is selected for execution (transition *Tsel*). *Cont*, if marked, indicates that an instruction is ready to be issued to the execution pipeline. Instruction execution is modeled by transition *Trun* which represents the first stage of the execution pipeline. It is assumed that once the instruction enters the pipeline, it will progress through the stages and, eventually, leave the pipeline; since these pipeline implementation details are not important for performance analysis of the processor, they are not represented here.

Done is another free-choice place which determines if the current instruction performs a long–latency access to memory or not. If the current instruction is a non–long–latency one, *Tnxt* occurs (with the corresponding probability), and another instruction is fetched for issuing. *Pnxt* is a free-choice place with three possible outcomes: *Tst0* (with the choice probability p_{s0}) represents issuing an instruction without any further delay; *Tst1* (with the

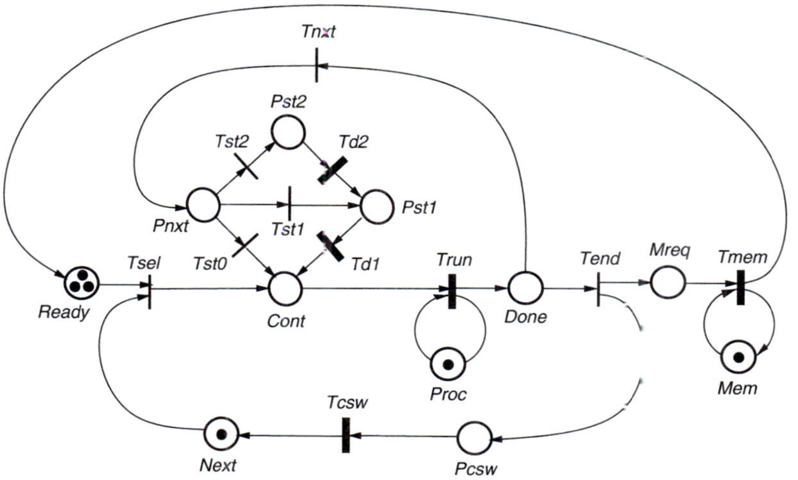

Figure 1. Petri net model of a multithreaded processor.

choice probability p_{s1}) represents a single-cycle pipeline stall (modeled by *Td1*), and *Tst2* (with the choice probability p_{s2}) represents a two–cycle pipeline stall (*Td2* and then *Td1*); other pipeline stalls could be represented in a similar way, if needed.

If long–latency operation is detected in the issued instruction, *Tend* initiates two concurrent actions: (i) context switching performed by enabling an occurrence of *Tcsw*, after which a new thread is selected for execution (if it is available), and (ii) a memory access request is entered into *Mreq*, the memory queue, and after accessing the memory (transition *Tmem*), the thread, suspended for the duration of memory access, becomes "ready" again and joins the pool of threads *Ready*. *Tmem* will typically represent a cache miss (with all its consequences); cache hits (at the first level cache memory) are not considered long-latency operations.

The choice probability associated with *Tend* determines the runlength of a thread, ℓ_t, i.e., the average number of instructions between two consecutive long–latency operations: if this choice probability is equal to 0.1, the runlength is equal to 10, if it is equal to 0.2, the runlength is 5, and so on.

Proc, which is connected to *Trun*, controls the number of pipelines. If the processor contains just one instruction execution pipeline, the initial marking assigns a single token to *Proc* as only one instruction can be issued in each processor cycle. In order to model a processor with two (identical) pipelines, two initial tokens are needed in *Proc*, and so on.

The number of memory ports, i.e., the number of simultaneous accesses to memory, is controlled by the initial marking of *Mem*; for a single port memory, the initial marking assigns just a single token to *Mem*, for dual-port memory, two tokens are assigned to *Mem*, and so on.

In a similar way, the number of simultaneous threads (or instruction issue units) is controlled by the initial marking of *Next*.

Memory hierarchy can be incorporated into the model shown in Fig.1 by refining the representation of memory. In particular, levels of memory hierarchy can be introduced by replacing the subnet *Tmem–Mem* by a number of subnets, each subnet for one level of the hierarchy, and adding a free–choice structure which randomly selects the submodel according

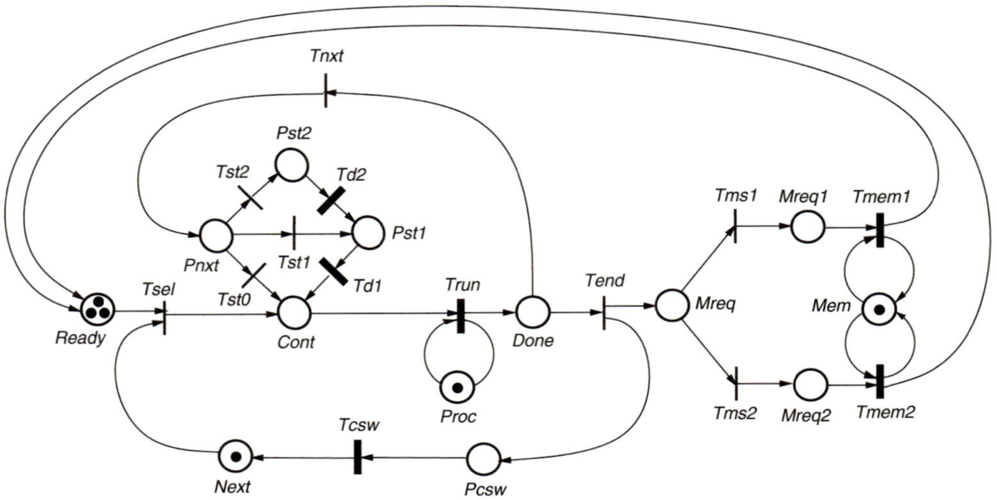

Figure 2. Petri net model of a multithreaded processor with a two–level memory.

to probabilities describing the use of the hierarchical memory. Such a refinement, for two levels of memory (in addition to the first-level cache), is shown in Fig.2, where *Mreq* is a free–choice place selecting either level–1 (submodel *Mem–Tmem1*) or level–2 (submodel *Mem–Tmem2*). More levels of memory can be easily added similarly, if needed.

The effects of memory hierarchy can be compared with a uniform, non–hierarchical memory by selecting the parameters in such a way that the average access time of the hierarchical model (Fig.2) is equal to the access time of the non–hierarchical model (Fig.1).

Processors with different numbers of instruction issue units and instruction execution pipelines can be described by a pair of numbers, the first number denoting the number of instruction issue units, and the second – the number of instruction execution pipelines. In this sense a 3-2 processor is a (multithreaded) processor with 3 instruction issue units and 2 instruction execution pipelines.

For convenience, all temporal properties are expressed in processor cycles, so, the occurrence times of *Trun*, *Td1* and *Td2* are all equal to 1 (processor cycle), the occurrence time of *Tcsw* is equal to the number of processor cycles needed for a context switch (which is equal to 1 for many of the following performance analyzes), and the occurrence time of *Tmem* is the average number of processor cycles needed for a long–latency access to memory.

The main modeling parameters and their typical values are shown in Table 1.

4. Performance exploration

The model developed in the previous section is evaluated for different combinations of modeling parameters. Performance results are obtained by event-driven simulation of timed Petri net models.

The utilization of the processor and memory, as a function of the number of available threads, for a 1-1 processor (i.e., a processor with a single instruction issue unit and a single instruction execution pipeline) is shown in Fig. 3.

symbol	*parameter*	*value*
n_t	number of available threads	1,...,10
n_p	number of execution pipelines	1,2,..
n_s	number of simultaneous threads	1,2,3,...
ℓ_t	thread runlength	10
t_m	average memory access time	5
t_{cs}	context switching time	1,3
p_{s1}	prob. of one–cycle pipeline stall	0.2
p_{s2}	prob. of two–cycle pipeline stall	0.1

Table 1. Simultaneous multithreading – modeling parameters and their typical values

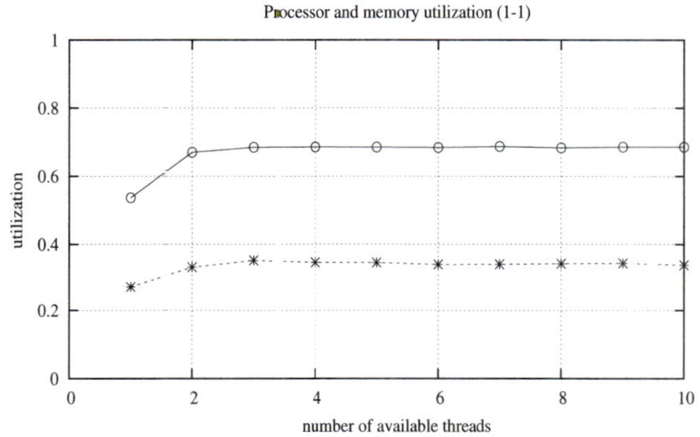

Figure 3. Processor (-o-) and memory (-x-) utilization for a 1-1 processor; $l_t = 10$, $t_m = 5$, $t_{cs} = 1$, $p_{s1} = 0.2$, $p_{s2} = 0.1$

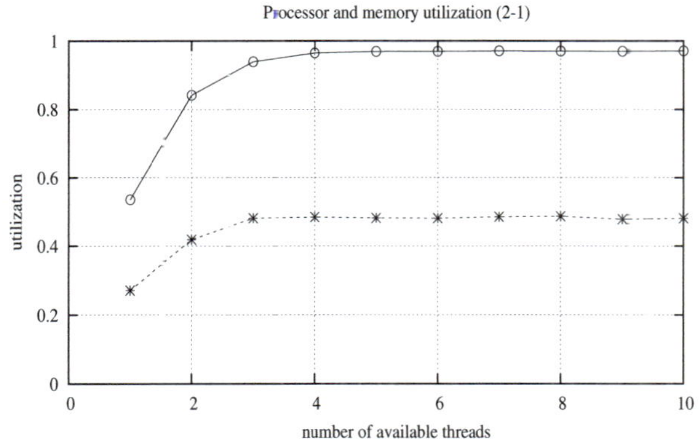

Figure 4. Processor (-o-) and memory (-x-) utilization for a 2-1 processor; $l_t = 10$, $t_m = 5$, $t_{cs} = 1$, $p_{s1} = 0.2$, $p_{s2} = 0.1$

The value of the processor utilization for $n_t = 1$ (i.e., for one thread) can be derived from the (average) number of unused instruction issuing slots. Since the probability of a single–cycle stall is 0.2, and probability of a two–cycle stall is 0.1, on average 40 % of issuing slots remain unused because of pipeline stalls (for all instructions except the first one in each thread). Processor utilization for one thread is thus $\ell_t/(\ell_t + (\ell_t - 1) * 0.4 + t_m) = 10/18.6 = 0.537$, which corresponds very well with Fig.3. For a large number of threads processor utilization is obtained similarly, but with the context switching time, t_{cs}, replacing t_m, so it is $\ell_t/(\ell_t + (\ell_t - 1) * 0.4 + t_{cs}) = 0.685$.

The utilization of the processor can be improved by introducing a second (simultaneous) thread which issues its instructions in the slots unused by the first slot. Fig.4 shows the utilization of the processor and memory for a 2-1 processor, i.e., a processor with two (simultaneous) threads (or two instruction issue units) and a single pipeline. The utilization of the processor is improved by almost 50 % and is within a few percent from its upper bound (of 100 %).

The influence of pipeline stalls (probabilities p_{s1} and p_{s2}) is shown in Fig.5 and Fig.6. Fig.5 shows that the performance actually depends upon the total number of stalls rather than specific values of p_{s1} and p_{s2}; in Fig.5 all pipeline stalls are single–cycle ones, so $p_{s1} = 0.4$ and $p_{s2} = 0$, and the results are practically the same as in Fig. 3.

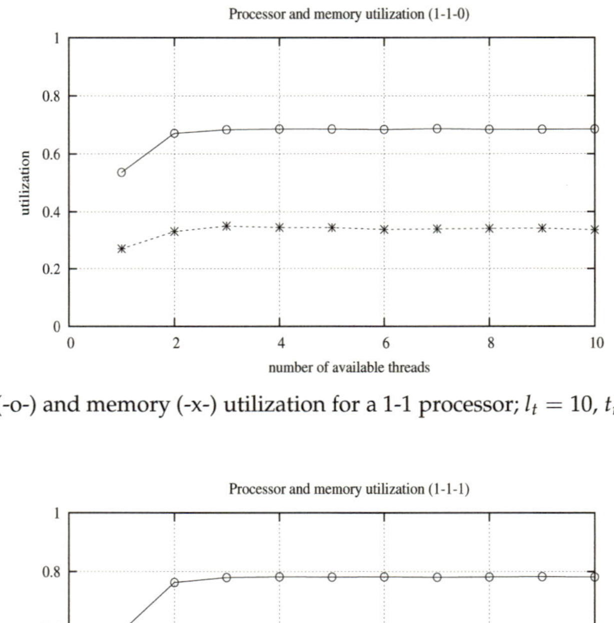

Figure 5. Processor (-o-) and memory (-x-) utilization for a 1-1 processor; $l_t = 10$, $t_m = 5$, $t_{cs} = 1$, $p_{s1} = 0.4$, $p_{s2} = 0$

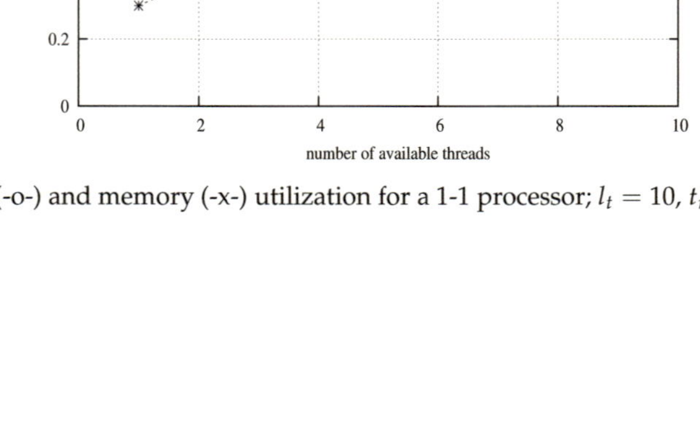

Figure 6. Processor (-o-) and memory (-x-) utilization for a 1-1 processor; $l_t = 10$, $t_m = 5$, $t_{cs} = 1$, $p_{s1} = 0.2$, $p_{s2} = 0$

Fig. 6 shows the utilizations of processor and memory for reduced probabilities of pipeline stalls, i.e., for $p_{s1} = 0.2$ and $p_{s2} = 0$. As is expected, the utilizations are higher than in Fig.3 and Fig.5.

A more realistic model of memory, that captures the idea of a two–level hierarchy, is shown in Fig.2. In order to compare the results of this model with Fig.3 and Fig.4, the parameters of the two–level memory are chosen in such a way that the average memory access time is equal to the memory access time in Fig.1 (where $t_m = 5$). Let the two levels of memory have access times equal to 4 and 20, respectively; then the choice probabilities are equal to 15/16 and 1/16 for level–1 and level–2, respectively, and the average access time is:

$$4 * \frac{15}{16} + 20 * \frac{1}{16} = 5.$$

The results for a 1-1 processor with a two–level memory are shown in Fig.7, and for a 2-1 processor in Fig.8.

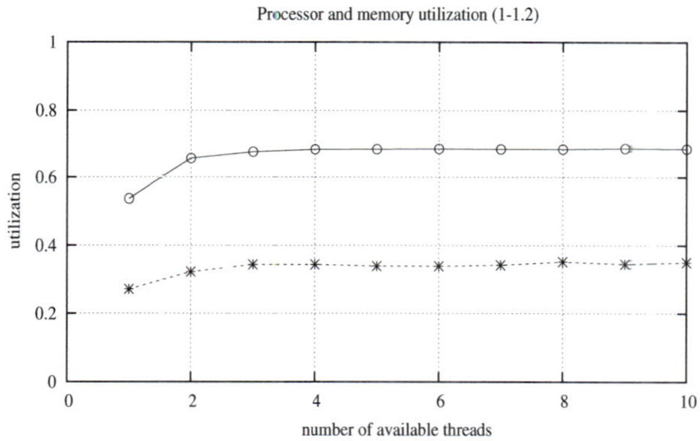

Figure 7. Processor (-o-) and memory (-x-) utilization for a 1-1 processor with 2-level memory; $l_t = 10$, $t_m = 4 + 20$, $t_{cs} = 1$, $p_{s1} = 0.2$, $p_{s2} = 0.1$

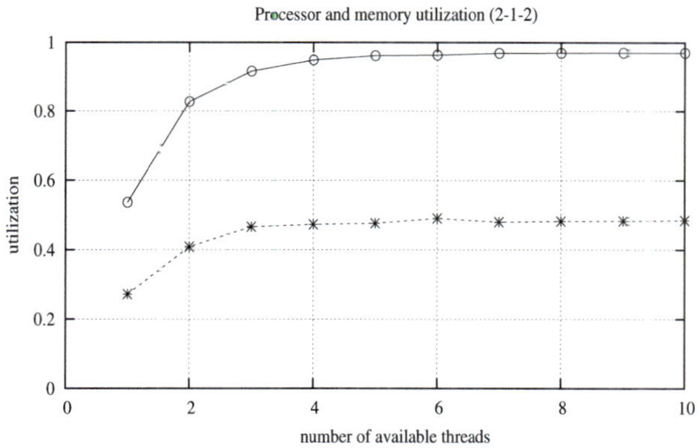

Figure 8. Processor (-o-) and memory (-x-) utilization for a 2-1 processor with 2-level memory; $l_t = 10$, $t_m = 4 + 20$, $t_{cs} = 1$, $p_{s1} = 0.2$, $p_{s2} = 0.1$

The results in Fig.7 and Fig.8 are practically the same as in Fig.3 and Fig.4. This is the reason that the remaining results are shown for (equivalent) one-level memory models; the multiple levels of memory hierarchy apparently have no significant effect on the performance results.

The effects of simultaneous multithreading in a more complex processor, e.g., a processor with two instruction issue units and two instruction execution pipelines, i.e., a 2-2 processor, can be obtained in a very similar way. The utilization of the processor (shown as the sum of the utilizations of both pipelines, with the values ranging from 0 to 2), is shown in Fig.9.

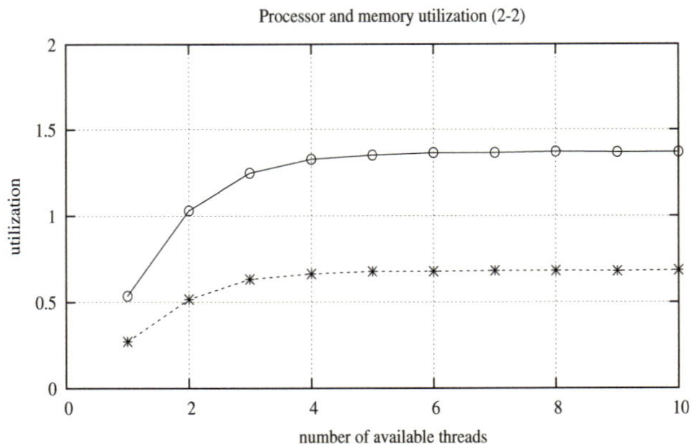

Figure 9. Processor (-o-) and memory (-x-) utilization for a 2-2 processor; $l_t = 10$, $t_m = 5$, $t_{cs} = 1$, $p_{s1} = 0.2$, $p_{s2} = 0.1$

When another instruction issue unit is added, the utilization increases by about 40 %, as shown in Fig.10.

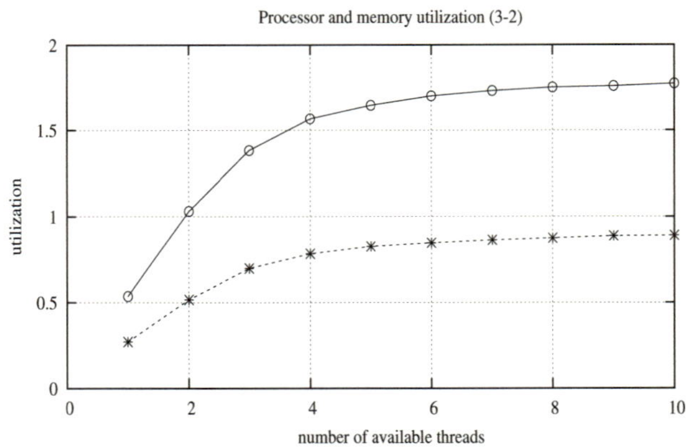

Figure 10. Processor (-o-) and memory (-x-) utilization for a 3-2 processor; $l_t = 10$, $t_m = 5$, $t_{cs} = 1$, $p_{s1} = 0.2$, $p_{s2} = 0.1$

Further increase of the number of the simultaneous threads (in a processor with 2 pipelines) can provide only small improvements of the performance because the utilizations of both, the processor and the memory, are quite close to their limits. The performance of the system can be improved by increasing the number of pipelines, but then the memory becomes the system bottleneck, so its performance also needs to be improved, for example, by introducing dual ports (which allow to handle two accesses at the same time). The performance of a 5-3 processor with a dual-port memory is shown in Fig.11 (the utilization of the processor is the sum of utilizations of its 3 pipelines, so it ranges from 0 to 3).

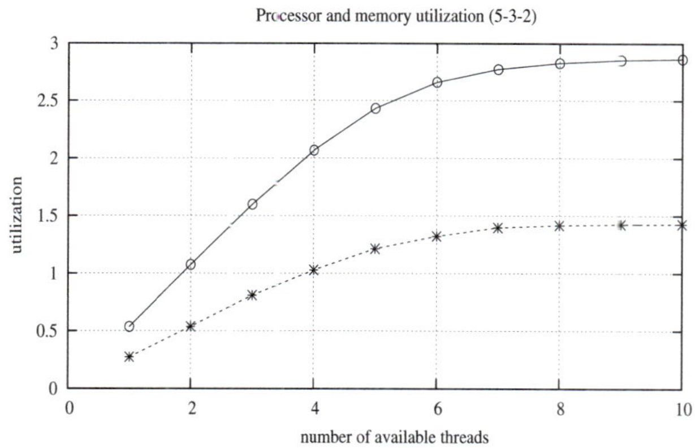

Figure 11. Processor (-o-) and memory (-x-) utilization for a 5-3 processor with dual–port memory; $l_t = 10$, $t_m = 5||2$, $t_{cs} = 1$, $p_{s1} = 0.2$, $p_{s2} = 0.1$

Fig.11 shows that for 3 pipelines and 5 simultaneous threads, the number of available threads greater than 6 provides the speedup that is almost equal to 3.

System bottlenecks can be identified by comparing service demands for different components of the system (in this case, the memory and the pipelines); the component with the maximum service demand is the bottleneck because it is the first component to reach its utilization limit and to prevent any increase of the overall performance. For a single runlength (of all simultaneous threads) the total service demand for memory is equal to $n_s * t_m$, while the service demand for each pipeline (assuming an ideal, uniform distribution of load over the pipelines) is equal to $n_s * \ell_t / n_p$. For a 4-2 processor, the service demands are equal (such a system is usually called "balanced"), so the utilizations of both the processor and the memory, tend to their limits in a "synchronous" way. For a 5-3 processor with a dual-port memory, the service demand for the pipelines is greater than the service demand for memory, so the number of pipelines could be increased (by one pipeline); for more than 4 pipelines, the memory again becomes the bottleneck.

Simultaneous multithreading is quite flexible with respect to context switching times because the (simultaneous) threads fill the instruction issuing slots which normally would remain empty during context switching. Fig.12 shows the utilization of the processor and memory in a 1-1 processor with $t_{cs} = 3$, i.e., context switching time 3 times longer than in Fig.3. The reduction of the processor's utilization is more than 10 %, and is due to the additional 2 cycles of context switching which remain empty (out of 17 cycles, on average).

Fig.13 shows utilization of the processor and memory in a 2-1 processor, also for $t_{cs} = 3$. The reduction of utilization is much smaller in this case and is within 5 % (when compared with Fig.4).

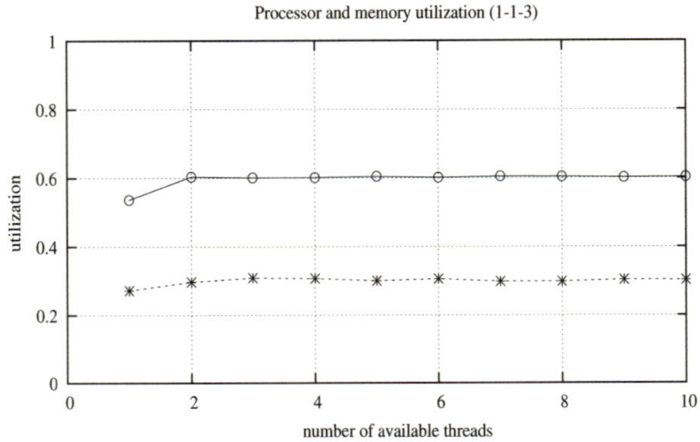

Figure 12. Processor (-o-) and memory (-x-) utilization for a 1-1 processor; $l_t = 10$, $t_m = 5$, $t_{cs} = 3$, $p_{s1} = 0.2$, $p_{s2} = 0.1$

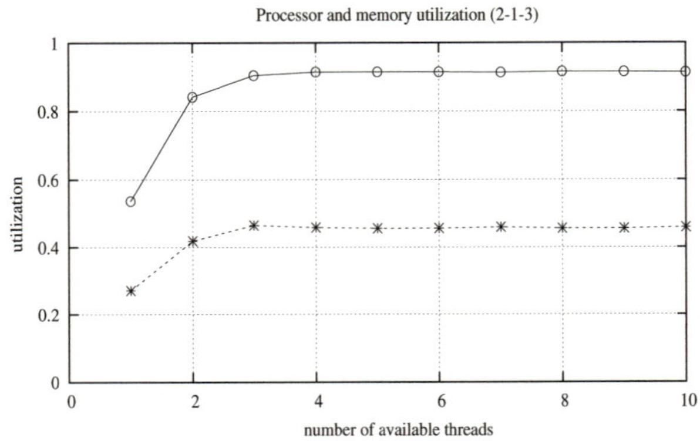

Figure 13. Processor (-o-) and memory (-x-) utilization for a 2-1 processor; $l_t = 10$, $t_m = 5$, $t_{cs} = 3$, $p_{s1} = 0.2$, $p_{s2} = 0.1$

5. Concluding remarks

Simultaneous multithreading discussed in this paper is used to increase the performance of processors by tolerating long–latency operations. Since the long–latency operations are playing increasingly important role in modern computer system, so is simultaneous multithreading. Its implementation as well as the required hardware resources are much simpler than in the case of out–of–order approach, and the resulting speedup scales well with the number of simultaneous threads. The main challenge of simultaneous multithreading is to balance the system by maintaining the right relationship between the number of simultaneous threads and the performance of the memory hierarchy.

All presented results indicate that the number of available threads, required for improved performance of the processor, is quite small, and is typically greater by 2 or 3 threads than the number of simultaneous threads. The results show that a larger number of available threads provides rather insignificant improvements of system's performance.

The presented models of multithreaded processors are quite simple, and for small values of modeling parameters (n_t, n_p, n_s) can be analyzed by the explorations of the state space. The following tables compare some results for the 1-1 processor and 3-2 processors:

n_t	*number of states*	*analytical utilization*	*simulated utilization*
1	11	0.538	0.536
2	52	0.670	0.671
3	102	0.684	0.685
4	152	0.685	0.686
5	202	0.685	0.686

Table 2. A comparison of simulation and analytical results for 1-1 processors.

n_t	*number of states*	*analytical utilization*	*simulated utilization*
1	11	0.538	0.536
2	80	1.030	1.031
3	264	1.384	1.381
4	555	1.568	1.568
5	951	1.655	1.647

Table 3. A comparison of simulation and analytical results for 3-2 processors.

The comparisons show that the results obtained by simulation of net models are very similar to the analytical results obtained from the analysis of states and state transitions.

A similar performance analysis of simultaneous multithreading, but using a slightly different model, was presented in [20]. All results presented there are very similar to results presented in this work which is an indication that the performance of simultaneous multithreaded systems is insensitive to (at least some) variations of implementation.

It should also be noted that the presented model is oversimplified with respect to the probabilities of pipeline stalls and does not take into account the dependence of stall probabilities on the history of instruction issuing. In fact, the model is "pessimistic" in this regard, and the predicted performance, presented in the paper, is worse than the expected performance of real systems. However, the simplification effects are not expected to be significant.

Acknowledgement

The Natural Sciences and Engineering Research Council of Canada partially supported this research through grant RGPIN-8222.

Author details

Wlodek M. Zuberek
Memorial University, St.John's, Canada,
University of Life Sciences, Warsaw, Poland

6. References

[1] Patterson, D.A., Hennessy, J.L. (2006). *Computer architecture – a quantitative approach* (4-th ed.); Morgan Kaufmann.

[2] Hamilton, S. (1999). "Taking Moore's law into the next century"; *IEEE Computer*, vol.32, no.1, pp.43-48.

[3] Wilkes, M.V. (2001). "The memory gap and the future of high-performance memories"; *ACM Architecture News*, vol.29, no.1, pp.2-7.

[4] Sinharoy B. (1997). "Optimized thread creation for processor multithreading"; *The Computer Journal*, vol.40, no.6, pp.388-400.

[5] Baer, J-L. (2010). *Microprocessor architecture: from simple pipelines to chip multiprocessors;* Cambridge University Press.

[6] Jesshope, C. (2003). "Multithreaded microprocessors – evolution or revolution"; in *Advances in Computer Systems Architecture* (LNCS 2823), pp.21-45.

[7] Tseng, J. & Asanovic, K. (2003). "Banked multiport register files for high–frequency superscalar microprocessor"; *Proc. 30-th Int. Annual Symp. on Computer Architecture*, San Diego, CA, pp.62-71.

[8] Burger, D. & Goodman, J.R. (2004). "Billion–transistor architectures: there and back again"; *IEEE Computer*, vol.37, no.3, pp.22-28.

[9] Byrd, G.T. & Holliday, M.A. (1995). "Multithreaded processor architecture"; *IEEE Spectrum*, vol.32, no.8, pp.38-46.

[10] Dennis, J.B. & Gao, G.R. (1994). "Multithreaded architectures: principles, projects, and issues"; in *Multithreaded Computer Architecture: a Summary of the State of the Art*, Kluwer Academic, pp.1-72.

[11] Ungerer, T., Robic, G. & Silc, J. (2002). "Multithreaded processors"; *The Computer Journal*, vol.43, no.3, pp.320-348.

[12] Eggers, S.J., Emer, J.S., Levy, H.M., Lo, J.L., Stamm, R.L. & Tullsen, D.M. (1997). "Simultaneous multithreading: a foundation for next-generation processors"; *IEEE Micro*, vol.17, no.5, pp.12-19.

[13] Mutlu, O., Stark, J., Wilkerson, C. & Patt, Y.N. (2003). "Runahead execution: an effective alternative to large instruction windows"; *IEEE Micro*, vol.23, no.6, pp.20-25.

[14] Zuberek, W.M. (1991). "Timed Petri nets – definitions, properties and applications"; *Microelectronics and Reliability* (Special Issue on Petri Nets and Related Graph Models), vol.31, no.4, pp.627-644.

[15] Murata, T. (1989). "Petri nets: properties, analysis, and applications"; *Proceedings of the IEEE*, vol.77, no.4, pp.541-580.

[16] Reisig, W. (1985). *Petri nets – an introduction* (EATCS Monographs on Theoretical Computer Science 4); Springer-Verlag.

[17] Zuberek, W.M. (1986). "M–timed Petri nets, priorities, preemptions, and performance evaluation of systems"; in *Advances in Petri Nets 1985* (LNCS 222), Springer-Verlag, pp.478-498.

[18] Zuberek, W.M. (1987). "D–timed Petri nets and modelling of timeouts and protocols"; *Transactions of the Society for Computer Simulation*, vol.4, no.4, pp.331-357.

[19] Zuberek, W.M. (1996). "Modeling using timed Petri nets – discrete–event simulation"; Technical Report #9602, Department of Computer Science, Memorial University, St. John's, Canada A1B 3X5.

[20] Zuberek, W.M. (2007). "Modeling and analysis of simultaneous multithreading"; *Proc. 14-th Int. Conf. on Analytical and Stochastic Modeling Techniques and Applications (ASMTA-07)*, a part of the *21-st European Conference on Modeling and Simulation (ECMS'07)*, Prague, Czech Republic, pp.115-120.

Chapter 14

A Petri Net-Based Approach to the Quantification of Data Center Dependability

Gustavo Callou, Paulo Maciel, Dietmar Tutsch, Julian Araújo,
João Ferreira and Rafael Souza

Additional information is available at the end of the chapter

http://dx.doi.org/10.5772/47829

1. Introduction

Data center availability and reliability have accomplished greater concern due to increased dependence on Internet services (e.g., Cloud computing paradigm, social networks and e-commerce). For companies that heavily depend on the Internet for their operations, service outages can be very expensive, easily running into millions of dollars per hour [15]. A widely used design principle in fault-tolerance is to introduce redundancy to enhance availability. However, since redundancy leads to additional use of resources and energy, it is expected to have a negative impact on sustainability and the associated cost.

Data center designers need to verify several trade-offs and select the feasible solution considering dependability metrics. In this context, formal models (e.g., Stochastic Petri nets and Reliability Block Diagrams) are important to provide estimates before implementing the data center system. Additionally, a growing concern of data center designers is related to the identification of components that may cause system failure as well as systems parts that must be improved before implementing the architecture.

In this work, we propose a set of formal models for quantifying dependability metrics for data center power infrastructures. The adopted approach takes into account a hybrid modeling technique that considers the advantages of both stochastic Petri nets (SPN) [22] and reliability block diagrams (RBD) [10] to evaluate system dependability. An integrated environment, namely, ASTRO [20] has been developed as one of the results of this work to automate dependability evaluation of data center architectures.

2. Preliminaries

This section briefly touches some fundamental concepts as a basis for a better understanding of this work.

2.1. Petri nets

Petri nets (PN) were introduced in 1962 by the PhD dissertation of Carl Adams Petri [16], at Technical University of Darmstandt, Germany. The original theory was developed as an approach to model and analyze communication systems. Petri Nets (PNs) [14] are a graphic and mathematical modeling tool that can be applied in several types of systems and allow the modeling of parallel, concurrent, asynchronous and non-deterministic systems. Since its seminal work, many representations and extensions have been proposed for allowing more concise descriptions and for representing systems feature not observed on the early models. Thus, the simple Petri net has subsequently been adapted and extended in several directions, in which timed, stochastic, high-level, object-oriented and coloured nets are a few examples of the proposed extensions.

2.2. Place-Transition nets

Place/Transition Petri nets are one of the most prominent and best studied class of Petri nets, and it is sometimes called just by Petri net (PN). A marked Place/Transition Petri net is a bipartite directed graph, usually defined as follows:

Definition 2.1. (Petri net) A Petri net [14] is a 5-tuple:

$$PN = (P, T, F, W, M_0)$$

where:

1. $P = \{p_1, p_2, ..., p_m\}$ is a finite set of places;
2. $T = \{t_1, t_2, ..., t_n\}$ is a finite set of transitions;
3. $F \subseteq (P \times T) \cup (T \times P)$ is a set of arcs (flow relation);
4. $W : F \rightarrow \{1, 2, 3, ...\}$ is a weight function;
5. $M_0 : P \rightarrow \{0, 1, 2, 3, ...\}$ is the initial marking;

This class of Petri net has two kinds of nodes, called places (P) represented by circles and transitions (T) represented by bars, such that $P \cap T =$ and $P \cup T \neq$. Figure 1 depicts the basic elements of a simple PN. The set of arcs F is used to denote the places connected to a transition (and vice-versa). W is a weight function for the set of arcs. In this case, each arc is said to have multiplicity k, where k represents the respective weight of the arc. Figure 2 shows multiple arcs connecting places and transitions in a compact way by a single arc labeling it with its weight or multiplicity k.

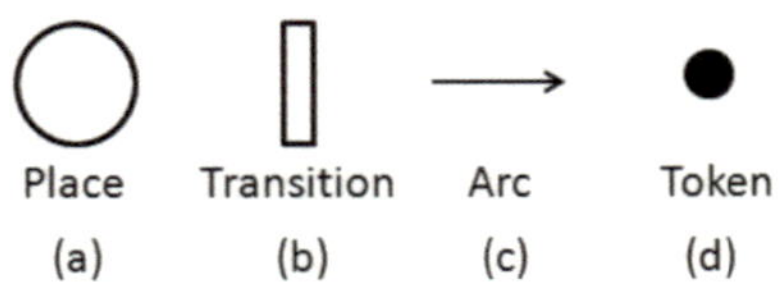

Figure 1. Petri net basic elements.

Places and transitions may have several interpretations. Using the concept of conditions and events, places represent conditions, and transitions represent events, such that, an event may have several pre-conditions and post-conditions. For more interpretations, Table 1 shows other meanings for places and transitions [14].

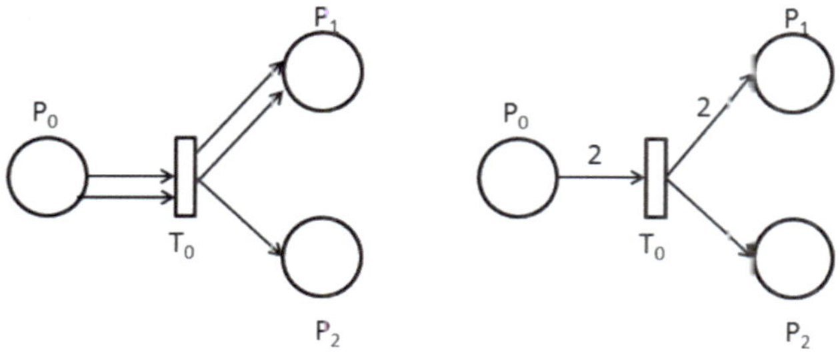

Figure 2. Compact representation of a PN

Input Places	Transitions	Output Places
pre-conditions	events	post-conditions
input data	computation step	output data
input signals	signal processor	output signals
resource needed	tasks	resource releasing
conditions	logical clauses	conclusions
buffers	processor	buffers

Table 1. Interpretation for places and transitions.

It is important to show that there are another way to represent PN's elements. As an example, the set of input and output places of transitions is shown in Definition 2.2. Similarly, the set of input and output transitions of determinate place is shown in Definition 2.3.

Definition 2.2. (Input and Output Transitions of a place) The set of input transitions (also called pre-set) of a place $p_i \in P$ is:

$$\text{label} = \bullet p_i = \{t_j \in T | (t_j, p_i) \in F\}.$$

and the set of output transitions (also called post-set) is:

$$\text{label} = p_i \bullet = \{t_j \in T | (p_i, t_j) \in F\}.$$

Definition 2.3. (Input and output places of a transition) The set of input places of a transition $t_j \in T$ is:

$$\text{label} = \bullet t_j = \{p_i \in P | (p_i, t_j) \in F\}.$$

and the set of output places of a transition $t_j \in T$ is:

$$\text{label} = t_j \bullet = \{p_i \in P | (t_j, p_i) \in F\}.$$

2.2.1. *Marked Petri nets*

A marking (also named token) has a primitive concept in PNs such as place and transitions. Markings are information attributed to places; the number and mark distributions consist of the net state in determined moment. The formal definitions are presented as follows.

Definition 2.4. (Marking) Considering the set of places P in a net N, the formal definition of marking is represented by a function that maps the set of places P into non negative integers $M : P \to \mathbb{N}$.

Definition 2.5. (Marking vector) Considering the set of places P in a net N, the marking can be defined as a vector $M = (M(p_1), ..., M(p_n))$, where $n = \#(P), \forall p_i \in P \ / \ M(p_i) \in \mathbb{N}$. Thus, such vector gives the number of tokens in each place for the marking M_i.

Definition 2.6. (Marked net) A marked Petri net is defined by a tupla $NM = (N; M_0)$, where N is the net structure and M_0 is the initial marking.

A marked Petri net contains tokens, which reside in places, travel along arcs, and their flow through the net is regulated by transitions. A peculiar distribution (M) of the tokens in the places, represents a specific state of the system. These tokens are denoted by black dots inside the places as shown in Figure 1 (d).

2.2.2. *Transition enabling and firing*

The behavior of many systems can be described in terms of system states and their changes. In order to simulate the dynamic behavior of a system, a state (or marking) in a Petri net is changed according to the following firing rule:

1. A transition t is said to be enabled, if each input place p of t is marked with at least the number of tokens equal to the multiplicity of its arc connecting p with t. Adopting a mathematical notation, an enabled transition t for given marking m_i is denoted by $m_i[t >$, if $m_i(p_j) \geq W(p_j, t), \forall p_j \in P$.
2. An enabled transition may or may not fire (depending on whether or not the respective event takes place).
3. The firing of an enabled transition t removes tokens (equal to the multiplicity of the input arc) from each input place p, and adds tokens (equal to the multiplicity of the output arc) to each output place p'. Using a mathematical notation, the firing of a transition is represented by the equation $m_j(p) = m_i(p) - W(p,t) + W(t,p), \forall p \in P$. If a marking m_j is reachable from m_i by firing a transition t, it is denoted by $m_i[t > m_j$.

Figure 3 (a) shows the mathematical representation of a Petri net model with three places (p_0, p_1, p_2) and one transition (t_0). Besides, there is one arc connecting the place p_0 to the transition t_0 with weight two, one arc from the place p_1 to the transition t_0 with weight one, and one arc connecting the transition t_0 to the place p_2 with weight two. The initial marking (m_0) is represented by three tokens in the place p_0 and one token in the place p_1. Figure 3 (b) outlines its respective graphical representation, and Figure 3 (c) provides the same graphical representation after the firing of t_0. For this example, the set of reachable markings is m = $\{m_0 = (3,1,0), m_1 = (1,0,2)\}$. The marking m_1 was obtained by firing t_0, such that, $m_1(p_0)$ = 3 - 2 + 0, $m_1(p_1)$ = 1 - 1 + 0, and $m_1(p_2)$ = 0 - 0 + 2.

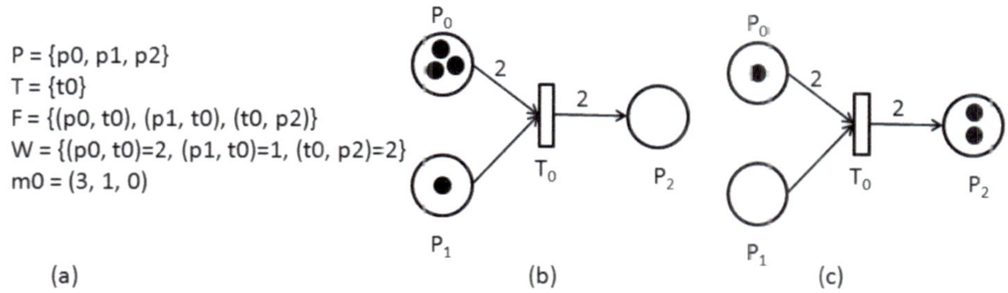

Figure 3. (a) Mathematical formalism; (b) Graphical representation before the firing of t_0; (c) Graphical representation after the firing of t_0.

There are two particular cases which the firing rule happens differently. The first one is a transition without any input place that is called as a *source* transition, and the other one is a transition without any output place, named *sink* transition. A *source* transition is unconditionally enabled, and the firing of a *sink* transition consumes tokens, but does not produce any. Figure 4 (a) shows a *source* transition, and Figure (b) 4 depicts a *sink* transition. In both, the markings are represented before and after their respective firing.

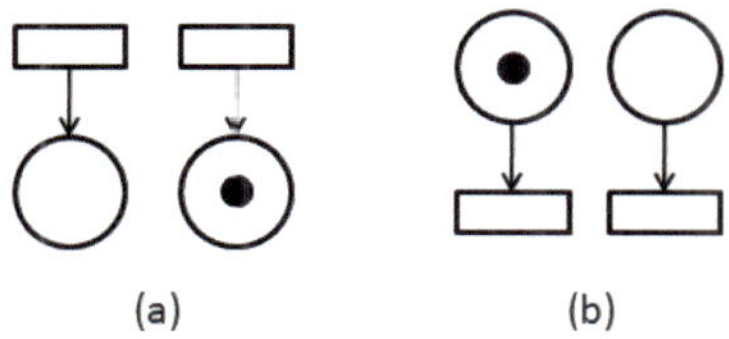

Figure 4. (a) *Source* transitions; (b) *Sink* transitions.

Definition 2.7. (Source transitions) A transition is said to be source if, and only if, $I(p,t) = 0$, $\forall p \in P$.

Definition 2.8. (Sink transitions) A transition is said to be sink if, and only if, $O(p,t) = 0$, $\forall p \in P$.

Definition 2.9. (Inhibitor arc) Originally not present in PN, the introduction of the concept of inhibitor arc increases the modeling power of PN, adding the ability of testing if a place does not have tokens. In the presence of an inhibitor arc, a transition is enabled to fire if each input place connected by a normal arc has a number of tokens equal to the arc weight, and if each input place connected by an inhibitor arc has no tokens. Figure 5 illustrates an inhibitor arc connecting the input place p_0 to the transition t_0, which is denoted by an arc finished with a small circle. In such Figure, the transition t_0 is enabled to fire.

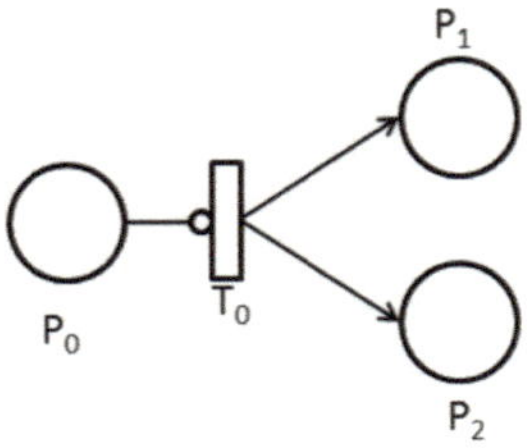

Figure 5. PN with an inhibitor arc.

Definition 2.10. (Pure net) A Petri net is said to be pure if it has no self-loops. A pair of a place p and transition t is called a self-loop if p is both an input and output place of t. Figure 6 shows a self-loop net.

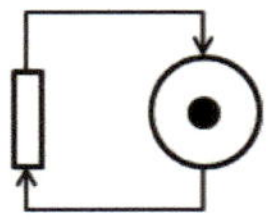

Figure 6. Self-Loop.

2.3. Elementary structures

Elementary nets are used as building blocks in the specification of more complex applications. Figure 7 shows five structures, namely, (a) sequence, (b) fork, (c) synchronization, (d) choice, and (e) merging.

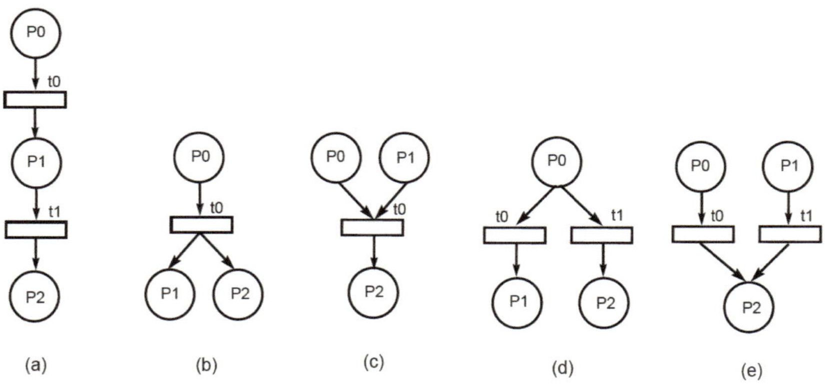

Figure 7. Elementary PN Structures.

Sequence

Sequence structure represents sequential execution of actions, provided that a condition is satisfied. After the firing of a transition, another transition is enabled to fire. Figure 7(a) depicts an example of this structure in which a mark in place p_0 enables the transition t_0. The firing of transition t_0 enables the transition t_1 (p_1 is marked).

Fork

Figure 7(b) shows an example of a fork structure that allows the creation of parallel processes.

Join

Generally, concurrent activities need to synchronize with each other. This net (Figure 7(c)) combines two or more nets, allowing that another process continues this execution only after the end of predecessor processes.

Choice

Figure 7(d) depicts a choice model, in which the firing of the transition $t0$ disables the transition t_1. This building block is suited for modeling if-then-else statement, for instance.

Merging

The merging is an elementary net that allows the enabling of the same transition by two or more processes. Figure 7(e) shows a net with two independent transitions (t_0 and t_1) that have an output place in common ($P2$). Therefore, firing of any of these two transitions, a condition is created (p_2 is marked) which allows the firing of another transition (not shown in the figure).

Confusions

The mixing between conflict and concurrency is called confusion. While conflict is a local phenomenon in the sense that only the pre-sets of the transitions with common input places are involved, confusion involves firing sequences. Figure 8 depicts two types of confusions: (a) symmetric confusion, where two transitions t_1 and t_3 are concurrent while each one is in conflict with transition t_2; and (b) asymmetric confusion, where t_1 is concurrent with t_2, but will be in conflict with t_3 if t_2 fires first.

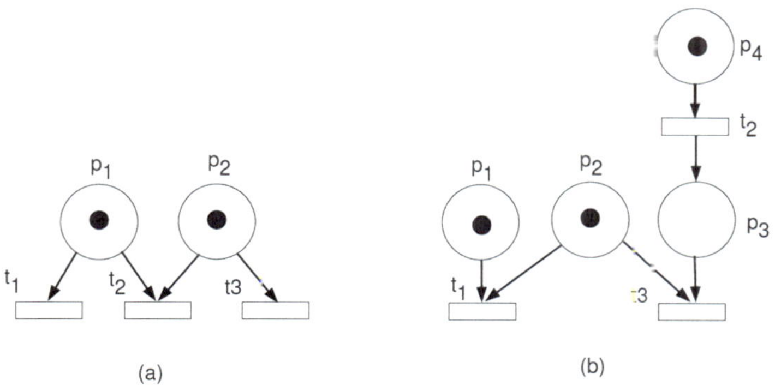

Figure 8. (a) symmetric confusion; (b) asymmetric confusion.

2.4. Petri nets modeling examples

In this section, several simple examples are given in order to introduce how to model some basic concepts such as parallel process and mutual exclusion in Petri nets.

Parallel processes

In order to represent parallel processes, a model may be obtained by composing the model for each individual process with a fork and synchronization models. Two transitions are said to be parallel (or concurrent), if they are causally independent, i.e., one transition may fire either before (or after) or in parallel with the other.

Figure 9 depicts an example of parallel process, where transitions t_1 and t_2 represent parallel activities. When transition t_0 fires, it creates marks in both output places (p_0 and p_1), representing a concurrency. When t_1 and t_2 are enabled for firing, each one may fire independently. The firing of t_3 depends on two pre-conditions, p_2 and p_3, implying that the system only continues if t_1 and t_2 have been fired.

Figure 9 presents a net in which each place has exactly one incoming arc and exactly one outgoing arc. Thus, such model represents a sub-class of Petri nets known as marked graphs. Marked graphs allow representation of concurrency but not decisions or conflicts.

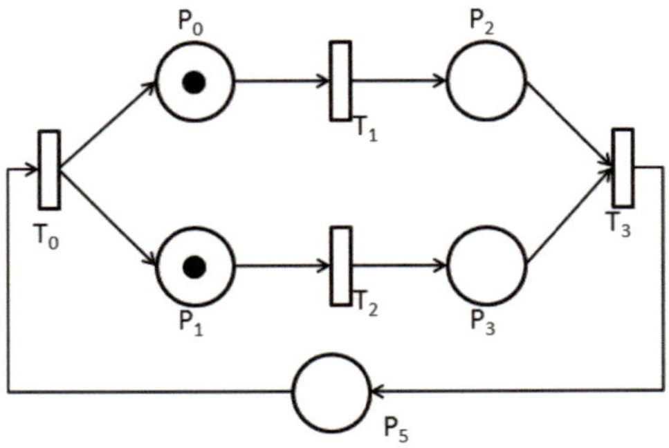

Figure 9. A Petri net representing parallel activities.

Mutual exclusion

The sharing of resources and/or data are common in many system applications, in which most of resources and data should be accessed in a mutual exclusive way. Resources (or data variable) may be modeled by a place with tokens representing the amount of resources. This place is seen as pre-conditions for all transitions that need such resource. After the use of one resource, it must be released. Figure 10 depicts an example of a machine that is accessed in a mutual exclusive way.

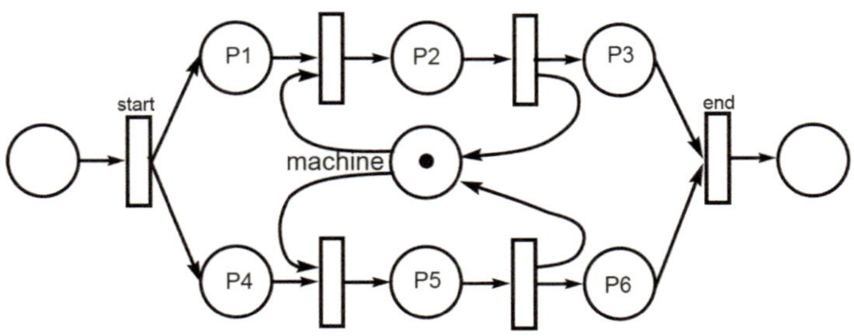

Figure 10. Mutual Exclusion.

Dataflow computation

Petri nets can be used to represent not only the control-flow but also the data-flow. The net shown in Figure 11 is a Petri net representation of a dataflow computation. A dataflow is characterized by the concurrent instruction execution (or transitions firing) as soon as the operands (pre-conditions) are available. In the Petri net representation, tokens may denote values of current data as well as the availability of data. The instructions are represented by transitions such as *Add* and *Subtract* that can be executed in parallel. After that, if the activity *Subtract* has computed a result different from zero, meaning that the pre-conditions to perform *divide* operation were satisfied. Afterwards, when the transition *divide* occur, the dataflow computation is completed.

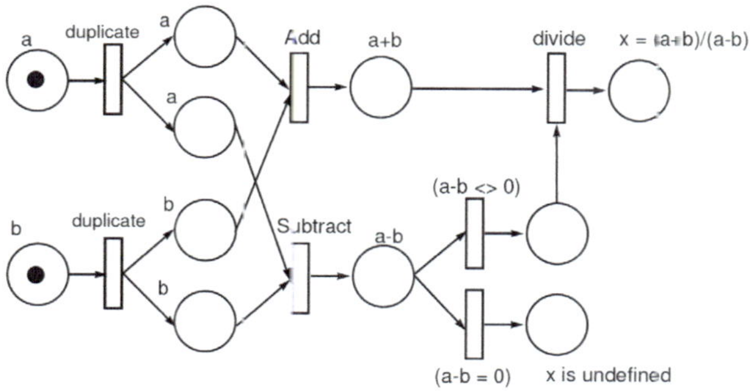

Figure 11. Dataflow example.

2.5. Petri nets properties

The PN properties allow a detailed analysis of the modeled system. For this, two types of properties have been considered in a Petri net model: behavioral and structural properties. Behavioral properties are those which depend on the initial marking. Structural properties, on the other hand, are those that are marking-independent.

2.5.1. Behavioral properties

This section, based on [14], describes some behavioral properties, since such properties are very important when analyzing a given system.

Reachability

The firing of an enabled transition changes the token marking in a Petri net, and a sequence of firings results in a sequence of markings. A marking M_n is said to be reachable from a marking M_0 if there exists a sequence of firings that transforms M_0 to M_n.

A firing (or occurrence) sequence is denoted by $\sigma = t_1, t_2, ..., t_n$. In this case, m_i is reachable from m_0 by σ, and it is denoted by $m_0[\sigma > m_i$. The set of all possible reachable markings from m_0 in a net (PN, m_0) is denoted by R(PN,m_0), or simply R(m_0). The set of all possible firing sequence from m_0 in a net (PN,m_0) is denoted by L(PN, m_0), or simply L(m_0).

Boundedness

A Petri net is said to be bounded if the number of tokens in each place does not exceed a finite number k for any marking reachable from M_0. In a formal way, $M(p) \leq k, \forall p \in P$ and $\forall M \in R(M_0)$.

Safe

When the number of tokens in each place does not exceed the number "1" (one), such Petri net is said to be safe. It is important to state that if a net is bounded or safe, it is guaranteed that there will be no overflows in any place, no matter the firing sequence adopted.

Deadlock freedom

A PN is said to be deadlock free if there is no reachable marking such that no transition is enabled.

Liveness

In an informal way, a Petri net is said to be live if it is guaranteed that no matter what firing sequence is chosen, it continues in deadlock-free operation. The formal definition, a Petri net (N,M_0) is said to be live if, no matter what marking has been reached from M_0, it is possible to ultimately fire any transition of the net.

Liveness is an ideal property for many real systems. However, it is very strong and too costly to verify. Thus, the liveness condition is relaxed in different levels. A transition t is said to be live at the following levels:

- L_0 Live (dead), if t can never be fired in any firing sequence in L(m_0), it is a dead transition.
- L_1-Live (potentially firable), if it can be fired at least once in some firing sequence in L(m_0).
- L_2-Live if, given any positive integer k, t can be fired at least k times in some firing sequence in L(m_0).
- L_3-Live if there is an infinite-length firing sequence in L(m_0) in which t is fired infinitely.
- L_4-Live (or simply live), if it is L1-Live for every marking m in R(m_0).

Persistence

A Petri net is said to be persistent if, for any two enabled transitions, the firing of one transition will not disable the other. Once a transition is enabled in a persistent net, it is continue to be enabled until it fires. Persistency is closed related to conflict-free nets. It is worth noting that all marked graph are persistent, but not all persistent nets are marked graphs. Persistence is a very important property when dealing with parallel system design and speed-independent asynchronous circuits.

2.5.2. Structural properties

Structural liveness

A PN N is said to be structurally live if there is a live initial marking for N.

Structural boundedness

A PN N is said to be structurally bounded if it is bounded for any finite initial marking M_0.

Structural conservativeness

A PN that provides a constant weighted sum of tokens for any reachable marking when considering any initial marking is said to be structural conservative.

Structural repetitiveness

A PN is classified as repetitive if there is an initial marking m_0 and an enabled firing sequence from m_0 such that every transition of the net is infinitely fired. On the other hand, if only some of these transitions are fired infinitely often in the sequence σ, this net is called partially repetitive.

Consistence

A net is classified as consistent if there is an initial marking m_0 and an enabled firing sequence from m_0 back to m_0 such that every transition of the net is fired at least once. If only some of these transitions are not fired in the sequence σ, this net is called partially consistent.

2.6. Stochastic Petri nets

Petri nets [17] are a classic tool for modeling and analyzing discrete event systems which are too complex to be described by automata or queueing models. Time (stochastic delays) and probabilistic choices are essential aspects for a performance evaluation model. We adopt the usual association of delays and weights with transitions [11] in this paper, and adopt the extended stochastic Petri net definition similar to [9]:

Let $SPN = (P, T, I, O, H, \Pi, G, M_0, Atts)$ be a stochastic Petri net, where

- $P = \{p_1, p_2, ..., p_n\}$ is the set of places, which may contain tokens and form the discrete state variables of a Petri net.
- $T = \{t_1, t_2, ..., t_m\}$ is the set of transitions, which model active components.
- $I \in (\mathbb{N}^n \to \mathbb{N})^{n \times m}$ is a matrix of marking-dependent multiplicities of input arcs, where i_{jk} entry of I gives the (possibly marking-dependent) arc multiplicity of input arcs from place p_j to transition t_k $[A \subseteq (P \times T) \cup (T \times P)$ — set of arcs$]$. A transition is only enabled if there are enough tokens in all input places.
- $O \in (\mathbb{N}^n \to \mathbb{N})^{n \times m}$ is a matrix of marking dependent multiplicities of output arcs, where o_{jk} entry of O specifies the possibly marking-dependent arc multiplicity of output arcs from transition t_j to place p_k. When a transition fires, it removes the number of tokens specified by the input arcs from input places, and adds the amount of tokens given by the output arcs to all output places.
- $H \in (\mathbb{N}^n \to \mathbb{N})^{n \times m}$ is a matrix of marking-dependent multiplicities describing the inhibitor arcs, where h_{jk} entry of H returns the possibly marking-dependent arc multiplicity of an inhibitor arc from place p_j to transition t_k. In the presence of an inhibitor arc, a transition is enabled to fire only if every place connected by an inhibitor arc contains fewer tokens than the multiplicity of the arc.
- $\Pi \in \mathbb{N}^m$ is a vector that assigns a priority level to each transition. Whenever there are several transitions fireable at one point in time, the one with the highest priority fires first and leads to a state change.

- $M_0 \in \mathbb{N}^n$ is a vector that contains the initial marking for each place (initial state).
- $Atts : (Dist, W, G, Policy, Concurrency)^m$ comprises a set of attributes for the m transitions, where
  - $Dist \in \mathbb{N}^m \rightarrow \mathcal{F}$ is a possibly marking dependent firing probability distribution function. In a stochastic timed Petri net, time has to elapse between the enabling and firing of a transition. The actual firing time is a random variable, for which the distribution is specified by $\mathcal{F}$. We differ between immediate transitions ($\mathcal{F} = 0$) and timed transitions, for which the domain of $\mathcal{F}$ is $(0, \infty)$.
  - $W \in \mathbb{R}^+$ is the weight function, that represents a firing weight w_t for immediate transitions or a rate λ_t for timed transitions. The latter is only meaningful for the standard case of timed transitions with exponentially distributed firing delays. For immediate transitions, the value specifies a relative probability to fire the transition when there are several immediate transitions enabled in a marking, and all have the same probability. A random choice is then applied using the probabilites w_t.
  - $G \in \mathbb{N}^n \rightarrow \{true, false\}$ is a function that assigns a guard condition related to place markings to each transition. Depending on the current marking, transitions may not fire (they are disabled) when the guard function returns false. This is an extension of inhibitor arcs.
  - $Policy \in \{prd, prs\}$ is the preemption policy (*prd* — *preemptive repeat different* means that when a preempted transition becomes enabled again the previously elapsed firing time is lost; *prs* — *preemptive resume*, in which the firing time related to a preempted transition is resumed when the transition becomes enabled again),
  - $Concurrency \in \{ss, is\}$ is the concurrency degree of transitions, where *ss* represents single server semantics and *is* depicts infinity server semantics in the same sense as in queueing models. Transitions with policy *is* can be understood as having an individual transition for each set of input tokens, all running in parallel.

In many circumstances, it might be suitable to represent the initial marking as a mapping from the set of places to natural numbers ($m_0 : P \rightarrow \mathbb{N}$), where $m_0(p_i)$ denotes the initial marking of place p_i. $m(p_i)$ denotes a reachable marking (reachable state) of place p_i. In this work, the notation $\#p_i$ has also been adopted for representing $m(p_i)$.

2.7. Dependability

Dependability of a computer system must be understood as the ability to deliver services with respect to some agreed-upon specifications of desired service that can be fully trusted [1, 13]. Indeed, dependability is related to disciplines such as fault tolerance and reliability. Reliability is the probability that the system will deliver a set of services for a given period of time, whereas a system is fault tolerant when it does not fail even when there are faulty components. Availability is also another important concept, which quantifies the mixed effect of both failure and repair process in a system. In general, availability and reliability are related concepts, but they differ in the sense that the former may consider maintenance of failed components [8] (e.g., a failed component is restored to a specified condition).

In many situations, modeling is the method of choice either because the system might not yet exist or due to the inherent complexity for creating specific scenarios under which the system should be evaluated. In a very broad sense, models for dependability evaluation can be classified as simulation and mathematical models. However, this does not mean that mathematical models cannot be simulated. Indeed, many mathematical models, besides being analytically tractable, may also be evaluated by simulation. Mathematical models can be characterized as being either state-based or non-state-based.

Dependability metrics (e.g., availability, reliability and downtime) might be calculated either by using RBD or SPN (to mention only the models adopted in this work). RBDs allow to one represent component networks and provide closed-form equations, so the results are usually obtained faster than using SPN simulation. Nevertheless, when faced with representing maintenance policies and redundant mechanisms, particularly those based on dynamic redundancy methods, such models experience drawbacks concerning the thorough handling of failures and repairing dependencies. On the other hand, state-based methods can easily consider those dependencies, so allowing the representation of complex redundant mechanisms as well as sophisticated maintenance policies. However, they suffer from the state-space explosion. Some of those formalism allow both numerical analysis and stochastic simulation, and SPN is one of the most prominent models of such class.

If one is interested in calculating the availability (A) of given device or system, he/she might need either the uptime and downtime or the time to failure (TTF) and time to repair (TTR). Considering that the uptime and downtime are not available, the later option is the mean. If the evaluator needs only the mean value, the metrics commonly adopted are Mean Time to Failure ($MTTF$) and Mean Time To Repair ($MTTR$) (other central values might also be adopted). However, if one is also interested in the availability variation, the standard deviation of time to failure ($sd(TTF)$), and the respective standard deviation of time to repair ($sd(TTR)$) allow one the estimate the availability variation.

The availability (A) is obtained by steady-state analysis or simulation, and the following equation expresses the relation concerning $MTTF$ and $MTTR$:

$$A = \frac{MTTF}{MTTF + MTTR} \quad (1)$$

Through transient analysis or simulation, the reliability (R) is obtained, and, then, the $MTTF$ can be calculated as well as the standard deviation of the Time To Failure (TTF):

$$MTTF = \int_0^\infty tf(t)dt = \int_0^\infty -\frac{dR(t)}{dt}tdt = \int_0^\infty R(t)dt \quad (2)$$

$$sd(TTF) = \sqrt{\int_0^\infty t^2 f(t)dt - (MTTF)^2} \quad (3)$$

Considering a given period t, $R(t)$ is the probability that the time to failure is greater than or equal to t. Regarding exponential failure distributions, reliability is computed as follows:

$$R(t) = exp\left[-\int_0^t \lambda(t')dt'\right] \quad (4)$$

where $\lambda(t')$ is the instantaneous failure rate.

One should bear in mind that, for computing reliability of a given system service, the repairing activity of the respective service must not be represented. Besides, taking into account $UA = 1 - A$ (unavailability) and Equation 1, the following equation is derived

$$MTTR = MTTF \times \frac{UA}{A} \tag{5}$$

As well, the standard deviation of the Time To Repair (TTR) can be calculated as follows:

$$sd(TTR) = sd(TTF) \times \frac{UA}{A} \tag{6}$$

Next, $\frac{MTTF}{sd(TTF)}$ (and $\frac{MTTR}{sd(TTR)}$) are computed for choosing the expolinomial distribution that best fits the TTF and TTR distributions [6, 22].

Figure 12 depicts the generic simple component model using SPN, which provides a high-level representation of a subsystem. One should notice the trapezoidal shape of transitions (high-level transition named s-transition). This shape means that the time distributions of such transitions are not exponentially distributed, instead they should be refined by subnets. The delay assigned to s-transition f is the TTF and the delay of s-transition r is the TTR. If the TTF and TTR are exponentially distributed, the shape of the transitions should be the regular one (white rectangles) and TTF and TTR should be summarized by the respective $MTTF$ and $MTTR$.

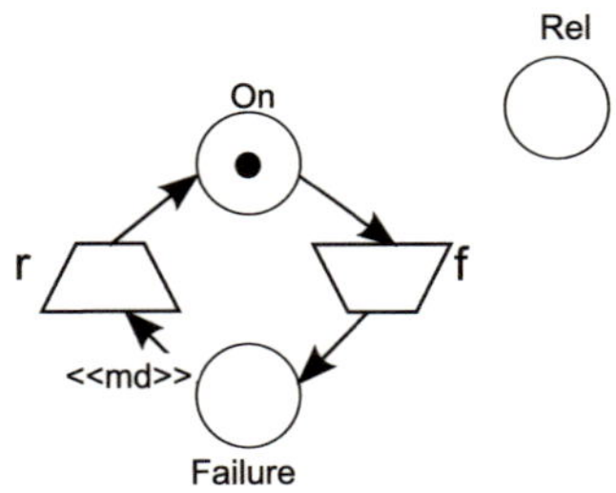

Figure 12. Generic simple model - SPN

A well-established method that considers *expolynomial distribution* random variables is based on distribution moment matching. The moment matching process presented in [6] takes into account that Hypoexponential and Erlangian distributions have the average delay (μ) greater than the standard-deviation (σ) -$\mu > \sigma$-, and Hyperexponential distributions have $\mu < \sigma$, in order to represent an activity with a generally distributed delay as an Erlangian or a Hyperexponential subnet referred to as s-transition[1]. One should note that in cases where these distributions have $\mu = \sigma$, they are, indeed, equivalent to an exponential distribution with parameter equal to $\frac{1}{\mu}$. Therefore, according to the coefficient of variation associated with an activity's delay, an appropriate s-transition implementation model could be chosen. For each s-transition implementation model (see Figure 13), a set of parameters should be configured for matching their first and second moments. In other words, an associated delay distribution (it might have been obtained by a measuring process) of the

[1] In this work, μ could be $MTTF$ or $MTTR$ and the σ could represent $sd(TTF)$ or $sd(TTR)$, for instance.

original activity is matched with the first and second moments of s-transition (*expolynomial distribution*). According to the aforementioned method, one activity with $\mu < \sigma$ is approximated by a two-phase Hyperexponential distribution with parameters

$$r_1 = \frac{2\mu^2}{(\mu^2 + \sigma^2)}, \tag{7}$$

$$r_2 = 1 - r_1 \tag{8}$$

and

$$\lambda = \frac{2\mu}{(\mu^2 + \sigma^2)}. \tag{9}$$

where λ is the rate associated to phase 1, r_1 is the probability of related to this phase, and r_2 is the probability assigned to phase 2. In this particular model, the rate assigned to phase 2 is assumed to be infinity, that is, the related average delay is zero.

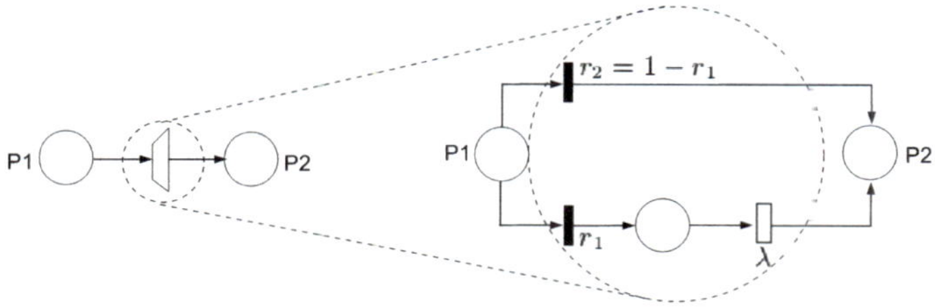

Figure 13. Hyperexponential Model

Activities with coefficients of variation less than one might be mapped either to Hypoexponential or Erlangian s-transi-
tions. If $\frac{\mu}{\sigma} \notin \mathbb{N}, \frac{\mu}{\sigma} \neq 1, (\mu, \sigma \neq 0)$, the respective activity is represented by a Hypoexponential distribution with parameters λ_1, λ_2 (exponential rates); and γ, the integer representing the number of phases with rate equal to λ_2, whereas the number of phases with rate equal to λ_1 is one. In other words, the s-transition is represented by a subnet composed of two exponential and one immediate transitions. The average delay assigned to the exponential transition t_1 is equal to μ_1 ($\lambda_1 = 1/\mu_1$), and the respective average delay assigned to the exponential transition t_2 is $\mu_2 (\lambda_2 = 1/\mu_2)$. γ is the integer value considered as the weight assigned to the output arc of transition t_1 as well as the input arc weight value of the immediate transition t_3 (see Figure 14). These parameters are calculated by the following expressions:

$$(\frac{\mu}{\sigma})^2 - 1 \leq \gamma < (\frac{\mu}{\sigma})^2, \tag{10}$$

$$\lambda_1 = \frac{1}{\mu_1} \, and_2 = \frac{1}{\mu_2}, \tag{11}$$

where

$$\mu_1 = \frac{u \pm \sqrt{\gamma(\gamma+1)\sigma^2 - \gamma\mu^2}}{\gamma + 1}, \tag{12}$$

$$\mu_2 = \frac{\gamma\mu \mp \sqrt{\gamma(\gamma+1)\sigma^2 - \gamma\mu^2}}{\gamma + 1} \tag{13}$$

If $\frac{\mu}{\sigma} \in \mathbb{N}, \frac{\mu}{\sigma} \neq 1, (\mu, \sigma \neq 0)$, an Erlangian s-transition with two parameters, $\gamma = (\frac{\mu}{\sigma})^2$ is an integer representing the number of phases of this distribution; and $\mu_1 = \mu/\gamma$, where $\mu_1(1/\lambda_1)$ is the average delay value of each phase. The Erlangian model is a particular case of a Hypoexponential model, in which each individual phase rate has the same value.

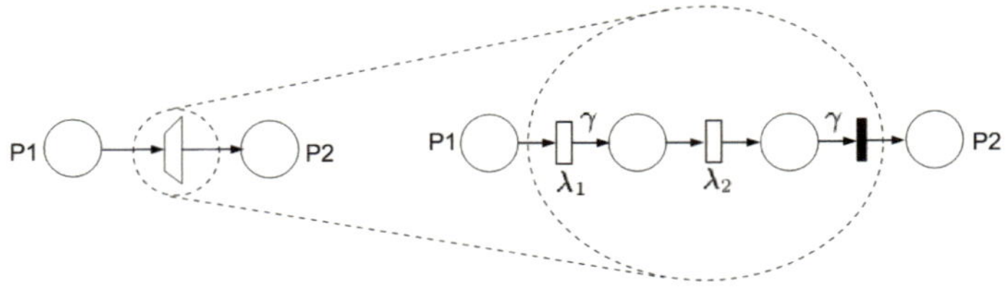

Figure 14. Hypoexponential Model

The reader should refer to [6] for details regarding the representation of expolinomial distributions using SPN. For the sake of simplicity, the SPN models presented in the next sections consider only exponential distributions.

Depending on the system characteristics, a RBD model (Figure 15) could be adopted instead of the SPN counterpart, whenever the former is more suitable.

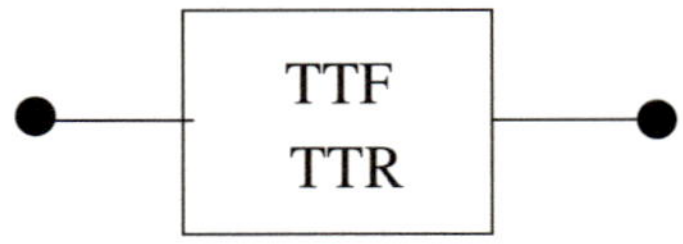

Figure 15. Generic simple model - RBD

3. Related works

In the last few years, some works have been developed to perform dependability analysis of data center systems [24][26][27]. Reliability (which encompasses both the durability of the data and its availability for access) correspond to the primary property that data center users desire [2], .

Robidoux [28] proposes Dynamic RBD (DRBD) model, an extension to RBD, which supports reliability analysis of systems with dependence relationships. The additional blocks (in relation to RBD) to model dependence, turned the DRBD model complex. The DRBD model is automatic converted to CPN model in order to perform behavior properties analysis which may certify the correctness of the model [18]. It seems that an interesting alternative would be to model the system directly using CPN or any other formalism (e.g., SPN) which is able to perform dependability analysis as well as to model dependencies between components.

Wei [25] presents an hierarchical method to model and analyze virtual data center (VDC). The approach combines the advances of both RBD and General SPN (GSPN) for quantifying availability and reliability. Data center power architectures are not the focus of their research and the proposed models are specific for modeling VDC.

Additionally, redundancies on components to increase system reliability are costly. [7] propose an approach for reliability evaluation and risk analysis of dynamic process systems using stochastic Petri nets.

Different from previous works, this paper proposes a set of models to the quantification of dependability metrics in the context of data center design. Furthermore, the adopted methodology for the quantification of those values takes into account a hybrid modeling approach, which utilizes RBD and SPN whenever they are best suited. The idea of mixing state (SPN) and non-state (RBD) based models is not new (e.g., [23]), but, as far as we are concerned, there is no similar work that applies such technique on the evaluation of data center infrastructures. Besides, a tool is proposed to automate several activities.

4. Dependability models

The following sections presents the adopted dependability models.

RBD Models

Reliability Block Diagram (RBD) [8] is a combinatorial model that was initially proposed as a technique for calculating reliability of systems using intuitive block diagrams. Such a technique has also been extended to calculate other dependability metrics, such as availability and maintainability [10]. Figure 16 depicts two examples, in which independent blocks are arranged through series (Figure 16(a)) and parallel (Figure 16(b)) compositions.

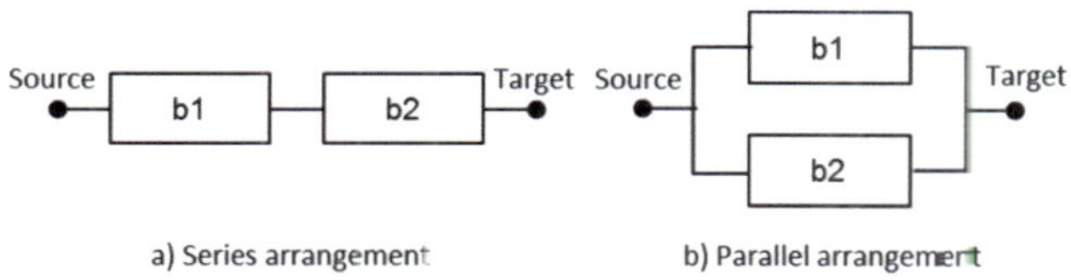

Figure 16. Reliability Block Diagram

In the series arrangement, if a single component fails, the whole system is no longer operational. Assuming a system with n independent components, the reliability (instantaneous availability or steady state availability) is obtained by

$$P_s = \prod_{i=1}^{n} P_i \tag{14}$$

where P_i is the reliability - $R_i(t)$ (instantaneous availability ($A_i(t)$) or steady state availability (A_i)) of block b_i.

For a parallel arrangement (see Figure 16(b)), if a single component is operational, the whole system is also operational. Assuming a system with n independent components, the reliability (instantaneous availability or steady state availability) is obtained by

$$P_p = 1 - \prod_{i=1}^{n} (1 - P_i) \tag{15}$$

where P_i is the reliability - $R_i(t)$ (instantaneous availability ($A_i(t)$) or steady state availability (A_i)) of block b_i.

A k-out-of-n system functions if and only if k or more of its n components are functioning. Let p be the success probability of each of those blocks. The system success probability (reliability or availability) is depicted by:

$$\Sigma_{i=k}^{n}\binom{n}{b}p^k(1-p)^{n-k} \tag{16}$$

For other examples and closed-form equations, the reader should refer to [10].

SPN Models
This section presents two proposed SPN building block for obtaining dependability metrics.

Simple Component. The simple component has two states: functioning or failed. To compute its availability, $MTTF$ and $MTTR$ should be represented. Figure 17 shows the SPN model of the "simple component", which has two parameters (not depicted in the figure), namely X_MTTF and X_MTTR, representing the delays associated to the transitions $X\_Failure$ and X_Repair, respectively.

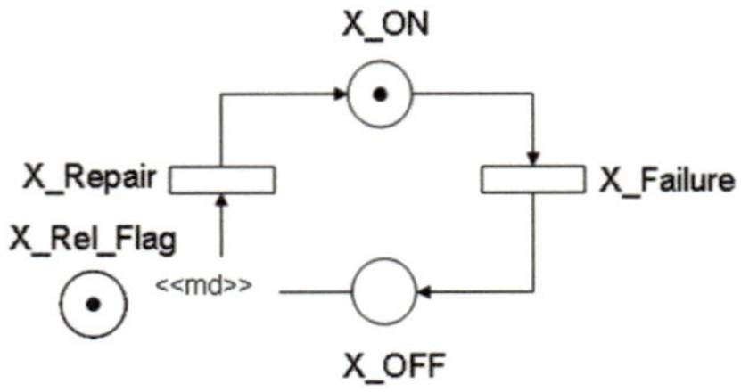

Figure 17. Simple component model

Places X_ON and X_OFF are the model component's activity and inactivity states, respectively. The simple component also includes an arc from X_OFF to X_Repair with multiplicity depending on place marking. The multiplicity is defined through the expression IF(#X_Rel_Flag = 1):2 ELSE 1, where place X_Rel_Flag models the evaluation of reliability/availability. Hence, if condition #$X\_Rel\_Flag = 1$ is true, then the evaluation refers to reliability. Otherwise, the evaluation concerns availability.

Besides, although simple component model has been presented using the exponential distribution, other expolinomial distributions that best fits the TTF and TTR may be adopted following the techniques presented in [22].

Cold standby. A cold standby redundant system is composed by a non-active spare module that waits to be activated when the main active module fails. Figure 18 depicts the SPN model of this system, which includes four places, namely X_ON, X_OFF, X_Spare1_ON, X_Spare1_OFF that represent the operational and failure states of both the main and spare modules, respectively. The spare module (Spare1) is initially deactivated, hence no tokens are initially stored in places X_Spare1_ON and $X\_Spare1\ \_OFF$. When the main module fails, the transition $X\_Activate\_Spare1$ is fired to activate the spare module.

Table 2 presents the attributes of each transition of the model. Once considering reliability evaluation (number of tokens (#) in the place $X\_Rel\_Flag = 1$), the X_Repair, $X\_Activate\_Spare1$ and X_Repair_Spare1 transitions receive a huge number (many times larger than the associated MTTF or MTActivate) to represent the absence of repair. The MTActivate corresponds to the mean time to activate the spare module. Besides, when considering reliability, the weight of the edge that connects the place X_Wait_Spare1 and the $X\_Activate\_Spare1$ transition is two; otherwise, it is one. Both availability and reliability may be computed by the probability $P\{\#X\_\ ON = 1 \text{ OR } \#X\_Spare1\ \_ON = 1\}$.

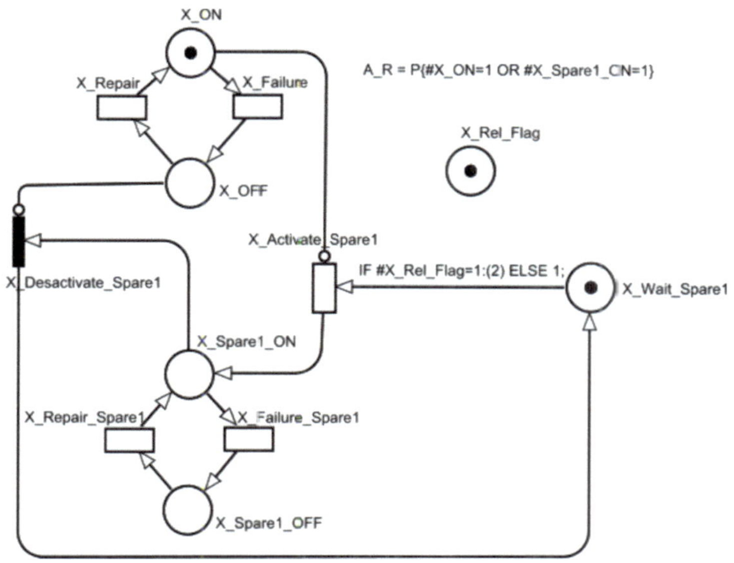

Figure 18. Cold standby model.

Transition	Priority	Delay or Weight
X_Failure	-	X_MTTF
X_Repair	-	IF #X_Rel_Flag=1:(10^{13} x X_MTTF) ELSE X_MTTR
X_Activate_Spare1	-	IF #X_Rel_Flag=1:(10^{13} x MTActivate) ELSE MTActivate
X_Failure_Spare1	-	X_MTTF_Spare1
X_Repair_Spare1	-	IF #X_Rel_Flag=1:(10^{13} x X_MTTF_Spare1) ELSE X_MTTR_Spare1
X_Desactivate_Spare1	1	1

Table 2. Cold standby model - Transition attributes.

5. Applications

This section focuses in presenting the applicability of the proposed models to perform dependability analysis of real-world data center power architectures (from HP Labs Palo Alto, U.S. [12]). The environment ASTRO was adopted to conduct the case study. ASTRO was validated through our previous work [5] [3] [4].

5.1. Architectures

Data center power infrastructure is responsible for providing uninterrupted, conditioned power at correct voltage and frequency to the IT equipments. Figure 19 (a) depicts a real-world power infrastructure. From the utility feed (i.e., AC Source), typically, the power goes through voltage panels, uninterruptible power supply (UPS) units, power distribution units (PDUs) (composed of transformers and electrical subpanels), junction boxes, and, finally, to rack PDUs (rack power distribution units). The power infrastructure fails (and, thus, the system) whenever both paths depicted in Figure 19 are not able to provide the power demanded (500 kW) by the IT components (50 racks). The reader should assume a path as a set of redundant interconnected components inside the power infrastructure. Another architecture is analyzed with an additional electricity generator (Figure 19 (b)) for supporting the system when both AC sources are not operational.

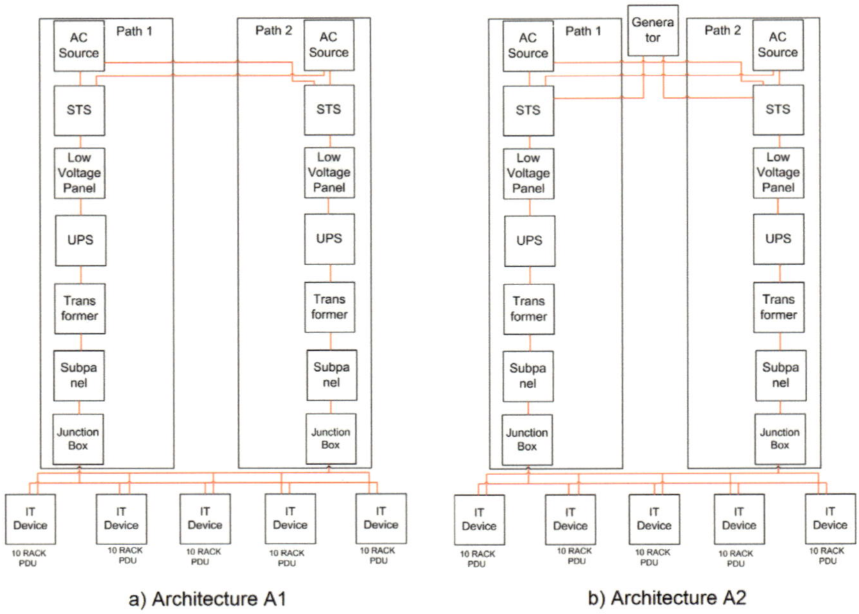

Figure 19. Data Center Power Architectures.

5.2. Models

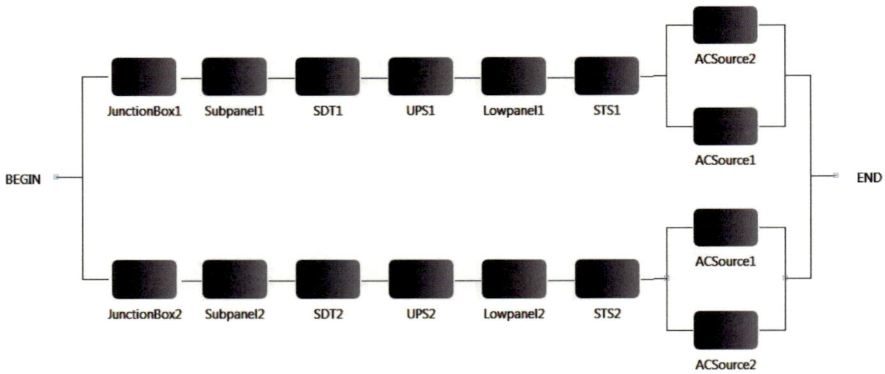

Figure 20. RBD of Architecture A1.

This work adopts a hierarchical methodology for conducting dependability evaluation of data center architectures. In general, the methodology aims at grouping related components in order to generate subsystem models, which are adopted to mitigate the complexity of the final system model evaluation. Thus, the final model is an approximation, but rather simpler, of a more intricate system model. One should bear in mind that the detailed model could be adopted instead, but at the expenses of complexity.

Following the adopted methodology, systems with no failure dependencies between components have been evaluated through RBD models. For instance, Figure 20 depicts the RBD model that represents the architecture A1.

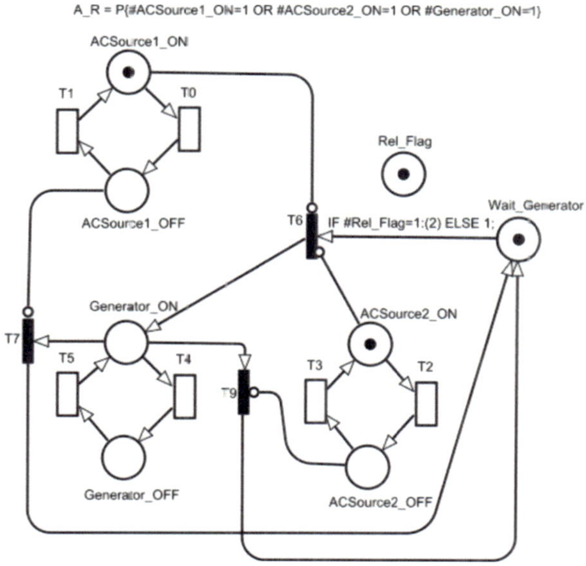

Figure 21. SPN of Architectures A2.

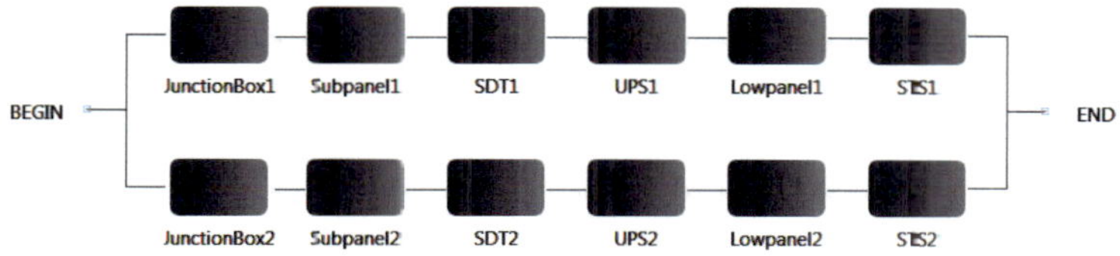

Figure 22. RBD of Architectures A2.

In architecture A2, the generator is only activated when both AC sources are not available. Therefore, a model that deal with dependencies must be adopted. Figure 21 shows the SPN model considering cold standby redundance to represent the subsystem composed of generator and two AC sources. Besides, we assume that UPS' batteries support the system during the generator activation. The reliability or availability is computed by the probability $P\{\#ACSource1\_ON = \text{OR } \#ACSource2\_ON = 1 \text{ OR } \#Generator\_ON = 1\}$.

The other components of the architecture A2 are modeled using RBD as shown in Figure 22. Once obtained the results of both models (RBD and the SPN model with dependencies), a RBD model with two blocks (considering the results of those models) in a serial arrangement is created. The RBD evaluation provides the dependability results of the architecture A2 system.

The adopted MTTF and MTTR values for the power devices were obtained from [21] [29] [19] and are shown in Table 3.

5.3. Results

Figure 23 depicts a graphical comparison between the reliability results (in number of 9's) of those two data center power architectures. The respective number of nines (-*log*[1 - A/100]) and the period of 8760 hours (1 year) are adopted. As the reader should note, the reliability of both architectures decreases when the time increases. Besides, it is also possible to notice that

Equipment	MTTF (hs)	MTTR (hs)
AC Source	4,380	8
Generator	2,190	8
STS	240,384	8
Subpanel	1,520,000	8
Transformer	1,412,908	8
UPS	250,000	8
Low Voltage Panel	1,520,000	8

Table 3. MTTF and MTTR values for power devices.

the generator has increased the reliability of the architecture A2. Considering the availability results, similar behavior happened. The availability has increased from 5.47 to 7.96 (in number of 9's).

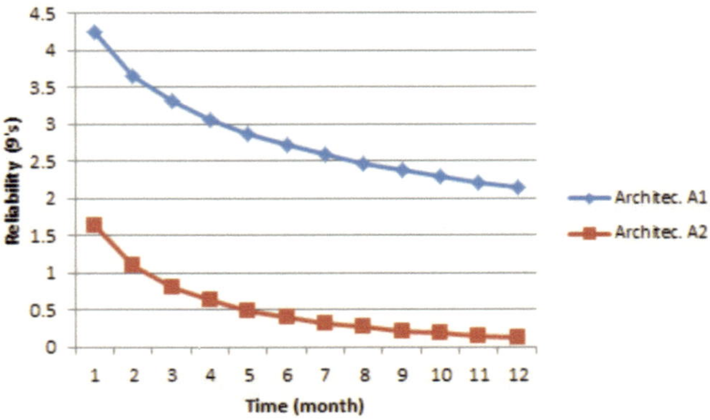

Figure 23. Reliability Comparison of Architectures A1 and A2.

6. Conclusion

This work considers the advantages of both Stochastic Petri Nets (SPN) and Reliability Block Diagrams (RBD) formalisms to analyze data center infrastructures. Such approach is supported by an integrated environment, ASTRO, which allows data center designers to estimate the dependability metrics before implementing the architectures. The methodology proposes that the system should be evaluated piecewisely to allow the composition of simpler models representing a data center infrastructure appropriately. Moreover, experiments demonstrate the feasibility of the environment, in which different architectures for a data center power infrastructures have been adopted.

Acknowledgments

The authors would like to thank CNPQ for financing the project (290018/2011-0) and supporting the development of this work.

Author details

Gustavo Callou, Paulo Maciel, Julian Araújo, João Ferreira and Rafael Souza
Informatics Center, Federal University of Pernambuco - Recife, Brazil

Dietmar Tutsch
Automation/Computer Science, University of Wuppertal, Wuppertal, Germany

7. References

[1] Avizienis, A., Laprie, J. & Randell, B. [2001]. Fundamental Concepts of Dependability, *Technical Report Series-University of Newcastle upon Tyne Computing Science* .

[2] Banerjee, P., Bash, C., Friedrich, R., Goldsack, P., Huberman, B. A., Manley, J., Patel, C., Ranganathan, P. & Veitch., A. [2011]. Everything as a service: Powering the new information economy, *IEEE Computer* pp. 36–43.

[3] Callou, G., Maciel, P., Magnani, F., Figueiredo, J., Sousa, E., Tavares, E., Silva, B., Neves, F. & Araujo, C. [2011]. Estimating sustainability impact, total cost of ownership and dependability metrics on data center infrastructures, *Sustainable Systems and Technology (ISSST), 2011 IEEE International Symposium on*, pp. 1 –6.

[4] Callou, G., Maciel, P., Tavares, E., Sousa, E., Silva, B., Figueiredo, J., Araujo, C., Magnani, F. & Neves, F. [2011]. Sustainability and dependability evaluation on data center architectures, *Systems, Man, and Cybernetics (SMC), 2011 IEEE International Conference on*, pp. 398 –403.

[5] Callou, G., Sousa, E., Maciel, P., Tavares, E., Silva, B., Figueirêdo, J., Araujo, C., Magnani, F. & Neves, F. [2011]. A formal approach to the quantification of sustainability and dependability metrics on data center infrastructures, *Proceedings of the 2011 Symposium on Theory of Modeling & Simulation: DEVS Integrative M&S Symposium*, TMS-DEVS '11, Society for Computer Simulation International, San Diego, CA, USA, pp. 274–281.
URL: *http://dl.acm.org/citation.cfm?id=2048476.2048512*

[6] Desrochers, A. & Al-Jaar, R. [1995]. *Applications of Petri Nets in Manufacturing Systems: Modeling, Control, and Performance Analysis*, IEEE Press.

[7] Dutuit, Y., Châtelet, E., Signoret, J. & Thomas, P. [1997]. Dependability modelling and evaluation by using stochastic Petri nets: application to two test cases, *Reliability Engineering & System Safety* 55(2): 117–124.

[8] Ebeling, C. [1997]. *An Introduction to Reliability and Maintainability Engineering*, Waveland Press.

[9] German, R. [2000]. *Performance Analysis of Communication Systems with Non-Markovian Stochastic Petri Nets*, John Wiley & Sons, Inc., New York, NY, USA.

[10] Kuo, W. & Zuo, M. J. [2003]. *Optimal Reliability Modeling - Principles and Applications*, Wiley.

[11] Marsan, M. A., Balbo, G., Conte, G., Donatelli, S. & Franceschinis, G. [1995]. *Modelling with Generalized Stochastic Petri Nets.*, John Wiley and Sons.

[12] Marwah, M., Maciel, P., Shah, A., Sharma, R., Christian, T., Almeida, V., Araújo, C., Souza, E., Callou, G., Silva, B., Galdino, S. & Pires, J. [2010]. Quantifying the sustainability impact of data center availability, *SIGMETRICS Perform. Eval. Rev.* 37: 64–68.
URL: *http://doi.acm.org/10.1145/1773394.1773405*

[13] Meyer, J. F. & Sanders, W. H. [1993]. Specification and construction of performability models., *Proceedings of the Second International Workshop on Performability Modeling of Computer and Communication Systems, Mont Saint-Michel, France.*

[14] Murata, T. [1989]. Petri nets: Properties, analysis and applications, *Proceedings of the IEEE* 77(4): 541 –580.

[15] Patterson, D. [2002]. A simple way to estimate the cost of downtime, *Proceedings of the 16th USENIX conference on System administration*, LISA '02, USENIX Association, Berkeley, CA, USA, pp. 185–188.
URL: *http://dl.acm.org/citation.cfm?id=1050517.1050538*

[16] Petri, C. A. [1962]. *Kommunikation mit Automaten*, PhD Dissertation, Darmstad University, Germany.

[17] Reisig, W. [1985]. *Petri nets: an introduction*, Springer-Verlag New York, Inc., New York, NY, USA.

[18] Robidoux, R., Xu, H., Member, S., Xing, L., Member, S. & Zhou, M. [2010]. Automated modeling of dynamic reliability block diagrams using colored petri nets, *IEEE Transactions on Systems, Man, and Cybernetics, Part A: Systems and Humans* 40(2): 337–351.

[19] *Service Level Agreement for Data Center Services* [2012]. http://www.earthlinkbusiness.com/_static/_files/_pdfs/legal/DataCenterServiceSLA.pdf.

[20] Silva, B., Maciel, P., Tavares, E., Araujo, C., Callou, G., Sousa, E., Rosa, N., Marwah, M., Sharma, R., Shah, A., Christian, T. & Pires, J. [2010]. Astro: A tool for dependability evaluation of data center infrastructures, *Systems Man and Cybernetics (SMC), 2010 IEEE International Conference on*, pp. 783 –790.

[21] std., I. [1997]. *Gold Book 473 Design of Reliable Industrial and Commercial Power Systems*, IEEE.

[22] Trivedi, K. [2002]. *Probability and Statistics with Reliability, Queueing, and Computer Science Applications*, 2 edn, Wiley Interscience Publication.

[23] Trivedi, K. & et al [1994]. Reliability analysis techniques explored through a communication network example, *International Workshop on Computer-Aided Design, Test, and Evaluation for Dependability*.

[24] Vilkomir, S. A., Parnas, D. L., Mendiratta, V. B. & Murphy, E. [2006]. Segregated failures model for availability evaluation of fault-tolerant system, *ACSC '06: Proceedings of the 29th Australasian Computer Science Conference*, Australian Computer Society, Inc., Darlinghurst, Australia, Australia, pp. 55–61.

[25] Wei, B., Lin, C. & Kong, X. [2011]. Dependability modeling and analysis for the virtual data center of cloud computing, *High Performance Computing and Communications (HPCC), 2011 IEEE 13th International Conference on*, pp. 784 –789.

[26] Wiboonrat, M. [2008a]. An empirical study on data center system failure diagnosis, *Internet Monitoring and Protection, 2008. ICIMP '08. The Third International Conference on*, pp. 103 –108.

[27] Wiboonrat, M. [2008b]. Risk anatomy of data center power distribution systems, *ICSET'08*.

[28] Xu, H., Xing, L. & Robidoux, R. [2008]. Drbd: Dynamic reliability block diagrams for system reliability modeling, *International Journal of Computers and Applications* .

[29] Zhou, L. & Grover, W. [2005]. A theory for setting the "safety margin" on availability guarantees in an sla, *Design of Reliable Communication Networks, 2005. (DRCN 2005). Proceedings.5th International Workshop on*, p. 7 pp.

Chapter 15

Grammars Controlled by Petri Nets

J. Dassow, G. Mavlankulov, M. Othman, S. Turaev, M.H. Selamat and R. Stiebe

Additional information is available at the end of the chapter

http://dx.doi.org/10.5772/50637

1. Introduction

Formal language theory, introduced by Noam Chomsky in the 1950s as a tool for a description of natural languages [8–10], has also been widely involved in modeling and investigating phenomena appearing in computer science, artificial intelligence and other related fields because the symbolic representation of a modeled system in the form of strings makes its processes by information processing tools very easy: coding theory, cryptography, computation theory, computational linguistics, natural computing, and many other fields directly use sets of strings for the description and analysis of modeled systems. In formal language theory a model for a phenomenon is usually constructed by representing it as a set of words, i.e., a *language* over a certain alphabet, and defining a generative mechanism, i.e., a *grammar* which identifies exactly the words of this set. With respect to the forms of their rules, grammars and their languages are divided into four classes of *Chomsky hierarchy*: *recursively enumerable*, *context-sensitive*, *context-free* and *regular*.

Context-free grammars are the most investigated type of Chomsky hierarchy which, in addition, have good mathematical properties and are extensively used in many applications of formal languages. However, they cannot cover all aspects which occur in modeling of phenomena. On the other hand, context-sensitive grammars, the next level in Chomsky hierarchy, are too powerful to be used in applications of formal languages, and have bad features, for instance, for context-sensitive grammars, the emptiness problem is undecidable and the existing algorithms for the membership problem, thus for the parsing, have exponential complexities. Moreover, such concepts as a derivation tree, which is an important tool for the analysis of context-free languages, cannot be transformed to context-sensitive grammars. Therefore, it is of interest to consider "intermediate" grammars which are more powerful than context-free grammars and have similar properties. One type of such grammars, called *grammars with regulated rewriting* (*controlled* or *regulated grammars* for short), is defined by considering grammars with some additional mechanisms which extract some subset of the generated language in order to cover some aspects of modeled phenomena. Due to the variety of investigated practical and theoretical problems, different additional mechanisms to grammars can be considered. Since Abraham [1] first defined matrix grammars in 1965, several grammars with restrictions such as programmed, random context, valence grammars, and etc., have been introduced (see [16]). However, the rapid developments in present day technology, industry, medicine and other areas challenge to deal with more and more new and complex problems, and to look for new suitable tools for the modeling and investigation of these problems. *Petri net controlled grammars*, which introduce *concurrently parallel control mechanisms* in formal language theory, were proposed as a theoretical model for some problems appearing in systems biology and automated manufacturing systems (see [18–23, 56, 59–62]).

Petri nets, which are graphical and mathematical modeling tools applicable to many concurrent, asynchronous, distributed, parallel, nondeterministic and stochastic systems, have widely been used in the study of formal languages. One of the fundamental approaches in this area is to consider Petri nets as language generators. If the transitions in a Petri net are labeled with a set of (not necessary distinct) symbols, a sequence of transition firing generates a string of symbols. The set of strings generated by all possible firing sequences defines a language called a Petri net language, which can be used to model the flow of information and control of actions in a system. With different kinds of labeling functions and different kinds of final marking sets, various classes of Petri net languages were introduced and investigated by Hack [34] and Peterson [46]. The relationship between Petri net languages and formal languages were thoroughly investigated by Peterson in [47]. It was shown that all regular languages are Petri net languages and the family of Petri net languages are strictly included in the family of context-sensitive languages but some Petri net languages are not context-free and some context-free languages are not Petri net languages. It was also shown that the complement of a free Petri net language is context-free [12].

Another approach to the investigation of formal languages was considered by Crespi-Reghizzi and Mandrioli [11]. They noticed the similarity between the firing of a transition and application of a production rule in a derivation in which places are nonterminals and tokens are separate instances of the nonterminals. The major difference of this approach is the lack of ordering information in the Petri net contained in the sentential form of the derivation. To accommodate it, they defined the commutative grammars, which are isomorphic to Petri nets. In addition, they considered the relationship of Petri nets to matrix, scattered-context, nonterminal-bounded, derivation-bounded, equal-matrix and Szilard languages in [13].

The approach proposed by Crespi-Reghizzi and Mandrioli was used in the following works. By extending the type of Petri nets introduced in [11] with the places for the terminal symbols and arcs for the control of nonterminal occurrences in sentential forms, Marek and Češka showed that for every random-context grammar, an isomorphic Petri net can be constructed, where each derivation of the grammar is simulated by some occurrence sequence of transitions of the Petri net, and vice versa. In [39] the relationship between vector grammars and Petri nets was investigated, partially, hybrid Petri nets were introduced and the equality of the family of hybrid Petri net languages and the family of vector languages was shown. By reduction to Petri net reachability problems, Hauschildt and Jantzen [35] could solve a number of open problems in regulated rewriting systems, specifically, every matrix language without appearance checking over one letter alphabet is regular and the finiteness problem for the families of matrix and random context languages is decidable; In several papers [2, 14, 25], Petri nets are used as minimization techniques for context-free (graph) grammars. For instance, in [2], algorithms to eliminate erasing and unit (chain) rules, algorithms to remove useless rules using the Petri net concept are introduced.

Control by Petri nets has also been introduced and studied in automata theory [26–28, 38] and grammar systems theory [6].

In this chapter we summarize the recent obtained results on Petri net controlled grammars and propose new problems for further research.

In Section 2 we recall some basic concepts and results from the areas formal languages and Petri nets: strings, grammars, languages, Petri nets, Petri net languages and so on, which will be used in the next sections.

In Section 3 we define a *context-free Petri net* (a *cf Petri net* for short), where places correspond to nonterminals, transitions are the counterpart of the production rules, the tokens reflect the occurrences of symbols in the sentential form, and there is a one-to-one correspondence between the application of (sequence of) rules and the firing of (sequence of) transitions. Further, we introduce grammars controlled by k-Petri nets, i.e., cf Petri nets with additional k places, and studies the computational power and closure properties of families of languages generated by k-Petri net controlled grammars.

In Section 4 we consider a generalization of the k-Petri net controlled grammars: we associate an arbitrary place/ transition net with a context-free grammar and require that the sequence of applied rules corresponds to an occurrence sequence of transitions in the Petri net. With respect to different labeling strategies and different definitions of final marking sets, we define various classes of Petri net controlled grammars. Here we study the influence of the labeling functions and the effect of the final markings on the generative power.

It is known that many decision problems in formal language theory are equivalent to the reachability problem in Petri net theory, which has been shown that it is decidable, however, it has exponential time complexity. The result of this has been the definition of a number of structural subclasses of Petri nets with a smaller complexity and still adequate modeling power. Thus, it is interesting to consider grammars controlled by such kind of subclasses of Petri nets. In Section 5 we continue our study of arbitrary Petri net controlled grammars by restricting Petri nets to their structural subclasses, i.e., special Petri nets such as state machines, marked graphs, and free-choice nets, and so on.

In Section 6 we examine Petri net controlled grammars with respect to dynamical properties of Petri nets: we use (cf and arbitrary) Petri nets with place capacities. We also investigate capacity-bounded grammars which are counterparts of grammars controlled by Petri nets with place capacities.

In Section 7 we draw some general conclusions and present suggestions for further research.

2. Preliminaries

In this section we recall some prerequisites, by giving basic notions and notations of the theories formal languages, Petri nets and Petri net languages which are used in the next sections. The reader is referred to [16, 34, 36, 42, 45, 47, 50, 52] for further information.

2.1 General notions and notations

Throughout the chapter we use the following general notations. $\in$ denotes the membership of an element to a set while the negation of set membership is denoted by $\notin$. The inclusion is denoted by $\subseteq$ and the strict (proper) inclusion is denoted by $\subset$. The symbol $\emptyset$ denotes the empty set. The set of positive (non-negative) integers is denoted by $\mathbb{N}$ ($\mathbb{N}_0$). The set of integers is denoted by $\mathbb{Z}$. The power set of a set X is denoted by 2^X, while the cardinality of a set X is denoted by $|X|$.

Let Σ be an *alphabet* which is a finite nonempty set of symbols. A *string* (sometimes a *word*) over the alphabet Σ is a finite sequence of symbols from Σ. The *empty* string is denoted by λ. The *length* of a word w, denoted by $|w|$, is the number of occurrences of symbols in w. The number of occurrences of a symbol a in a string w is denoted by $|w|_a$. The set of all strings over the alphabet Σ is denoted by Σ^*. The set of nonempty strings over Σ is denoted by Σ^+, i.e., $\Sigma^+ = \Sigma^* - \{\lambda\}$. A subset of Σ^* is called a *language*. A language $L \in \Sigma^*$ is λ*-free* if $\lambda \notin L$. For two languages $L_1, L_2 \subseteq \Sigma^*$ the *operation shuffle* is defined by

$$\begin{aligned}\mathrm{Shuf}(L_1, L_2) = \{&u_1v_1u_2v_2\cdots u_nv_n \mid u_1u_2\cdots u_n \in L_1, v_1v_2\cdots v_n \in L_2,\\ &u_i, v_i \in \Sigma^*, 1 \leq i \leq n\}\end{aligned}$$

and for $L \subseteq \Sigma^*$, $\mathrm{Shuf}^*(L) = \bigcup_{k\geq 1} \mathrm{Shuf}^k(L)$ where

$$\mathrm{Shuf}^1(L) = L \text{ and } \mathrm{Shuf}^k(L) = \mathrm{Shuf}(\mathrm{Shuf}^{k-1}(L), L), k \geq 2.$$

2.2 Grammars

A *phrase structure* (*Chomsky*) grammar is a quadruple $G = (V, \Sigma, S, R)$ where V and Σ are two disjoint alphabets of *nonterminal* and *terminal* symbols, respectively, $S \in V$ is the *start symbol* and $R \subseteq (V \cup \Sigma)^*V(V \cup \Sigma)^* \times (V \cup \Sigma)^*$ is a finite set of (*production*) *rules*. Usually, a rule $(u, v) \in R$ is written in the form $u \to v$. A rule of the form $u \to \lambda$ is called an *erasing rule*.

A phrase structure grammar $G = (V, \Sigma, S, R)$ is called a *GS grammar* (a phrase structure grammar due to Ginsburg and Spanier [31]) if $R \subseteq V^+ \times (V \cup \Sigma)^*$.

The families of languages generated by GS grammars and by phrase structure grammars are denoted by **GS** and **RE**, respectively. It is well-known that the family **GS** is equal to the family **RE**.

A string $x \in (V \cup \Sigma)^*$ *directly derives* a string $y \in (V \cup \Sigma)^*$ in G, written as $x \Rightarrow y$ if and only if there is a rule $u \to v \in R$ such that $x = x_1ux_2$ and $y = x_1vx_2$ for some $x_1, x_2 \in (V \cup \Sigma)^*$. The reflexive and transitive closure of the relation $\Rightarrow$ is denoted by $\Rightarrow^*$. A derivation using the sequence of rules $\pi = r_1r_2\cdots r_k$, $r_i \in R$, $1 \leq i \leq k$, is denoted by $\stackrel{\pi}{\Rightarrow}$ or $\xrightarrow{r_1r_2\cdots r_k}$. The *language* generated by G, denoted by $L(G)$, is defined by $L(G) = \{w \in \Sigma^* \mid S \Rightarrow^* w\}$.

A phrase-structure grammar $G = (V, \Sigma, S, R)$ is called *context-sensitive* if each rule $u \to v \in R$ has $u = u_1Au_2$, $v = u_1xu_2$ for $u_1, u_2 \in (V \cup \Sigma)^*$, $A \in V$ and $x \in (V \cup \Sigma)^+$ (in context sensitive grammars $S \to \lambda$ is allowed, provided that S does not appear in the right-hand members of rules in R); *context-free* if each rule $u \to v \in R$ has $u \in V$; *linear* if each rule $u \to v \in R$ has $u \in V$ and $v \in \Sigma^* \cup \Sigma^*V\Sigma^*$; *regular* if each rule $u \to v \in R$ has $u \in V$ and $v \in \Sigma \cup \Sigma V$.

The families of languages generated by context-sensitive, context-free, linear and regular grammars are denoted by **CS**, **CF**, **LIN** and **REG**, respectively. Further we denote the family of finite languages by **FIN**. The next strict inclusions, named *Chomsky hierarchy*, hold (for details, see [52]):

Theorem 1. **FIN** $\subset$ **REG** $\subset$ **LIN** $\subset$ **CF** $\subset$ **CS** $\subset$ **RE**.

2.3 Regulated grammars

The idea of regulated rewriting consists of restricting the application of the rules in a context-free grammar in order to avoid some derivations and hence obtaining a subset of the context-free language generated in usual way. The computational power of some context-free grammars with regulated rewriting turns out to be greater than the power of context-free grammars.

A *regularly controlled grammar* is a quintuple $G = (V, \Sigma, S, R, K)$ where V, Σ, S, R are specified as in a context-free grammar and K is a regular set over R. The language generated by G consists of all words $w \in \Sigma^*$ such that there is a derivation $S \xRightarrow{r_1 r_2 \cdots r_n} w$ where $r_1 r_2 \cdots r_n \in K$.

A *matrix grammar* is a quadruple $G = (V, \Sigma, S, M)$ where V, Σ, S are defined as for a context-free grammar, M is a finite set of *matrices* which are finite strings over a set R of context-free rules (or finite sequences of context-free rules). The language generated by the grammar G is $L(G) = \{w \in \Sigma^* \mid S \xRightarrow{\pi} w \text{ and } \pi \in M^*\}$.

A *vector grammar* is a quadruple $G = (V, \Sigma, S, M)$ whose components are defined as for a matrix grammar. The language generated by the grammar G is defined by

$$L(G) = \{w \in \Sigma^* \mid S \xRightarrow{\pi} w \text{ and } \pi \in \mathrm{Shuf}^*(M)\}.$$

An *additive valence grammar* is a quintuple $G = (V, \Sigma, S, R, v)$ where V, Σ, S, R are defined as for a context-free grammar and v is a mapping from R into $\mathbb{Z}$. The language generated by G consists of all strings $w \in \Sigma^*$ such that there is a derivation $S \xRightarrow{r_1 r_2 \cdots r_n} w$ where $\sum_{i=1}^{n} v(r_i) = 0$.

A *positive valence grammar* is a quintuple $G = (V, \Sigma, S, R, v)$ whose components are defined as for additive valence grammars. The language generated by G consists of all strings $w \in \Sigma^*$ such that there is a derivation $S \xRightarrow{r_1 r_2 \cdots r_n} w$ where $\sum_{i=1}^{n} v(r_i) = 0$ and for any $1 \leq j < n$, $\sum_{i=1}^{j} v(r_i) \geq 0$.

The families of languages generated by regularly controlled, matrix, vector, additive valence and positive valence grammars (with erasing rules) are denoted by **rC**, **MAT**, **VEC**, **aV**, **pV** ($\mathbf{rC}^\lambda$, $\mathbf{MAT}^\lambda$, $\mathbf{VEC}^\lambda$, $\mathbf{aV}^\lambda$, $\mathbf{pV}^\lambda$), respectively.

Theorem 2. *The following inclusions and equalities hold (for details, see [16]):*

$$(1)\ \mathbf{CF} \subset \mathbf{aV} = \mathbf{aV}^\lambda \subset \mathbf{MAT} = \mathbf{rC} = \mathbf{pV};$$
$$(2)\ \mathbf{MAT} \subseteq \mathbf{VEC} \subset \mathbf{CS};$$
$$(3)\ \mathbf{MAT} \subseteq \mathbf{MAT}^\lambda = \mathbf{rC}^\lambda = \mathbf{VEC}^\lambda = \mathbf{pV}^\lambda \subset \mathbf{RE}.$$

2.4 Petri nets

A *Petri net* (PN) is a construct $N = (P, T, F, \phi)$ where P and T are disjoint finite sets of *places* and *transitions*, respectively, $F \subseteq (P \times T) \cup (T \times P)$ is the set of *directed arcs*, $\phi : F \to \mathbb{N}$ is a *weight function*.

A Petri net can be represented by a bipartite directed graph with the node set $P \cup T$ where places are drawn as *circles*, transitions as *boxes* and arcs as *arrows*. The arrow representing an arc $(x, y) \in F$ is labeled with $\phi(x, y)$; if $\phi(x, y) = 1$, then the label is omitted.

An *ordinary net* (ON) is a Petri net $N = (P, T, F, \phi)$ where $\phi(x, y) = 1$ for all $(x, y) \in F$. We omit ϕ from the definition of an ordinary net, i.e., $N = (P, T, F)$.

A mapping $\mu : P \to \mathbb{N}_0$ is called a *marking*. For each place $p \in P$, $\mu(p)$ gives the number of *tokens* in p. Graphically, tokens are drawn as small solid *dots* inside circles. ${}^\bullet x = \{y \mid (y, x) \in F\}$ and $x^\bullet = \{y \mid (x, y) \in F\}$ are called *pre-* and *post-sets* of $x \in P \cup T$, respectively. For $t \in T$ ($p \in P$), the elements of ${}^\bullet t$ (${}^\bullet p$) are called *input* places (transitions) and the elements of $t^\bullet$ ($p^\bullet$) are called *output* places (transitions) of t (p).

A transition $t \in T$ is *enabled* by marking μ if and only if $\mu(p) \geq \phi(p, t)$ for all $p \in {}^\bullet t$. In this case t can *occur* (*fire*). Its occurrence transforms the marking μ into the marking μ' defined for each place $p \in P$ by $\mu'(p) = \mu(p) - \phi(p, t) + \phi(t, p)$. We write $\mu \xrightarrow{t} \mu'$ to indicate that the firing of t in μ leads to μ'. A marking μ is called *terminal* if in which no transition is enabled. A finite sequence $t_1 t_2 \cdots t_k$, $t_i \in T, 1 \leq i \leq k$, is called *an occurrence sequence* enabled at a marking μ and finished at a marking μ_k if there are markings $\mu_1, \mu_2, \ldots, \mu_{k-1}$ such that $\mu \xrightarrow{t_1} \mu_1 \xrightarrow{t_2} \ldots \xrightarrow{t_{k-1}} \mu_{k-1} \xrightarrow{t_k} \mu_k$. In short this sequence can be written as $\mu \xrightarrow{t_1 t_2 \cdots t_k} \mu_k$ or $\mu \xrightarrow{\nu} \mu_k$ where $\nu = t_1 t_2 \cdots t_k$. For each $1 \leq i \leq k$, marking μ_i is called *reachable* from marking μ. $\mathcal{R}(N, \mu)$ denotes the set of all reachable markings from a marking μ.

A *marked* Petri net is a system $N = (P, T, F, \phi, \iota)$ where (P, T, F, ϕ) is a Petri net, ι is the *initial marking*.

A Petri net *with final markings* is a construct $N = (P, T, F, \phi, \iota, M)$ where (P, T, F, ϕ, ι) is a marked Petri net and $M \subseteq \mathcal{R}(N, \iota)$ is set of markings which are called *final* markings. An occurrence sequence ν of transitions is called *successful* for M if it is enabled at the initial marking ι and finished at a final marking τ of M. If M is understood from the context, we say that ν is a successful occurrence sequence.

A Petri net N is said to be *k-bounded* if the number of tokens in each place does not exceed a finite number k for any marking reachable from the initial marking ι, i.e., $\mu(p) \leq k$ for all $p \in P$ and for all $\mu \in \mathcal{R}(N, \iota)$. A Petri net N is said to be *bounded* if it is k-bounded for some $k \geq 1$.

A Petri net with *place capacity* is a system $N = (P, T, F, \phi, \iota, \kappa)$ where (P, T, F, ϕ, ι) is a marked Petri net and $\kappa : P \to \mathbb{N}_0$ is a function assigning to each place a number of maximal admissible tokens. A marking μ of the net N is valid if $\mu(p) \leq \kappa(p)$, for each place $p \in P$. A transition $t \in T$ is *enabled* by a marking μ if additionally the successor marking is valid.

2.5 Special Petri nets

It is known that many decision problems are equivalent to the reachability problem [33], which has been shown to be decidable. However, it has exponential space complexity [40], thus from a practical point of view, Petri nets may be too powerful to be analyzed. The result of this has been the definition of a number of subclasses of Petri nets in order to find a subclass with a smaller complexity and still adequate modeling power for practical purposes. These subclasses are defined by restrictions on their structure intended to improve their analyzability. We consider the following main structural subclasses of Petri nets.

A *state machine* (SM) is an ordinary Petri net such that each transition has exactly one input place and exactly one output place, i.e., $|^{\bullet}t| = |t^{\bullet}| = 1$ for all $t \in T$. This means that there can not be concurrency but there can be conflict.

A *generalized state machine* (GSM) is an ordinary Petri net such that $|^{\bullet}t| \leq 1$ and $|t^{\bullet}| \leq 1$ for all $t \in T$.

A *marked graph* (MG) is an ordinary Petri net such that each place has exactly one input transition and exactly one output transition, i.e., $|^{\bullet}p| = |p^{\bullet}| = 1$ for all $p \in P$. This means that there can not be conflict but there can be concurrency.

A *generalized marked graph* (GMG) is an ordinary Petri net such that $|^{\bullet}p| \leq 1$ and $|p^{\bullet}| \leq 1$ for all $p \in P$.

A *casual net* (CN) is a generalized marked graph each subgraph of which is not a a cycle.

A *free-choice* net (FC) is an ordinary Petri net such every arc is either the only arc going from the place, or it is the only arc going to a transition, i.e., that if $p_1^{\bullet} \cap p_2^{\bullet} \neq \emptyset$ then $|p_1^{\bullet}| = |p_2^{\bullet}| = 1$ for all $p_1, p_2 \in P$. This means that there can be both concurrency and conflict but not the same time.

An *extended free-choice* net (EFC) is an ordinary Petri net such that if $p_1^{\bullet} \cap p_2^{\bullet} \neq \emptyset$ then $p_1^{\bullet} = p_2^{\bullet}$ for all $p_1, p_2 \in P$.

An *asymmetric choice net* (AC) is an ordinary Petri net such that if $p_1^{\bullet} \cap p_2^{\bullet} \neq \emptyset$ then $p_1^{\bullet} \subseteq p_2^{\bullet}$ or $p_1^{\bullet} \supseteq p_2^{\bullet}$ for all $p_1, p_2 \in P$. In asymmetric choice nets concurrency and conflict (in sum, confusion) may occur but not asymmetrically.

3. *k*-Petri net controlled grammars

Since a context-free grammar and its derivation process can also be described by a Petri net (see [11]), where places correspond to nonterminals, transitions are the counterpart of the production rules, and the tokens reflect the occurrences of symbols in the sentential form, and there is a one-to-one correspondence between the application of (sequence of) rules and the firing of (sequence of) transitions, it is a very natural and very easy idea to control the derivations in a context-free grammar by adding some features to the associated Petri net. In this section we introduce a Petri net associated with a context-free grammar (i.e., a *context-free Petri net*), construct Petri net control mechanisms from cf Petri nets by adding new places, and define the corresponding grammars, called *k-Petri net controlled grammars*.

The construction of the following type of Petri nets is based on the idea of using similarity between the firing of a transition and the application of a production rule in a derivation in which places are nonterminals and tokens are separate occurrences of nonterminals.

Definition 1. A *context-free Petri net* (in short, a *cf Petri net*) w.r.t. a context-free grammar $G = (V, \Sigma, S, R)$ is a septuple $N = (P, T, F, \phi, \beta, \gamma, \iota)$ where

- (P, T, F, ϕ) is a Petri net;
- labeling functions $\beta : P \to V$ and $\gamma : T \to R$ are bijections;
- there is an arc from place p to transition t if and only if $\gamma(t) = A \to \alpha$ and $\beta(p) = A$. The weight of the arc (p, t) is 1;

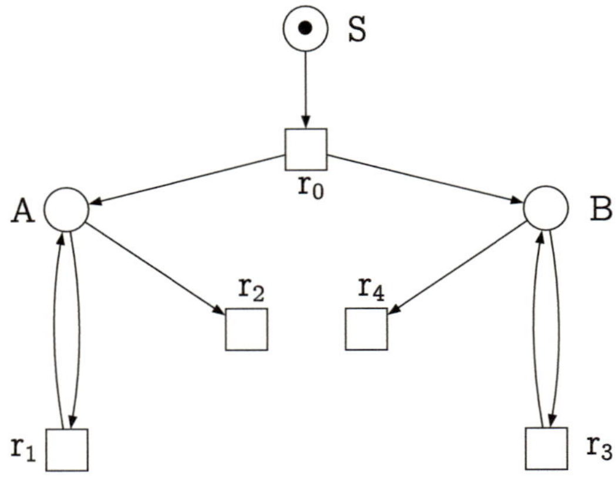

Figure 1. A cf Petri net N_1

- there is an arc from transition t to place p if and only if $\gamma(t) = A \to \alpha$ and $\beta(p) = x$ where $|\alpha|_x > 0$. The weight of the arc (t, p) is $|\alpha|_x$;
- the initial marking ι is defined by $\iota(\beta^{-1}(S)) = 1$ and $\iota(p) = 0$ for all $p \in P - \{\beta^{-1}(S)\}$.

Example 1. Let G_1 be a context-free grammar with the rules:

$$r_0 : S \to AB,\ r_1 : A \to aAb,\ r_2 : A \to ab,\ r_3 : B \to cB,\ r_4 : B \to c$$

(the other components of the grammar can be seen from these rules). Figure 1 illustrates a cf Petri net N_1 with respect to the grammar G_1. Obviously, $L(G_1) = \{a^n b^n c^m \mid n, m \geq 1\}$.

The following proposition shows the similarity between terminal derivations in a context-free grammar and successful occurrences of transitions in the corresponding cf Petri net.

Proposition 3. *Let $N = (P, T, F, \phi, \iota, \beta, \gamma)$ be the cf Petri net with respect to a context-free grammar $G = (V, \Sigma, S, R)$. Then $S \xrightarrow{r_1 r_2 \cdots r_n} w$, $w \in \Sigma^*$ is a derivation in G iff $t_1 t_2 \cdots t_n$, $\iota \xrightarrow{t_1 t_2 \cdots t_n} \mu_n$, is an occurrence sequence of transitions in N such that $\gamma(t_1 t_2 \cdots t_n) = r_1 r_2 \cdots r_n$ and $\mu_n(p) = 0$ for all $p \in P$.*

Now we define a *k-Petri net*, i.e., a cf Petri net with additional k places and additional arcs from/to these places to/from transitions of the net, the pre-sets and post-sets of the additional places are disjoint.

Definition 2. Let $G = (V, \Sigma, S, R)$ be a context-free grammar with its corresponding cf Petri net $N = (P, T, F, \phi, \beta, \gamma, \iota)$. Let k be a positive integer and let $Q = \{q_1, q_2, \ldots, q_k\}$ be a set of new places called *counters*. A *k-Petri net* is a construct $N_k = (P \cup Q, T, F \cup E, \varphi, \zeta, \gamma, \mu_0, \tau)$ where

- $E = \{(t, q_i) \mid t \in T_1^i, 1 \leq i \leq k\} \cup \{(q_i, t) \mid t \in T_2^i, 1 \leq i \leq k\}$ such that $T_1^i \subset T$ and $T_2^i \subset T$, $1 \leq i \leq k$ where $T_l^i \cap T_l^j = \emptyset$ for $1 \leq l \leq 2$, $T_1^i \cap T_2^j = \emptyset$ for $1 \leq i < j \leq k$ and $T_1^i = \emptyset$ if and only if $T_2^i = \emptyset$ for any $1 \leq i \leq k$.
- the weight function $\varphi(x, y)$ is defined by $\varphi(x, y) = \phi(x, y)$ if $(x, y) \in F$ and $\varphi(x, y) = 1$ if $(x, y) \in E$,

- the labeling function $\zeta : P \cup Q \to V \cup \{\lambda\}$ is defined by $\zeta(p) = \beta(p)$ if $p \in P$ and $\zeta(p) = \lambda$ if $p \in Q$,
- the initial marking μ_0 is defined by $\mu_0(\beta^{-1}(S)) = 1$ and $\mu_0(p) = 0$ for all $p \in P \cup Q - \{\beta^{-1}(S)\}$,
- τ is the final marking where $\tau(p) = 0$ for all $p \in P \cup Q$.

Definition 3. A *k-Petri net controlled grammar* (*k-PN controlled grammar* for short) is a quintuple $G = (V, \Sigma, S, R, N_k)$ where V, Σ, S, R are defined as for a context-free grammar and N_k is a k-PN with respect to the context-free grammar (V, Σ, S, R).

Definition 4. The *language* generated by a k-Petri net controlled grammar G consists of all strings $w \in \Sigma^*$ such that there is a derivation

$$S \xrightarrow{r_1 r_2 \cdots r_n} w \text{ where } t_1 t_2 \cdots t_n = \gamma^{-1}(r_1 r_2 \cdots r_n) \in T^*$$

is an occurrence sequence of the transitions of N_k enabled at the initial marking ι and finished at the final marking τ.

We denote the family of languages generated by k-PN controlled grammars (with erasing rules) by $\mathbf{PN}_k$ ($\mathbf{PN}_k^\lambda$), $k \geq 1$.

Example 2. Let G_2 be a 2-PN controlled grammar with the production rules:

$$\begin{array}{lll} r_0 : S \to A_1 B_1 A_2 B_2, & r_1 : A_1 \to a_1 A_1 b_1, & r_2 : A_1 \to a_1 b_1, \\ r_3 : B_1 \to c_1 B_1, & r_4 : B_1 \to c_1, & r_5 : A_2 \to a_2 A_2 b_2, \\ r_6 : A_2 \to a_2 b_2, & r_7 : B_2 \to c_2 B_2, & r_8 : B_2 \to c_2 \end{array}$$

and the corresponding 2-Petri net N_2 is given in Figure 2. Then it is easy to see that G_2 generates the language

$$L(G_2) = \{a_1^n b_1^n c_1^n a_2^m b_2^m c_2^m \mid n, m \geq 1\}.$$

Theorem 4. *The language*

$$L = \prod_{i=1}^{k+1} a_i^{n_i} b_i^{n_i} c_i^{n_i}$$

where $k \geq 1$ and $n_i \geq 1$, $1 \leq i \leq k+1$, cannot be generated by a k-PN controlled grammar.

The following theorem presents the relations of languages generated by k-Petri net controlled grammars to context-free, (positive) additive valence and vector languages.

Theorem 5.

$$\mathbf{CF} \subset \mathbf{PN}_1^{[\lambda]} \subseteq \mathbf{pV}^{[\lambda]}, \ \mathbf{aV}^{[\lambda]} \subset \mathbf{PN}_2^{[\lambda]} \ \textit{and} \ \mathbf{PN}_n^{[\lambda]} \subseteq \mathbf{VEC}^{[\lambda]}, n \geq 1.$$

The next theorem shows that the language families generated by k-Petri net controlled grammars form infinite hierarchy with respect to the numbers of additional places.

Theorem 6. *For* $k \geq 1$, $\mathbf{PN}_k^{[\lambda]} \subset \mathbf{PN}_{k-1}^{[\lambda]}$.

The closure properties of the language families generated by k-PN controlled grammars are given in the following theorem.

Theorem 7. *The family of languages* $\mathbf{PN}_k$, $k \geq 1$, *is closed under union, substitution, mirror image, intersection with regular languages and it is not closed under concatenation.*

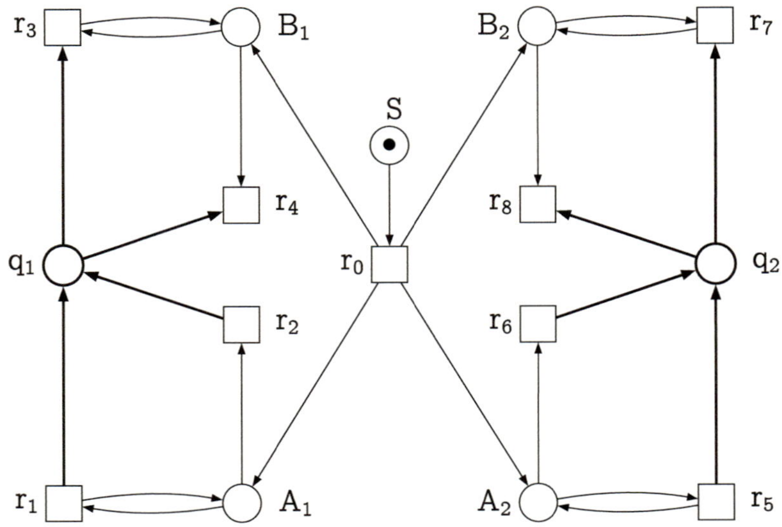

Figure 2. A 2-Petri net N_2

4. Arbitrary Petri net controlled grammars

In this section we consider a generalization of regularly controlled grammars: instead of a finite automaton we associate a Petri net with a context-free grammar and require that the sequence of applied rules corresponds to an occurrence sequence of the Petri net, i.e., to sequences of transitions which can be fired in succession. However, one has to decide what type of correspondence is used and what concept is taken as an equivalent of acceptance. Since the sets of occurrence sequences form the language of a Petri net, we choose the correspondence and the equivalent for acceptance according to the variations which are used in the theory of Petri net languages.

Therefore as correspondence we choose a bijection (between transitions and rules) or a coding (any transition is mapped to a rule) or a weak coding (any transition is mapped to a rule or the empty word) which agree with the classical three variants of Petri net languages (see e.g. [34, 57, 58]).

We consider two types of acceptance from the theory of Petri net languages: only those occurrence sequences belonging to the languages which transform the initial marking into a marking from a given finite set of markings or all occurrence sequences are taken (independent of the obtained marking). If we use only the occurrence sequence leading to a marking in a given finite set of markings we say that the Petri net controlled grammar is of *t*-type; if we consider all occurrence sequences, then the grammar is of *r*-type. We add a further type which can be considered as a complement of the *t*-type. Obviously, if we choose a finite set M of markings and require that the marking obtained after the application of the occurrence sequence is smaller than at least one marking of M (the order is componentwise), then we can choose another finite set M' of markings and require that the obtained marking belongs to M'. The complementary approach requires that the obtained marking is larger than at least one marking of the given set M. The corresponding class of Petri net controlled grammars is called of *g*-type. Therefore, we obtain nine classes of Petri net controlled grammars since we have three different types of correspondence and three types of the set of admitted occurrence sequences. These types of control are generalizations of those types of control considered in the previous chapter, too, where instead of arbitrary Petri nets only such Petri nets have been considered where the places and transitions correspond in a one-to-one manner to nonterminals and rules, respectively.

We now introduce the concept of control by an arbitrary Petri net.

Definition 5. An *arbitrary Petri net controlled grammar* is a tuple $G = (V, \Sigma, S, R, N, \gamma, M)$ where V, Σ, S, R are defined as for a context-free grammar and $N = (P, T, F, \varphi, \iota)$ is a (marked) Petri net, $\gamma : T \to R \cup \{\lambda\}$ is a transition labeling function and M is a set of final markings.

Definition 6. The *language* generated by a Petri net controlled grammar G, denoted by $L(G)$, consists of all strings $w \in \Sigma^*$ such that there is a derivation $S \xrightarrow{r_1 r_2 \cdots r_k} w \in \Sigma^*$ and an occurrence sequence $\nu = t_1 t_2 \cdots t_s$ which is successful for M such that $r_1 r_2 \cdots r_k = \gamma(t_1 t_2 \cdots t_s)$.

Example 3. Let $G_3 = (\{S, A, B, C\}, \{a, b, c\}, S, R, N_3, \gamma, M)$ be a Petri net controlled grammar where R consists of

$$S \to ABC,$$

$$A \to aA, \quad B \to bB, \quad C \to cC,$$

$$A \to a, \quad B \to b, \quad C \to c$$

and N_3 is illustrated in Figure 3. If M is the set of all reachable markings, then G_3 generates the language

$$L(G_3) = \{a^n b^m c^k \mid n \geq m \geq k \geq 1\}.$$

If $M = \{\mu\}$ with $\mu(p) = 0$ for all $p \in P$, then it generates the language

$$L(G_3) = \{a^n b^n c^n \mid n \geq 1\}.$$

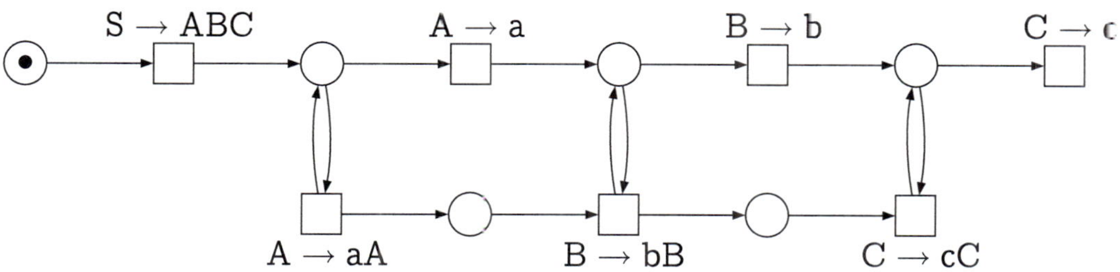

Figure 3. A labeled Petri net N_3

Different labeling strategies and different definitions of the set of final markings result in various types of Petri net controlled grammars. We consider the following types of Petri net controlled grammars.

Definition 7. A Petri net controlled grammar $G = (V, \Sigma, S, R, N, \gamma, M)$ is called *free* (abbreviated by f) if a different label is associated to each transition, and no transition is labeled with the empty string; λ-*free* (abbreviated by $-\lambda$) if no transition is labeled with the empty string; *extended* (abbreviated by λ) if no restriction is posed on the labeling function γ.

Definition 8. A Petri net controlled grammar $G = (V, \Sigma, S, R, N, \gamma, M)$ is called *r-type* if M is the set of all reachable markings from the initial marking ι, i.e., $M = \mathcal{R}(N, \iota)$; *t-type* if $M \subseteq \mathcal{R}(N, \iota)$ is a finite set; *g-type* if for a given finite set $M_0 \subseteq \mathcal{R}(N, \iota)$, M is the set of all markings such that for every marking $\mu \in M$ there is a marking $\mu' \in M_0$ such that $\mu \geq \mu'$.

We use the notation (x, y)*-PN controlled grammar* where $x \in \{f, -\lambda, \lambda\}$ shows the type of a labeling function and $y \in \{r, t, g\}$ shows the type of a set of final markings. We denote by $\mathbf{PN}(x, y)$ and $\mathbf{PN}^\lambda(x, y)$ the families of languages generated by (x, y)-PN controlled grammars without and with erasing rules, respectively, where $x \in \{f, -\lambda, \lambda\}$ and $y \in \{r, t, g\}$.

The following theorem shows that the labeling strategy does not effect on the generative capacity of arbitrary Petri net controlled grammars.

Theorem 8. *For* $y \in \{r, t, g\}$,

$$\mathbf{PN}^{[\lambda]}(f, y) = \mathbf{PN}^{[\lambda]}(-\lambda, y) = \mathbf{PN}^{[\lambda]}(\lambda, y).$$

Not surprisingly, arbitrary Petri net controlled grammars generate matrix languages. Moreover, in [65] it was proven that the erasing rules in arbitrary Petri net controlled grammars can be eliminated without effecting on the generative power of the grammars. If we take into consideration this result, we obtain the following inclusions and equalities:

Theorem 9. *For* $x \in \{f, -\lambda, \lambda\}$ *and* $y \in \{r, t, g\}$,

$$\mathbf{MAT} \subseteq \mathbf{PN}(x, r) = \mathbf{PN}(x, g) \subseteq \mathbf{PN}(x, t) = \mathbf{PN}^\lambda(x, y) = \mathbf{MAT}^\lambda.$$

5. Grammars controlled by special Petri nets

In the previous section we investigated arbitrary Petri net controlled grammars in dependence on the type of labeling functions and on the definitions of final markings, and showed that Petri net controlled grammars have the same power as some other regulating mechanisms such as matrices, finite automata. If we consider these matrices and finite automata in terms of control mechanisms, special types of matrices and special regular languages are widely investigated in literature, for instance, as control, simple matrices ([37]) or some subclasses of regular languages ([15, 17]) are considered. Thus, it is also natural to investigate grammars controlled by some special classes of Petri nets. We consider (generalized) state machines, (generalized) marked graphs, causal nets, (extended) free-choice nets, asymmetric choice nets and ordinary nets. Similarly to the general case we also investigate the effects of labeling policies and final markings to the computational power, and prove that the family of languages generated by (arbitrary) Petri net controlled grammars coincide with the family of languages generated by grammars controlled by free-choice nets.

Let $G = (V, \Sigma, S, R, N, \gamma, M)$ be an arbitrary Petri net controlled grammar. The grammar G is called a (generalized) state machine, (generalized) marked graph, causal net, (extended) free-choice net, asymmetric choice net or ordinary net controlled grammar if the net N is a (generalized) state machine, (generalized) marked graph, causal net, (extended) free-choice net, asymmetric choice net or ordinary net, respectively.

We also use a notation an (x,y)-(generalized) state machine, ((generalized) marked graph, causal net, (extended) free-choice net, asymmetric choice net and ordinary net) controlled grammar where $x \in \{f, -\lambda, \lambda\}$ shows the type of a labeling function γ and $y \in \{r,t,g\}$ shows the type of a set of final markings.

We denote the families of languages generated by grammars controlled by state machines, generalized state machines, marked graphs, generalize marked graphs, causal nets, free-choice nets, extended free-choice nets, asymmetric nets, ordinary nets and Petri nets

$$\mathbf{SM}^{[\lambda]}(x,y),\ \mathbf{GSM}^{[\lambda]}(x,y),\ \mathbf{MG}^{[\lambda]}(x,y),\ \mathbf{GMG}^{[\lambda]}(x,y),\ \mathbf{CN}^{[\lambda]}(x,y),$$
$$\mathbf{FC}^{[\lambda]}(x,y),\ \ \mathbf{EFC}^{[\lambda]}(x,y),\ \ \mathbf{AC}^{[\lambda]}(x,y),\ \ \mathbf{ON}^{[\lambda]}(x,y),\ \ \ \mathbf{PN}^{[\lambda]}(x,y)$$

where $x \in \{f, -\lambda, \lambda\}$ and $y \in \{r,t,g\}$.

The inclusion $\mathbf{X}(x,y) \subseteq \mathbf{X}^{\lambda}(x,y)$ immediately follows from the definition where

- $\mathbf{X} \in \{\mathbf{SM}, \mathbf{GSM}, \mathbf{MG}, \mathbf{GMG}, \mathbf{CN}, \mathbf{FC}, \mathbf{EFC}, \mathbf{AC}, \mathbf{ON}\}$,
- $x \in \{f, -\lambda, \lambda\}$ and $y \in \{r,t,g\}$.

Example 4. Let $G_4 = (\{S,A,B\}, \{a,b\}, S, R, N_4, \gamma, M)$ be a SM controlled grammar where R consists of

$$S \to AB,$$
$$A \to aA, \quad A \to bA, \quad A \to \lambda,$$
$$B \to aB, \quad B \to bB, \quad B \to \lambda,$$

the Petri net N_4 illustrated in Figure 4 is a labeled state machine and $M = \{\mu\}$ where $\mu(p_0) = 1$ and $\mu(p) = 0$ for all $p \in P - \{p_0\}$, then

$$L(G_4) = \{ww \quad w \in \{a,b\}^*\} \in \mathbf{SM}^{\lambda}(\lambda, t).$$

Example 5. Let $G_5 = (\{S,A,B\}, \{a,b\}, S, R, N_5, \gamma', M')$ be a MG controlled grammar where R is as for the grammar G_1 in Example 4, a labeled marked graph N_5 is illustrated in Figure 5 and $M' = \{\mu\}$ where $\mu(p) = 0$ for all $p \in P$. Then

$$L(G_5) = \{ww' \mid w \in \{a,b\}^* \text{ and } w' \in \mathrm{Perm}(w)\} \in \mathbf{MG}^{\lambda}(\lambda, t).$$

We have the same result on the labeling strategies as that in the previous section: the labeling of transitions of special Petri nets do not effect on the generative powers of the families of languages generated by grammars controlled by these nets.

Theorem 10. *For* $\mathbf{X} \in \{\mathbf{SM}, \mathbf{GSM}, \mathbf{MG}, \mathbf{GMG}, \mathbf{CN}, \mathbf{FC}, \mathbf{EFC}, \mathbf{AC}, \mathbf{ON}\}$, *and* $y \in \{r,t,g\}$.

$$\mathbf{X}^{[\lambda]}(f,y) = \mathbf{X}^{[\lambda]}(-\lambda,y) = \mathbf{X}^{[\lambda]}(\lambda,y).$$

The following theorem shows the relations of families of languages generated by special Petri net controlled grammars.

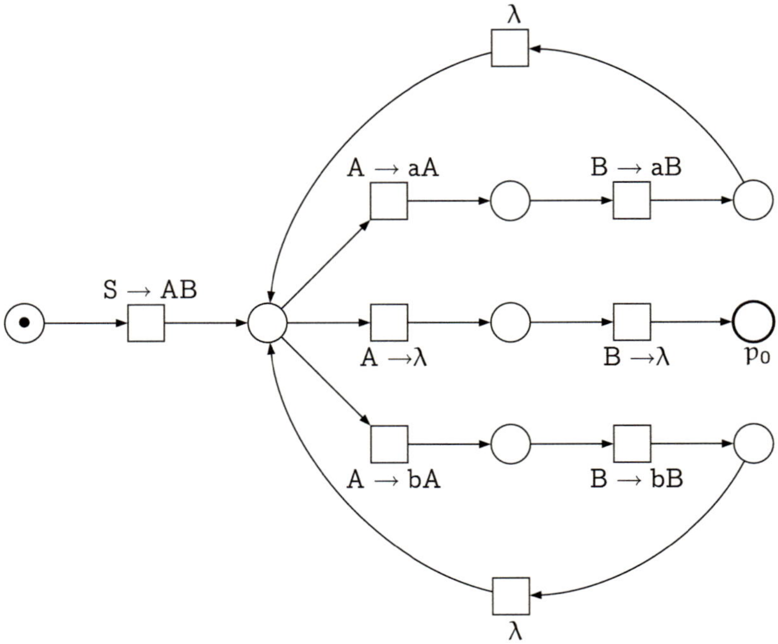

Figure 4. A labeled state machine N_4

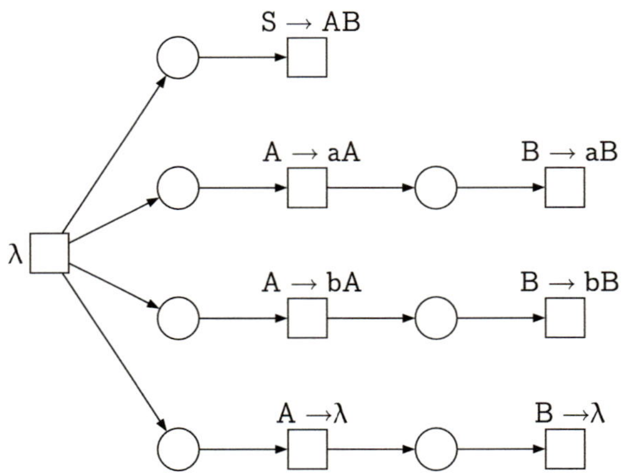

Figure 5. A labeled marked graph N_5

Theorem 11. *The following inclusions and equalities hold:*

$$(1)\ \mathbf{MG}^{[\lambda]}(x,y) = \mathbf{GMG}^{[\lambda]}(x,y) \ \textit{and}\ \mathbf{PN}(x,y') = \mathbf{X}(x,y'),$$

$$(2)\ \mathbf{CN}(x,y') \subseteq \mathbf{MG}(x,y') \subseteq \mathbf{PN}(x,y') \subseteq \mathbf{MAT}^{\lambda},$$

$$(3)\ \mathbf{MAT} \subseteq \mathbf{GSM}(x,y') \subseteq \mathbf{PN}(x,y') \subseteq \mathbf{MAT}^{\lambda},$$

$$(4)\ \mathbf{CF} \subset \mathbf{MAT} = \mathbf{SM}(x,y) \subseteq \mathbf{VEC} \subseteq \begin{cases} \mathbf{GSM}(x,t) \\ \mathbf{CN}(x,t) \subseteq \mathbf{MG}(x,t) \end{cases} \subseteq \mathbf{MAT}^{\lambda},$$

$$(5)\ \mathbf{MAT}^{\lambda} = \mathbf{PN}^{\lambda}(x,y) = \mathbf{PN}(x,t) = \mathbf{X}^{\lambda}(x,t) = \mathbf{Y}^{\lambda}(x,t) = \mathbf{Z}^{\lambda}(x,y),$$

where $x \in \{f,-\lambda,\lambda\}$, $y \in \{r,g,t\}$, $y' \in \{r,g\}$ *and* $\mathbf{X} \in \{\mathbf{FC},\mathbf{EFC},\mathbf{AC},\mathbf{ON}\}$, $\mathbf{Y} \in \{\mathbf{MG},\mathbf{GMG},\mathbf{CN}\}$, $\mathbf{Z} \in \{\mathbf{SM},\mathbf{GSM},\mathbf{FC},\mathbf{EFC},\mathbf{AC},\mathbf{ON}\}$.

6. Capacity-bounded grammars

In this section we continue the research in this direction by restricting to (context-free, extended or arbitrary) Petri nets with place capacities. Quite obviously, a context-free Petri net with place capacity regulates the defining grammar by permitting only those derivations where the number of each nonterminal in each sentential form is bounded by its capacity. Similar mechanisms have been introduced and investigated by several authors. Grammar with *finite index* (the index of a grammar is the maximal number of nonterminals simultaneously appearing in its complete derivations (considering the most economical derivations for each string)) were first considered by Brainerd [7]. *Nonterminal-bounded* grammars (a grammar a nonterminal-bounded if the total number of nonterminals in every sentential form does not exceed an upper bound) were introduced by Altman and Banerji in [3–5]. A "weak" variant of nonterminal-bounded grammars (only the complete derivations are required to be bounded) were defined by Moriya [44]. Ginsburg and Spanier introduced *derivation-bounded* languages in [32] (all strings which have complete derivation in a grammar G consisting of sentential forms each of which does not contain more than k nonterminals collected in the set $L_k(G)$). There it was shown that grammars regulated in this way generate the family of context-free languages of finite index, even if arbitrary nonterminal strings are allowed as left-hand sides of production rules. Finite index restrictions to regulated grammars have also been investigated [29, 30, 48, 49, 51, 53–55]. There it was shown that the families of most regulated languages are collapse.

In this section we show that capacity-bounded context-free grammars have a larger generative power than context-free grammars of finite index while the family of languages generated by capacity-bounded phrase structure grammars (due to Ginsburg and Spanier) and several families of languages generated by grammars controlled by extended cf Petri nets with place capacities coincide with the family of matrix languages of finite index.

We will now introduce capacity-bounded grammars and show some relations to similar concepts known from the literature.

Definition 9. A *capacity-bounded* grammar is a tuple $G = (V,\Sigma,S,R,\kappa)$ where $G' = (V,\Sigma,S,R)$ is a grammar and $\kappa : V \to \mathbb{N}$ is a capacity function. The derivation relation $\Rightarrow_G$ is defined as $\alpha \Rightarrow_G \beta$ iff $\alpha \Rightarrow_{G'} \beta$ and $|\alpha|_A \leq \kappa(A)$ and $|\beta|_A \leq \kappa(A)$, for all $A \in V$. The language of G is defined as $L(G) = \{w \in \Sigma^* \mid S \Rightarrow_G^* w\}$.

The families of languages generated by capacity-bounded GS grammars and by context-free capacity-bounded grammars are denoted by $\mathbf{GS}_{cb}$ and $\mathbf{CF}_{cb}$, respectively. The capacity function mapping each nonterminal to 1 is denoted by **1**. The notions of finite index and bounded capacities can be extended to matrix, vector and semi-matrix grammars. The corresponding language families are denoted by

$$\mathbf{MAT}_{fin}^{[\lambda]},\ \mathbf{VEC}_{fin}^{[\lambda]},\ \mathbf{sMAT}_{fin}^{[\lambda]},\ \mathbf{MAT}_{cb}^{[\lambda]},\ \mathbf{VEC}_{cb}^{[\lambda]}.$$

Capacity-bounded grammars are very similar to derivation-bounded grammars, which were studied in [32]. A *derivation-bounded* grammar is a quintuple $G = (V, \Sigma, S, R, k)$ where $G' = (V, \Sigma, S, R)$ is a grammar and $k \in \mathbb{N}$ is a bound on the number of allowed nonterminals. The language of G contains all words $w \in L(G')$ that have a derivation $S \Rightarrow^* w$ such that $|\beta|_V \leq k$, for each sentential form β of the derivation.

Other related concepts are nonterminal-bounded grammars and grammars of finite index. A context-free grammar $G = (V, \Sigma, S, R)$ is *nonterminal-bounded* if $|\beta|_V \leq k$ for some fixed $k \in \mathbb{N}$ and all sentential forms β derivable in G. The *index* of a derivation in G is the maximal number of nonterminal symbols in its sentential forms. G is of *finite index* if every word in $L(G)$ has a derivation of index at most k for some fixed $k \in \mathbb{N}$. The family of context-free languages of finite index is denoted by $\mathbf{CF}_{fin}$.

Note that there is a subtle difference between the first two and the last two concepts. While context-free nonterminal-bounded and finite index grammars are just context-free grammars with a certain structural property (and generate context-free languages by definition), capacity-bounded and derivation-bounded grammars are special cases of *regulated rewriting* (and could therefore generate non-context-free languages). However, it has been shown that the family of derivation bounded languages is equal to $\mathbf{CF}_{fin}$, even if arbitrary grammars due to Ginsburg and Spanier are permitted [32]. We will now give an example of capacity-bounded grammars generating non-context-free languages.

Example 6. Let $G = (\{S, A, B, C, D, E, F\}, \{a, b, c\}, S, R, \mathbf{1})$ be the capacity-bounded grammar where R consists of the rules:

$$\begin{array}{llll} r_1 : S \to ABCD, & r_2 : AB \to aEFb, & r_3 : CD \to cAD, & r_4 : EF \to EC, \\ r_5 : EF \to FC, & r_6 : AD \to FD, & r_7 : AD \to ED, & r_8 : EC \to AB, \\ r_9 : FD \to CD, & r_{10} : FC \to AF, & r_{11} : AF \to \lambda, & r_{12} : ED \to \lambda. \end{array}$$

The possible derivations are exactly those of the form

$$\begin{aligned} S &\xRightarrow{r_1} ABCD \\ &\xRightarrow{(r_2 r_3 r_4 r_6 r_8 r_9)^n} a^n ABb^n c^n CD \\ &\xRightarrow{r_2 r_3} a^{n+1} EFb^{n+1} c^{n+1} AD \\ &\xRightarrow{r_5 r_7} a^{n+1} FCb^{n+1} c^{n+1} ED \\ &\xRightarrow{r_{10} r_{11} r_{12}} a^n b^n c^n \end{aligned}$$

(in the last phase, the sequences $r_{10} r_{12} r_{11}$ and $r_{12} r_{10} r_{11}$ could also be applied with the same result). Therefore,

$$L(G) = \{a^n b^n c^n \mid n \geq 1\}.$$

The above example shows that capacity-bounded grammars – in contrast to derivation bounded grammars – can generate non-context-free languages. Moreover, any context-free language generated by a grammar of G of finite index is also generated by the capacity-bounded grammar (G, κ) where κ is capacity function constantly k.

Let $\mathbf{CF}^1_{cb}$ and $\mathbf{GS}^1_{cb}$ be the language families generated by context-free and arbitrary grammars with capacity function $\mathbf{1}$. Then,

Lemma 12. $\mathbf{CF}_{cb} = \mathbf{CF}^1_{cb}$ *and* $\mathbf{GS}_{cb} = \mathbf{GS}^1_{cb}$.

On the other hand, capacity-bounded GS grammars generate exactly the family of matrix languages of finite index. This is in contrast to derivation bounded grammars which generate only context-free languages of finite index [32].

Lemma 13. $\mathbf{GS}_{cb} = \mathbf{MAT}_{fin}$.

It turns out that capacity-bounded context-free grammars are strictly between context-free languages of finite index and matrix languages of finite index.

Theorem 14. $\mathbf{CF}_{fin} \subset \mathbf{CF}_{cb} \subset \mathbf{GS}_{cb} = \mathbf{MAT}_{fin}$.

The next theorem shows that the families of capacity bounded matrix and vector languages are exactly the family of matrix languages with finite index.

Theorem 15. $\mathbf{MAT}_{fin} = \mathbf{VEC}^{[\lambda]}_{cb} = \mathbf{MAT}^{[\lambda]}_{cb}$.

As regards closure properties, we remark that the constructions showing the closure of **CF** under homomorphisms, union, concatenation and Kleene closure can be easily extended to the case of capacity-bounded languages.

Theorem 16. $\mathbf{CF}_{cb}$ *is closed under homomorphisms, union, concatenation and Kleene closure.*

Regarding intersection with regular sets and inverse homomorphisms, we can show non-closure properties.

Theorem 17. $\mathbf{CF}_{cb}$ *is neither closed under intersection with regular sets nor under inverse homomorphisms.*

Control by Petri nets can in a natural way be adapted to Petri nets with place capacities. A context-free grammar is controlled by its context-free Petri net with place capacity by only allowing derivations that correspond to valid firing sequences respecting the capacity bounds. The (trivial) proof for the equivalence between context-free grammars and grammars controlled by cf Petri nets can be immediately transferred to context-free grammars and Petri nets with capacities:

Theorem 18. *Grammars controlled by context-free Petri nets with place capacity functions generate the family of capacity-bounded context-free languages.*

Let us now turn to grammars controlled by arbitrary Petri nets with capacities. Let $G = (V, \Sigma, S, R, N, \gamma, M)$ be an arbitrary Petri net controlled grammar. G is called a grammar controlled by an arbitrary Petri net with place capacity if N is a Petri net with place capacity. The families of languages generated by grammars controlled by arbitrary Petri nets with place capacities (with erasing rules) is denoted by $\mathbf{PN}_{cb}(x, y)$ ($\mathbf{PN}^{\lambda}_{cb}(x, y)$) where $x \in \{f, -\lambda, \lambda\}$ and $y \in \{r, t, g\}$.

The next statement indicates that the language generated by a grammar controlled by an arbitrary Petri net with place capacities iff it is generated by a matrix grammar (for details, see [56]).

Theorem 19. *For $x \in \{f, -\lambda, \lambda\}$ and $y \in \{r, t, g\}$,*

$$\mathbf{PN}_{cb}(x, y) = \mathbf{MAT} \subseteq \mathbf{PN}^{\lambda}_{cb}(x, y) = \mathbf{MAT}^{\lambda}.$$

We summarize our results in the following theorem.

Theorem 20. *The following inclusions and equalities hold:*

$$\begin{aligned} \mathbf{CF}_{fin} \subset \mathbf{CF}_{cb} &= \mathbf{CF}^{1}_{cb} \\ &\subset \mathbf{MAT}_{fin} = \mathbf{MAT}^{[\lambda]}_{cb} = \mathbf{VEC}^{[\lambda]}_{cb} = \mathbf{GS}_{cb} = \mathbf{GS}^{1}_{cb} \\ &\subset \mathbf{MAT} = \mathbf{PN}_{cb}(x, y) \subseteq \mathbf{MAT}^{\lambda} = \mathbf{PN}^{\lambda}_{cb}(x, y) \end{aligned}$$

where $x \in \{f, -\lambda, \lambda\}$ and $y \in \{r, t, g\}$.

7. Conclusions and future research

The chapter summarizes the recent results on Petri net controlled grammars presented in [18–23, 56, 59–62] and the close related topic: capacity-bounded grammars. Though the theme of regulated grammars is one of the classic topics in formal language theory, a Petri net controlled grammar is still interesting subject for the investigation for many reasons. On the one hand, this type of grammars can successfully be used in modeling new problems emerging in manufacturing systems, systems biology and other areas. On the other hand, the graphically illustrability, the ability to represent both a grammar and its control in one structure, and the possibility to unify different regulated rewritings make this formalization attractive for the study. Moreover, control by Petri nets introduces the concept of *concurrency* in regulated rewriting systems.

We should mention that there are some open problems, the study of which is of interest: one of them concerns to the classic open problem of the theory of regulated rewriting systems – the strictness of the inclusion $\mathbf{MAT} \subseteq \mathbf{MAT}^{\lambda}$. We showed that language families generated by (arbitrary) Petri net controlled grammars are between the families $\mathbf{MAT}$ and $\mathbf{MAT}^{\lambda}$. Moreover, the work [65] of G. Zetzsche shows that the erasing rules in Petri net controlled grammars with finite set of final markings can be eliminated without effecting on the generative power, which gives hope that one can solve this problem.

There is also another very interesting topic in this direction for the future study. If we notice the definitions of derivation-bounded [32] or nonterminal-bounded grammars [3–5] only nonterminal strings are allowed as left-hand sides of production rules. Here, an interesting question is emerged, what kind of languages can be generated if we derestrict this condition, i.e., allow any string in the left-hand side of the rules?

In all investigated types of Petri net controlled grammars, we only used the sequential firing mode of transitions. The consideration of simultaneous firing of transitions, another fundamental feature of Petri nets, opens a new direction for the future research: one can study *grammars controlled by Petri nets under parallel firing strategy*, which introduces concurrently parallelism in formal language theory.

Grammar systems can be considered as a formal model for a phenomenon of solving a given problem by dividing it into subproblems (grammars) to be solved by several parts in turn (CD grammar systems) or in parallel (PC grammar systems). The control of derivations in grammar systems also allows increasing computational power grammar systems. We can extend the regulation of a rule by a transition to the regulation a set of rules by a transition, which defines a new type of grammar systems: the firing of a transition allows applying several (assigned) rules in a derivation step parallelly and different modes.

In [19–22, 41, 62] it was shown that by adding places and arcs which satisfy some structural requirements one can generate well-known families of languages as random context languages, valence languages, vector languages and matrix languages. Thus, the control by Petri nets can be considered as a unifying approach to different types of control. On the other hand, Petri nets can be transformed into *occurrence nets*, i.e., usually an infinite, tree-like structure whose nodes have the same labels as those of the places and transitions of the Petri net preserving the relationship of adjacency, using *unfolding technique* introduced in [43] and given in [24] in detail under the name of *branching processes*. Any *finite initial* part, i.e., *prefix* of the occurrence net of a cf Petri net can be considered as a derivation tree for the corresponding context-free grammar as it has the same structure as a usual derivation tree, here we can also accept the rule of reading "leaf"-places with tokens from the left to the right as in usual derivation trees. We can also generalize this idea for regulated grammars considering prefixes of the occurrences nets obtained from cf Petri nets with additional places. Hence, we can take into consideration the grammar as well as its control, and construct (Petri net) derivation trees for regulated grammars, which help to construct effective parsing algorithms for regulated rewriting systems. Though the preliminary results (general parsing algorithms, Early-like parsing algorithm for deterministic extended context-free Petri net controlled grammars, etc.) were obtained in [63, 64], the problem of the development of the effective parsing algorithms for regulated grammars remain open.

Acknowledgements

This work has been supported by Ministry of Higher Education of Malaysia via Fundamental Research Grant Scheme FRGS /1/11/SG/UPM/01/1 and Universiti Putra Malaysia via RUGS 05-01-10-0896RU/F1.

Author details

Jürgen Dassow and Ralf Stiebe
Fakultät für Informatik, Otto-von-Guericke-Universität Magdeburg, Magdeburg, Germany

Gairatzhan Mavlankulov, Mohamed Othman, Mohd Hasan Selamat and Sherzod Turaev
Faculty of Computer Science and Information Technology, Universiti Putra Malaysia, UPM Serdang, Selangor, Malaysia

8. References

[1] Abraham, A. [1965]. Some questions of phrase-structure grammars, *Comput. Linguistics* 4: 61–70.

[2] Al-A'ali, M., Khan, A. & Al-Shamlan, N. [1996]. Simplification of context-free grammar through Petri net, *Computers and Structures* 58: 1055–1058.

[3] Altman, E. [1964]. The concept of finite representability, *Systems Research Center Report SRC 56-A-64-20*, Case Institute of Technology.

[4] Altman, E. & Banerji, R. [1965]. Some problems of finite representability, *Information and Control* 8: 251–263.

[5] Banerji, R. [1963]. Phrase structure languages, finite machines, and channel capacity, *Information and Control* 6: 153–162.

[6] Beek, M. t. & Kleijn, H. [2002]. Petri net control for grammar systems, *Formal and Natural Computing*, Vol. 2300 of *LNCS*, Springer, pp. 220–243.

[7] Brainerd, B. [1968]. An analog of a theorem about context-free languages, *Information and Control* 11: 561–567.

[8] Chomsky, N. [1956]. Three models for the description of languages, *IRE Trans. on Information Theory* 2(3): 113–124.

[9] Chomsky, N. [1957]. *Syntactic structure*, Mouton, Gravenhage.

[10] Chomsky, N. [1959]. On certain formal properties of grammars, *Information and Control* 2: 137–167.

[11] Crespi-Reghizzi, S. & Mandrioli, D. [1974]. Petri nets and commutative grammars, *Internal Report 74-5*, Laboraterio di Calcolatori, Instituto di Elettrotecnica ed Elettromca del Politecnico di Milano, Italy.

[12] Crespi-Reghizzi, S. & Mandrioli, D. [1975]. Properties of firing sequences, *Proc. MIT Conf. Petri Nets and Related Methods*, MIT, Cambridge, Mass., pp. 233–240.

[13] Crespi-Reghizzi, S. & Mandrioli, D. [1977]. Petri nets and Szilard languages, *Inform. and Control* 33: 177–192.

[14] Darondeau, P. [2001]. On the Petri net realization of context-free graphs, *Theor. Computer Sci.* 258: 573–598.

[15] Dassow, J. [1988]. Subregularly controlled derivations: Context-free case, *Rostock. Math. Kolloq.* 34: 61–70.

[16] Dassow, J. & Păun, G. [1989]. *Regulated rewriting in formal language theory*, Springer-Verlag, Berlin.

[17] Dassow, J. & Truthe, B. [2008]. Subregularly tree controlled grammars and languages, *in* E. Csuhaj-Varjú & Z. Esik (eds), *Proc. the 12th International Conference AFL 2008*, Balatonfured, Hungary, pp. 158–169.

[18] Dassow, J. & Turaev, S. [2008a]. Arbitrary Petri net controlled grammars, *in* G. Bel-Enguix & M. Jiménez-López (eds), *Linguistics and Formal Languages. Second International Workshop on Non-Classical Formal Languages In Linguistics, Tarragona, Spain*, pp. 27–39. ISBN 978-84-612-6451-3.

[19] Dassow, J. & Turaev, S. [2008b]. *k*-Petri net controlled grammars, *in* C. Martín-Vide, F. Otto & H. Fernau (eds), *Language and Automata Theory and Applications. Second*

International Conference, LATA 2008. Revised Papers*, Vol. 5196 of *LNCS*, Springer, pp. 209–220.

[20] Dassow, J. & Turaev, S. [2009a]. Grammars controlled by special Petri nets, *in* A. Dediu, A.-M. Ionescu & C. Martín-Vide (eds), *Language and Automata Theory and Applications, Third International Conference, LATA 2009*, Vol. 5457 of *LNCS*, Springer, pp. 326–337.

[21] Dassow, J. & Turaev, S. [2009b]. Petri net controlled grammars: the case of special Petri nets, *Journal of Universal Computer Science* 15(14): 2808–2835.

[22] Dassow, J. & Turaev, S. [2009c]. Petri net controlled grammars: the power of labeling and final markings, *Romanian Jour. of Information Science and Technology* 12(2): 191–207.

[23] Dassow, J. & Turaev, S. [2010]. Petri net controlled grammars with a bounded number of additional places, *Acta Cybernetica* 19: 609–634.

[24] Engelfriet, J. [1991]. Branching processes of petri nets, *Acta Informatica* 28: 575–591.

[25] Erqing, X. [2004]. A Pr/T-Net model for context-free language parsing, *Fifth World Congress on Intelligent Control and Automation*, Vol. 3, pp. 1919–1922.

[26] Farwer, B., Jantzen, M., Kudlek, M., Rölke, H. & Zetzsche, G. [2008]. Petri net controlled finite automata, *Fundamenta Informaticae* 85(1-4): 111–121.

[27] Farwer, B., Kudlek, M. & Rölke, H. [2006]. Petri-net-controlled machine models, *Technical Report 274*, FBI-Bericht, Hamburg.

[28] Farwer, B., Kudlek, M. & Rölke, H. [2007]. Concurrent Turing machines, *Fundamenta Informaticae* 79(3-4): 303–317.

[29] Fernau, H. & Holzer, M. [1997]. Conditional context-free languages of finite index, *New Trends in Formal Languages – Control, Cooperation, and Combinatorics (to Jürgen Dassow on the occasion of his 50th birthday)*, Vol. 1218 of *LNCS*, pp. 10–26.

[30] Fernau, H. & Holzer, M. [2008]. Regulated finite index language families collapse, *Technical Report WSI-96-16*, Universität Türbingen, Wilhelm-Schickard-Institut für Informatik.

[31] Ginsburg, S. & Spanier, E. [1968a]. Contol sets on grammars, *Math. Syst. Th.* 2: 159–177.

[32] Ginsburg, S. & Spanier, E. [1968b]. Derivation bounded languages, *J. Comput. Syst. Sci.* 2: 228–250.

[33] Hack, M. [1975a]. *Decidablity questions for Petri nets*, PhD thesis, Dept. of Electrical Engineering, MIT.

[34] Hack, M. [1975b]. Petri net languages, *Computation Structures Group Memo, Project MAC 124*, MIT, Cambridge Mass.

[35] Hauschildt, D. & Jantzen, M. [1994]. Petri nets algorithms in the theory of matrix grammars, *Acta Informatica* 31: 719–728.

[36] Hopcroft, J. & Ullman, J. [1990]. *Introduction to automata theory, languages, and computation*, Addison-Wesley Longman Publishing Co., Inc.

[37] Ibarra, O. [1970]. Simple matrix grammars, *Inform. Control* 17: 359–394.

[38] Jantzen, M., Kudlek, M. & Zetzsche, G. [2008]. Language classes defined by concurrent finite automata, *Fundamenta Informaticae* 85(1-4): 267–280.

[39] Jiang, C. [1996]. Vector grammar and PN machine, *Sci. Chin. (Ser. A)* 24: 1315–1322.

[40] Liptop, R. [1976]. The reachability problem requires espcnential space, *Technical Report 62*, Yale University.

[41] Marek, V. & Češka, M. [2001]. Petri nets and random-context grammars, *Proc. of the 35th Spring Conference: Modelling and Simulation of Systems*, MARQ Ostrava, Hardec nad Moravicí, pp. 145–152.

[42] Martín-Vide, C., Mitrana, V. & Păun, G. (eds) [2004]. *Formal languages and applications*, Springer-Verlag, Berlin.

[43] McMillan, K. [1995]. A technique of a state space search based on unfolding, *Formal Methods in System Design* 6(1): 45–65.
[44] Moriya, E. [1973]. Associate languages and derivational complexity of formal grammars and languages, *Information and Control* 22: 139–162.
[45] Murata, T. [1989]. Petri nets: Properties, analysis and applications, *Proceedings of the IEEE* 77(4): 541–580.
[46] Peterson, J. [1976]. Computation sequence sets, *J. Computer and System Sciences* 13: 1–24.
[47] Peterson, J. [1981]. *Petri net theory and modeling of systems*, Prentice-Hall, Englewood Cliffs, NJ.
[48] Păun, G. [1977]. On the index of grammars and languages, *Inf. Contr.* 35: 259–266.
[49] Păun, G. [1979]. On the family of finite index matrix languages, *JCSS* 18(3): 267–280.
[50] Reisig, W. & Rozenberg, G. (eds) [1998]. *Lectures on Petri Nets I: Basic Models*, Vol. 1491 of *LNCS*, Springer, Berlin.
[51] Rozenberg, G. [1976]. More on ET0L systems versus random context grammars, *IPL* 5(4): 102–106.
[52] Rozenberg, G. & Salomaa, A. (eds) [1997]. *Handbook of formal languages*, Vol. 1–3, Springer.
[53] Rozenberg, G. & Vermeir, D. [1978a]. On ET0L systems of finite index, *Inf. Contr.* 38: 103–133.
[54] Rozenberg, G. & Vermeir, D. [1978b]. On the effect of the finite index restriction on several families of grammars, *Inf. Contr.* 39: 284–302.
[55] Rozenberg, G. & Vermeir, D. [1978c]. On the effect of the finite index restriction on several families of grammars; Part 2: context dependent systems and grammars, *Foundations of Control Engineering* 3(3): 126–142.
[56] Selamat, M. & Turaev, S. [2010]. Grammars controlled by petri nets with place capacities, *2010 International Conference on Computer Research and Development*, pp. 51–55.
[57] Starke, P. [1978]. Free Petri net languages, *Mathematical Foundations of Computer Science 1978*, Vol. 64 of *LNCS*, Springer, Berlin, pp. 506–515.
[58] Starke, P. [1980]. *Petri-Netze*, Deutscher Verlag der Wissenschaften.
[59] Stiebe, R. & Turaev, S. [2009a]. Capacity bounded grammars, *Journal of Automata, Languages and Combinatorics* 15(1/2): 175–194.
[60] Stiebe, R. & Turaev, S. [2009b]. Capacity bounded grammars and Petri nets, *EPTCS* 3: 193–203.
[61] Stiebe, R. & Turaev, S. [2009c]. Capacity bounded grammars and Petri nets, *in* J. Dassow, G. Pighizzini & B. Truthe (eds), *Eleventh International Workshop on Descriptional Complexity of Formal Systems, Magdeburg, Germany*, pp. 247–258.
[62] Turaev, S. [2007]. Petri net controlled grammars, *Third Doctoral Workshop on Mathematical and Engineering Methods in Computer Science, MEMICS 2007*, Znojmo, Czechia, pp. 233–240. ISBN 978-80-7355-077-6.
[63] Turaev, S., Krassovitskiy, A., Othman, M. & Selamat, M. [2011]. Parsing algorithms for grammars with regulated rewriting, *in* A. Zaharim, K. Sopian, N. Mostorakis & V. Mladenov (eds), *Recent Researches in Applied Informatics and Remote Sensing. The 11th WSEAS International Conference on APPLIED COMPUTER SCIENCE*, pp. 103–109.
[64] Turaev, S., Krassovitskiy, A., Othman, M. & Selamat, M. [2012]. Parsing algorithms for regulated grammars, *Mathematical Models & Methods in Applied Science* . (to appear).
[65] Zetzsche, G. [2009]. Erasing in petri net languages and matrix grammars, *Proceedings of the 13th International Conference on Developments in Language Theory*, DLT '09, Springer-Verlag, Berlin, Heidelberg, pp. 490–501.

Chapter 16

Timed Petri Nets

José Reinaldo Silva and Pedro M. G. del Foyo

Additional information is available at the end of the chapter

http://dx.doi.org/10.5772/50117

1. Introduction

In the early 60's a young researcher in Darmstadt looked for a good representation for communicating systems processes that were mathematically sound and had, at the same time, a visual intuitive flavor. This event marked the beginning of a schematic approach that become very important to the modeling of distributed systems in several and distinct areas of knowledge, from Engineering to biologic systems. Carl Adam Petri presented in 1962 his PHD which included the first definition of what is called today a Petri Net. Since its creation Petri Nets evolved from a sound representation to discrete dynamic systems into a general schemata, capable to represent knowledge about processes and (discrete and distributed) systems according to their internal relations and not to their work domain. Among other advantages, that feature opens the possibility to reuse some experiences acquired in the design of known and well tested systems while treating new challenges.

In the conventional approach, the key issue for modeling is the partial ordering among constituent events and the properties that arise from the arrangement of state and transitions once some basic interpretation rules are preserved. Such representation can respond from several systems of practical use where the foundation for analysis is based in reachability and other property analysis. However, there are some cases where such approach is not enough to represent processes completely, for instance, when the assumption that all transitions can fire instantaneously is no longer a good approximation. In such cases a time delay can be associated to firing transitions. This is absolutely equivalent (in a broader sense) to say that firing pre-conditions must hold for a time delay before the firing is completed. The first approach is called T-time Petri Net and the second P-time Petri Nets.

Thus, what we have in conclusion is that even in a hypothesis that we should consider only firing pre-conditions[1] [31][19] a time delay is associated with a transition location and consequently to its firing. Several applications in manufacturing, business, workflow and

[1] In many text books and review articles the enabling condition is presented using only firing pre-conditions as a requirement. This can be justified since the use of this week firing condition is sufficient if a complete net that is, that includes its dual part, is used

other processes can use this approach to represent processes in a more realistic way. It is also true tat even with a simple approach a strong representation power can be derived, including the possibility to make some direct performance analysis [29][42]. This is called a time slice or a time interval approach. In general, this augmented nets with time delay (P-time, T-time or even both) are called Timed Petri Nets[2].

There are also cases where it is necessary to use more than time delays. In such cases the time is among the variables that describes the state (a set of places in Petri Nets). Notice that raising the number of variables that characterize a state would make untreatable the enumeration of a net state space. Therefore, a more direct approach is adopted, where each transition is associated to a time interval t_{min} and t_{max} where the first would stand for the minimal waiting time since the enabling until a firing can occur. Similarly, t_{max} stands for the maximum waiting time allowed since enabling up to a firing.

If the time used in the model is a real number, then we call that a Time Petri Net. It should be also noticed that if $t_{min} = t_{max}$ the situation is reduced to the previous one where a deterministic time interval is associated to a transition. Thus, Time Petri Net is the more general model which can be used to model real time systems in several work domains, from electronic and mechatronic systems to logistic a business domains.

In this chapter we focus in the timed systems and its application which are briefly described in section 2. In section 3 we will present a perspective and demand for a framework to model, analysis and simulation of timed (and time) systems mentioning the open discussion about algorithms and approaches to represent the state space. That discussion will be oriented by the recent advances to establish a standard to Petri Nets in general that includes Timed and Time Petri Nets as a extension. Such standard is presented in ISO/IEC 15.909 proposal launched for the first time in 2004. A short presentation of what could be a general formalization to Time Petri Nets is done in section 4. Concluding remarks are in section 5.

2. A schematic description of time dependent systems

Petri Nets are an abstract formal model for describing and studying information processing systems that are characterized as being concurrent, asynchronous, distributed, parallel, non-deterministic and/or stochastic [31]. Since its creation the formalism has been extended by practitioners and theoreticians for dealing with complex systems attached to many application fields. One of those important extensions were proposed to deal with timed systems.

Among several proposed extensions to deal with time we detach two basic models: Ranchamdani's *Timed Petri nets* [34] and Merlin *Time Petri nets* [30]. These two temporal Petri net models are included in t-time nets because time inscriptions are always associated to transitions. Other time extensions have been published including some approaches where time is associated to places or even to both places and arcs (see [13] for a survey).

Formally, Petri Nets can defined as:

---

[2] Some authors also include another possibility where time is associated to the arcs, that is, to a pair (x, y) where $x, y \in X = S \subseteq T$ where S and T denotes the set of places and transitions, respectively.

Definition 1. [Petri Net] A Petri net structure is a directed weighted bipartite graph

$$N = (P, T, A, w)$$

where

P is the finite set of places, $P \neq \emptyset$

T is the finite set of transitions, $T \neq \emptyset$

$A \subseteq (P \times T) \cup (T \times P)$ is the set of arcs from places to transitions and from transitions to places

$w : A \rightarrow \{1, 2, 3, \ldots\}$ is the weight function on the arcs.

We will normally represent the set of places by $P = \{p_1, p_2, \ldots, p_n\}$ and the set of transitions $T = \{t_1, t_2, \ldots, t_m\}$ where $|P| = n$ and $|T| = m$ are the cardinality of the respective sets. A typical arc is of the form (p_i, t_j) or (t_j, p_i) according to arc direction, where its weight w is a positive integer greater than zero.

Definition 2. [Marked Petri Net] A marked Petri net is a five-tuple (P, T, A, w, M) where (P, T, A, w) is a Petri Net and M is a marking, defined as a mapping $M : P \rightarrow \mathbb{N}^+$

Thus, a marking is a row vector with $|P|$ elements. Figure 1 shows a possible marking for a simple Petri Net.

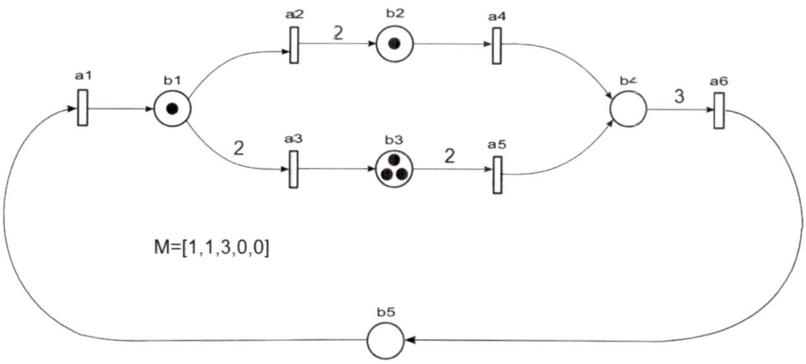

Figure 1. A marked Petri net and it respective marking vector M

The relational functions $Pre, Pos : P \times T \rightarrow \mathbb{N}$ are defined to obtain the number of tokens in places p_i, p_j which are preconditions or postconditions of a transition $t \in T$, that is, there exists arcs $(p_i, t), (p_j, t) \in A$ for the Pre function or $(t, p_i), (t, p_j) \in A$ for the Pos function. In Fig. 1 for instance we have $Pre(b1, a3) = 1$ and $Pos(b3, a3) = 3$.

Using Petri nets to model systems imply in associate net elements (places or transitions) to some components and actions of the modeled system, turning out in what is called "labeled" or "interpreted" nets. The evolution of marking in a labeled Petri nets describes the dynamic behavior of the modeled system.

We restrict the definition of Labeled Petri Net to associate labels only to events or actions similarly to the formalism of automata.

Definition 3. [Labeled Petri Net] A labeled Petri net is a seven-tuple

$$N = (P, T, A, w, E, l, M_0)$$

where

$$(P, T, A, w) \text{ is a Petri net structure}$$
$$E \subseteq \mathbb{P}(T) \ , E \neq \emptyset$$
$$l : T \to E \text{ is the transition labeling function}$$
$$M_0 : P \to \mathbb{N}^+ \text{ is the initial state of the net}$$

Labeled Petri Nets has been proved to be an efficient tool for the modeling, analysis and control of Discrete Event System (DES). Petri Nets is a good option to model these DES systems for wide set of applications, from manufacturing, traffic, batch chemical processes, to computer, communications, database and software systems [27]. From now on we shall refer to "labeled Petri nets" simply as "Petri nets".

The state transition mechanism in Petri nets is provided by moving tokens through the net and hence changing to a new state. When a transition is enabled, we say that it can fire or that it can occur.

Definition 4. [Enabled Transition] A transition $t_j \in T$ in a Petri net is said to be enabled if

$$\forall p \in P, \quad M(p) \geq Pre(p, t_j)$$

In other words, a transition t_j in the Petri net is enabled when the number of tokens in p is greater then or equal to the weight of the arc connecting p to t_j , for all places p that are input to transition t_j.

The set of all enabled transition at some marking M is defined as $enb(M)$. In Fig. 1 only transitions $a2$, $a4$ and $a5$ are enabled, then $enb(M) = \{a2, a4, a5\}$.

Definition 5. [State Transition] A Petri net evolves from a marking M to a marking M′ through the firing of a transition $t_f \in T$ only if $t_f \in enb(M)$. The new marking M′ can be obtained by

$$\forall p \in P | (p, t_f) \vee (t_f, p) \in A, M'(p) = M(p) - Pre(p, t_f) + Pos(p, t_f)$$

The reachable markings in a Petri net can be computed using an algebraic equation. Two incidence matrices must be defined (A^- for incoming arcs, and A^+ for outgoing arcs) and a firing vector u which is a (unimodular) row vector containing "1" in the corresponding position of the firing transition and "0" in all other positions.

The new marking can be obtained using the state equation:

$$M' = M + u(A^+ - A^-) \tag{1}$$

This formalism is sufficient to represent a great amount of dynamic discrete systems, based only in partial order sequence of transitions. However, "untimed"[3] Petri nets are not powerful enough to deal with performance evaluations, safety determination, or behavioral properties in systems where time appears as a quantifiable and continuous parameter.

Ramchandani's timed Petri nets were derived from Petri nets by associating a firing finite duration to each transition in the net. Timed Petri nets and related equivalent models have been used mainly to performance evaluation [7].

Definition 6. [Timed Petri Net] A timed Petri net is a six-tuple

$$N = (P, T, A, w, M_0, f)$$

where

(P, T, A, w, M_0) is a marked Petri net

$f : T \rightarrow \mathbb{R}^+$ is a firing time function that assigns a positive real number to each transition on the net

Therefore, the firing rule has to be modified in order to consider time elapses in the transition firing. If an enabled transition $t_j \in enb(M)$ then it will fire after $f(t_j)$ times units since it became enabled. The system state is not only determined by the net marking but also by a timer attached to every enabled transition in the net.

Definition 7. [Clock State] The clock state is a pair (M, V), where M is a marking and V is a clock valuation function, $V : enb(M) \rightarrow \mathbb{R}^+$

For a clock state (M, V) and $t \in enb(M)$, $V(t)$ is the value of the clock associated with a transition t. The initial clock state is $s_0 = (M_0, V_0)$ where $V_0(t) = f(t), \forall t \in enb(M_0)$.

Definition 8. [New Enabled Transition] A transition $t \in T$ is said new enabled, after firing transition t_f at marking M which leads to marking M', if it is enabled at marking M' and it was not enabled at M or, if it was enabled at M, it is the former fired transition t_f. Formally:

$$new(M') = \{t \in enb(M') | t = t_f \vee \exists p, (M'(p) - Pos(p, t_f)) \leq Pre(p, t)\}$$

We denote as $new(M')$ the set of transitions new enabled at marking M'.

The reachability graph of a timed Pedri net can be computed using the definition of firable transition, that is, those transitions that can be fired in a certain marking.

Definition 9. [Firable Transition] A transition $t_f \in T$ can fire in a marking M yielding a marking M' if:

$t_f \in enb(M)$

$V_M(t_f) \leq V_M(t_i) \; \forall t_i \in enb(M)$

[3] A Petri Net where there is no event depending directly or parametrically of the time

We denote as $Y(M)$ the set of transitions firable at a marking M. Assuming that the firing of transition t_f leads to a new marking M', we denote it as $(M, V_M) \xrightarrow{\tau} (M', V_{M'})$ where $\tau = V_M(t_f)$ is the time elapsed in state transition, M′ is computed using equation 1 and $V_{M'}$ is computed as follows:

$$V_{M'} = \begin{cases} f(t) & \text{se } t \in new(M'); \\ V_M(t) - \tau & \text{se } t \in enb(M') \setminus new(M') \end{cases}$$

The reachability tree can be built including all feasible firing sequences of the timed Petri net. Notice that in M_0 all transition are new enabled, $enb(M_0) = new(M_0)$. However, finite reachability trees can be built only for bounded Petri nets (see bounded property in [31], and an equivalent result for Time Petri in [6]).

Paths or runs in a reachability tree are sequences of state transitions in a timed Petri net. Then, the time elapsed in some path can be computed as the summation of all the elapsed times in the firing schedule. If a path $\omega = s_0 \xrightarrow{\tau_1} s_1 \xrightarrow{\tau_2} s_2 \xrightarrow{\tau_3} s_3$ exists, then the time elapsed between states s_0 and s_3 is $\tau = \tau_1 + \tau_2 + \tau_3$.

The reachabitity tree approach has been successfully used in communication protocols validation and in performance analyses [38, 45]. Moreover, these tests require known computation times for the tasks (often referred by WCET as "Worst Case Execution Time") or process durations. Besides the difficulty to measure or estimate such times, taking into consideration a deterministic time (even in the longest path) does not lead necessarily to the worst case [36].

More realistic analysis can be done on communication protocols using Merlin approach, since some network time durations or even software routines cannot be completed always in the same time [6, 30].

Merlin defined Time Petri Nets (TPN) as nets with a time interval associated to each transition. Assuming that a time interval $[a, b]$ $(a, b \in \mathbb{R}^+)$ is associated with a transition t_i, and that such transition has been enabled at a marking M_i and is being continuously enabled since then in all successive markings $M_{i+1}, \ldots, M_{i+k}$, we define:

- a $(0 \leq a)$, as the minimal time that transition t_i must remain continuously enabled, until it can fire. This time is also known as Early Firing Time (EFT)
- b $(0 \leq b \leq \infty)$, as the maximum time that transition can remain continuously enabled without fire. This time is also known as Latest Firing Time (LFT)

Times a and b for transition t_i are relative to the moment in which transition t_i became last enabled. If transition t_i became enabled at time τ, and remains continuously enabled at $\tau + a$ then it can be fired. After time $\tau + a$, transition t_i can remains continuously enabled without fire until $\tau + b$, in which it must be fired. Note that transitions with time intervals $[0, \infty]$ correspond to the classical "untimed" (no deterministic) Petri net behavior.

The firing semantic described here is called "strong semantic". There also exists a called "weak semantic" in which transitions must not necessarily be fired at its LFT, and after that time it can no longer be fired [35]. In this chapter we will used the strong semantic.

Time Petri nets then can model systems in which events has non-deterministic durations. State transitions in that kind of systems may occur not in an exact time but in some time interval. Real-time systems are examples of this kind of system.

Definition 10. [Time Petri Net] A time Petri net is a six-tuple

$$N = (P, T, A, w, M_0, I)$$

where

(P, T, A, w, M_0) is a marked Petri net

$I : T \rightarrow \{\mathbb{R}^+, \mathbb{R}^+ \cup \{\infty\}\}$ associates with each transition t an interval $[\downarrow I(t), \uparrow I(t)]$ called its static firing interval. The bounds of the time interval are also known as EFT and LFT respectively.

The enabling condition remains the same as in the timed Petri Net but the firing rule must be redefined. The possibility to fire in a time interval rather than an exact time lead to the existence of infinite clock states. Then, even for bounded Petri nets the state space will be infinite, turning intractable any analysis technique based on that model formalism. To overcome this problem, Berthomieu and Menasche [7] proposed a new definition for state.

Definition 11. [Interval State] A state in a TPN is a pair (M, θ) where

M is a marking

θ is a firing interval function $\theta : enb(M) \rightarrow \{\mathbb{R}^+, \mathbb{R}^+ \cup \{\infty\}\}$.

The firing interval associated with transition $t \in enb(M)$ is $\theta(t) = [\downarrow \theta(t), \uparrow \theta(t)]$.

Using that approach, a bounded TPN yields a finite number of states [6]. Note that each Interval state contains infinite clock states, then the new state definition allow us to group infinite clock states into one interval state satisfying the condition:

$$(M, V) \in (M', \theta) \text{ iff } (M = M') \wedge \forall t \in enb(M), \downarrow \theta(t) \leq f(t) - V(t) \leq \uparrow \theta(t)$$

An enumerative analysis technique was introduced in [7] based in what is called "state classes". An algorithm for enumeration of these state classes was proposed for bounded TPNs and then used to the analysis of system. Since then, many algorithm has been proposed to build system state space based on the state class approach [6, 9, 11, 17, 22, 44].

Definition 12. [Firable Transition] Assuming that transition $t_f \in T$ becomes enabled at time τ in state (M, θ), it is firable at time $\tau + \lambda$ iff:

$t_f \in enb(M)$: t_f is enabled at (M, θ).

$\forall t_i \in enb(M), \downarrow t_f \leq \lambda \leq min(\uparrow t_i)$

We denote as $\Upsilon(s)$ the set of transitions firable at state $s = (M, \theta)$ and as $(M, \theta) \xrightarrow{t_f, \lambda} (M', \theta')$ the behavior "transition t_f is firable from state (M, θ) at time λ and its firing leads to state (M', θ')"

The first condition is the usual one for Petri nets and the second results from the necessity of firing transitions according to their firing interval. According to the second condition, a transition t_f, enabled by a marking M at absolute time τ, could be fired at the firing time λ iff λ is not smaller than the EFT of t_f and not greater than the smallest of the LFT's of all the transitions enabled by marking M.

Each firable transition will have its own time interval in which it can be fired. That time depends of its EFT and of the time elapsed since it became last enabled, and of the time in which the rest of the the enabled transitions will reach its LFTs, also according to the time elapsed since each one became last enabled.

Definition 13. [State Class] A state class is a pair $C = (M, D)$ where:

M is a marking;

D is the firing domain of the class.

The state class marking is shared by all states in the class and the firing domain is defined as the union of the firing domains of all the states in the class. The domain D is a conjunction of atomic constraints of the form $(t - t' \prec c)$, $(t \prec c)$ or $(-t \prec c)$, where $c \in \mathbb{R} \cup \{\infty, -\infty\}$, $\prec \in \{=, \leq, \geq\}$ and $t, t' \in T$.

The domain of D is therefore convex and has a unique canonical form defined by:

$$\bigwedge_{(t,t') \in enb(M)^2} t - t' \leq Sup_D(t - t') \wedge \bigwedge_{(t \in enb(M))} t \leq Sup_D(t) \wedge -t \leq Sup_D(-t)$$

where $Sup_D(t - t')$, $Sup_D(t)$, and $Sup_D(-t)$ are respectively the supremum of $t - t'$, t, and $-t$ in the domain of D.

In [12] was proposed an implementation for the firing rule, which directly computes the canonical form of each reachable state class in $O(n^2)$. The firing sequences beginning at some state s_i has the form:

$$\omega = s_i \overset{t_1,[l_{i+1},u_{i+1}]}{\longrightarrow} s_{i+1} \overset{t_2,[l_{i+2},u_{i+2}]}{\longrightarrow} s_{i+2} \ldots s_{i+n-1} \overset{t_j,[l_{i+n},u_{i+n}]}{\longrightarrow} s_{i+n} \tag{2}$$

where the intervals $[l_n, u_n]$ for each t_n are respectively the minimum and maximum time in which the transition can fire.

Once the state space is built, different verifications can be done, including model-checking techniques which determine if some temporal formulas are true or false over the state space. There are severals tools that use such approach [8, 17, 20, 21, 44].

In the special case where EFT and LFT has the same value, the behavior of the TPN reproduce the one of timed Petri Nets. Note that in paths over the graph which is built using the timed Petri net firing rule, the elapsed time in state transitions is fixed while in the TPN it is a time interval. In timed Petri nets states are clock states while in TPN they are interval states or state classes that contain infinite clock states.

The Timed Automaton (TA) with guards [3] is an automaton to which is adjoined a set of continuous variables whose dynamical evolution is time-driven. This formalism has been used to modeling and to a formal verification of real-time systems with success. Some tools as KRONOS [16] and UPPAAL [28] are available for such purposes. The state space yielded using Timed Automaton with guards is quite similar of that of TPN regarding the differences on their constructions.

3. Towards a unified PN system framework

In spite of the great theoretical importance and applicability of Time (or Timed) Petri Nets the PN theory was develop since the early 60's in different directions, always seeking for a way to face combinatorial explosion or to approximate to Fuzzy Logic or object-oriented systems. Several extensions were developed to fit practical applications or to attend the need to treat a new class of distributed systems, such as real-time systems. The new century started with a good amount of work published in this area but also with some confusion about concepts and representations. On the other hand, the raising complexity of distributed systems demanded a unified approach that could handle from abstract models down to the split of these general schemas in programs addressed to specific devices. In fact, integrated and flexible systems depend on that capacity.

A ISO/IEC project were launched in the beginning of this century to provide a standard to Petri Nets: the ISO/IEC 15909. Briefly, this project consists of three phases, where the first one defined P/T nets and High Level Nets in a complementary view, that is, taken P/T nets as a reduced set of the High Level Nets (HLPNs) when we reduce the color set to only one type. That is equivalent to unfold the net. Therefore, the proposed standard provides a comprehensive documentation of the terminology, the semantical model and graphic notations for High-level Petri nets. It also describes different conformance levels. Technically, the part 1 of the standard provides mathematical definitions of High-level Petri Nets, called semantic model, and a graphical form, known as High-level Petri Net Graphs (HLPNGs), as well as its mapping to the semantic model [23, 24].

Similarly to other situations where advances in technology and engineering demands a standardization, the introduction of a Petri Net standard also put in check the capacity of exchanging models among different modeling environments and tools. Thus, a Petri Net Markup Language (PNML) was introduced as an interchange format for the Petri nets defined in part 1 of the standard [25]. That composes the Part 2 of the standard and was published in February 2011, after a great amount of discussion, defining a transfer format to support the exchange of High-level Petri Nets among different tool environments [24]. The standard defined also a transfer syntax for High-level Petri Net Graphs and its subclasses defined in the first part of the standard, capturing the essence of all kinds of colored, high-level and classic Petri nets.

Part 3 is of the standard is devoted to Petri nets extensions, including hierarchies, time and stochastic nets, and is still being discussed, with a estimated time to be launched in 2013. The main requirement is that extensions be built upon developments over the core model, providing a structured and sound description. That also would allow user defined extensions based on built-in extensions and would reduce the profusion of nets attached to application domains. At least two main advantages would come out from that:

- a simple, comprehensive and structured definition of PN which would make it easier the modeling and design of distributed systems;
- a wide range of possible applications will be using the same representation which facilitate the re-use of modeling inside work domains;
- the expansion of reusability to cases among different work domains, reinforcing the use of PNs as a general schema;
- the extension of the use of Petri Nets beyond the modeling phase of design, including requirements analysis and validation.

Thus, it is very important to insert Timed Petri Nets in the proper context of the net standard, and in the context of PN extensions. During the last years a design environment has been built, in parallel with our study of Timed nets and its application to the design of automated and real time systems: the General Hierarchical Enhanced Net System (GHENeSys), where timed Petri Nets were included in a complementary way. That is, the time definition - which could be a proposal to part 3 of the standard - is made associating to each transition (place) a time interval, as proposed by Merlin [30] to model dense time. In the special case of deterministic transition (place) time it suffices to make the interval collapse by making the extremes equal to the same constant. For the case of a deterministic time PN, this imply in modifying Definition 6 to have the mapping $f : T \rightarrow \{\mathbb{R}^+ \times \mathbb{R}^+ \cup \{\infty\}\}$.

Besides the time extension, GHENeSys is also a hierarchical, object-oriented net which has also the following extended elements:

- **Gates:** which stands for elements propagating only information and preserving the marking in its original place. It could be an enabling gate, that is, one that send information if is marked or an inhibitor gate, if propagates information when is not marked. Of course GHENeSys does not allow internal gates. Thus gates should have always an original place, a special place called pseudo-box.
- **Pseudo-boxes:** denotes an observable condition that is not controlled by the modeled system. During the course of the modeling pseudo-boxes could also stand for control information external to the hierarchical components and could be collapsed when components are put together. Thus, pseudo-boxes must be considered in the structure of the net but should not affect its properties or the rank of the incidence matrix.

The graphic representation of the elements followed the schema shown in the Fig. 2 bellow,

Since our focus in this work is time extensions we illustrate hierarchy with a simple example net shown in the Fig. 3 Notice that hierarchical elements are such that the border is composed of only place or transition elements and has a unique entrance element and a unique output element. Besides, we require that each hierarchical element be simply live, that is, there is at least one live path from the entrance to the output. This is called a proper element in the theory of structured systems.

Definition 14.[GHENeSys] GHENeSys is tuple $G = (L, A, F, K, \Pi, C_0, \tau)$ where (L, A, F, K, Π) represents a net structure, C_0 is a set of multisets representing the initial marking, and τ is a function that maps time intervals to each element of the net.

Figure 2. Graphic representation GHENeSys graphic elements.

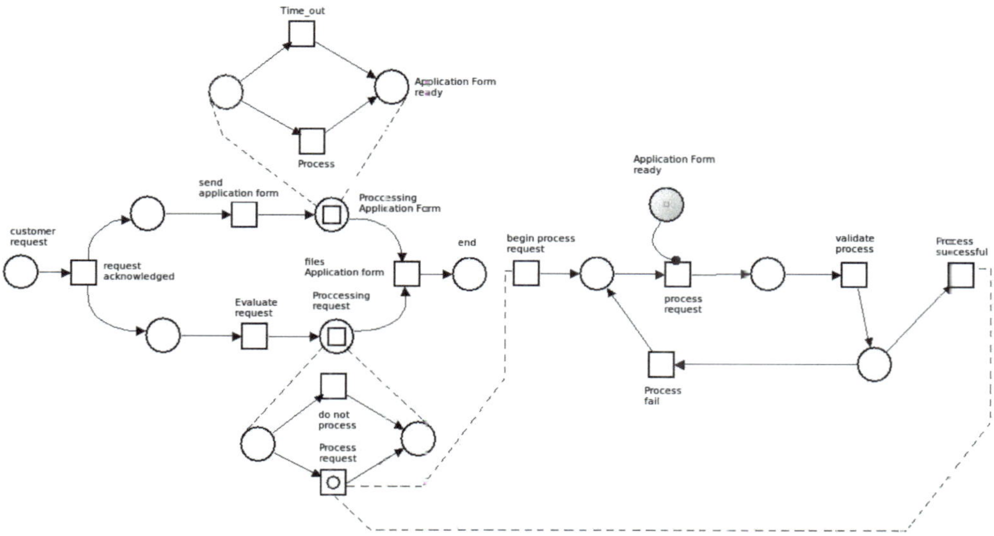

Figure 3. Example of hierarchical proper elements or macro-boxes and macro-transitions.

- $L = B \cup P$, are sets of places denoted by *Boxes* and *pseudo-boxes;*
- A is a set of activities;
- $F \subseteq (L \times A \rightarrow N) \cup (A \times L \rightarrow N)$ is the flux relation;
- $K : L \rightarrow N^+$ is a capacity function;
- $\Pi : (B \cup A) \rightarrow \{0, 1\}$ is a mapping that identifies the macro elements;
- $C_0 = \{(l, \sigma_j) | l \in L, \sigma_j \in R^+ \ |l| \leq K(l)\}$ is the marking of the initial state;
- $\tau : (B \cup A) \longrightarrow \{\mathbb{R}^+, \mathbb{R}^+ \cup \{\propto\}\}$ is a mapping that associates time intervals to each element of the net

3.1. A simple example of verification with GHENeSys

As mentioned before the main advantage of GHENeSys is to facilitate the verification of requirements and restrictions in the modeling and design of distributed systems. Therefore the environment should be able to related the elements and verify the interpretation of formulas that could involve deterministic time (explicitly or not). In the simple example that follow we show how this verification is performed in the GHENeSys system.

Besides the illustration of the use of deterministic time and the GHENeSys net, the example also shows a method adopted to the modeling with Petri Nets, which is based on eliciting requirements in UML and then (if the target is a dynamic system) transforming the semantic diagrams of UML in classic Petri Nets[4]. A Petri Net with some extensions is created in the GHENeSys which also allows the insertion of formulas in CTL that can be verified. Figure 4 [5] shows the UML class diagram to this problem. In a cycle time three drives come to the station which has only two independent pumps.

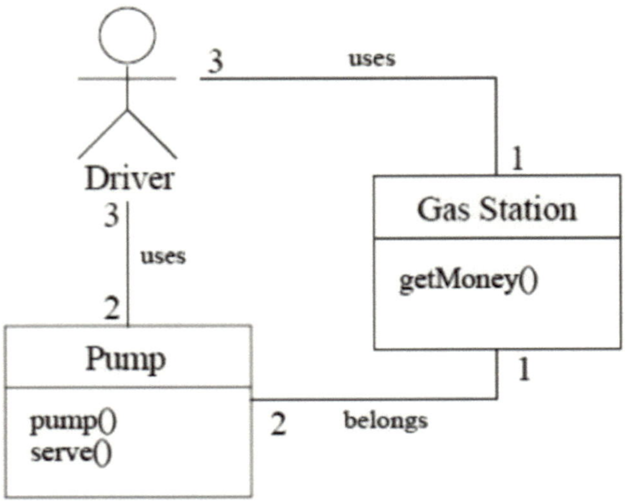

Figure 4. Class diagram to the problem of gas station.

In the gas station problem three different agents are identified: i) the gas station management who is responsible for charging the users, ii) the pumps that are supposed to serve gasoline to the costumers, and iii) the costumers, that is, drivers who are supposed to pay for a proper amount of gasoline and them help themselves. In this simple event we follow the model proposed in Baresi [5] where three drivers depends of only one cashier to pay for the gas and can use two different pumps to fill their cars. First of all we can guarantee that the proper process is followed and them we could insert a characteristic time in the basic operations. We used GHENeSys to provide the model using a classic P/T net. The resulting model is shown in the Fig. 5. This problem is to simple to use extensions but even in that case it would be possible to simply verify if the payment was done (using a gate) to enable the pump with the proper amount of gas instead or carrying the mark. For this problem it would be no significant difference in the size of the graph or in the resulting model.

The important feature here is to follow a modeling approach, which is implied in the steps described so far. Before modeling, requirements should be modeled in UML by semantic

[4] It would also be possible to synthesize a high level net, but this is not in the scope of the present work

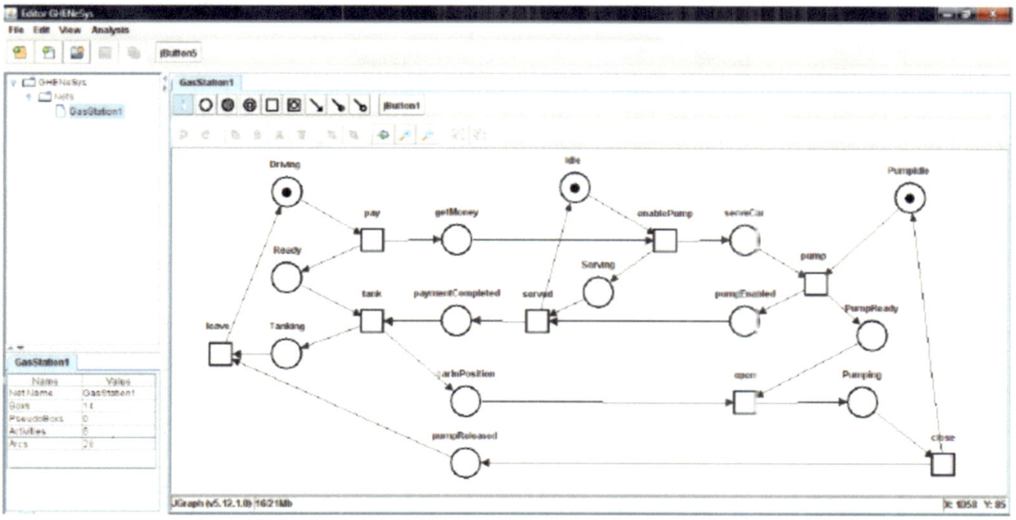

Figure 5. Classic model to the gas problem.

diagrams. There is a good discussion in the academy about the choice of the diagrams to each class of problem. Some authors prefer to go directly to SysML [4] while others just leave open the question about which diagrams should be used and invest in the analysis of this diagrams using Petri Nets [5, 10, 18, 39, 40].

Proceeding with our example let us suppose that we desire to verify some properties of the model such as

$$getMoney \longrightarrow \forall \diamond Pumping \tag{3}$$

$$\forall \Box (getMoney \longrightarrow \forall \diamond Pumping) \tag{4}$$

Using GHENeSys, formulas 3 and 4 can be evaluated by the Timed Petri Net modeling as we can see in the following.

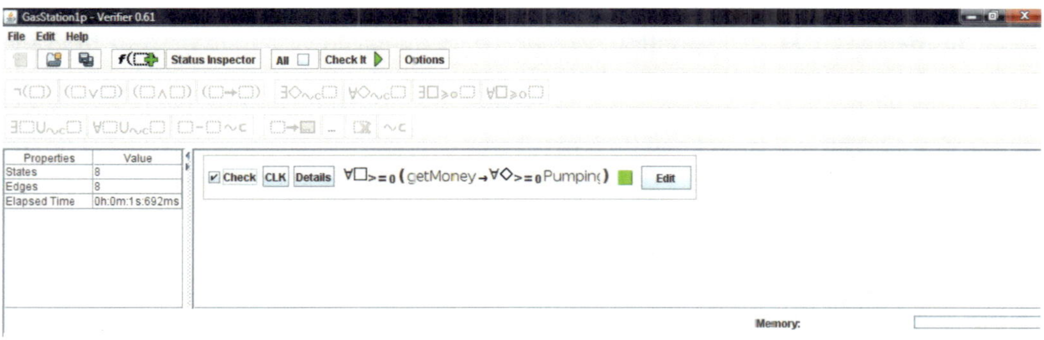

Figure 6. Sanpshot of the GHENeSys verifier for property 4.

The introduction of deterministic time (transition) would add more detail about the process, with the characteristic time for processing the payment or to fill a car. An organized queue would fail (even if works quite fine in the model) since this time can be modified depending of the user or to unpredictable events during the payment or during the supply process. However if specific (and deterministic)intervals such as 3 min for the payment and 5 min for the filling of gas are stablished, the system could handle 9 drivers in 25 min with a waiting time of at most 2 min for some drivers.

More convincing examples can be found in business, manufacturing or computer networks. More challenge problems emerged in the spatial applications or satellite control, but what is important is that even deterministic time approach can be used to solve a diversified set of problems. However, it could be stressed that the timed approach should be supported for tools and environments that rely in a sound and complementary approach to Timed Nets including Time Petri Nets. The approach shown here, inserted in the GHENeSys environment is exactly one of this cases. Besides, GHENeSys is an implementation of a unified net, that follows the specifications in ISO/IEC 15909 standard.

In the next section we go further in the discussion of using Petri Nets and specifically Timed Petri Nets to fit requirements that come in the new version of UML, which includes time diagrams and timelines.

4. PN as a general system representation framework

As pointed in the beginning of this work, Petri Nets has developed for the last fifty years to become a general schema for systems modeling.

In the previous section, we showed that a modeling discipline should be followed to achieve good results with Petri Nets formal representation, specially when time is an important variable to consider, either by deterministic time or using continuous dense time intervals. However, in the example above time does not appear explicitly at the beginning, since we started with the class diagram where there was no reference to duration time of the processes (supplying or payment). The problem them begins with a demand to a proper representation of time duration in UML that could later be transformed in a timed net.

To fit this demand UML 2.0 specification inserted an interaction diagram derived from the sequence diagram where time intervals or time duration are very important issues. Thus, once identified the actors and sub-systems in the model, their interaction could be viewed and modeled taking in account that it occurs during a running time where specific events can cause a change in the status of that interaction. Thus, the full relation can be described in what is called a state lifetime where several timelines show the evolution of the interacting components.

OMG (www.omg.org) shows a very appealing example of time diagram to model

In Figure 7 we can see a hierarchical superposition of levels and the action derived from the interaction between a user and a web system. Sub-systems invoked by this action and the time they spent to provide a proper action are explicitly depicted. As in the previous problem

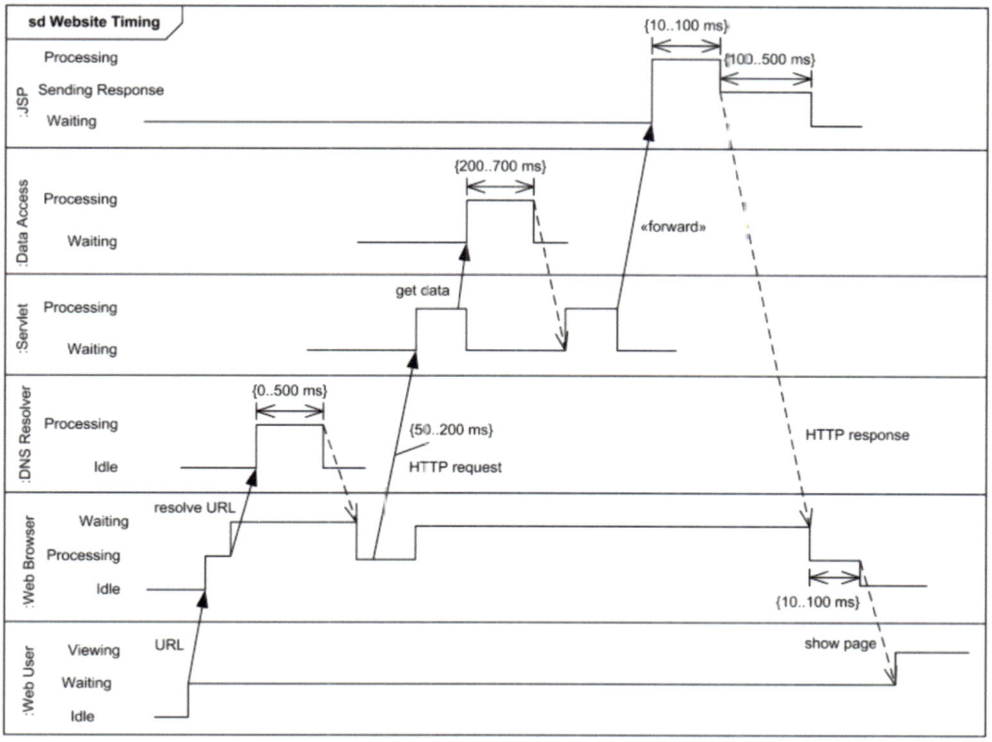

Figure 7. Time diagram for the web user latency.

of the gas station, the total time interval spent to serve one or nine users is the summation of the not superposed time intervals required for each dependent action.

Thus, the complete process would be to elicit the requirements using UML diagrams - including time diagrams - synthesize a Timed Petri Net from this model, and them perform the requirement analysis and final synthesis of a model for the problem. In fact, the final results for the example of the gas station were obtained following this approach.

Formally, the timelines are drawn according the behavior of *state variables*, defined in the following.

Definition 15.[State Variables] A state variable is a triple (V, T, D) where:

$V = v_i$ is a finite set of state values;

$T : V \rightarrow V$ specify each atomic transition or change in value.

$D : V \rightarrow \mathbb{N} \times \mathbb{N}$ is the time duration for each state value.

A timeline is the tracking of all changes in state value in a interval $[0, \tau)$ where τ is the observed time horizon. A timeline is said to be completely closed if the union of its not superposed values is exactly τ. In that case the transitions occur in deterministic time.

If the transitions occur in a time interval $[t_{min}, t_{max}]$ the timeline is said to be flexible. In this case we can represent the transition in a Timed Petri Net by an interval, as proposed in the first section. If we want to deal with deterministic time transition it is enough to make $t_{min} = t_{max}$ and the same net framework could be used.

Timeline models can be very useful in some critical problem applications such as intelligent planning and scheduling. Some of those applications could be used in spatial projects [14][5]. In other applications Petri Nets were used to perform requirements analysis including deterministic time, as in the one proposed by Vaquero et al.[40][41]. In that case the idea of solving real life planning problems starts with the elicitation and specification of requirements using UML, goes through the analysis of this requirements using Timed Petri Nets, synthesizes a model also in Petri Nets and finally uses a specific language, PDDL, to transfer the model to software planners which will provide the final result. Also, a modeling design environment were developed to perform this process[41][40].

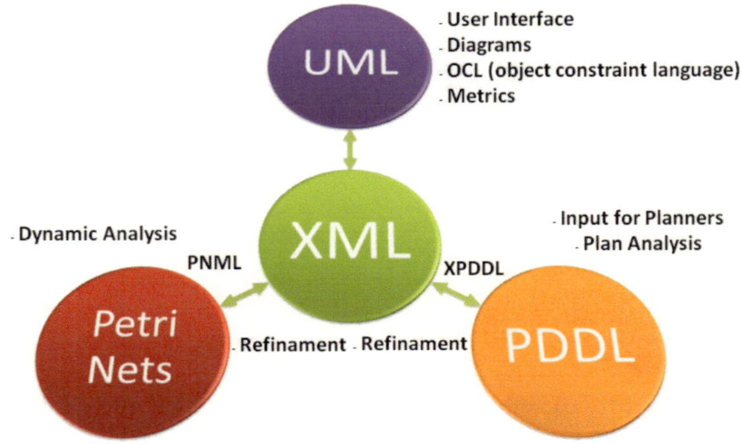

Figure 8. Language structure in itSIMPLE 3.1

A specific state lifetime were developed to model and analyze the timelines for the agents and objects that would compose the plan, as shown in Figure 8.

Based on this time diagram Petri Nets could be synthesized to make the proper validation of the model. It is important to notice that there are a large number of approaches and tools that claim to perform a good analysis of models directly associated to a planer software with good results. However, most of this systems address only model problems which are well behaved and/or have a limited size and complexity. When the challenge is to model a large system, such as the space project mentioned before or a port to get and deliver petroleum, the challenge could be too big to be faced by these proposals.

Therefore the combination UML/Timed Petri Nets could be successful in the modeling of large and complex problems also in the planning area, with the possibility to be applied in practice to real systems.

[5] See also the Mexar 2 Project and the use of intelligent software application in the link mexar.istc.cnr.it/mexar2.

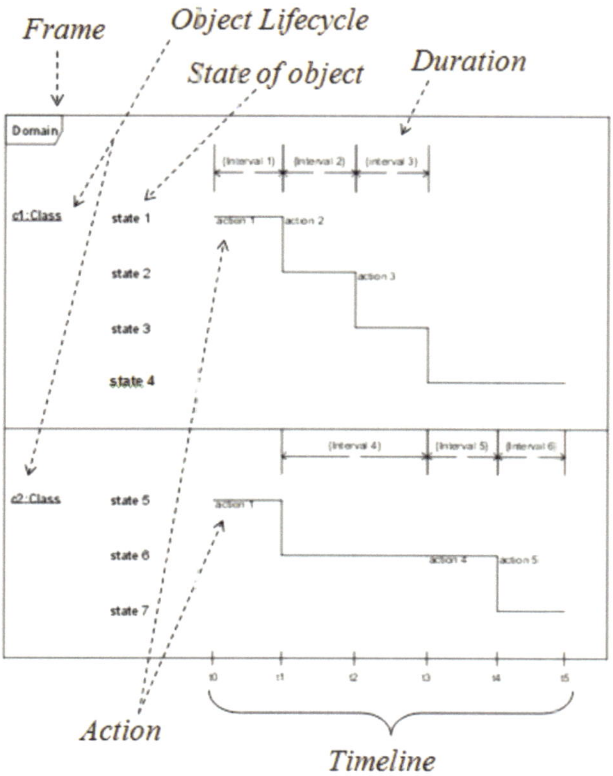

Figure 9. Time diagram in the itSIMPLE system.

5. Conclusions

In conclusion it is important to remark that the evolution of Petri Nets towards a formal representation, capable to treat complex systems should be based in two basis: the extension to model timed systems; and the development of a unified net that includes all extensions besides the timed approach - hierarchy, gates, not controled elements, always respecting the recent published ISO/IEC standard and its next release to appear in 2013. This is the fundamental concepts to have new environments that could support a complementary treatment of timed systems, that is, that could deal with deterministic timed net as well as with time PN in the same environment. That is the focus of the present work.

Besides, it would be advisable that the same environment could deal, also in a complementary way, with classic P/T nets as well as with high level (HLPN) nets or even with simetric nets, which is also part of the ISO/IEC standard. The novelty would be to use a unified net system as a platform to reach the further challenge which would be the introduction of abstract nets.

In what concerns the unified net to treat time intervals and dense time, we achieve a good point with the system GHENeSys where the present work focus most in the first part. However, in [17] a more detailed description of the state class algorithm is given and the basic concepts that lead to a modeling and simulation approach to dense time nets. Therefore the unification with timed PN is a promising result in the near future. Also the system GHENeSys is being developed to implement a unified net as we described above, dealing with P/T and HLPN in the same environment. That is a good combination, capable to model and simulate timed and time nets (in that case using model checking) in the same environment, with the advantage to have a sound and formal representation supporting all process.

Thus, it would be possible to have performance analysis that really fits the complexity of the problem addressed, adapting very easily to discrete or dense time approach.

Acknowledgements

The authors acknowledge to all members of the Design Lab in Mechatronic Department for their work who are present in every part of this article be in the background, in the implementation of tools, in the search for new applications in the analysis of the problems already solved. Particularly we thank the work of Gustavo Costa, Arianna Salmon and Jose Armando S. P. Miralles.

Author details

Silva, José Reinaldo
University of São Paulo, Mechatronics Department, Escola Politécnica, São Paulo, Brazil

Del Foyo, Pedro M. G.
Federal University of Pernambuco, Department of Mechanical Engineering, Recife, Brazil

6. References

[1] Aalst, W van der (2002) Workflow Management: Models, Methods, and Systems, MIT Press, 365 p.

[2] Aalst, W van der (2004) Business Process Management Demystified: A Tutorial on Models, Systems and Standards for Workflow Mangement , LNCS 3098 pp 1-65.

[3] Alur, R. and Dill, D. (1990) Automata for modeling real-time systems, *Lecture Notes in Computer Science* 443: 322–335.

[4] Andrade, E, Maciel, P, Callou, G, Nogueira, B, Araujo, C (2011) An Approach Based in Petri Nets for Requirements Analysis, in in Petri Nets Applications, Pauwel Pawlewski (ed.), InTech, 752 p.

[5] Baresi, L, Pezze, M (2001) Uniform Approaches to Graphical Process Specification Techniques, Electronic Notes in Theoretical Computer Science, vol. 44, pp. 107-119.

[6] Berthomieu, B. and Diaz, M. (1991). Modelling and verification of time dependent systems using time petri nets, *IEEE Trans. on Software Engineering* 17(3): 259–273.

[7] Berthomieu, B. and Menasche, M. (1983) . An enumerative approach for analyzing time Petri nets, *in* R. E. A. Mason (ed.), *Information Processing: proceedings of the IFIP congress 1983*, Vol. 9, Elsevier Science Publishers, Amsterdam, pp. 41–46.

[8] Berthomieu, B., Ribet, P. O. and Vernadat, F. (2004). The tool tina - construction of abstract state spaces for petri nets and time petri nets, *Int. J. Prod. res.* 42(14): 2741–2756.

[9] Berthomieu, B. and Vernadat, F. (2003). State class constructions for branching analysis of time petri nets, *Lecture Notes in Computer Science* 2619: 442–457.

[10] Bodbar, B, Giacomini, L, Holding, DJ (2000) UML and Petri Nets for the Design and Analysis of Distributed Systems, Proc. of the IEEE Int. Conf. on Control Applications, pp. 610-615.

[11] Boucheneb, H., Alger, U. and Berthelot, G. (1993) . Towards a simplified building of time petri nets reachability graph, *Proc. 5th International Workshop on Petri Nets and Performance Models*, Toulouse, France, pp. 46–55.

[12] Boucheneb, H. and Mullins, J. (2003). Analyse des réseaux temporels. calcul des classes en o(n2) et des temps de chemin en o(m x n), *Technique et Science Informatiques* 22(4): 435–459.

[13] Cerone, A. and Maggiolo-Schettini. A. (1999). Time-based expressivity of time petri nets for system specification, *Theoretical Computer Science* 216(1): 1–53.

[14] Cesta, A, Finzi, A, Fratini, S, Orlandini, A, Ronci, E (2010) Validation and verification issues in a temiline-bsed planning system, Knowledge Engineering Review, vol. 25, no. 3, pp. 299-318.

[15] Ciufudean C, Filote C (2010) Workflow Diagnosis Using Petri Net Charts, in Petri Nets Applications, Pauwel Pawlewski (ed.), InTech, 752 p.

[16] Daws, C., Olivero, A., Tripakis, S. and Yovine, S. (1995). The tool KRONOS, *Hybrid Systems III: Verification and Control*, Vol. 1066, Springer, Rutgers University, New Brunswick, NJ, USA, pp. 208–219.

[17] del Foyo, P. M. G. and Silva, J. R. (2011). Some issues in real-time systems verification using time petri nets, *Journal of the Braz. Soc. of Mech. Sci. & Eng.* XXXIII(4): 467–474.

[18] del Foyo, P. M. G., Salmon, A. Z. O., Silva, J. R. (2011) Requirements Analysis of Automated Projects Using UML/Petri Nets, Proc. of COBEM 2011.

[19] Girault, C, Valk, R (2003) Petri Nets for System Engineering, Springer, 607 p.

[20] Gardey, G., Lime, D., Magnin, M. and Roux, O. H. (2005). Romeo: A tool for analyzing time petri nets, *in* K. Etessami and S. Rajamani (eds), *CAV2005*, Vol. 3576, Springer-Verlag, pp. 418–423.

[21] Hadjidj, R. and Boucheneb, H. (2006). On-the-fly tctl model checking for time petri nets using state class graphs, *acsd* 0: 111–122.

[22] Hadjidj, R. and Boucheneb, H. (2008). Improving state class constructions for ctl* model checking of time petri nets, *STTT* 10(2): 167–184.

[23] ISO/IEC (2002) High-Level Petri Nets: Concepts, Definitions and Graphical Notation, International Standard Final Draft, ISO/IEC 15909.

[24] ISO/IEC (2005) Software and Systems Engineering - High-Level Petri Nets, Part 2: Transfer Format, International Standard WD ISO/IEC 15909.

[25] Kindler, E (2006) PNML: Concepts, Status and Future Directions, Invited paper, Proc. of EKA 2006, pp. 35-55.

[26] Kordic, V (ed.) (2008) Petri Nets: Theory and Applications, I-Tech Education and Pub, 208 p.

[27] Lafortune, S. and Cassandras, C. G. (2008). *Introduction to Discrete Event Systems*, second edn, Springer, 233 Spring Street, New York, NY 10013, USA.

[28] Larsen, K. G., Pettersson, P. and Yi, W. (2000). Uppaal - validation and verification of real time systems - status & developments.

[29] Marsan MA, Bobbio, A, Donatelli S (1998) Petri Nets in Performance Analysis: an Introduction, LNCS 1491, pp. 211-256.

[30] Merlin, P., Faber, D. (1976) Recoverability on communication protocols - implications of a theoretical study, IEEE Trans. on Communications, vol. 4, no. 9, pp. 1036-1043.

[31] Murata, T (1989) Petri Nets: Properties, Analysis and Applications, Proceedings of IEEE, vol. 77, pp 541-580.

[32] Patrice B (2010) A New Control Synthesis Approach of P-Time Petri Nets, in Petri Nets Applications, Pawel Pawlewski (ed.), InTech, 752 p.

[33] Pawlewski P (2010) Using Petri Nets to Model and Simulation Production Systems in Process Reengineering, in Petri Nets Applications, Pawel Pawlewski (ed.), InTech, 752 p.

[34] Ramchandani, C. (1973) Analysis of Asynchronous Concurrent Systems by Timed Petri Nets, PHD thesis, MIT, 220 p.

[35] Riviere, N., Valette, R., Pradin-Chezalviel, B. and Ups, I. A. . (2001). Reachability and temporal conflicts in t-time petri nets, *PNPM '01: Proceedings of the 9th international Workshop on Petri Nets and Performance Models (PNPM'01)*, IEEE Computer Society, Washington, DC, USA, p. 229.

[36] Roux, O. H. and Déplanche, A. M. (2002) . A T-time petri net extension for real time-task scheduling modeling, *European Journal of Automation* 36: 973–987.

[37] Salmon, A. Z. O., Miralles, J. A. S. P., del Foyo, P. M. G., Silva, J. R. (2011) Towards a Unified View of Modeling and Design with GHENeSys, Proc. of COBEM 2011.

[38] Sifakis, J. (1980). Performance evaluation of systems using nets, *Proceedings of the Advanced Course on General Net Theory of Processes and Systems*, Springer-Verlag, London, UK, pp. 307–319.

[39] Tierry-Mieg, Y, Hilah, L-M (2008) UML Behavioral Consistency Checking Using Instantiable Petri Nets, Workshop UML in Formal Methods, 10th. Int. Conf. on Formal Engineering Methods.

[40] Vaquero, T.S., Silva, J.R., Ferreira, M., Tonidandel, F., Bech, J.C. (2009) From Requirements and Analysis to PDDL in itSIMPLE 3.0, Proc. of Int. Conf. in Artificial Planning and Scheduling, AAAI.

[41] Vaquero, T.S., Silva, J.R., Bech, J.C. (2011) A Brief Review of Tools and Methods for Knowledge Engineering for Planning and Scheduling, Proc. of Int. Conf. in Artificial Planning and Scheduling, AAAI.

[42] Wang, J (1998) Timed Petri Nets: Theory and Applications, Kluwer Academic Pub. 281 p.

[43] Wang, J, Deng, Y, Xu, G (2000) Reachability Analysis of Real-time Systems Using Timed Petri Nets, IEEE Trans. on Syst. Man and Cybernetics, vol 30 no. 5, pp. 725-736.

[44] Yoneda, T. and Ryuba, H. (1998). CTL model checking of time petri nets using geometric regions, *IEICE Trans. on Information and Systems* E81-D(3): 297–396.

[45] Zuberek, W. M. (1980). Timed petri nets and preliminary performance evaluation, *ISCA '80: Proceedings of the 7th annual symposium on Computer Architecture*, ACM Press, New York, NY, USA, pp. 88–96.

Section 3

Theory

Chapter 17

Boolean Petri Nets

Sangita Kansal, Mukti Acharya and Gajendra Pratap Singh

Additional information is available at the end of the chapter

http://dx.doi.org/10.5772/50354

1. Introduction

Petri net is a graphical tool invented by Carl Adam Petri [13]. These are used for describing, designing and studying discrete event-driven dynamical systems that are characterized as being concurrent, asynchronous, distributed, parallel, random and/or nondeterministic. As a graphical tool, Petri net can be used for planning and designing a system with given objectives, more practically effective than flowcharts and block diagrams. As a mathematical tool, it enables one to set up state equations, algebraic equations and other mathematical models which govern the behavior of discrete dynamical systems. Still, there is a drawback inherent in representing discrete event-systems. They suffer from the state explosion problem as what will happen when a system is highly populated, i.e., initial state consists of a large number of places that are nonempty. This phenomenon may lead to an exponential growth of its reachability graph. This makes us to study the safe systems. The aim of this chapter is to present some basic results on 1-safe Petri nets that generate the elements of a Boolean hypercube as marking vectors. Complete Boolean hypercube is the most popular interconnection network with many attractive and well known properties such as regularity, symmetry, strong connectivity, embeddability, recursive construction, etc. For brevity, we shall call a 1-safe Petri net that generates all the binary n-vectors as marking vectors a *Boolean Petri net*. *Boolean Petri nets* are not only of theoretical interest but also are of practical importance, required in practice to construct control systems [1]. In this chapter, we will consider the problems of characterizing the class of Boolean Petri nets as also the class of *crisp* Boolean Petri nets, viz., the Boolean Petri nets that generate all the binary n-vectors exactly once. We show the existence of a disconnected Boolean Petri net whose reachability tree is homomorphic to the n-dimensional complete lattice L_n. Finally, we observe that characterizing a Boolean Petri net is rather intricate.

We begin by showing that a 1-safe *Star Petri net* S_n [5], with $|P| = n$ and $|T| = n+1$, having a central transition, is a Boolean Petri net; here, P is the set of its places and T is the set of its transitions. Often, it is desirable to have a crisp Boolean Petri net because one may possibly explore for existence of certain sequences of enabled transitions to fire toward initiating and completing a prescribed process that uses specified nodes of the Boolean lattice.

For example, in the design of generalized switches such as those used to control automatic machines [1], suppose that we have a sequence of n terminals each of which can be either at a prescribed low-voltage (denoted by zero '0') or at a prescribed high-voltage (denoted by unity, '1'). It is required to arrange them so that every one of the 2^n sequences of n bits, corresponding to the 2^n binary n-tuples, can appear on the terminals [1]. Now that Q_n, the binary n-cube, is known to be Hamiltonian (in the sense that there exists an all-vertex covering cycle) one can design a "Hamiltonian switch" using a crisp Boolean Petri net that triggers operation of a machine exactly once after 2^n successive switching moves along the prescribed Hamiltonian cycle in Q_n. The 'switch design' may be imagined to be an arbitrary connected graph of order 2^n, where connection between a pair (u, v) of nodes would mean that v is to be the terminal that needs to be turned on after the terminal corresponding to u (which may or may not be in an active state depending on the machine design). Therefore, a good characterization of such Boolean Petri nets is needed. This problem is still open. Many specific classes of such 1-safe Petri nets have been found [5–7]. Also, many fundamental issues regarding Boolean Petri nets emerge from this study.

2. Preliminaries

To keep this chapter self-contained as far as possible, we present some of the necessary definitions and concepts. For standard terminology and notation on Petri net theory and graph theory, we refer the reader to Peterson [12] and Harary [3], respectively. In this chapter, we shall adopt the definition of Jenson [4] for Petri nets:

Definition 1. *A Petri net is a 5-tuple* $C = (P, T, I^-, I^+, \mu^0)$, *where*

(a) P *is a nonempty set of 'places',*

(b) T *is a nonempty set of 'transitions',*

(c) $P \cap T = \emptyset$,

(d) $I^-, I^+ : P \times T \longrightarrow \mathbf{N}$, *where* **N** *is the set of nonnegative integers, are called the negative and the positive 'incidence functions' (or,'flow functions') respectively,*

(e) $\forall\, p \in P, \exists t \in T : I^-(p,t) \neq 0 \;\; or \;\; I^+(p,t) \neq 0$ *and*
$\forall t \in T, \exists p \in P : I^-(p,t) \neq 0 \;\; or \;\; I^+(p,t) \neq 0$,

(f) $\mu^0 : P \rightarrow \mathbf{N}$ *is the initial marking.*

In fact, $I^-(p,t)$ and $I^+(p,t)$ represent the number of arcs from p to t and t to p respectively, and some times referred to a 'flow relations'. I^-, I^+ and μ^0 can be viewed as matrices of size $|P| \times |T|$, $|P| \times |T|$ and $|P| \times 1$, respectively.

The quadruple (P, T, I^-, I^+) in the definition of the Petri net is called the *Petri net structure*. The *Petri net graph* is a representation of the Petri net structure, which is essentially a bipartite directed multigraph, in which any pair of symmetric arcs (p_i, t_j) and (t_j, p_i) is called a *self-loop*.

As in many standard books (e.g., see [14]), Petri net is a particular kind of directed graph [3], together with an initial marking μ^0. The underlying graph of a Petri net is a directed, weighted, bipartite graph consisting of two kinds of nodes, called places and transitions, where arcs are either from a place to a transition or from a transition to a place. No two of the same kind being adjacent. Hence, Petri nets have a well known graphical representation in which transitions are represented as boxes and places as circles with directed arcs interconnecting places and transitions, to represent the flow relations. The initial marking is represented by placing a token, shown as a black dot, in the circle representing a place p_i, whenever $\mu^0(p_i) = 1,\ 1 \leq i \leq n = |P|$. In general, a *marking* μ is a mapping $\mu : P \longrightarrow \mathbf{N}$. A marking μ can hence be represented as a vector $\mu \in \mathbf{N}^n$, $n = |P|$, such that the ith component of μ is the value $\mu(p_i)$, viz., the number of tokens placed at p_i.

Definition 2. *Let $C = (P, T, I^-, I^+, \mu)$ be a Petri net. A transition $t \in T$ is said to be enabled at μ if and only if $I^-(p,t) \leq \mu(p), \forall p \in P$. An enabled transition may or may not 'fire' (depending on whether or not the event actually takes place). After firing at μ, the new marking μ' is given by the rule*

$$\mu'(p) = \mu(p) - I^-(p,t) + I^+(p,t), \text{for all } p \in P.$$

We say that *t fires at* μ to yield μ' (or, that *t fires* μ to μ'), and we write $\mu \xrightarrow{t} \mu'$, whence μ' is said to be *directly reachable* from μ. Hence, it is clear, what is meant by a sequence like

$$\mu^0 \xrightarrow{t_1} \mu^1 \xrightarrow{t_2} \mu^2 \xrightarrow{t_3} \mu^3 \cdots \xrightarrow{t_k} \mu^k,$$

which simply represents the fact that the transitions

$$t_1, t_2, t_3, \ldots, t_k$$

have been successively fired to transform the *initial marking* μ^0 into the *terminal* marking μ^k. The whole of this sequence of transformations is also written in short as $\mu^0 \xrightarrow{\sigma} \mu^k$, where $\sigma = t_1, t_2, t_3, \ldots, t_k$ is called the corresponding *firing sequence*.

A marking μ is said to be *reachable from* μ^0, if there exists a firing sequence of transitions which successively fire to reach the state μ from μ^0. The set of all markings of a Petri net C reachable from a given marking μ is denoted by $M(C, \mu)$ and, together with the arcs of the form $\mu^i \xrightarrow{t_r} \mu^j$, represents what in standard terminology is called the *reachability graph* of the Petri net C, denoted by $R(C, \mu^0)$. In particular, if the reachability graph has no semicycle then it is called the *reachability tree* of the Petri net.

A place in a Petri net is *safe* if the number of tokens in that place never exceeds one. A Petri net is *safe* if all its places are safe.

The *preset* of a transition t is the set of all input places to t, i.e., $^\bullet t$=$\{p \in P : I^-(p,t) > 0\}$. The *postset* of t is the set of all output places from t, i.e., $t^\bullet$=$\{p \in P : I^+(p,t) > 0\}$. Similarly, p's preset and postset are $^\bullet p$=$\{t \in T : I^+(p,t) > 0\}$ and $p^\bullet$=$\{t \in T : I^-(p,t) > 0\}$, respectively.

Definition 3. *Let $C = (P, T, I^-, I^+, \mu^0)$ be a Petri net with $|P| = n$ and $|T| = m$, the incidence matrix $I = [a_{ij}]$ is an $n \times m$ matrix of integers and its entries are given by $a_{ij} = a^+_{ij} - a^-_{ij}$ where a^+_{ij}=$I^+(p_i, t_j)$ is the number of arcs from transition t_j to its output place p_i and a^-_{ij}=$I^-(p_i, t_j)$ is the number of arcs from place p_i to its output transition t_j i.e., in other words, $I = I^+ - I^-$.*

3. 1-safe star Petri net is Boolean

We shall now define *1-safe star* Petri net. The notion of a *star* is from graph theory (see [3]); it is the *complete bipartite graph* $K_{1,n}$ which consists of exactly one vertex c, called the *center*, joined by a single edge cv_i to the pendant vertex v_i (i.e. the degree of v_i is 1) for each $i \in \{1,2, \ldots, n\}, n \geq 1$. A *1-safe star Petri net* S_n is obtained by *subdividing* every edge of the graph $K_{1,n}$, $n \geq 1$, so that every subdividing vertex is a place node and the original vertices of $K_{1,n}, n \geq 1$, are the $(n+1)$ transition nodes, $(n+1)^{th}$ being the central node. Further, every arc incident to the central node is directed towards it, and every arc incident to a pendent node is directed towards the pendent node (See Figure 1).

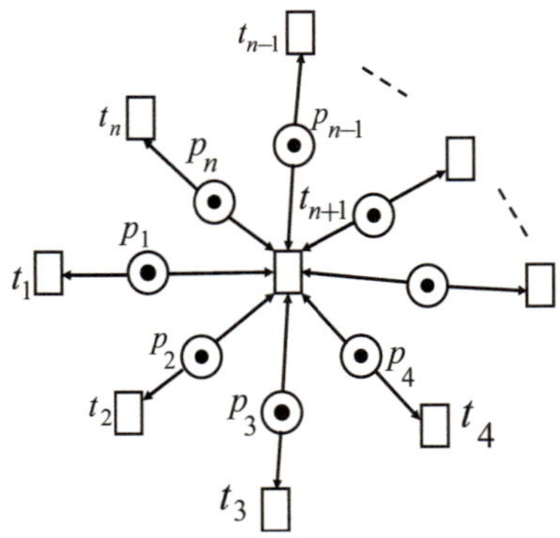

Figure 1. 1-safe star Petri net S_n

Theorem 1. *[5] The reachability tree of* S_n *with* $\mu_0 = (1, 1, 1, 1, \ldots, 1)$ *as the initial marking contains every binary* n*-vector* $(a_1, a_2, a_3, \ldots, a_n)$, $a_i \in \{0, 1\}$.

Proof. We shall prove this result by using the Principle of Mathematical Induction (PMI). Clearly, the reachability tree $R(S_1, \mu^0)$ of S_1 generates both the binary 1-vectors (1) and (0) as shown in Figure 2. Next, consider the 1-safe star Petri net S_2 as shown in Figure 3 and its reachability tree $R(S_2, \mu^0)$ displayed in Figure 4.

It is clear from Figure 4 that $R(S_2, \mu^0)$ has all the $4 = 2^2$, binary 2-vectors (a_1, a_2), $a_1, a_2 \in \{0, 1\}$. We can construct $R(S_2, \mu^0)$ from $R(S_1, \mu^0)$ as follows. Take two copies of $R(S_1, \mu^0)$. In the first copy, augment each vector of $R(S_1, \mu^0)$, by putting a 0 entry at the second position of every marking vector and denote the resulting labeled tree as $R_0(S_1, \mu^0)$. Similarly, in the second copy, augment each vector by putting 1 at the second position of every marking and let $R_1(S_1, \mu^0)$ be the resulting labeled tree (See Figure 5). Now, using the following steps we construct the reachability tree $R(S_2, \mu^0)$ of S_2 from $R_0(S_1, \mu^0)$ and $R_1(S_1, \mu^0)$.

1. Clearly, the set of binary 2-vectors in $R_0(S_1, \mu^0)$ is disjoint with the set of those appearing in $R_1(S_1, \mu^0)$ and together they contain all the binary 2-vectors.

2. In $R_0(S_1, \mu^0)$, transition t_2 does not satisfy the enabling condition, since $I^-(p_i, t) \leq \mu(p_i)$, for each $p_i \in S_1$ is violated. So, we can ignore this transition at this stage.

3. In $R_1(S_1, \mu^0)$, transition t_2 is enabled and the marking obtained after firing of t_2 is actually (1, 0) whereas the augmented vector attached to this node is (0,1). So, we concatenate

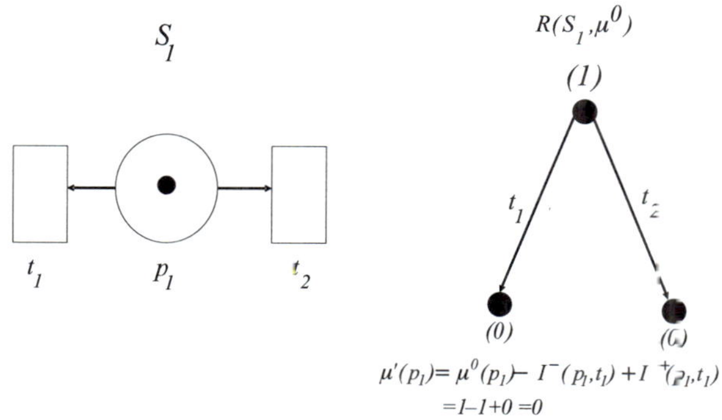

Figure 2. 1−safe star Petri net S_1 and $R(S_1, \mu^0)$

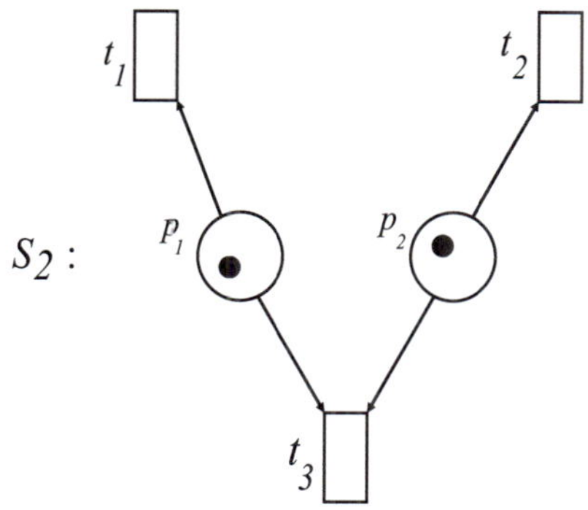

Figure 3. 1-safe star Petri net S_2

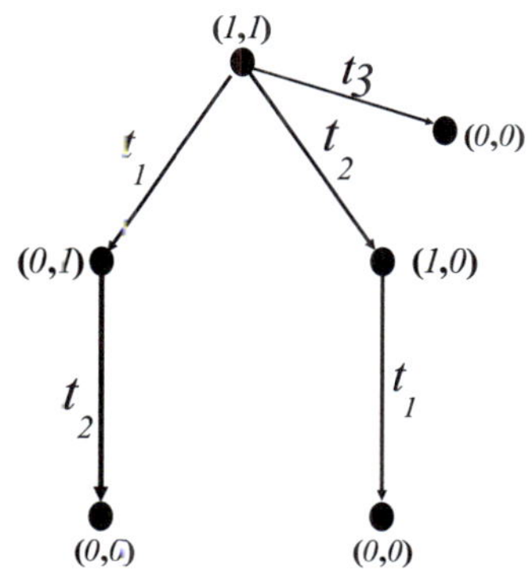

Figure 4. $R(S_2, \mu^0)$, $\mu^0 = (1,1)$

$R_0(S_1, \mu^0)$ by fusing the node labeled (1, 0) with the node labeled (0, 1) in $R_1(S_1, \mu^0)$ and replacing (0, 1) by the label (1, 0) which is the initial marking of $R_0(S_1, \mu^0)$.

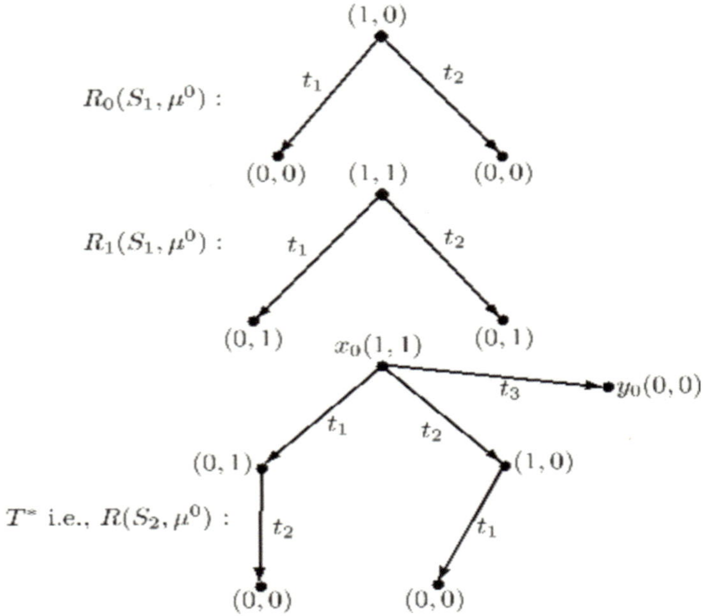

Figure 5. Augmented reachability trees and resulting labeled tree T^*

4. We then augment an extra pendent node labeled y_0 joined to the new root node x_0, labeled by the 2-vector (1, 1), by the new arc $(x_0,\ y_0)$ labeled as t_3 and complete this tree by firing transitions(s) at the marking vector(s) where nonzero components appear, till all the transitions become dead. Then the resulting labeled tree T^* is shown in Figure 5. This has all the binary 2-vectors as its node labels, possibly with repetitions. It remains to show that it is the reachability tree $R(S_2,\mu^0)$ of S_2 with 2-vector (1, 1) as its initial marking μ^0. For this, consider an arbitrary 2-vector $\mu = (a_1,\ 1)$, where $a_1 \in \{0,1\}$. When transition t_2 is enabled, this yields

$$\mu'(p_i) = \mu(p_i) - I^-(p_i,\ t_2) + I^+(p_i,\ t_2)$$

$$= 1 - 1 + 0 = 0$$

Then, we get a new marking $\mu' = (a_1,\ 0)$, where $a_1 \in \{0,\ 1\}$. The marking μ' is found in $R_0(S_2,\ \mu^0)$. If all a_i's are zero then μ' is a dead marking. Hence, suppose some $a_i \neq 0$. In this case, t_i is enabled and in the next new marking μ'', the ith component is reduced to zero. Eventually, this process will lead to a dead marking. Further, the marking vectors of the form $\mu = (a_1,\ 0)$ are already obtained as a result of firing $t_1,\ t_2$, through some subsequences. Thus, T is indeed the reachability tree $R(S_2,\mu^0)$ of S_2.

Now, we assume that the result is true for all the 1-safe star Petri nets S_k having k places, $k \leq n$. We will prove the result for the 1-safe star Petri net S_{n+1} having $(n+1)$ places. For this purpose, consider two copies of the reachability tree $R(S_n,\mu^0)$ of S_n. In the first copy, we extend each vector by augmenting a 0 entry at the $(n+1)^{th}$ position and let $R_0(S_n,\ \mu^0)$ denote the resulting labeled tree. Next, in the second copy of $R(S_n,\mu^0)$, we augment the entry 1 to the $(n+1)^{th}$ position in every marking vector and let $R_1(S_n,\ \mu^0)$ be the resulting labeled tree. Hence, using the following steps we construct the reachability tree of the 1-safe star Petri net S_{n+1} having $(n+1)$ places.

1. Clearly, the set of binary $(n+1)$-vectors in $R_0(S_n, \mu^0)$ is disjoint with the set of those appearing in $R_1(S_n, \mu^0)$ and together they contain all the binary $(n+1)$-vectors.

2. In $R_0(S_n, \mu^0)$, transition t_{n+1} does not satisfy the enabling condition, $I^-(p_i, t) \leq \mu(p_i)$, for each $p_i \in S_n$. So, we can ignore this transition for the moment.

3. In $R_1(S_n, \mu^0)$, transition t_{n+1} is enabled and the marking obtained after firing of t_{n+1} is actually $(1, 1, \ldots, 0)$. So we concatenate $R_0(S_n, \mu^0)$ at this node with the $(n+1)$-vector $(0, 0, \ldots, 1)$ replaced by the actual marking $(1, 1, \ldots, 0)$ being the initial marking of $R_0(S_n, \mu^0)$.

4. We then augment an extra pendent node labeled y_0 joined to the new root node x_0, labeled by the $(n+1)$-vector $(1, 1, \ldots, 1)$ by the new arc (x_0, y_0) labeled as t_{n+2} and complete this tree by firing transition(s) at the marking vector(s) where nonzero components appear till all the transitions become dead. In this way, the tree T^* so obtained has all the binary $(n+1)$-vectors as its node labels, possibly with repetitions. It remains to show that T^* is indeed the reachability tree $R(S_{n+1}, \mu^0)$ of S_{n+1} with binary $(n+1)$-vector $(1, 1, 1, \ldots, 1)$ as its initial marking μ^0. For this, consider an arbitrary $(n+1)$-vector $\mu = (a_1, a_2, a_3, \ldots, a_n, 1)$, where $a_i \in \{0,1\}, \forall\, i$. When transition t_{n+1} is enabled, this yields

$$\mu'(p_i) = \mu(p_i) - I^-(p_i, t_{n+1}) + I^+(p_i, t_{n+1}) \; = 1 - 1 + 0 = 0$$

Then, we get a new marking $\mu' = (a_1, a_2, a_3, \ldots, a_n, 0)$, where $a_i \in \{0, 1\}$. The marking μ' is found in $R_0(S_{n+1}, \mu^0)$. If all a_i's are zero, then μ' is a dead marking. Hence, suppose some $a_i \neq 0$. In this case, t_i is enabled and in the next new marking μ'', the ith component is reduced to zero. Eventually, this process will lead to a dead marking. Further, the marking vectors of the form $\mu = (a_1, a_2, a_3, \ldots, a_n, 0)$ are already obtained as a result of firing $t_1, t_2, t_3, \ldots, t_n$ through some subsequences by virtue of the induction hypothesis. Thus, T^* is precisely the reachability tree $R(S_{n+1}, \mu^0)$ of S_{n+1}. Hence, the result follows by PMI. □

4. Some general questions and a necessary condition

The above theorem opens not only the general problem of determining all such Petri nets but also raises the question of determining such optimal Petri nets ; for example, one can ask

1. Precisely which Petri nets produce the set of all binary n-vectors with minimum repetitions?

2. Precisely which Petri nets produce all the binary n-vectors in the smallest possible number of steps? As pointed out, these questions could be quite important from practical application point of view.

3. Do there exist Petri nets that generate every binary n-vector exactly once?

4. Is it not possible to take any marking other than $(1, 1, 1, \cdots, 1)$ as an initial marking for such a Petri net?

The following proposition and theorem answer the last two questions.

Proposition 1. *[6] If a Petri net is Boolean then* $\mu^0(p) = 1, \forall p \in P$.

Proof. Suppose $C = (P, T, I^-, I^+, \mu^0)$ is a Petri net which is Boolean and $\mu^0(p_i) \neq 1$ for some $p_i \in P$. By the definition of a Petri net, no place can be isolated. Therefore p_i has to be connected to some $t_i \in T$. Now, three cases arise for consideration:

Case-1: $p_i \in t_i^{\bullet}$,
Case-2: $p_i \in {}^{\bullet}t_i \cap t_i^{\bullet}$, and
Case-3: $p_i \in {}^{\bullet}t_i$

In Case 1, since the given Petri net C is safe, ${}^{\bullet}t_i \neq \emptyset$ [2]. Therefore, $\exists\, p_j \in {}^{\bullet}t_i$ for some $p_j \in P$. p_j will have either one token or no token. If p_j has one token then t_i is enabled and hence fires. After firing of t_i, p_j will have no token and p_i will receive one token. So, both the places cannot have one token simultaneously. Hence, we will not get the marking vector whose components are all equal to 1. Again, if p_j has no token then t_i cannot fire, whence p_i will never receive a token, which contradicts the assumption of the case.

Case 2 follows from the arguments given for Case 1 above since, in particular, $p_i \in t_i^{\bullet}$.

Also, in Case 3, as in the proof of Case 1 $p_i \in {}^{\bullet}t_i$ implies that we cannot have the marking vector whose components are all equal to 1.

Thus, if a Petri net generates all the binary n-vectors then $\mu^0(p_i) = 1\ \forall\ p_i \in P$. □

5. Crisp Petri nets

Theorem 2. *[6] There exists a 1-safe Petri net with the initial marking $\mu^0(p) = 1, \forall p \in P$ which generates each of the 2^n binary n-vectors*

$$(a_1, a_2, a_3, \cdots, a_n),\ a_i \in \{0,1\},\ n = |P|,$$

as one of its marking vectors, exactly once.

Proof. We shall prove this result again by using the PMI on $n = |P|$.

For $n = 1$, we construct a Petri net C_1 as shown in Figure 6. In this Petri net C_1,

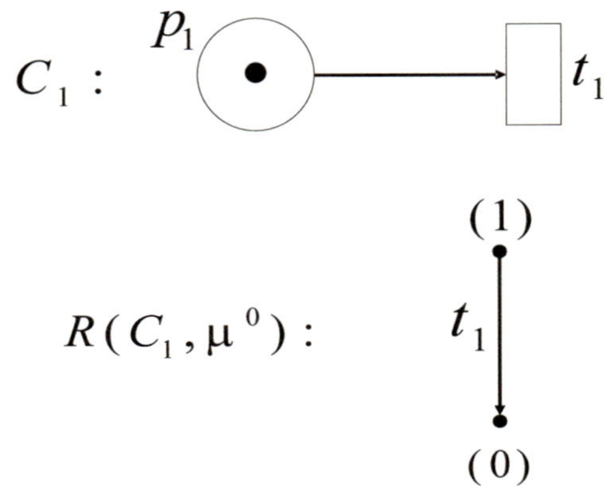

Figure 6. Petri net C_1 and $R(C_1, \mu^0)$

the total number of transitions $= 2^1 - 1 = 1$,

$|p_1^{\bullet}| = 2^1 - 1 = 1$,

$|^{\bullet}p_1| = 2^{1-1} - 1 = 0$,

$|^{\bullet}t_1| = 1$.

Total number of transitions whose post-sets having no element $= {}^1C_0 = 1$ and this transition is t_1. Clearly, $R(C_1, \mu^0)$ of C_1 generates both the binary 1-vectors (1) and (0) as shown in Figure 6 in the first step and after this step, transition becomes dead.

Next, for $n = 2$, the Petri net C_2 shown in Figure 7 has two places. In C_2, we have

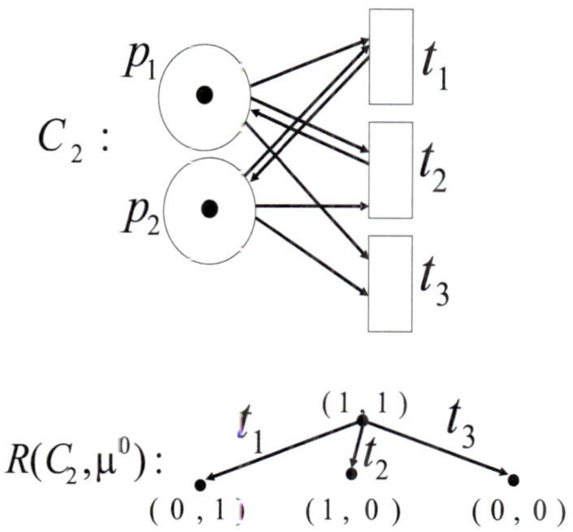

Figure 7. Petri net C_2 and $R(C_2, \mu^0)$

the total number of transitions $= 2^2 - 1 = 4 - 1 = 3$,

$|p^{\bullet}| = 2^2 - 1 = 3, \forall\, p$,

$|^{\bullet}p| = 2^{2-1} - 1 = 1, \forall\, p$,

$|^{\bullet}t| = 2, \forall\, t$.

The total number of transitions whose post-sets have one element $= {}^2C_1 = 2$ and these transitions are t_1, t_2.

The total number of transitions whose post-sets have no element $= {}^2C_0 = 1$ and this transition is t_3.

It is clear from Figure 7 that $R(C_2, \mu^0)$ has exactly $4 = 2^2$ binary 2-vectors (a_1, a_2), $a_1, a_2 \in \{0, 1\}$ in the first step and after this step, all the transitions become dead.

We can construct $R(C_2, \mu^0)$ from $R(C_1, \mu^0)$ as follows: Take two copies of $R(C_1, \mu^0)$. In the first copy, augment each vector of $R(C_1, \mu^0)$ by the adjunction of a '0' entry at the second coordinate of every marking vector and denote the resulting labeled tree as $R_0(C_1, \mu^0)$. Similarly, in the second copy, augment each vector by the adjunction of a '1' at the second coordinate of every marking vector and let $R_1(C_1, \mu^0)$ be the resulting labeled tree (see Figure 8). Now, using

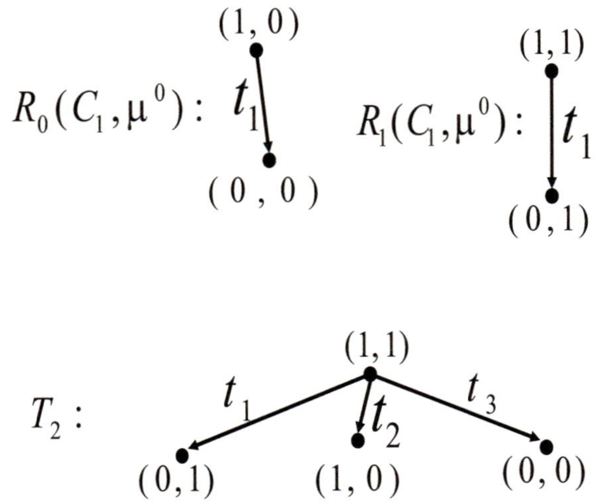

Figure 8. Augmented reachability trees and resulting labeled tree T_2

the following steps we construct the reachability tree $R(C_2, \mu^0)$ of C_2 from $R_0(C_1, \mu^0)$ and $R_1(C_1, \mu^0)$.

Step-1. Clearly, the binary 2-vectors in $R_0(C_1, \mu^0) \cup R_1(C_1, \mu^0)$ are all distinct and are exactly $2^2 = 4$ in number.

Step-2. In $R_0(C_1, \mu^0)$, none of the transitions t_j is enabled at $(1, 0)$.

Step-3. In $R_0(C_1, \mu^0)$, the root node $(1, 0)$ has the marking obtained after firing of transition t_2 in C_2. Hence, we join the root node $(1, 0)$ of $R_0(C_1, \mu^0)$ to the root node $(1, 1)$ of $R_1(C_1, \mu^0)$ by an arc labeled t_2 so that $(1, 0)$ would become the 'child node' obtained by firing t_2 in C_2. Next, we join the child node $(0, 0)$ of $R_0(C_1, \mu^0)$ to the root node $(1, 1)$ of $R_1(C_1, \mu^0)$ by an arc labeled t_3 so that $(0, 0)$ would become the child node obtained by firing t_3 in C_2. Then, the resulting labeled tree T_2 has exactly 2^2 binary 2-vectors as its set of nodes. T_2 is indeed the reachability tree of C_2 because in C_2 all the transitions t_1, t_2 and t_3 are enabled at the initial marking $(1, 1)$ and fire. Further, after firing of each transition, the new markings obtained by the rule

$$\mu'(p_i) = \mu^0(p_i) - I^-(p_i, t_j) + I^+(p_i, t_j)$$

are $(0, 1), (1, 0)$ and $(0, 0)$ respectively and no further firing takes place as the enabling condition fails to hold for these marking vectors; i.e., we get exactly $2^2 = 4$ binary 2-vectors in the first step only.

Next, suppose this result is true for $n = k$. That is, C_k is the 1-safe Petri net having k-places and $2^k - 1$ transitions $t_1, t_2, t_3, \cdots$, generating each of the 2^k binary k-vectors exactly once and having the structure as schematically shown in Figure 9 which has the following parameters:

$|p^\bullet| = 2^k - 1, \; \forall \, p,$
$|^\bullet p| = 2^{k-1} - 1, \; \forall \, p,$
$|^\bullet t| = k, \; \forall \, t.$

The total number of transitions whose post-sets have $k - 1$ elements $= {}^kC_{k-1} = {}^kC_1 = k$ and these transitions are $t_1, t_2, t_3, \cdots, t_k$.

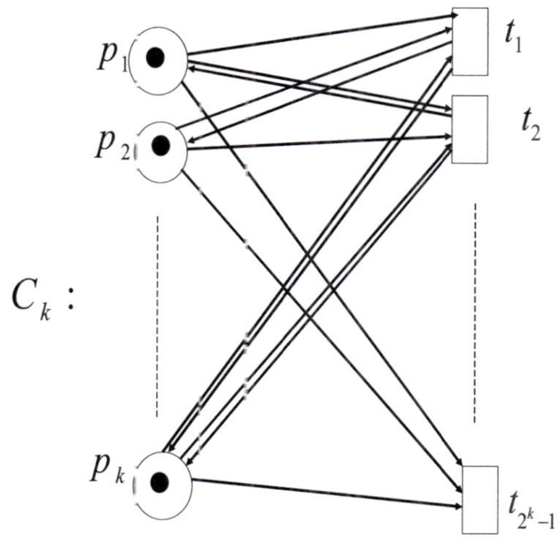

Figure 9. Petri net C_k for k places

The total number of transitions whose post-sets have $k-2$ elements $= {}^kC_{k-2} = {}^kC_2 = \frac{k(k-1)}{2}$ and these transitions are $t_{k+1}, t_{k+2}, t_{k+3}, \cdots, t_{\frac{k^2+k}{2}}$.

The total number of transitions whose post-sets have $k-3$ elements $= {}^kC_{k-3} = {}^kC_3 = \frac{k(k-1)(k-2)}{6}$ and these transitions are $t_{\frac{k^2+k+2}{2}}, t_{\frac{k^2+k+4}{2}}, t_{\frac{k^2+k+6}{2}}, \cdots, t_{\frac{k^3+5k}{6}}$.

⋮ ⋮ ⋮ ⋮ ⋮

The total number of transitions whose post-sets have one element $= {}^kC_1 = k$ and these transitions are $t_{2^k-k-1}, t_{2^k-k}, t_{2^k-k+1}, \cdots, t_{2^k-2}$.

The total number of transitions whose post-sets have no element $= {}^kC_0 = 1$ and this transition is t_{2^k-1}.

We will now prove the result for the 1-safe Petri net C_{k+1} having $k+1$ places and $t_{2^{k+1}} - 1$ transitions and having the structure shown schematically in **Figure-9**. For this purpose, take two copies of $R(C_k, \mu^0)$. In the first copy, augment each vector of $R(C_k, \mu^0)$ by the adjunction of a '0' entry at the $(k+1)^{th}$ coordinate of every marking vector and denote the resulting labeled tree as $R_0(C_k, \mu^0)$. Similarly, in the second copy, augment each vector by the adjunction of a '1' at the $(k+1)^{th}$ coordinate of every marking vector and let $R_1(C_k, \mu^0)$ be the resulting labeled tree. Now, using the following steps we construct the reachability tree $R(C_{k+1}, \mu^0)$ of C_{k+1} from $R_0(C_k, \mu^0)$ and $R_1(C_k, \mu^0)$.

Step-1. The induction hypothesis implies that the binary $(k+1)$-vectors in $R_0(C_k, \mu^0) \cup R_1(C_k, \mu^0)$ are all distinct and they are exactly $2^k + 2^k = 2^{k+1}$ in number.

Step-2. In $R_0(C_k, \mu^0)$, none of the transitions is enabled at $(1, 1, 1, \cdots 0)$.

Step-3. In $R_0(C_k, \mu^0)$, the root node $(1, 1, 1, \cdots, 0)$ is the marking obtained after firing of transition t_{k+1} in C_{k+1}. Hence, we join the root node $(1, 1, 1, \cdots, 0)$ of $R_0(C_k, \mu^0)$ to the root node $(1,1,1,\cdots,1)$ of $R_1(C_k,\mu^0)$ by an arc labeled t_{k+1} so that $(1,1,1,\cdots,0)$ would become the child node obtained by firing t_{k+1} in C_{k+1} and in $R_1(C_k,\mu^0)$ the child node $(0,0,0,\cdots,1)$ is the marking obtained after firing of the transition t_{k+2} at the root node $(1,1,1,\cdots,1)$ of $R_1(C_k,\mu^0)$; so, we replace the arc labeled as t_{k+1} by t_{k+2} in $R_1(C_k,\mu^0)$. Next, we join the remaining $(2^{k+1}-1)-\overline{k+2}$ child nodes $(0,1,0,\cdots,0)$, $(1,0,0,\cdots,0)$, $\cdots,(0,0,0,\cdots,0)$ of $R_0(C_k,\mu^0)$ to the root node $(1,1,1,\cdots,1)$ of $R_1(C_k,\mu^0)$ by an arc each, labeled $t_{k+3},t_{k+4},t_{k+5},\cdots,t_{2^k-1}$ respectively, so that $(0,1,0,\cdots,0)$, $(1,0,0,\cdots,0)$, $\cdots$, $(0,0,0,\cdots,0)$ would become the marking vector obtained after firing of t_{k+3}, t_{k+4}, t_{k+5}, $\cdots$, t_{2^k-1} respectively in C_{k+1}. Then the resulting labeled tree T_{k+1} has exactly 2^{k+1} binary $(k+1)$-vectors. T_{k+1} is indeed the reachability tree of C_{k+1} because in C_{k+1} all the transitions are enabled at the initial marking $(1,1,1,\cdots,1)$ and fire. After firing, the new markings obtained by the rule

$$\mu'(p_i)=\mu^0(p_i)-I^-(p_i,t_j)+I^+(p_i,t_j)$$

are

$$(0,1,1,\cdots,1),(1,0,1,\cdots,1),(1,1,0,\cdots,1),\cdots,(0,0,0,\cdots,0)$$

respectively and no further firing takes place as the enabling condition fails to hold for these marking vectors; i.e., we get exactly 2^{k+1} binary $(k+1)$-vectors, each generated exactly once in the first step itself.

It is clear that the Petri net constructed above generates each of the 2^n binary n-vectors exactly once in the very first step and, hence, is the smallest number of steps because no firing will take place after that step.

Hence, the result follows by the PMI. □

Hence, we shall call a Boolean Petri net *crisp* if it generates every binary $n-$vector exactly once.

It may be observed from the above proof that the Petri net constructed therein yields all the binary n-vectors as marking vectors in the least possible number of steps. Such a Boolean Petri net will be called *optimal.*

6. Uniqueness of minimal crisp Petri net

The problem of characterizing 1-safe Petri nets generating all the 2^n binary n-vectors as marking vectors exactly once is an open problem [6]. We completely settle a part of this problem, viz., to determine minimal such Petri nets, 'minimal' in the sense that the depth of their reachability tree is minimum possible, where the *depth* of a rooted tree is defined as the maximum distance of any vertex in it from the root. In fact, we show here that such a 1-safe Petri net has a unique structure.

Theorem 3. *[8] The Petri net $C=(P,T,I^-, I^+,\mu^0)$ constructed in theorem 2 is the only minimal Crisp Petri net and the underlying graph of its reachability tree is isomorphic to the star $\downarrow K_{1,2^n-1}$, where '$\downarrow$' indicates the fact that arcs of the reachability tree of C are oriented downward from its root which is the center of $K_{1,2^n-1}$.*

Proof. The existence of C has already been established in Theorem 2. We will establish here the uniqueness of C. Suppose there exists a Petri net

$$C' = (P', T', I'^{-}, I'^{+}, \mu^0)$$

satisfying the hypothesis of the theorem. This implies, in particular that the reachability graph $R(C', \mu^0)$ of C' is isomorphic to the reachability graph $R(C, \mu^0)$ of C, i.e.,

$$R(C', \mu^0) \cong R(C, \mu^0) \cong\downarrow K_{1,2^n-1}.$$

Now, we need to show that $C' \cong C$.

Toward this end, define a map $\psi : P' \cup T' \longrightarrow P \cup T$ satisfying $\psi(p_i') = p_i$ and $\psi(t_i') = t_i$. Clearly, ψ is a bijection. We shall now show that it preserves the directed adjacency of C' onto C. For this, consider any isomorphism $\varphi : M(C', \mu^0) \longrightarrow M(C, \mu^0)$ from the reachability set $M(R(C', \mu^0))$ of C' onto the reachability set of C; this has the property that

$$(\mu^0, \mu^i) \in \mathcal{A}(R(C', \mu^0)) \Leftrightarrow (\varphi(\mu^0), \varphi(\mu^i)) \in \mathcal{A}(R(C, \mu^0)), \tag{1}$$

where $\mathcal{A}(D)$ denotes the set of arcs of any digraph D (in this case, D is the reachability graph of the corresponding Petri net).

Let (p_i', t_j') be an arc in C', we will show then that $(\psi(p_i'), \psi(t_j'))$ is an arc in C. Suppose, on the contrary $(\psi(p_i'), \psi(t_j')) = (p_i, t_j)$ is not an arc in C. This implies in C that the marking vector μ^i whose i^{th} component is zero does not get generated by firing t_j or when $t_j^\bullet = \emptyset$ the marking vector obtained by firing t_j is repeated. The latter case does not arise due to the hypothesis that every marking vector is generated exactly once in C. But, then the former statement implies $\varphi(\mu^0)$ does not form the arc $(\varphi(\mu^0), \varphi(\mu^i))$ in $R(C, \mu^0)$ and hence, from (1), it follows that (μ^0, μ^i) does not form an arc in the reachability tree $R(C', \mu^0)$. This is a contradiction to our assumption that C' generates all the binary n-vectors exactly once. Similarly, one can arrive at a contradiction by assuming $(\psi(t_j'), \psi(p_i'))$ is not an arc in C. Thus, $C' \cong C$ follows, because the choice of the arcs (p_i', t_j') and (t_j', p_i') was arbitrary in each case. □

7. A Boolean Petri net whose reachability graph is homomorphic to the complete lattice

As mentioned already, Boolean Petri nets generating all the 2^n binary n-vectors as their marking vectors are not only of theoretical interest but also are of practical importance. We demonstrate the existence of a disconnected 1-safe Petri net whose reachability tree is homomorphic to the n-dimensional complete lattice L_n. This makes the problem of characterizing the crisp Boolean Petri nets appear quite intricate.

Definition 4. *Given any graph $G = (V, E)$, by a homomorphism of G we mean a partition $\{V_1, V_2, \ldots, V_t\}$ of its vertex-set $V(G) := V$ such that for any $i \in \{1, 2, \ldots, t\}$ no two distinct vertices in V_i are adjacent; in other words, V_i is an independent set of G. In general, given any partition $\pi = \{V_1, V_2, \ldots, V_t\}$ (not necessarily a homomorphism) of G, the partition graph with respect to π of G, denoted $\pi(G)$, is the graph whose vertex-set is π and any two vertices V_i and V_j are adjacent whenever there exist vertices $x \in V_i$ and $y \in V_j$ such that x and y are adjacent in G, that is, whenever, $xy \in E(G)$. If, in particular, π is a homomorphism then $\pi(G)$ is called a homomorphic image of G; further, a graph H is homomorphic to a graph G if there exists a homomorphism π of H such that $\pi(H) \cong G$ (read as "$\pi(H)$ is 'isomorphic to' G").*

Theorem 4. *[7] Let $C_n = (P, T, I^-, I^+, \mu^0)$ be the 1-safe Petri net consisting of n connected components, each isomorphic to $C^\star := \odot \longrightarrow \square$. Then the reachability tree of C_n is homomorphic to the n-dimensional complete lattice L_n.*

Proof. We prove this result by using the PMI on the number of connected components each isomorphic to $C^\star$.

Let $n = 1$. That is, C_1 has only one connected component $C^\star$, whence $C_1 = C^\star$. Then, the reachability tree of C_1 is the 1-dimensional complete lattice L_1, in which the direction of the 'link' (or, 'arc') $((1), (0))$ between the two 1-dimensional marking vectors (1) and (0) is shown as the 'vertical' one, as in Figure 10. The arc $((1), (0))$ in L_1, labeled as t_1, signifies the fact that the transition t_1 fires at (1), moving the only token out of the place p_1 resulting in the next state of the Petri net in which t_1 is 'dead' in the sense that it no longer fires at (0). Therefore, the next state of the Petri net C_1 is determined by the *zero vector* (0) as the marking vector of C_1. Thus, C_1 has just two states, viz., the 'active' one represented by the 1-dimensional 'unit vector' (1) and the 'dead' one represented by the 1-dimensional zero vector (0). Hence, the entire 'dynamics' of C_1 is completely represented by L_1. Next, consider $n = 2$. That is, we

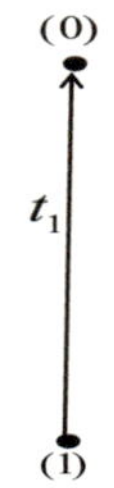

Figure 10. Lattice L_1

have the 1-safe Petri net C_2, consisting of two connected components, each isomorphic to $C^\star$ as shown in Figure 11, along with its reachability tree (seen as a connected acyclic digraph) that is isomorphic to the 2-dimensional complete lattice L_2. In C_2, the transitions t_1 and t_2 are

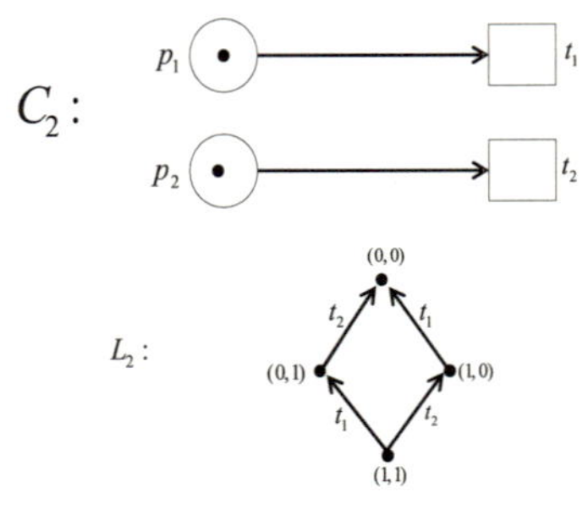

Figure 11. Petri net C_2 and its directed reachability tree L_2

both enabled. After firing t_1 and t_2 at the node $(1, 1)$ successively, in the first step, we get the marking vectors $(0, 1)$ and $(1, 0)$ respectively. Here, we fix the direction of t_2 to be 'orthogonal' to that of t_1 in L_2. Further, at $(0, 1)$ the transition t_2 is enabled, which fires in the same direction as in the first step giving the marking $(0,0)$. Subsequently, at $(1,0)$ transition t_1 is enabled, which fires in the same direction as in its previous step of firing giving the marking $(0,0)$. After this second step of firing, both the transitions t_1 and t_2 become dead at $(0,0)$. Thus, it is clear from Figure 11 that the reachability tree L_2 of C_2, seen as a connected acyclic digraph, has exactly $4 = 2^2$ binary vectors (a_1, a_2), $a_1, a_2 \in \{0,1\}$ as the marking vectors of C_2.

We can construct L_2 tactically from L_1 as follows.

Step1. Take two copies of L_1. In the first copy, augment each vector of L_1 by one extra coordinate position on the right by putting a 0 entry in that position and denote the resulting labeled copy of L_1 as L_1^0. Similarly, in the second copy, augment each vector by one extra coordinate position on the right by filling it with 1 and denote the resulting labeled copy of L_1 as L_1^1.

Step2. Take the union $L_1^0 \cup L_1^1$ and augment the new 'edges' (i.e., undirected line segments) joining those pairs of nodes whose marking vectors are at unit Hamming distance from each other. Direct each of these edges from the node, represented by its marking vector, at which t_2 fires to the node whose label (i.e., marking vector) gives the result of that firing. Accordingly, label each of such arcs by the label t_2.

Thus, the directed arcs labeled t_2 join every node of L_1^1 to exactly one node in L_1^0 in a bijective manner as shown in Figure 12. In this way, we see that the resulting discrete structure L_2^* has $4 = 2^2$ nodes which correspond to 2^2 binary vectors (a_1, a_2), $a_1, a_2 \in \{0,1\}$. Clearly, L_2^* is nothing but the reachability tree L_2 of C_2, seen as a connected acyclic digraph. Next, consider

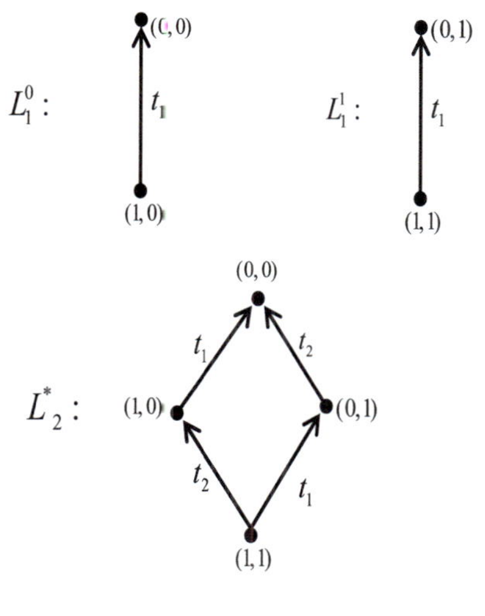

Figure 12. Augmented lattices and resulting complete lattice for 2 places

$n = 3$. That is, we have the 1-safe Petri net C_3 consisting of three connected components each isomorphic to C^* as shown in Figure 13. In C_3, all the three transitions t_1, t_2, t_3 are enabled. Hence, after firing the transitions t_1, t_2 and t_3 successively at $(1,1,1)$ we get the marking vectors $(0,1,1), (1,0,1)$ and $(1,1,0)$ respectively, in first step. Right here, we fix the directions of t_1, t_2 and t_3 so as to be orthogonal to each other. Further, at $(0,1,1)$ the transitions

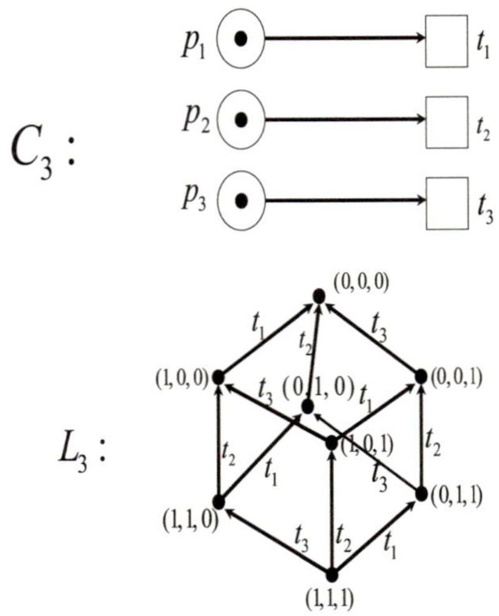

Figure 13. Petri net C_3 with 3 places and its complete lattice

t_2 and t_3 are enabled. After firing them successively we get the marking vectors $(0, 0, 1)$ and $(0, 1, 0)$, respectively. Subsequently, firing t_1 and t_3 at $(1, 0, 1)$ will give the marking vectors $(0, 0, 1)$ and $(1, 0, 0)$ respectively, whereas the firing of t_1 and t_2 at $(1, 1, 0)$ give the marking vectors $(0, 1, 0)$ and $(1, 0, 0)$. On continuing the process of firing in the next (i.e., the third) step we get the marking vector $(0, 0, 0)$ at which no transition is enabled. So, we have the reachability tree L_3 of C_3, which is isomorphic to the 3-dimensional complete lattice L_3, seen as a connected acyclic digraph.

We can construct L_3 from L_2 as follows.

Step1. Take two copies of L_2. In the first copy, augment each vector of L_2 by one extra coordinate position on the extreme right by putting a 0 entry in that position; denote the resulting labeled copy of L_2 as L_2^0. Similarly, in the second copy, augment each vector by one extra coordinate position on the extreme right by filling it with 1; denote the resulting labeled copy of L_2 as L_2^1.

Step2. Take the union $L_2^0 \cup L_2^1$ and augment the new 'edges' (i.e., undirected line segments) joining those pairs of nodes whose marking vectors are at unit Hamming distance from each other. Direct each of these edges from the node, represented by its marking vector, at which t_3 fires, to the node whose label (i.e., marking vector) gives the result of that firing. Accordingly, label each of such arcs by the label t_3.

Thus, the directed arcs labeled t_3 join every node of L_2^1 to exactly one node in L_2^0 in a bijective manner as shown in Figure 14. In this way, we see that the resulting discrete structure L_3^* has $8 = 2^3$ nodes which correspond to 2^3 binary vectors (a_1, a_2, a_3), $a_1, a_2, a_3 \in \{0, 1\}$. Clearly, L_3^* is nothing but the reachability tree L_3 of C_3, seen as a connected acyclic digraph. Hence, let us assume that the result is true for $n = k$. That is, we have the 1-safe Petri net C_k consisting of k connected components each isomorphic to C^* and L_k is isomorphic to the reachability

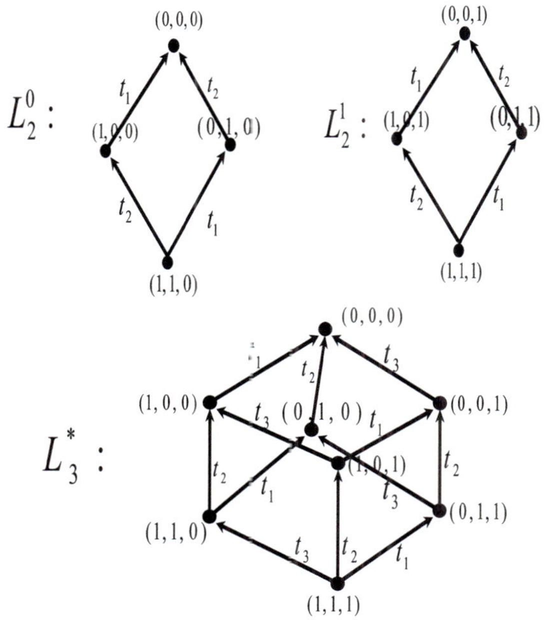

Figure 14. Augmented lattices and resulting complete lattice

tree of C_k, seen as a connected acyclic digraph. Now, we will prove that the result is true for $n = k + 1$.

Note that, in C_k, all the k transitions $t_1, t_2, \ldots, t_k$ are enabled at the k-dimensional unit vector $(1, 1, \ldots, 1)$.

Step1. Take two copies of L_k. In the first copy, augment each vector of L_k by one extra coordinate position on the extreme right by putting a 0 entry in that position; denote the resulting labeled copy of L_k as L_k^0. Similarly, in the second copy, augment each vector by one extra coordinate position on the extreme right by filling it with 1; denote the resulting labeled copy of L_k as L_k^1.

Step2. Take the union $L_k^0 \cup L_k^1$ and augment the new 'edges' (i.e., undirected line segments) joining those pairs of nodes whose marking vectors are at unit Hamming distance from each other. Direct each of these edges from the node, represented by its marking vector, at which t_{k+1} fires, to the node whose label (i.e., marking vector) gives the result of that firing. Accordingly, label each of such arcs by the label t_{k+1}.

It is now enough to show that L_{k+1} is indeed isomorphic to the reachability tree of C_{k+1}, seen as a connected acyclic digraph. Towards this end, consider the sets $A_0 = \{(a_1, a_2, \ldots, a_{k+1}) : a_{k+1} = 0\}$ and $A_1 = \{(a_1, a_2, \ldots, a_{k+1}) : a_{k+1} = 1\}$ Clearly, the subdigraph induced by A_0 is 'label-isomorphic' to L_k^0 whose nodes are labeled by the 2^k $(k+1)$-dimensional vectors in A_0 and the subdigraph induced by A_1 is 'label-isomorphic' to L_k^1 whose nodes are labeled by the 2^k $(k+1)$-dimensional vectors in A_1. Every arc in $L_k^0 \cup L_k^1$ is labeled by one of the transitions $t_1, t_2, \ldots, t_k$ in such a way that for any two indices $i, j \in \{1, 2, \ldots, k\}$ t_i and t_j are in orthogonal or parallel directions in each of L_k^0 and L_k^1 according to whether $i \neq j$ or $i = j$; thus, by Step 1 and the induction hypothesis, each of the $k2^{k-1}$ arcs in L_k^0 (respectively, in L_k^1) represents one of the transitions $t_1, t_2, \ldots, t_k$ fired in accordance with the firing rule, yielding the next state marking vector from its previous state marking vector that is at unit Hamming distance from the former. Now, by Step 2, the edges joining those pairs of nodes whose marking vectors are at unit Hamming distance from each other are directed in such a way that each of the resulting arcs represents the firing of a new transition t_{k+1} at the node, represented by its marking vector in the reachability tree of C_{k+1}, yielding the node of the reachability tree of C_{k+1} whose label (i.e., marking vector) gives the result of that firing. Accordingly, label each of such arcs by the label t_{k+1}. Since no two marking vectors in A_0 or in A_1 are interconnected by an arc labeled t_{k+1} in the above scheme, it follows that every arc labeled t_{k+1} has its initial node in A_1 and terminal node in A_0, signifying the fact that t_{k+1} fires at its initial node in A_1 and yields the next state marking vector that belongs to A_0. Further, no two of these arcs have a common node (whence we say that they are *independent*). Also, every node in A_1 is joined to a unique node in A_0 at Hamming distance one by an arc labeled t_{k+1} in a bijective way and, therefore, the number of such arcs is 2^k.

Next, consider the node labeled $(0,0,\ldots,0)$ in L_{k+1}. The only arcs incoming at this node are from the nodes that are at unit Hamming distance from it, viz., those that are labeled by the elementary coordinate vectors $(1,0,0,\ldots,0)$, $(0,1,0,\ldots,0)$, $(0,0,1,\ldots,0)$, $\ldots$, $(0,0,0,\ldots,1)$ and, hence, the corresponding arcs are labeled $t_1, t_2, \ldots, t_k, t_{k+1}$. Consequently, all these transitions become dead at the node labeled by the $(k+1)$-dimensional zero vector $(0,0,\ldots,0)$ as its marking vector.

The foregoing arguments imply that L_{k+1} indeed represents the reachability tree of C_{k+1}, being a connected acyclic digraph, invoking the PMI.

Now, for any arbitrary positive integer n, construct the partition π_H of the reachability tree $R(C_n, \mu^0)$ by defining its 'parts' (which are subsets of the nodes of $R(C_n, \mu^0)$) by letting $V_0 = \{(1,1,\ldots,1)\}$ and $V_i = \{(a_1, a_2, \ldots, a_n) : d_H((1,1,\ldots,1),(a_1,a_2,\ldots,a_n)) = i\}$, for each $i \in \{1,2,\ldots,n\}$, where $d_H(A,B)$ denotes the Hamming distance between the vectors A and B of the same dimension. Clearly, $|V_i| = {}^nC_i$ for each $i \in \{0,1,2,\ldots,n\}$, where ${}^nC_k = \frac{n!}{k!(n-k)!}$ will in general denote the number of ways in which k objects can be selected out of n given objects. Now, consider the mapping $\eta^{\mu^0} : V(R(C_n, \mu^0)) \to \{0,1\}^n$ that assigns to each node $u \in R(C_n, \mu^0)$ the marking vector derived by the sequence of transitions fired starting from the initial marking vector μ^0 as specified by the unique path from the root vertex u_0 whose marking vector is μ^0. Hence, we consider the *refinement* π'_H of π_H defined as follows: For each $i \in \{0,1,2,\ldots,n\}$ and for each $(a_1, a_2, \ldots, a_n) \in V_i$, let $U^i_{(a_1,a_2,\ldots,a_n)} = \{u \in V(R(C_n,\mu^0)) : \eta^{\mu^0}(u) = (a_1,a_2,\ldots,a_n)\}$. Then, clearly, U^i's form a partition of the set V_i for each $i \in \{0,1,2,\ldots,n\}$. It may be easily verified that no two marking vectors in V_i are adjacent in $R(C_n, \mu^0)$, whence π'_H is a homomorphism of $R(C_n, \mu^0)$. Further, the homomorphic image $\pi'_H(R(C_n, \mu^0)) \cong L_n$ because (V_i, V_{i+1}) is an arc in L_n if and only if there is an arc from a marking vector in V_i to a marking vector in V_{i+1} in $R(C_n, \mu^0)$.

This completes the proof. □

In the above theorem, we have shown that by fixing the sequence of transitions in a Petri net for firing tactfully, one can produce the complete Boolean lattice as a homomorphic image of its reachability tree. One can perhaps produce many such interesting results like, for instance, getting the vertices of a regular polyhedron in terms of marking vectors and using them for analysis of Boolean circuits with given properties. This raises another new question, viz., to characterize 1-safe Petri nets whose reachability trees have a given property $\mathcal{P}$.

Note that given any 1-safe Petri net C of order n, its reachability tree $R(C,\mu)$, with an arbitrary binary n-dimensional vector μ as its root, is essentially finite (cf.: [11]) and has all its nodes labeled by the function η^{μ} into the vertex set of the Boolean complete lattice L_n, possibly with repetitions of marking vectors. Consider the *Hamming distance partition* $\pi_H := \pi_H(V(R(C,\mu)))$ of the vertex-set of $R(C,\mu)$ defined by letting $V_0 = \{\mu\}$ and

$$V_i = \{(a_1, a_2, \ldots, a_n) : d_H(\mu, (a_1, a_2, \ldots, a_n)) = i\},$$

for each $i \in \{1, 2, \ldots\}$. Then, its refinement $\pi'_H = \{V_0, V_1, V_2, \ldots, V_n\}$ is a homomorphism of $R(C,\mu)$ into a connected sublattice of L_n. Thus, we are lead to the problem of determining 1-safe Petri nets whose reachability trees are homomorphic to a given sublattice of L_n. First of all, we have the question whether for any arbitrarily given connected sublattice L of L_n there exists a 1-safe Petri net whose usual reachability tree is homomorphic to L. We have a conjecture that the answer to this question is in the affirmative.

Next, given a connected sublattice L of L_n, let $\mathcal{C}^n_L$ denote the set of all 1-safe Petri nets of order n whose reachability trees are homomorphic to L. Let $\mathcal{L}_n$ denote the set of all pairwise nonisomorphic connected sublattices of L_n. Clearly, $\{\mathcal{C}^n_L : L \in \mathcal{L}_n\}$ is a partition of the set $\mathcal{S}_1$ of all 1-safe Petri nets of order n. In other words, 1-safe Petri nets in any one of the sets in $\mathcal{C}^n_L$ are all 'equivalent' in the sense that the dynamics of any two of them are in accordance with the given connected sublattice L of L_n; thus, it is enough to pick any one of them so that we have an option to choose the 'required' one as per our practical constraints.

8. Towards characterizing Boolean Petri nets

We discuss here some necessary and sufficiency conditions for a 1-safe Petri net to be Boolean.

Lemma 1. *[9] If a 1-safe Petri net $C = (P, T, I^-, I^+, \mu^0)$, $|P| = n$ is Boolean then $p \in t^\bullet \Rightarrow p \in {}^\bullet t$.*

Proof. Suppose $p \in t^\bullet$ and $p \notin {}^\bullet t$. Since C is 1-safe, ${}^\bullet t \neq \emptyset \; \forall \; t \in T$ (see [2]). This means that there exists at least one place $p_i \in P$ such that $p_i \in {}^\bullet t$. Further, since C is Boolean, $\mu^0(p)=1$ $\forall \; p \in P$ (Proposition 1) and, therefore, every transition is enabled. In particular, t is enabled. After firing of t the place p will receive 2 tokens ($\because \mu'(p) = \mu(p) - I^-(p,t) + I^+(p,t)$), which contradicts the fact that the Petri net is 1-safe. Hence, $p \in t^\bullet \Rightarrow p \in {}^\bullet t$. □

Lemma 2. *[9] If a 1-safe Petri net $C = (P, T, I^-, I^+, \mu^0)$, $|P| = n$ is Boolean then $|P| \leq |T|$.*

Proof. Since C generates all the binary n-vectors, it generates the marking vectors of the type $(0,1,\cdots,1), (1,0,1,\cdots,1), \cdots, (1,1,\cdots,0)$, each having the Hamming distance 1 from the initial marking vector μ^0=$(1,1,\cdots,1)$. These n marking vectors can be obtained only in the very first step of firing because the marking vector whose Hamming distance is 1 from the initial marking cannot be obtained from any other marking vector whose Hamming distance is greater than or equal to 2 from the initial marking. These n marking vectors can be generated only if for every place $p_i \in P$, $i = 1,2,3,\cdots,n$, there exist n distinct transitions say t_1,t_2,t_3,$\cdots$,t_n such that $p_i \in^\bullet t_i$ and $p_i \notin t_i^\bullet$, $\forall \; i = 1,2,3,\cdots,n$. Hence, $|P| \leq |T|$. □

Lemma 3. *[9] If a 1-safe Petri net $C = (P, T, I^-, I^+, \mu^0)$, $|P| = n$ is Boolean then the incidence matrix I of C contains $-I_n$, the identity matrix of order n as a submatrix.*

Proof. Since C is Boolean, $\mu^0(p)$=1 $\forall\ p \in P$ (Proposition 1). Again, because of the generation of all the binary n-vectors, the vectors of the type $(0, 1, \cdots, 1), (1, 0, 1, \cdots, 1), \cdots, (1, 1, \cdots, 0)$ each at a Hamming distance 1 from the initial marking, have also been generated. These vectors can be obtained only in the first step of firing, as shown in Lemma 2. Therefore, $\forall$ $p_i \in P$, $i = 1, 2, 3, \cdots, n$, there exist n distinct transitions, say t_1,t_2,t_3,$\cdots$,t_n such that $p_i \in {}^\bullet t_i$ and $p_i \notin t_i^\bullet$ and hence $I^-(p_i, t_j)$=1 if i=j and 0 if $i \neq j$ and also $I^+(p_i, t_i) = 0\ \forall\ i = 1, 2, 3, \cdots, n$. Since I=I^+-I^-, I contains $-I_n$ as a submatrix. □

Lemma 4. *[9] If a 1-safe Petri net $C = (P, T, I^-, I^+, \mu^0)$, $|P| = n$ is Boolean then there exists at least one transition t such that $t^\bullet = \emptyset$.*

Proof. Suppose, under the hypothesis, there does not exist any $t \in T$ such that $t^\bullet = \emptyset$; i.e., $t^\bullet \neq \emptyset$ for every $t \in T$. Since $t^\bullet \neq \emptyset$, $p \in t^\bullet$ for some $p \in P$. Then, by Lemma 1, $p \in {}^\bullet t$. Then, at p, the number of tokens remains one throughout the dynamic states of C. This implies that the vector $(0, 0, \cdots, 0)$ would never occur as a marking vector, a contradiction to the hypothesis. Therefore, the lemma follows by contraposition. □

Now, we will study necessary and sufficient conditions for a 1-safe Petri net that generates all the binary n-vectors as its marking vectors.

Theorem 5. *[9] A 1-safe Petri net $C = (P, T, I^-, I^+, \mu^0)$, $|P| = n$ with $t^\bullet = \emptyset\ \forall\ t \in T$ is Boolean if and only if*

1. $\mu^0(p) = 1\ \forall\ p \in P$
2. $|P| \leq |T|$
3. *The incidence matrix I of C contains $-I_n$ as a submatrix.*

Proof. Necessity: This follows from Proposition 1, Lemma 2 and Lemma 3 above.

Sufficiency: Given the hypothesis and conditions (1), (2) and (3), we claim that C is Boolean. Since $I = I^+ - I^-$ and $t^\bullet = \emptyset, \forall\ t \in T, I^+ = 0$. This implies that $I = -I^-$. Since I contains $-I_n$ as a submatrix, $\forall\ p_i \in P, \exists\ t_i \in T$ such that $p_i \in {}^\bullet t_i\ \forall\ i = 1, 2, \cdots, n$. Also, $\mu^0(p) = 1\ \forall p \in P$. Therefore, all the n transitions $t_1, t_2, \cdots, t_n$ are enabled and fire. After firing, we get distinct ${}^nC_1 = n$ marking vectors whose Hamming distance is 1 from the initial marking vector. At these n new marking vectors, $n - 1$ transitions are enabled and give at least ${}^nC_2$ distinct marking vectors, each of whose Hamming distance is 2 from the initial marking. Therefore this set of new vectors contains at least ${}^nC_2$ new distinct binary $n-$vectors.

In general, at any stage j, $3 \leq j \leq n$, we get a set of at least ${}^nC_j$ new distinct binary n-vectors whose Hamming distance is j from the initial marking, which are also distinct from the sets of ${}^nC_r$ distinct marking vectors for all r, $2 \leq r \leq j - 1$. Therefore, at the nth stage we would have obtained at least ${}^nC_1 +^n C_2 + \cdots +^n C_n$=$2^n - 1$ distinct binary n-vectors. Together with the initial marking $(1, 1, \cdots, 1)$, we thus see that all the 2^n binary n-vectors would have been obtained as markings vectors, possibly with repetitions. □

Theorem 6. *[9] A 1-safe Petri net $C = (P, T, I^-, I^+, \mu^0)$, $|P| = n$ with $I^-(p_i, t_j) = 1\ \forall\ i, j$ is Boolean if and only if there exist at least ${}^nC_r$, $r = 1, 2, \cdots, n$ distinct transitions $t \in T$ such that $|t^\bullet| = n - r$, where r is the Hamming distance of any binary n-vector from the initial marking $(1, 1, \cdots, 1)$.*

Proof. Necessity: Since C generates all the binary n-vectors, we have binary n-vectors $(0, 1, 1, \cdots, 1)$, $(1, 0, 1, \cdots, 1)$, $(1, 1, 0, \cdots, 1)$, $\cdots$, $(1, 1, 1, \cdots, 0)$, whose Hamming distance is 1 from the initial marking $(1, 1, 1, \cdots 1)$. They are n in number. Since $I^-(p_i, t_j) = 1\ \forall i, j$, these vectors can be obtained only if $I^+(p_i, t_j) = 0$ for $i = j$ and 1 for $i \neq j$, $1 \leq j \leq n$. This implies that there are at least ${}^nC_1$ distinct transitions say t_1, t_2, $\cdots$, t_n such that $|t^\bullet| = n - 1$. After firing, they become dead. Further, we also have the binary n-vectors $(0, 0, 1, \cdots, 1)$, $(1, 0, 0, 1, \cdots, 1)$, $(1, 0, 1, 0, 1, \cdots, 1)$, $\cdots$, $(1, 1, \cdots, 1, 0, 0)$ whose Hamming distance is 2 from $(1, 1, 1, \cdots 1)$, $r = 1, 2, \ldots, n$. These vectors are ${}^nC_2$ in number and can be obtained only if there exist at least ${}^nC_2$ distinct transitions with $|t^\bullet| = n - 2$. In general, there are at least ${}^nC_r$ distinct transitions t such that $|t^\bullet| = n - r$, that yield ${}^nC_r$ binary n-vectors at Hamming distance r from $(1, 1, 1, \cdots 1)$, $r = 1, 2, \ldots, n$.

Sufficiency: Since $\mu^0(p) = 1\ \forall p$, all the transitions are enabled and fire. After firing they all become dead as $I^-(p_i, t_j) = 1\ \forall\ i, j$. This implies that the matrix I^- is of order $n \times m$ where $m \geq 2^n - 1$ and the matrix I^+ gets constructed as follows. By hypothesis, there are at least ${}^nC_1 = n$ distinct transition in C say t_1, t_2, $\cdots$, t_n which on firing generate all the binary n-vectors each having exactly one zero because $|t_i^\bullet| = n - 1$ (w.l.o.g., we assume that there is no arc from t_i to p_i i.e., $I^+(p_i, t_i) = 0$ for $i = 1, 2, \cdots, n$). Thus, we place the transpose of these binary n-vectors as the first n-columns in I^+ matrix. Next, by hypothesis, we have ${}^nC_2$ distinct transitions, say $t_{n+1}, t_{n+2}, \cdots, t_{{}^nC_2}$, such that $|t_j^\bullet| = n - 2$. Since they all become dead after firing and $|t_j^\bullet| = n - 2$ for all $n + 1 \leq j \leq {}^nC_2$ these must generate all the distinct binary n-vectors each having exactly two zeros. Hence, the transpose of these ${}^nC_2$ vectors are placed as columns in the matrix I^+ immediately after the previous $n = {}^nC_1$ columns. We are thus enabled by the hypothesis to construct the submatrix H of order $n \times (2^n - 1)$ of I^- which contains all the $2^n - 1$ distinct binary n-vectors, the last column of H being the all zero n-vector. We may augment to H the initial all-one n-vector as a column either on the extreme left or on the extreme right of H in I^+. Let the so augmented submatrix of I^+ have more columns. That means, each one of them is a repetition of some column in H. Thus, we see that the Petri net C generates all the binary n-vectors as its marking vectors. □

Definition 5. *A Petri net C=(P, T, I^-, I^+, μ^0) is said to have a* ***Strong chain cycle*** *(SCC) Z if Z is a subnet satisfying $|{}^\bullet t|$=2, $|p^\bullet|$=2 and $|t^\bullet|$=1 $\forall$ p,t$\in$ Z (See Figure 15). Any SCC is said to become a* ***strong chain*** *after the removal of the arcs of any one of its self loops.*

Theorem 7. *[9] A 1-safe Petri net $C = (P, T, I^-, I^+, \mu^0)$, $|P| = n$ having an SCC Z, covering all the places, is Boolean if and only if*

1. $\mu^0(p) = 1\ \forall\ p \in P$
2. *there exists at least one transition t outside Z such that $t^\bullet = \emptyset$.*

Proof. Necessity: Suppose that the 1-safe Petri net C with an SCC covering all the places is Boolean.

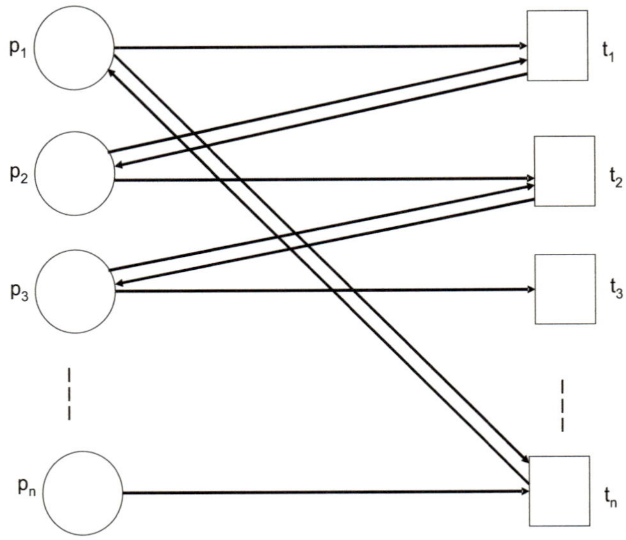

Figure 15. Strong Chain Cycle

In part 1 of the statement of the theorem, let $\mu^0(p_i) \neq 1$ for some $p_i \in P$. Then, $\mu^0(p_i) = 0$. Since C has an SCC, we cannot get one token in the place p_i. So, we cannot get all the binary n-vectors, which is a contradiction to the hypothesis.

In part 2 of the theorem, since C generates all the binary n-vectors, we have $(0,0,\cdots,0)$ as a marking vector. This vector can be obtained only if there is a transition t such that $t^\bullet$=$\emptyset$, by virtue of Lemma 4. We claim that such a transition t does not belong to Z. Suppose $t \in Z$=$(p_1, t_1, p_2, t_2, p_3, t_3, \cdots, p_{n-1}, t_{n-1}, p_n, t_n, p_1)$ where (p_i, t_i) is a single arc in C and (t_i, p_{i+1}) is a symmetric arc in C. This means, $t = t_i$ for some i, $1 \leq i \leq n$. This implies, $|t^\bullet|$=$|t_i^\bullet|$=1, which is a contradiction to our assumption that $t^\bullet$=$\emptyset$. Therefore, t does not belong to any SCC.

Sufficiency: Since $\mu^0(p) = 1 \; \forall \; p \in P$, all the transitions belonging to Z are enabled and fire. After firing, they give ${}^nC_1$ distinct binary n-vectors $a_1 = (0,1,1,\cdots,1)$, $a_2 = (1,0,1,\cdots,1)$, $\cdots$, $a_i = (1,1,\cdots,1,0,1,\cdots,1)$, $\cdots$, $a_n = (1,1,\cdots,1,0)$, whose Hamming distance is 1 from μ^0, since $p_i^\bullet$=$\{t_{i-1}, t_i\}$ for $i > 1$ and $p_1^\bullet$=$\{t_1, t_n\}$, at each of these vectors a_i, exactly $(n-2)$ remaining transitions on Z are enabled and fire. After firing them, we get at least ${}^nC_2$ distinct marking vectors each of whose Hamming distance from μ^0 is 2 because in this second stage of firing there are $n(n-2)$ binary n-vectors in each of which there are exactly two zeros. In the third stage, at least ${}^nC_3$ distinct marking vectors are obtained by firing the above n-vectors obtained in the second stage and each of these vectors contains exactly three zeros. Continuing in this manner in the rth stage we get at least ${}^nC_r$ distinct marking vectors, each containing exactly r zeros, by firing all the n-vectors obtained in the $(r-1)$ stage. Since r ranges from $1, 2, \cdots, (n-1)$, we thus obtain at least ${}^nC_1$+${}^nC_2$+${}^nC_3$+$\cdots$+${}^nC_{n-1}$ which is equal to 2^n-${}^nC_0$-${}^nC_n$=2^n-2 distinct n-marking vectors. Since all of them are distinct from μ^0 as well as from the zero vector $(0,0,\cdots,0)$, which is obtained due to the hypothesis that there exists a transition t outside Z such that $t^\bullet = \emptyset$. Thus, we see that all the 2^n distinct binary n-vectors are generated by C. $\square$

Lemma 5. *Let $C = (P, T, I^-, I^+, \mu^0)$, $|P| = n$ be a 1-safe Petri net with $\mu^0(p) = 1\ \forall\ p \in P$ and let Z be an SCC that passes through all the n places. Then any Petri net C' obtained from C by the deletion of any of the self loops belonging to Z generates all the binary n-vectors.*

Proof. First, we note that the removal of any self-loop from C results in a Petri net C' with $\mu^0(p) = 1\ \forall\ p \in P$ and a transition t such that $t^\bullet = \emptyset$. Now, if C' has an SCC Z' then by Theorem 7, C' is Boolean and hence there is nothing to prove. Hence, without loss of generality, we may assume that the given Petri net C has an SCC, say Z. We shall then prove the result by invoking the PMI on $n = |P|$. First, let $n = 1$. Then C does not contain any SCC and, therefore $C' = C$. Further, it is easy to verify that C' generates all the binary 1-vectors, namely (1), (0) as shown in Figure 16. Next, let $n = 2$. Then C' contains the following

$$p_1 \odot \longrightarrow \square\ t_1$$

Figure 16. Petri net $C' =:\cong C$ for 1 place

structure, shown in Figure 17. Here, $t_2^\bullet = \emptyset$. Since $\mu^0(p) = 1\ \forall\ p \in P$, t_2 is enabled and it

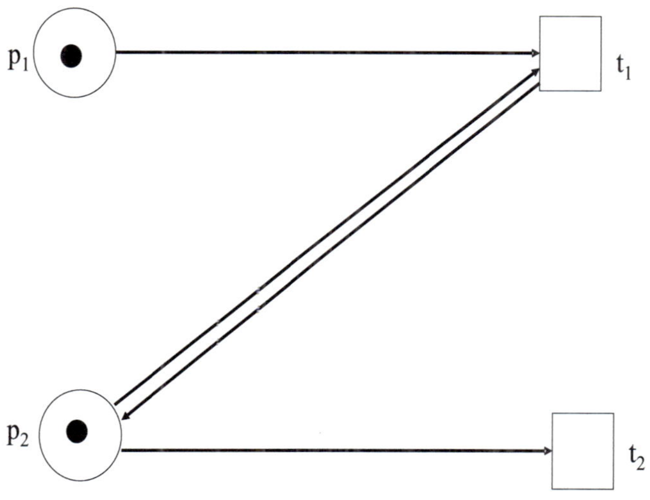

Figure 17. Petri net C' for 2 places

fires. After firing t_2, we get the marking vector $\mu^1 = (1, 0)$. Since t_1 fires simultaneously with t_2, we get the marking vector $\mu^2 = (0, 1)$. At this stage, t_2 is enabled and after firing, it gives the marking vector $\mu^3 = (0, 0)$. Hence we can obtain these marking vectors procedurally by taking two marking vectors obtained in the previous case namely, (1), (0) as follows.

Step-1. Augment 1 in the second position (corresponding to the case $t_2^\bullet = \emptyset$) in each of these vectors.

Step-2. In each case, t_2 fires and after firing, we get the marking vectors $(1, 0)$ and $(0, 0)$, respectively.

Next, take $n = k \geq 3$ and assume the validity by the above procedure to get all the 2^k binary k-vectors.

Let $n = k + 1$. Then, apply the following procedure.

Step-I. Augment 1 to each of the marking vectors $(a_1, a_2, \cdots, a_k)$ at its right most end to get the $(k+1)$-vector $(a_1, a_2, \cdots, a_k, 1)$.

Step-II. In this case, t_{k+1} fires and after firing we get the marking vectors $(a_1, a_2, \cdots, a_k, 0)$.

By the induction hypothesis, we have all the 2^k marking vectors to which Step-I has been applied to obtain the 2^k binary $(k+1)$-vectors as marking vectors (because of firing at each stage), having 1 in the $(k+1)^{th}$ coordinate. Further, each of these 2^k binary $(k+1)$-vectors has been fired using Step-II to obtain the binary $(k+1)$-vectors of the form $(a_1, a_2, \cdots, a_k, 0)$ which are all distinct from those obtained in Step-I. Together, therefore, we have obtained $2^k + 2^k = 2^{k+1}$ binary $(k+1)$-vectors as marking vectors from C'. Thus, the proof follows by PMI. □

9. An embedding theorem and complexity

The following is a "frustration theorem" due to the negative fact it reveals, to the effect that one cannot hope to have a "forbidden subgraph characterization" of a Boolean Petri net.

Theorem 8. *[10]: Every 1-safe Petri net $C = (P, T, I^-, I^+, \mu^0)$, $|P| = n$ with $\mu^0(p) = 1 \;\forall\; p \in P$ can be embedded as an induced subnet of a Boolean Petri net.*

Proof. Let $C = (P, T, I^-, I^+, \mu^0)$, $|P| = n$ be a 1-safe Petri net. If C is a Boolean Petri net then there is nothing to prove. Hence, assume that C is not a Boolean Petri net. Then, we have the following steps to obtain a Boolean Petri net C' in which C is one of its induced subnets.

Step-1: First of all, find those places in C each of whose postsets has single distinct sink transition (if the postset of a place has more than one distinct sink transitions then choose only one transition giving K_2). Suppose such places are $p_1, p_2, \cdots, p_k$, $1 \leq k < n$. If there is no sink transition in C, then augment one sink transition to each place in C.

Step-2: Augment $n-k$ new transitions and join each of them to the remaining $n-k$ places in C by an arc from a place to a new transition creating $n-k$ new active transitions.

Step-3: Thus, in C' we have n-copies of K_2 as its subgraph. Since $\mu^0(p) = 1 \;\forall p \in P$, all the transitions are enabled. Firing of n transitions forming n 'pendant transitions' will produce ${}^nC_1$ distinct binary n-vectors whose Hamming distance is 1 from the initial marking vector. At these marking vectors, $n-1$ transitions out of those n transitions are enabled, and after firing give at least ${}^nC_2$ distinct marking vectors, each of whose Hamming distance is 2 from the initial marking.

In general at any stage j, $3 \leq j \leq n$, we get a set of at least ${}^nC_j$ new distinct binary n-vectors whose Hamming distance is j from the initial marking, which are also distinct from the sets of ${}^nC_r$ distinct marking vectors for all r, $2 \leq r \leq j-1$. Therefore, at the nth stage we would have obtained at least ${}^nC_1 +^n C_2 + \cdots +^n C_n = 2^n - 1$ distinct binary n-vectors. Together with the initial marking $(1, 1, \cdots, 1)$, we thus see that all the 2^n binary n-vectors would have been obtained as marking vectors, possibly with repetitions. Thus C' is Boolean.

Therefore, every 1-safe Petri net C can be embedded as an induced subgraph of a Boolean Petri net. □

10. Scope for research

Precisely which Petri nets generate all the binary n-vectors as their marking vectors, or the so-called Boolean Petri net? This has been a hotly pursued research problems. We have shown in this chapter some necessary and sufficient conditions to characterize a Boolean Petri net, containing an SCC. However, the general problem of characterizing such a 1-safe Petri net C, when C does not contain an SCC or a strong chain, is still open. A Petri net containing an SCC is strongly connected, in the graph-theoretical sense that any two nodes in it are mutually reachable. However, the converse is not true; that is, if the underlying digraph of a Petri net is strongly connected, it need not contain an SCC. So, even a characterization of strongly connected Boolean Petri net is an open problem. Further, in general, characterizing crisp Boolean Petri nets is open too. If we relax the condition on the depth of the reachability tree in our original definition of minimality of a 'minimal' crisp Boolean Petri net and require instead that the number of enabled transitions be kept at minimum possible, the reachability graphs of such Petri nets may not have their underlying graph structures isomorphic to $K_{1,2^n-1}$, whence they would all be trees of the same order 2^n. Since they would be finite in number, determination of the structures of such Petri nets and their enumeration would be of potential practical interest. It involves orienting trees of order 2^n (in general, for theoretical purposes, trees of any order as such) that admit an orientation of their edges to make them the reachability trees of minimal $1-$safe crisp Boolean Petri nets.

11. Concluding remarks

As pointed out, many fundamental issues regarding Boolean Petri nets emerge from the above study. For example, it is found and established that the reachability tree of a 1-safe Petri net can be homomorphically mapped on to the n-dimensional complete Boolean lattice, thereby yielding new techniques to represent the dynamics of these Petri nets. One can expect to bring out in the near future some salient features of 1-safe Petri nets in general as a part of a theory that is likely to emerge even in our work.

Following our first discovery of an infinite class of 1-safe star Petri nets that are Boolean, we came across crisp Boolean Petri nets, viz., that generate every binary n-vector as marking vector exactly once. This motivated us to move towards a characterization of such 1-safe Petri nets in general. Our work towards this end revealed to our surprise that there can be even such disconnected 1-safe Petri nets. We demonstrated the existence of a disconnected 1-safe Petri net which was obtained by removing the central transition from the star Petri net S_n whose reachability tree can be tactically represented as an n-dimensional complete lattice L_n [7]. In this disconnected Petri net, the firing of transitions in a particular way (which we may regard as a 'tact' or 'strategy'), gives exactly 2^n marking vectors, repetitions occurring possibly only within a level, that can be arranged as a homomorphic image of the reachability tree of the Petri net, forming the n-dimensional complete Boolean lattice L_n.

The results of this chapter can perhaps be used gainfully in many purely theoretical areas like mathematics, computer science, universal algebra and order theory, the extent and effectiveness of its utility in solving the practical problem requiring the design of multi-functional switches for the operation of certain discrete dynamical systems of common use such as washing machines and teleprinters (e.g., see [1]).

Acknowledgement

The authors deeply acknowledge with thanks the valuable suggestions and thought-provoking comments by Dr. B.D. Acharya from time to time while carrying out the work reported in this chapter.

Author details

Sangita Kansal, Mukti Acharya and Gajendra Pratap Singh
Department of Applied Mathematics, Delhi Technological University, Shahbad Daulatpur, Main Bawana Road, Delhi-110042, India

12. References

[1] Acharya, B.D (2001). *Set-Indexers of a Graph and Set-Graceful Graphs*, Bull. Allahabad Math. Soc. 16, pp. 1-23.
[2] Best, E. and Thiagarajan, P.S. (1987). Some Classes of Live and Safe Petri Nets, Concurrency and Nets, Vol. 25, pp. 71-94.
[3] Harary, F. (1969).Graph Theory, Addison-Wesley, Reading, Massachusettes.
[4] Jensen, K. (1986). Coloured Petri nets, Lecture Notes in Computer Science, Vol. 254, Springer-Verlag, Berlin, pp. 248-299.
[5] Kansal, S., Singh, G.P. and Acharya, M. (2010). On Petri Nets Generating all the Binary n-Vectors, Scientiae Mathematicae Japonicae, 71, No. 2, pp. 209-216.
[6] Kansal, S., Singh, G.P. and Acharya, M. (2011). 1-Safe Petri Nets Generating Every Binary $n-$Vectors Exactly Once, Scientiae Mathematicae Japonicae, 74, No. 1, pp. 29-36.
[7] Kansal, S., Singh, G.P. and Acharya, M. (2011). A Disconnected 1-Safe Petri Net Whose Reachability Tree is Homomorphic to a Complete Boolean Lattice, proceeding of PACC-2011, IEEE Xplore, Catalog Number: CFP1166N-PRT ISBN: 978-1-61284-762-7.
[8] Kansal, S., Acharya, M. and Singh, G.P. (2012). Uniqueness of Minimal 1-Safe Petri Net Generating Every Binary n-Vectors as its Marking Vectors Exactly Once, Scientiae Mathematicae Japonicae, pp., e-2012, 75-78.
[9] Kansal, S., Acharya, M. and Singh, G.P. (2012). On the problem of characterizing 1-safe Petri nets that generate all the binary n-vectors as their marking vectors, Preprint.
[10] Singh, G.P., Kansal, S. and Acharya, M. (2012). Embedding an Arbitrary 1-Safe Petri Net in a Boolean Petri Net, Research Report, Deptartment of Applied Mathematics, Delhi Technological University, Delhi, India.
[11] Nauber, W. (2010). *Methods of Petri Net Analysis.* Ch.5 In: Lectures on Design and Analysis With Petri Nets, <http://www.tcs.inf.tu-dresden.de/nauber/dapn.shtml>
[12] Peterson, J.L. (1981). Petri Net Theory and the Modeling of Systems, Prentice-Hall, Inc., Englewood Cliffs, NJ.
[13] Petri, C.A. (1962). Kommunikation Mit Automaten, Schriften des Institutes fur Instrumentelle Mathematik, Bonn.
[14] Reisig, W. (1985). Petri nets, Springer-Verleg, New York.

Chapter 18

Performance Evaluation of Timed Petri Nets in Dioid Algebra

Samir Hamaci, Karim Labadi and A.Moumen Darcherif

Additional information is available at the end of the chapter

http://dx.doi.org/10.5772/48498

1. Introduction

The theory of Discrete Event Dynamic Systems focuses on the analysis and conduct systems. This class essentially contains man-made systems that consist of a finite number of resources (processors or memories, communication channels, machines) shared by several users (jobs, packets, manufactured objects) which all contribute to the achievement of some common goal (a parallel computation, the end-to-end transmission of a set of packets, the assembly of a product in an automated manufacturing line).

Discrete Event Dynamic Systems can be defined as systems in which state variables change under the occurrence of events. They are usually not be described, like the classical continuous systems, by differential equations due to the nature of the phenomenon involved, including the synchronization phenomenon or mutual exclusion. These systems are often represented by state-transition models. For such systems, arise, among others, three problems: Performance evaluation (estimate the production rate of a manufacturing system), resource optimization (minimizing the cost of some resources in order to achieve a given rate of production). To deal with such problems, it is necessary to benefit of models able to take into account all dynamic characteristics of these systems. However, the phenomena involved by Discrete Event Dynamic Systems, and responsible for their dynamics, are much and of diverse natures: sequential or simultaneous, delayed tasks or not, synchronized or rival. From this variety of phenomena results the incapacity to describe all Discrete Event Dynamic Systems by a unique model which is faithful at once to the reality and exploitable mathematically.

The study of Discrete Event Dynamic Systems is made through several theories among which we can remind for example the queuing theory, for the evaluation of performances of timed systems, or the theory of the languages and the automatons, for the control of other systems. The work presented here is in line with theory of linear systems on dioids. This theory involves subclass of Timed Discrete Event Dynamic Systems where the evolution of the state is representable by linear recurrence equations on special algebraic structures called diod algebra. The behavior of systems characterized by delays and synchronization can be described by such recurrences [1]. These systems are modeled by Timed Event Graphs (TEG). This latter constitute a subclasses of Timed Petri Nets with each place admits an upstream transition and downstream transition. When the size of model becomes very significant, the techniques of analysis developed for TEG reach their limits. A possible alternative consists in using Timed Event Graphs with Multipliers denoted TEGM. Indeed, the use of multipliers associated with arcs is natural to model a large number of systems, for example, when the achievement of a specific task requires several units of a same resource, or when an assembly operation requires several units of a same part.

This chapter deals with the performance evaluation of TEGM in dioid algebra. Noting that these models do not admit a linear representation in dioid algebra. This nonlinearity is due to the presence of weights on arcs. To mitigate this problem of nonlinearity and to apply the results used to evaluate the performances of linear systems, we use a linearization method of mathematical model reflecting the behavior of a Timed Event Graphs with Multipliers in order to obtain a linear model.

Few works deal with the performance evaluation of TEGM. Moreover, the calculation of cycle time is an open problem for the scientific community. In the case where the system is modeled by a TEGM, in the most of works the proposed solution is to transform the TEGM into an ordinary TEG, which allows the use of well-known methods of performances evaluation. In [12] the initial TEGM is the object of an operation of expansion. Unfortunately, this expansion can lead to a model of significant size, which does not depend only on the initial structure of TEGM, but also on initial marking. With this method, the system transformation proposed under *single* server semantics hypothesis, or in [14] under *infinite* server semantics hypothesis, leads to a TEG with $|\theta|$ transitions.

Another linearization method was proposed in [17] when each elementary circuit of graph contains at least one *normalized* transition (*i.e.,* a transition for which its corresponding elementary T-invariant component is equal to one). This method increases the number of transitions. Inspired by this work, a linearization method without increasing the number of transition was proposed in [8]. A calculation method of cycle time of a TEGM is proposed in [2] but under restrictive conditions on initial marking. We use a new method of linearization without increasing the number of transition of TEGM [6].

This chapter is organized as follows. After recalling in Section 2 some properties of Petri nets, we present in Section 3, modeling the dynamic behavior of TEGM, which are a class of Petri nets, in dioid algebra, precisely in $(min, +)$ algebra. In this section we will show that TEGM are nonlinear in this algebraic structure, unlike to TEG. This nonlinearity prevents us to use the spectral theory developed in [5] for evaluate the performances of TEG in $(min, +)$ algebra. To mitigate this problem of nonlinearity, we will encode the mathematical equations governing the dynamic evolution of TEGM in a dioid of operators developed in [7], inspired by work presented in [3]. The description of this dioid and the new state model based on operators will be the subject of Section 4. To exploit the mathematical model obtained, a linearization method of this model will be presented in Section 5, in order to obtain a linear model in $(min, +)$ algebra and to apply the theory developed for performance evaluation. This latter will be the subject of Section 6. Before concluding, w e give a short example to illustrate this approach for evaluate the performances of TEGM in dioid algebra.

2. Petri Net

2.1. Definitions and notations

Petri Nets (PN) are a graphical and mathematical tool, introduced in 1962 by Carl Adam Petri [15]. They allow the modeling of a large number of Discrete Event Dynamic Systems. They are particularly adapted to the study of complex processes involving properties of synchronization and resource sharing.

The behavior over time of dynamical systems, including evaluation of their performance (cycle time, ...), led to introduce the notion of time in models Petri Net. Several models Petri Net incorporating time have been proposed. These models can be grouped into two classes: deterministic models and stochastic models. The former consider the deterministic values for durations of activity, whereas the latter consider probabilistic values.Among the existing Timed Petri Net include: the Temporal Petri Net [11] associating a time interval to each transition and each place, the T-Timed Petri Net [4] associating a positive constant (called firing time of transition) at each transition and P-Timed Petri Net ; [4], [9] associating a positive constant (called holding time in the place) at each place of graph. It has been shown that P-Timed Petri Net can be reduced to T-Timed Petri Net and vice versa [13]. In the next, for consistency with the literature produced on the dioid algebra, we consider that P-Timed Petri Net.

A *P-Timed Petri Net* is a valued bipartite graph given by a 5-tuple (P, T, M, m, τ).

1. P is the finite set of places, T is the finite set of transitions.
2. $M \in \mathbb{N}^{P\times T \cup T\times P}$. Given $p \in P$ and $q \in T$, the multiplier $M_{pq'}$ (resp. M_{qp}) specifies the weight of the arc from transition $n_{q'}$ to place p (resp. from place p to transition n_q).
3. $m \in \mathbb{N}^P$: m_p assigns an initial number of tokens to place p.
4. $\tau \in \mathbb{N}^P$: τ_p gives the minimal time a token must spend in place p before it can contribute to the enabling of its downstream transitions.

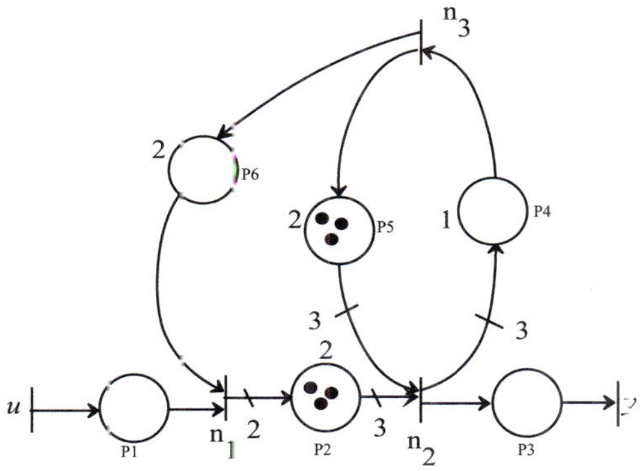

Figure 1. Example of a P-Timed Petri Net.

More generally, for a Petri Net, we denote $W^- = [M_{qp}]$ (input incidence matrix), $W^+ = [M_{pq}]$ (output incidence matrix), $W = W^+ - W^-$ (incidence matrix) and considering S a possible firing sequence from a marking m_i to the marking m_k, then a fundamental equation reflecting the dynamic behavior of Petri Net, is obtained:

$$m_k = m_i + W \times \underline{S}. \tag{1}$$

$\underline{S}$ is the characteristic vector of the firing sequence S. In Figure 1, the firing sequence $S = \{n_2\}$, the characteristic vector is equal to $\underline{S}^t = (0,1,0,0)$, and from marking $m_0^t = (0,3,0,0,3,0)$, is reached the marking $m_1^t = (0,0,0,3,0,0)$ by firing of the transition n_2, after a stay of 2 time units of tokens in the places P_2 and P_5.

2.2. Invariants of a Petri Net

There are two types of invariants in a Petri Net; *Marking Invariants*, also called P-invariant and *Firing Invariant*, also called T-invariant [4].

Definition 1. (P-invariant)

Marking Invariants illustrate the conservation of the number of tokens in a subset of places of a Petri Net.

A vector, denoted Y, which has a dimension equal to the number of places of a Petri Net is a P-invariant, if and only if it satisfies the following equation:

$$Y^t \times W = \vec{0}, \qquad Y \neq \vec{0}. \tag{2}$$

From Equation 1, we deduce that if Y is a P-invariant, then for a given marking, denoted m_i, obtained from an initial marking m_0, we have:

$$Y^t \times m_i = Y^t \times m_0 = k, \quad k \in \mathbb{N}^*. \tag{3}$$

This equation represents an invariant marking, it means that if Y is a P-invariant of Petri Net then the transpose of the vector Y multiplied by the marking vector m_i of the Petri Net is an integer constant regardless of the m_i marking reachable from the initial marking m_0. All the places for which the associated component in the P-invariant is nonzero, is called the conservative component of the Petri Net.

Definition 2. (T-invariant)

A nonzero vector of integers θ of dimension $\mid T \mid \times 1$ is a T-invariant of Petri Net if and only if it satisfies the following equation:

$$W \times \theta = \vec{0}. \tag{4}$$

From Equation 1, the evolution from a marking m_i to a sequence whose characteristic vector θ back the graph to same marking $m_k = m_i$. The set of transitions for which the associated component in the T-invariant is nonzero is called the support of T-invariant. A T-invariant corresponding to a firing sequence is called feasible repetitive component.

Definition 3. (Consistent Petri Net)

A Petri Net is said *consistent* if it has a T-invariant θ covering all transitions of graph. A Petri Net which has this property is said *repetitive*.

The graph reaches a periodic regime when there is a firing sequence achievable with θ as characteristic vector.

Definition 4. (Conservative Petri Net)

A Petri Net is said conservative if all places in the graph form a conservative component.

The Petri Nets considered here are *consistent* (*i.e.*, there exists a T-invariant θ covering all transitions: $\{q \in T|\theta(q) > 0\} = T$) and *conservative* (*i.e.*, there exists a P-invariant Y covering all places: $\{p \in P|Y(p) > 0\} = P$). Such graphs verify the next properties [13]:

- A PNPetri Net allows a live and bounded initial marking m *iff* it is consistent and conservative.
- A consistent Petri Net is strongly connected *iff* it is conservative.
- A consistent Petri Net has a unique elementary T-invariant.
- The product of multipliers along any circuit of a conservative Petri Net is equal to one.

In the next, we denote by ${}^\bullet q$ (resp. $q^\bullet$) the set of places upstream (resp. downstream) transition q. Similarly, ${}^\bullet p$ (resp. $p^\bullet$) denotes the set of transitions upstream (resp. downstream) place p.

3. Dynamic behavior of Timed Petri Nets in dioid algebra

Definition 5. An ordinary *Timed Event Graph* (TEG) is a Timed Petri Net such that each place has exactly one upstream transition and one downstream transition. Weights of arcs are all unit.

These graphs are well adapted to model synchronization phenomena occurring in Discrete Event Dynamic Systems. They admit a linear representation on a particular algebraic structure called the *dioid* algebra [1].

Definition 6. *A dioid* $(\mathcal{D}, \oplus, \otimes)$ is a semiring in which the addition $\oplus$ is idempotent ($\forall a,\ a \oplus a = a$). Neutral elements of $\oplus$ and $\otimes$ are denoted ε and e respectively.

- A dioid is *commutative* when $\otimes$ is commutative. The symbol $\otimes$ is often omitted. Due to idempotency of $\oplus$, a dioid can be endowed with a natural order relation defined by $a \preceq b \Leftrightarrow b = a \oplus b$ (the least upper bound of {a,b} is equal to $a \oplus b$).
- A dioid $\mathcal{D}$ is *complete* if every subset A of $\mathcal{D}$ admits a least upper bound denoted $\bigoplus_{x \in A} x$, and if $\otimes$ distributes at left and at right over infinite sums. The greatest element denoted T of a complete dioid $\mathcal{D}$ is equal to $\bigoplus_{x \in \mathcal{D}} x$. The greatest lower bound of every subset X of a complete dioid always exists and is denoted $\bigwedge_{x \in X} x$.

Example 1. The set $\mathbb{Z} \cup \{\pm\infty\}$, endowed with ($min$) as $\oplus$ and usual addition as $\otimes$, is a complete dioid denoted $\overline{\mathbb{Z}}_{\min}$ and usually called $(min, +)$ algebra with neutral elements $\varepsilon = +\infty$, $e = 0$ and $T = -\infty$.

Example 2. The set $\mathbb{Z} \cup \{\pm\infty\}$, endowed with ($max$) as $\oplus$ and usual addition as $\otimes$, is a complete dioid denoted $\overline{\mathbb{Z}}_{\max}$ and usually called $(max, +)$ algebra with neutral elements $\varepsilon = -\infty$, $e = 0$ and $T = +\infty$.

Definition 7. A *signal* is an increasing map from $\mathbb{Z}$ to $\mathbb{Z} \cup \{\pm\infty\}$. Denote $S=(\mathbb{Z} \cup \{\pm\infty\})^{\mathbb{Z}}$ the set of signals.

This set is endowed with a kind of module structure, called *min-plus semimodule,* the two associated operations are:

- pointwise minimum of time functions to add signals: $\forall t \in \mathbb{Z},(x \oplus y)(t) = x(t) \oplus y(t) = \min(x(t), y(t))$;
- addition of a constant to play the role of external product of a signal by a scalar: $\forall t \in \mathbb{Z}, \forall \rho \in \mathbb{Z} \cup \{\pm\infty\},(\rho.x)(t) = \rho \otimes x(t) = \rho + x(t)$.

Definition 8. An operator Ψ is a mapping defined from $\mathbb{Z} \cup \{\pm\infty\}$ to $\mathbb{Z} \cup \{\pm\infty\}$ is *linear* in $(min, +)$ algebra if it preserves the min-plus semimodule structure, *i.e.*, for all signals x, y and constant ρ,

$$\Psi(x \oplus y) = \Psi(x) \oplus \Psi(y) \ \text{(additive property)},$$
$$\Psi(\rho \otimes x) = \rho \otimes \Psi(x) \ \text{(homogeneity property)}.$$

To study a TEG in $(min, +)$ algebra, considered state variable is a *counter* , denoted $x_q(t)$. This latter denotes the cumulated number of firings of transition x_q up to time t ($t \in \mathbb{Z}$). To illustrate the evolution of a counter associated with the transition x_q of a TEG, we consider the following elementary graph:

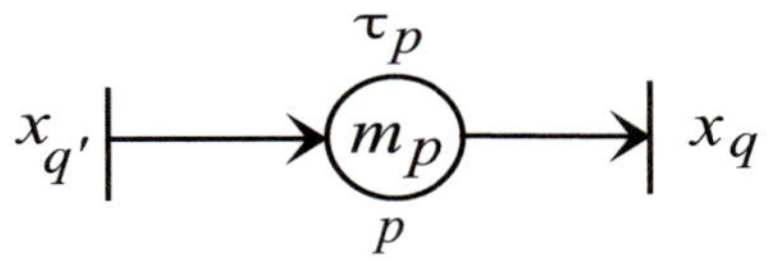

Figure 2. Elementary TEG

$$x_q(t) = \min_{p \in {}^\bullet q, q' \in {}^\bullet p} (m_p + x_{q'}(t - \tau_p)). \tag{5}$$

Note that this equation is nonlinear in usual algebra. This nonlinearity is due to the presence of the (min) which models the synchronization phenomena [1] in the transition x_q. However, it is linear equation in $(min, +)$ algebra:

$$x_q(t) = \bigoplus_{p \in {}^\bullet q, q' \in {}^\bullet p} (m_p \otimes x_{q'}(t - \tau_p)). \tag{6}$$

In the case where weight of an arc is greater than one, TEG becomes weighted. This type of model is called Timed Event Graph with Multipliers, denoted TEGM.

The *earliest* functioning rule of a TEGM is defined as follows. A transition n_q fires as soon as all its upstream places $\{p \in {}^\bullet q\}$ contain enough tokens (M_{qp}) having spent at least τ_p units of time in place p. When transition $n_{q'}$ fires, it produces $M_{pq'}$ tokens in each downstream place $p \in q'^\bullet$.

[1] Synchronization phenomena occurs when multiple arcs converge to the same transition.

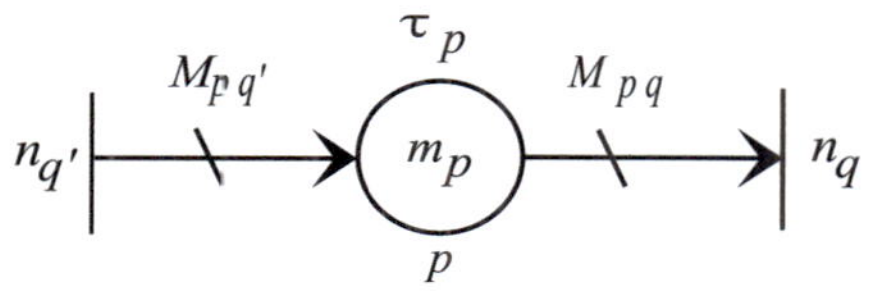

Figure 3. Elementary TEGM.

Assertion 1. The counter variable associated with the transition n_q of an elementary TEGM (under the earliest firing rule) satisfy the following *transition to transition* equation:

$$n_q(t) = \min_{p \in {}^\bullet q, q' \in {}^\bullet p} \lfloor M_{qp}^{-1}(m_p + M_{pq'} n_{q'}(t - \tau_p)) \rfloor. \tag{7}$$

The inferior integer part is used to preserve the integrity of Equation 7. In general, a transition n_q may have several upstream transitions $\{n_{q'} \in {}^{\bullet\bullet}q\}$ which implies that the associated counter variable is given by the *min* of *transition to transition* equations obtained for each upstream transition.

Example 3. Let us consider TEGM depicted in Figure 4.

$$\begin{cases} n_1(t) &= \lfloor \frac{4+3n_2(t-1)}{2} \rfloor, \\ n_2(t) &= \min(\lfloor \frac{2n_1(t-1)}{3} \rfloor, 2 + 2n_3(t-1)), \\ n_3(t) &= \lfloor \frac{n_2(t-1)}{2} \rfloor. \end{cases}$$

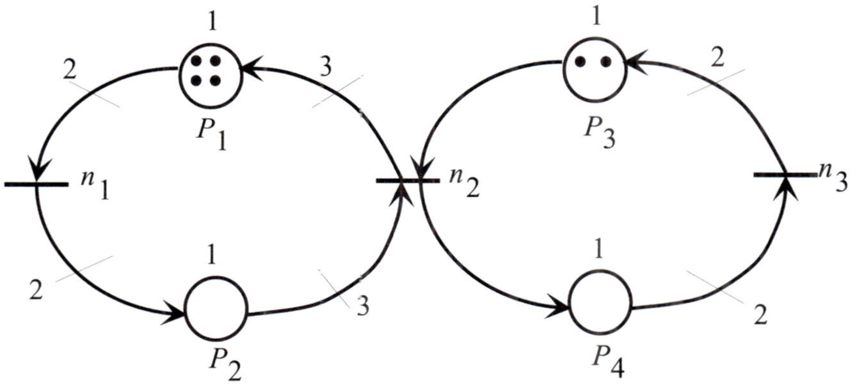

Figure 4. Timed Event Graph with Multipliers.

The mathematical model representing the behavior of this TEGM does not admit a linear representation in $(min, +)$ algebra. This nonlinearity is due to the presence of the integer parts generated by the presence of the weights on the arcs. Consequently, it is difficult to use $(min, +)$ algebra to tackle, for example, problems of control and the analysis of performances. As alternative, we propose another model based on operators which will be linearized in order to obtain a $(min, +)$ linear model.

4. Operatorial representation of TEGM

We now introduce three operators, defined from $\mathbb{Z} \cup \{\pm\infty\}$ to $\mathbb{Z} \cup \{\pm\infty\}$, which are used for the modeling of TEGM.

- **Operator** γ^{ν} to represent a shift of ν units in counting ($\nu \in \mathbb{Z} \cup \{\pm\infty\}$). It is defined as follows:

$$\forall t \in \mathbb{Z}, \ \forall\, n_{q'} \in \overline{\mathbb{Z}}^{\mathbb{Z}}, \qquad n_q(t) = \gamma^{\nu} n_{q'}(t) = n_{q'}(t) + \nu.$$

Property 1. Operator γ^{ν} satisfies the following rules:

$$(\gamma^{\nu} \oplus \gamma^{\nu'}) n'_q(t) = \gamma^{min(\nu,\nu')} n'_q(t).$$

$$(\gamma^{\nu} \otimes \gamma^{\nu'}) n'_q(t) = \gamma^{\nu+\nu'} n'_q(t).$$

Indeed, we have

- $(\gamma^{\nu} \oplus \gamma^{\nu'}) n'_q(t) = min(n'_q(t) + \nu, n'_q(t) + \nu') = n'_q(t) + min(\nu, \nu') = \gamma^{min(\nu,\nu')} n'_q(t).$
- $(\gamma^{\nu} \otimes \gamma^{\nu'}) n'_q(t) = \gamma^{\nu}(n'_q(t) + \nu') = n'_q(t) + \nu' + \nu = \gamma^{\nu+\nu'} n'_q(t).$

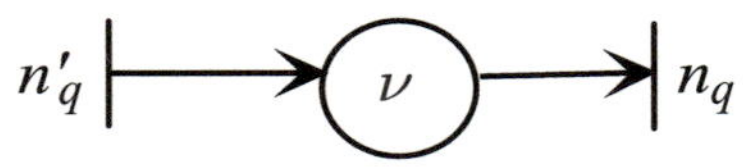

Figure 5. Operator γ^{ν}

- **Operator** δ^{τ} to represent a shift of τ units in dating ($\tau \in \mathbb{Z} \cup \{\pm\infty\}$). It is defined as follows:

$$\forall t \in \mathbb{Z}, \ \forall\, n_{q'} \in \overline{\mathbb{Z}}^{\mathbb{Z}}, \qquad n_q(t) = \delta^{\tau} n_{q'}(t) = n_{q'}(t - \tau).$$

Property 2. Operator δ^{τ} satisfies the following rules:

$$(\delta^{\tau} \oplus \delta^{\tau'}) n'_q(t) = \delta^{max(\tau,\tau')} n'_q(t).$$

$$(\delta^{\tau} \otimes \delta^{\tau'}) n'_q(t) = \delta^{\tau+\tau'} n'_q(t).$$

- Knowing that the signal $n_q(t)$ is non decreasing, we have :

$$(\delta^{\tau} \oplus \delta^{\tau'}) n'_q(t) = min(n'_q(t - \tau), n'_q(t - \tau')) = n'_q(t - max(\tau, \tau')) = \delta^{max(\tau,\tau')} n'_q(t).$$

$$(\delta^{\tau} \otimes \delta^{\tau'}) n'_q(t) = \delta^{\tau} n'_q(t - \tau') = n'_q(t - \tau' - \tau) = \delta^{\tau'+\tau} n'_q(t).$$

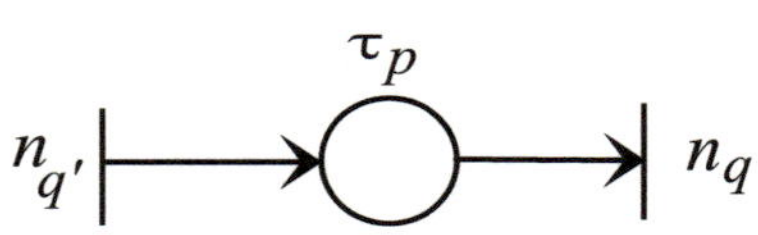

Figure 6. Operator δ^{τ}

- **Operator** μ_r to represent a scaling of factor r ($r \in \mathbb{Q}^+$). It is defined as follows:

$$\forall t \in \mathbb{Z},\ \forall n_{q'} \in \overline{\mathbb{Z}}^{\mathbb{Z}}, \qquad n'_q(t) = \mu_r n'_{q'}(t) = \lfloor r \times n'_{q'}(t) \rfloor,$$

with $r \in \mathbb{Q}^+$(r is equal to a ratio of elements in $\mathbb{N}$).

Property 3. Operator μ_r satisfies the following rules when composed with operators δ^τ *and* γ^ν *:*

$$(\mu_r \otimes \delta^\tau)n'(t) = (\delta^\tau \otimes \mu_r)n'(t),$$

$$(\mu_r \otimes \gamma^\nu)n'(t) = (\gamma^{\nu \times r} \otimes \mu_r)n'(t), \text{for } \nu \in r^{-1} \times \mathbb{N}.$$

Indeed, we have:

- $(\mu_r \otimes \delta^\tau)n'(t) = \lfloor r \times n'(t-\tau) \rfloor = (\delta^\tau \otimes \mu_r)n'(t)$.
- $\forall \nu \in r^{-1} \times \mathbb{N}, \quad (\mu_r \otimes \gamma^\nu)n'(t) = \lfloor r \times \nu + r \times n'(t) \rfloor = r \times \nu + \lfloor r \times n'(t) \rfloor = (\gamma^{\nu \times r} \otimes \mu_r)n'(t)$, since $\nu \times r \in \mathbb{N}$.

Figure 7. Operator $\mu_r(r = \frac{a}{b})$

Denote by $\mathcal{D}_{\min}$ the (noncommutative) dioid of finite sums of operators $\{\mu_r, \gamma^\nu\}$ endowed with pointwise *min* ($\oplus$) and composition ($\otimes$) operations, with neutral elements equal to $\varepsilon = \mu_{+\infty}\gamma^{+\infty}$ and $e = \mu_1\gamma^0$ respectively. Thus, an element in $\mathcal{D}_{\min}$ is a map $p = \bigoplus_{i=1}^{k} \mu_{r_i}\gamma^{\nu_i}$ defined from S to S such that $\forall t \in \mathbb{Z}$, $p(n(t)) = \min_{1 \le i \le k}(\lfloor r_i(\nu_i + n(t)) \rfloor)$.

Let a map $h : \mathbb{Z} \to \mathcal{D}_{\min}$, $\tau \mapsto h(\tau)$ in which $h(\tau) = \bigoplus_{i=1}^{k_\tau} \mu_{r_i^\tau}\gamma^{\nu_i^\tau}$. We define the power series $H(\delta)$ in the indeterminate δ with coefficients in $\mathcal{D}_{\min}$ by: $H(\delta) = \bigoplus_{\tau \in \mathbb{Z}} h(\tau)\delta^\tau$.

The set of these formal power series endowed with the two following operations:
$F(\delta) \oplus H(\delta)$: $(f \oplus h)(\tau) = f(\tau) \oplus h(\tau) = \min(f(\tau), h(\tau))$,
$F(\delta) \otimes H(\delta) : (f \otimes h)(\tau) = \bigoplus_{i \in \mathbb{Z}} f(i) \otimes h(\tau - i) = \inf_{i \in \mathbb{Z}}(f(i) + h(\tau - i))$,
is a dioid denoted $\mathcal{D}_{\min}[\![\delta]\!]$, with neutral elements $\varepsilon = \mu_{+\infty}\gamma^{+\infty}\delta^{-\infty}$ and $e = \mu_1\gamma^0\delta^0$.

Elements of $\mathcal{D}_{\min}[\![\delta]\!]$ allow modeling the transfer between two transitions of a TEGM. A formal series of $\mathcal{D}_{\min}[\![\delta]\!]$ can also represent a signal n as $N(\delta) = \bigoplus_{\tau \in \mathbb{Z}} n(\tau)\,\delta^\tau$, simply due to the fact that it is also equal to $n \otimes e$ (by definition of neutral element e of $\mathcal{D}_{\min}$).

Assertion 2. The counter variables of an elementary TEGM satisfies the following equation in dioid $\mathcal{D}_{\min}[\![\delta]\!]$:

$$N_q(\delta) = \bigoplus_{p \in {}^\bullet q,\, q' \in {}^\bullet p} \mu_{M_{qp}^{-1}}\gamma^{m_p}\delta^{\tau_p}\mu_{M_{pq'}}N_{q'}(\delta). \tag{8}$$

• $N_q(\delta)$ is the counter $n_q(t)$ associated with the transition n_q, encoded in $\mathcal{D}_{\min}[\![\delta]\!]$. It is equal to the counter $N_{q'}(\delta)$ shifted by the composition of operators $\mu_{M_{pq'}}, \delta^{\tau_p}, \gamma^{m_p}$ and $\mu_{M_{qp}^{-1}}$ connected in series. Let us express some properties of operators γ, δ, μ in dioid $\mathcal{D}_{\min}[\![\delta]\!]$.

Proposition 1. Let $a,\ b \in \mathbb{N}$, we have:

1. $\gamma^a\delta^b = \delta^b\gamma^a$, $\mu_a\delta^b = \delta^b\mu_a$ (commutative properties).
2. $\mu_{a^{-1}}\mu_b = \mu_{(a^{-1}b)}$.
3. Let $N(\delta)$ such that, $\forall t \in \mathbb{Z}$, $n(t)$ *is a multiple of* a, *then* $\mu_{a^{-1}}\gamma^b N(\delta) = \gamma^{\lfloor a^{-1}b \rfloor}\mu_{a^{-1}}N(\delta)$.
4. $\gamma^b\mu_a = \mu_a\gamma^{a^{-1}b}$, or equivalently, $\mu_a\gamma^b = \gamma^{ab}\mu_a$.

Proof:

- Point 1 is obvious.
- Point 2: $\mu_{a^{-1}}\mu_b N(\delta)$ corresponds to $\lfloor a^{-1}\lfloor b\,n(t)\rfloor\rfloor = \lfloor a^{-1}b\,n(t)\rfloor$ which leads to $\mu_{(a^{-1}b)}N(\delta)$.
- Point 3: $\mu_{a^{-1}}\gamma^b N(\delta)$ correspond to $\lfloor a^{-1}(b+n(t))\rfloor = \lfloor a^{-1}b\rfloor + a^{-1}n(t)$ since $n(t) \in \mathbb{Z} \cup \{\pm\infty\}$ is a multiple of a, which leads to $\gamma^{\lfloor a^{-1}b\rfloor}\mu_{a^{-1}}N(\delta)$.
- Point 4: $\gamma^b\mu_a N(\delta)$ corresponds to $b + \lfloor a\,n(t)\rfloor = \lfloor a(a^{-1}b + n(t))\rfloor$ which leads to $\mu_a\gamma^{a^{-1}b}N(\delta)$.

Example 4. The TEGM depicted in Figure 4 admits the following representation in $\mathcal{D}_{\min}[\![\delta]\!]$:

$$\begin{pmatrix} N_1 \\ N_2 \\ N_3 \end{pmatrix} = \begin{pmatrix} \varepsilon & \mu_{1/2}\gamma^4\delta^1\mu_3 & \varepsilon \\ \mu_{1/3}\delta^1\mu_2 & \varepsilon & \gamma^2\delta^1\mu_2 \\ \varepsilon & \mu_{1/2}\delta^1 & \varepsilon \end{pmatrix} \begin{pmatrix} N_1 \\ N_2 \\ N_3 \end{pmatrix}$$

5. Linearization of TEGM

The presence of integer part modeled by operator μ induces a nonlinearity in Equation 8 used to represent a TEGM. So, as far as possible, we seek to represent a TEGM with linear equations in order to apply standard results of linear system theory developed in the dioid setting, which leads to transform a TEGM into a TEG (represented without operator μ).

5.1. Principle of linearization

A consistent TEGM has a unique elementary T-invariant in which components are in $\mathbb{N}^*$. The used method is based on the use of commutation rules of operators and the impulse inputs (Proposition 1 and 2).

In the next, we suppose that all tokens in a TEGM are "frozen" before time 0 and are available at time 0 which is a classical assumption in Petri Nets theory. Hence, with each counter variable of a TEGM is added a counter variable corresponding to an impulse input e (*i.e.*, $e(t) = 0$ for $t < 0$ and $e(t) = +\infty$ for $t \geq 0$). These initial conditions are weakly compatible. For more details, see [10].

To linearize the expression of counters variables written as Equation 8, one expresses each counter according to an entry impulse. This latter will permit to linearize the mathematical model reflecting the behavior of a TEGM in order to obtain a linear model in (min, +) algebra.

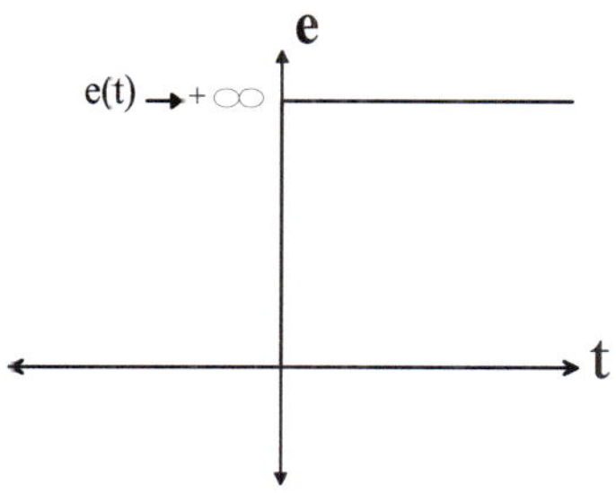

Figure 8. Impulse (Point of view of counter).

Proposition 2. let E an impulse input, we have : $\forall a \in \mathbb{N}, \beta \in Q^+$,

$$\mu_\beta \gamma^a \delta^\tau E(\delta) = \gamma^{\lfloor \beta a \rfloor} \delta^\tau E(\delta). \tag{9}$$

Proof: Thanks to Proposition 1.3, $\mu_\beta \gamma^a \delta^\tau E(\delta)$ corresponds to $\lfloor \beta \times (a + e(t-\tau)) \rfloor = \lfloor \beta \times a \rfloor - e(t-\tau)$ since for $t \geq 0 \;\; e(t) \mapsto +\infty$, hence $e(t)$ is a multiple of β, which leads to $\gamma^{\lfloor \beta a \rfloor} \delta^\tau E(\delta)$

We now give the state model associated to the dynamic of counters of a TEGM. Consider the vector N composed of the counter variable. The counter variables corresponding to impulse input e added with each transition n_i:

$$N(\delta) = A \otimes N(\delta) \oplus E(\delta). \tag{10}$$

Knowing that such equation admits the following earliest solution:

$$N(\delta) = A^* \otimes E(\delta), \tag{11}$$

$A^* = e \oplus A \oplus A^2 \oplus \cdots$.

Proposition 3. For initial conditions *weakly compatible*, consistent and conservative TEGM is linearizable without increasing the number of its transitions.

Proof: Consider a consistent and conservative TEGM represented by the equation $A(\delta) = A \otimes N(\delta) \oplus E(\delta)$. Using Equation 11, and then apply the Proposition 2, we obtain a linear equation between transitions of graph (corresponding to a linear TEG). This linearization method may be applied to all transitions of graph, since for any transition, one can involve an impulse input.

Example 5. The TEGM depicted in Figure 9 admits the elementary T-invariant $\theta^t = (3, 2, 1)$.

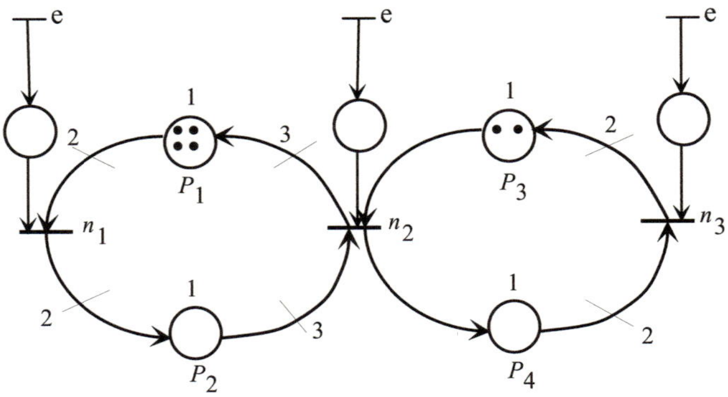

Figure 9. TEGM with impulse inputs added to each transition.

The inputs e correspond to the impulse inputs. They have not influence on the evolution of the model. Indeed, $\forall t \geq 0, \forall n_q \in \mathcal{T}, \min(n_q(t), e(t)) = n_q(t)$, since $e(t) \mapsto +\infty$.

$$\begin{pmatrix} N_1 \\ N_2 \\ N_3 \end{pmatrix} = \begin{pmatrix} \varepsilon & \mu_{1/2}\gamma^4\delta^1\mu_3 & \varepsilon \\ \mu_{1/3}\delta^1\mu_2 & \varepsilon & \gamma^2\delta^1\mu_2 \\ \varepsilon & \mu_{1/2}\delta^1 & \varepsilon \end{pmatrix} \begin{pmatrix} N_1 \\ N_2 \\ N_3 \end{pmatrix} \oplus \begin{pmatrix} E \\ E \\ E \end{pmatrix}.$$

Using Equation 11, $N(\delta) = A^*E(\delta)$. The Proposition 2 allows to calculate $A^*E(\delta)$:

$$\begin{aligned} A^*E(\delta) &= (e \oplus A \oplus A^2 \oplus A^3 \oplus ...)E(\delta) \\ &= (\,E(\delta) \oplus A\,E(\delta) \oplus \underbrace{A \otimes AE(\delta)}_{A^2E(\delta)} \oplus \underbrace{A \otimes A^2E(\delta)}_{A^3E(\delta)} \oplus ...). \end{aligned}$$

$$A^*\,E(\delta) = \begin{pmatrix} (\gamma^2\delta^2)(\gamma^3\delta^4)^* \\ \delta^1(\gamma^1\delta^2)^* \\ \delta^4(\gamma^1\delta^4)^* \end{pmatrix} E(\delta),$$

which is the earliest solution of the following equations:

$$\begin{pmatrix} N_1(\delta) \\ N_2(\delta) \\ N_3(\delta) \end{pmatrix} = \begin{pmatrix} \gamma^3\delta^4 \\ \gamma^1\delta^2 \\ \gamma^1\delta^4 \end{pmatrix} \begin{pmatrix} N_1(\delta) \\ N_2(\delta) \\ N_3(\delta) \end{pmatrix} \oplus \begin{pmatrix} \gamma^2\delta^2 \\ \delta^1 \\ \delta^4 \end{pmatrix} E(\delta).$$

Let us express these equations in usual counter setting (dioid $\overline{\mathbb{Z}}_{\min}$), we have, $\forall t \in \mathbb{Z}$:

$$\begin{cases} n_1(t) = 3 \otimes n_1(t-4) \bigoplus 2 \otimes e(t-2), \\ n_2(t) = 1 \otimes n_2(t-2) \bigoplus e(t-1), \\ n_3(t) = 1 \otimes n_3(t-4) \bigoplus e(t-4). \end{cases}$$

These equations are quite $(min, +)$ linear. It turns out that the TEG depicted in Figure 10, composed of three elementary circuits: (n_1, n_1), (n_2, n_2), (n_3, n_3), is a possible representation of the previous equations.

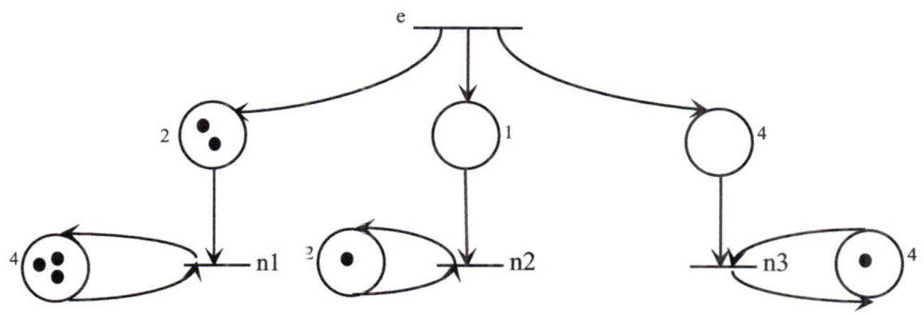

Figure 10. TEG (Linearized TEGM).

6. Performance evaluation of TEGM

• **General case**: To evaluate the performance of a TEGM returns to calculate the cycle time and firing rate associated with each transition of a graph.

Definition 9. [16] The cycle time, TC_m, of a TEGM is the average time to fire once the T-invariant under the earliest firing rule (i.e., transitions are fired as soon as possible) from the initial marking.

This cycle time is equivalent to the average time between two successive firing of a transition. It is calculated by the following relation:

$$TC_m = \frac{\theta_q}{\lambda_{m_q}}. \tag{12}$$

• θ_q is the component of T-invariant associated with transition n_q, and λ_{m_q} is the firing rate associated with transition n_q of TEGM corresponding to the average number of firing of one transition per unit time.

• For an industrial system, the cycle time corresponds to the average manufacturing time of a piece, and the firing rate is the average number of pieces produced per unit of time.

• **Particular case**: Elements of performance evaluation for TEG. We recall main results characterizing an ordinary TEG modeled in the dioid $\mathbb{Z}_{min}$. Knowing that a TEG is a TEGM with unit weights on the arcs, and their components of T-invariant are all equals 1.

Definition 10. A matrix A is said *irreducible* if for any pair *(i,j)*, there is an integer m such that $(A^m)_{ij} \neq \varepsilon$.

Theorem 1. [5] Let A be a square matrix with coefficient in $\mathbb{Z}_{min}$. The following assertions are equivalent:

- Matrix A is irreducible,
- The TEG associated with matrix A is strongly connected.

One calls *eigenvalue* and *eigenvector* of a matrix A with coefficients in $\mathbb{Z}_{min}$, the scalar λ and the vector v such as:

$$A \otimes v = \lambda \otimes v.$$

Theorem 2. [5] Let A be a square matrix with coefficients in $\mathbb{Z}_{min}$. If A is irreducible, or equivalently, if the associated TEG is strongly connected, then there is a single eigenvalue denoted λ. The eigenvalue can be calculated in the following way:

$$\lambda = \bigoplus_{j=1}^{n} (\bigoplus_{i=1}^{n} (A^j)_{ii})^{\frac{1}{j}}. \tag{13}$$

λ corresponds to the firing rate which is identical for each transition. This eigenvalue λ can be directly deduced from the TEG by:

$$\lambda = \min_{c \in C} \frac{M(c)}{T(c)}, \tag{14}$$

- C is the set of elementary circuits of the TEG.
- T(c) is the sum of holding times in circuit c.
- M(c) is the number of tokens in circuit c.

In the case of Ordinary TEG strongly connected, The inverse of eigenvalue λ is equivalent to cycle time, denoted TC.

$$TC = \frac{1}{\lambda}, \tag{15}$$

Example 6. The TEG depicted in Figure 10, which is not strongly connected, is composed of three circuits : (n_1, n_1), (n_2, n_2) and (n_3, n_3). Each circuit admits a T-invariant composed of one component equals 1.

Using the Definition 9 and Equation 15, one deduce that each circuit, which is an elementary TEG strongly connected, admits the following cycle time:

- Circuit (n_1, n_1), $TC = \frac{4}{3}$.
- Circuit (n_2, n_2), $TC = \frac{2}{1}$.
- Circuit (n_3, n_3), $TC = \frac{4}{1}$.

The cycle time of TEGM depicted in Figure 4, corresponds to the time required to fire each transition a number of times equal its corresponding elementary T-invariant component. Hence

$$TC_1 = 3 \times \frac{4}{3}, \qquad TC_2 = 2 \times \frac{2}{1}, \qquad TC_3 = 1 \times \frac{4}{1}.$$

Note that the cycle time is identical for all transitions of the graph which is equal to 4 time units. This means that each transition is asymptotically fired once every four time units.

About the firing rate associated with each transition of the graph, using the relation (12):

$$\lambda_{m_1} = \frac{3}{4}, \qquad \lambda_{m_2} = \frac{1}{2}, \qquad \lambda_{m_3} = \frac{1}{4}.$$

Confirmation of these results can be deducted directly to the following marking graph of the initial TEGM.

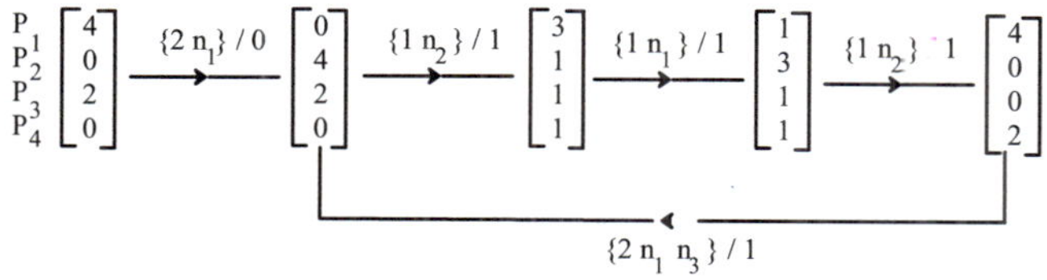

Figure 11. Marking graph of the initial TEGM.

- kn_i/t: after t time units, the transition n_i is firing k time.

7. Conclusion

Performance evaluation of TEGM is the subject of this chapter. These graphs, in contrast to ordinary TEG, do not admit a linear representation in $(min, +)$ algebra. This nonlinearity is due to the presence of weights on the arcs. For that, a modeling of these graphs in an algebraic structure, based on operators, is used. The obtained model is linearized, by using of pulse inputs associated with all transitions of graphs, in order to obtain representation in linear $(min+)$ algebra, and apply some results basic spectral theory, usually used to evaluate the performance of ordinary TEG. The work presented in this chapter paves the way for other development related to evaluation of performance of these models. In particular, the calculation of cycle time for any timed event graph with multipliers is, to our knowledge, an open problem to date.

Author details

Samir Hamaci, Karim Labadi and A.Moumen Darcherif
EPMI, 13 Boulvard de l'Hautil, 95092, Cergy-Pontoise, France

8. References

[1] Baccelli, F., Cohen, G., Olsder, G.-J. & Quadrat, J.-P. [1992]. *Synchronization and Linearity: An Algebra for Discrete Event Systems*, Wiley and Sons.

[2] Chao, D., Zhou, M. & Wang, D. [1993]. Multiple weighted marked graphs, *IFAC 12th Triennial World Congress*, Sydney, Australie, pp. 371–374.

[3] Cohen, G., Gaubert, S. & Quadrat, J.-P. [1998]. Timed-event graphs with multipliers and homogenous min-plus systems, *IEEE Transaction on Automatic Control* Vol.43(No.9): 1296–1302.

[4] David, R. & Alla, H. [1992]. *Du Grafcet au réseaux de Petri*, Editions Hermès, Paris.

[5] Gaubert, S. [1995]. Resource optimization and (min,+) spectral theory, *IEEE Transaction on Automatic Control* 40(11): 1931–1934.

[6] Hamaci, S., Benfekir, A. & Boimond, J.-L. [2011]. Dioid approach for performance evaluation of weighted t-systems, *16th IEEE International Conference on Emerging Technologies and Factory Automation (ETFA)*, Toulouse, France, pp. 1–8.

[7] Hamaci, S., Boimond, J.-L. & Lahaye, S. [2006]. On modeling and control of hybrid timed event graphs with multipiers using (min,+) algebra, *Journal of Discrete Event Dynamic Systems* Vol.16(No.2): 241–256.

[8] Hamaci, S., Boimond, J.-L., Lahaye, S. & Mostefaoui, M. [2004]. On the linearizability of discrete timed event graphs with multipliers using (min,+) algebra, *7th international Workshop on Discrete Event Systems (WODES)*, Reims, France, pp. 367–372.

[9] Hillion, H. [1989]. *Modélisation et analyse des systèmes de production discrets par les réseaux de Petri temporisés*, Thèse, Université de Paris IV, France.

[10] Lahaye, S. [2000]. *Contribution à l'étude des systèmes linéaires non stationnaires dans l'algèbre des dioïdes*, Thèse, LISA - Université d'Angers.

[11] Merlin, P. [1979]. Methodology for the Design and Implementation of Communication Protocole, *IEEE Transaction on Communication* Vol.24(No.6).

[12] Munier, A. [1993]. Régime asymptotique optimal d'un graphe d'événements temporisé généralisé: application à un problème d'assemblage, *APII* Vol.5(No.5): 487–513.

[13] Murata, T. [1989]. Petri nets: Properties, analysis and applications, *IEEE Proceedings* Vol.77(No.4): 541–580.

[14] Nakamura, M. & Silva, M. [1999]. Cycle time computation in deterministically timed weighted marked graphs, *IEEE-International Conference on Emerging Technologies and Factory Automation (ETFA)*, Universitat Politècnica de Catalunya, Barcelona, Spain, pp. 1037–1046.

[15] Petri, C. [1962]. *Kommunikation mit Automaten*, Phd thesis, Institut für Instrumentelle Mathematik, Bonn, Germany.

[16] Sauer, N. [2003]. Marking optimization of weighted marked graphs, *Journal of Discrete Event Dynamic Systems* Vol.13: 245–262.

[17] Trouillet, B., Benasser, A. & Gentina, J.-C. [2001]. Sur la modélisation du comportement dynamique des graphes d'événements pondérés, *in* G. Juanole & R. Valette (eds), *Conférence, Modélisation des Systèmes Réactifs (MSR),*, Hermès, Toulouse, France, pp. 447–462.

Chapter 19

Reachability Criterion with Sufficient Test Space for Ordinary Petri Net

Gi Bum Lee, Han Zandong and Jin S. Lee

Additional information is available at the end of the chapter

http://dx.doi.org/10.5772/50518

1. Introduction

Petri nets (PN) are widely recognized as a powerful tool for modelling and analyzing discrete event systems, especially systems are characterized by synchronization, concurrency, parallelism and resource sharing [1, 2]. One of the major advantages of using Petri net models is that the PN model can be used for the analysis of behaviour properties and performance evaluation, as well as for systematic construction of discrete-event simulators and controllers [3, 4]. The reachability from an initial marking to a destination marking is the most important issue for the analysis of Petri nets. Many other problems such as liveness and coverability can be deduced from this reachability problem [5, 6].

Two basic approaches are usually applied to solve the reachability problem. One is the construction of reachability tree [7, 8]. It can obtain all the reachable markings, but the computation complexity is exponentially increased with the size of a PN. The other is to solve the state equation [9]. The solution of the matrix equation provides a firing count vector that describes the relation between initial marking and reachable markings. Its major problem is the lack of information of firing sequences and the existence of spurious solutions.

Many researchers have investigated the reachability problem [10, 11]. Iko Miyazawa *et al.* have utilized the state equation to solve the reachability problem of Petri nets with parallel structures [12]. Tadashi Matsumoto *et al.* have presented a formal necessary and sufficient condition on reachability of general Petri nets with known firing count vectors [13]. Tadao Murata's paper has concentrated on presenting and analyzing Petri nets as discrete time systems. Controllability and reachability are analyzed in terms of the matrix representation of a Petri net [14].

In most cases, it is not necessary to find all reachable markings. One of the most important things is to know whether a given marking is reachable or not. If the destination marking

$\mathbf{M}_d$ is reachable from the initial marking $\mathbf{M}_0$, it is significant to find a firing sequence, which is an ordered sequence of transitions that lead $\mathbf{M}_0$ to $\mathbf{M}_d$. The following method can be utilized to find a reachable marking [15].

i. Solve the equation $\mathbf{AX}=\mathbf{M}_d-\mathbf{M}_0$ to ascertain all the solutions $\mathbf{X}_1$, $\mathbf{X}_2$, … and construct the set X={$\mathbf{X}_1$, $\mathbf{X}_2$, …}.
ii. Test if $\mathbf{X}_i$ in X is an executable solution from $\mathbf{M}_0$, i.e. there is at least one sequence S($\mathbf{X}_i$) that is a firing sequence under $\mathbf{M}_0$.
iii. If an executable solution exists, then $\mathbf{M}_d$ is reachable. On the contrary, if X=Φ or all solutions are spurious, then $\mathbf{M}_d$ is not reachable.

However, this approach is theoretic rather than practical, because there are two problems: One is that the solution of the fundamental equation $\mathbf{AX}=\mathbf{M}_d-\mathbf{M}_0$ is infinite in some cases. In that case, it is impossible to test all solution $\mathbf{X}_i$. The other is that the computation complexity of testing $\mathbf{X}_i$ increases at least exponentially as the length of S($\mathbf{X}_i$) increases.

In this chapter, the above two problems will be solved as follows: First, we construct a sufficient test space to include at least one executable solution within set X. An approach is secondly proposed to test whether there is an executable solution within the sufficient test space or not. A systematic method to search an executable solution in a sufficient test space and to enumerate the associated firing sequence is presented.

The remainder of the chapter is arranged as follows: Definitions and notations required in this chapter are given in Section 2. Section 3 describes how to determine the sufficient test space for the reachability problem. In Section 4, an algorithm is developed to determine if $\mathbf{X}_i$ is a executable solution under $\mathbf{M}_0$ and gives the associated firing sequence S($\mathbf{X}_i$). The illustrative examples are given in Section 3, Section 4, and Section 5.

2. Preliminaries

In this section, we present some definitions and notations to be necessary in the following sections.

Definition 1. Let PN=(P, T, I, O, M_0) be a marked Petri net. P={p_1, p_2, …, p_n} is the finite set of places. T={t_1, t_2, …, t_m} is the finite set of transitions. I is the input function. O is the output function. M_0 is the initial marking.

A PN is an ordinary Petri net iff I(p, t)→{0, 1} and O(t, p)→{0, 1} for any p∈P and t∈T. **A**=**O**-**I** is the incidence matrix, where **O** and **I** are the output and input function matrices [16]. Let $\mathbf{X}=[x_1\ x_2\ \dots\ x_m]^T$ be a column vector. If **X** is the firing count vector of S(**X**), the sequence S(**X**) is called the transition sequence associated with **X.** The transition set T(**X**) is called the support of **X** if it is composed of transitions associated with positive elements of **X**, i.e. T(**X**)={t_i|x_i>0}. p° is the set of output transitions of p, $^\circ p$ is the set of input transitions of p, t° is the set of output places of t, and $^\circ t$ is the set of input places of t.

Definition 2. C_i=<p, T_{ci}> is called a conflict structure [17] if it satisfies the following condition: T_{ci}={t|t∈p°} and |T_{ci}|≥2, where |T_{ci}| is the cardinality of T_{ci}. We note that C={C_1, C_2, …} is the set of all C_i and T_c=T_{c1}∪T_{c2}∪…. is the set of all conflict transitions.

Definition 3. For transition t_j and **X**, the sub-vector $\mathbf{H}(t_j|\mathbf{X})$ is defined as: $\mathbf{H}(t_j|\mathbf{X})=e[t_j]\cdot x_j$. $e[t_j]$ is the unit m-vector which is zero everywhere except in the j-th element.

Definition 4. For the conflict structure C_i=<p, T_{ci}> and **X**, the sub-vector $\mathbf{H}(C_i|\mathbf{X})$ is defined as follows:

$$\mathbf{H}(C_i \mid \mathbf{X}) = \sum_{t_j \in T_{ci}} \mathbf{H}(t_j \mid \mathbf{X}) \quad (1)$$

Definition 5. C_i=<p, T_{ci}> is in a spurious conflict state for **X** under **M** if there exists a firing sequence $S(\mathbf{H}(C_i|\mathbf{X}))$ under **M**, i.e. the mathematic criterion is $\mathbf{M}\geq\mathbf{I}\cdot\mathbf{H}(C_i|\mathbf{X})$.

Otherwise, C_i is in an effective conflict state for **X** under **M**, and the transition in T_{ci} is called the effective conflict transition for **X** under **M**.

Notation 1. $N(t_j|S(\mathbf{X}))=x_j$ is the number of occurrence times of t_j in $S(\mathbf{X})$.

Notation 2. If $q=\min\{\mathbf{M}(p_i), p_i\in{}^{\circ}t_j\}$, we call t_j q-enabled under marking **M.** This q is denoted as $E(t_j|\mathbf{M})$.

Definition 6. $\mathbf{F}=[f_1\ f_2\ \ldots\ f_m]^T$ is called an actual firing vector whose j-th element is $f_j=\min\{N(t_j|S(\mathbf{X})), E(t_j|\mathbf{M})\}$. **F** can be partitioned into two parts as follows: $\mathbf{F}=\mathbf{F}_o+\mathbf{F}_c$, where $\mathbf{F}_c=[f_{c1}\ f_{c2}\ \ldots\ f_{cm}]^T$ is associated with effective conflict transitions, $\mathbf{F}_o=[f_{o1}\ f_{o2}\ \ldots\ f_{om}]^T$ is associated with the other transitions. $\mathbf{F}_o$ and $\mathbf{F}_c$ satisfy the following conditions:

a. If t_j is an effective conflict transition for **X** under **M**, then $f_{oj}=0$ and $f_{cj}=f_j$.
b. Otherwise, $f_{cj}=0$ and $f_{oj}=f_j$.

3. Determination of the sufficient test space

If all the solutions of the equation $\mathbf{AX}=\mathbf{M}_d-\mathbf{M}_0$ are tested, It can be found whether M_d is reachable or not. But in some case, the solutions are infinite. Therefore, the tested range is determined in order to keep the method practical. This range must be finite and include at least one executable solution if it exists. This section will discuss how to determine the tested range.

Definition 7. Given the initial marking $\mathbf{M}_0$ and the destination marking $\mathbf{M}_d$ of a PN, **X** is a solution of $\mathbf{AX}=\mathbf{M}_d-\mathbf{M}_0$. If $\mathbf{M}_d$ is reachable from $\mathbf{M}_0$ under **X**, then **X** is called an executable solution. Otherwise, **X** is called a spurious solution.

Definition 8. $X=\{\mathbf{X}_1, \mathbf{X}_2, \ldots\}$ is the set of a solution **X**, the subset $X_e=\{\mathbf{X}_{e1}, \mathbf{X}_{e2}, \ldots\}$ of X is called the sufficient test space if it satisfies following conditions:

i. If $\mathbf{M}_d$ is reachable from $\mathbf{M}_0$, there must exist at least one element in X_e which is executable solution; in other words, if all elements in X_e are not executable, then all the elements in X are not executable either.
ii. X_e is a finite set.

Definition 9. The vector **X** which is a solution of $\mathbf{AX}=0$ is known as a T-invariant [18]. A solution **X** is called positive if every element of **X** is nonnegative.

Definition 10. The positive T-invariant solution **U** of **AU=0** is minimal if it satisfies the following condition: for any other T-invariant $\mathbf{U}_i$, at least one element of $\mathbf{U}$-$\mathbf{U}_i$ is negative. The set of minimal T-invariant solutions is U={$\mathbf{U}_1$, $\mathbf{U}_2$, …, $\mathbf{U}_s$}.

Definition 11. The positive particular solution **V** of $\mathbf{AV}$=$\mathbf{M}_d$-$\mathbf{M}_0$ is minimal if it satisfies the following condition: for any T-invariant **U** of PN, there must be at least one element in **V-U** which is negative, i.e. {**U**|**V-U**≥0, **U** is a T-invariant}=Φ. The set of minimal particular solutions is V={$\mathbf{V}_1$, $\mathbf{V}_2$, …, $\mathbf{V}_q$}.

The general solution of $\mathbf{AX}$=$\mathbf{M}_d$-$\mathbf{M}_0$ must be expressed by the form of one minimal particular solution and the arbitrary linear combination of the T-invariant solutions as follows:

$$\mathbf{X} = \mathbf{V}_i + \sum_{j=1}^{r} k_j U_j \tag{2}$$

where $\mathbf{V}_i \in V$, k_j is nonnegative integer.

Algorithm 1. Interpretation of the computation for X_e.

Step 1. Solve the equation **AX=0**, get all the positive integer solutions U={$\mathbf{U}_1$, $\mathbf{U}_2$, …, $\mathbf{U}_s$}, where each $\mathbf{U}_j$ ($1 \le j \le s$) is a minimal T-invariant.

Step 2. Solve the equation $\mathbf{AX}$=$\mathbf{M}_d$-$\mathbf{M}_0$, get all the positive integer particular solutions V={$\mathbf{V}_1$, $\mathbf{V}_2$, …, $\mathbf{V}_q$}, where each $\mathbf{V}_i$ ($1 \le i \le q$) is a minimal particular solution. B={$\mathbf{B}_1$, $\mathbf{B}_2$, …, $\mathbf{B}_n$} is a subset of V.

If V= Φ, $\mathbf{M}_d$ is not reachable, then end.

Step 3. Initialization: Let X_e=V={$\mathbf{V}_1$, $\mathbf{V}_2$ …, $\mathbf{V}_q$} and X_{temp}= Φ.

If U= Φ, then end.

Otherwise, for every $\mathbf{V}_i$, if $T(\mathbf{V}_i) \subset T(\mathbf{U}_j)$, then $\mathbf{V}_i \notin B$. If $T(\mathbf{V}_i) \not\subset T(\mathbf{U}_j)$, then $\mathbf{V}_i \in B$.

Go to Step 4.

Step 4. For each pair of ($\mathbf{B}_i$, $\mathbf{U}_j$), where i=1, 2, … |B|, j=1, 2, … s, and |B| is the cardinality of set B, carry out the following operations:

If $^{\circ}T(\mathbf{B}_i) \cap T(\mathbf{U}_j)^{\circ} = \Phi$, choose the next pair of ($\mathbf{B}_i$, $\mathbf{U}_j$).

If $^{\circ}T(\mathbf{B}_i) \cap T(\mathbf{U}_j)^{\circ} \neq \Phi$ and $T(\mathbf{U}_j) \subset T(\mathbf{B}_i)$, choose the next pair of ($\mathbf{B}_i$, $\mathbf{U}_j$).

If $^{\circ}T(\mathbf{B}_i) \cap T(\mathbf{U}_j)^{\circ} \neq \Phi$ and $T(\mathbf{U}_j) \not\subset T(\mathbf{B}_i)$, then $\mathbf{D}_i = \mathbf{B}_i - \max(\mathbf{B}_i) \cdot \mathbf{U}_j$, where $\max(\mathbf{B}_i)$ is the maximum value of elements in $\mathbf{B}_i$.

Let $\mathbf{D}_i(r)$ be the r-th elememt of $\mathbf{D}_i$.

$\mathbf{W}_i(r)=f(\mathbf{D}_i(r))$, where $f(x) = \begin{cases} \mathbf{D}_i(r), & \text{if } \mathbf{D}_i(r) > 0 \\ 0, & \text{if } \mathbf{D}_i(r) \le 0 \end{cases}$, r=1, 2, … m.

$\sum_{r=1}^{m} (\mathbf{W}_i(r) \cdot \left| \{p \mid p \in {}^{\circ}t_r \cap T(\mathbf{U}_j)^{\circ}\} \right|) = \beta$, where $\mathbf{W}_i(r)$ is the r-th element of $\mathbf{W}_i$, m=|T|.

Add $\mathbf{B}_i+k\cdot\mathbf{U}_j$, k=1, 2, … β, to X_{temp}

When all pairs of ($\mathbf{B}_i$, $\mathbf{U}_j$) have been tested, go to Step 5.

Step 5. If $X_{temp}=\Phi$, then end.

Otherwise, Let B=X_{temp}, $X_e=X_e\cup B$, $X_{temp}=\Phi$, go to Step 4.

Step 1 and Step 2 are to determine all the positive integer solutions **X** for equation $\mathbf{AX}=\mathbf{M}_d-\mathbf{M}_0$. The firing count vector of any firing sequence from $\mathbf{M}_0$ to $\mathbf{M}_d$ belongs to **X**. In Step 4, if $\mathbf{B}_i$ is not an executable solution, then there must be some transitions in T($\mathbf{B}_i$) which aren't enable it, i.e. some places in °T($\mathbf{B}_i$) are lack of tokens. In this case, if {p|p∈°T($\mathbf{B}_i$)∩T($\mathbf{U}_j$)° and T($\mathbf{U}_j$) ⊄ T($\mathbf{B}_i$)}≠ Φ, then T($\mathbf{U}_j$)° may provide tokens for °t, where t∈T($\mathbf{B}_i$). Consequently, $\mathbf{B}_i+k\cdot\mathbf{U}_j$ may be an executable solution, where k=1, 2, … β. Since the number of places and transitions in PN is finite, Step 4 and Step 5 only add finite elements to X_e. Since the number of minimal T-invariants is finite, the finishing condition $X_{temp}=\Phi$, i.e. |{p|p∈°T($\mathbf{B}_i$)∩T($\mathbf{U}_j$)° and T($\mathbf{U}_j$) ⊄ T($\mathbf{B}_i$)}|= Φ, is satisfied after all the related T-invariants have been considered. As a result of the iterative process of Step 4→Step 5→Step 4, X_e includes at least one executable solution if it exists.

The following examples show how to implement the computation algorithm. These examples illustrate that suppressing any k_i in $\mathbf{B}_i+k\cdot\mathbf{U}_j$, k=1, 2, … β, may eliminate some possible executable solutions.

Example 1. When the initial marking is $\mathbf{M}_0$=(1,0,0,0,0,1,0,0,0) and the destination marking is $\mathbf{M}_d$=(1,0,0,0,0,0,0,0,1) in Figure 1, calculate the sufficient test space X_e. The • and ○ symbols are represented as the initial and destination markings respectively.

Step 1. Solve the equation **AX**=0, get the positive integer minimal T-invariant $\mathbf{U}_1$=(1,1,1,1,0,0,0,0).

Step 2. Solve the equation $\mathbf{AX}=\mathbf{M}_d-\mathbf{M}_0$, get the positive integer minimal particular solution V={**V**}=(0,0,0,0,1,1,1,1)

Step 3. Initialization: Let X_e=V, $X_{temp}=\Phi$, B=X_e

Step 4-1. For (**V**, $\mathbf{U}_1$),

If T($\mathbf{U}_1$) ⊄ T(**V**), then $\mathbf{D}=\mathbf{V}-\max(\mathbf{V})\cdot\mathbf{U}_1$, **W**(r)=f(**D**(r)),

$$\sum_{r=1}^{8}\left(\mathbf{W}(r)\cdot\left|\{p\,|\,p\in {}^{\circ}t_r\cap T(\mathbf{U}_1)^{\circ}\}\right|\right)=3.$$

Then add $\mathbf{V}+\mathbf{U}_1$, $\mathbf{V}+2\cdot\mathbf{U}_1$, $\mathbf{V}+3\cdot\mathbf{U}_1$ to the set of X_{temp},

Therefore, X_{temp}={$\mathbf{V}+\mathbf{U}_1$, $\mathbf{V}+2\cdot\mathbf{U}_1$, $\mathbf{V}+3\cdot\mathbf{U}_1$}

Step 5-1. If $X_{temp}\neq\Phi$, then let B=X_{temp}={$\mathbf{V}+\mathbf{U}_1$, $\mathbf{V}+2\cdot\mathbf{U}_1$, $\mathbf{V}+3\cdot\mathbf{U}_1$}

$X_e=X_e\cup B$={**V**, $\mathbf{V}+\mathbf{U}_1$, $\mathbf{V}+2\cdot\mathbf{U}_1$, $\mathbf{V}+3\cdot\mathbf{U}_1$}, $X_{temp}=\Phi$.

Go to Step4 in Algorithm 1.

Step 4-2. For any pair of ($\mathbf{B}_i$, $\mathbf{U}_1$), $T(\mathbf{U}_1) \subset T(\mathbf{B}_i)$ is satisfied. Therefore, $X_{temp}=\Phi$

Step 5-2. If $X_{temp}=\Phi$, then end.

As a result of above sequence, $\mathbf{M}_d$ is reachable from $\mathbf{M}_0$. The firing sequence is $t_5*t_1*t_2*t_6*t_7*t_3*t_4*t_8$. Its firing count vector corresponds to $\mathbf{V}+\mathbf{U}_1=(1,1,1,1,1,1,1,1)$ in the sufficient test space X_e. This example shows that suppressing $\mathbf{B}_i+k\cdot\mathbf{U}_j$ (k=1) in X_e may eliminate some possible executable solution.

Example 2. Consider the PN of Figure 2, given the initial marking $\mathbf{M}_0=(1,0,0,0,0,0,0,0,1,0)$ and the destination marking $\mathbf{M}_d=(0,0,0,1,0,0,0,0,1,0)$, calculate the sufficient test space X_e.

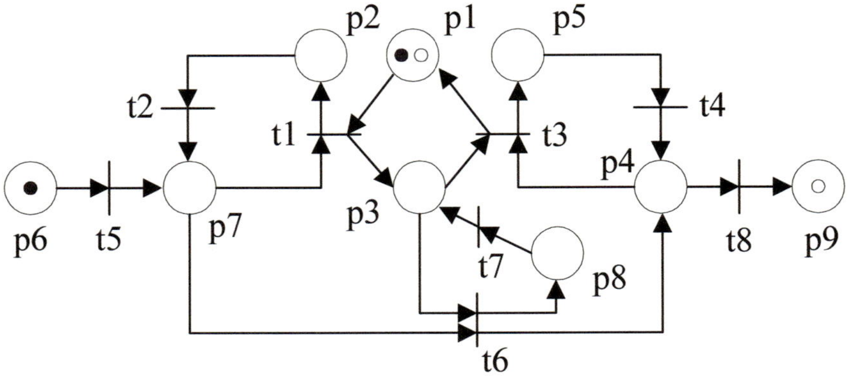

Figure 1. Petri net structure

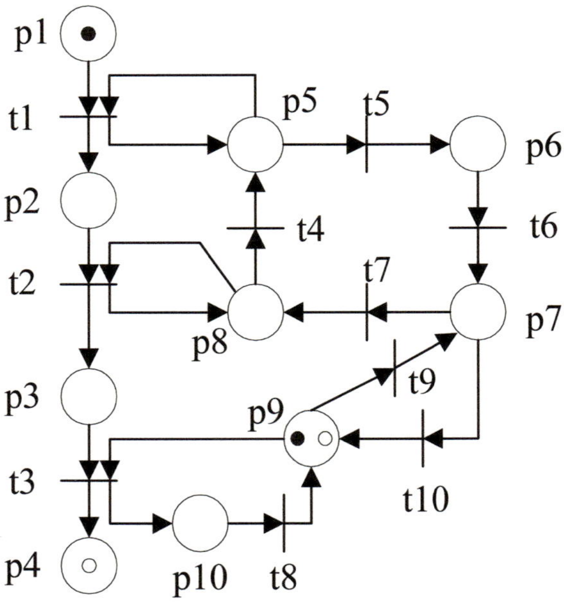

Figure 2. Petri net structure

Step 1. Solve the equation **AX**=0, two positive integer minimal T-invariants are obtained: $\mathbf{U}_1$=(0,0,0,1,1,1,1,0,0,0), $\mathbf{U}_2$=(0,0,0,0,0,0,0,0,1,1)

Step 2. Solve the equation **AX**=$\mathbf{M}_d$-$\mathbf{M}_0$, get the positive integer minimal particular solutions V={**V**}={(1,1,1,0,0,0,0,1,0,0)}

The general solution can be expressed as follows:

$$\mathbf{X} = (1,1,1,0,0,0,0,1,0,0) + k_1 \cdot (0,0,0,1,1,1,1,0,0,0) + k_2 \cdot (0,0,0,0,0,0,0,0,1,1)$$

k_1 and k_2 are nonnegative integer.

Step 3. Initialization: Let X_e=V, X_{temp}=Φ, B=X_e

Step 4-1. For (**V**, $\mathbf{U}_1$),

If $T(\mathbf{U}_1) \not\subset T(\mathbf{V})$, then **D**=**V**-max(**V**)·$\mathbf{U}_1$, **W**(r)=f(**D**(r)),

$$\sum_{r=1}^{10}(\mathbf{W}(r)\cdot\left|\{p \mid p \in {}^{\circ}t_r \cap T(\mathbf{U}_1)^{\circ}\}\right|) = 2.$$

Then add **V**+$\mathbf{U}_1$, **V**+2·$\mathbf{U}_1$ to X_{temp}. So X_{temp}={**V**+$\mathbf{U}_1$, **V**+2$\mathbf{U}_1$}

For (**V**, $\mathbf{U}_2$),

If $T(\mathbf{U}_2) \not\subset T(\mathbf{V})$, then **D**=**V**-max(**V**)·$\mathbf{U}_2$, **W**(r)=f(**D**(r)),

$$\sum_{r=1}^{10}(\mathbf{W}(r)\cdot\left|\{p \mid p \in {}^{\circ}t_r \cap T(\mathbf{U}_2)^{\circ}\}\right|) = 1.$$

Then add **V**+$\mathbf{U}_2$ to X_{temp}. So X_{temp}={**V**+$\mathbf{U}_1$, **V**+2$\mathbf{U}_1$, **V**+$\mathbf{U}_2$}

Step 5-1. If X_{temp}≠Φ, then let B=X_{temp}={**V**+$\mathbf{U}_1$, **V**+2$\mathbf{U}_1$, **V**+$\mathbf{U}_2$},

X_e=X_e∪B={**V**, **V**+$\mathbf{U}_1$, **V**+2$\mathbf{U}_1$, **V**+$\mathbf{U}_2$}. Let's put X_{temp}=Φ.

Go to Step 4 in Algorithm 1.

Step 4-2. For (**V**+$\mathbf{U}_1$, $\mathbf{U}_1$), because $T(\mathbf{U}_1) \subset T(\mathbf{V}+\mathbf{U}_1)$, choose the next pair.

For (**V**+$\mathbf{U}_1$, $\mathbf{U}_2$),

If $T(\mathbf{U}_2) \not\subset T(\mathbf{V}+\mathbf{U}_1)$, then $\mathbf{D}_1$=(**V**+$\mathbf{U}_1$)-max(**V**+$\mathbf{U}_1$)·$\mathbf{U}_2$, $\mathbf{W}_1$(r)=f($\mathbf{D}_1$(r)),

$$\sum_{r=1}^{10}(\mathbf{W}_1(r)\cdot\left|\{p \mid p \in {}^{\circ}t_r \cap T(\mathbf{U}_2)^{\circ}\}\right|) = 2.$$

Then add **V**+$\mathbf{U}_1$+$\mathbf{U}_2$ and **V**+$\mathbf{U}_1$+2$\mathbf{U}_2$ to X_{temp}. So X_{temp}={**V**+$\mathbf{U}_1$+$\mathbf{U}_2$, **V**+$\mathbf{U}_1$+2$\mathbf{U}_2$}

For (**V**+2$\mathbf{U}_1$, $\mathbf{U}_1$), because $T(\mathbf{U}_1) \subset T(\mathbf{V}+2\mathbf{U}_1)$, choose the next pair.

For (**V**+2$\mathbf{U}_1$, $\mathbf{U}_2$),

If $T(\mathbf{U}_2) \not\subset T(\mathbf{V}+2\mathbf{U}_1)$, then $\mathbf{D}_2$=(**V**+2$\mathbf{U}_1$)-max(**V**+2$\mathbf{U}_1$)·$\mathbf{U}_2$, $\mathbf{W}_2$(r)=f($\mathbf{D}_2$(r)),

$$\sum_{r=1}^{10}(\mathbf{W}_2)(r)\cdot\left|\{p \mid p\in {}^{\circ}t_r \cap T(\mathbf{U}_2)^{\circ}\}\right|) = 3.$$

Then add $\mathbf{V}+2\mathbf{U}_1+\mathbf{U}_2$, $\mathbf{V}+2\mathbf{U}_1+2\mathbf{U}_2$, and $\mathbf{V}+2\mathbf{U}_1+3\mathbf{U}_2$ to X_{temp}. So $X_{temp}=\{\mathbf{V}+\mathbf{U}_1+\mathbf{U}_2, \mathbf{V}+\mathbf{U}_1+2\mathbf{U}_2, \mathbf{V}+2\mathbf{U}_1+\mathbf{U}_2, \mathbf{V}+2\mathbf{U}_1+2\mathbf{U}_2, \mathbf{V}+2\mathbf{U}_1+3\mathbf{U}_2\}$

For $(\mathbf{V}+\mathbf{U}_2, \mathbf{U}_2)$, because $T(\mathbf{U}_2)\subset T(\mathbf{V}+\mathbf{U}_2)$, choose the next pair.

For $(\mathbf{V}+\mathbf{U}_2, \mathbf{U}_1)$,

If $T(\mathbf{U}_1)\not\subset T(\mathbf{V}+\mathbf{U}_2)$, then $\mathbf{D}_3=(\mathbf{V}+\mathbf{U}_2)-\max(\mathbf{V}+\mathbf{U}_2)\cdot\mathbf{U}_1$, $\mathbf{W}_3(r)=f(\mathbf{D}_3(r))$,

$$\sum_{r=1}^{10}(\mathbf{W}_3(r)\cdot\left|\{p \mid p\in {}^{\circ}t_r \cap T(\mathbf{U}_1)^{\circ}\}\right|) = 3.$$

Then add $\mathbf{V}+\mathbf{U}_2+\mathbf{U}_1$, $\mathbf{V}+\mathbf{U}_2+2\mathbf{U}_1$, and $\mathbf{V}+\mathbf{U}_2+3\mathbf{U}_1$ to X_{temp}. So $X_{temp}=\{\mathbf{V}+\mathbf{U}_1+\mathbf{U}_2, \mathbf{V}+\mathbf{U}_1+2\mathbf{U}_2, \mathbf{V}+2\mathbf{U}_1+\mathbf{U}_2, \mathbf{V}+2\mathbf{U}_1+2\mathbf{U}_2, \mathbf{V}+2\mathbf{U}_1+3\mathbf{U}_2, \mathbf{V}+\mathbf{U}_2+3\mathbf{U}_1\}$

Step 5-2. If $X_{temp}\neq\Phi$, then let $B=X_{temp}=\{\mathbf{V}+\mathbf{U}_1+\mathbf{U}_2, \mathbf{V}+\mathbf{U}_1+2\cdot\mathbf{U}_2, \mathbf{V}+2\cdot\mathbf{U}_1+\mathbf{U}_2, \mathbf{V}+2\cdot\mathbf{U}_1+2\cdot\mathbf{U}_2, \mathbf{V}+2\cdot\mathbf{U}_1+3\cdot\mathbf{U}_2, \mathbf{V}+\mathbf{U}_2+3\mathbf{U}_1\}$.

So, $X_e=X_e+B=\{\mathbf{V}, \mathbf{V}+\mathbf{U}_1, \mathbf{V}+2\cdot\mathbf{U}_1, \mathbf{V}+\mathbf{U}_2, \mathbf{V}+\mathbf{U}_1+\mathbf{U}_2, \mathbf{V}+\mathbf{U}_1+2\cdot\mathbf{U}_2, \mathbf{V}+2\cdot\mathbf{U}_1+\mathbf{U}_2, \mathbf{V}+2\cdot\mathbf{U}_1+2\cdot\mathbf{U}_2, \mathbf{V}+2\cdot\mathbf{U}_1+3\cdot\mathbf{U}_2, \mathbf{V}+\mathbf{U}_2+3\mathbf{U}_1\}$. Let's put $X_{temp}=\Phi$.

Go to Step 4 in Algorithm 1.

Step 4-3. For any pair of $(\mathbf{B}_i, \mathbf{U}_j)$, because $T(\mathbf{U}_j)\subset T(\mathbf{B}_i)$, $X_{temp}=\Phi$
Step 5-3. If $X_{temp}=\Phi$, then end

$\mathbf{M}_d$ is reachable from $\mathbf{M}_0$. The firing sequence is $t_9{*}t_7{*}t_4{*}t_1{*}t_5{*}t_6{*}t_7{*}t_2{*}t_4{*}t_5{*}t_6{*}t_{10}{*}t_3{*}t_8$. Its firing count vector corresponds to $\mathbf{V}+2\cdot\mathbf{U}_1+\mathbf{U}_2=(1,1,1,2,2,2,2,1,1,1)$ in the sufficient test space X_e. This example illustrates that suppressing $\mathbf{B}_i+k\cdot\mathbf{U}_j$ $(k=\beta)$ in X_e may eliminate some possible executable solution.

4. Search of a firing sequence

Given the initial marking $\mathbf{M}_0$ and the destination marking $\mathbf{M}_d$ of a PN, a solution $\mathbf{X}_{ei}$ is solved from $\mathbf{A}\mathbf{X}=\mathbf{M}_d-\mathbf{M}_0$. Then, an algorithm is developed to determine whether $\mathbf{M}_d$ is reachable from $\mathbf{M}_0$ under $\mathbf{X}_{ei}$ or not. If $\mathbf{M}_d$ is reachable from $\mathbf{M}_0$, the algorithm gives the associated firing sequence $S(\mathbf{X}_{ei})$.

Definition 12. Let $S= t_1t_2\ldots t_r$ be a finite transition sequence. The transitions appearing in S are defined by the set $Z(S) =\{t_1, t_2, \ldots, t_r\}$. The set of transitions $Z(S)$ is called a sequence component. $Z(S)$ is the set of elements that appear in a transition sequence S.

Algorithm 2. Search of a firing sequence $S(\mathbf{X}_{ei})$ under $\mathbf{M}_0$

Step 1. According to $\mathbf{I}$, determine all the conflict structure $C_i=\langle p, T_{ci}\rangle$, and construct T_c and C.

Step 2. Initialization: Let M=$\mathbf{M}_0$, X=$\mathbf{X}_{ei}$, S=λ (λ is the sequence of length zero)

Step 3. Under M and X, calculate $\mathbf{F}$=$\mathbf{F}_o$−$\mathbf{F}_c$ from Definition 6.

If $\mathbf{F}_o\neq\mathbf{0}$, go to Step 4.

If $\mathbf{F}_o$ =$\mathbf{0}$ and $\mathbf{F}_c\neq 0$, go to Step 5.

If $\mathbf{F}$=$\mathbf{0}$, go to step 6.

Step 4. If $\mathbf{F}_o\neq 0$, then there exists an S($\mathbf{F}_o$) that has a firing sequence under M. Therefore, S($\mathbf{F}_o$) can be fired. The reachable marking is calculated by $\mathbf{M}'$=M-$\mathbf{A}\cdot\mathbf{F}_o$,

Let M=$\mathbf{M}'$, X=X−$\mathbf{F}_o$, S=S*S($\mathbf{F}_o$), where * is concatenation operation and S*S($\mathbf{F}_o$) means S followed by S($\mathbf{F}_o$). Go to Step 3.

Step 5. $\mathbf{F}_o$ =0 and $\mathbf{F}_c\neq 0$ means that all transitions in S($\mathbf{F}_c$) are effective conflict transitions. Therefore, branching occurs and the number of branches is |T($\mathbf{F}_c$)|. From here, the computation has to consider all |T($\mathbf{F}_c$)| branches.

After selecting a transition $t_j\in$T($\mathbf{F}_c$), fire it, then the reachable marking is calculated by $\mathbf{M}'$=M-$\mathbf{A}\cdot e[t_j]$.

Let M=$\mathbf{M}'$, X=X−$e[t_j]$, S=S*t_j.Go to Step 3

Step 6. If X=0, then $\mathbf{M}_d$ is reachable from $\mathbf{M}_0$ and S=S($\mathbf{X}_{ei}$) is one of the firing sequences, end. Otherwise, go to Step 7.

Step 7. If all the branches in Step 5 have been implemented, then $\mathbf{M}_d$ is not reachable, end. Otherwise, go to Step 5 and implement the remaining branches.

The validity of the above algorithm is proved as the following four cases:

Base: Let $\mathbf{X}$ be a solution of $\mathbf{AX}$=$\mathbf{M}_d$-$\mathbf{M}_0$. The actual firing vector $\mathbf{F}$=$\mathbf{F}_o$+$\mathbf{F}_c$ is obtained with $\mathbf{M}$ and $\mathbf{X}$. Let $t_o\in$T($\mathbf{F}_o$) and $t_c\in$T($\mathbf{F}_c$).

Case 1: If $\mathbf{F}_o\neq\mathbf{0}$ and $\mathbf{F}_c$=$\mathbf{0}$, then multiple firing of S($\mathbf{F}_o$) doesn't affect a firing sequence associated with $\mathbf{X}$ under $\mathbf{M}_0$, for the input places of T($\mathbf{F}_o$) don't affect the enabling condition of other transitions in T($\mathbf{X}$) except transitions in T($\mathbf{F}_o$).

Case 2: If $\mathbf{F}_o$=$\mathbf{0}$ and $\mathbf{F}_c\neq\mathbf{0}$, then the firing of each transition in S($\mathbf{F}_c$) is considered as a branch and implemented with respect to all branches. It means that all possibilities are involved. So, Algorithm 2 doesn't eliminate any possible firing sequence.

Case 3: If $\mathbf{F}_o$=$\mathbf{0}$ and $\mathbf{F}_c$=$\mathbf{0}$, then no transition is enabled.

Case 4: If $\mathbf{F}_o\neq\mathbf{0}$ and $\mathbf{F}_c\neq\mathbf{0}$, then the multiple firing of S($\mathbf{F}_o$) can be implemented before S($\mathbf{F}_c$). It doesn't eliminate any probability of finding a firing sequence associated with $\mathbf{X}$ under $\mathbf{M}_0$. It is proven in Proposition 1.

Proposition 1. If $\sigma\in$S($\mathbf{X}$) is a firing sequence under $\mathbf{M}_0$, then (S($\mathbf{F}_o$)*σ')$\in$S($\mathbf{X}$) is a firing sequence under $\mathbf{M}_0$ for any sequence σ'.

Proof:

Step 1. Let $T(\mathbf{F_o})=\{t_{o1}, t_{o2}, \ldots, t_{on}\}$. For a transition $t_{o1}\in T(\mathbf{F_o})$, σ can be represented as $\sigma=\sigma_1{*}t_o{*}\sigma_2$, where $t_{o1}\notin Z(\sigma_1)$. Then $\mathbf{M_0}\xrightarrow{\sigma_1}\mathbf{M_1}\xrightarrow{t_{o1}}\mathbf{M_2}\xrightarrow{\sigma_2}\mathbf{M_d}$ is a firing sequence. Since $T(\mathbf{F_o})$ is the set of transitions possible to be enabled under $\mathbf{M_0}$, $\mathbf{M_0}$ enables t_{o1}. Therefore it is possible to put $\mathbf{M_0}\xrightarrow{t_{o1}}\mathbf{M_3}$. By the definition of $\mathbf{F_o}$, we have $M_3(p)\geq M_0(p)$ for any $p\in{}^{\circ}Z(\sigma_1)$. So σ_1 is enabled under M_3 because σ_1 is enabled under M_0 (Monotonicity Lemma). After σ_1 firing, $\mathbf{M_2}$ is reachable from $\mathbf{M_3}$. Therefore, we have $\mathbf{M_0}\xrightarrow{t_{o1}}\mathbf{M_3}\xrightarrow{\sigma_1}\mathbf{M_2}$. Since σ_2 is enabled under M_2, $t_{o1}{*}\sigma_1{*}\sigma_2$ is a firing sequence under $\mathbf{M_0}$.

Step 2. Under $\mathbf{M_3}$, let's consider the new $T(\mathbf{F_o})=\{t_{o2}, \ldots, t_{on}\}\cup T(\mathbf{F_o}')$, where $T(\mathbf{F_o}')$ is the set of transition generated after t_{o1} firing and may be empty. For a transition $t_{o2}\in T(\mathbf{F_o})$, $\sigma_1{*}\sigma_2$ can be represented as $\sigma_1{*}\sigma_2=\sigma_3{*}t_{o2}{*}\sigma_4$, where $t_{o2}\notin Z(\sigma_3)$. Then $\sigma_3{*}t_{o2}{*}\sigma_4$ is a firing sequence. By the same way described in Step 1, we can prove that $t_{o2}{*}\sigma_3{*}\sigma_4$ is a firing sequence under $\mathbf{M_3}$.

Step 3. By Step 1 and Step 2, $t_{o1}{*}t_{o2}{*}\sigma_3{*}\sigma_4$ is a firing sequence under $\mathbf{M_0}$.

Step 4. In the same way, it is proven that $t_{o1}{*}t_{o2}{*}\ldots{*}t_{on}{*}\sigma_i{*}\sigma_j$ is a firing sequence under $\mathbf{M_0}$. According to the definition of $\mathbf{F_o}$, all transitions in $\{t_{o1}, t_{o2}, \ldots, t_{on}\}$ can fire simultaneously under $\mathbf{M_0}$. Let's put $\sigma'=\sigma_i{*}\sigma_j$, then $(S(\mathbf{F_o}){*}\sigma')\in S(\mathbf{X})$ is a firing sequence under $\mathbf{M_0}$.

Example 3. Let us now apply the proposed algorithm to the PN of Figure 3. Given $\mathbf{M_0}$=(0,0,0,0,0,0,1,0,0), $\mathbf{M_d}$=(0,0,0,0,1,0,1,0,0) and $\mathbf{X}$=(1,2,1,1,1,1,1), determine if $\mathbf{M_d}$ is reachable or not under $\mathbf{M_0}$ and $\mathbf{X}$.

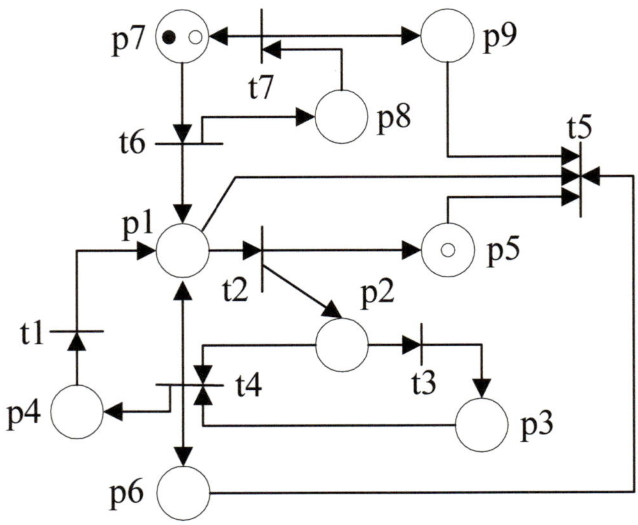

Figure 3. Petri net structure

Step 1. There are two conflict structures, C_1=<p_1, {t_2, t_5}>, C_2=<p_2, {t_3, t_4}>, T_c={t_2, t_3, t_4, t_5}.
Step 2. Initialization: *M*=**M**$_0$= (0,0,0,0,0,0,1,0,0), *X*=**X**=(1,2,1,1,1,1,1), *S*=λ
Step 3. Under *M* and *X*, only t_6 is 1-enabled. Then, **F**$_o$=(0,0,0,0,0,1,0).
Step 4. Fire S(**F**$_o$)= t_6. Then the reachable marking **M′** becomes (1,0,0,0,0,0,0,1,0)

Let *M*=**M′**, *X*=*X*-**F**$_o$=(1,2,1,1,1,0,1), *S*=t_6. Go to Step 3 in Algorithm 2.

Step 3-1. Under *M* and *X*, **F**$_o$=(0,0,0,0,0,0,1).
Step 4-1. Fire S(**F**$_o$)=t_7. Then, the reachable marking becomes **M′**=(1,0,0,0,0,0,1,0,1)

Let *M*=**M′**, *X*=*X*-**F**$_o$=(1,2,1,1,1,0,0), *S*=t_6*t_7. Go to Step 3 in Algorithm 2.

Step 3-2. Under ***M*** and ***X***, **F**$_o$=(0,1,0,0,0,0,0). Go to Step 4 in Algorithm 2.
Step 4-2. Fire S(**F**$_o$)=t_2 (t_2 is not an effective conflict transition because t_5 cannot enable),

then the reachable marking becomes **M′**=(0,1,0,0,1,0,1,0,1)

Let *M*=**M′**, *X*=*X*-**F**$_o$=(1,1,1,1,1,0,0). *S*= t_6*t_7*t_2. Go to Step 3 in Algorithm 2.

Step 3-3. Under ***M*** and ***X***, **F**$_o$=(0,0,1,0,0,0,0). Go to Step 4 in Algorithm 2.
Step 4-3. Fire S(**F**$_o$)=t_3 (t_3 is not an effective conflict transition because t_4 cannot enable),

then the reachable marking becomes **M′**=(0,0,1,0,1,0,1,0,1)

Let *M*=**M′**, *X*=*X*-**F**$_o$=(1,1,0,1,1,0,0). *S*= t_6*t_7*t_2*t_3. Go to Step 3 in Algorithm 2.

Step 3-4. Under ***M*** and ***X***, **F=0,** go to Step 6 in Algorithm 2.

Step 6. Because ***X*≠0,** go to Step 7 in Algorithm 2.

Step 7. There is no effective conflict transition i.e., no branch. Consequently, **M**$_d$ is not reachable under **X** because ***X*≠0.**

The above implementing process can be presented by a firing path tree as shown in Figure 4.

5. Application of Reachability Criterion

An example will be given to illustrate how to use the proposed method of Algorithm 1 and Algorithm 2 to solve the reachability problem.

Example 4. When the initial marking is **M**$_0$=(1,0,0,0,0,0,0,0,1) in the PN of Figure 5, is the destination marking **M**$_d$=(0,0,1,0,1,0,0,0,1) reachable from **M**$_0$?

First, calculate sufficient test space using the following steps:

Step 1. Solve the equation **AX**=0, get one positive integer minimal T-invariant **U**=(0,0,0,0,0,0,1,1).
Step 2. Solve the equation **AX**=**M**$_d$-**M**$_0$, get the positive integer minimal particular solutions **V**$_1$=(0,2,1,0,2,2,0,0), **V**$_2$=(2,2,1,2,0,0,0,0) and **V**$_3$=(1,2,1,1,1,1,0,0)
Step 3. Initialization: Let X_e={**V**$_1$, **V**$_2$, **V**$_3$}, X_{temp}=Φ, B=X_e
Step 4-1. For (**V**$_1$, **U**),

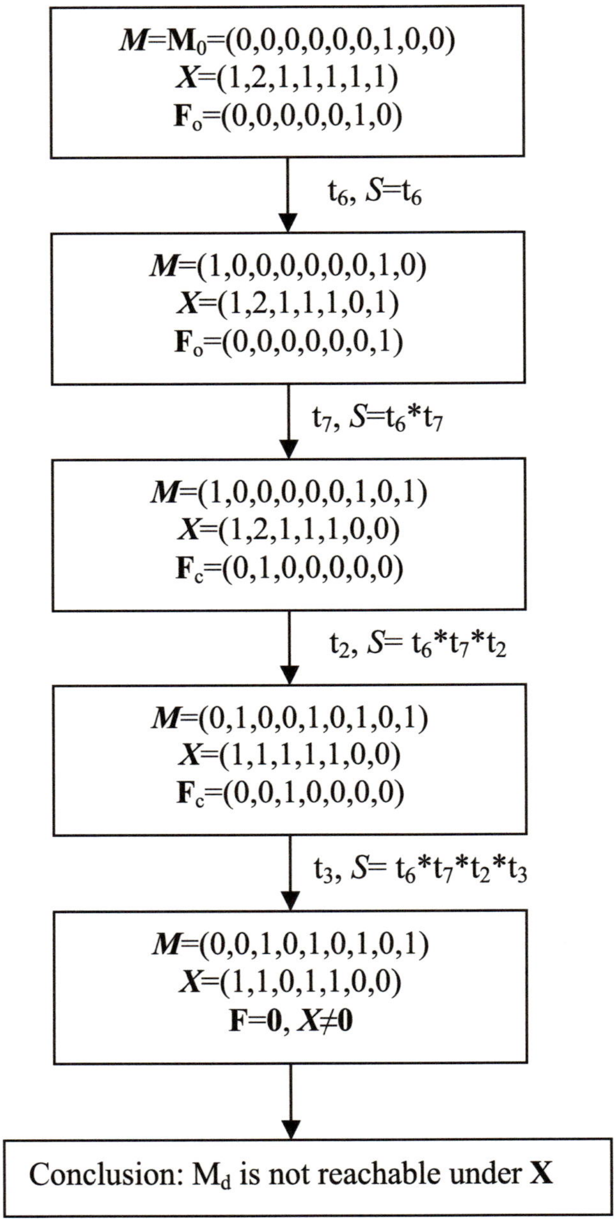

Figure 4. Firing path tree on reachability of Figure 3.

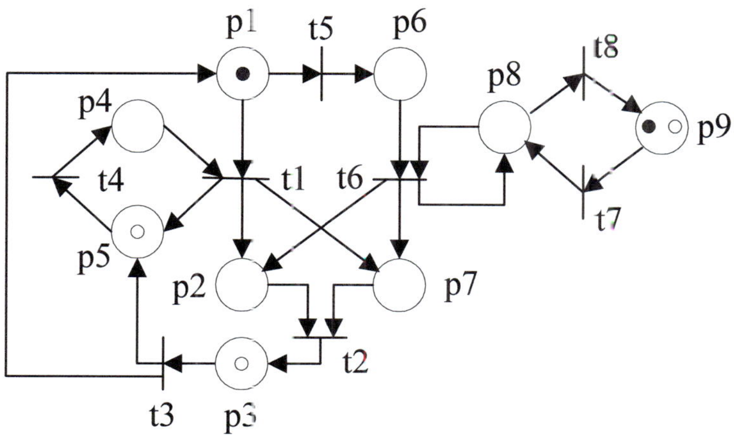

Figure 5. Petri net structure

If T(**U**) $\not\subset$ T(**V**$_1$), then **D**$_1$=**V**$_1$-max(**V**$_1$)·**U**, **W**$_1$(r)=f(**D**$_1$(r)),

$$\sum_{r=1}^{8}(\mathbf{W}_1(r)\cdot\left|\{p\,|\,p\in {}^{\circ}t_r\cap T(\mathbf{U})^{\circ}\}\right|)=2$$

Then add **V**$_1$+**U**, **V**$_1$+2·**U** to X$_{temp}$. Then, X$_{temp}$={**V**$_1$+**U**, **V**$_1$+2·**U** }

For (**V**$_2$, **U**), because °T(**V**$_2$)∩T(**U**) °=Φ, choose the next pair.

For (**V**$_3$, **U**),

If T(**U**) $\not\subset$ T(**V**$_3$), then **D**$_3$=**V**$_3$-max(**V**$_3$)·**U**, **W**$_3$(r)=f(**D**$_3$(r)),

$$\sum_{r=1}^{8}(\mathbf{W}_3(r)\cdot\left|\{p\,|\,p\in {}^{\circ}t_r\cap T(\mathbf{U})^{\circ}\}\right|)=1$$

Then add **V**$_3$+**U** to X$_{temp}$, X$_{temp}$={**V**$_1$+**U**, **V**$_1$+2·**U**, **V**$_3$+**U**}

Step 5-1. If X$_{temp}$≠Φ, then let B=X$_{temp}$={**V**$_1$+**U**, **V**$_1$+2·**U**, **V**$_3$+**U**},

X$_e$=X$_e$∪B={**V**$_1$, **V**$_2$, **V**$_3$, **V**$_1$+**U**, **V**$_1$+2·**U**, **V**$_3$+**U** }. Let's put X$_{temp}$=Φ. Go to Step 4 in Algorithm 1.

Step 4. For any pair of (**B**$_i$, **U**), because T(**U**$_j$) ⊂ T(**B**$_i$), X$_{temp}$=Φ.

Step 5. If X$_{temp}$=Φ, then end.

Consequently, the sufficient test space becomes X$_e$={**V**$_1$, **V**$_2$, **V**$_3$, **V**$_1$+**U**, **V**$_1$+2·**U**, **V**$_3$+**U**}.

Second, calculate a firing sequence in order to test if M(d) is reachable from M(0) under some element in X$_e$

The elements of the sufficient test space X$_e$ are calculated separately as follows:

Step 1. For **X**=**V**$_1$=(0,2,1,0,2,2,0,0)

The implementing process is shown in Figure 6.

Step 2. For $\mathbf{X}=\mathbf{V}_2=(2,2,1,2,0,0,0,0)$

Carrying out the same process, the conclusion is as follows: M_d is not reachable under $\mathbf{V}_2$.

Step 3. For $\mathbf{X}=\mathbf{V}_3=(1,2,1,1,1,1,0,0)$

Carrying out the same process, the conclusion is as follows: M_d is not reachable under $\mathbf{V}_2$.

Step 4. For $\mathbf{X}=\mathbf{V}_1+\mathbf{U}=(0,2,1,0,2,2,1,1)$

Carrying out the same process shown in Figure 7, the conclusion is as follows: M_d is reachable from M_0 under $\mathbf{V}_1+\mathbf{U}$. $\mathbf{V}_1+\mathbf{U}$ is an executable solution in X_e, and the firing sequence is $t_5*t_7*t_6*t_2*t_3*t_5*t_6*t_2*t_8$.

As a result of calculating each element of the sufficient test space $X_e=\{\mathbf{V}_1, \mathbf{V}_2, \mathbf{V}_3, \mathbf{V}_1+\mathbf{U}, \mathbf{V}_1+2\cdot\mathbf{U}, \mathbf{V}_3+\mathbf{U}\}$ individually, a firing sequence is finally found at the fourth element ($\mathbf{V}_1+\mathbf{U}$) of X_e. Therefore, the elements $\mathbf{V}_1+2\cdot\mathbf{U}$ and $\mathbf{V}_3+\mathbf{U}$ don't need to be calculated. Consequently, the structure of the Petri net (Figure 5) is shown to possess at least one reachable firing sequence.

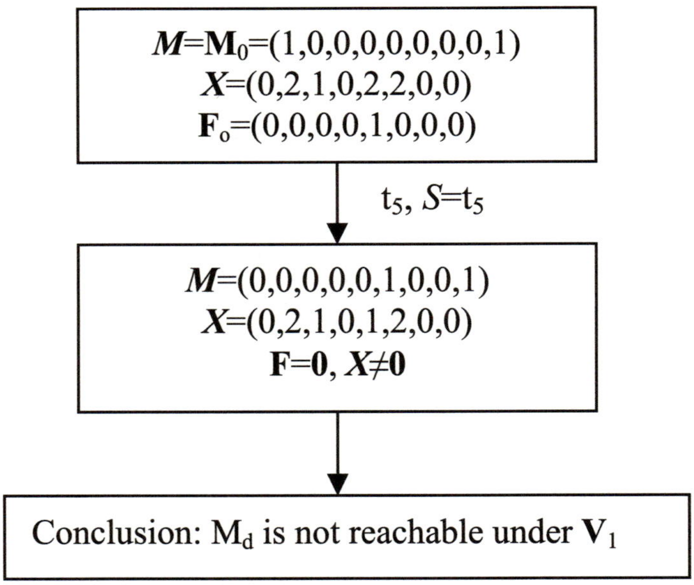

Figure 6. Firing path tree for $\mathbf{V}_1$.

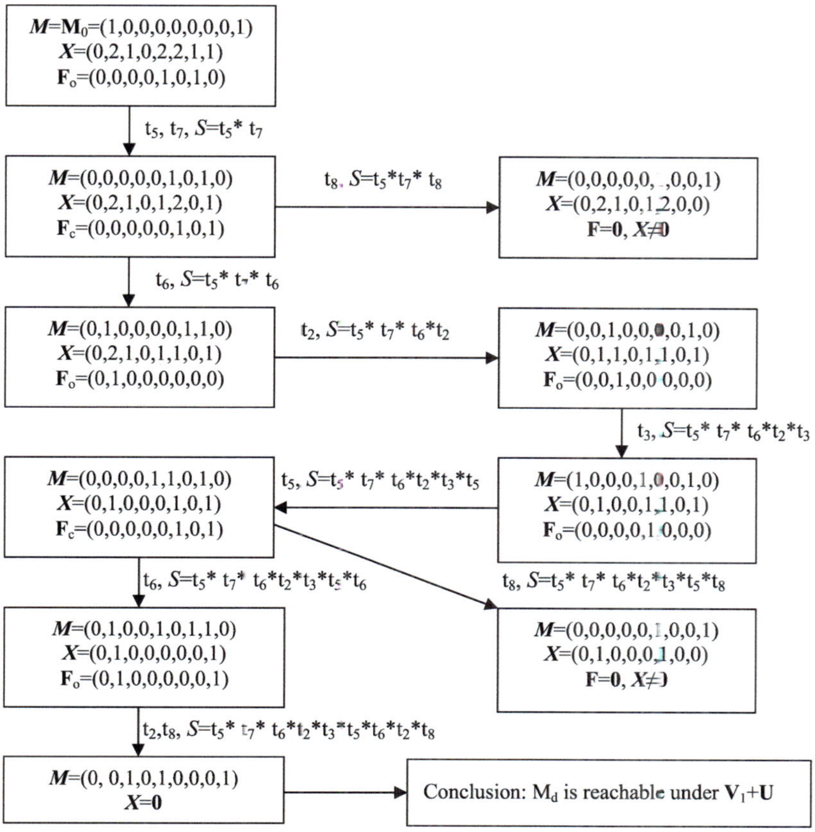

Figure 7. Firing path tree for $\mathbf{V}_1$+**F**.

6. Conclusions

In this chapter, a new general criterion has been created to solve the reachability problems for ordinary Petri nets. This criterion is based on two processes: (i) Calculating the sufficient test space. (ii) Testing whether or not the destination marking is reachable from the initial marking under the sufficient test space. The sufficient test space significantly reduces the quantity of computation needed to search for an executable solution in X. The firing path tree shows the firing sequence of an executable solution. Consequently, if the destination marking is reachable from the initial marking, this method gives at least one firing sequence that leads from the initial marking to the destination marking. Some examples are given to illustrate how to use this method to solve the reachability problem. This algorithm can be utilized in the following fields: Path searching, auto routing, and reachability between any places in a complicated network.

Author details

Gi Bum Lee

Research Institute of Industrial Science & Technology, Pohang, Korea

Han Zandong
Tsinghua University, Beijing, P.R. China

Jin S. Lee
Pohang University of Science and Technology, Pohang, Korea

7. References

[1] Frank L. Lewis, Ayla Gurel, Stjepan Bogdan, Alper Doganalp and Octavian C. Pastravanu (1998) Analysis of deadlock and circular waits using a matrix model for flexible manufacturing systems. Automatica. 34(9): 1083-1100.
[2] Tadao Murata (1989) Petri Nets: Properties, Analysis and Applications. Proceedings of the IEEE . 77: 541-580.
[3] Gi Bum Lee, Han Zandong, Jin S. Lee (2004) Automatic generation of ladder diagram with control Petri Net. Journal of Intelligent Manufacturing. 15(2): 245-252.
[4] MengChu Zhou (1995) Petri nets in flexible and agile automation [M]. Boston: Kluwer Academic Publishers Group.
[5] Ernst W. Mayr (1984) An algorithm for the general Petri net reachability problem. SIAM J. COMPUT. 13(3): 441-449.
[6] Jeng S. Huang and Tadao Murata (1997) Classifications of Petri Net Transitions and Their Application to Firing Sequence and Reachability Problems. IEEE International Conference on Systems, Man, and Cybernatics. 1: 263-268.
[7] Jorg Desel and Javier Esparza (1995) Free choice Petri nets: Cambridge University Press.
[8] Kunihiko Hiraishi (2000) An Efficient Algorithm for Exploring State Spaces of Petri Nets with Large Capacities. IEICE Trans. Fundamentals. E83-A(11): 2188-2195.
[9] Karsten Schmidt (2001) Narrowing Petri Net State Spaces Using the State Equation. Fundamenta Informaticae. 47: 325-335.
[10] Alexander E. Kostin and Svetlana A. Tchoudaikina (1998) Yet Another Reachability Algorithm for Petri nets. SIGACT News. 29(4): 98-110.
[11] Toshiro ARAKI and Tadao KASAMI (1977) Some Decision Problems Related to the Reachability Problem for Petri nets. Theoretical Computer Science. 3: 85-104.
[12] Iko Miyazawa, Haruki Tanaka, and Takashi Sekiguchi (1996) Classification of solutions of matrix equation related to parallel structure of a Petri Net. IEEE Conference on Emerging Technologies and Factory Automation: 446-452.
[13] Tadashi Matsumoto and Yasushi Miyano (1998) Reachability criterion for Petri Nets with known firing count Vectors. IEICE Trans. Fundamentals. E81-A(4): 628-634.
[14] Jaegeol Yim, Peter C. Nelson, and Tadao Murata (1994) Predicate-Transition Net Reachability Testing Using Heuristic Search. T. IEE Japan. 114-C(9): 907-913.
[15] David (1992) Petri net and Grafcet: Prentice Hall International Ltd.
[16] Gi Bum Lee, Jin S. Lee (2002) Conversion of LD program into augmented PN graph. International Journal of Modelling & Simulation. 22(4): 201-212.
[17] Gi Bum Lee, Han Zandong, Jin S. Lee (2003) Generalized State Equation of Petri nets with Priority. International Journal of Intelligent Systems. 18(11): 1145-1153.
[18] Peterson (1981) Petri net theory and the modeling of systems: London: Prentice Hall international (UK) Ltd.

Chapter 20

A Forward On-The-Fly Approach in Controller Synthesis of Time Petri Nets

Parisa Heidari and Hanifa Boucheneb

Additional information is available at the end of the chapter

http://dx.doi.org/10.5772/47744

1. Introduction

Controller synthesis refers to finding a controller which is running in parallel with the system under study and preventing any violation from the given properties. Such a controller guarantees satisfaction of the desired properties; a controller makes an open-loop system to be closed-loop.

Controller synthesis can also be explained by game theory as a timed game with two players: environment and the controller. The strategy of the game determines the sequence of actions to be executed. In this context, the objective of controller synthesis is to find a strategy such that no matter what action is executed by the environment, the controller wins absolutely the game. Two main questions arise for the controller: the existence and possibility of implementation. The first question, *Control Problem* says given a system $\mathcal{S}$ and a property φ, does a controller C exist for the system $\mathcal{S}$ such that C running in parallel with $\mathcal{S}$ satisfies the property φ ($\mathcal{S}||C \models \varphi$). And the second one is the *Controller Synthesis Problem*; if the mentioned controller exists, is there a solution to implement it? First, a system should be modeled and then, synthesized regarding the desired property.

Among various models used to describe the behavior of $\mathcal{S}$, Timed Automata (*TA* in short) and Time Petri Nets (*TPN* in short) are the well-known. The properties studied in the TPN and TA for control purposes are classified in two main categories:

1. Safety properties: Whatever path is traveled, for all situations, a given set of forbidden states (or bad states) are never reached.
2. Reachability properties: Whatever path is traveled, for all situations, a state of a given set of states (good states) will eventually be reached.

Some research has been done to find algorithms to control these kinds of properties for timed models (TA and TPN), such as [10, 11, 20]. Two known methods in the literature are the backward *fix point* method and the backward/forward *on-the-fly* method. Both methods are based on computing controllable predecessors of abstract states (state zones). This computation involves some expensive operations such as computing differences between abstract states (state zones).

In this chapter, we discuss an efficient approach to check whether a safety / reachability controller in time Petri nets exists or not [13]. Our approach is a completely forward on-the-fly algorithm based on the state class graph method. Unlike approaches proposed in [10, 11, 20] based on the state zone graph method, our approach does not need to compute controllable predecessors. It consists of exploring the state class graph while extracting sequences leading to undesired states and determining subclasses to be avoided. The state class graph is a suitable choice for the forward on-the-fly exploration. Using the state class graph method, the exploration algorithm converges fast and does not need any over-approximation operation to enforce the convergence.

This chapter is organized as follows: The definition of time Petri nets and its semantics as well as the state graph method come in Section 2. In Section 3, after a short survey on the control theory, previous algorithms and related work are discussed. The algorithm proposed in this chapter is developed in Section 4. Finally, Section 5 presents the conclusion and future work.

2. Time Petri nets

2.1. Definition and behavior

A time Petri net [14] is a Petri net augmented with time intervals associated with transitions. Among the different semantics proposed for time Petri nets [18], here we focus on the classical one, called intermediate semantics in [18], in the context of mono-server and strong-semantics [7].

Formally, a *TPN* is a tuple $(P, T, Pre, Post, M_0, Is)$ where:
- P and T are finite sets of places and transitions such that $(P \cap T = \emptyset)$,
- Pre and $Post$ are the backward and the forward incidence functions $(Pre, Post : P \times T \rightarrow \mathbb{N}, \mathbb{N}$ is the set of nonnegative integers),
- M_0 is the initial marking $(M_0 : P \rightarrow \mathbb{N})$, and
- Is is the static interval function $(Is : T \rightarrow \mathbb{Q}^+ \times (\mathbb{Q}^+ \cup \{\infty\}))$. $\mathbb{Q}^+$ is the set of nonnegative rational numbers. Is associates with each transition t an interval called the static firing interval of t. Bounds $\downarrow Is(t)$ and $\uparrow Is(t)$ of the interval $Is(t)$ are respectively the minimum and maximum firing delays of t.

In a controllable time Petri net, transitions are partitioned into controllable and uncontrollable transitions, denoted T_c and T_u, respectively (with $T_c \cap T_u = \emptyset$ and $T = T_c \cup T_u$). For the sake of simplicity and clarification, in this manuscript the controllable transitions are depicted as white bars, while the uncontrollable ones as black bars.

A TPN, is called bounded if for every reachable marking M, there is a bound $b \in \mathbb{N}^p$ where $M \leq b$ holds. In this condition p stands for the number of places in P.

Let M be a marking and t a transition. Transition t is enabled for M iff all required tokens for firing t are present in M, i.e., $\forall p \in P, M(p) \geq Pre(p, t)$. In this case, the firing of t leads to the marking M' defined by: $\forall p \in P, M'(p) = M(p) - Pre(p,t) + Post(p,t)$. We denote $En(M)$ the set of transitions enabled for M:

$$En(M) = t \in T | \forall p \in P, Pre(p,t) \leq M(p). \quad (1)$$

For $t \in En(M)$, we denote $CF(M,t)$ the set of transitions enabled in M but in conflict with t:

$$CF(M,t) = t' \in En(M) | t' = t \vee \exists p \in P, M(p) < Pre(p,t') + Pre(p,t). \quad (2)$$

Let $t \in En(M)$ and M' the successor marking of M by t, a transition t' is said to be newly enabled in M' iff t' is not enabled in the intermediate marking (i.e., $M - Pre(.,t)$) or $t' = t$. We denote $New(M',t)$ the set of transitions newly enabled M', by firing t from M:

$$New(M',t) = \{t' \in En(M') | t = t' \vee \exists p \in P, M'(p) - Post(p,t) < Pre(p,t')\}. \quad (3)$$

There are two known characterizations for the TPN state. The first one, based on clocks, associates with each transition t_i of the model a *clock* to measure the time elapsed since t_i became enabled most recently. The TPN clock state is a couple (M,ν), where M is a marking and ν is a clock valuation function, $\nu : En(M) \rightarrow \mathbb{R}^+$. For a clock state (M,ν) and $t_i \in En(M)$, $\nu(t_i)$ is the value of the clock associated with transition t_i. The initial clock state is $q_0 = (M_0, \nu_0)$ where $\nu_0(t_i) = 0$, for all $t_i \in En(M_0)$. The TPN clock state evolves either by time progression or by firing transitions. When a transition t_i becomes enabled, its clock is initialized to zero. The value of this clock increases synchronously with time until t_i is fired or disabled by the firing of another transition. t_i can fire, if the value of its clock is inside its static firing interval $Is(t_i)$. It must be fired immediately, without any additional delay, when the clock reaches $\uparrow Is(t_i)$. The firing of a transition takes no time, but may lead to another marking (required tokens disappear while produced ones appear).

Let $q = (M,\nu)$ and $q_0 = (M_0,\nu_0)$ be two clock states of the TPN model, $\theta \in \mathbb{R}^-$ and $t_f \in T$. We write $q \xrightarrow{\theta} q'$, also denoted $q + \theta$, iff state q' is reachable from state q after a time progression of θ time units, i.e.:

$$\bigwedge_{t' \in En(M)} \nu(t) + \theta \leq \uparrow Id(t_i), M' = M, and\, \forall t_j \in En(M'), \nu'(t_j) = \nu(t_j) + \theta. \quad (4)$$

We write $q \xrightarrow{t_f} q'$ iff state q' is immediately reachable from state q by firing transition t_f, i.e.: $t_f \in En(M)$, $\nu(t_f) \geq \downarrow Is(t_f)$, $\forall p \in P, M'(p) = M(p) - Pre(p,t_f) + Post(p,t_f)$, and $\forall t_i \in En(M'), \nu'(t_i) = 0$, if $t_i \in New(M',t_f)$, $\nu'(t_i) = \nu(t_i)$ otherwise.

The second characterization, based on intervals, defines the TPN state as a marking and a function which associates with each enabled transition the time interval in which the transition can fire [5].

The TPN state is defined as a pair (M, Id), where M is a marking and Id is a firing interval function $(Id : En(M) \rightarrow \mathbb{Q}^+ \times (\mathbb{Q}^+ \cup \{\infty\}))$. The initial state is (M_0, Id_0) where M_0 is the initial marking and $Id_0(t) = Is(t)$, for $t \in En(M_0)$.

Let (M, Id) and (M', Id') be two states of the TPN model, $\theta \in \mathbb{R}^+$ and $t \in T$. The transition relation $\longrightarrow$ over states is defined as follows:

- $(M, Id) \xrightarrow{\theta} (M', Id')$, also denoted $(M, Id) + \theta$, iff from state (M, Id), we will reach the state (M', Id') by a time progression of θ units, i.e., $\bigwedge_{t' \in En(M)} \theta \leq \uparrow Id(t'), M' = M$, and $\forall t'' \in En(M'), Id'(t'') = [Max(\downarrow Id(t'') - \theta, 0), \uparrow Id(t'') - \theta]$.
- $(M, Id) \xrightarrow{t} (M', Id')$ iff the state (M', Id') is reachable from state (M, Id) by firing immediately transition t , i.e., $t \in En(M), \downarrow Id(t) = 0$, $\forall p \in P, M'(p) = M(p) - Pre(p,t) + Post(p,t)$, and $\forall t' \in En(M'), Id'(t') = Is(t')$, if $t' \in New(M', t), Id'(t') = Id(t')$, otherwise.

The TPN state space is the structure $(\mathcal{Q}, \longrightarrow, q_0)$, where $q_0 = (M_0, Id_0)$ is the initial state of the TPN and $\mathcal{Q} = \{q | q_0 \xrightarrow{*} q\}$($\xrightarrow{*}$ being the reflexive and transitive closure of the relation $\longrightarrow$ defined above) is the set of reachable states of the model.

A *run* in the TPN state space $(\mathcal{Q}, \longrightarrow, q_0)$, of a state $q \in \mathcal{Q}$, is a maximal sequence $\rho = q_1 \xrightarrow{\theta_1} q_1 + \theta_1 \xrightarrow{t_1} q_2 \xrightarrow{\theta_2} q_2 + \theta_2 \xrightarrow{t_2} q_3 ...$, such that $q_1 = q$. By convention, for any state q_i, relation $q_i \xrightarrow{0} q_i$ holds. The sequence $\theta_1 t_1 \theta_2 t_2 ...$ is called the timed trace of ρ. The sequence $t_1 t_2 ...$ is called the firing sequence (untimed trace) of ρ. A marking M is reachable iff $\exists q \in \mathcal{Q}$ s.t. its marking is M. Runs (resp. timed / untimed traces) of the TPN are all runs (resp. timed / untimed traces) of the initial state q_0.

To use enumerative analysis techniques with time Petri nets, an extra effort is required to abstract their generally infinite state spaces. Abstraction techniques aim to construct by removing some irrelevant details, a finite contraction of the state space of the model, which preserves properties of interest. For best performances, the contraction should also be the smallest possible and computed with minor resources too (time and space). The preserved properties are usually verified using standard analysis techniques on the abstractions [16].

Several state space abstraction methods have been proposed, in the literature, for time Petri nets like the *state class graph (SCG)* [4], the *zone based graph (ZBG)* [6], and etc. These abstractions may differ mainly in the characterization of states (interval states or clock states), the agglomeration criteria of states, the representation of the agglomerated states (abstract states), the kind of properties they preserve (markings, linear or branching properties) and their size.

These abstractions are finite for all bounded time Petri nets. However, if only linear properties are of interest, abstractions based on clocks are less interesting than the interval based abstractions. Indeed, abstractions based on intervals are finite for bounded TPN with unbounded intervals, while this is not true for abstraction based on clocks. The finiteness is enforced using an approximation operation, which may involve some overhead computation.

2.2. Zone Based Graph

In the Zone Based Graph (ZBG)[6], all clock states reachable by runs supporting the same firing sequence are agglomerated in the same node and considered modulo some over-approximation operation [2, 12]. This operation is used to ensure the finiteness of the ZBG for Bounded TPNs with unbounded firing intervals. An abstract state, called state zone, is defined as a pair $\beta = (M, FZ)$ combining a marking M and a formula FZ which characterizes the clock domains of all states agglomerated in the state zone. In FZ, the clock of each enabled transition for M is represented by a variable with the same name. The domain of FZ is convex and has a unique canonical form represented by the pair (M, Z), where Z is a DBM of order $|En(M) \cup \{o\}$ defined by: $\forall (x, y) \in (En(M) \cup \{o\})^2$, $z_{xy} = Sup_{FZ}(x - y)$, where o represents the value 0. State zones of the ZBG are in relaxed form.

The initial state zone is the pair $\beta_0 = (M_0, FZ_0)$, where M_0 is the initial marking and $FZ_0 = \bigwedge_{t_i, t_j \in En(M_0)} 0 \leq ti = tj \leq \bigwedge_{t_u \in En(M_0)} \uparrow I_s(t_u)$.

As an example, consider the TPN given in [11] and reported at Figure 1, its state zone graph is reported at Figure 2 and its state zones are reported in Table 1.

In this document, we consider the state class method and study the possibility to enforce the behavior of a given TPN so that to satisfy a safety / reachability property. The idea is to construct on-the-fly the reachable state classes of the TPN while collecting progressively firing subintervals to be avoided so that to satisfy the properties of interest.

2.3. The state class graph method

In the state class graph method [4], all states reachable by the same firing sequence from the initial state are agglomerated in the same node and considered modulo the relation of equivalence defined by: Two sets of states are equivalent iff they have the same marking and the same firing domain. The firing domain of a set of states is the union of the firing domains of its states. All equivalent sets are agglomerated in the same node called a *state class* defined as a pair $\alpha = (M, F)$, where M is a marking and F is a formula which characterizes the firing domain of α. For each transition t_i enabled in M, there is a variable $\underline{t}_i$, in F, representing its firing delay. F can be rewritten as a set of atomic constraints of the form[1]: $\underline{t}_i - \underline{t}_j \leq c$, $\underline{t}_i \leq c$ or $-\underline{t}_j \leq c$, where t_i, t_j are transitions, $c \in \mathbb{Q} \cup \{\infty\}$ and $\mathbb{Q}$ is the set of rational numbers.

Though the same domain may be expressed by different conjunctions of atomic constraints (i.e., different formulas), all equivalent formulas have a unique form, called canonical form that is usually encoded by a difference bound matrix (DBM) [3]. The canonical form of F is encoded by the DBM D (a square matrix) of order $|En(M)| + 1$ defined by: $\forall t_i, t_j \in En(M) \cup \{t_0\}, d_{ij} = (\leq, Sup_F(\underline{t}_i - \underline{t}_j))$, where t_0 ($t_0 \notin T$) represents a fictitious transition whose delay is always equal to 0 and $Sup_F(\underline{t}_i - \underline{t}_j)$ is the largest value of $\underline{t}_i - \underline{t}_j$ in the domain of F. Its computation is based on the shortest path *Floyd-Warshall*'s algorithm and is considered as the most costly operation (cubic in the number of variables in F). The canonical form of a DBM makes easier some operations over formulas like the test of equivalence. Two formulas are equivalent iff the canonical forms of their DBMs are identical.

The initial state class is $\alpha_0 = (M_0, F_0)$, where $F_0 = \bigwedge_{t_i \in En(M_0)} \downarrow Is(t_i) \leq \underline{t}_i \leq \uparrow Is(t_i)$.

Let $\alpha = (M, F)$ be a state class and t_f a transition and $succ(\alpha, t_f)$ the set of states defined by:

$$succ(\alpha, t_f) = \{q' \in \mathcal{Q} \mid \exists q \in \alpha, \exists \theta \in \mathbb{R}^+ \text{ s.t. } q \xrightarrow{\theta} q + \theta \xrightarrow{t_f} q'\} \tag{5}$$

[1] For economy of notation, we use operator $\leq$ even if $c = \infty$.

$\beta_0 : p_1 + p_2$	$0 \leq \underline{t_1} = \underline{t_2} \leq 3$
$\beta_1 : p_2 + p_3$	$0 \leq \underline{t_2} \leq 3 \wedge 0 \leq \underline{t_3} \leq 3 \wedge 0 \leq \underline{t_2} - \underline{t_3} \leq 3$
$\beta_2 : p_1 + p_4$	$2 \leq \underline{t_1} \leq 4$
$\beta_3 : p_3 + p_4$	$0 \leq \underline{t_3} \leq 3 \wedge 0 \leq \underline{t_4} \leq 1 \wedge 0 \leq \underline{t_3} - \underline{t_4} \leq 3$
$\beta_4 : p_2$	$2 \leq \underline{t_2} \leq 3$
$\beta_5 : p_3 + p_4$	$0 \leq \underline{t_3} = \underline{t_4} \leq 2$
$\beta_6 : p_4$	

Table 1. State zones of the TPN presented at Figure 2

The state class α has a successor by t_f (i.e. $succ(\alpha, t_f) \neq \emptyset$), iff t_f is enabled in M and can be fired before any other enabled transition, i.e., the following formula is consistent[2]: $F \wedge (\bigwedge_{t_i \in En(M)} \underline{t_f} \leq \underline{t_i})$. In this case, the firing of t_f leads to the state class $\alpha' = (M', F') = succ(\alpha, t_f)$ computed as follows [4]:

1. $\forall p \in P, M'(p) = M(p) - Pre(p, t_f) + Post(p, t_f)$.
2. $F' = F \wedge (\bigwedge_{t_i \in En(M)} \underline{t_f} - \underline{t_i} \leq 0)$
3. Replace in F' each $\underline{t_i} \neq \underline{t_f}$, by $(\underline{t_i} + \underline{t_f})$.
4. Eliminate by substitution $\underline{t_f}$ and each $\underline{t_i}$ of transition conflicting with t_f in M.
5. Add constraint $\downarrow Is(t_n) \leq \underline{t_n} \leq \uparrow Is(t_n)$, for each transition $t_n \in New(M', t_f)$.

Formally, the SCG of a TPN model is a structure $(CC, \longrightarrow, \alpha_0)$, where $\alpha_0 = (M_0, F_0)$ is the initial state class, $\forall t_i \in T, \alpha \xrightarrow{t_i} \alpha'$ iff $\alpha' = succ(\alpha, t_i) \neq \emptyset$ and $CC = \{\alpha | \alpha_0 \xrightarrow{*} \alpha\}$.

The SCG is finite for all bounded TPNs and preserves linear properties [5]. As an example, Figure 2 shows the state class graph of the TPN presented at Figure 1. Its state classes are reported in Table 2. For this example, state class graph and state zone based graph of the system are identical while classes and zones are different.

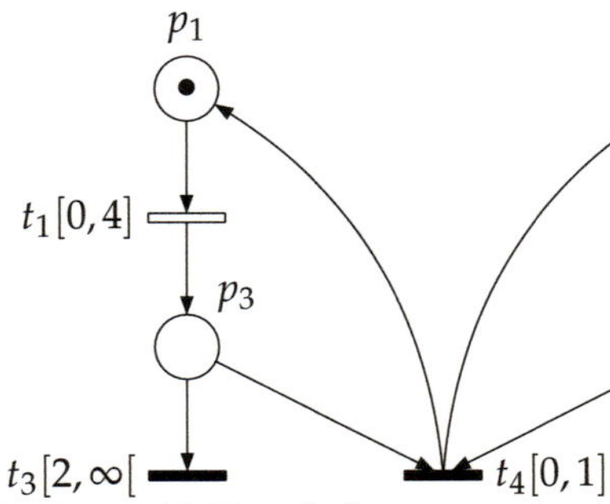

Figure 1. A simple Petri net with $T_c = \{t_1\}$

[2] A formula F is consistent iff there is, at least, one tuple of values that satisfies, at once, all constraints of F.

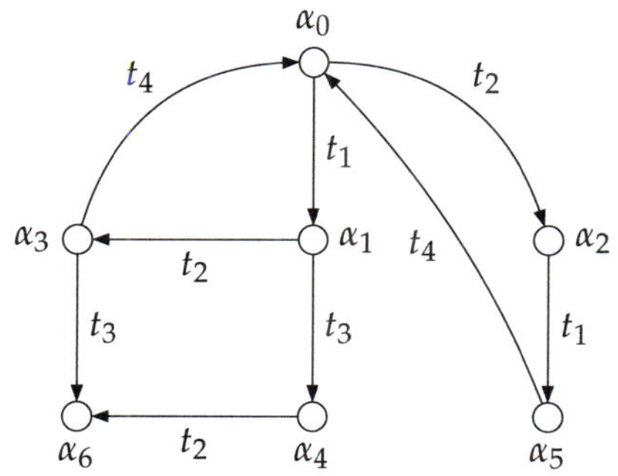

Figure 2. The State Graph of the TPN presented at Figure 1

$\alpha_0 : p_1 + p_2$	$0 \leq \underline{t}_1 \leq 4 \wedge 2 \leq \underline{t}_2 \leq 3$
$\alpha_1 : p_2 + p_3$	$0 \leq \underline{t}_2 \leq 3 \wedge 2 \leq \underline{t}_3$
$\alpha_2 : p_1 + p_4$	$0 \leq \underline{t}_1 \leq 2$
$\alpha_3 : p_3 + p_4$	$0 \leq \underline{t}_3 \wedge 0 \leq \underline{t}_4 \leq 1$
$\alpha_4 : p_2$	$0 \leq \underline{t}_2 \leq 1$
$\alpha_5 : p_3 + p_4$	$2 \leq \underline{t}_3 < \infty \wedge 0 \leq \underline{t}_4 \leq 1$
$\alpha_6 : p_4$	

Table 2. The state classes of the TPN presented at Figure 2

2.4. A forward method for computing predecessors of state classes

Let $\alpha = (M, F)$ be a state class and $\omega \in T^+$ a sequence of transitions firable from α. We denote $succ(\alpha, \omega)$ the state class reachable from α by firing successively transitions of ω. We define inductively this set as follows: $succ(\alpha, \omega) = \alpha$, if $\omega = \epsilon$ and $succ(\alpha, \omega) = succ(succ(\alpha, \omega'), t_i)$, if $\omega = \omega'.t_i$.

During the firing of a sequence of transitions ω from α, the same transition may be newly enabled several times. To distinguish between different enabling of the same transition t_i, we denote t_i^k for $k > 0$ the transition t_i (newly) enabled by the kth transition of the sequence; t_i^0 denotes the transition t_i enabled in M. Let $\omega = t_1^{k_1}....t_m^{k_m} \in T^+$ with $m > 0$ be a sequence of transitions firable from α (i.e., $succ(\alpha, \omega) \neq \emptyset$). We denote $Fire(\alpha, \omega)$ the largest subclass α' of α (i.e., $\alpha' \subseteq \alpha$) s.t. ω is firable from all its states, i.e.,

$$Fire(\alpha, \omega) = \{q_1 \in \alpha \mid \exists \theta_1, ..., \theta_m, q_1 \xrightarrow{\theta_1} q_1 + \theta_1 \xrightarrow{t_1^{k_1}} q_2 ... q_m + \theta_m \xrightarrow{t_m^{k_m}} q_{m+1}\} \quad (6)$$

Proposition 1. *$Fire(\alpha, \omega)$ is the state class (M', F') where $M' = M$ and F' can be computed as follows*[3]*: Let $M_1 = M$ and M_{f+1}, for $f \in [1, m]$, be the marking reached from M by the subsequence $t_1^{k_1}....t_f^{k_f}$ of ω.*

1. *Initialize F' with the formula obtained from F by renaming all variables $\underline{t}_i$ in $\underline{t}_i^0$.*

[3] We suppose that the truth value of an empty set of constraints is always *true*.

2. *Add the following constraints:*

$$\bigwedge_{f\in[1,m]} \Big(\bigwedge_{t_i \in (En(M_1) - \bigcup_{j\in[1,f[} CF(M_j,t_j))} \underline{t}_f^{k_f} - \underline{t}_i^0 \leq 0 \wedge$$
$$\bigwedge_{j\in[1,f[, t_n \in (New(M_{j+1},t_j) - \bigcup_{k\in]j,f[} CF(M_k,t_k))} \underline{t}_f^{k_f} - \underline{t}_n^j \leq 0 \wedge \quad (7)$$
$$\bigwedge_{t_n \in New(M_{f+1},t_f)} \downarrow Is(t_n) \leq \underline{t}_n^f - \underline{t}_f^{k_f} \leq \uparrow Is(t_n) \Big)$$

3. *Put the resulting formula in canonical form and eliminate all variables $\underline{t}_i^j$ such that $j > 0$, rename all variables $\underline{t}_i^0$ in $\underline{t}_i$.*

Note that $Fire(\alpha, \omega) \neq \emptyset$ (i.e., ω is firable from α) iff ω is feasible in the underlying untimed model and the formula obtained at step 2) above is consistent.

Proof. By step 1) all variables associated with transitions of $En(M)$ are renamed ($\underline{t}_i$ is renamed in $\underline{t}_i^0$). This step allows us to distinguish between delays of transitions enabled in M from those that are newly enabled by the transitions of the firing sequence.

Step 2) adds the firing constraints of transitions of the sequence (for $f \in [1, m]$). For each transition $t_f^{k_f}$ of the sequence, three blocks of constraints are added. The two first blocks mean that the delay of $t_f^{k_f}$ must be less or equal to the delays of all transitions enabled in M_f (i.e., transitions of $En(M)$ and those enabled by t_j ($New(M_{j+1}, t_j), 1 \leq j < f$) that are maintained continuously enabled at least until firing $t_f^{k_f}$). Transitions of $En(M)$ that are maintained continuously enabled at least until firing $t_f^{k_f}$ are transitions of $En(M)$ which are not in conflict with $t_1^{k_1}$ in M_1, and, ..., and not in conflict with $t_{f-1}^{k_{f-1}}$ in M_{f-1}. Similarly, transitions of $New(M_j, t_j)$ (with $1 \leq j < f$) that are maintained continuously enabled at least until firing $t_f^{k_f}$ are transitions of $New(M_{j+1}, t_j)$ which are not in conflict with $t_{j+1}^{k_{j+1}}$ in M_{j+1}, and, ..., and not in conflict with $t_{f-1}^{k_{f-1}}$ in M_{f-1}. The third block of constraints specifies the firing delays of transitions that are newly enabled by $t_f^{k_f}$.

Step 3) isolates the largest subclass of α such that ω is firable from all its states. □

As an example, consider the TPN depicted at Figure 1 and its state class graph shown at Figure 2. Let us show how to compute $Fire(\alpha_0, t_1^0 t_2^0 t_3^1)$. We have $En(M_0) = \{t_1, t_2\}$, $CF(M_0, t_1) = \{t_1\}$, $CF(M_1, t_2) = \{t_2\}$, $New(M_0, t_1) = \{t_3\}$ and $New(M_1, t_2) = \{t_4\}$. The subclass $(p_1 + p_2, F') = Fire(\alpha_0, t_1^0 t_2^0 t_3^1)$ is computed as follows:

1. Initialize F' with the formula obtained from $0 \leq \underline{t}_1 \leq 4 \wedge 2 \leq \underline{t}_2 \leq 3$ by renaming all variables $\underline{t}_i$ in $\underline{t}_i^0$: $0 \leq \underline{t}_1^0 \leq 4 \wedge 2 \leq \underline{t}_2^0 \leq 3$

2. Add the firing constraints of t_1 before t_2, t_2 before t_3 and constraints on the firing intervals of transitions enabled by these firings (i.e., t_3 and t_4):

$$\underline{t}_1^0 - \underline{t}_2^0 \leq 0 \wedge \underline{t}_2^0 - \underline{t}_3^1 \leq 0 \; \wedge \; 2 \leq \underline{t}_3^1 - \underline{t}_1^0 \; \wedge \; 0 \leq \underline{t}_4^2 - \underline{t}_2^0 \leq 1$$

3. Put the resulting formula in canonical form and eliminate all variables $\underline{t}_i^j$ such that $j > 0$, rename all variables $\underline{t}_i^0$ in $\underline{t}_i$: $0 \leq \underline{t}_1 \leq 2 \wedge 2 \leq \underline{t}_2 \leq 3 \wedge 1 \leq \underline{t}_2 - \underline{t}_1 \leq 3$.

The subclass $Fire(\alpha_0, t_1^0 t_2^0 t_3^1)$ consists of all states of α_0 from which the sequence $t_1 t_2 t_3$ is firable. If t_1 is controllable, to avoid reaching the marking p_4 by the sequence $t_1 t_2 t_3$, it suffices to choose the firing interval of t_1 in α_0 outside its firing interval in $Fire(\alpha_0, t_1^0 t_2^0 t_3^1)$ (i.e., $]2, 4]$).

Note that this forward method of computing predecessors can also be adapted and applied to the clock based abstractions. For instance, using the zone based graph, the initial state zone of the TPN shown at Figure 1 is $\beta_0 = (p_1 + p_2, 0 \leq \underline{t}_1 = \underline{t}_2 \leq 3)$. The sub-zone β_0' of β_0, from which the sequence $t_1 t_2 t_3$ is firable, can be computed in a similar way as the previous procedure where delay constraints are replaced by clock constraints:

$\beta_0' = (p_1 + p_2, 0 \leq \underline{t}_1 = \underline{t}_2 \leq 2)$. To avoid reaching by the sequence $t_1 t_2 t_3$ the marking p_4, it suffices to delay the firing of t_1 until when its clocks overpasses 2, which means that its firing interval should be $]2, 4]$.

3. Related work

The theory of control was initially introduced by Ramadge and Worham in [17]. They have formalized, in terms of formal languages, the notion of control and the existence of a controller that forces a discrete event system (DES) to behave as expected. The concept of control has been afterwards extended to various models such as timed automata [21] and time Petri nets [19], where the control specification is expressed on the model states rather than the model language. Thus, for every system modeled by a controllable language, timed automata or time Petri nets, controller synthesis is used to restrict the behavior of the system making it to satisfy the desired safety or reachability properties. The typical procedure is: a system is modeled, the desired properties are defined, then, the existence and the implementation of the appropriate controller (control problem and controller synthesis problem respectively [1]) are investigated.

Several approaches of controller synthesis have been proposed in the literature. They may differ in the model they are working on (various types of Petri nets or automata), the approach they are based on (analytical as in [22], structural as in [9], semantic as in [10, 11, 20]), and finally the property to be controlled.

In [22], the authors have considered a particular type of capacity timed Petri net, where timing constraints are associated with transitions and some places, and all transitions are controllable. This timed Petri net is used to model a cluster tool with wafer residency time constraints. The wafers and their time constraints are represented by timed places. Using analytical approaches of schedulability and the particular structure of their model (model of the cluster tool), the authors have established an algorithm for finding, if it exists, an optimal periodic schedule which respects residency time constraints of wafers. The control consists

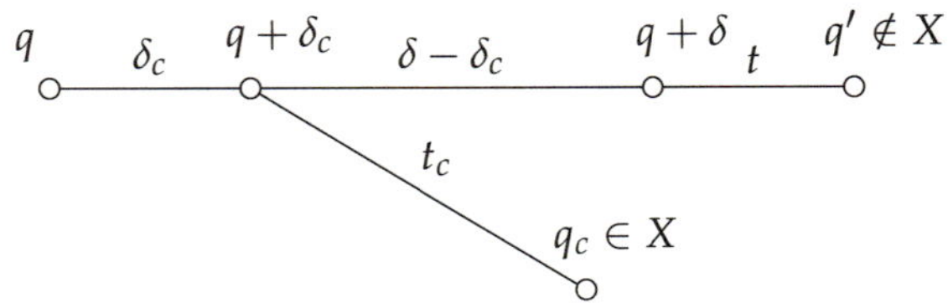

Figure 3. Controllable Predecessors

of limiting timing constraints of transitions and some places so as to respect residency time constraints of wafers.

In [8, 9], the authors have considered safe and live time Petri nets where deadlines can be associated with some transition firings. The control consists of enforcing the model to meet deadlines of transition firings. The controller has the possibility to disable any transition t which prevents to meet the deadline of a transition t_d. A transition t is allowed to fire only if its latency (the maximum delay between firing t and the next firing of t_d) is not greater than the current deadline of t_d. The latencies of transitions are computed by constructing an unfolding Petri net of the underlying untimed Petri net. This approach does not need to explore the state space. However, in general, the resulting controller is not maximally permissive (i.e. meaning that the controller may disable a net behavior that does not violate the properties of interest).

In [10, 11, 20], the authors have considered timed models (TA or TPN) with two kinds of transitions (controllable and uncontrollable) and investigated the control problem for safety or reachability properties. To prevent some undesired states, the controller can act on any firable and controllable transition by delaying or forcing its firing but it cannot disable transitions. The control problem is addressed by computing the winning states of the model, i.e. states which will not lead, by an uncontrollable transition, to an undesired state. The computation of the winning states is based on the concept of controllable predecessors of states. In the literature, the set of controllable predecessors is usually denoted by $\pi(X)$, where X is a set of states satisfying the desired property (safe/goal states). The set $\pi(X)$ is defined by [11]:

$$\begin{aligned}
&\pi(X) = \{q \in \mathcal{Q} | ((\exists\, \delta \in \mathbb{R}_{\geq 0}, t \in T\; q' \in X\; q \xrightarrow{\delta}\xrightarrow{t} q') \vee \\
&(\exists\, \delta \in \mathbb{R}_{\geq 0}, q' \in X\; q \xrightarrow{\delta} q')) \wedge \\
&\forall\, \delta \in \mathbb{R}_{\geq 0}\; if\; \exists\, t \in T, q' \notin X\; q \xrightarrow{\delta}\xrightarrow{t} q' \\
&then\; \exists\, \delta_c < \delta, t_c \in T_c,\; q_c \in X\; q \xrightarrow{\delta_c}\xrightarrow{t_c} q_c\}
\end{aligned} \tag{8}$$

Intuitively, $\pi(X)$ is the set of predecessors of X which will not bring the system out of X. Figure 3 clarifies this concept. If the environment can execute an uncontrollable transition after δ time units, leading the system out of X (denoted by $\bar{X}$), then the controller should be able to execute a controllable action to keep the system in X before δ time units. In addition, in the context of timed models with strong semantics (a transition must be fired, without any additional delay, when the upper bound of its firing interval is reached), the controller should not be forced to execute a controllable transition leading the system out of X.

Let $AG\,\phi$ be a safety property and $X_0 = Sat(\phi)$ the set of states which satisfy the property ϕ (safe states). The fix point of $X_{i+1} = h(X_i) = X_i \cap \pi(X_i), i \geq 0$ gives the largest set of safe states whose behaviors can be controlled so as to maintain the system inside this set of states (i.e., winning states). If the largest fix point of h includes the initial state then, it gives a controller which forces the system to stay in safe states (i.e., a winning strategy).

Similarly, the fix point method is also used for reachability properties. Let $AF\ \psi$ be a reachability property and $X_0 = Sat(\psi)$ the set of goal states. The least fix point of $X_{i+1} = h(X_i) = X_i \cup \pi(X_i), i \geq 0$ is the set of states whose behaviors can be controlled so as to reach one of the goal states (i.e., winning states) [10, 20].

In the context of a timed model, this technique is applied on a state space abstraction of the timed model. In this case, X_i is a set of abstract states. If X_i is a finite set of abstract states, then the controllable predecessors of X_i is also a finite set of abstract states. The computation of the fix point of h will converge after a finite number of steps if the state space abstraction is finite [10, 11, 20].

Note that the state space abstractions used in [10, 11, 20] are based on clocks but the state space abstraction used in [11] is not necessarily complete. The fix point method cannot guarantee to give the safety controller when it exists, unless the state space abstraction is both sound and complete. A state space abstraction of a given model is sound and complete iff it captures all firing sequences of the model and each firing sequence in the state space abstraction reflects a firing sequence of the model. Indeed, a synthesis may fail because of some unreachable states, while for the reachable state space the safety controller exists. However, the cost of processing is increased as a sound and complete state space abstraction should be entirely calculated before applying the fix point algorithm.

Let us explain by means of an example how to compute the fix point of h for a safety property. Consider the TPN given in [11] and reported in Figure 1. The state class graph (SCG) and the zone based graph (ZBG) of this TPN are equal, except that nodes are defined differently (state classes or state zones). The state class graph is depicted in Figure 2. Its state zones and state classes are reported in Table 1 and Table 2, respectively.

Consider the state zone graph and suppose that we are interested to force the following safety property: $AG\ \Sigma_{i=1}^{4} p_i = 2$ which means that the number of tokens in the TPN is always 2. The transition t_1 is the only controllable transition and the forbidden markings is determined by $\Sigma_{i=1}^{4} p_i \neq 2$. As the state class graph shows, if t_2 happens before t_1 the right path happens which is safe and the controller has nothing to do. On the other hand, if t_1 happens before t_2, two state classes having forbidden markings may be reached (α_4, α_6).

To verify whether or not there is a controller for such a property, we compute the fix point of $X_{i+1} = h(X_i) = X_i \cap \pi(X_i)$, where $X_0 = \{\beta_0, \beta_1, \beta_2, \beta_3, \beta_5\}$ is the set of state zones which satisfy the property *not* $p_1 + p_3 = 0$. Such a controller exists iff the initial state of the model is a winning state (i.e., belongs to the fix point of h). The fix point is computed, in 3 iterations, as follows:

1) Iteration 1: $X_1 = X_0 \cap \pi(X_0) = \{\beta_0, \beta_1', \beta_2, \beta_3', \beta_5\}$. In this iteration, all states of β_1 and β_3, which are uncontrollable predecessors of bad state classes β_4 and β_6 are eliminated:

$\beta_1' = (p_2 + p_3, 1 < \underline{t}_2 \leq 3 \wedge 0 \leq \underline{t}_3 < 2 \wedge 1 < \underline{t}_2 - \underline{t}_3 \leq 3)$ and

$\beta_3' = (p_3 + p_4, 1 \leq \underline{t}_3 <\leq 3 \wedge 0 < \underline{t}_4 \leq 1 \wedge 1 \leq \underline{t}_3 - \underline{t}_4 \leq 3)$.

2) Iteration 2: $X_2 = X_1 \cap \pi(X_1) = \{\beta_0, \beta_1'', \beta_2, \beta_3', \beta_5\}$. This iteration eliminates from β_1' all states, which are uncontrollable predecessors of bad states of $\beta_3 - \beta_3'$:

$\beta_1'' = \{p_2 + p_3, 2 < \underline{t}_2 \leq 3 \wedge 0 \leq \underline{t}_3 < 1 \wedge 2 \leq \underline{t}_2 - \underline{t}_3 \leq 3\}$.

3) Iteration 3: $X_2 = X_2 \cap \pi(X_2) = \{\beta_0, \beta_1'', \beta_2, \beta_3', \beta_5\}$. The fix point X_2 is then the set of winning states. Since the initial state zone belongs to X_2, there is a controller for forcing the property *AG not* $p_1 + p_3 = 0$. To keep the model in safe states (in states of X_2), the controller must delay, in β_0, the firing of t_1 until its clock overpasses the value 2. Doing so, the successor of β_0 by t_1 will be β_1''.

This approach needs however to construct a state space abstraction before computing the set of winning states. To overcome this limitation, in [10, 20], the authors have investigated the use of on-the-fly algorithms besides the fix point to compute the winning states for timed game automata (timed automata with controllable and uncontrollable transitions). We report, in Fig 4, the on-the-fly algorithm given in [10] for the case of reachability properties and timed game automata. This algorithm uses three lists *Passed* containing all state zones explored so far, *Waiting*, containing the set of edges to be processed and *Depend* indicating, for each state zone S, the set of edges to be reevaluated in case the set of the winning states in S ($Win[S]$) is updated. Using this on-the-fly method, in each step, a part of the state zone graph is constructed and an edge $e = (S, a, S')$ of the *Waiting* list is processed. If the state zone S' is not in *Passed* and there is, in S', some states which satisfy the desired reachability property, then these states are added to the winning states of S' ($Win[S']$). The winning states of S will be recomputed later (the edge e is added to the *Waiting* list). If S' is in *Passed*, the set of the winning states of S ($Win[S]$) is recomputed and possibly those of its predecessors and so on. The set $Win[S]$ is the largest subset of S which is included in the controllable predecessors of the winning states of all its successors.

This on-the-fly algorithm, based on computing controllable predecessors, requires some expensive operations such as the difference between abstract states (state zones). The difference between two state zones is not necessarily a state zone and then may result in several state zones which need to be handled separately.

In this chapter, we propose another on-the-fly approach which does not need this expensive operation. Our approach differs from the previous ones by the fact it computes bad states (i.e.: states which may lead to an undesired state) instead of computing the winning states and it constructs a state class graph instead of a state zone graph. In addition, the bad states are computed, using a forward approach, for only state classes containing at least a controllable transition.

4. An on-the-fly algorithm for investigating the existence of a controller for a TPN

This chapter aims to propose an efficient forward on-the-fly method based on the state class graph for checking the existence of a safety/reachability controller for a TPN. As discussed earlier, the state class graph is a good alternative for the on-the-fly algorithms as the exploration converges fast and does not need any over-approximation operation to enforce the convergence. The method, proposed here, is completely a forward and does not compute

Initialization:

$Passed \leftarrow \{S_0\}$ **where** $S_0 = \{(\ell_0, \vec{0})\}^{\nearrow}$;
$Waiting \leftarrow \{(S_0, \alpha, S') \mid S' = \mathsf{Post}_\alpha(S_0)^{\nearrow}\}$;
$Win[S_0] \leftarrow S_0 \cap (\{\mathsf{Goal}\} \times \mathbb{R}^X_{\geq 0})$;
$Depend[S_0] \leftarrow \emptyset$;

Main:

while $((Waiting \neq \emptyset) \wedge (s_0 \notin Win[S_0]))$ **do**
  $e = (S, \alpha, S') \leftarrow pop(Waiting)$;
  if $S' \notin Passed$ **then**
    $Passed \leftarrow Passed \cup \{S'\}$;
    $Depend[S'] \leftarrow \{(S, \alpha, S')\}$;
    $Win[S'] \leftarrow S' \cap (\{\mathsf{Goal}\} \times \mathbb{R}^X_{\geq 0})$;
    $Waiting \leftarrow Waiting \cup \{(S', \alpha, S'') \mid S'' = \mathsf{Post}_\alpha(S')^{\nearrow}\}$;
    if $Win[S'] \neq \emptyset$ **then** $Waiting \leftarrow Waiting \cup \{e\}$;
  else (* **reevaluate** *)[a]
    $Win^* \leftarrow \mathsf{Pred}_t(Win[S] \cup \bigcup_{S \xrightarrow{c} T} \mathsf{Pred}_c(Win[T]),$
      $\bigcup_{S \xrightarrow{u} T} \mathsf{Pred}_u(T \setminus Win[T])) \cap S$;
    if $(Win[S] \subsetneq Win^*)$ **then**
      $Waiting \leftarrow Waiting \cup Depend[S]$; $Win[S] \leftarrow Win^*$;
    $Depend[S'] \leftarrow Depend[S'] \cup \{e\}$;
  endif
endwhile

[a] When $T \notin Passed, Win[T] = \emptyset$

Figure 4. On-the-fly algorithm for timed game automata proposed in [10]

controllable predecessors (which is considered as an expensive operation). To explain the method, we start with safety properties.

Let us introduce informally the principle of our approach by means of the previous example. Consider the TPN shown in Figure 1, its state class graph depicted in Figure 2 and its state classes reported in Table 2. Our goal is to avoid to reach bad states (i.e., state classes α_4 and α_6) by choosing appropriately the firing intervals for controllable transitions.

From the initial state class α_0, there are two elementary paths $\alpha_0 t_1 \alpha_1 t_3 \alpha_4$ and $\alpha_0 t_1 \alpha_1 t_2 \alpha_3 t_3 \alpha_6$ that lead to bad states. In both paths, there is only one state class (α_0) where the controllable transition t_1 is firable. To avoid these bad paths, we propose to compute all states of α_0 from which $t_1 t_3$ or $t_1 t_2 t_3$ is firable, i.e., $B(\alpha_0) = Fire(\alpha_0, t_1 t_3) \cup Fire(\alpha_0, t_1 t_2 t_3)$, where:

$Fire(\alpha_0, t_1 t_3) = (p_1 + p_2, 0 \leq \underline{t_1} \leq 1 \wedge 2 \leq \underline{t_2} \leq 3 \wedge 2 \leq \underline{t_2} - \underline{t_1} \leq 3)$ and

$Fire(\alpha_0, t_1 t_2 t_3) = (p_1 + p_2, 0 \leq \underline{t_1} \leq 2 \wedge 2 \leq \underline{t_2} \leq 3 \wedge 1 \leq \underline{t_2} - \underline{t_1} \leq 3)$.

To avoid these bad states, it suffices to replace in α_0, the firing interval of t_1 with $]2,4]$. This interval is the complement of $[0,2] \cup [0,1]$ in the firing interval of t_1 in α_0 ($[0,4]$).
The approach we propose in the following section, is a combination of this principle with a forward on-the-fly method.

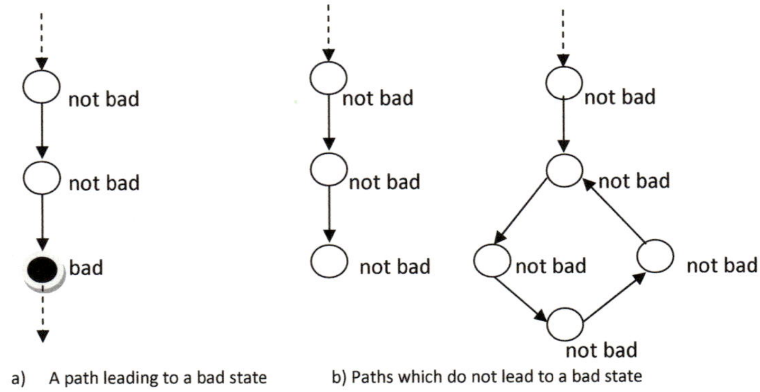

Figure 5. Path satisfying or not a safety property. Black states should be avoided.

4.1. Controller for safety properties

A controller for safety properties running in parallel with the system should satisfy the property *'AG not bad'* where 'bad' stands for the set of states having a forbidden marking and it means that 'bad' states will never happen. We introduce here an algorithm to re-constrain the controllable transitions and reach a safe net.

The idea is to construct, using a forward on-the-fly method, the state class graph of the TPN to determine whether controllable transitions have to be constrained, in order to avoid forbidden markings. This method computes and explores, path by path, the state class graph of a TPN looking for the sequences leading the system to any forbidden marking (bad sequences or bad paths). And using Proposition 1, we get the subclasses causing the bad states happening later through the found sequences (bad subclasses). We restrict the domain of controllable transitions in the state class where they were enabled so as to avoid its bad subclasses. The restriction of the interval of a controllable transition t of a state class α is obtained by subtracting from its interval in α ($INT(\alpha, t)$), intervals of t in its bad subclasses.

Before describing the procedure formally, we define an auxiliary operation over intervals to be used in the algorithm. Let I and I' be two nonempty (real) intervals. We denote $I \oplus I'$ intervals defined by:

$$\forall a \in \mathbb{R}, a \in I \oplus I' iff \exists b \in I, \exists c \in I', a = b + c. \tag{9}$$

As an example, for $I = [1,4]$ and $I' =]2,5]$, $I \oplus I' =]3,9]$. And also

$$LI(\alpha) = \{(t_c, t_s, BI) | t_c \in En_c(M), t_s \in En_c^0(M); BI = \bigcup_{\omega \in \Omega(\alpha)} INT(Fire(\alpha,\omega), \underline{t}_c - \underline{t}_s) \neq INT(\alpha, \underline{t}_c - \underline{t}_s)\} \tag{10}$$

This method is presented in the algorithms 1 and 2. The symbol T_c refers to the set of controllable transitions and all forbidden markings of the net are saved in a set called, *bad*. The list *Passed* is used to retrieve the set of state classes processed so far, their bad sequences, and the bad intervals of controllable transitions (their domains in bad subclasses). Function *main* consists of an initialization step and a calling to the recursive function *explore*. The call $explore(\alpha_0, \emptyset, \{\alpha_0\})$ returns the set of bad sequences that cannot be avoided, from α_0, by restricting firing domains of controllable transitions. If this set is nonempty, it means that such a controller does not exist. Otherwise, it exists and the algorithm guarantees that for each state class α with some bad sequences, there is a possibility to choose appropriately the firing intervals of some controllable transitions so as to avoid all bad subclasses of α. The control of α consists of eliminating, from the firing intervals of such controllable transitions, all parts figuring in its bad subclasses. The restriction of domains is also applied on firing delays between two controllable transitions of α. We get in $Ctrl$, all possibilities of controlling each state class. In case there is only one controllable transition in α, its delay with a fictitious transition whose time variable is fixed at 0 is considered.

Each element of *Passed* is a triplet $(\alpha, \Omega(\alpha), LI(\alpha))$ where $\alpha = (M, F)$ is a state class s.t $M \notin bad$, $\Omega(\alpha)$ is the set of bad sequences of α, which cannot be avoided, independently of α, from its successors, and $LI(\alpha)$ gives the intervals of controllable transitions in bad subclasses of α (bad intervals). The set $LI(\alpha)$ allows to retrieve the safe intervals of controllable transitions, by computing the complements, in α, of the forbidden intervals (i.e., all possibilities of controlling α, $Ctrl(\alpha)$).

The function *explore* receives parameters α being the class under process, t the transition leading to α and C the set of traveled classes in the current path. It uses functions $succ(\alpha, t)$ and $Fire(\alpha, \omega)$ already explained by equations 5 and 6 (in sections 2.3 and 2.4, respectively). It distinguishes 3 cases:

1) α has been already processed (i.e., α is in *Passed*): In this case, there is no need to explore it again. However, its bad sequences have to be propagated to its predecessor by t, in case the control needs to be started before reaching α in order to avoid bad states of its predecessors. The control of α is independent of its predecessors along the path if all possibilities of control in α are limited to the newly enabled transitions. In case there is, in α, a possibility of control, which limits the firing interval of some controllable transition not newly enabled in α, it means that the predecessor of α by t has some bad states that must be avoided. The condition $Dep(\alpha, t, LI)$, used in Algorithm 2, is to control α independently of its predecessor by t.

2) α has a forbidden marking (i.e., α is a bad state class): In this case, the transition t is returned, which means that this sequence needs to be avoided before reaching α.

3) In other cases, the function *explore* is called for each successor of α, not already encountered in the current path (see Figure 5), to collect, in Ω, the bad sequences of its successors. Once all successors are processed, Ω is checked:

3.1) If $\Omega = \emptyset$, it means that α does not lead to any bad state class or its bad sequences can be avoided later by controlling its successors, then $(\alpha, \emptyset, \emptyset)$ is added to *Passed* and the function returns with $\emptyset$.

3.2) If $\Omega \neq \emptyset$, the function *explore* determines intervals of controllable transitions in bad subclasses, which do not cover their intervals in α. It gets such intervals, identifying states to be avoided, in LI (bad intervals). It adds (α, Ω, LI) to *Passed* and then verifies whether or not α is controllable independently of its predecessor state class in the current path. In such a case, there is no need to start the control before reaching α and then the empty set is returned by the function. Otherwise, it is needed to propagate the control to its predecessor by t. The set of sequences, obtained by prefixing with t sequences of Ω, is then returned by the function.

This algorithm tries to control the system behavior starting from the last to the first state classes of bad paths. If it fails to control a state class of a path, so as to avoid all bad state classes, the algorithm tries to control its previous state classes. If it succeeds to control a state class, there is no need to control its predecessors. The aim is to limit as little as possible the behavior of the system (more permissive controller).

Algorithm 1 On-the-fly algorithm for safety control problem of TPN- Part A

Function $main(TPN\ \mathcal{N},\ Markings\ bad)$
Where $\mathcal{N}$ **is a TPN**
bad **is a set of bad markings.**
Let T_c **be the set of controllable transitions of** $\mathcal{N}$ **and**
α_0 **the initial state class of** $\mathcal{N}$**.**
$Passed = \emptyset$
if $(explore(\alpha_0, \epsilon, \{\alpha_0\}) \neq \emptyset)$ **then**
  {Controller does not exist}
  return
end if
for all $((\alpha, \Omega, LI) \in Passed)$ **do**
  $Ctrl[\alpha] = \bigcup_{(t_c,t_s,BI) \in LI} \{(t_c, t_s, INT(\alpha, \underline{t}_c - \underline{t}_s) - BI)\}$
end for

(*)
$\alpha = (M, F);$
$En_c(M) = En(M) \cap T_c;$
$En_c^0(M) = En_c(M) \cup \{t_0\};$
$New_c(M,t) = New(M,t) \cap T_c;$
$New(M_0, \epsilon) = En(M_0);$
t_0 is a fictitious transition whose time variable is fixed at 0.
$Dep(\alpha, t, LI) \equiv$
$\exists (t_c, t_s, BI) \in LI, t_c \notin New(M,t) \wedge (t_s \notin New(M,t) \vee$
$INT(\alpha, \underline{t}_c - \underline{t}_0) \not\subseteq \bigcap_{I \in BI} (I \oplus INT(\alpha, \underline{t}_s - \underline{t}_0)))$

4.2. Example

To explain the procedure, we trace the algorithm on the TPN shown in Figure 1. Its SCG and its state classes are reported in Figure 2 and Table 2, respectively. For this example, we have $T_c = \{t_1\}$, $bad = \{p_2, p_4\}$, $Passed = \emptyset$ and $\alpha_0 = (p_1 + p_2, 0 \leq \underline{t}_1 \leq 4 \wedge 2 \leq \underline{t}_2 \leq 3)$.

The process starts by calling $explore(\alpha_0, \epsilon, \{\alpha_0\})$ (see Figure 6). Since α_0 is not in *Passed* and its marking is not forbidden, *explore* is successively called for the successors of α_0: $explore(\alpha_1, t_1, \{\alpha_0, \alpha_1\})$ and $explore(\alpha_2, t_2, \{\alpha_0, \alpha_2\})$. In *explore* of α_1, function *explore* is successively called for α_3 and α_4. In *explore* of α_3, function *explore* is called for the successor α_6 of α_3 by t_3: $explore(\alpha_6, t_3, \{\alpha_0, \alpha_1, \alpha_3, \alpha_6\})$. For the successor of α_3 by t_4 (i.e., α_0), there is no need to call *explore* as it belongs to the current path. Since α_6 has a forbidden marking, *explore* of α_6 returns to *explore* of α_3 with $\{t_3\}$, which, in turn, adds $(\alpha_3, \{t_2 t_3\}, \emptyset)$ to *Passed* and returns to *explore* of α_1 with $\{t_2 t_3\}$.

Algorithm 2 On-the-fly algorithm for safety control problem of TPN- Part B

Function $Traces\ explore(Class\ \alpha, Trans\ t,\ Classes\ \mathcal{C})$
if $(\exists \Omega, LI$ **s.t.** $(\alpha, \Omega, LI) \in Passed)$ **then**
  if $(\Omega \neq \emptyset \wedge Dep(\alpha, t, LI))$ **then**
    return $\{t.\omega | \omega \in \Omega\}$
  end if
  return $\emptyset$
end if
if $(M \in bad)$ **then**
  return $\{t\}$
end if
$Traces\ \Omega = \emptyset;$
for all $t' \in En(M)$ **s.t** $succ(\alpha, t') \neq \emptyset \wedge succ(\alpha, t') \notin \mathcal{C}$ **do**
  $\Omega = \Omega \cup explore(succ(\alpha, t'), t', \mathcal{C} \cup \{succ(\alpha, t')\})$
end for{Ω **contains all bad sequences of** α.}
if $(\Omega = \emptyset)$ **then**
  $Passed = Passed \cup \{(\alpha, \emptyset, \emptyset)\}$
  return $\emptyset$
end if
$LI = \{(t_c, t_s, BI) | (t_c, t_s) \in En_c(M) \times En_c^0(M) \wedge$

$$BI = \bigcup_{\omega \in \Omega} INT(Fire(\alpha, \omega), \underline{t}_c - \underline{t}_s) \subset INT(\alpha, \underline{t}_c - \underline{t}_s)\}$$

$Passed = Passed \cup \{(\alpha, \Omega, LI)\}$
if $(Dep(\alpha, t, LI))$ **then**
  return $\{t.\omega | \omega \in \Omega\}$
end if
return $\emptyset$

In *explore* of α_1, function *explore* is called for α_4 ($explore(\alpha_4, t_3, \{\alpha_0, \alpha_1, \alpha_4\})$). This call returns, to *explore* of α_1, with $\{t_3\}$, since α_4 has a forbidden marking. In *explore* of α_1, the tuple $(\alpha_1, \{t_2t_3, t_3\}, \emptyset)$ is added to *Passed* and $\{t_1t_2t_3, t_1t_3\}$ is returned to *explore* of α_0. Then, *explore* of α_0 calls $explore(\alpha_2, t_2, \{\alpha_0, \alpha_2\})$, which in turn calls $explore(\alpha_5, t_1, \{\alpha_0, \alpha_2, \alpha_5\})$. Since α_5 has only one successor (α_0) and this successor belongs to the current path, the call of *explore* for α_5 adds $(\alpha_5, \emptyset, \emptyset)$ to *Passed* and returns to *explore* of α_2 with $\emptyset$, which, in turn, returns to *explore* of α_0.

After exploring both successors of α_0, in *explore* of α_0, we get in $\Omega = \{t_1t_2t_3, t_1t_3\}$ the set of bad paths of α_0. As the state class α_0 has a controllable transition t_1, its bad subclasses are computed: $Fire(\alpha_0, t_1t_2t_3) = \{(p_1 + p_2, 0 \leq \underline{t}_1 \leq 2 \wedge 2 \leq \underline{t}_2 \leq 3 \wedge 1 \leq \underline{t}_2 - \underline{t}_1 \leq 3)$ and $Fire(\alpha_0, t_1t_3) = (p_1 + p_2, 0 \leq \underline{t}_1 \leq 1 \wedge 2 \leq \underline{t}_2 \leq 3 \wedge 2 \leq \underline{t}_2 - \underline{t}_1 \leq 3)\}$. The firing interval of t_1 in α_0 ($[0,4]$) is not covered by the union of intervals of t_1 in bad subclasses of α_0 ($[0,2] \cup [0,1] \neq [0,4]$). Then, $(\alpha_0, \{t_1t_2t_3, t_1t_3\}, \{(t_1, t_0, \{[0,2]\})\})$ is added to *Passed*. As t_1 is newly enabled, the empty set is returned to the function *main*, which concludes that a controller

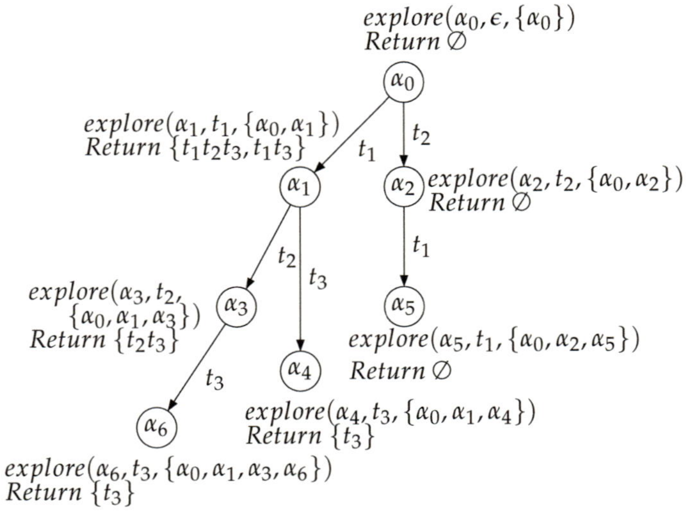

Figure 6. Applying Algorithms 1 & 2 on the TPN at Figure 1 for $AG\ not\ p_1 + p_3 = 0$

exists. According with the list *Passed*, α_0 needs to be controlled ($Ctrl[\alpha_0] = \{(t_1, t_0, \{[0,4] - [0,2]\})\}$). For all others, there is nothing to do.

Note that for this example, it is possible to carry out a static controller, which is, in this case, a mapping over controllable transitions. Indeed, it suffices to replace the static interval of t_1 with $]2,4]$. Such a controller is in general less permissive than the state dependent controller. However, its implementation is static and very simple as if the model is corrected rather than controlled.

It is also possible to carry out a marking dependent controller (a mapping over markings). Such a controller can be represented by duplicating t_1, each of them being associated with an interval and conditioned to a marking (see Table 3 and Figure 7).

This algorithm is able to determine whether a safety controller exists or not. If the algorithm fails to determine a controller, then the controller does not exist. This failure may have two

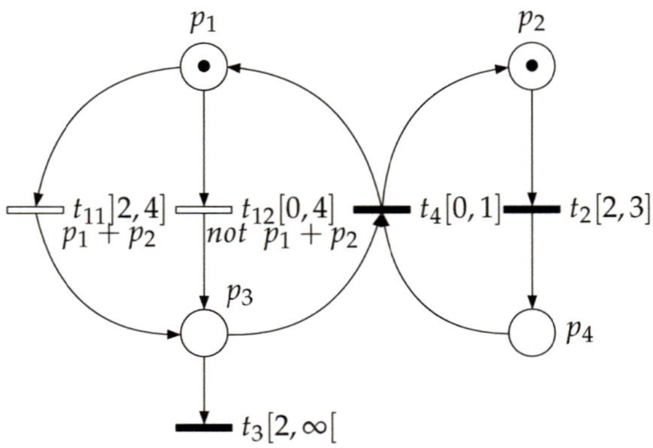

Figure 7. The controlled TPN obtained for the TPN at Figure 1 for $AG\ not\ p_1 + p_3 = 0$

Marking	Constraint to be applied on t_1
$p_1 + p_2$	$2 < t_1 \leq 4$
Others	$0 \leq t_1 \leq 4$

Table 3. A marking dependent controller for the TPN at Figure 1

reasons: no class having enabled controllable transitions exists in a bad path; or, calculated bad subclasses covers entire domain of controllable transitions. Note that, in a time Petri net[15] it is impossible to cancel a transition. Thus, if the entire domain of a controllable transition leads to bad states, as it cannot be canceled or delayed, the state class cannot be controlled so as to avoid bad states.

In the algorithms presented here, a state class is declared to be uncontrollable if it does not contain controllable transitions or it cannot be controlled so as to avoid all bad state classes. Note that if a state class cannot be controlled to avoid all bad classes, it can be however controlled to avoid some bad classes. To limit as little as possible the behavior of the system, the set of bad sequences of a state class α can be partitioned in two subsets: the set of bad sequences that can be avoided from α and the set of bad sequences that cannot to be avoided from α. The former set is avoided from α while the latter is let to be controlled by the predecessors of α. The function *explore* in this case should return the set of bad sequences that cannot be controlled from α. In this way, we increase the permissiveness of the controller.

The most significant advantage of this algorithm is the possibility of choosing the level of control. Three levels of control can be carried out:

1) Static controller: The control is independent of markings and states of the system. For each controllable transition, the intersection of all safe intervals is considered. Let t_c be a controllable transition whose interval needs to be restricted and $SIr(t_c) = \{Ir | \forall(\alpha, \Omega, L) \in Passed, \exists(t_c, SI) \in Ctrl[\alpha], Ir \subseteq SI \wedge Ir \neq \emptyset\}$. The static firing interval of t_c should be replaced with any interval of $SIr(t_c)$. Note that $SIr(t_c)$ may be empty. In this case, such a controller does not exist. Otherwise, it exists and its implementation is static as if the model is corrected rather than controlled. On the other hand, the permissiveness is sacrificed for the sake of simplicity of implementation. Albeit being simple, the controller has a high impact on performance of the system. For the previous example, such a controller exists and consists of replacing the static interval of t_1 with $[2, 4]$.

2) Marking dependent controller: The controller is a function of marking. The intersection of all safe intervals of controllable state classes with the same marking is considered, causing loss of permissiveness. Let t_c be a controllable transition whose interval needs to be restricted and $SIm(M, t_c) = \{Im | \forall((M, I), \Omega, L) \in Passed, \exists(t_c, SI) \in Ctrl[(M, I)], Im \subseteq SI \wedge Im \neq \emptyset\}$. For each marking M, the firing interval of each controllable transition t_c enabled in M should be any interval of $SIm(M, t_c)$. The set $SIm(M, t_c)$ may be empty and then such a controller does not exist. Otherwise, it exists and can be represented by duplicating some controllable transitions, each of them being associated with an interval and conditioned to a marking. Such a controller exists for the previous example and is given in Table 3 and the controlled TPN is what comes in Figure 7.

3) State dependent controller: The third level is the most permissive. A controllable transition is limited depending on the class the system is. In fact, making decision is delayed as much as possible. When the algorithm is being synthesized, different scenarios are considered. During the execution, the controller decides upon the scenario the system is (the current state class).

4.3. Controller for reachability properties

The algorithm proposed here for the safety properties, is also adaptable to reachability properties. A reachability controller running in parallel with the system should satisfy the property $AFgoal$ meaning that a goal state will certainly be reached, where 'goal' is an atomic proposition specifying the goal states (Figure 8). For reachability properties, the controller should prevent all paths which terminates without reaching a goal state, or contains a loop on none goal states (Figure 8.b). Then, if we define state classes leading to such cases as bad states, a safety controller is able to control this system to satisfy the given reachability property. Thus, the algorithm proposed to safety properties is extensible to reachability properties with some minor modification and is presented in the algorithms 3 and 4. Note that, in this case, the set $goal$ stands for the set of markings of goal states.

Algorithm 3 On-the-fly algorithm for the reachability control of TPN- Part A

Function $main(TPN\ \mathcal{N}, Markings\ goal)$
Where $\mathcal{N}$ **is a TPN and**
$goal$ **is a set of goal markings.**
Let T_c **be the set of controllable transitions of** $\mathcal{N}$ **and**
α_0 **the initial state class of** $\mathcal{N}$**.**

$Passed = \emptyset$
if $(explore(\alpha_0, \epsilon, \{\alpha_0\}) \neq \emptyset)$ **then**
  {Controller does not exist}
  return
end if

for all $((\alpha, \Omega, LI) \in Passed)$ **do**
  $Ctrl[\alpha] = \bigcup_{(t_c,t_s,BI)\in LI} \{(t_c, t_s, INT(\alpha, \underline{t}_c - \underline{t}_s) - BI)\}$
end for
return

(*)
$\alpha = (M, F)$;
$En_c(M) = En(M) \cap T_c$;
$En_c^0(M) = En_c(M) \cup \{t_0\}$;
$New_c(M,t) = New(M,t) \cap T_c$;
$New(M_0, \epsilon) = En(M_0)$; $New^0(M_0, \epsilon) = En(M_0) \cup \{t_0\}$;
t_0 is a fictitious transition whose time variable is fixed at 0.
$Dep(\alpha, t, LI) \equiv$
$\exists (t_c, t_s, BI) \in LI, t_c \notin New(M,t) \wedge (t_s \notin New(M,t) \vee$
$INT(\alpha, \underline{t}_c - \underline{t}_0) \not\subseteq \bigcap_{I\in BI} (I \oplus INT(\alpha, \underline{t}_s - \underline{t}_0)))$

Algorithm 4 On-the-fly algorithm for the reachability control of TPN-Part B

Function $Traces\ explore(Class\ \alpha, Trans\ t,\ Classes\ \mathcal{C})$
if $(\exists \Omega, LI$ **s.t.** $(\alpha, \Omega, LI) \in Passed)$ **then**
  if $(\Omega \neq \emptyset \wedge Dep(\alpha, t, LI))$ **then**
    return $\{t.\omega | \omega \in \Omega\}$
  end if
  return $\emptyset$
end if
if $(M \in goal)$ **then**
  return $\emptyset$
end if
if $(En(M) = \emptyset)$ **then**
  return $\{t\}$
end if
$Traces\ \Omega = \emptyset$
for all $t' \in En(M)$ **s.t** $succ(\alpha, t') \neq \emptyset$ **do**
  if $succ(\alpha, t') \in \mathcal{C}$ **then**
    $\Omega = \Omega \cup \{t'\}$
  else
    $\Omega = \Omega \cup explore(succ(\alpha, t'), t', \mathcal{C} \cup \{succ(\alpha, t')\})$
  end if
end for
if $(\Omega = \emptyset)$ **then**
  $Passed = Passed \cup \{(\alpha, \Omega, \emptyset)\}$
  return $\emptyset$
end if
$LI = \{(t_c, t_s, BI) | (t_c, t_s) \in En_c(M) \times En_c^0(M) \wedge$

$$BI = \bigcup_{\omega \in \Omega} INT(Fire(\alpha, \omega), \underline{t}_c - \underline{t}_s) \subset INT(\alpha, \underline{t}_c - \underline{t}_s)\}$$

$Passed = Passed \cup \{(\alpha, \Omega, LI)\}$
if $(Dep(\alpha, t, LI))$ **then**
  return $\{t.\omega | \omega \in \Omega\}$
end if
return $\emptyset$

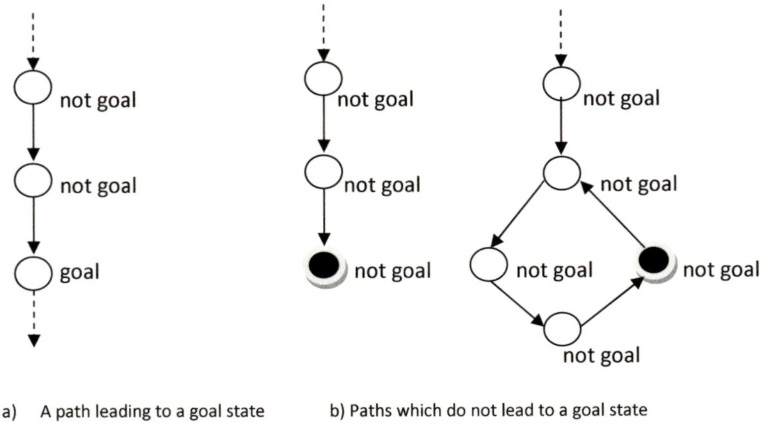

Figure 8. Paths satisfying or not a reachability property. Black states should be avoided.

5. Conclusion

In this chapter, we have proposed a completely forward on-the-fly algorithm for synthesizing safety and reachability controllers for time Petri nets. This approach guarantees to find a controller if it exists as it explores all possible state classes in the state graph and collects paths which do not satisfy the properties (bad paths).

To limit as little as possible the behavior of the system (more permissive controller), this algorithm tries to control the system behavior starting from the last to the first state classes of bad paths. If it fails to control a state class of a path, so as to avoid all bad paths, the algorithm tries to control its previous state classes. If it succeed to control a state class, there is no need to control its predecessors. The control of a state class consists of restricting the firing intervals of controllable transitions and does not need to compute any controllable predecessor.

Computing controllable predecessors involves some expensive operations such as the difference between time domains. Three levels of control can be carried out from the algorithm: the first level being independent from marking and state is static but not permissive. Second and third levels being dependent of marking and state, respectively are more permissive. One can choose to control the system during execution (third level), modify the model and make transitions conditioned to marking (second level), or re-constraining the intervals, correct the system statically before execution(first level). Correcting the system statically before the execution can reduce the impact of controller interference and solve the problem of synchronization between the controller and system.

The algorithm proposed here is decidable for a bounded TPN because the state class graph is finite and the algorithm explores, path by path, the state class graph (the exploration of a path is abandoned as soon as a loop is detected or a bad state class is reached).

One perspective of this work is the investigation of the use of more compact abstraction (abstraction by inclusion, abstraction by convex-combination) and then, extend the devised and optimized algorithm to large scale and modular systems.

Author details

Parisa Heidari and Hanifa Boucheneb
École Polytechnique de Montréal, Canada

6. References

[1] Altisen, K., Bouyer, P., Cachat, T., Cassez, F. & Gardey, G. [2005]. Introduction au contrôle des systèmes temps-réel, *Journal Européen des Systemes Automatises* 39(1-3): 367–380.

[2] Behrmann, G., Bouyer, P., Larsen, K. & Pelanek, R. [2006]. Lower and upper bounds in zone-based abstractions of timed automata, *International Journal on Software Tools for Technology Transfer* 8(3): 204 – 15.

[3] Bengtsson, J. [2002]. *Clocks, DBMs and states in timed systems.*, dissertation, Uppsala Universitet (Sweden).

[4] Berthomieu, B. & Diaz, M. [1991]. Modeling and verification of time dependent systems using time Petri nets, *IEEE Transactions on Software Engineering* 17(3): 259–273.

[5] Berthomieu, B. & Vernadat, F. [2003]. State class constructions for branching analysis of time Petri nets, *9th International Conference on Tools and Algorithms for the Construction and Analysis of Systems (TACAS)*, pp. 442–457.

[6] Boucheneb, H., Gardey, G. & Roux, O. H. [2009]. TCTL model checking of time Petri nets, *Journal of Logic and Computation* 6(19): 1509–1540.

[7] Boyer, M. & Vernadat, F. [2000]. Language and bisimulation relations between subclasses of timed petri nets with strong timing semantic, *Technical report, LAAS* .

[8] Buy, U. & Darabi, H. [2003]. Deadline-enforcing supervisory control for time Petri nets., *IMACS Multiconference on Computational Engineering in Systems Applications (CESA)*.

[9] Buy, U., Darabi, H., Lehene, M. & Venepally, V. [2005]. Supervisory control of time Petri nets using net unfolding, Vol. 2, pp. 97–100.

[10] Cassez, F., David, A., Fleury, E., Larsen, K. G. & Lime, D. [2005]. Efficient on-the-fly algorithms for the analysis of timed games, *16th International Conference on concurrency theory*, pp. 66–80.

[11] Gardey, G., Roux, O. E. & Roux, O. H. [2006a]. Safety control synthesis for time Petri nets, *8th International Workshop on Discrete Event Systems*, pp. 22–28.

[12] Gardey, G., Roux, O. & Roux, O. [2006b]. State space computation and analysis of time petri nets, *Theory and Practice of Logic Programming* 6: 301 – 20.

[13] Heidari, P. & Boucheneb, H. [2010]. Efficient method for checking the existence of a safety/ reachability controller for time Petri nets, *10th International Conference on Application of Concurrency to System Design(ACSD)*, pp. 201–210.

[14] Merlin, P. M. [1974]. *A study of the recoverability of computing systems*, Ph.d. dissertation, University of California, Irvine, United States.

[15] Merlin, P. M. & Farver, D. [1976]. Recoverability of communications protocols-implication of a theoretical study., *IEEE Trans. on Communications* 24(9): 1036–1043.

[16] Penczek, W. & Polrola, A. [2004]. Specification and model checking of temporal properties in time Petri nets and timed automata, *25th International conference on application and theory of Petri nets*, Vol. 3099 of LNCS, pp. 37–76.

[17] Ramadge, P. J. & Wonham, W. M. [1987]. Supervisory control of a class of discrete event processes, *SIAM Journal on Control and Optimization* 25(1): 206–230.

[18] Roux, O.-H., Lime, D., Haddad, S., Cassez, F. & Bérard, B. [2005]. Comparison of different semantics for time Petri nets, *3rd Automated Technology for Verification and Analysis* Volume 3707 of LNCS: 293–307.

[19] Sathaye, A. S. & Krogh, B. H. [1993]. Synthesis of real-time supervisors for controlled time Petri nets, *32nd Conference on Decision and Control*, Vol. 1, pp. 235–236.

[20] Tripakis, S. [1998]. *L'Analyse Formelle des Systèmes Temporisés en Pratique*, PhD thesis, Université Joseph Fourier - Grenoble 1 Sciences et Geographie.

[21] Wong-Toi, H. & Hoffmann, G. [1991]. The control of dense real-time discrete event systems, *30th IEEE Conference on Decision and Control Part 2 (of 3)*, Vol. 2, pp. 1527–1528.

[22] Wu, N., Chu, C., Chu, F. & Zhou, M. [2008]. Modeling and schedulability analysis of single-arm cluster tools with wafer residency time constraints using Petri net, pp. 84–89.

Section 4

Other

Chapter 21

Petri Nets Models for Analysis and Control of Public Bicycle-Sharing Systems

Karim Labadi, Taha Benarbia, Samir Hamaci
and A-Moumen Darcherif

Additional information is available at the end of the chapter

http://dx.doi.org/10.5772/47774

1. Introduction

Public Bicycle-Sharing Systems (PBSS), also known as self-service public bicycle systems, are available in numerous big cities in the world (Vélib' in Paris, Bicing in Barcelona, Call-a-Bicycle in Munich, OyBicycle in London, etc.). Since its inception, Bicycle-sharing programs have grown worldwide. There are now programs in Europe, North America, South America, Asia, and Australia. A still growing list of cities which provides such green public transportation mode can be found at the Bicycle-sharing world map (http://Bike-sharing.blogspot.com) as shown in Figure 1. As a good complementary to other urban transportation modes, bicycle use entails a number of benefits including environmental, mobility and economic benefits. The public bicycle sharing systems are especially useful for short-distance city transport trips and to face many public transport problems, including growing traffic congestion, pollution, greater car dependency, buses caught in city congestion, and ageing transport infrastructure.

A PBS system can be described as a bank of bicycles that can be picked up and dropped off at numerous stations (service points) across an urban area. The bicycle stations are usually located 300 meters apart, consisting of terminals and stands for fastening the bicycles. Every station is equipped with roughly twenty bicycle stands (the number can be estimated depending on the location of the service point and the estimated level of use). A customer uses a bicycle to travel from one station to another. A bicycle can be taken out from any station and returned to the same or any other station, provided that there is an available locking berth. A PBS system requires more than just bicycles and stations; a variety of other equipment is needed to keep the bicycles and stations functioning at adequate level of service. Particularly, this includes a fleet of vehicles for redistribution of bicycles between stations in order to balance the network (see Figures 2 to 4).

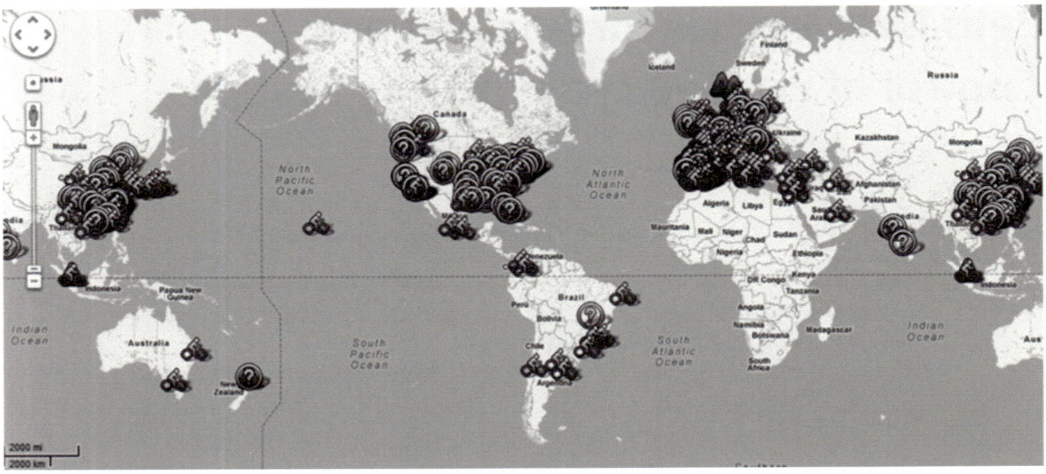

Figure 1. Bike-Sharing world map (source http://Bike-sharing.blogspot.com).

Figure 2. Full station, (http://www.velib.paris.fr/)

Figure 3. Empty station, (http://www.velib.paris.fr/)

Figure 4. Redistribution vehicle (http://www.velib.paris.fr/)

Over the recent years, public bicycle-sharing schemes have developed from being interesting experiments in urban mobility to mainstream public transport options in cities as large and complex as Paris and London (http://www.velib.paris.fr/). PBS schemes have evolved dramatically since their introduction in the 1960s and undergone various changes. These changes can be categorized into three key phases, known as Bicycle sharing generations [9]-[8]. These include the first generation, called white Bicycles (or free Bicycles); the second generation, coin-deposit systems; and the third generation, or information technology based systems. Potential "fourth generation" design innovations are already under development including electric bicycles, movable docking stations, solar-powered docking stations, and mobile phone and iPhone real time availability applications. Of these innovations, the introduction of electric bicycles is likely to be the most significant in terms of attractiveness. The Table 1 gives a survey of some significant public bicycle-sharing programs over the world since the first generation schemes that were introduced in Amsterdam.

A crucial question for the success of a PBS system is its ability to meet the fluctuating demand for bicycles at each station and to provide enough vacant lockers to allow the renters to return the bicycles at their destinations. Indeed, some stations have more demand than others, especially during peak hours. In addition, not surprisingly stations located at the top of hills are chronically empty of bicycles, as the customers ride down the hill but do not wish to make the return trip uphill. Bicycles also tend to collect in stations in the city centres and stay there. In some cases, the *imbalance is temporary*, e.g., high return rate in a suburban train station in the morning and high renting rate in the afternoon. In other cases, the *imbalance is persistent*, e.g., relatively low return rate in stations located on top of hills [30]. If no action is taken by the service provider they rapidly fill or empty, thus preventing other users from collecting or delivering bicycles.

Thus, the system requires constant monitoring to balance the network. The monitoring system dispatches motorized redistribution vehicles (trucks) to rebalance bicycles between stations that are emptying out and those that are filling up. This operation can be carried out in two different modes [30]:

- *Static mode* — The bicycle redistribution operation can be carried out during the night when the usage rate of the PBS system is very low. The bicycle repositioning is performed based on the status of the system at that time and the demand forecast for the next day.

- *Dynamic mode* — The bicycle redistribution operation can be carried out during the day when the usage rate of the PBS system is significant. The bicycle repositioning is performed based on the current state of the station as well as aggregate statistics of the station's usage patterns [16].

Year	City	Bicycle-sharing program
1960	Amsterdam (Netherlands)	The first Bicycle sharing system in the world appeared in Amsterdam, the Netherlands on July 28, 1965. Bicycles were painted white and offered to the public who would like to use them. Due to theft and abuse, unfortunately the program only survived for several days.
1995	Copenhagen (Denmark)	In 1995 in Copenhagen, Bycyklen or City Bicycles was operated as the first large-scale second generation Bicycle sharing program. The system had improved in many aspects. The bicycles are specifically designed for intensive urban use and stations were set up with each equipped with a coin deposit.
1998	Rennes (France)	Rennes launched "Vélo à la Carte" in 1998, which was the first computerized system in the world and the first one in France, and was also operated by ClearChannel, a private company. In 2009, the operator changed to EFFIA and shifted to a new system called "VéloStar".
2005	Lyon (France)	Lyon started its Bicycle sharing system Vélo'V with an unusually large scale in 2005. The city of Lyon and JC Decaux funds the system together through an advertisement contract, which the latter one operates the scheme. Vélo'V is based on stations and has long and short term subscription available with first 30 minutes free.
2007	Paris (France)	Velib' was introduced to Paris in 2007. With the similar operation scheme as Lyon, city of Paris and Cycocity fund the system together and the latter one operates it. Velib' has fixed stations and requires registration beforehand.
2008	Hangzhou (China)	In May, 2008, the first Bicycle sharing program in China started its operation in Hangzhou, a city 180 km southwest of Shanghai, with 4.2 million inhabitants in the metropolitan area, 8 districts included.
2008	Washington (USA)	SmartBicycle DC was a bicycle sharing system implemented in August 2008 with 120 bicycles and 10 automated rental locations in the central business district of Washington, D.C. The network was the first of its kind in North America.
2009	Canada (Quebec)	Bixi is a public bicycle sharing system serving Montreal, Quebec, Canada. The system was launched on May 12 2009, with 3000 bicycles and 300 stations located around Montreal's central core, and it expanded to 5,000 bicycles and 400 stations later that summer.

Table 1. Summary of some PBS systems over the world

Vogel et al., (2011) [38] identify three management and design measures alleviating these imbalances divided into different planning horizons: *(1) Strategic (long-term)* network design comprising decisions about the location, number and size of stations, *(2) Tactical (mid-term)* incentives for customer based distribution of bicycles. For example, the Vélib in Paris grants some extra minutes for returning bicycles at uphill stations, *(3) Operational (short-term)* provider based repositioning of bicycles. The most important issues for the success of a PBS system are summarized in Table 2.

Stage	Questions
Before deployment (Strategic / Tactical)	• *How many bicycles and stations?* • *Where to locate stations?* • *What is the size of each station?* • *How should the bicycles be distributed?* • *How many vehicles (and what sizes) are needed for bicycle redistribution?* • ...
After deployment (Operational)	• *How often should the bicycles be redistributed?* • *Is the current number of redistribution vehicles and projections sufficient?* • *Should more bicycles be purchased?* • *More stations needed?* • *Regular or preventative maintenance required?* • ...

Table 2. Management and design measures of a PBS system

To help planners and decision makers answer these crucial questions, modelling and performance analysis and optimization methods and tools for PBS systems are needed. A literature review describing some existing works developed in this research area is dressed in the section 2. After, the rest of this chapter deals with an original Petri net approach dedicated for PBS systems modelling for control purposes [2]-[19]-[20]-[21]. The section 3 provides an introduction for Petri nets with the "marking dependent weights" concept [17] as it is used throughout this chapter to model PBS systems for control purposes. In the sections 4 to 6, a modular framework based on Petri nets with marking dependent weights is developed for modelling and performance evaluation of PBS systems. The concluding section 7 gives some remarks and perspectives of this work. Our approach is intended to help planners and decision makers in determining how to implement, and operate successfully these complex dynamical systems.

2. A review of the literature

Public Bicycle-sharing systems have attracted a great deal of attention in recent years. Although the growth of the system has been rapid following the development of better tracking technology, most of the studies related to PBS systems in the literature have focused on their history, development and some practical advises [9]-[31]-[39]. There are, however, relatively few studies addressing strategic and operational issues that arise in such systems.

About strategic issues, Lin and Yang (2011) [22] and Lin et al., (2011) [23] address the strategic problem of finding optimal stations using mathematical programming techniques. The problem is formulated as a hub location inventory model. The key design decisions considered are: the number and locations of bicycle stations in the system, the creation of bicycle lanes between bicycle stations, the selection of paths of users between origins and destinations, and the inventory levels of sharing bicycles to be held at the bicycle stations. The design decisions are made with consideration for both total cost and service levels. Dell'Olio et al. (2011) [7] present a complete methodology for the design and implementing of bicycle sharing systems based on demand estimates considering the stations and the fares. Vogel et al. (2011) [38] develop a methodology for strategic and operational planning using data mining. A case study shows how Data Mining applied to operational data offers insight into typical usage patterns of bike-sharing systems and is used to forecast bike demand with the aim of supporting and improving strategic and operational planning.

Regarding operational issues, besides the work presented in [38], the static balancing problem studying the repositioning of bicycles among bicycle stations where the customer demand is assumed to be negligible is addressed in [5]-[30]. Several mathematical formulations of the problem can be found in [30] and an exact algorithm based on column generation and a suitable pricing algorithm based on dynamic programming are given by Chemla et al.; (2011) [5]. From an OR perspective, the bicycle repositioning problem bears great similarities to some other routing problems which have been largely studied in the literature. As an example from this point of view, Forma et al. (2010) [12] consider the bicycle repositioning problem as a variation of the Pickup and Delivery problem (PDP). Naturally, some similarities between bicycle-sharing and car-sharing systems can be explored in order to adapt some existing results in this field (see, for example [26]-[36]).

Besides OR approaches developed, particularly by using mathematical programming techniques [5]-[12]-[22]-[23]-[30] to support decision making in the design and management of PBS systems, Data Mining techniques receives attention in academia as well as in practice. Data Mining is particularly suitable to analyze and to predict the dynamics of a PBS system. By exploring and analyzing the temporal and geographic human mobility data in an urban area using the amount of available bicycles in the stations of a PBS system [3], statistical and prediction models can be developed [13]-[16] for tactical and operational management of such systems.

As noted in [37], although extensive analysis of bicycle data or customer surveys can be applied to predict future bicycle demand at stations, the demand still has to be considered stochastic and not deterministic. Moreover various points in time have to be incorporated in a suitable mathematical optimization models. Such a stochastic and dynamic model can be computational intractable. In addition, customer behavior cannot be modelled in these mathematical optimization models. According to our knowledge, unlike our work [2]-[19]-[20]-[21], no other studies has been undertaken on the dynamics modelling and performance evaluation of such dynamical systems. In addition to their self-service mode, PBS systems are dynamic, stochastic, and complex systems, this makes their modelling and analysis very complicated. Among the formalisms used to model the dynamic systems, Petri nets are one of the graphical and formal specification techniques for the description of the operational behavior of the systems. They are widely used in a number of different disciplines including engineering, manufacturing, business, chemistry, mathematics, and even within the judicial system [17]-[18]-[40]-[32]-[42]-[41]. They have been accepted as a powerful formal specification tool for a variety of systems including concurrent, distributed, asynchronous, parallel, deterministic and non-deterministic.

However, although Petri nets have been widely used in various domains, they played a relatively minor role in modelling and analysis of urban transportation systems. According to some existing works, the modelling of the systems by using Petri nets formalisms can be considered from either a discrete and/or a continuous point of view. Continuous Petri nets for the macroscopic and microscopic traffic flow control are used in [15]-[34], while hybrid Petri nets are used in [11] to provide a valuable model of urban networks of signalized intersections. Recently, batch Petri nets with controllable batch speed are used [10] to study a portion of the A12 highway in The Netherlands. From a discrete point of view, generalized stochastic Petri nets are used [1]-[4] for modelling and planning of public transportation systems. The two complementary tools, Petri nets and (max, +) algebra, have been used [28]-[29] to deal with the modelling and the performance evaluation of a public transportation system. For the modelling of passenger flows at a transport interchange, as shown in [33] colored Petri nets are able to incorporate some specific parameters and data in the model such as the variation of walking speeds between passengers and the restricted capacity of features of the interchange infrastructure.

These are a few works that demonstrate the high potential of Petri nets as a tool for modelling and performance analysis of urban transportation systems, but also on the other hand, it is shown that the application of Petri nets is still in its early stage and particularly limited to intersection traffic control [11]-[14]-[15]-[25]-[35]-[34] and to some studies dealing with the modelling of urban transportation systems for planning purposes [28]-[29]-[33]. In addition, according to our knowledge, unlike traditional urban transportation systems, no work has been undertaken on PBS systems modelling and performances analysis by using Petri net models. Our contribution in this context is the first one in the literature [18]-[19]-[20]-[21].

3. Petri nets with variable arc weights

In its basic form, a Petri net may be defined as a particular bipartite directed graph consisting of places, transitions, and arcs. Input arcs are ones connecting a place to a transition, whereas output arcs are ones connecting a transition to a place. A positive weight may be assigned to each arc. A place may contain tokens and the current state (the marking) of the modelled system is specified by the number of tokens in each place. Each transition usually models an activity whose occurrence is represented by its firing. A transition can be fired only if it is enabled, which means that all preconditions for the corresponding activity are fulfilled (there are enough tokens available in the input places of the transition). When the transition is fired, tokens will be removed from its input places and added to its output places. The number of tokens removed/added is determined by the weight of the arc connecting the transition with the corresponding place. Graphically, places are represented by circles, transitions by bars or thin rectangles (filled or not filled), tokens by dots. For a comprehensive introduction of Petri nets, see for example [27].

Formally, a Petri net can be defined as $PN = (P, T, Pré, Post, Inhib, M^0)$, where: $P = \{p_1, p_2, \ldots, p_n\}$ is a finite and non-empty set of places; $T = \{t_1, t_2, \ldots, t_m\}$ is a finite and non-empty set of transitions; *Pre*: $(P\times T)\rightarrow N$ is an input function that defines directed weighted arcs from places to transitions, where N is a set of nonnegative integers; *Post*: $(P\times T)\rightarrow N$ is an output function which defines directed weighted arcs from transitions to places; *Inhib*: $(P\times T)\rightarrow N$ is an inhibitor function which defines inhibitor weighted arcs (circle-headed weighted arcs) from places to transitions; and M_0 is called initial marking (initial distribution of the tokens in the places). A place connected with a transition by an arc is referred to as input, output, and inhibitor place, depending on the type of the arc. The set of input places, the set of output places, and the set of inhibitor places of a transition t are denoted by $^\bullet t$, $t^\bullet$, and $^\circ t$, respectively. The weights of the input arc from a place p to a transition t, of the output arc from t to p, and of the inhibitor arc from p to t are denoted by $Pre(p, t)$, $Post(p, t)$, and $Inhib(p, t)$, respectively.

The behavior of many systems can be described in terms of system states and their changes. In order to simulate the dynamic behavior of a system, a state or marking in a Petri net is changed according to the following transition rules:

- A transition t is said to be enabled if each of its input places contains at least a number of tokens equal to the weight of the corresponding input arc, and each of its inhibitor places contains tokens less than the weight of its corresponding inhibitor arcs.

Formally:

$$\forall p \in {}^\bullet t,\ M(p) \geq \mathrm{Pre}(p,t) \tag{1}$$

$$\forall p \in {}^\circ t,\ M(p) < Inhib(p,t) \tag{2}$$

- An enabled transition t fires by removing from each of its input places a number of tokens corresponding to the weight of the corresponding input arc, and adding a number of tokens in each of its output places corresponding to the weight of the corresponding output arc.

Formally:

$$\forall p \in P, M'(p) = M(p) - \mathrm{Pre}(p,t) + Post(p,t) \tag{3}$$

The firing of transitions in a Petri net model corresponds to the occurrence of events that changes the state of the modelled system. This change of state can be due to (*i*) the completion of some activity or/and (*ii*) the verification of some logical condition in the system. Since transitions are often used to model activities (production, delivery, order...), transition enabling durations correspond to activity executions and transition firings correspond to activity completions. Hence, deterministic or stochastic temporal specifications can be naturally associated with transitions [24].

In addition of the concept of time and the introduction of inhibitor arcs, which are not given in the original definition of Petri nets, the modelling of the complex dynamic of a PBS system requires the use of Petri nets models with *"variable arc weights depending on its marking"* and possibly on some decision parameters of the system. The same modelling concept is introduced for modelling inventory control systems and supply chains in [17]-[6]. Precisely, the Petri net model of an inventory control system whose inventory replenishment decision is based on the inventory position of the stock and the reorder and order-up-to-level parameters. Similarly, in the case of a PBS system, the redistribution operation of the bicycles between stations depends on the number of the available bicycles in each station when controlled.

By allowing the weights of some arcs of a Petri net to depend on its marking, control policies of the stations can be easily described in the PBS model. Therefore, we consider in this chapter that for any arc (*i, j*), its weight *w(i, j)* is now defined as a linear function of the marking *M* with integer coefficients α and β. The weight *w(i, j)* is assumed to take a positive value.

$$w(i,j) = \alpha_{ij} + \sum_{p_i \in P} \left(\beta_{ij}\right)_{P_i} \cdot M\left(p_i\right) \quad (4)$$

To understand the mathematical and intuitive meaning of this concept, consider the Petri net shown in Figure 5.

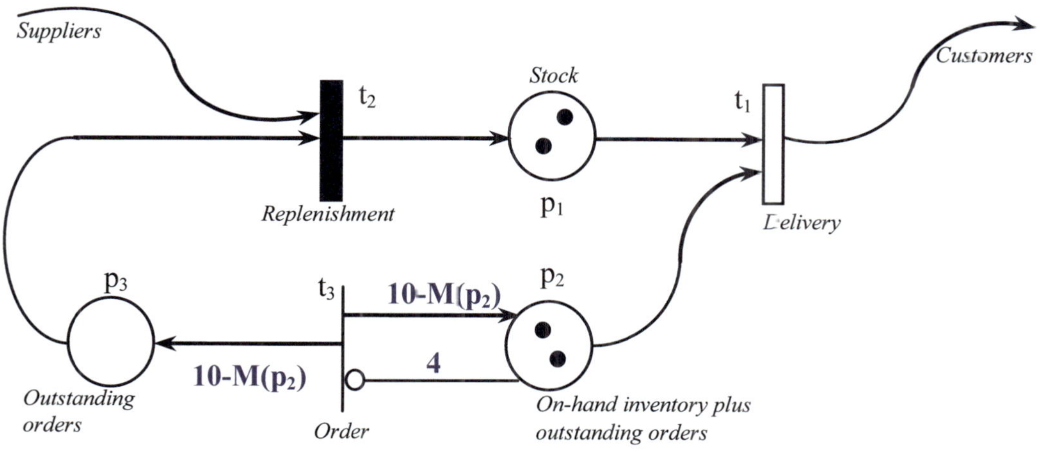

Figure 5. Illustration of a Petri net with variable arc weights depending on its marking

The model represents an inventory control system with continue review (s, S) policy (here $s = 4$ and $S = 10$) [17]. The different operations of the system are modelled by using a set of transitions: generation of replenishment orders (t_3); inventory replenishment (t_2); and order delivery (t_1). In the model, the weights of the arcs (t_3, p_2), (t_3, p_3) are variable and depend on the parameters s and S of the system and on the marking of the model (S - $M(p_2)$; s).

- According to the current marking $M_i = (2, 2, 0)$ of the net, the transition t_3 is enabled, since the following condition is satisfied:

$$M(p_2) = 2 < Inhib(p_2, t_3) = 4$$

- After the firing of t_3, 10 - $M(p_2)$ = 10–2 = 8 tokens are added into the places p_2 and p_3. In other words, the firing of the transition t_3 from the initial marking M_i leads to a new marking $M_f = (2, 10, 8)$ as the following:

$$M_f(p_2) = M_i(p_2) + \left[10 - M_i(p_2)\right] = 2 + \left[10 - 2\right] = 10.$$

$$M_f(p_3) = M_i(p_3) + \left[10 - M_i(p_3)\right] = 0 + \left[10 - 2\right] = 8.$$

4. Modelling of a PBS system

As mentioned in the second section of this chapter, modelling, analysis and performance evaluation of PBS systems is crucial not only for their successful implementation and performance improvement but also for ensuring an effective regulation of bicycle traffic flows. This section deals with our original Petri net approach dedicated for PBS system modelling and analysis for control purposes. We consider a PBS system with N stations noted by $S = \{S_1, S_2, \ldots, S_N\}$. Each station $S_i \in S$ is equipped with C_i bicycle stands (the capacity of a station S_i). In practice, the number C_i depends on the location of the service point and the estimated level of use. The system requires a constant control which consists in transporting bicycles from stations having excess of bicycles to stations that may run out of bicycles soon. In the general way, the main objective of the control system, performed by using redistribution vehicles as shown in Figure 4, is to maintain R_i (reorder point) bicycles per station S_i to ensure bicycles are available for pick up and thus ($C_i - R_i$) vacant berths available for bicycle drop off at every station.

4.1. The Petri net model

Firstly, for the sake of clarity, we consider a PBS system with only three stations and then we design a Petri model of the system as shown in Figure 6. The designation of the elements and parameters of the Petri net model are given in Tables 3, 4 and 5. Thereafter, as will be shown in this section, according to the modular structure of the resulting Petri net model, its generalization to represent PBS systems with N stations will be straightforward and intuitive.

Before a formal description and analysis of the model in the next sub-sections, the Figure 6 and the Tables 3, 4, and 5 allow readers to quickly gain an understanding of the Petri net model of the system. A closer look at the Petri net model shows three subnets (modules) representing three different functions named as follows: (*1*) the "station control" subnet; (*2*) the "bicycle flows" subnet; and (*3*) the "redistribution circuit" subnet. The main function of each subnet is described in the following:

- The "bicycle flows" subnet represents the bicycle traffic flows between the different stations of the network. A customer uses a bicycle to travel from one station to another. In other words, a bicycle can be taken out from any station and returned to the same or any other station, provided that there is an available locking berth.
- The "station control" subnet represents the control function of the stations to ensure bicycles are available for pick up and vacant berths available for bicycle drop off at every station S_i. The purpose of this function is two-fold: First, the control of the state of the station in terms of the number of bicycles available for new users; and second, according to the state of the controlled station, take one decision among three alternatives: (*i*) Add bicycles in the station, or (*ii*) Remove bicycles from the station, or (*iii*) Take no action.
- The "redistribution circuit" subnet represents the path (circuit) to be followed by the redistribution vehicle in order to visit the different stations of the network. Its objective is to rebalance bicycles between stations that are emptying out and those that are filling up.

Place	*Interpretation*
PS_i	Represents a station S_i. Its marking $M(PS_i)$ correspond to the number of bicycles available in the station S_i.
PR_i	Represents a redistribution vehicle used to regulate the stations. Its marking $M(PR_i)$ correspond to the number of bicycles available in this redistribution vehicle when the station S_i is visited in order to be controlled.
PO_i	Specify whether the number of bicycles in a station S_i is greater than the reorder point R_i. It is indicated when $M(PO_i) = 1$.
PC_i	Specify the end of the control of a station S_i by the redistribution vehicle. $M(PC_i) = 1$ means that the control of the station S_i is completed and indicates that the redistribution vehicle is liberated to go to the next station.

Table 3. Interpretation of places of the PN model

Transition	*Interpretation*
TR_i	Test and add (if necessary) bicycles into a station S_i.
TO_i	Test if the number of bicycles available in a station S_i is greater than the reorder point R_i.
TS_i	Remove bicycles from a station S_i if the number of bicycles available in this station is judged less than the reorder point R_i
TE_i	Test if the number of bicycles available in a station S_i is equal to the reorder point R_i

Table 4. Interpretation of transitions of the PN model

Parameter	*Interpretation*
R_i	Reorder point fixed for each station S_i. It is the minimum level of available bicycles in the station S_i when a decision should be made to adding or removing bicycles into (from) the station (redistribution of bicycles between stations)
C_i	Capacity of each station S_i. More precisely, C_i corresponds to the maximal number of bicycle stands in a station S_i.

Table 5. Decision parameters of the PN model

Thanks to the modularity of the developed model, its generalization for a system with *N* stations is simple to make according to the different functions cited previously. For example, to model *N* stations S_i (i = 1, 2, …, *N*), we need to *N* places denoted by PS_i and the control subnet is duplicated for each station similarly to the model represented for three stations (see Figure 6). Finally, by considering all the modules, the Petri net model representing a PBS system with *N* stations should contain:

$|T| = N^2 + 5 * N$ transitions; $|P| = 4 * N$ places; $|A_d| = 2 * N^2 + 21 * N$ directed arcs, and $|A_i| = N^2 + 7 * N$ inhibitors arcs.

4.2. Description of the Petri net model

4.2.1. The "control stations" subnet

The subnet representing the control function of each station S_i is indicated in Figure 6. As shown in the model, the considered subnet is duplicated for each station S_i. We recall that, the main objective of the control function is to rebalance bicycles between stations that are emptying out and those that are filling. The control function of the system is realized by using three places denoted by PS_i, PC_i, PR_i; for transitions denoted by TE_i TR_i, TS_i, TO_i. As indicated in the tables 3 and 4, the place PS_i represents a station S_i; the place PR_i represents the redistribution vehicle when visiting the station S_i; and the place PC_i means to indicate the end of the control operation of the station S_i. When the redistribution vehicle arrives at a station S_i, the state of this station is controlled. According to the number of bicycles available in the station, the decision to be made is either (*a*) to put bicycles in the station, or (*b*) to take bicycles from the station, or (*c*) take no action. The different operations are described and illustrated as follows.

a. **"Addition of bicycles to a station" operation**: The decision to add bicycles in a station S_i is performed by the transition TR_i connected by the corresponding arcs to the places PR_i and PS_i. Indeed, the transition TR_i means to verify the current number of bicycles in the station and to add (if necessary!) a given number (R_i – $M(PS_i)$) of bicycles to the station S_i. When the transition TR_i is fired, R_i - $M(PS_i)$ tokens (bicycles) will be removed from the place PR_i (the regulation vehicle) and at the same time, R_i - $M(PS_i)$ tokens (bicycles) will be added to the place PS_i (the station S_i). At the same time, one token will be deposited in the place PC_i to indicate the end of the control of the station S_i, and then the redistribution vehicle can travel to the next section S_{i+1}.

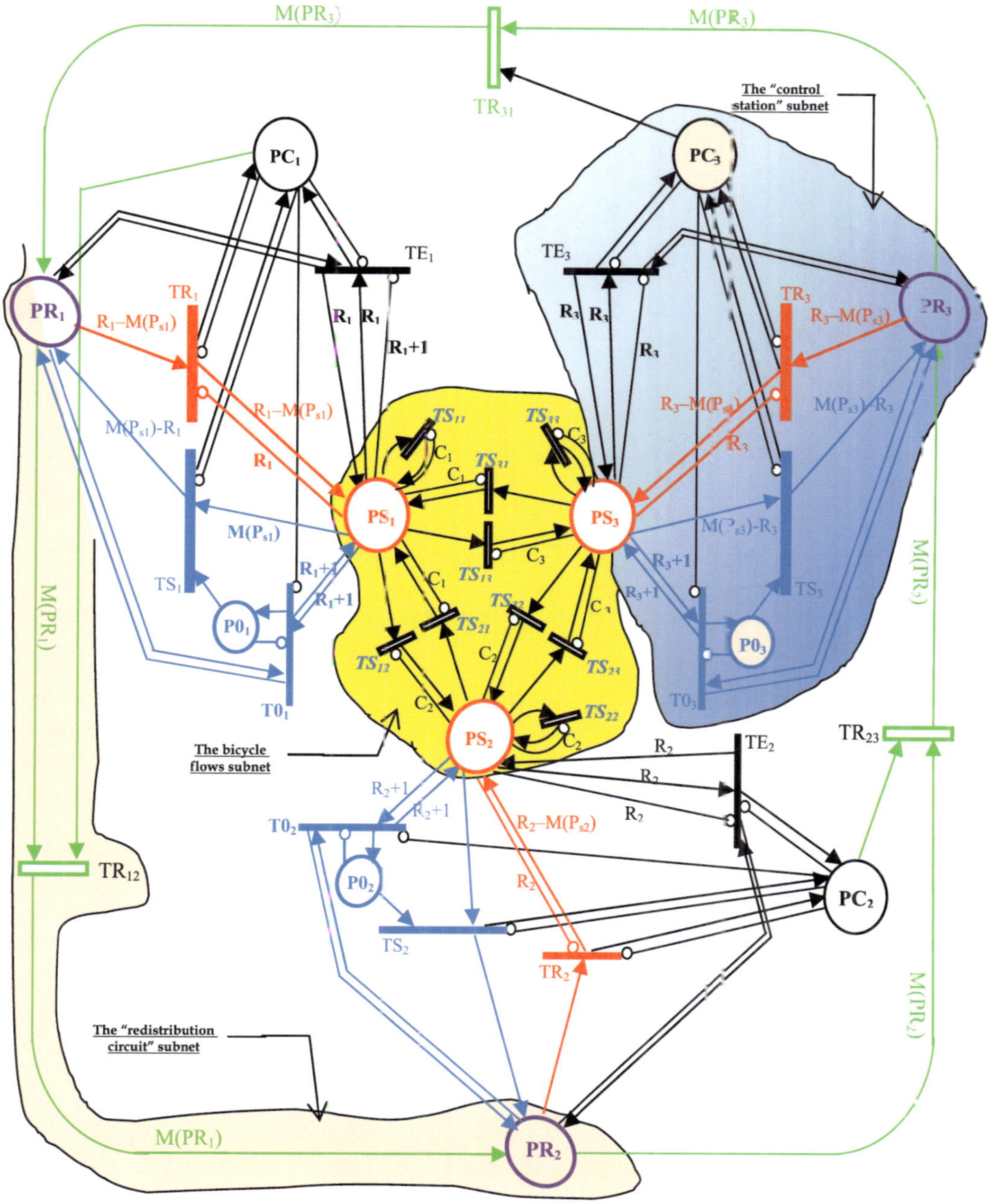

Figure 6. The Petri net model of a self-service public bicycles system (with three stations)

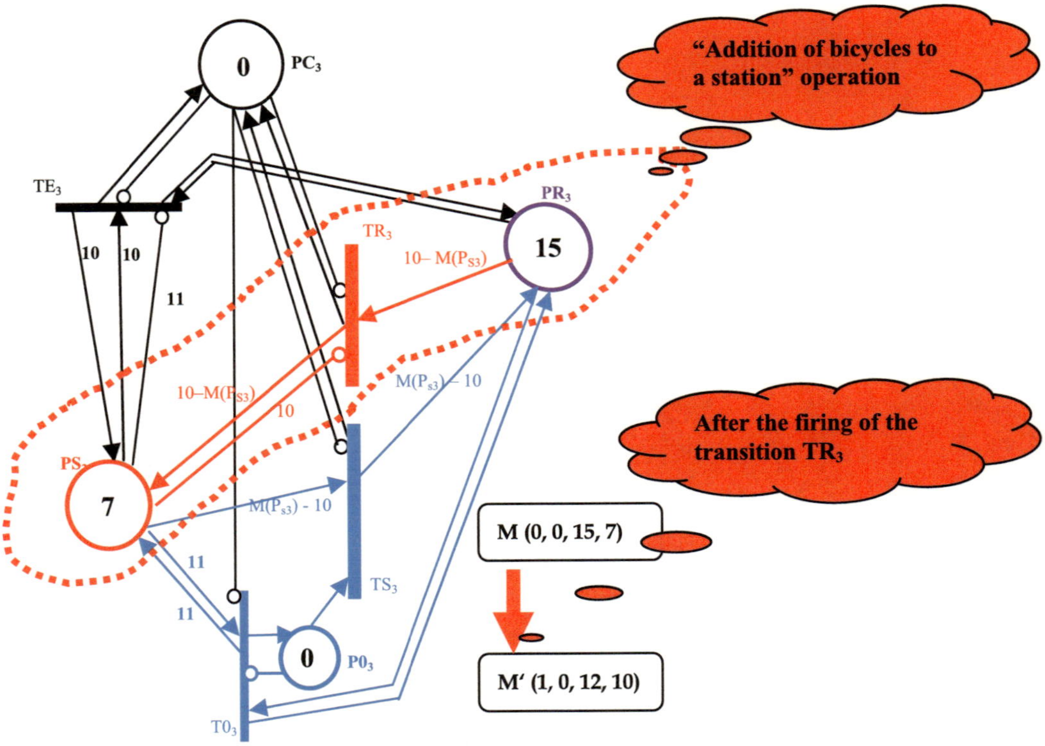

Figure 7. "Control station" subnet illustration: The number of available bicycles in the station S_i is less than R_i *(i.e., $M(S_i) < R_i = 10$)*

- **Illustrative example 1**.— As shown in Figure 7, consider that initially there are 7 available bicycles in the station S_3 (i.e. $M(PS_3) = 7$); 15 available bicycles in the redistribution vehicle (i.e. $M(PR_3) = 15$); $M(PC_3) = 0$; and the reorder point R_3 is fixed to 10. For this marking, only the transition TR_3 is enabled since the following enabling equations are satisfied:

$$M(PS_3) = 7 < 10 \ ; M(PR_3) = 15 \geq 10 - M(PS_i) = 3 \ ; \ M(PC_3) = 0 < 1 \ .$$

After the firing of the transition TR3, the marking of the corresponding places changes in this way:

$$M'(PS_3) = M(PS_3) + \left[10 - M(PS_3)\right] = 7 + \left(10 - 7\right) = 10. \ ;$$

$$M'(PR_3) = M(PR_3) - \left[10 - M(PS_3)\right] = 15 - \left(10 - 7\right) = 12. \ ;$$

$$M'(PC_3) = M(PC_3) + 1 = 0 + 1 = 1.$$

b. **"Remove bicycles from a station" operation:** The decision to remove bicycles (superfluous) from a station S_i is made by the two transitions TO_i and TS_i. More precisely, the transition TO_i means to test if the current number of bicycles in the station

S_i is greater than the reorder point R_i and the transition TS_i allows us to remove bicycles (if necessary!) from the station S_i and put them in the regulation vehicle. When the transition TO_i is enabled, its firing will add a token into the place PO_i to indicate that the current number of bicycles in the station S_i is greater than the reorder point R_i fixed for the station S_i. This indication (i.e. $M(PO_i) =1$) is one of the enabling conditions of the transition TS_i. When the transition TS_i is enabled, its firing leads to remove $M(PS_i)-R_i$ bicycles (superfluous) will be removed from the station S_i and, at the same time, they are deposited in the place PR_i which represents the redistribution vehicle.

- **Illustrative example 2.**— Now, as illustrated in Figure 8, consider that initially there are *15* available bicycles in the station S_3 (*i.e.* $M(PS_3) = 15$); *22* available bicycles in the redistribution vehicle (i.e. $M(PR_3) = 15$); $M(PC_3) = 0$; and the reorder point R_3 is fixed to *10*. For the current marking of the subnet, the transition TO_3 is enabled, since:

$$M(PS_3)=15\geq 11 \ ; \ M(PO_3)=0<1 \ ; \ M(PC_3)=0<1 \, .$$

After the firing of the immediate transition TO_3, a token will be placed in PC_3 indicating that the current number of bicycles in the station S_3 is greater than R_3 = *10* ($M(PS_3)>10$). That is: $M'(PO_3)=M(PO_3)+1=1$. With this indication, the transition TS_3 is systematically enabled, according to the following satisfied enabling equations:

$$M(PS_3)=15\geq 15 \ ; M(PO_3)=1\geq 1 \ M(PC_3)=0<1 \ ; M(PR_3)=22\geq 10 \, .$$

Then, after the firing of the transition TR_3, the state of the subnet will change as follows:

$$M'(PS_3)=M(PS_3)+\left[10-M(PS_3)\right]=10 \ ;$$

$$M'(PR_3)=M(PR_3)-10+M(PS_3)=22-10+15=27 \ ;$$

$$M'(PC_3)=M(PC_3)+1=1 \, ; M'(PO_3)=M(PO_3)-1=0.$$

c. **"No action" operation:** Contrarily to the two previous actions corresponding "to remove" or "to add" bicycles from (resp. into) the station S_i, the "not action" function will be performed when the current number of bicycles in the controlled station S_i is equal to the reorder point R_i. Testing that $M(PS_i) = R_i$ is made by the transition TE_i with its corresponding arcs connecting the places PS_i and PC_i with the transition. The firing of TE_i will not change the marking of the place PS_i which represents the number of bicycles in the controlled station S_i. Similarly to the two previous functions, after the firing of TE_i one token will be deposited in the place PC_i. This is to indicate the end of the control of the station S_i and then the redistribution vehicle can travel at the next section by the firing a transition TR_{ij} in the Petri net model. This case is illustrated in Figure 9 where we consider $M(PS_3) = 10$.

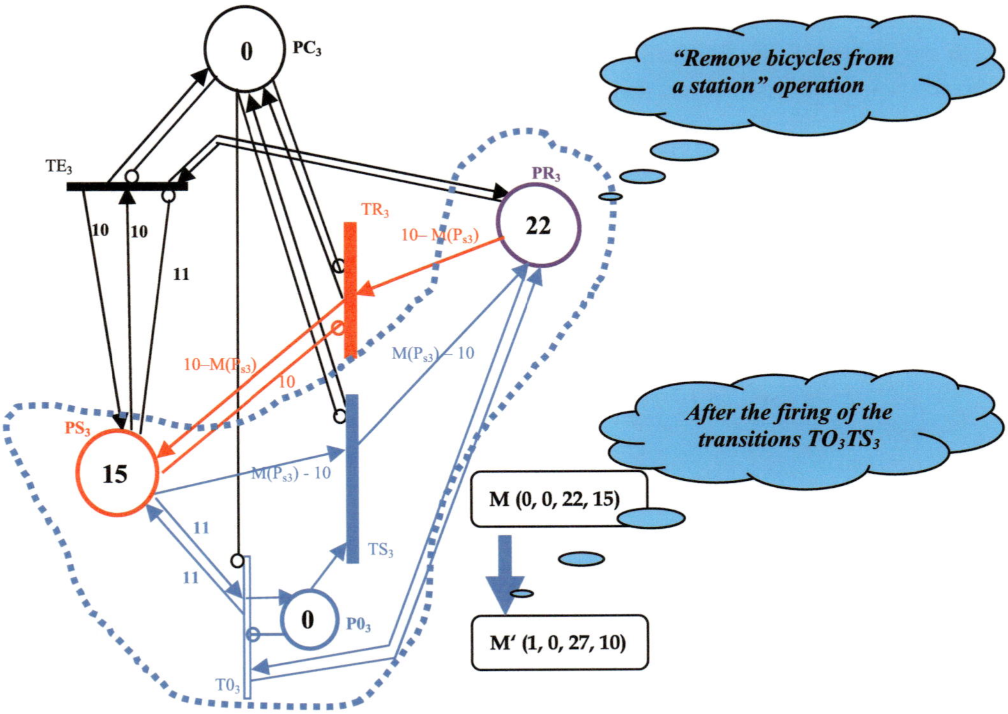

Figure 8. "Control station" subnet illustration: The number of available bicycles in the station S_i is greater than R_i *(i.e.,* $M(S_i) > R_i = 10$*)*

4.2.2. The "bicycle flows" subnet

A public bicycle system is a bank of bicycles which are continuously used by users to travel from one station to another. Thus, each bicycle of the system can be taken out from any station and returned to the same or any other station, provided that there is an available locking berth. The subnet representing the displacements of the bicycles between the different stations of the system is represented in Figure 10 and indicated in Figure 2. Each station S_i of the system is modelled by using a place denoted by PS_i. The bicycle flows is represented by the multiple token displacements from any place to the same or any other place by firing transitions denoted by TS_{ij} (possibly TS_{ii}) connecting the different places of the subnet. Each station S_i is equipped with C_i bicycle stands. It is the capacity of each place PS_i in the subnet. The parameter C_i represents the weight of the inhibitor arcs connecting the places PS_i with the transition TS_{ij}. The inhibitor arcs are used in order to respect the capacity C_i of each station. According to the stochastic behavior of the bicycle flows between the different stations, the transitions of the subnet must be stochastic transitions.

4.2.3. The "redistribution circuit" subnet

As noted previously, the PBS system requires constant control which consists in transporting bicycles from stations having excess of bicycles to stations that may run out of bicycles soon. In our model, we consider that the vehicle(s) used to rebalance bicycles between stations visits successively stations $S_1, S_2, \ldots, S_N$.

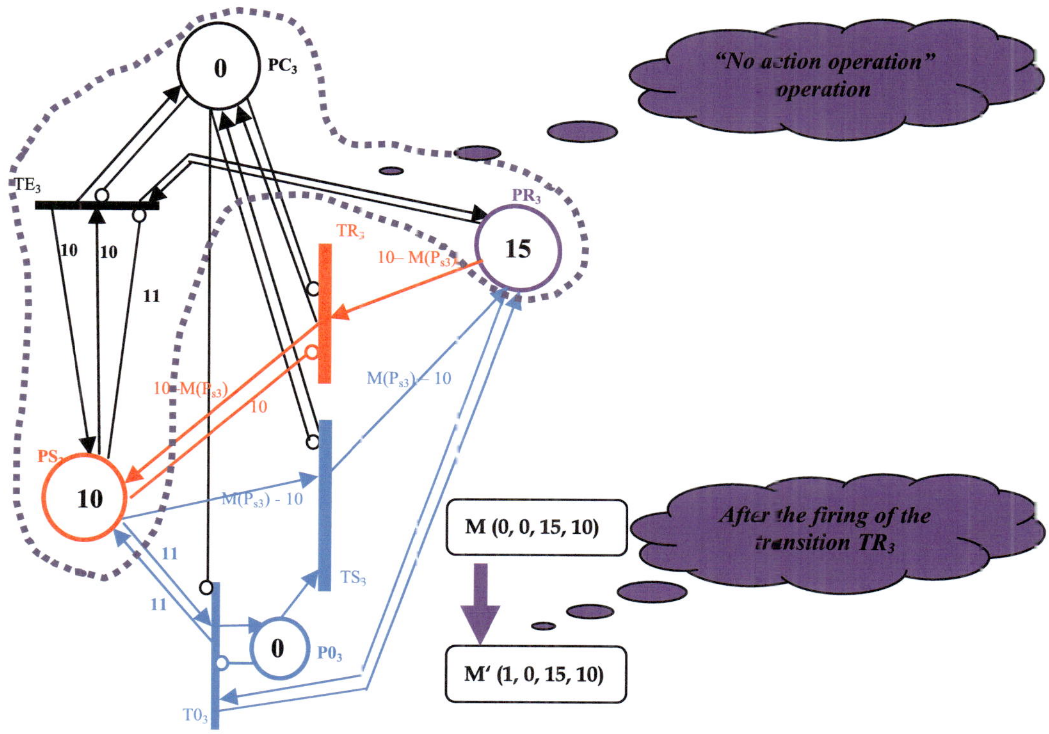

Figure 9. "Control station" subnet illustration: The number of available bicycles in the station S_i is equal to R_i (i.e., $M(S_i) = R_i = 10$)

As can be seen in the Figure 6, the places denoted by PR_i ($i = 1, 2, \ldots, N$), the transitions denoted by TR_{ij} ($i \neq j$ and $i, j = 1, 2, \ldots, N$) and all of the corresponding arcs form a closed path. The resulting subnet represents a circuit which the redistribution vehicle follows in order to visit and to control successively the different stations of the network. When the redistribution vehicle arrives at a given station S_i, the marking of the place PR_i (i.e., $M(PR_i)$) indicates the current available bicycles in the vehicle. The displacement of the vehicle from a station S_i to another station S_j is modelled by the transition TR_{ij}. Obviously, the circuit is connected to the control subnet of the system. Indeed, each place PR_i is connected to the three transitions TS_i, TE_i, and TR_i in order to execute the control function of the station S_i. The connection is made by the corresponding arcs.

Now, suppose that the control of a given station S_i is finished. Then, the redistribution vehicle leaves the station S_i and goes to the next section S_j. The firing of the enabled transition TR_{ij} leads to a new marking the place PC_i, $M'(PC_i) = 0$, indicating that the redistribution vehicle is arrived at the next station S_j with $M(PR_i)$ bicycles in its trailer. $M(PR_i)$ corresponds to the rest of bicycles just after the control of the previous station S_i.

In the presented Petri net model (for three stations), we used a single redistribution vehicle for the control of the stations. Obviously, in practice, for a system with N stations implemented in a given city, the regulation can be performed by several redistribution vehicles which can be affected to different districts of the city. Thus, in the Petri net model, several redistribution vehicles and their circuits can be represented similarly to the example presented with one redistribution vehicle.

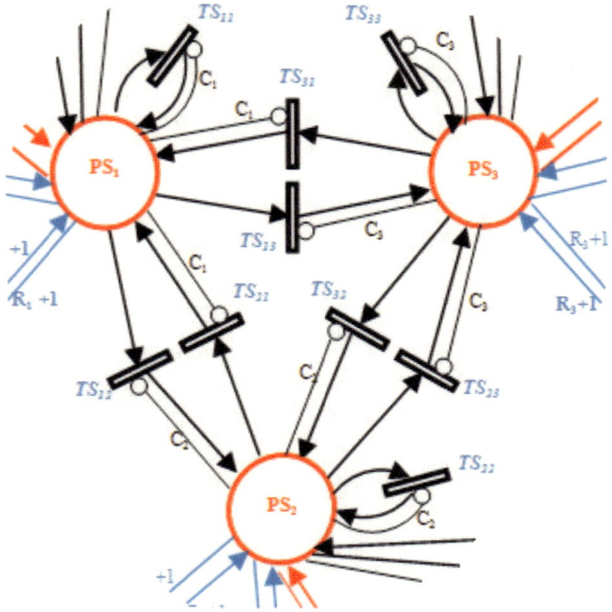

Figure 10. The "bicycle flows" subnet.

5. Performance evaluation with simulation

Real systems are large and complex and so are the Petri nets used for their modelling and analysis. As the model complexity increases, the use of analytical techniques for analysis and performance evaluation becomes harder for many real-life applications or case studies. Despite the many free software tools available for Petri nets simulation and analysis, we had to develop our specific simulation tool in order to validate and analyze the performance of the models presented in this chapter. In fact, the "marking dependent weights" concept, which is an important feature to model self-service public bicycle systems, does not exist anywhere in the existing Petri nets simulation tools.

Our simulation tool has been developed by exploiting the *BDSPN* simulator recently realized by us [17]-[6] for the simulation of *BDSPN* models developed for the modelling and performance evaluation of inventory control systems and logistic systems where we also used the "marking dependent weights" concept. The developed simulation tool provides functions for calculating some important perfomance indices of the Petri net model. These indices can then be mapped to the system's performance indices by the modeler. At the end of the simulation, some performance indices for places and transitions can be obtained. Some of them are formulated and interpreted for the performance evaluation of PBS systems as follows:

a. Average number of tokens in a place P (M_{avr}(P)):

$$M_{avr}(P) = \frac{\sum M(P) * \tau}{T_s} \tag{5}$$

where *M(P)* is the number of tokens at the beginning of the cycle; T_s is the total simulation time and τ is the duration of the cycle. This performance indice can be used particulary to get the mean number of bicycles in each station S_i and in the regulation vehicle(s) by computing the average marking of the corresponding places PS_i and PR_i.

b. Mean sojourn time of tokens in a place (Savr(P)):

$$S_{avr}(P) = \frac{\sum M(P) * \tau}{N_t} \tag{6}$$

where N_t is the number of different tokens that have passed through the place until the current cycle. The value of N_t can be obtained by incrementing a counter each time an input transition fires and put tokens in the place. *M(P)* is the number of tokens in the place *P* and τ is the duration of the cycle. By calculating the mean sejourn times of the places PS_i, we get important informations about the the turnover (rotation) of bicycles between the different stations of the transport network.

c. Effective firing rate of a transition T (Favr(T)):

$$F_{avr}(T) = \frac{NF(T)}{T_s} \tag{7}$$

where T_s is the total simulation time; *NF(T)* is the number of firings of the transition. The firing rates of some transitions of the Petri net model, such as the transitions TR_i, TS_i, and TR_{ij}, measure some operations rates of the regulation function in order to quantify the dynamics of the system or some rates of specific activities.

d. Rates of empty and full places (REmpty(P); RFull(P)):

$$R_{empty\%}(P) = 100 \cdot \frac{T_s - \sum(\tau_k - \tau_{k+1})_{M(P)=0}}{T_s} \tag{8}$$

$$R_{full(\%)}(P) = 100 \cdot \frac{T_s - \sum(\tau_k - \tau_{k+1})_{M(P)=Cp}}{T_s} \tag{9}$$

where T_s is the simulation time ($T_s \rightarrow \infty$); (τ_k - τ_{k+1}) represente the the duration of the cycle where the place *P* is empty (resp. full) (i.e., $M(P) = 0$ resp. $M(P) = C_p$ where C_p is the capacity of the place *P*). The performance indices are particularly interesting to measure the rates of two uncomfortable situations that can occur in the system. That is the case of empty and full stations which have necessary to be avoided.

6. Simulation and validation of the model

Now, the relevance of the Petri net model represented in Figure 6 and described in the previous sections is demonstrated through several simulations made for different interesting configurations of the system. They are defined according to the functions to be activated (or not) in the Petri net model of the PBS system.

1. *Configuration (a).— The dynamic model with the regulation system:* In this case, we consider the general functioning of the system. That is, stations are available for users and the system is under control to rebalance bicycles between stations that are emptying out and those that are filling up. The Petri net model represented in Figure 6 reproduces this case when all of its subnets are not disabled as it is the case in the following configurations (case *b* and case *c*).
2. *Configuration (b).— The dynamic model without the regulation system*: Unlike the first case, here, we consider that the regulation system is unavailable. So, the stations remain operational for users but without any control of the bicycle flows. According to the Petri net model, this configuration is obtained when the initial marking of all the places PR_i is equal to zero. This configuration deactivates the redistribution vehicle path and the whole control function of each station.
3. *Configuration (c).— The static model:* This case represents the behavior of the system when the frequentation of the stations is very low (functioning of the system during night, for example). In terms of the Petri net model, this situation can be simulated by increasing considerably the transition firing delays of the transitions TS_{ij} which represent the displacements of bicycles between different stations. Similarly to the case B, the stations remain operational for users but without any control because (for the case *c*) of the limited bicycle flows.

6.1. Simulation of the PBS model under the configuration (a)

Let us consider the configuration (a) with the parameters given in the Table 6. The first part of the Table 6 gives the initial marking of the Petri net where we consider that initially there are 15 bicycles available in each station S_i. In the second part of the table, we read the parameters R_i and C_i of the control function of the system. It is assumed that the reorder point R_i (resp. the capacity C_i) of each station is the same and fixed to 10 (resp. 20) bicycles. Finally, the table gives the parameters of the transitions of the Petri net model. For each transition, are indicated its nature which can be an immediate transition (I); a deterministic transition (D); or an exponential transition (E); its rule policy namely continue process (C) or restart process (R); and also its firing delay given in minutes (constant firing delay for deterministic transitions; zero firing delay for immediate transitions, and mean firing delay for stochastic transitions).

Configuration Of The Initial Marking Of The Model					
$M_0(PS_1)$	$M_0(PS_2)$	$M_0(PS_3)$	$M_0(PR_1)$	$M_0(PR_2)$	$M_0(PR_3)$
15	15	15	10	0	0
$M_0(PS_1)$	$M_0(PS_2)$	$M_0(PS_3)$	$M_0(PR_1)$	$M_0(PR_2)$	$M_0(PR_3)$
0	0	0	0	0	0
Configuration Of The Parameters R_i And C_i Of The Petri Net Model					
R^1	R^2	R^3	C^1	C^2	C^3
10	10	10	20	20	20
Configuration Of The Transitions Of The Model					
TS_{11}	TS_{12}	TS_{13}	TS_{21}	TS_{22}	TS_{23}
E, C, 20	E, C, 5	E, C, 10	E, C, 5	E, C, 20	E, C, 5
TS_{31}	TS_{32}	TS_{33}	TR_1	TO_1	TS_1
E, C, 10	E, C, 5	E, C, 20	E, C, 3	I, 0	E, C, 3
TR_2	TO_2	TS_2	TR_3	TO_3	TS_3
E, C, 3	I, 0	E, C, 3	E, C, 3	I, 0	E, C, 3
TR_{12}	TR_{23}	TR_{31}	TE_1	TE_2	TE_3
E, C, 15	E, C, 15	E, C, 15	I, 0	I, 0	I, 0

Table 6. Configuration data of the Petri net model

Considering all the parameters of this configuration, evolution graphs and some performances of the system can be established thanks to our simulation tool. We focus our attention on the behavior of the time evolution of the number of available bicycles in the stations which can be observed in Figure 11. According to the control function integrated in the model, it can be observed that the number of bicycles (marking the places PS_i) in the three stations "oscillates" around the reorder point R_i (=10) and the capacity C_i (= 20) of each station is respected. Obviously, the dynamic behavior of this part of the system is similar to the one of inventory control systems [17].

As shown in Figure 12, the dynamic behavior of the redistribution vehicle can also be observed through the time evolution of the marking of the places PR_i together. For the chosen parameters of the system, we see that there are always enough bicycles in the redistribution vehicle.

6.2. Simulation of the PBS model under the configuration (b)

As defined previously, in this configuration, we consider the dynamic model without the regulation system. Here, the initial markings of all the places $M(PR_i)$ are equal to zero. That is the only modification to be made in the Table 6 to obtain this situation. Thanks to this change, the redistribution vehicle path and all of the control function of each station are not available in the Petri net model (see Figure 6). Formally, for $M(PR_i) = 0$ and $M(PC_i) = 0$, the transitions TE_i, TS_i, TO_i, TR_i (control function) and TR_{ij} (displacement of the redistribution vehicle) are never enabled for this configuration. Consequently, the stations remain operationnal for users but whitout any control.

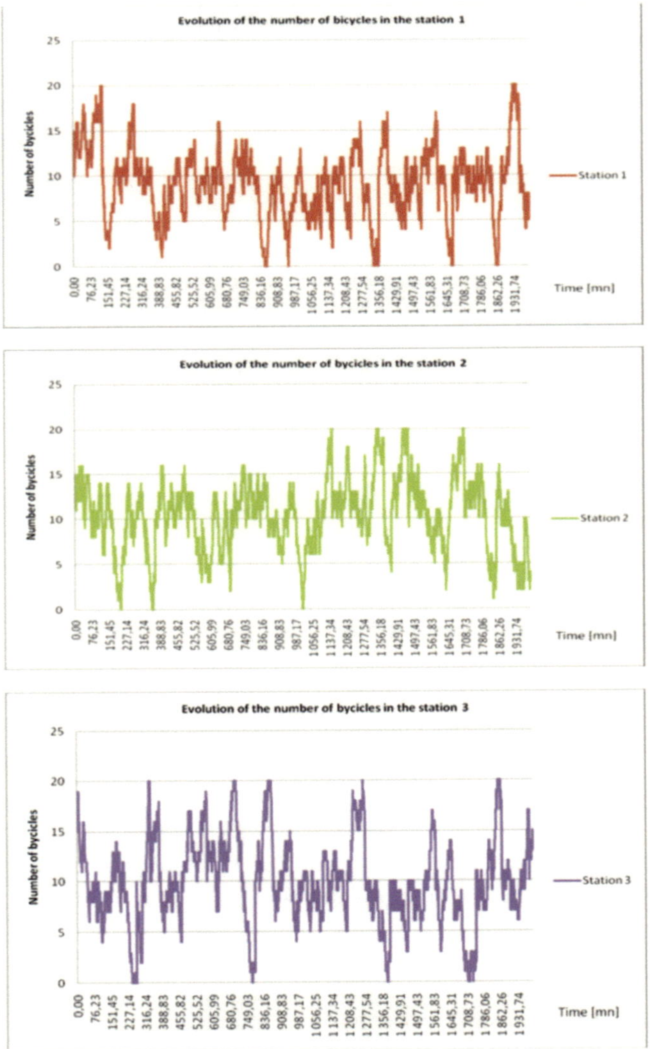

Figure 11. Evolution of the number of available bicycles in the stations (configuration a)

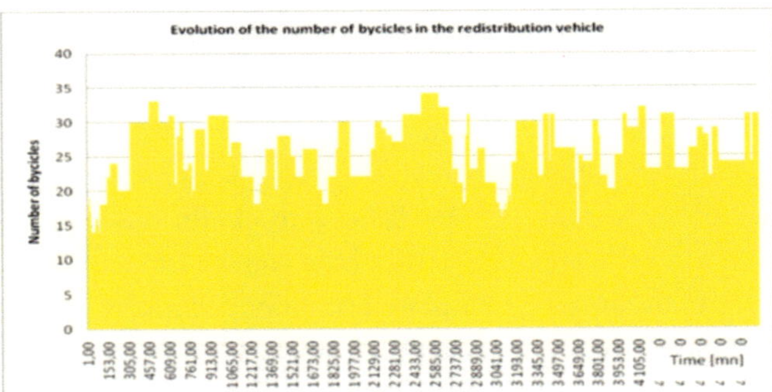

Figure 12. Evolution of the number of bicycles in the redistribution vehicle (configuration a).

Thanks to our simulator, the evolution time of the number of bicycles in the different stations is given in Figure 13. With regard to the first configuration (a), here, we see clearly the absence of the control functions of the system. It is observed that the stations are very frequently full. In contrast, empty stations are not observed in this configuration. This is only due to the parameters chosen for this case. Indeed, recall that we have 15 bicycles in each station (there are a total of 45 bicycles in the system) and the capacity of each station is fixed to 20. Thus, the minimal number of bicycles which can be found in a given station is 5 bicycles (Indeed, 45 - 20*2 (two full stations) = 5) which can be observed in the graphs.

Finally, the Table 7 gives some performances of the system for the two configurations obtained by computing the equations (5-9). The average number of available bicycles in each station is represented by the average marking of the places PS_i. For the configuration A, $M_{avr}(PS_i)$ is approximately equal to 10 which is coherent with the reorder point R_i fixed to 10 for this configuration. In contrast, for the configuration B where the system is without the regulation function, the average number of bicycles in the stations is over 15. The rates of empty and full stations are also given in the table. The rate of empty and full stations (together), $R_{F/F}(PS_i)=R_{Full}(PS_i)+R_{Empty}(PS_i)$, is estimated to 6.80% in the case of the configuration (a), and 51% in the case of the configuration (b) for each station.

Perf. evaluation of the configuration (a)		
$M_{avr}(PS_1)$	$M_{avr}(PS_2)$	$M_{avr}(PS_3)$
10,18	10,14	10,21
$R_{Empty}(PS_1)$	$R_{Empty}(PS_2)$	$R_{Empty}(PS_3)$
3.33%	3.30%	3.31%
$R_{Full}(PS_1)$	$R_{Full}(PS_1)$	$R_{Full}(PS_1)$
3.52%	3.50%	3.51%
$R_{E/F}(PS_1)$	$R_{F/E}(PS_1)$	$R_{F/E}(PS_1)$
6.85%	6.80%	6.82%
Perf. evaluation of the configuration (b)		
$M_{avr}(PS_1)$	$M_{avr}(PS_2)$	$M_{avr}(PS_3)$
15,72	15,57	15,53
$R_{Empty}(PS_1)$	$R_{Empty}(PS_2)$	$R_{Empty}(PS_3)$
0%	0%	0%
$R_{Full}(PS_1)$	$R_{Full}(PS_1)$	$R_{Full}(PS_1)$
51.0%	51.1%	50.8%
$R_{F/E}(PS_1)$	$R_{F/E}(PS_1)$	$R_{F/E}(PS_1)$
51.0%	51.1%	50.8%

Table 7. Some performances indices of the model (for the considered parameters)

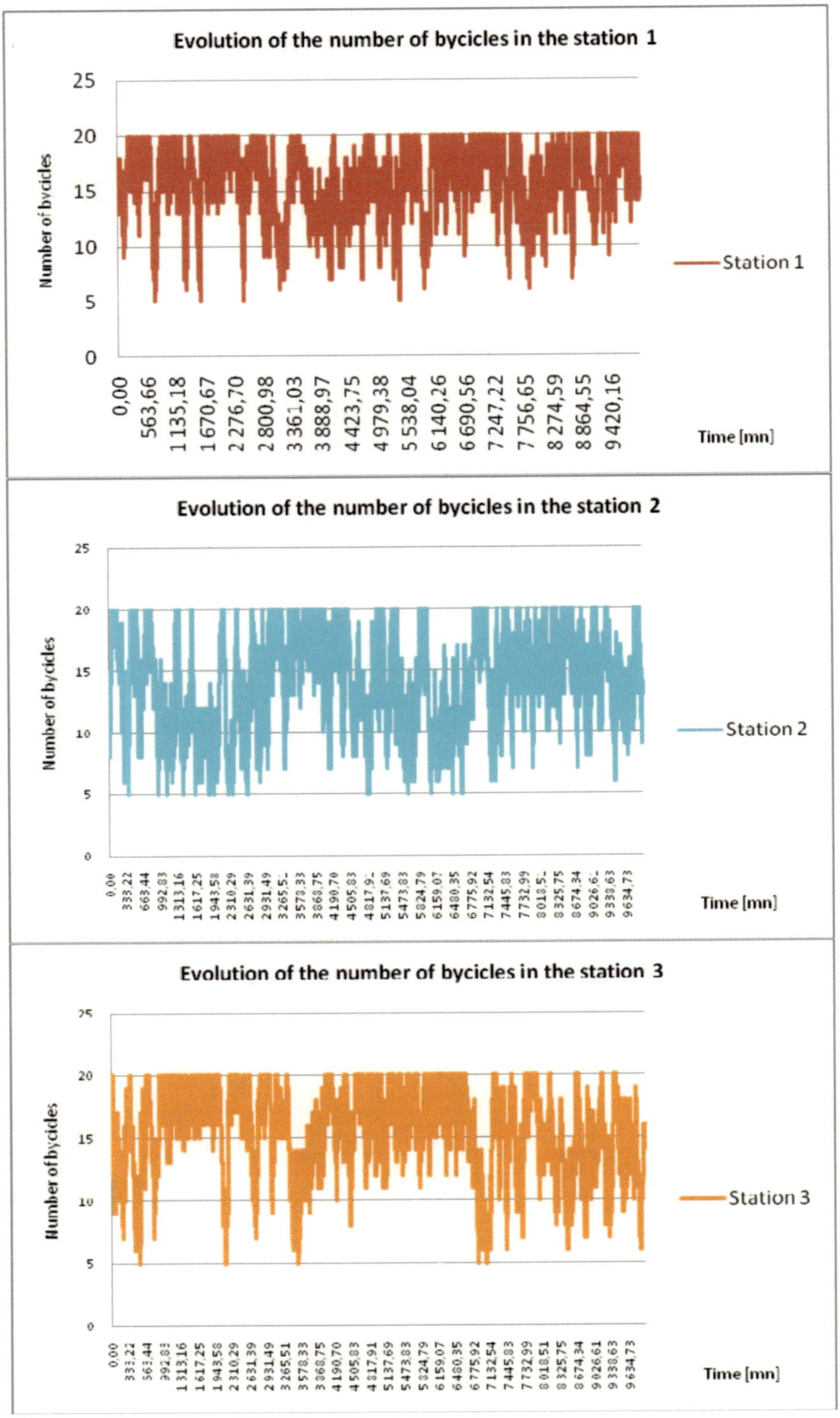

Figure 13. Evolution of the number of available bicycles in the station 3 (configuration b)

As noted previously, to obtain the configuration c, the Petri net model shown in Figure 6 must be parameterized as in the configuration b but by increasing considerably the transition firing delays of the transitions TS_{ij}. Contrary to the behavior of the system shown in Figure 13, in this situation, we obtain a static model with very low (negligible) evolution of the distribution of the bicycles in the network.

7. Conclusion

In this chapter, we have presented an original Petri net approach for public bicycle sharing systems modelling and performance evaluation for control purposes. A modular dynamic model based on Petri nets with marking dependent weights is proposed and a simulation approach is developed and used to simulate and validate models described in this chapter. Very likely, this approach is the first one in the literature dedicated to this urban transportation mode by using Petri nets. The authors believe that this new area of research has significant promise for the future to help planners and decision makers in determining how to implement, and operate successfully these complex dynamical systems. Now, we are working in the following directions: (1) Development of some natural extensions of the models including more complex modelling features such as the application of other control strategies used for the latest systems which operate with smart technologies and provide users and controllers with real-time bike availability information; (2) Development of optimization methods for optimal control purposes. For example, the objective is how to search optimal values of the decision parameters R_i, C_i of the model in order to minimize the two uncomfortable situations $M(PS_i) = 0$ (empty station) and $M(PS_i) = C_i$ (full station) that may occur in the different stations of the system.

Author details

Karim Labadi, Taha Benarbia, Samir Hamaci and A-Moumen Darcherif
EPMI, Ecole d'Electricité, de Production et Management Industriel, France

8. References

[1] Abbas-Turki A.; Bouyekhf R.; Grunder O.; El Moudni A.; (2004) "On the line planning problems of the hub public-transportation networks", *International journal of systems science*, Vol. 35, No. 12, pp. 693-706.

[2] Benarbia, T., Labadi, K., and Darcherif, M., (2011) "A Petri Net Approach for Modelling, Performance Evaluation and Control of Self-Service Public Bicycle Systems", *16th International IEEE conference on Emerging Technologies on Factory Automation*, ETFA'2011, September 5-9 2011, Toulouse, France.

[3] Borgnat, P., Abry, P., Flandrin, P., Robardet, C., Rouquier, J-B., Fleury, E., (2011), "Shared Bicycles in a City: a Signal Processing and Data Analysis Perspective", *Advances in Complex Systems*, Vol. 14, No. 3, pp. 415-438.

[4] Bouyekhf R., Abbas-Turki A., Grunder O., El Moudni A., (2003) "Modelling, performance evaluation and planning of public transport systems using generalized stochastic Petri nets", *Transport reviews,* Vol. 23, No. 1, pp.51-69.

[5] Chemla, D., Meunier, F., Wolfler-Calvo, R., "Balancing the stations of a self-service bike scharing system", *Working paper, 2011.*

[6] Chen H., Amodeo L., Chu F., and Labadi K., (2005)"Performance evaluation and optimization of supply chains modelled by Batch deterministic and stochastic Petri net", *IEEE transactions on Automation Science and Engineering,* Vol. 2, No. 2, pp. 132-144.

[7] Dell'Olio, L., Ibeas, A., Moura, J.-L, (2011) *"Implementing bike-sharing systems",* Proceedings of the ICE-Municipal Engineer, Volume 164, Issue 2, pp. 89 –101

[8] DeMaio, P., (2003). "Smart Bicycles: Public transportation for the 21st century", *Transportation Quarterly,* Vol. 57, No.1, pp. 9–11.

[9] DeMaio, P., (2009) "Bicycle-sharing: History, Impacts, Model of Provision, and Future", *Journal of Public Transportation,* Vol. 12, No.4, pp. 41-56.

[10] Demongodin I., (2009) "Modelling and Analysis of Transportation Networks using Batches Petri Nets with controllable Batch Speed", *in Proc. 30th Int. Conf. Applications and Theory of Petri Nets, Giuliana Franceschinis, Karsten Wolf, Ed. Paris, France.*

[11] Di Febrarro, A., Giglio, D., Sacco, N., (2004) "Urban traffic control structure based on hybrid Petri nets", *IEEE Transactions on Intelligent Transportation systems,* Vol. 5, No. 4, pp. 224-237.

[12] Forma, I.; Raviv, T.; Tzur, M., (2010), "The Static Repositioning Problem in a Bike-Sharing System", *In the proceeding of the 7th Treinnial Symposium on Transportation Analysis* (TRISTAN 2010), Tromso, Norway, pp. 279-282.

[13] Froehlich, J., Neumann, J. & Oliver, N. (2009), "Sensing and Predicting the Pulse of the City through Shared Bicycling", *Proceedings of the International Workshop on Urban", Community and Social Applications of Networked Sensing Systems.*

[14] Gallego J.L., Farges J.L., Henry J.J., (1996) "Design by Petri nets of an intersection signal controller" *Transportation Research, part. C,* Vol. 4, No. 4, pp. 231–248.

[15] Júlvez J., Boel R.K., (2010) "A continuous Petri net approach for model predictive control of traffic systems" *IEEE Transactions on Systems, Man, and Cybernetics, Part A: Systems and Humans,* Vol. 40, No. 4, pp. 686 – 697.

[16] Kaltenbrunner, A., Meza, R., Grivolla, J., Condina, J. & Banchs, R. (2010), "Urban cycles and mobility patterns: Exploring and predicting trends in a bicycle-based public transport system", *Pervasive and Mobile Computing,* Vol.6, No.4, pp. 455–466.

[17] Labadi K., Chen H., Amodeo L., (2007) "Modelling and Performance Evaluation of Inventory Systems using Batch deterministic and stochastic Petri nets", *IEEE Transactions on Systems, man and Cybernetics, Part C: Applications and review,* Vol. 37, No. 6, pp. 1287-1302.

[18] Labadi, K. and Chen, H., (2010) "Modelling, analysis, and optimisation of supply chains by using Petri net models: the state-of-the-art", *Int. J. Business Performance and Supply Chain Modelling,* Vol. 2, No. ¾, pp.188-215.

[19] Labadi, K., Benarbia, T., Darcherif, M., (2010) « Sur la régulation des systèmes de vélos en libre-service : approche basée sur les réseaux de Petri (avec des arcs a poids

variables) », *8th ENIM IFAC International Conference of Modeling and Simulation*, MOSIM'10, 10 au 12 mai 2010 - Hammamet – Tunisie.

[20] Labadi, K., Benarbia, T., Darcherif, M., and Chayet, M., (2012) "Modelling and Control of Self-Service Public Bicycle Systems by Using Petri Nets", *International Journal of Modelling, Identification and Control*, Vol. x, No. x, xxxx Vol. x, No. x, 2012 (accepted, to appear)

[21] Labadi, K., Hamaci, S., Benarbia, T., (2010) "Un modèle dynamique pour la régulation des systèmes de vélos en libre-service", *ROADEF 2010, 11e Congrès annuel de la société française de Recherche Opérationnelle et d'Aide à la Décision*, 24-26 février 2010, Toulouse.

[22] Lin, J.-R., Yang, T.-H. (2011), "Strategic design of public bicycle sharing systems with service level constraints", *In Transportation Research Part E: Logistics and Transportation Review*, Vol. 47, No.2, pp. 284–294.

[23] Lin, J.-R., Yang, T-H., Chang, Y-C., (2011) "A hub location inventory model for bicycle sharing system design: Formulation and solution", *Article in Press, Computers & Industrial Engineering xxx (2011) xxx–xxx.*

[24] Lindemann C., (1998) "Performance modelling with deterministic and stochastic Petri nets", *John Wiley and Sons Edition.*

[25] List, G.F.; Cetin, M.; (2004) *"Modeling traffic signal control using Petri nets"*. IEEE Transactions on Intelligent Transportation Systems, Vol. 5, No. 3, pp. 177–187.

[26] Mukai, N., Watanabe T., (2005) "Dynamic location management for on-demand car sharing system", *KES'05 Proceedings of the 9th international conference on Knowledge-Based Intelligent Information and Engineering Systems*, Melbourne, Australia, pp. 768-774.

[27] Murata T., (1989) "Petri nets: Properties, analysis, and applications," *in Proc. of the IEEE*, Vol. 77, No. 4, pp. 541-580.

[28] Nait-Sidi-Moh A., Manier M-A., El Moudni A., (2005) "max-plus algebra Modeling for a Public Transport System", *Journal of Cybernetics and Systems, Vol. 36/2, pp.165-180.*

[29] Nait-Sidi-Moh A., Manier M-A., El Moudni A., Manier H., (2003) *"Performance Analysis of a Bus Network Based on Petri Nets and (max, +) Algebra"*. International Journal of Systems Science (ex. SAMS: Systems Analysis Modelling Simulation), Vol. 43, No 5. pp. 639-669.

[30] Raviv T., Tzur M., Forma I., (2011), *"Static Repositioning in a Bike-Sharing System: Models and Solution Approaches"*, Working paper.

[31] Shaheen, S., Guzman, S., & Zhang, H. (2010). *"Bikesharing in Europe, the Americas, and Asia: Past, Present, and Future"*, Journal of the Transportation Research Board, 2143, pp. 159–167.

[32] Silva M., Teruel E., (1997) "Petri nets for the design and operation of manufacturing systems", *European Journal of Control*, Vol. 3, No. 3, pp. 182-199

[33] Takagi R., Goodman C.J., Roberts C., (2003) *"Modelling passenger flows at a transport interchange using Petri nets"*, Proceedings of the Institution of Mechanical Engineers, Part F: Journal of Rail and Rapid Transit, Vol. 217, No. 2, pp. 125-134.

[34] Tolba C., D. Lefebvre, Thomas P., El Moudni A., (2005) "Continuous and timed Petri nets for the macroscopic and microscopic traffic flow control", *Simulation Modelling Practice and Theory,* Vol. 13, No. 5, pp. 407-436.

[35] Tzes A., Seongho K., and McShane W. R., (1996) "Application of Petri networks to transportation network modeling" *IEEE Transactions on Vehicular Technology*, Vol. 45, pp. 391–400.

[36] Uesugi K., Mukai, N., and Watanabe T., (2007) "Optimization of Vehicle Assignment for Car Sharing System", *Lecture Notes in Computer Science, Knowledge-Based Intelligent Information and Engineering Systems*, Vol. 4693/2007, pp. 1105-1111.

[37] Vogel, P., & Mattfeld, D. (2010). *"Modeling of repositioning activities in bike-sharing systems"*. Proceedings of 12th WCTR.

[38] Vogel, P., Greisera, T., Mattfelda, D., (2011) "Understanding Bicycle-Sharing Systems using Data Mining: Exploring Activity Patterns", *Procedia Social and Behavioral Sciences*, Vol. 20, pp. 514–523.

[39] Wang Shang, Zhang Jiangman; Liu Liang, Duan Zheng-yu (2010),"Bike-Sharing-A new public transportation mode: State of the practice & prospects", *IEEE International Conference on Emergency Management and Management Sciences*, (ICEMMS 2010), pp. 222-225

[40] Zhou Mengchu and Kurapati Venkatesh., (1999) "Modeling, simulation, and control of flexible manufacturing systems: A Petri net approach", Vol. 6 of Series in Intelligent Control and Intelligent Automation, World Scientific.

[41] Zhou MengChu, and DiCesare Frank., (1993) "Petri net synthesis for discrete control of manufacturing systems", *Kluwer Academic Publishers*.

[42] Zurawski, R., and Zhou Mengchu., (1994) "Petri nets and industrial applications: A tutorial", *IEEE Transactions on Industrial Electronics*, Vol. 41, No. 6, pp. 567-583.